Children's Representation

Australia
The Law Book Company
Brisbane, Sydney, Melbourne, Perth

Canada
Carswell
Ottawa, Toronto, Calgary, Montreal, Vancouver

AGENTS

India
N.M. Tripathi (Private) Ltd
Bombay

Eastern Law House (Private) Ltd
Calcutta

M.P.P. House
Bangalore

Universal Book Traders
Delhi

Aditya Books
Delhi

Israel
Steimatzky's Agency Ltd
Tel Aviv

Japan
Macmillan Shuppan KK
Tokyo

Pakistan
Pakistan Law House
Karachi, Lahore

Children's Representation

A Practitioner's Guide

Judith E. Timms

Director, IRCHIN
Honorary Research Fellow, Department of Law,
University of Liverpool

LONDON
SWEET & MAXWELL
1995

Published by Sweet & Maxwell Limited of
South Quay Plaza, 183 Marsh Wall, London E14 9FT
Typeset by MHL Typesetting Ltd, Coventry
Printed by Hobbs the Printers, Southampton

A CIP catalogue record for this book is available from
the British Library

ISBN 0 421 49720 3

To Joff
and our children,
Becky, Matthew and Dan

Acknowledgments

In writing this book I would like to acknowledge the help and support I have received from many friends and colleagues involved in children's representation. In particular I would like to thank Jim Richards (Director of Catholic Children's Society, Westminster), Sue Hardy (Training Co-ordinator for the National Association of Guardians *ad Litem* and Reporting Officers), Janet Ollier (Guardian *ad Litem*, Cheshire) and His Honour Judge Peter Urquhart, for their constructive comments on individual chapters; and Guy Mitchell (Senior Guardian *ad Litem*, Boys and Girls Welfare Society, Cheadle, Cheshire, formerly editor of *Panel News*) and Professor Christina Lyon (Professor of Common Law at the University of Liverpool) for their generous contribution of time and experience in being willing to attempt the marathon task of reading the drafts.

I owe a great debt of gratitude to Trisha Knapman, IRCHIN's Administrator, for her consistent support and patience in typing the manuscript, and to my nephew Edward Maude and my daughter Rebecca Timms for their practical help and encouragement. Lastly I would like to thank all my family, Becky, Matthew and Dan and particularly my husband Jonathan Timms for their unfailing love, support and good humour in accepting *Children's Representation* as an additional member of the household during many months' gestation.

JET

Foreword

I am pleased to have been asked to write the foreword to this important and challenging work which brings together an impressive range of information and experience relating to children's representation. It draws on both substantial practical experience of representing children's views and a comprehensive knowledge of social policy and child care legislation affecting children. It is innovative in combining together a body of information about the guardian *ad litem* service in England and Wales, and in incorporating discussion on the representation of the child in private law proceedings and in non-judicial decision making, such as local authority complaints proceedings. The work also provides a comprehensive overview of the law and practice relating to representing children since the implementation of the Children Act 1989. A new area of work for guardians *ad litem* covered by this book is their involvement in proceedings under S.30 Human Fertilisation and Embryology Act 1990 and, as such, this is a timely contribution to the available literature. The question of how children's voices can be heard in litigation is one which will increasingly preoccupy children's representatives in the coming decade and beyond. I therefore strongly recommend this book to all those involved in representing children, both as a source of valuable information and as a practical guide to children's rights.

Christina M. Lyon
Professor of Common Law
Director of the Centre for the Study of the Child, The Family and the Law
University of Liverpool

2 February 1995

Introduction

This book is an examination of the current state of children's rights to representation in family proceedings in England and Wales, and a discussion of how separate and independent representation makes a direct contribution to the welfare of children.

The major part of the book, in Part II, examines and contrasts the representation of children in both public and private law proceedings, focusing particularly on the role of the guardian *ad litem* as an independent social work representative of the child. Chapter 8 looks at the recent and controversial area of involvement for guardians *ad litem* in S.30 of the Human Fertilisation and Embryology Act 1990, Surrogacy Arrangements. Chapter 10 examines the representation of children in quasi- or non-judicial proceedings, and acknowledges that judicial decision making, even when children are separately represented, constitutes only the tip of the iceberg in terms of the thousands of decisions made daily by adults on behalf of children for whom they are responsible. Parts I and III look respectively at rights and welfare, and at how their respective interaction determines both positive and negative outcomes for the child.

Practical experience confirms that planning for children is most successful when the children themselves have been involved in the decision making, and can commit themselves to making plans work. Consulting young people does not commit responsible adults to comply with their wishes, if to do so would be detrimental to long term health, protection and welfare. It does mean that the child's wishes may be incorporated as a major, but not necessarily overriding, element in the decision making.

The UN Convention on the Rights of the Child, together with the Children Act 1989, provides a framework which considerably strengthens the position of the child, and which may facilitate the development of new services to children and families, based on principles of participation and an acknowledgment of children's rights. However the emerging tensions between children's rights and children's welfare, and the scale of change of culture required to empower children, within both legal and social services departments, should not be under-estimated, and could emerge as one of the key practice issues in the next ten years. As Michael Freeman pointed out:

> the framework for children's rights is very different from those of welfare, which provides for protection, and is essentially paternalistic. A children's rights framework sees children as active participants in social processes. Rights are valuable commodities, important moral coinage. They enable us to stand with dignity, if necessary to demand what is our due without having to grovel, plead or beg. A world with claim rights is one in which all persons are dignified objects of

respect. Love, compassion, having the child's best interests in mind are important values but they are no substitute for rights.[1]

Such rights are free-standing and are not within the gift of any individual or local authority. They make adults, carers, parents and professionals uneasy because they threaten the ability of adults to make unchallenged decisions. The weakness of children's rights is that they remain dependent on the goodwill of adults to enforce them, and so are particularly fragile.

The view here is essentially pragmatic. It reinforces the view of Dame Elizabeth Butler-Sloss, reporting on events in Cleveland, that children are people, not objects of concern. It is based on the belief that a clear working knowledge of the rights of children and young people can act as the necessary corrective to imprecise definitions of best interest, and that best practice is that which incorporates a core curriculum of rights within definitions of welfare at every stage of decision making, both in and out of court.

Independent and effective representation is the mechanism through which a healthy synthesis of rights and welfare may be achieved. It is also the powerful force in motion which acts as the catalyst for change, debate and review.

---

1   Freeman, 'Children's Charters and Children's Acts' *Panel News*, December 1989, Vol.9, IRCHIN (Independent Representation for Children in Need). See also Bandman 'Do Children have any Natural Rights?', *Proceedings of 29th Annual Meeting of Philosophy of Education Society* (1973), at 234 to 236, and Joel Feinberg, 'Duties, Rights and Claims', (1966) *American Philosophical Quarterly* 3, 137.

Contents

Part III Welfare

Table of Cases

Table of Statutes

Table of Statutory Instruments

Table of Conventions and Declarations

Part I
Rights

Chapter 1

The Children Act 1989

A Change of Culture

The implementation of the Children Act 1989 on October 14 1991 (appropriately a century after the first Prevention of Cruelty to Children Bill in 1889) represented a major overhaul of the patchwork of new, old and reconstituted legislation which had provided the framework for child care law and practice. There had been many previous Acts — including the Children and Young Persons Act 1933, the Children Act 1948 (which established Children's Departments with designated children's officers), the Children and Young Persons Act 1963 and the Children and Young Persons Act 1969 (both of which carried substantial commitments to the establishment of preventative support services for children and families, as well as providing a framework for protection from abuse and neglect).

More recently the Children Act 1975, hailed as a 'Children's Charter', diminished the importance of the blood tie philosophy in child care social work and facilitated the expansion of fostering and adoption services for many children (particularly older children) deprived of families of their own, while the Child Care Act 1980 was rationalising legislation, which attempted to co-ordinate existing child care law, introducing new measures to allow parents to challenge local authority decision making. In particular, parents were enabled to initiate proceedings, following written notification of the cessation of access by the local authority, and guardians *ad litem* could be appointed, to represent the child's interests.[1] The Children Act 1989, however, amalgamated public and private law in one statute for the first time, dealing with major aspects of children's lives and well-being.

In 1984 The Short Committee announced that:

the time has arrived — indeed it arrived some time ago — for a thorough-going review of the body of statute law, regulations and judicial decisions relating to

---

1 S.12F, Child Care Act 1980 as inserted by Schedule 1 of the Health and Social Security Adjudications Act 1983.

children with a view to the production of a simplified and coherent body of law, comprehensible not only to those operating it but also to those affected by its operation · · ·[2]

In response to the Short Committee's recommendations, the Department of Health and Social Security set up a major review of child care law, to be carried out by an inter-departmental working party. The aim was to produce proposals for changes to child care law, which would provide a framework for developing the best child care practice and meeting more effectively the needs of children and their families.[3] The Review was wide-ranging, but specifically did not include arrangements for dealing with young offenders under the criminal law, nor did it review the case for a unified family court, which was to be the subject of a separate official working party established by the Lord Chancellor and the Home Secretary. The view was that there was a considerable urgency in the need for a review of child care law and that these 'desirable changes' should not be held back pending decisions on a family court. The Review was followed by the publication of a White Paper, *The Law on Child Care and Family Services*.[4]

In the same year that the Short Committee reported, the Law Commission commenced a wide-ranging review of private law as part of a co-ordinated family law programme.[5] The simultaneous reviewing of both public and private law provided an opportunity to bring together both aspects in one comprehensive piece of legislation.

Meanwhile, in the field of social work, four major child abuse enquiries made a significant impact on the child care law review recommendations. They were The Field Fisher Report, The Report of the Committee of Enquiry into the Care and Supervision provided in relation to Maria Colwell (1974), *A Child in Trust*, The Report of the Panel of Enquiry into the circumstances surrounding the death of Jasmine Beckford (1985), The Report of the Review Panel into the death of Heidi Koseda, Hillingdon Area Review Committee (1986) and *A Child in Mind*, the Report of the Commission of Enquiry into the circumstances surrounding the death of Kimberley Carlile (1987).

All four reports raised fundamental concerns about decision making processes in child care social work. Writing in *A Child in Trust*, the Panel of Enquiry was critical of social work philosophies which sought to establish 'a consistent trusting professional relationship with families, rather than emphasising the statutory authority of their role'. As with the Maria Colwell Enquiry in 1974, the reports emphasised the accountability of social services for their work with children and families.

We think, in fact, we have identified and isolated one fundamental aspect of professional response to child abuse that has been overlooked or discarded by modern social work training and practice. It is that the making of a Care Order invests social services with pervasive parental powers. By such a judicial act, society

---

2   House of Commons Second Report from the Social Services Committee, Session 1983/84 *Children in Care*, Vol.1, para. 119, published March 28, 1984.
3   *Review of Child Care Law*, Report to Ministers of an Inter-departmental Working Party, September 1985, DHSS.
4   Cm. 62 (1987).
5   See 'Facing the Future', a discussion paper published by the Law Commission, May 1988, and 'The Ground for Divorce', Law Commission, November 1990.

expects that a child at risk from abuse by its parents will be protected by social services personnel, exercising parental powers effectively and authoritatively on behalf of society. Such a child is a child in trust.[6]

Social workers were made uncomfortably aware of their vulnerability and, just as the number of place of safety orders trebled between 1973 and 1977, following the criticism of social workers' delayed actions in the Maria Colwell Enquiry Report in 1974, so, following subsequent reports enquiring into the deaths of Kimberley Carlile, Tyra Henry, Jasmine Beckford and others, social workers became involved in more interventionist, controlling and authoritarian practice, in which the phrase 'at risk' came to mean at risk from parents, rather than at risk of coming into care. Wardship was used increasingly by local authorities, thus giving other parties few opportunities to challenge decision making and effectively by-passing the scrutiny of the guardian *ad litem*. In this context, the case of *F. v. Wirral Metropolitan Borough Council*[7] was particularly compelling illustrating the powerlessness of parents to challenge local authority decision making or to obtain any redress for what amounted to alienation of their children's affections. This case took more than 10 years to reach the Court of Appeal, during which time, the children involved had grown up.

The pendulum swung wildly between rescue and rehabilitation. The social work profession became polarised increasingly between what Fox called 'kinship defenders' (those who defend the autonomy of the family from state intervention) and 'society as parent protagonists' (child rescuers intervening to save the child from abusing families).[8] In the process, professionals sometimes lost sight of the fact that rehabilitation and rescue are not mutually exclusive, but are different stages along the same continuum.

The *Report of the Enquiry into Child Abuse in Cleveland in 1987*[9] was published amidst a furore of publicity and implied that, once again, social workers had got it wrong. They were accused of removing children unnecessarily and conducting a child sexual witch-hunt.[10] Attention was drawn to the 'secondary' abuse suffered by children in the process of protecting them, and public debate focused, as never before, on the criteria for, and the manner of, state intervention into family life.

The Enquiry strongly endorsed the proposals set out in the White Paper *The Law on Child Care and Family Services*[11] and underlined the urgency of implementing the proposals in the White Paper. However, when the Children Bill was published, there were those who felt that the delicate balance between family and state autonomy achieved in the review, had been disturbed by what was seen as the anti-interventionist lessons of Cleveland. The introduction of S.1(5) in particular — the principle of minimum intervention — was seen as

---

6   *A Child in Trust*, the Report of the Panel of Enquiry into the circumstances surrounding the death of Jasmine Beckford (1985), p.297.
7   [1991] Fam.69, C.A.; 2 All E.R. 648.
8   Fox, 'Two Value Positions in Recent Child Care Law and Practice', June 1982, *British Journal of Social Work*, British Association of Social Workers (BASW) Vol.12, No.3, 265.
9   Cm. 412 (1988).
10 See 'When Salem came to the Boro': *The True Story of the Cleveland Child Abuse Crisis* (1988).
11 Cm.67 (1987).

potentially sacrificing some elements of child protection. The resultant Children Bill was introduced by Lord Mackay in the House of Lords as 'the most comprehensive and far-reaching reform of child law which has come before parliament in living memory'.[12] It passed through both Houses with a very high degree of all party support and was implemented in full (in itself unusual for child care legislation) on 14 October 1991.

The Provisions of the 1989 Act

The 1989 Act provided a unified jurisdiction for a wide range of family proceedings, including both public and private law. It incorporates measures which seek to empower children and provide an appropriate balance between family and state autonomy, by facilitating the establishment of services to help parents fulfil their responsibilities, rather than claim their rights, in relation to their children. It was intended that the centrality of the child should be recognised in all proceedings.

Guiding principles

The 1989 Act contained a number of guiding principles, to be applied to all provisions under the 1989 Act, which together created a new culture for child care law and practice. These principles are as follows:

- the welfare of the child is the paramount consideration;
- wherever possible, the children should be brought up and cared for within their own families;
- parents with children in care should be helped to resume the care of those children as soon as possible;
- this help should be provided as a service to the child and his or her family and should:
  - be provided in partnership with the parents;
  - meet each child's identified needs;
  - be appropriate to the child's race, culture, religion and language;
  - be open to effective independent representations in complaints procedures; and
  - draw upon effective partnership between the local authority and other agencies, including voluntary agencies.
- children should be safe and be protected by effective intervention if they are in danger;
- when dealing with children, courts should ensure that delay is avoided and an order is made only if to do so is better than making no order at all;
- children should be kept informed about what is happening to them and should participate when decisions are made about their future;
- parents will continue to have parental responsibility for their children, even when their children are no longer living with them; parents should be kept

---

12   *Hansard* H.L. Vol. 502, col. 488.

informed and participate when decisions are made about their children's lives;
- there will be an assumption of reasonable contact between parents and children, from the point at which they are received into care. The assumption of reasonable contact is implicit in all proceedings under the 1989 Act.

The welfare checklist

For the first time, the 1989 Act introduced a welfare checklist in S.1(3), which applies to public law cases under Part IV of the 1989 Act and contested private law cases.

Section 1(3) stated that, in considering whether or not to make an order, the court shall have regard to:

(a) the ascertainable wishes and feelings of the child concerned (considered in light of his age and understanding);
(b) his physical, emotional and educational needs;
(c) the likely effect on the child of any change in his circumstances;
(d) the age, sex and background of the child and other characteristics of his which the court considers relevant. [This includes the child's race, ethnic origin, culture and religion];
(e) any harm which he has suffered or is at risk of suffering;
(f) how capable each of his parents, and any other person in relation to whom the court considers the question to be relevant, is of meeting his needs;
(g) the range of powers available to the court under this Act in the proceedings in question.

Core provisions

The 1989 Act is in 12 parts:

Part I   Introduction.
Part II   Orders with respect to children in family proceedings.
Part III   Local authority support for children and families.
Part IV   Care and supervision.
Part V   Protection of children.
Part VI   Community homes.
Part VII   Voluntary homes and voluntary organisations.
Part VIII   Registered children's homes.
Part IX   Private arrangements for fostering children.
Part X   Child minding and day care for young children.
Part XI   The Secretary of State's supervisory functions and responsibility.
Part XII   Miscellaneous and general, including the effect and duration of orders, the amendments of adoption legislation and jurisdiction and procedure.

The legislation is supported by nine volumes of the Children Act 1989 Guidance and Regulations (ten including the index):

Volume 1   Court Orders
Volume 2   Family Support; Day Care and Educational Provision for
           Young Children
Volume 3   Family Placements
Volume 4   Residential Care
Volume 5   Independent Schools
Volume 6   Children with Disabilities
Volume 7   Guardians *ad litem* and other Court-related Issues
Volume 8   Private Fostering and Miscellaneous
Volume 9   Adoption Issues

Significant Changes Brought About by the 1989 Act

Children's rights to make applications of their own volition

The 1989 Act gave children the right to apply directly to the court for leave to apply for any one of the new range of S.8 orders available. The power of the court to make S.8 orders is dealt with in S.10. Where the leave of the court is required to bring any relevant proceedings, the person seeking leave shall file:

● a written request for leave, setting out the reasons for the application, and
● a draft of the application for the making of which leave is sought in the appropriate form in Schedule 1 to the Family Proceedings Courts (Children Act 1989) Rules 1991[13] or, where there is no such form, in writing, together with sufficient copies for one to be served on each respondent.

On considering the request for leave, the court shall:

● grant the request, whereupon the Justices' Clerk shall inform the person making the request of the decision; or
● direct that a date be fixed for a hearing of the request, whereupon the Justices' Clerk shall fix such a date and give such notice as the court directs to the person making the request and to such other persons as the court requires to be notified of the date so fixed.[14]

Where the person applying for leave to make an application for a S.8 order is not the child concerned, the court shall, in deciding whether or not to grant leave, have particular regard to:

● the nature of the proposed application for the S.8 order,
● the applicant's connection with the child,
● any risk there might be of that proposed application disrupting the child's life to such an extent that he would be harmed by it, and
● where the child is being looked after by a local authority:
  ● the authority's plans for the child's future, and

---

13   S.I. 1991 No.1395 (L.17).
14   Family Proceedings Courts (Children Act 1989) Rules 1991, r. 3, see also rr. 1 and 2.

- the wishes and feelings of the child's parents.[15]

Theoretically, the child does not need a guardian *ad litem* or next friend in order to make an application. Rule 9.2A of the Family Proceedings Rules 1991 makes it clear that the child may act alone. However, where the person applying for leave to make an application for a S.8 order is the child concerned, the court may only grant leave if it is satisfied that he has sufficient understanding to make the proposed application for a S.8 order.[16] The court may grant leave, either with or without a hearing, but if they intend to refuse an application, there must be a hearing. Interestingly, the child's welfare is not the paramount consideration at this stage. That question only arises if, and when, the court hear the substantive application.[17]

Listening to children

The 1989 Act emphasised the need to listen to children and involve them in decision making, where they have sufficient understanding. There is also a responsibility, both for the court[18] and for the local authority, to attempt to ascertain the child's wishes and feelings.[19]

Consideration to be given to the child's religious persuasion, racial origin and cultural and linguistic background[20]

For the first time, local authorities were required to give consideration to key matters of race, culture and religion in making any decision with respect to a child, whom they are looking after, or proposing to look after.

Parental responsibility

Parental responsibility means all the rights, duties, powers , responsibilities and authority which, by law, a parent of a child has in relation to the child and his property.[21] The concept of parental responsibility for children, rather than rights in relation to them, is fundamental to the ethos of the 1989 Act. Parental responsibility derives from a concept of a collection of obligations in relation to children, rather than a holding of powers over them. The 1989 Act firmly buried the Victorian concept of children as chattels or possessions, who owe duties to parents, and placed the obligation firmly on the parents, who must consider their responsibilities in relation to their children.

The Act did not provide a list of those responsibilities, but these were fully examined in the Law Commission's Family Law Review of Child Law

---

15   Children Act 1989, S.10(9)(a)–(d).
16   Children Act 1989, S.10(8).
17   See *J.R. v. Merton London Borough* [1992] 2 F.C.R. 174, C.A.
18   S.1.(3)(a).
19   S.22(4)(a) and S.22(5)(a).
20   S.22(5)(c).
21   S.3(1).

Guardianship and Custody, and have been helpfully collated by Brenda Hoggett.[22]

Duties of parents to children before birth. This remains a vexed area of the law, as there are complex conflicts of interests between mothers and children during the gestation period. In certain situations, the High Court have been prepared to take steps to safeguard the life of an unborn baby against the mother's will.[23]

Choosing the child's name. It is the prerogative of the parent to choose the child's name, when registering the child's birth.

Parental responsibility for care and upbringing. It is the responsibility of parents to either look after their children themselves or make adequate arrangements for them to be looked after by others. Parents also have a responsibility to maintain the child financially. Parental responsibility may no longer be lost through passage of time (as was the case under the 1975 Children Act when parents whose children had been in voluntary care for more than three years automatically forfeited their rights in relation to them, in favour of the local authority), nor can parents have their rights removed through a purely administrative process (as was the case in the local authorities' assumption of parental rights, in previous legislation).

Discipline. The question of appropriate and acceptable discipline is particularly fraught. The shocking murder of James Bulger on Merseyside in February 1993, by two 10-year-old boys, focused attention on the perceived need for parents to take on more responsibility for the behaviour of their children. The case of *Sutton London Borough Council v. Davis*[24] confirmed the right of parents to determine arrangements for their children, including arrangements for discipline, regardless of existing local authority guidelines to the contrary. In this case, the mother gave permission to her child minder to smack the child. The Council refused to register the child minder under S.71(7)(a) of the Children Act 1989. EPOCH (End Physical Punishment of Children) launched as a national campaign in 1989 and supported by many child care organisations, continue to campaign vigorously to abolish the physical punishment of children. Discipline patterns are determined largely by the familial and cultural norms prevalent within any group. There is a peculiarly British attitude to corporal punishment, which seems to suggest that it is somehow character building and good for the soul.

Medical treatment. Medical treatment is normally the responsibility of parents, who are required to give consent to the treatment of their child, who is under 16. S.8 of the Family Law Reform Act 1969 gave children over 16 the right to consent to treatment. However, the emergence of the Gillick

---

22   The Law Commission Law Com. 172 (1988), Part 2, paragraphs 2.1–2.30; Hoggett, *Parents and Children* (4th ed., 1993), p. 11.
23   Re. S. (Adult: Refusal of Treatment), [1992] 3 W.L.R. 806.
24   *The Times* March 17, 1994.

competent child[25] established that a child under 16, if of sufficient age and understanding to appreciate what treatment is being proposed, may give his own consent, provided, of course, that the treatment is in his best interests. The provisions of S.44(7), S.43(7) and S.38(6) of the 1989 Act give a child, of sufficient understanding, the right to refuse to submit to examination, or other assessment, which may precede treatment. The right of the child to refuse treatment has been less clear, even when the child appears to have sufficient understanding or has reached the age of 16. The state will listen to the child's views, but will not allow him to die, or to suffer serious harm, through lack of treatment.[26]

Re K., W. and H. (Minors) (Medical Treatment)[27] appears to indicate that anyone with parental responsibility may be able to override the child's views, while *South Glamorgan County Council v. W. and B.*[28] showed the high court ready to exercise its discretion in a non-life threatening situation and, more importantly, apparently to deny the statutory right given by Parliament in the Children Act 1989.

This is an area which clearly illustrates the potential conflict between the right of the child to make an informed decision (and this begs the question of where or from whom the child is to obtain the necessary information), and the right of the state or the parent to make a decision in the child's best interest.[29]

Leaving the country. It is the responsibility of parents to determine whether or when a child may leave the country.

Education. It is the responsibility of the parents to see that children receive both adequate and appropriate education, in order for them to achieve their full educational potential. This frequently brings parents into conflict with local authorities who, in attempting to meet the needs of children in general, may find it difficult to meet the needs of a particular child in a particular area.

Religion. Even where children are being looked after by the local authority, social services departments must give due consideration to the child's religious persuasion, racial origin, cultural and linguistic background.[30] The making of a care order does not transcend the right of the parent to have a say in the child's religious upbringing. Children who are in care must be brought up in the same religion in which they would have been reared, had they not come into care.[31]

---

25   *Gillick v. West Norfolk and Wisbech Area Health Authority and the D.H.S.S.*, [1986] A.C. 112.
26   *Re W. (A Minor)* (Medical Treatment: Court's Jurisdiction) [1993] Fam. 64, C.A. and *Re R. (A Minor)* (Wardship:Consent to Treatment) [1992] Fam. 11, C.A.
27   [1993] 1 F.L.R. 854.
28   [1993] 1 F.L.R. 574.
29   S.8 of the Family Law Reform Act 1987 deals with consent by minors over the age of 16 to surgical, medical and dental treatment. In effect they are to be treated as of full age. Failure to gain consent constitutes a trespass on the person. See further Barbara Mitchels and Alister Prince, *Children Act and Medical Practice* (1st ed., 1992).
30   Children Act 1989, S.22(5)(c).
31   Children Act 1989, S.33(6)(a).

Finance and Property. Parents are financially responsible for the maintenance of their children. The Child Support Act 1991 established the responsibility of both parents, whether or not they have parental responsibility, to support the child. Initial concerns about the effect of the Act on mothers was swiftly replaced by the indignation of fathers who found that, having made a 'clean break' financial arrangement, they were now being reassessed by the Child Support Agency. The establishment of the Agency, designed to ensure that parents shoulder their financial responsibilities in respect of their children, has aroused concerns that questions about the financial upkeep of the child may distort appropriate decision making about where the child is to live. Social services departments have expressed concern that information relating to parents which they hold on their files may be used by the Child Support Agency. To counter this, it has been agreed between the local authority associations and the Agency, that the Agency's officers will not look to social services to provide any information relating to parents which they hold on their files. The agreement covers both information which would enable the Agency to trace an absent parent and information to support what a client has told the Agency, when interviewed about possible reduction in benefit. Any information volunteered by a social worker (for example, to help a client's case) will be treated in the strictest of confidence. However, the regulations do permit the Agency to enquire of a local authority whether or not a child is in their care. Where this information is held in social work records, there is a requirement for it to be passed on. The concern of the social work profession about access to their files by the Agency reflects, in part, concern about being seen as agents of social control rather than social support.[32]

Representation. Many parents advocate very effectively on behalf of their children. However, in cases where there is a conflict of interest between parents and children, there is a need for separate and independent representation. In public law proceedings, both a solicitor and a guardian *ad litem* represent the interests of the child before the court. There is no provision for such dual representation in private law proceedings, although in certain cases the child will have their own solicitor or the official solicitor appointed to represent him.

Marriage. It is part of the responsibility of a parent to give consent for marriage, if the child is 16 or 17. In the past, parents have made children wards of court in order to prevent a marriage taking place. This is little used, now.

In summary, Christina Lyon has identified parental responsibility as responsibilities in relation to:

● the physical care of the child
● discipline
● protection
● maintenance

---

32   See Bird, *Child Maintenance — The Child Support Act 1991* (2nd ed., 1993).

- contact
- education
- religious upbringing
- medical treatment
- agreement to adoption
- appointment of a guardian
- determining a child's surname
- removal of the child out of the jurisdiction
- legal representation
- burial of the child
- consent to marriage.[33]

Parental responsibility is not limited to the biological or legal parents of the child, but may be acquired by those who have an interest in the child's welfare, through application to the court. This list would include uncles, aunts, grandparents and other concerned people. An unmarried father may acquire parental responsibility by making an application to the court to do so and unmarried parents may make a parental responsibility agreement, which allows for both to have parental responsibility. Clearly, the acquiring of parental responsibility constitutes an acceptance of paternity, or maternity, and has accompanying responsibilities under the provisions of the Child Support Act 1991. Parental responsibility and custody do not go together. Parental responsibility is established by the granting of a Parental Responsibility Order and it is perfectly possible for persons to have parental responsibility for a child who never lives with them. The 1989 Act, therefore, created a much larger reservoir of parental responsibility on which a child may potentially draw. It also created some complex situations, particularly in care proceedings, when all those who have parental responsibility must be notified and consulted about what is in the child's best interests.

Accommodating the child near the family home

The 1989 Act directed local authorities providing accommodation for children to ensure that the accommodation is near the child's home. It also directed (S.23(7)(b)) that siblings should be accommodated together.

Contact

The 1989 Act emphasised the importance of contact between parents, children, siblings and the extended family. The assumption of reasonable contact permeates all proceedings under the 1989 Act, even, and perhaps most particularly, during the initial period of removal of the child, following emergency proceedings. The new, wider, concept of access includes indirect contacts, for example, telephone calls, birthday cards and letters. Arguably, new attitudes to contact and the presumption in its favour have led to a significant reappraisal of current practice.

---

33   Lyon, *The Law Relating to Children* (1993), chap.4, paras. 79–97.

Preventing family breakdown

Local authorities have responsibilities, under Part III of the 1989 Act, to prevent family breakdown through the provision of a variety of services. For the first time, children with disabilities are included in the definitions of children in need. Schedule 2 of the 1989 Act should be read in conjunction with Part III, as it provides considerable detail about the range and scope of the services which local authorities are called upon to provide.[34]

Partnership with parents

The *Review of Child Care Law* emphasised the importance of monitoring family links 'to care for the child in partnership, rather than in opposition to, his parents and to work towards his return to them.'[35] This approach is endorsed in *The Care of Children — Principles and Practice in Regulations and Guidance*,[36] a summary of principles governing the care of children published by the Department of Health as part of their guidance (for a full list of these principles, see Chapter 11, Appendix 1). Public care should be a supplement of, rather than a substitute for, family life. Although the idea of a shared care order was not included in the Act, nevertheless the underlying ethos is of partnership, rather than compulsion.

The introduction of representation and complaints procedures

Section 26 of the 1989 Act required local authorities to establish representations, including complaints procedures. The introduction of the new procedures reflected a change of ethos, also found in the National Health Service and Community Care Act 1990. The aim was to emphasise the accountability of service providers to service users in all health and social service provision, and reflected a move towards more consumer-led services. The question of how effective complaints procedures are is examined in Chapter 10.

One criterion for care

The 1989 Act established one route into care, through one set of criteria. Section 31(2) included not only the harm that the child is suffering, but any significant harm that the child is likely to suffer in the future. Looking to the future will allow care proceedings to cover many situations which would formerly have been heard in wardship proceedings in the High Court. The threshold criteria laid down at S.1.5 for making the care or supervision order are:

---

34   See also Jane Gibbins *The Children Act 1989 and Family Support: Principles into Practice* (1992), Department of Health, London HMSO.
35   *Review of Child Care Law* (1985), Department of Health and Social Security, para. 2.8.
36   *The Care of Children — Principles and Practice in Regulations and Guidance* (1989), HMSO, p. 18.

(a) that the child concerned is suffering, or is likely to suffer, significant harm; and
(b) that the harm, or likelihood of harm, is attributable to:
   (i) the care given to the child, or likely to be given to him if the order were not made, not being what it would be reasonable to expect a parent to give him; or
   (ii) the child being beyond parental control; and
(c) that making the order or any order would be better for the child than making no order at all.

'Harm' means ill-treatment or the impairment of health or development, which in turn means physical, intellectual, emotional, social or behavioural development. 'Health' includes both physical and mental health and 'ill-treatment' includes sexual abuse and forms of ill-treatment which are not physical. In situations where the question of significant harm is considered in relation to the child's health or development, that health or development shall be compared with that which could reasonably be expected of a similar child.

The question of the precise interpretation of 'is suffering or is likely to suffer' was extensively examined in *Re M. (A Minor) Care Orders: Threshold Condition*.[37] In supporting the approach taken by Eubank J in *Northamptonshire County Council v S and Others*,[38] the House of Lords supported the decision of Bracewell J that the correct approach is that which relates 'is suffering' to the period immediately before child protection procedures were first mobilised. Only then should the court move on to examine the range of Section 8 orders available as alternatives.

The principle of minimum intervention

Section 1(5) stipulates that 'where a court is considering whether or not to make one or more orders under this Act with respect to the child, it shall not make the order or any of the orders unless it considers that doing so would be better for the child than making no order at all.' This provision is intended not as a deterrent to the making of care orders, but as an opportunity to make a realistic assessment of the likely relevant outcomes for the child.

Substantial extension of the role and powers of guardians ad litem in public law proceedings

Guardians *ad litem* are appointed earlier and more often, in a wider range of specified proceedings and, in addition, take on a significant new case management role, as set out in S.41 of the 1989 Act and the Family Proceedings Courts (Children Act 1989) Rules 1991. In particular, guardians are appointed in applications for Emergency Protection and Secure Accommodation Orders.[39]

---

37   September [1994] Fam. Law 501.
38   [1993] 1 FLR 554, at 557.
39   S.44 and S.25 respectively.

A unified jurisdiction

The Children Act created a concurrent jurisdiction for a wide range of family proceedings in Magistrates' Courts, Family Proceedings Courts, County Courts and the High Courts. The majority of cases start in the Family Proceedings Court, but from there they may be transferred upwards to the County or High Court or sideways to other Family Proceedings Courts in different areas, usually for the purpose of avoiding delay.

Restricted use of wardship

Section 7 of the Family Law Reform Act 1969, giving the High Court power to place a ward of court in care or under supervision of a local authority has ceased to have effect.[40] No court shall exercise the High Court's inherent jurisdiction with respect to children:

(a) so as to require a child to be placed in the care, or put under the supervision of a local authority;

(b) so as to require the child to be accommodated by or on behalf of a local authority;

(c) so as to make a child who is the subject of a care order a ward of court; or

(d) for the purpose of conferring, on any local authority, power to determine any question that has arisen, or which may arise, in connection with any aspect of parental responsibility for a child.

No application for any exercise of the court's inherent jurisdiction with respect to children may be made by a local authority, unless the authority has obtained the leave of the court.[41]

The introduction of apprehended or likely harm in the future as grounds for care proceedings, together with the package of S.8 orders mean that the need for cases to be heard in wardship is substantially reduced. The 1989 Act made wardship and care incompatible and local authorities are no longer allowed to invoke the inherent jurisdiction of the High Court as an alternative to public law proceedings, except as set out in S.100(4).

Designation of adoption as family proceedings

Under the 1989 Act, adoption and freeing for adoption have become family proceedings, in which any of the orders available under the Children Act 1989 may be made as an alternative to the order applied for.

Other remedies

Judicial review An application for judicial review may only be made with the leave of the court or by someone who can demonstrate sufficient interest in the

---

40 S.100(1).
41 S.100(3).

matter. The Wednesbury principle[42] established that local authorities must abide by the law and should not act unlawfully or unreasonably. They should also follow proper procedures in reaching their decisions. However, the precise criteria for judicial review are not clear. Before the Children Act was implemented, it was thought that there might well be increased applications for judicial review, partly because of the responsibilities of local authorities for children in need are potentially very wide-ranging. In the event, the predicted spate of judicial review did not happen and indeed has been discouraged by the courts in favour of pursuing representation and complaints procedures under S.26. However, it is an avenue well worth exploring, and potential applicants now have a wealth of guidelines to cite in support of cases. Cretney and Masson[43] have identified three areas in which courts have been willing to review decisions taken. They are where the authority:

- has failed to consider issues as required by statute;[44]
- has fettered its discretion;[45]
- has acted without adequate enquiry.[46]

It is probable that the full possibilities of judicial review, as a mechanism to challenge post Children Act practice, have not been fully explored.

Judicial review may be appropriate in three situations, as outlined by Christina Lyon:

> *Firstly*, if the complaint is that the decision reached is unreasonable, rather than that it is the result of procedural irregularity, judicial review is the only means of challenge. The duty to consult under Section 22(4) does not make judicial review redundant.
> *Secondly*, the duty to consult only applies to a child whom the local authority is looking after, and so would not apply to situations where a case conference never considered a proposal to look after the child concerned, if the child was not in need.
> *Thirdly*, Judicial Review may continue to provide a means of challenging whether a decision taken, by a parent or local authority, paid due regard to the child's welfare.[47]

However, as Lyon and Cruz point out, there may be a greater possibility of challenging local authority decision making following the decision in *Re B. (Minors) (Children in Care: Contact, Local Authority Plans)*.[48]

The Ombudsman The local Commissioner for Administration, or Ombudsman, investigates complaints of maladministration. The drawbacks of the procedure are the length of time that it takes to carry out the investigation and the lack of clear sanctions. However, the resultant report does have to be

---

42 *Associated Provincial Picture Houses Ltd v. Wednesbury Corporation* [1948] 1 K.B. 223.
43 Cretney and Masson, *Principles of Family Law* (1990), p.654, Wardship and Judicial Review.
44 *Att.-Gen., ex rel. Tilley v. Wandsworth London Borough Council* [1981] 1 W.L.R. 854.
45 *Liddle v. Sunderland Borough Council* (1983) 13 Fam. Law and *R. v. Avon County Council, ex p.K.* [1986] 1 F.L.R. 443, both cases regarding decisions being made about the closure of children's homes, without due regard for the welfare of the child.
46 *R. v. Bedfordshire County Council, ex p.C.* [1987] 1 F.L.R. 239 and *R. v. Wandsworth Borough Council, ex p.P.* [1989] C.O.D. 262.
47 Lyon and de Cruz, *Child Abuse* (2nd ed., 1993) para 9.9.1.
48 [1993] 1 F.L.R. 543.

published and may provide the impetus for changes to be made. In January 1986 IRCHIN (Independent Representation for Children in Need) made a complaint to the Ombudsman about Rochdale Metropolitan Borough Council's administration of their panel of guardians *ad litem* and reporting officers. The resultant discontinuation report, based on the Council's acknowledgement and full apology for the matters identified, was published in April 1989.[49] The matter complained about was the local authority's maladministration in withholding from the court (at the request of the National and Local Government Officers' Association (NALGO) the names of duly appointed sessional panel members not employed by the local authority.

Orders

Section 8 Orders

The 1989 Act introduced four new Orders under section 8, Residence Orders, Contact Orders, Prohibited Steps Orders and Specific Issue Orders.

A *Residence Order* is an Order settling the arrangements to be made as to the person with whom the child is living. It is possible to make joint Residence Orders[50] and, in these cases, the court may specify the periods for which the child is to live in the different households concerned.

A *Contact Order* is an Order requiring the person with whom the child lives or is to live to allow the child to visit or stay with the person named in the Order or for that person and the child otherwise to have contact with each other. Contact can include indirect contact, letters, telephone calls and birthday and Christmas cards and it may allow for contact with extended family members, siblings and friends as well as parents. It is also for stopping contact.

A *Prohibited Steps Order* is an Order which stipulates the steps which may not be taken by a parent in meeting his parental responsibility for a child, and which also specifies the steps which may not be taken by any person, without the consent of the court. The Order does not impose an absolute prohibition. The steps specified may still be taken with the leave of the court. *Nottinghamshire County Council v. P.*[51] makes it clear that a Prohibited Steps Order may not be used to obtain a Residence or Contact Order 'by the back door'.

A *Specific Issue Order* is an Order giving directions for the purpose of determining a specific question which has arisen, or which may arise, in connection with any aspect of parental responsibility for a child. Examples of specific issues would be concerning the education or health of the child.

The four S.8 Orders are available in all private law proceedings. However, they are subject to a number of restrictions in public law proceedings. A local

---

49   Discontinuation Report by the local Ombudsman on an investigation into complaint no.
     1440/C/85 against Rochdale Metropolitan Borough Council.
50   S.11(4).
51   [1993] 2 F.L.R. 134, C.A.

authority cannot apply for a Contact or Residence Order or have either Order made in its favour. A child in care may apply for a Residence Order, but for none of the other S.8 Orders. No court may make any S.8 Order, other than a Residence Order, with respect to a child who is in the care of a local authority.[52] It could be said that S.9 effectively filters the right of parents and children to question local authority decision making.

The Emergency Protection Order[53]

The Emergency Protection Order replaces the Place of Safety Order. Anyone may apply for an Emergency Protection Order, but an Order may only be made if the court is satisfied that:

(a) there is reasonable cause to believe that the child is likely to suffer significant harm if:
  (i) he is not removed to accommodation provided by, or on behalf of, the applicant; or
  (ii) he does not remain in the place in which he is then being accommodated;
(b) in the case of an application made by a local authority:
  (i) enquiries are being made with respect to the child under S.47(1)(b); and
  (ii) those enquiries are being frustrated by access to the child being unreasonably refused to a person authorised to seek access and the applicant has reasonable belief that access to the child is required as a matter of urgency; or
(c) in the case of an application made by an authorised person:
  (i) the applicant has reasonable cause to suspect that a child is suffering, or is likely to suffer, significant harm;
  (ii) the applicant is making enquiries with respect to the child's welfare; and
  (iii) those enquiries are being frustrated by access to the child being unreasonably refused to a person authorised to seek access and the applicant has reasonable cause to believe that access to the child is required as a matter of urgency.[54]

The Order:

● lasts for eight days, with one possible extension of seven days, making a maximum duration of 15 days;
● may only be extended once;
● may be sought either to remove or to detain a child;
● assumes reasonable contact will be allowed between parents and children;

---

52 S.9. See the controversial *A. v. Liverpool City Council* [1982] A.C. 363, which prevented parents using wardship to question local authority decision making.
53 S.44. See Fricker, Adams, Pearce, Salter, Stevens and Whybrow, *Family Courts — Emergency Remedies and Procedures: Preparing, Making and Enforcing Family and Child Law Applications*, (2nd ed., 1993).
54 S.44(1).

● allows parents and children to challenge the order at any time although the challenge will only be heard after 72 hours.

The application may be heard *ex parte* or on notice. The purpose of the application is to protect the child from significant harm, by removing him to a place of safety. Emergency Protection Orders are not family proceedings, so the other Orders available under the Children Act 1989 do not apply, nor do the provisions of the welfare checklist in S.1(3). However, the child, like the parents, has the right to apply to discharge the Order and local authorities should inform children of their rights in relation to discharge.

The Child Assessment Order[55]

This Order had not existed in previous legislation and was introduced at a late stage in the debate on the Bill, after considerable discussion. It is designed to cover situations where there is reasonable cause to suspect that a child is suffering significant harm, but is not at immediate risk and the applicant believes that a medical, psychiatric or other assessment is required. If the parents are unwilling to co- operate, the local authority can apply for a Child Protection Order.

The Order lasts for a maximum of seven days and directs the type and nature of the assessment which is to be carried out and whether the child should be kept away from home for the purposes of the assessment.

The Education Supervision Order[56]

Under the 1989 Act, non-school attendance is no longer a ground for care proceedings. Instead, the Education Supervision Order, which is applied for by the local education authority rather than the social services department, places a child of compulsory school age, who is not being properly educated, under the supervision of the local education authority. Any Care Order made subsequently automatically ends the Education Supervision Order.

The Family Assistance Order[57]

This is a voluntary Order which offers short-term advice, assistance and befriending to families involved in situations of conflict, such as divorce.

Supervision Orders

The threshold criteria for Supervision Orders are the same as those for Care Orders. Supervision Orders are flexible, in that requirements can be attached

---

55   S.43.
56   S.36.
57   S.17.

to the Orders to contribute to their effective use. While the Supervision Order is in force, it shall be the duty of the supervisor:

(a) to advise, assist and befriend a supervised child;
(b) to take such steps as are reasonably necessary to give effect to the order; and
(c) to consider whether or not to apply to the court for a variation or discharge[58] where:
     (i) the order is not wholly complied with; or
     (ii) the supervisors consider that the order may no longer be necessary.

Section 38 provides for the making of interim Supervision Orders.

In making any of these Orders, and in all cases, the court must give paramount consideration to the child's welfare[59], shall not make an Order unless it thinks that to do so would be better for the child than making no Order at all[60] and shall have regard to the requirements of the welfare checklist, as laid out in S.1(3).

The court must also have regard to the general principle that any delay in proceedings is likely to prejudice the child's welfare and must draw up a timetable giving appropriate directions for keeping to the stated programme.[61]

What the 1989 Act does not do

The 1989 Act does not:

● provide a non-adversarily based family court;
● deal with children as offenders, or offer any philosophical reconciliation of 'troubled' and 'troublesome'. The general lack of clarity and more robust approach by the courts was illustrated by Mann LJ in *C v DPP*[62] when he announced that there was no longer a presumption in English law that a young person between the ages of 10 and 14 was incapable of telling the difference between right and wrong.
● provide the resources to underpin the service provisions necessary to implement the 1989 Act.

The lack of resources is particularly worrying in relation to the provision of family support services to children and families. Part III and Schedule 2 of the 1989 Act outline the very considerable responsibilities placed on local authorities to attempt to prevent family breakdown. The concept of family support goes beyond that of prevention (particularly of prevention of reception into care) to that of promoting children's welfare within their families, encompassing a very wide range of service provision and including services which improve the general quality of life for children, such as toy libraries, drop-in centres and appropriate day care facilities.

---

58 S.35(1).
59 S.1.
60 S.1(5).
61 S.1(1) and S.11.
62 *The Times* March 30, 1994.

In addition, the definition of children in need in S.17(10) is very wide and includes all children with disabilities. There are approximately 360,000 children under 16 with physical and learning disabilities in Britain.[63] Local authorities face very great demands on their time and resources and both policies and practices will have to change to ensure that family support is given the priority it demands. An Audit Commission report which looked at co-ordinating community child health care and social services for children in need confirmed earlier impressions that there has been a comparative over-emphasis of resources on child protection procedures and statutory interventions rather than on substantial support services.[64]

Areas of concern

Children's Rights The Children Act 1989 contains substantial measures which confer specific rights on children and young people. These are:

- the right to seek leave to initiate proceedings,[65]
- the right to have their wishes and feelings considered in decision making,[66]
- the right to refuse medical treatment, or other examination,[67]
- the right to give unsworn evidence,[68]
- the right to have their race, culture, religion and first language considered in decision making,[69]
- the right to make representations or complaints about services received from local authorities.[70]

However, some of these 'rights' appear to have been circumscribed by the judiciary, who appear to be concerned about both the potential increase in precocious challenges to adult authority and the inadvisability of exposing children to court proceedings. The landmark decision in *Gillick v. West Norfolk and Wisbech Area Health Authority and the DHSS*[71] established the right of the competent child to override parental decisions, subject to a satisfactory level of age or understanding of the matter to be decided — in this case the right of a teenage girl to receive confidential contraceptive advice. Matters have moved further since then, and the courts (who are, of course, well aware of public opinion) are apparently increasingly prepared to override

---

63 Bone and Meltzer, *The Prevalence of Disability among Children* (1989), Office of Population Censuses and Surveys, HMSO.
64 See *Children in Need and their Families. A New Approach — A Guide to Part III of the Children Act 1989 for Local Authority Councillors*, 1990, Booklet, University of Leicester, School of Social Work and Faculty of Law and the Department of Health; *Seen but not Heard: Co-ordinating Community Child Health and Social Services for Children in Need — Detailed Evidence and Guidelines for Managers and Practitioners*, The Audit Commission, HMSO, 1994.
65 S.10.
66 S.1(3) and S.22(4) and (5).
67 S.38(6), S.43(8) and S.44(7).
68 S.96(2).
69 S.22(5)(c).
70 S.26.
71 [1986] A.C. 112.

the wishes of the competent child, whether in life-threatening,[72] or non-life-threatening situations.[73]

It is very difficult for children to initiate proceedings on their own account (see Chapter 9) and, although the court has a duty to listen to children, the practical interpretation of that duty leaves much to be desired. Some children have had difficulty in being allowed to attend court, or, once there , in having their views heard. In this respect, children involved in public law proceedings are much better served than those in private law applications, who have no party status, no guardian *ad litem* and no solicitor. The Act is silent on why there should be such sharp differentiation between representational rights of the child in different proceedings under the same Act.

Concerns have also been expressed[74] that public and media antagonism to children heightened, influenced by the murder of James Bulger in Liverpool by two ten-year-old boys in February 1993 and by what appears to be a well orchestrated media emphasis on juvenile crime, particularly crimes committed by those under the age of criminal responsibility. The calls for stronger discipline may have had some bearing on the decision in the Sutton child minding case, in which the right of a parent to give permission for a child minder to smack her charge, in defiance of local authorities' guidelines to the contrary, was upheld.[75]

On the positive side, the decision by Thorpe J in *Re H. (A Minor)*[76] upheld the right of a fifteen-year-old to instruct his own solicitor, when he disagreed with the views of the guardian. Solicitors must ensure adequate representation for children by taking instructions from them, rather than the guardian in a divergence situation. Under rule 11(3) of the Family Proceedings Courts (Children Act 1989) Rules 1991,[77] the guardian must inform the court when the child is instructing the solicitor direct, as the guardian may then be given leave to have legal representation, as well as the child. In this case, the child was intelligent but disturbed, yet as there was no expert evidence to suggest that the child was suffering from any disorder leading to a lack of sufficient understanding, the solicitor was in error and the child had not been properly represented. As a subsidiary issue, the judgment indicated that the level of competence required by the child to refuse medical examination is greater than that required to give separate instructions. (See further Chapter 5, Representation in Action.)

Problems in full party status for children Throughout the consultation period, the passage of the Bill through the House of Lords and, subsequently the passage through the House of Commons, constant reassurances were given that children would have full party status in all proceedings under the new Act. The fact that children were enabled to initiate proceedings on their own

---

72   *Re W. (A Minor) (Medical Treatment)* [1992] Fam. Law 541.
73   *South Glamorgan County Council v. W. and B.* [1993] 1 F.L.R. 574.
74   The Gulbenkian Foundation, Children's Rights Development Unit, Children's Legal Centre and others.
75   *Sutton London Borough Council v. Davis, The Times* March 17, 1994.
76   [1992] 2 F.C.R. 330.
77   S.I. 1991 No. 1395.

account was a considerable step forward. However, in practice, there are a number of other problems. Children do not have an automatic right to full party status, but have to apply for leave to make applications for any of the S.8 Orders, which the courts may refuse, on the grounds that the child must have a sufficient understanding of the proceedings and matters in question in order for leave to be granted. In addition, the court must be satisfied that the application *is* in the best interests of the child. The right to apply, therefore, is subordinate to judgment about both the child's competence and welfare. Fears arising from a number of cases in which children have sought to 'divorce their parents' led to a practice direction requiring applications by children to be transferred to the High Court, which may prove to be a deterrent for both children and solicitors. Children may be overawed by the formality of the High Court, while solicitors may be reluctant to test out their skills over relatively new ground, in such a high profile arena. Further, there is no provision, or suggestion, as to how children are to be informed of these rights.

On February 22, 1993, Sir Stephen Brown issued the following President's direction on applications by children:

> Under section 10 of the 1989 Act, the prior leave of the court is required in respect of applications by the child concerned for section 8 Orders. Rule 4.3 of the Family Proceedings Rules 1991 (S.I. 1991 No. 1247) and rule 3 of the Family Proceedings Courts (Children Act 1989) Rules (S.I. 1991 No. 1395) set out the procedure to be followed when applying for leave. Such applications raise issues which are more appropriate for determination in the High Court and should be transferred there for hearing.[78]

The deficiencies in leaving care provisions for young people[79]   Section 24 imposes no direct duty on local authorities to provide specific resources, either in cash or in kind, to the 11,000 young people leaving care each year. The 1989 Act was criticised for its lack of cross referencing with other relevant pieces of legislation, most notably those relating to housing and social security. (See further Chapter 11, Children in Need, Children at Risk and Children in Care.)

Risk of drift in care for children in accommodation[80]   Concerns were expressed about the practical difficulties in negotiating agreements with parents, in a situation in which no notice of removal of the child from accommodation was required. This was seen as a regressive step and a retreat from the situation under the Children Act 1975, which established the principle that parents could lose their parental rights, not through any offence, but purely through the passage of time. This came about because of research findings which indicated that large numbers of children were 'drifting' into and out of care without clear and permanent decisions being made about their lives.[81]

---

78   Practice Direction [1993] 1 All. E.R. 820.
79   S.24.
80   S.20.
81   See Rowe and Lambert, *Children Who Wait* (1973), Association of British Adoption and Fostering Agencies publications.

In practice, the new arrangements have provided an impetus for social service departments to work in partnership with parents and to involve them in planning for their child's future. Support services should be offered, under Part III of the Act, before consideration is given to proceeding to Parts IV and V. However, the new arrangements have also given rise to a large increase in the numbers of informal contractual agreements entered into between families and local authorities. Arguably, all children, whether in or out of care, have the right to some notice about imminent changes in their lives, whether these involve going to visit grandparents at the weekend or being prepared for a move of house, a change of family routine or a holiday. Many practitioners considered that 48 hours notice would not be unreasonable and would not be detrimental to the much welcomed new climate of partnership with parents.[82] Local authorities would have parental responsibility during those 48 hours.

Doubts about a Child Assessment Order   Opinion has been divided about the necessity for the new Child Assessment Order, with the National Society for the Prevention of Cruelty to Children (NSPCC) advocating strongly for its inclusion during the passage of the Bill through the House of Lords and the Association of Directors of Social Services expressing concern about the possibility of such an Order lowering the level of state intervention into family life, by requiring lower threshold criteria for the making of the Order than that required by S.31 Care Orders or S.44 Emergency Protection Orders. In the event, the NSPCC view prevailed, but in practice the Order has not been used extensively.

Lack of an 'Ouster' Order   The Act contains no provision which would provide for the removal of the alleged perpetrator of an abuse, rather than the child, from the family home. However, where it appears to a local authority that a child living in particular premises is suffering, or is likely to suffer, ill treatment at the hands of another person who is living on those premises, and that other person proposes to move from the premises, the authority may assist that other person to obtain alternative accommodation. Assistance given under this paragraph may be in cash.[83] It is unlikely that a Prohibited Steps Order may be used to oust one partner from the matrimonial home.[84]

Discretion in the provision of services to children in need   Section 17(1) sets out the duty of each local authority to provide services to children and their families:

> it shall be general duty of every local authority (in addition to the other duties imposed on them by this Part):
> (a) to safeguard and promote the welfare of children within their area who are in need; and

---

82   See further Thoburn and Lewis, Partnership with Parents in Need of Protection in *The Children Act 1989 and Family Support: Principles into Practice* (1992), HMSO, chap. 4.
83   Scheds. 2, 5, para 1(1) and (2).
84   *Nottinghamshire County Council v. P.* [1994] Fam. 18.

(b) so far as is consistent with that duty, to promote the upbringing of such children by the said families, by providing a range and level of services appropriate to those children's needs.

In practice, each local authority has written its own 'children in need' document, stating what it is able to provide, rather than what it is statutorily required to provide. Inevitably, in a situation where preventive services to children and families are resource rather than needs led, some rather large gaps in service provision have appeared. The question of the sanctions which may be imposed on local authorities who fail to provide services is problematic. *R v Barnet LBC ex parte B and others*[85] is typical in reinforcing the view that it is essentially a matter for each local authority to determine how it shall discharge its duties, and that remedies should be sought through S.26 complaints procedures rather than judicial review.

The lack of an independent guardian *ad litem* and reporting officer service   Although the role of the guardian *ad litem* is considerably extended under the 1989 Act, panels continue to be administered and funded by local authorities. The lack of central funding and the conflicts of interest inherent in the administration of the service by one party to the proceedings continue to be areas of great concern, despite assurances from the Lord Chancellor that the restructuring of the guardian *ad litem* service is part of his rolling programme of reform of the family jurisdiction. An amendment to the Children Bill put down by the British Association of Social Workers, which sought to establish an independent service, received an overwhelming consensus of support, not just from all the national child care organisations, but also the local government bodies — the Association of Directors of Social Services, the Association of County Councils and the Association of Metropolitan Authorities. In the event, the house of Lords accepted the Lord Chancellor's assurances that the independence of the guardian would be a matter of high and continuing priority. The inclusion of rule 10(7)(a) of the Family Proceedings Courts (Children Act 1989) Rules 1991,[86] which allows an ex-local authority employed social worker to be appointed as a guardian *ad litem* in that same local authority, somewhat undermines the assurances which were given before implementation. Certainly, guardians have felt compromised by these arrangements and the 'independence' of their views may be critically viewed by parents and other parties (see Chapter 3).

Potential weaknesses of the new guiding principle for local authorities' child care social work   Section 22 gives a commitment to safeguard the welfare of the child, but not to safeguard the welfare of the child *throughout its childhood*, as was the case in S.18 of the Child Care Act 1980, which it supersedes. Local authorities have to attend to the child's wishes and feelings, but they also have to attend to the wishes and feelings of a fairly extensive list

---

85   [1994] 2 FCR 781.
86   S.I. 1991 No. 1395.

of other people, some of whose interests may conflict with those of the child. However, the welfare of the child should be paramount.[87]

Shortage of adequately trained staff   Approximately 55,000 people were given training on the provision of the 1989 Act. The combined effects of the implementation of the 1989 Act, closely followed by implementation of the National Health Service and Community Care Act 1990, which introduced new arrangements for care management, mean that local authority social services departments have experienced a period of hiatus. There are considerable increases in the number of social workers needed, as well as increasing pressures to develop new skills of care management and assessment. There is a need for an expanded and nationally co-ordinated programme of training at both pre- qualifying and post-qualifying levels, particularly bearing in mind that the lack of a three-year qualifying course debars all but Southern Irish social workers from working in many countries outside the UK.

Concern about the detail of the 1989 Act   There was concern among child care law professionals about the extent to which the detail of the 1989 Act was left to rules and regulations. In the event, the Department of Health, with creditable speed, produced volumes of Regulations and Guidance, which together provide a sound and comprehensive framework for future child care social work.

The avoidance of delay   When the Children Act 1989 was implemented in October 1991 it was anticipated that cases would be completed within a twelve week timetable. Three years later, delay was endemic at all levels of the court system, with particular problems at County Court level, and an average completion period of 23.2 weeks per case.

Adoption and the Children Act 1989

Adoption law is under review[88] and in November 1993 a White Paper '*Adoption: The Future*' was published.[89] However, the 1989 Act introduced some changes in both law and practice as it relates to adoption and freeing for adoption applications.[90]

Amendments to adoption law are to be found in Schedule 10 to the 1989 Act; some important repeals of the Adoption Act 1976 are found in Schedule 15. The changes fall into three groups:

(a) amendments consequent upon changes in concepts and terminology introduced by the 1989 Act;

---

87   S.1(1).
88   *Review of Adoption Law: Report to the Ministers of an interdepartmental working group*, October 1992, Department of Health and Welsh Office.
89   For information on the impact of the Children Act 1989 on adoption laws see Children Act 1989 Guidance and Regulations Vol.9, Adoption Issues. There is a discussion of some of these issues in the Inter-departmental Review of Adoption Law, Discussion Paper No.1, *The Nature and Effect of Adoption*, Department of Health, September 1991 (para.57).
90   Cm. 2288 (1993).

(b) amendments designed to harmonise adoption law across the jurisdiction of England, Wales, Scotland and Northern Ireland;
(c) a small number of substantive changes, designed to remedy particular defects in adoption law or to introduce improvements, for which an opportunity had been awaited.

Changes introduced by the Children Act 1989

The introduction of S.8 Orders   Adoption proceedings are designated family proceedings so the court can make S.8 Orders of its own motion, at any stage of the adoption proceedings and without the need for a formal application for one of the relevant Orders by the parties concerned. This extends the court's powers, compared with S.14(3) of the 1976 Adoption Act (repealed by the Children Act 1989, Sched. 15). S.8 Orders may be made in favour of any individual, in respect of any child who is the subject of adoption proceedings. The court will be able to make S.8 Orders as an alternative to adoption, where parental agreement has been withheld. A court may make a Residence Order in favour of the prospective adopters, even though the parents have not agreed to the adoption and the court has not dispensed with their agreement. The scope of the proceedings is therefore considerably widened. Prospective adopters, who apply for an Adoption Order, may find their proceedings joined with a natural parent's S.8 or S.34 application for residence or contact, in a hearing in which the court may choose from the much enlarged range of Orders, rather than being restricted to either making or refusing the particular Order for which application is made.

Contact   The availability of S.8 Contact Orders in adoption signals a move away from the traditional clean-break concept of adoption. In the 1950s, 1960s and 1970s, the majority of adoptions involved the placement of very young infants, whose natural parents were not opposing the Adoption Order. With the growth in the numbers of older children being adopted from care, there has been a corresponding growth in the numbers of parents who oppose a final break with their children, even in situations where they may be painfully aware that they themselves are unable to provide the consistent care that the child needs. In particular, relinquishing parents often crave for news of the child, confirmation that he is well and happy and notification about significant events in his life, for example when he leaves school, when he marries or has children of his own. The availability of S.8 Contact Orders opens up a whole spectrum of choices, ranging from totally closed to totally open adoption situations. Of all the new provisions the S.8 Contact Orders have had the most impact on practice.

The possibility of adoption with contact is only feasible if it is underpinned by good practice and reasonable contact, starting from the time of the child's emergency reception into care and ending with the S.8 Contact Order in adoption. This has significant implications for the recruitment and training of prospective foster and adoptive parents, who must be prepared to work on sustaining and maintaining important links for the child, both with adoptive agencies and with natural parents. Conditions may be attached to the Contact Order, which provide either direct or indirect contacts such as telephone calls, Christmas and birthday cards, letters and photographs. Contact Orders can be made in addition to an Adoption Order, for example in favour of the birth mother, of grandparents or between separated siblings. The Contact Order may be made at the same time as the child is freed for adoption. Conditions can be attached to the Order, which must be adhered to by the person in whose favour the Order is made and also by any other person with parental responsibility for the child.

First or paramount consideration   Under S.1(1) of the 1989 Act, courts are directed to give paramount consideration to the welfare of the child. Adoption legislation is different, in that it directs the court to give first consideration to the welfare of the child throughout its childhood and, so far as is practical, ascertain the child's own wishes and feelings about the decision, giving due consideration to them having regard to his age and understanding.[91] 'First consideration' implies that the child's welfare is not paramount, but is just the first consideration, amongst other considerations, including the dictates of natural justice, the passage of time or public safety.

In considering the implications of the availability of Contact Orders in adoption, it must be remembered that courts previously had powers to attach conditions to Adoption Orders, including, if the court wished, conditions about contact. There is, therefore, little substantive change in this respect. However, courts were traditionally reluctant to impose such conditions, except where all the parties, including the adoptive parents, agreed. Adoption Orders with access conditions have been rare and it cannot be assumed that the availability of the new Orders will revolutionise all practice. Whatever Order is made, it is unlikely to be successful if it does not have the commitment of all the adults involved in the situation, as well as the child. Preparation of both adoptive parents and children for an open adoption must be painstaking and thorough. Much will depend on the circumstances and undertakings given at the time of the child's original placement. Courts will be reluctant to make adoption subject to Contact Orders in situations where the adoptive parents are unwilling to co-operate or are unhappy about the proposed arrangements, or where there is no post- adoption support forthcoming from the adoption agency.

The right to S.8 applications does not extend to the natural parents of a child who has been freed for adoption[92] nor do the provisions apply to a child who has actually been adopted.[93] Such parents or children would need to seek leave to apply.

The Adoption Contact Register   Schedule 10, para.21 of the 1989 Act introduces the Adoption Contact Register (the Register) established in England and Wales on May 1, 1991. The Register is kept at the General Register Office by the Registrar General. It is in two parts, one for adoptees and one for

---

91   Adoption Act 1976, S.6.
92   *Re C. (Minors)* (Adoption: Residence Order) [1992] 1 F.L.R. 115, C.A.
93   *Re S. (A Minor) The Times*, March 8, 1993.

relatives. Through the Register, relatives, as well as birth mother and fathers, are able to register interest in a particular child in a safe and confidential manner. The decision about whether or not to establish contact is left to the adoptee. Beyond recording in the Register whether they would prefer to be contacted or not to be contacted, relinquishing relatives have no control over the process (Adoption Act 1976. S.51(1)-(9). The Register is confidential and is not available to the public. Anyone wishing to register must pay a fee of £35, a cost which may well provide a deterrent to young mothers, with little income, who might otherwise consider using the Register. The Register is very similar to the Birth-Link Register already established in Scotland.

Since 1975, adopted adults, from the age of 18 have been able to apply for access to their original birth record. The Register does nothing to change that situation; it does however make possible an exchange of significant information between the birth family and the child, without committing either side to a face to face meeting. It is a way of being able to test the water. If, for example, it were clear from the relinquishing mother's entry in the Register that she would welcome contact from the child, then that is a considerable reassurance to the adoptee seeking to trace his origins. However, it does nothing to protect a relinquishing mother from what might be an unwelcome intrusion into her own settled family situation, as the right of the child to information about his background is put before the right of the mother to her own privacy.

Volume 9 of the Children Act 1989 Guidance and Regulations deals with adoption issues and reproduces a series of five booklets emphasising the Register, how to obtain access to birth records and providing advice to counsellors. The Register is only open to individuals who are at least 18 years of age.

Concurrent jurisdiction in family proceedings   Adoption and S.8 applications may now be heard at the same time by the same court. This is a considerable improvement on the former situation where, for example, an adoption application could be made to the County Court at the same time as an access application may have been made by the parents to the Juvenile Court. Such a situation could lead to the vexed question of which application should be heard first, without pre-empting the outcome of the second hearing.

Adoption applications   The provisions introduce relaxation on the age limit, which formerly prevented adoption applications from anyone under the age of 21. S.14 of the Adoption Act 1976, as amended, allows a step-parent and a spouse, who is the natural parent of the child, to apply for an adoption order, where the natural parent of the child is at least 18 years of age and the step-parent at least 21.

Freeing Orders   Children are no longer treated as being in the 'voluntary care' of a local authority. The 1989 Act provides for arrangements to be made for a child to be accommodated by a local authority, or on their behalf. Such arrangements can be terminated at any time, without notice. Similarly, a child is no longer in the 'care of' a voluntary organisation. The new measures are designed, in part, to enable parents to have confidence in the voluntary nature of 'accommodation'.

These changes have led to a corresponding restriction of the right to apply to free a child for adoption. Under the old law, an application could be made without the consent of a parent or guardian, if the child was 'in the care of an adoption agency'. This phrase was not defined in the 1976 Act, but was taken to include a child in voluntary care. Now, however, an adoption agency cannot apply for a freeing order without the consent of a parent or guardian, unless the agency is a local authority in whose care the child is, by virtue of a care order.[94] Other points to note in relation to freeing applications are:

- a Freeing Order does not end any duty to make payments in respect of the child's maintenance or upbringing arising by virtue of an agreement that constitutes a trust or which expressly provides that the duty is not extinguished by the making of an Adoption Order.
- When making a Freeing Order, courts must be satisfied that a father, who has no parental responsibility, has no intention of applying either for a Parental Responsibility Order or a S.8 Residence Order or that, if he did make such an application, it would be likely to be refused.
- Where the court varies a Freeing Order, to transfer parental responsibility from one agency to another, the new agency will assume all the responsibilities of the adoption agency, including progress reports to former parents, from the date of the original Freeing Order.

Protected children   The protected status of a child comes to an end if no Adoption Order is made within two years from the giving of the notice.[95] Under the old law, it was possible for a child to be a protected child until he reached the age of 18 years if applicants applied for an Adoption Order and subsequently allowed the application to lapse, without formally withdrawing it.

Unmarried fathers   In situations where unmarried fathers have acquired parental responsibility through S.4 of the 1989 Act, the court have to seek their agreement to adoption or, if grounds exist, dispense with such agreement as appropriate.

Abolition of Custodianship Orders   The court may no longer make Custodianship Orders, but instead may make a Residence Order, which settles the arrangements as to the person with whom the child is to live. Where the Residence Order is made in favour of someone who is not the child's parent or guardian, that person is given parental responsibility, but the extent of parental responsibility is restricted by S.12(3) of the 1989 Act. That is:

he shall not have the right — to consent, or refuse to consent, to the making of an application with respect to the child under S.18 of the Adoption Act 1976 or to agree, or refuse to agree, to the making of an adoption order or an order under S.55

---

94   Children Act 1989 Guidance and Regulations Vol.9, Adoption Issues, paras.1.18 and 1.19.
95   See S.32 of the Adoption Act 1976, as amended by the Children Act 1989, Sched.10.

of the Adoption Act 1976 with respect to the child or to appoint a guardian for the child.

Adoption allowances Adoption allowances are no longer paid under individual schemes approved by the Secretary of State. Instead payments are subject to the regulations as set out in Chapter 2 of Volume 9, Adoption Issues, *The Children Act 1989 Guidance and Regulations*, and in the Adoption Allowances Regulations 1991[96] Guidance. However, the central principle is still that an adoption allowance may be payable to help secure a suitable adoption, in cases where a child cannot be readily adopted because of a financial obstacle.

Harmonising provisions The 1989 Act harmonised certain aspects of adoption law within the United Kingdom and Northern Ireland. The main provisions are that:

• approved adoption societies in Scotland and Northern Ireland are able to operate in England and Wales;
• children who are 'protected children' under the law in Scotland and Northern Ireland are also protected in England and Wales;
• courts in England and Wales are able to order the return of a child who has been removed in defiance of adoption law in Scotland and Northern Ireland; and
• the provision of counselling services in connection with applications from adopted people for information about their birth records is to be made available in Scotland and Northern Ireland, for people whose adoption took place in England and Wales.

Adoption Law Review/White Paper

Adoption law is in a transitional phase. The 1989 Act brought about significant changes, but adoption legislation itself now requires substantial amendment to bring it into line with the provisions, ethos and spirit of the 1989 Act.

The Court and Administrative Arrangements

The courts which have jurisdiction to hear proceedings under the 1989 Act are the Magistrates' Family Proceedings Court, the County Court and the High Court Family Division. The allocation of cases is governed by the Children (Allocation of Proceedings) Order 1991.[97]

---

96 S.I. 1991 No. 2030.
97 S.I. 1991 No.1677.

Courts[98]

Magistrates Family Proceedings Courts All public law cases generally start here. Magistrates hear applications for Care and Supervision Orders, Emergency Protection Orders, Child Assessment Orders, applications for adoption and freeing for adoption, maintenance and domestic violence. In certain specified circumstances, cases may be transferred up to the County Court. Appeals under the 1989 Act from this court are heard in the Family Division of the High Court.

County Courts There are four tiers of County Court. Ninety-six non-divorce County Courts have no family jurisdiction, except for domestic violence injunctions. Seventy-two divorce County Courts issue all private law family proceedings, but matters which are contested will transfer to one of the 102 family hearing centres. Fifty-one of the family hearing centres are designated as 'care centres' and have full jurisdiction in public law matters transferred up from the Magistrates' Courts. Each care centre has a designated family judge, who is specially selected and trained in public law work.

Appeals from the County Court under the 1989 Act go to the Civil Division of the Court of Appeal and then on to the House of Lords, which is the final appeal court on matters of law.

High Court Family Division The High Court has full jurisdiction to hear all cases regarding children, including private wardship proceedings and appeals under the 1989 Act from the Magistrates' Family Proceedings Court. Appeals are heard in the Civil Division of the Court of Appeal.

Transfer Criteria

In order to expedite proceedings at all levels, both lateral and vertical transfers are available, according to the criteria set out in the Children (Allocation of Proceedings) Order 1991.

The two principles which apply to the transfer of any case are that:

- transfer must be in the best interests of the child;
- delay must be avoided, if it is likely to prejudice the welfare of the child.

Transfer of public law proceedings

Three criteria exist:

- *exceptional gravity, importance or complexity*, for example a case involving complicated or conflicting evidence, novel or difficult points of law or a question of general public interest;
- *consolidation* with other pending proceedings;
- *urgency*, where no other Family Proceedings Court can take the case.

It should be noted that applications for Emergency Protection Orders cannot be transferred, but can be issued in the higher courts, if public law proceedings are already under way in those courts.

---

98 See *The Court User Guide*, 1991, Lord Chancellor's Department and the Home Office.

The criteria for transfer to the High Court are:

● the proceedings are appropriate for determination in the High Court; and
● transfer would be in the interests of the child.

Transfer of private law proceedings

What the *Court User Guide* euphemistically refers to as 'the free market' on commencement of private law proceedings should make it less necessary to transfer such cases. However, a Family Proceedings Court may order transfer if the proceedings could be dealt with more appropriately in the County Court. County Courts may not transfer cases downwards, but may transfer them to the High Court on the same criteria as apply in public law proceedings.

Administrative and monitoring arrangements

The Lord Chancellor's Department established a committee structure to monitor the operation of the Children Act 1989 and to identify court-related issues that arose from its implementation. There are four levels of committee, all of which relate to each other, but not necessarily within a hierarchical structure:

The Children Act Advisory Committee The Children Act Advisory Committee advises the Lord Chancellor, the Home Secretary, the Secretary of State of Health and the President of the Family Division on whether the guiding principles of the 1989 Act are being achieved and whether the court procedures and the guardian *ad litem* service are operating satisfactorily. The Committee produces an annual report which monitors applications, outcomes and issues.

The Circuit Conference An annual one-day conference is held on each circuit (including the principal Registry of the Family Division), chaired by the Family Division Liaison Judge. The conference provides a forum for inter-disciplinary discussion of issues relating to family proceedings.

Family Court Business Committee The Family Court Business Committee makes sure that arrangements are working properly at local level, in particular allocation and transfer arrangements, and meeting agreed targets, where appropriate. The Committee:

● seeks to achieve administrative consistency between the two tiers of courts;
● ensures that the guardian *ad litem* and the probation services are aware of the needs of the court, while avoiding making unreasonable demands on those services;
● liaises with the area Family Court Services Committee. The Committee is chaired by the designated family judge, and the deputy chairman is the court's administrator, who is responsible for all the administrative arrangements on the circuit. The membership of the Family Court Business

Committee has been structured to provide representation from all the agencies whose management policies might affect the litigation process. They include representatives from the Justices' Clerk's Department, the local authority social services department, the local authority legal department, the local guardian *ad litem* panel and the Legal Aid Board.

Family Court Services Committee (After July 1994: **The Family Court Forum**)   This Committee promotes discussion and encourages co- operation between the professions, agencies and organisations involved in family proceedings. It considers and makes recommendations for the resolution of problematic issues which arise in the conduct of family proceedings, with particular reference to the practice of the courts, the legal profession, the medical profession, the health authorities, the social services, the education authorities and the police. It identifies any necessary improvements to the service provided to the parties to family proceedings by the courts or other agencies and professionals. It liaises with the Family Court Business Committee.

In July 1994, the Family Court Services Committee was re-named the Family Court Forum with an extended membership including a health visitor, a GP or NSPCC representative, representation of voluntary groups, a Citizens' Advice Bureau representative, a family law academic, a mediator and an education administrator or teacher as well as a solicitor, a barrister, a probation officer, a police representative, a justices' clerk, a district judge, a district health authority representative, a medical representative, a guardian *ad litem* and a social worker. In addition, the designated family judge may invite representatives according to local needs, interests or problem areas. Individuals may also be invited to attend particular meetings, if they have a specialist area of expertise to offer. The Family Court Forum is also chaired by the designated Judge, and the Children Act Advisory Committee suggest that the Family Court Forum should focus on a specific inter-disciplinary issue at each meeting in order to draw upon a wide range of professional opinion. The Forum also identifies areas of work of multi-disciplinary concern and arranges short seminars, study days and conferences on a local basis.

In essence, the difference between the Family Court Business Committee and the Family Court Forum is that the Family Court Business Committee considers whether the framework laid down by the 1989 Act and the rules of court are working efficiently and within resource constraints, whereas the Family Court Forum considers whether the framework has been correctly defined or whether other definitions should have been adopted. Any problems, issues or suggestions for change may be taken up by the designated judge and may be cross-referenced between the two Committees, who work very closely together. They may also be brought to the attention of the Children Act Advisory Committee, who may be able to pursue a particular issue at national level (see Figure 1, Family Court Committee Structure).

The Family Court Structure provides a very effective framework for the early identification of problems at a regional and local level. It provides a forum for discussion and for extremely valuable inter-agency and inter-disciplinary co-operation. It means that child care professionals from all

SECRETARY OF STATE

Annual Report

CHILDREN ACT
ADVISORY COMMITTEE

Annual Circuit Conference

52 FAMILY COURT BUSINESS COMMITTEES (Operational and court matters)	FAMILY COURT SERVICES (OR USERS) COMMITTEE (operational and welfare matters) from July 1994 THE FAMILY COURT FORUM
Chair: Designated Family Judge	**Chair:** Designated Family Judge
Deputy Chair: Courts Administrator	**Core Members:**[2] Solicitor in private practice Solicitor from the local authority legal department
Members: District Judge Representative of judges' clerks from courts operating family panels Representative from local authority social services department Representative from local authority legal department Representative from local Guardian *ad litem* panel Local Representative of Legal Aid Board[1]	Barrister Probation officer (appointed as a welfare officer) District health authority representative Police representative Magistrate from a family panel Justices' clerk District judge Child psychiatrist Guardian *ad litem* (rather than a panel manager) Social worker Health visitor GP Mediator[3]
Secretariat: Courts' Administrator's Office	**Secretariat:** Court Administrator's Office
Function: 1 Monitor efficiency of local arrangements; especially concerning allocation and transfer arrangements 2 Ensure efficient administration between courts 3 Ensure reporting services GALRO panel and FCWOs are meeting the courts' need, without overload 4 Liaise with family court users' services committee	**Function:** 1 Promote multi-disciplinary liaison and discussion 2 Identify and resolve problematic issues and areas of inter-agency co-operation 3 Identify areas where improvements in the service are possible and desirable 4 Liaise with Family Court Business Committee 5 Arrange multi-disciplinary conferences and seminars on matters of concern in relation to children and families.

Notes
1 Additional committee members may be: health visitor; GP; education welfare officer.
2 In contrast with FCBCs, which have a small, fixed membership, representing the main agencies involved in the litigation process, a more flexible approach is suggested to FCSC membership. The Lord Chancellor's Department suggested the 'core' membership given here.
3 Additional committee members may be: NSPCC representative; voluntary groups; Citizens Advice Bureau representative; Family Law academic; education administrator; teacher.

Figure 1   **Family Court Committee Structure**

disciplines can have an impact on the local arrangements and it provides welcome scope for flexibility.

Summary

Usually the law lags behind philosophy and practice, but in the case of the 1989 Act, the opposite is true. The range and flexibility of the new orders provides a 'menu', which enables the courts to select a combination which will meet the needs of a particular child, rather than fitting the child around constraining legislation. Proactive practitioners can mix and match and push the boundaries of legislation to improve the outcomes for children. The 1989 Act provides one user friendly document, which is available to all children and child care law professionals. The statute, together with the body of regulations and guidance, provide a strong framework for the potential development of constructive child care law and effective social work services. However, the realisation of that very considerable potential is still in doubt, as the courts and local authorities strive to match the ethos of statute with the reality and restrictions of service delivery.

Chapter 2
Children's Rights and the UN Convention on the Rights of the Child

Children's Rights

Rights and Welfare

The Children Act 1989 and the UN Convention on the Rights of the Child together provide a clear framework for the development of children's rights services. Services put the meat on the bones of idealism by incorporating the principle of rights, participation and consultation into organisational planning and thinking. These developments bring into sharp relief the potential for, at best, a creative tension between rights and welfare orientated services and, at worst, a mutual exclusivity. Children's rights, in the sense of claims, are often interpreted through the medium of welfare, and the conflicts inherent in such approach may conveniently be glossed over. Both the 1989 Act and the UN Convention espouse a 'best interests' approach.[1] Within this, however, both documents lay great emphasis on the importance of paying careful attention to the wishes and feelings of the child concerned, and to incorporating them into the decision making process.[2] The problem lies in incorporating the wishes and feelings of the child into the decision making, without sacrificing any aspect of the child's welfare, or imposing inappropriate burdens of responsibility on the child. The extent to which adults are willing, or able, to do this

---

1   S.1(1) Children Act 1989 and Article 3 of the UN Convention.
2   S.1(3)(a) and S.22(4)(a) of the Children Act 1989 and Article 12 of the UN Convention on
    the Rights of the Child.

depends not just on an intellectual acceptance of the ideological concepts of children's rights, but on an emotional acceptance of the benefits of listening to children and allowing them to participate in plans for their future. This requires a change in culture, as well as a change in ideology. Any casual questioning of a random group of adults will reveal that very few of them have had any experience of participating in decision making as children themselves. Many have raw memories of being excluded from family discussions of any real import. It is the functional shift in attitude which is required, as well as the ideological acceptance of a concept of children's rights, which together provide the necessary climate of change.

Listening to children and ascertaining their wishes and feelings is not an end in itself. It is the means to an end. The object is to listen with an understanding which will enable the child's views to be taken into consideration and which will inform decisions made about their welfare. It is an exercise of mutual respect, not patronage. It has been argued that a so-called 'right' to have welfare done to one is not a right in any meaningful sense.[3] However, as some have commented, the fact that a discretion-based welfare system seems to have failed children in many respects does not mean that a rights-based welfare regime will suffer the same fate.[4] John Eekelaar suggests that we have now reached the point where:

> general theories of what comprises children's best interests will not in themselves suffice as grounds for decision making. Also, since children mature gradually, it will always be necessary to observe the child closely for indications of what is important for that child, and why. This is in direct opposition to the devastating neglect of children's own opinions which has characterised much of the welfarist approach hitherto.[5]

The development of children's rights

Children's rights have their roots in the protectionist approaches of the late nineteenth century, when philanthropists led moral crusades against the exploitation of children in factories, down mines, and up chimneys. Dr Barnardo 'rescued' hundreds of children and sent them to a fresh start in a new world. The Cruelty to Children Act 1889 was passed 70 years after similar legislation for dogs. Until then, what parents did, or didn't do, with children was a matter of little public concern. Legislation in respect of children originally related to the need to control the property interests of minors. Children were not even objects of concern — they were possessions. The 1908 Children Act provided for the state education of children relieved from the burdens of exploitation by those seeking cheap labour. At that time, the right to education itself was seen as an infringement of parental rights in respect of their children. It was not until the Second World War that the evacuation programmes and large numbers of displaced children in Europe highlighted the needs of children as the raw material necessary to rebuild nations. The

---

3   Eekelaar, 'Importance of Thinking that Children have Rights' in *Children, Rights and the Law* (Alston and Parker ed. 1992).
4   Alston, Parker and Seymour (eds.), *Children, Rights and the Law* (1992), Introduction, p.x.
5   Eekelaar, op. cit p.229.

work of John Bowlby laid the foundations for a recognition of the constituents of healthy emotional as well as physical growth.[6] Children had needs and they had the right to have those needs met. Until the last 25 years, state concerns about children were essentially paternalistic, children were not regarded as persons of autonomy with their own powers of self-determination. In particular there was no concept of children as the bearers of rights which may override those exercised within the context of the family.

In the early 1970s the child liberationists, such as Holt and Farson, recognised the integrity of children as people in their own right, as distinct from the property of others. However, in doing so they espoused a view of childhood which many found difficult to accept. For example, the idea that children should assume all the responsibility of adulthood — voting, sexual freedom, freedom to design their own education — appears to be a contradiction and certainly an unhappy interpretation of children's rights to protection from potential abuse in the adult world. Carried to the logical conclusion, child liberationists deny the idea of childhood altogether, presenting instead the concept of a mini-adult. If both the concepts of child salvation and child liberation[7] are fundamentally flawed, then what is left is what is an essentially pragmatic approach to children's rights which attempts to incorporate both the right of the child to protection and the right of self-determination and autonomy.[8] Such an approach seeks to empower children, without burdening them at an immature or precocious stage of development. Pragmatic approaches are based upon the plight of individual children facing particular experiences of abuse, alienation or exploitation, rather than a more limited exploitation of ideologies. The approach is not limited to the securing of rights for the child to exercise for either good or ill, but seeks to involve the child in an interactive process of empowerment, based on a mutual respect between trusted adults, and children's own awareness of the responsibility to do one's best, both for oneself and for others. The proper exercise of responsibility is a learned activity. Children have a fine sense of justice. If treated fairly they will treat others fairly for the rest of their lives. That is the essence of society's investment in their future. If both the protectionist and liberationist approaches are found wanting, then it is through the grass roots development of rights-based children's services,[9] built on the solid foundation of statute, convention and regulations and guidance which now exists, that the key to the future must be found. Essential components of such services are the availability of accurate information to children and young people, practitioners' sound working knowledge of the

---

6 See Bowlby, 'Maternal Care and Mental Health', address to the World Health Organisation, Geneva (1951) and in *Child Care and the Growth of Love* (1953).

7 See Platt, *The Child Savers*, (1977); Pinchbeck and Hewitt, *Children in English Society* (1969); Goldstein, Freud and Solnit, *Beyond the Best Interests of the Child*, (1980); Farson *Birthrights* (1978); and Holt, *Escape from Childhood* (1975).

8 See further *Children, Rights and the Law op. cit.*; Freeman, *The Rights and Wrongs of Children*, (1983); *The Rights of Children* (Franklin, ed., 1986); Archard, *Children, Rights and Childhood* (1993); and Rodham, 'Children Under the Law', (1973) 43 *Harvard Educational Review*.

9 NAYPIC (National Association of Young People in Care), IRCHIN (Independent Representation for Children in Care) and CLC (The Children's Legal Centre) are examples of organisations who have adopted this approach.

national and international framework of children's rights and welfare, and effective independent spokespersons, both at national and international level. Effective advocacy services at local level, and a children's rights commissioner to safeguard the position of children nationally would be healthy developments of such an approach. In 1984 the Short Committee predicted that 'the growing conviction that children have, or should have, enforceable rights as individuals, even within the general tradition of liberal paternalism, can be expected to have a major impact on the whole field of child care over years to come.'[10]

Judith Masson identifies three sorts of rights in law. Positive or enforceable rights (these would include rights of direct representation), neutral rights (the right to be consulted in decision making, but not necessarily to determine the outcome), and negative rights (the right to have one's welfare considered). Negative rights are non-specific and may be enforceable, for example, in relation to the provision of services relating to the health and welfare of the child.[11]

Children need all three sorts of rights:

● rights to representation;
● rights to participation; and
● rights to protection and to have their best interests considered.

What is remarkable is the inconsistency of the present arrangements, in which some children have rights in some situations, whereas others do not even have the right to have their welfare considered, for example, 17-year-old offenders. The largest area of discrepancy is the limited representation of children in private law proceedings, as contrasted with the legal and social work representation of children in public law proceedings, although they may apply for leave to make applications under the Children Act 1989, and others may make applications on their behalf. Nevertheless their automatic access to the dual representation they have in public proceedings is sadly lacking.

The debates on the moral foundation of children's rights will undoubtedly continue in tandem with the debates about their practical application. Ripe areas for debate are whether or not children's positive rights should be based on the idea of moral obligations owed to children[12] or exist in their own right and give rise to moral obligations.[13] What is the purpose of rights — are they to empower the rights holder to exercise their powers of self-determination, or to protect their rights, as recognised by law? If the former, then can young children who are not 'competent' be said to have rights? If the answer is 'No', then some responsible adult or organisation must exercise those rights on their behalf, so inevitably the debate hinges on how adults interpret the rights of vulnerable children, in their best interest. There is no escaping the fact that

---

10   House of Commons, Second Report from the Social Services Committee, Session 1983/84, *Children in Care*, para. 18.
11   Masson, 'Children's Rights and The Children Bill', paper given at a Children's Rights and Action Conference held at the University of Leicester on April 19, 1989, published by Leicestershire County Council Social Services Department.
12   O'Neill, discussed in Alston, Parker and Seymour (eds), *Children, Rights and the Law* (1992).
13   Campbell, Freeman and Eekelaar, *ibid*.

rights and welfare are inextricably mixed, both philosophically and practically. The only answer is a working synthesis, not the mutual exclusivity which has characterised some socio-legal approaches to this fraught subject. As Michael Freeman has said:

> dichotomy as another classification should not divert us away from the fact that true protection of children does protect their rights.It is not a question of whether child savers or liberationists are right — they are both correct in emphasising part of what needs to be recognised, and both wrong in failing to address the claims of the other side. To take children's rights seriously requires us to take seriously both welfare and self-determination. It demands of us that we adopt policies, institutional structures, laws and practices which will both protect children and their rights.[14]

The UN Convention on the Rights of the Child

The UN Convention on the Rights of the Child is remarkable in that it exists at all. It is, inevitably, a compromise document which was not, according to Alston and Parker:

> conductive to a detailed or nuanced understanding of many of the key issues that arise. These issues include, for example, the philosophical underpinnings of the concept of children's rights, the practical difficulties in giving substance to concepts such as 'the best interests of the child', the problems that arise in seeking to balance competing and conflicting rights and the most appropriate mix of responsibilities to be accorded respectively to the child, the family, the community and the government.[15]

Nevertheless, the degree of international consensus achieved by the Convention in a relatively short space of time is remarkable. The ratification of the Convention by the UK, however, commits the government to a systematic analysis of law, policy and practice in relation to children in the UK as tested against the standards and principles of the Convention.

Background

In 1923, Eglantyne Jebb, founder of the Save the Children Fund, said, 'I believe we should claim certain rights for children and labour for their universal recognition'. In 1924, the League of Nations adopted the Declaration of Rights of the Child. The Declaration emphasised the physical needs of children, rather than addressing philosophical issues of rights or freedom. After the Second World War, the League of Nations was replaced by the United Nations, who, in 1948, produced a Universal Declaration of Human Rights. It was followed by the Declaration on the Rights of the Child, announced on November 20 1959, based on the principle that mankind owes to the child the best it has to give. Although these were significant steps forward for children's rights, the declarations were really only statements of general principles to be accepted by governments, and carried no specific

---

14 Michael Freeman, 'Whither Children: Protection, Participation, Autonomy?' (March 1994) Vol. 4 *Seen and Heard*, the Journal of the National Association of Guardians *ad litem* and Reporting Officers, p.12.
15 Alston and Parker in *Children's Rights and The Law* Introduction p.vii.

obligations. Conventions, on the other hand, require active decisions by states to ratify them and, once ratified, become binding international instruments. Accordingly, during the International Year of the Child, in 1979, Poland proposed that there should be a Convention on the rights of the child. A working group, composed of representatives of the 43 member states of the UN Commission on Human Rights, was set up. Once a working document had been agreed, it was forwarded to the UN Economic and Social Council. On November 20, 1989, exactly 30 years after the adoption of the first declaration on the rights of the child, the general assembly of the UN unanimously adopted the Convention. To date, it has been ratified by 154 countries, including the UK, who ratified on December 16, 1991. The Convention came into force in the UK on January 15, 1992. The process of ratification commits governments to report regularly to the UN Committee on the Rights of the Child (the UN Committee), outlining the progress towards full implementation that has been made by the member countries. Although the UN Convention does not have the force of law, in the UK it does provide a yardstick by which services and facilities for young people can be judged. Having ratified the UN Convention the UK government is obliged to implement it, subject only to the reservations it made when ratifying. The UK entered reservations in three main areas, firstly, those articles which dealt with nationality and immigration law, secondly, those dealing with employment safeguards for 16- to 18-year-olds; and thirdly, the UK reserved the right not to apply Article 37(c) in so far as those provisions require children who are detained to be accommodated separately from adults.

Following ratification, a Children's Rights Development Unit was established to work towards the fullest possible implementation of the UN Convention. The government was required to report to the UN Committee in January 1994, two years after ratifying the UN Convention, and thereafter each five years. These reports are to be given widespread distribution as part of the obligation to promote awareness of the UN Convention. The UN Committee monitors the progress of those who have ratified the UN Convention in fulfilling their obligations. In making an assessment of those obligations, the UN Committee will not depend solely on the governmental report. Views will also be sought from specialised agencies, such as UNICEF (United Nations International Children's Emergency Fund), and from a wide range of non-governmental organisations. Accordingly, at the same time as the Government was preparing its first report to the UN, the Children's Rights Development Unit was preparing a National Agenda for Children.

The UN Convention is, in essence, a human rights treaty. As Geraldine Van Bueren has pointed out, human rights law treaties are capable of being utilised on three levels:

● as educational instruments;
● as evidence of the need for national law reform; and
● as tools for advocates.

Unlike other European states, for example the Netherlands and Spain, the UK does not have a tradition of incorporating human rights treaties directly into national law. The majority of UK judges will only consider the provisions of a treaty, where the wording of the statute is ambiguous.[16] The UN Convention is much more broadly based than the Children's Act 1989, in that it includes articles dealing with children's economic and cultural, as well as civil and social, rights. However, the 1989 Act constitutes a major reform and review of child care law and it is unlikely that another such review, which might incorporate the provisions of the UN Convention, will be undertaken this century. One weakness of the UN Convention is that, although it deals with both the general and specific rights of children, it does not contain a right of individual petition or have the jurisdiction to respond to individual children's complaints.

Principles and content of the UN Convention and the Rights of the Child

The UN Convention consists of 54 articles. There are three key principles:

- that all the rights guaranteed by the Convention must be available to all children, without discrimination of any kind;[17]
- that the best interests of the child must be the primary consideration in all actions concerning children;[18] and
- that children's views must be considered and taken into account in all matters affecting them,[19] the principle of representation and participation in decision making.

Of these three, Article 12 is seen as the lynchpin of the Convention:

- parties shall assure to the child who is capable of forming his or her own views, the right to express those views freely in all matters affecting the child, the views of the child being given due weight, in accordance with the age and maturity of the child.
- for this purpose the child shall, in particular, be provided the opportunity to be heard in any judicial and administrative proceedings affecting the child, either directly or through a representative or an appropriate body in a manner consistent with the procedural rules of national law.

For the purposes of the UN Convention, the child means every human being below the age of 18 years unless, under the law applicable to a particular child, majority is attained earlier.[20] The Convention provides a set of minimum standards for children and young people's civil, political, economic, social and cultural rights.

The preamble recalls the basic principles of the United Nations and specific provisions of certain relevant human rights treaties and proclamations. It reaffirms the fact that children, because of their vulnerability, need special care and protection and places a special emphasis on the primary caring and

---

16 Van Bueren, 'The United Nations Convention on the Rights of the Child: The Necessity of Incorporation into United Kingdom Law' [1992] Fam. Law 373–375.
17 Art. 2.
18 Art. 3.
19 Art. 12.
20 Art. 1.

protective responsibility of the family, the need for legal and other protection of the child before and after birth, the importance of respect for the cultural values of the child's community and the vital role of international co-operation in achieving the realisation of children's rights.

The minimum standards established by the articles in the UN Convention can be broken down into three main categories — provision, protection and participation.

The provision sections deal with the rights to minimum standards of health, education, social security, physical care, family life, play, recreation, culture and leisure alongside maintenance of adequate standards of living.

The protection sections deal with the rights of children to be safe from discrimination, physical abuse, exploitation, substance abuse, injustice and conflict.

The participation sections describe the rights of children to their name and identity, to be consulted and taken account of, to have information, freedom of speech and opinion and to challenge decisions made on their behalf.

Children have both general and specific rights. General rights include the right to the highest possible standard of health and to medical facilities.[21] Parents have the primary responsibility for providing an adequate standard of living but states, too, have a role to play, particularly in ensuring that children are adequately nourished, clothed and housed.[22] All children have the right to primary education and states must ensure that free and compulsory education is available to all children; education should be designed to develop the child's talents, fostering basic human rights and developing respect for the child's own cultural values and those of others.[23] All children have the right to leisure, play and participation in cultural and artistic activities.[24]

Every child has the right to protection from all forms of exploitation and abuse, including sexual exploitation and abuse.[25]

Specific rights include the right to a name and nationality. The state has the obligation to protect the basis for a child's identity, including name, nationality and family ties.[26]

Children with special needs, for example, refugee and handicapped children, are entitled respectively to special protection and special care.[27] This special protection also extends to children without families.[28] Children also have specific rights to privacy[29] and to express an opinion and to have that opinion taken into account in any matter of procedure affecting the child.[30]

The UN Convention is remarkable in its scope and for the high degree of consensus that it commands. It achieves an enabling, rather than a critical tone. Clearly there are wide variations in the state of children's services across

---

21   Art. 24.
22   Art. 27.
23   Arts. 28 and 29.
24   Art. 31.
25   Art. 34.
26   Art. 7.
27   Arts. 22 and 23.
28   Art. 20.
29   Art. 16.
30   Art. 12.

the signatory states. For some, lack of resources or expertise mean that they are still struggling to provide basic standards of health and education. The important thing is the commitment to work towards full implementation and the establishment of an agreed framework on which to build.

The UN Convention as a vehicle for change

The UN Convention does not have the status of domestic law and legal sanctions are not available through the courts. In order to be effective, its principles must be accepted and incorporated into the provisions of services for children, creating a new awareness of children's rights and needs. In that way, the UN Convention can act as a powerful catalyst for change. Ratification provides the green light that is needed for private individuals and non-government organisations to apply pressure in the right directions. The obligation of the ratifying states is not limited to their own children, but effectively to the world's children. The UK is rich in comparison with many other countries, where millions of children have inadequate standards of living, health care and education. The amount of aid given by the UK to UNICEF, which is specifically mandated to meet the needs of children world-wide, fell from £15.4 million in 1987/88 to £9.3 million in 1989/90.[31]

Newall identifies two major obstacles to implementation of the UN Convention in the UK. First is a lack of information. There is only patchy monitoring of the state of the UK's children, the lack of consistently collected information making it hard to judge precisely how changes in social and economic polices are affecting children and young people. Newall points out that reforms for children often come about as a result of reactive, rather than proactive, policies, for example as a result of some scandal or exposed abuse, rather than through a comprehensive look at existing policies and practices. This can lead to haphazard and inconsistent changes.

The second major obstacle to effective change is the lack of co-ordination of policy at central government level, where many different departments are responsible for different services or different parts of the same service for children. A similar lack of co-ordination is reflected at local level. The main advantage of the UN Convention is that it does provide internationally accepted minimum standards, which can be used, if necessary, to exhort, encourage or embarrass governments, authorities, institutions and individuals who fail to meet them.[32]

In September 1990, a World Summit for Children was held in New York. Seventy-one heads of state or government took part. In June 1992, the Foreign and Commonwealth Office published a *Report on United Kingdom Implementation of the Goals agreed by the World Summit for Children.* Hopefully this report signals the beginning of a political commitment to underpin the principles of the Convention.

The introduction of the report paints a broad canvas of general principles:

---

31 Newall, *UN Convention and Children's Rights in the UK* (1991).
32 *Ibid.*, Introduction. Newall also makes a detailed examination of each of the 44 Articles which make up the UN Convention on the Rights of the Child.

The Government believes that the part played by the state should be complementary to, and supportive of, the role of the family. A stable home environment is the best foundation for the emotional and physical development of children. The Government, for its part, has a responsibility to ensure that the potential of each child is fulfilled, by the provision of good education and health services. It also has a special duty to protect children in certain situations, for example where family breakdown occurs or child abuse is suspected.[33]

In specific terms, the UK legislation in relation to children compares very favourably with that of most other countries. Theoretically, children have greatly enhanced rights both to be represented and to have their welfare considered. The reality for individual children is less satisfactory.

In February 1993 the Department of Health, in conjunction with the Children's Rights Development Unit, published a booklet for children entitled *The Rights of the Child: A Guide to the UN Convention*. The booklet identifies three main rights: the right to non-discrimination; the right for children to have their best interests considered; and the right to be listened to carefully.

The European Convention on Human Rights

Human rights encompass the rights of children and young people, as well as adults, and local authority decisions can be challenged as being in breach of the European Convention on Human Rights (the European Convention). In practical terms, the applicant must be able to show breach of either Article 8 (the right to respect for private and family life) or Article 6 (the right to take a civil matter before a court). The local authority cannot have its decision changed by the decision of the European Court, but the local authority can be required to pay compensation.

In *Gaskin v. United Kingdom*,[34] Graham Gaskin was awarded the sum of £5,000 for non-pecuniary damage and £11,000 for legal fees and expenses, on the grounds that the procedures followed had failed to secure respect for Mr Gaskin's private and family life, as required by Article 8 of the European Convention. Specifically the Article states that:

> everyone has a right to respect for his private and family life, his home and his correspondence. There shall be no interference by a public authority with the exercise of this right, except such as is in accordance with the law and is necessary in a democratic society, in the interests of national security, public safety or the economic well-being of the country for the prevention of disorder or crime, for the protection of health or morals or for the protection of the rights and freedoms of others.

Graham Gaskin was born on December 2, 1959 and, following the death of his mother, was received into care by the Liverpool City Council under S.1 of the Children Act 1948, on September 1, 1960. He was in voluntary care until

---

33   *Report on United Kingdom Implementation of the Goals agreed by the World Summit for Children* (1992), Foreign and Commonwealth Office. See further Goldrick 'Rights of the Child: UK Implementation of the Goals Agreed by the World Summit for Children' [1993] Fam. Law 536.
34   [1990] 1 F.L.R. 167.

June 18, 1974, when a care order was made under S.7 of the Children and Young Persons Act 1969. He remained in care until he was 18 on December 2, 1977. The applicant contended that he was ill-treated during those 17 years in care and, since his majority, wished to obtain details of where he was kept, by whom and in what conditions, in order to be able to help him overcome his problems and learn about his past. It is interesting that the Commission differentiated between the right of Gaskin to claim access to his file as an adult rather than as a child, on the grounds that 'claims to have access to the file must be viewed in a different light after his majority, than it would have been during the period spent as a minor in the local authority's care.'

Any earlier application by Graham Gaskin would have been refused on the basis of his age. The reality of the present situation is, therefore, that, for any practical purposes, children and young people will only be able to seek redress retrospectively. Under the UN Convention, all children are guaranteed the right to seek information. It is unlikely however that either the European Commission or the European Court will, in present circumstances, be able to assist a particular child, although they have had more success in general matters, for example being instrumental in bringing about the prohibition of corporal punishment in UK state schools.

In the case of *H. v. United Kingdom*[35] the court held that both Articles 6 and 8 of the European Convention had been violated. Mrs H., a British citizen, complained about the length of proceedings dealing with access to her child, who was in public care, and with the child's adoption. She was paid the sum of £12,000 for non-pecuniary damage.

In the case of *R. v. United Kingdom*[36] the European Court of Human Rights found that the UK was in breach of both Article 8 and Article 6 of the European Convention.

The European Court of Human Rights has jurisdiction to declare UK legislation to be incompatible with the terms of the European Convention. However, the judgments of the European Court are not binding on courts in this country and do not have a direct impact on English law. Nevertheless, where the European Court decides that English law is incompatible with the European Convention, Her Majesty's government is obliged to secure the enactment of the necessary amending legislation.

Graham Gaskin's case hung on whether or not he had the right of access to his own social services department file. On April 1, 1989 the Access to Personal Files Act 1987 came into force. The accompanying regulations stated that, except for certain specified exemptions, information should be given on request, within a specified period of time, provided that consent is obtained to the release of third party information and sources. A fundamental principle of the Act is to enable people to know what is recorded about them and it is envisaged that the withholding of information on grounds of serious harm would be most exceptional. The guidance sets out criteria for establishing whether or not children have the capacity for making informed requests for access to their personal files and states that this should not be determined by

35 (Judgment No. 3/1986/101/149) [1986] 10 H.R.R. 29.
36 (Judgment No. 6/1986/104/152) [1988] 2 F.L.R. 445.

any age limit. Applications by children must be in writing, but it does not have a set form. Children do not have absolute rights of access, as the authority may ask to interview them in order to decide whether or not they have the maturity to understand the nature of the requests. In the case of postal applications, the authority may request certificates from parent or other adults who may apply for access to information on their children's behalf, provided that this is in the best interests of the children. The Data Protection Act 1984 adopts a similar approach.

In *Re R.* a natural mother sought to question local authority decision making about her child in care. Since then, the 1989 Act has given parents much improved rights to representation and to challenge decisions at a much earlier stage, in the case of an Emergency Protection Order after only 72 hours.

There have been no recorded applications to the European Court since implementation of the 1989 Act, although it is worth remembering that the European Court is there to protect the rights of children, as well as those of adults. In practical terms, it would need an extremely astute young person, coupled with a tenacious solicitor and a great deal of patience, to follow the lengthy European route. The pecuniary benefit, in itself, would be unlikely to be sufficient motivation, as was evidenced in Graham Gaskin's case[37] where the amount of the final award was less than half the final legal costs. The main value of the European Court lies in bringing a matter under international scrutiny and in achieving a victory of principle, which can change domestic legislation.[38]

The Hague Convention on the Civil Aspects of International Child Abduction

The Hague Convention was ratified by the UK in January 1994, thus giving effect to Schedule 1, Article 8 of the Child Abduction and Custody Act 1985. The Hague Convention has a wider application than the European Convention, which is restricted to countries within Europe, and applies to Australasia and the Middle East as well as Europe. It deals with the recovery of children and child abduction, and is based on the assumption that the welfare of the child will best be determined by returning that child to the country of origin and submitting the matter to the domestic laws of the country involved. The criteria for the wrongful removal of children from one country to another, bearing in mind the provisions of the Children Act 1989, in relation to shared parental responsibility, can be less than clear.[39]

---

37   See MacVeigh, *Gaskin* (1982).
38   See also *H. v. United Kingdom* [1986] 10 H.R.R. 29, dealing with the unacceptable effects of delay (in this case two and a half years) in affecting contact between parent and child and subsequent loss of family life.
39   See *Re H.* and *Re. S.* (Abduction — Custody Rights) [1991] 2 F.L.R. 262 and see further Everall, 'The Hague Convention, The Children Act and other Recent Developments' [1992] Fam.Law. 164. See also Waite J. in *Re V. (Minors)* (Hague Convention) No.1 [1994] 1 F.C.R. 394, child abduction, the relationship between the jurisdiction under the Hague Convention and the jurisdiction for residence and contact.

A Children's Rights Commissioner

Children are a particulary vulnerable group. They are the future of our society. As such they deserve special consideration, special nurturing and special protection. One practical proposal is to create a Children's Rights Commissioner, a proposal supported by a consensus of leading child care organisations:

> Creating a Children's Rights Commissioner would be an important reform for the UK's 13.2 million children and young people. Its work would improve law, policy and practice affecting children and young people; raise the status of children and young people in policy making; and ensure that politicians, policy makers and practitioners take children's rights and interests more seriously. Policy affecting children would take more account of children's rights and interests and the need for co-ordination, and would be based on a better understanding of its impact on children and young people and their perspective. The commissioner's work would also result in better systems for children who are victims of injustice to obtain redress, and in less ill-treatment. Finally it would help the UK fulfil its obligations to its 13.2 million children and young people, under the UN Convention on the Rights of the Child.[40]

It is significant that the proposal for a Children's Rights Commissioner talks consistently of children's rights and interests, as well as the need to influence and co-ordinate central government responsibilities which affect children and young people and which are distributed across a wide variety of different government departments.

> A Children's Rights Commissioner would not only be able to concentrate on the problems of individual children, but be able to ensure that the needs of children, in general, are taken into consideration in policy decisions affecting housing, health, social security, as well as social welfare. The proposal for a Children's Rights Commissioner is not new, or exclusive to Britain. Norway has had a Children's Ombudsperson since September 1981, New Zealand appointed a Commissioner for Children in July 1989, while Australia established a Children's Interests Bureau in 1983. The Council of Europe is currently examining the possibility of a Council of Europe Legal Instrument on Children's Rights to complement the UN Convention. This would take the form of additional protocol to the European Convention on Human Rights, possibly containing some of the UN Convention's principles, for example, the obligation to take account of children's views on matters affecting them, and the requirement that the best interests of the child should be a primary consideration in decision making.[41]

The UN Convention has acted as a springboard for various new initiatives, addressing the needs and rights of children and young people. The mission of the Children's Rights Commissioner, as set out in the proposal, would be to promote children's rights throughout the UK by:

- influencing policy makers and practitioners to take greater account of children's rights and interest;
- promoting compliance with the minimum standards set by the United Nations Convention on the Rights of the Child and other relevant international treaties or agreements;

---

40 Rosenbaum and Newall, *Taking Children Seriously: A Proposal for a Children's Rights Commissioner* (1991) p.5.
41 *Ibid.*, p.48.

● seeking to ensure that children have effective means of redress, when their
rights are disregarded.

The Commissioner would take, as guiding principles, the 54 Articles of the
UN Convention and these, along with other international agreements, would
provide a base-line of minimum standards. However the Commissioner would
advocate further rights specific to the UK.

Although established by government, the Commissioner would be
independent in action and policy stances from government and all other
bodies. The Commissioner would adopt a broad perspective, cutting across
departments and agencies and consistently seeking input from children and
young people, co-operating with other organisations with similar interests.

The Commissioner would have a wide range of functions in respect of the
UK's 13.2 children and young people. The aims would be to improve law,
policy and practice affecting children and young people, to raise the status of
children and young people in policy making and to ensure that politicians,
policy makers and practitioners take children's rights and interests seriously.
Policies affecting children would take greater account of children's rights and
interests and of the need for co-ordination and would be based on a better
understanding of the perspective of children and young people. The
Commissioner's work would result in better systems for children who are
victims of injustice to obtain redress and less ill-treatment. Centrally the office
would help the UK fulfil its obligations under the UN Convention.[42]

The Norwegian Experience

Norway was the first country to appoint an Ombudsman for Children in
1981. The appointment of an Ombudsman for Children is a very practical
example of how national governments can engage with the reality of providing
services for children. The decision to appoint an Ombudsman was not carried
without opposition. The arguments against the establishment of an
Ombudsman's office are pertinent at a time when proposals for a similar office
in England are gaining momentum. It was thought in Norway in 1981 that:

● the Ombudsman would be a threat to parental authority;
● the Ombudsman might become an excuse for other groups and bodies
responsible for children to diminish or relinquish their responsibilities;
● the funds allocated should rather be used to strengthen other existing
efforts or services for children.

The role of the Ombudsman is to protect and improve the interests of
children. In pursuing his duties, the Commissioner works to ensure that the
needs, rights and interests of children are given the necessary consideration in
all areas of society. In 1989 the Norwegian Ombudsman attempted to
reconcile children's rights and responsibilities in a pamphlet which is
illuminating, as it attempts to integrate practical children's rights and interests
with state policies in relation to children:

---

42   *Ibid.*

7 years	● right and obligations to go to school; ● right to see films for children.
12 years	● legal right to express opinion on matters that concern him/her personally. The importance of the child's opinion gains with increasing age; ● the child must agree if he/she is to be adopted;[43] ● right to see films for adolescents.
13 years	● right to take a job that does not affect health or school, *e.g.* in vacations or as a newspaper boy/girl; ● right to be exempted from payment of taxes (within certain limits).
14 years	● right to be heard by parents/guardians in financial questions considering the young person; ● right to take job as part of education or vocational training; ● right to be warned and given opportunity to state opinion in cases concerning him/herself being handled by public services (school, child welfare committees); ● can be arrested, tried and imprisoned.
15 years	● right to decide choice of education; ● right to decide membership in organisation, including church; ● right to appeal or go to court to change decisions made by the child welfare board against the will of the parents; ● right to use money he/she has earned as he/she wishes (if the income is high the child may reasonably be expected to share expenses for his/her upkeep); ● right to work for pay as described in the Labour Conditions Act, as long as health and eduction do not suffer; ● must have own passport to go abroad. Parents must give permission for the young person to obtain passport.
16 years	● right to go to adult films; ● right to buy tobacco; ● right to demand confidentiality (including parents from doctors); ● right to buy and get licensed for motorised bicycle; ● age of sexual consent. When both parties are over 16 sexual activity is legal, as long as it is voluntary; ● public child allowance stops.
Up to 18	● children can be held financially responsible for damage done purposely or through negligence. Parents are required to cover damages up to 1,000 Norwegian Kroner, if the child is unable to pay;

43 There is a similar proposal in the White Paper on reform of adoption law, *Adoption: The Future* CM. 2288 London, HMSO, 1993.

- right to public child pension, if one parent dies;
- forbidden to work night-shifts;
- can become a ward of the child welfare system;
- must have parental consent to get married.

18 years
- age of majority. Can make all personal and financial decisions;
- right to vote;
- right to get driver's licence for automobiles and heavy motorcycles;
- right to buy wine and beer;
- right to apply for extended child support when completing secondary education.

The Norwegian list is interesting, especially in comparison with some aspects of British law, for example the age at which children can be arrested and imprisoned (14 years) and the age of heterosexual, as well as homosexual, consent being fixed at over 16.[44]

The Norwegian Ombudsman has been effective, particularly in co-ordinating national policies in relation to children's everyday lives. Access to adult videos and pornographic material, dealing with children's complaints and, in particular, focusing attention on the physical conditions necessary for the healthy development of children are all aspects of national policy tackled by the Ombudsman; for example integrating considerations of children's rights to open spaces into rural and urban planning and providing safe conditions for outdoor play.

One significant practical power which the Ombudsman has in Norway is the power to freeze bureaucratic and judicial decision making for up to one month, thus allowing time for an investigation of the child's case, and the opportunity to influence events in a central, rather than peripheral, manner.

There are significant lessons to be learned from the Norwegian experience, in terms of translation of statute and ideology into the reality of children's rights-based services.

The UK's First Report to the UN Committee on the Rights of the Child

Having ratified the UN Convention on the Rights of the Child, the UK assumed a responsibility to implement the principles and standards set out in the Convention. Under the terms of the Convention, the government is required to report after two years, and subsequently every five years, to a UN Committee on the Rights of the Child who have international responsibility for monitoring governments' respect for children's rights, in line with the Convention. Accordingly, in February 1994, the UK produced its first Report

---

44   Flekkøy, *A Voice for Children: Speaking out as their Ombudsman* (1991) commissioned by the United Nations Children's Fund (UNICEF), Children's Rights and Responsibilities at Appendix 4.

to the UN Committee on the Rights of the Child. The purpose of the report was to prepare an audit of practice and policy in relation to children in the UK, as measured against the standards laid down in the Convention. The implementation of the Children Act 1989 is identified as a considerable step forward in current legislation governing the care and upbringing of children in England and Wales. The Report claimed that the Act accorded closely with the principles of the Convention, in particular the two 'over-arching' principles, namely the best interests of the child shall be the first consideration and the voice for the child should be heard.

In general, the Report concentrated on identifying positives, rather than identifying problem areas. In particular it glossed over the issue of children involved in crime, making no mention of proposals in the Criminal Justice Bill to restrict the liberty of children under the age of 10 in a new network of secure units. Consideration of Article 12, and respect for the views of the child, occupies a disappointingly small section of the Report, giving the erroneous impression that the court welfare officer or the Official Solicitor acts as a representative of the child in 'many' private law proceedings, just as in 'most' public law proceedings a guardian *ad litem* will be appointed. It fails to identify the fact that children in private law proceedings have limited rights to separate legal or social work representation. Considering that Article 12, which deals with the participation of children in decision making, is regarded as central to the successful implementation of the Convention, there is a very limited examination of issues of participation in the first Report. The vexed question of corporal punishment is dealt with in a few contradictory lines, which justify the retainment of corporal punishment for privately funded pupils in independent schools (on grounds of parental choice),[45] at the same time as drawing attention to the government's guidance that corporal punishment has no place in the child care setting.

The Report does identify the fact that some authorities 'had been slow to develop adequate initiatives for children in need. Other authorities needed to improve their arrangements for preparing children for leaving care and their after care services.'[46]

The Report is generally unsatisfactory, in that it concentrates almost exclusively on what has been achieved. It does not contain a comprehensive audit of where services or legislation in the UK fail to comply with the UN Convention, or identify a clear programme of implementation for the next five years. Consequently there is no stated programme for the future development of children's rights, in accordance with the requirements of the Convention.

It is fair to say that, in comparison with other European countries, the UK has cause to feel proud of its statutes in relation to children. What is more debatable is the Report's statement that the principles of the Children Act 1989 are being increasingly reflected in practice, and that the welfare of children is being safeguarded and promoted more effectively than before. Services, however, still leave something to be desired.

---

45   The UK's First Report to the UN Committee on the Rights of the Child (February 1994), HMSO, para. 7.37, Corporal Punishment.
46   *Ibid.*, para. 1.9.

In January 1995 the UN Committee on the Rights of the Child was critical of the UK Government's record, attitude and policy to children's rights since it became a signatory to the Convention. In particular, the imprisonment of children was against the Convention. Welfare measures should be followed instead.

The UK Agenda for Children: An Agenda for Change

If one contrasts the UK's First Report to the UN Committee with the All Party Parliamentary Group for Children's Messages to Parliament concerning Children, and with the Children's Rights Development Unit's *UK Agenda for Children* one receives a different picture and a more focused approach.

In May 1994 the Children's Rights Development Unit, set up by the government to monitor the implementation of the UN Convention on the Rights of the Child in the UK, produced its own Agenda for Change,[47] identifying areas in which the UK met, or failed to meet, the criteria laid down by the UN. The simultaneous production of an independent report on the state of the UK's provision for children emphasises the importance of having an organisation or structure outside government which can serve as a centre for the collation and dissemination of information about children's issues.

The *UK Agenda for Children* consists of 14 reports, which together cover the whole spectrum of children's health and welfare. Each is impressive in its depth and detail.

Report 1: Personal freedoms. Freedom from discrimination; freedom of expression, of association and of thought, conscience and religion; the right to an identity of thought, conscience and religion; the right to an identity and to express views; preservation of a child's identity; protection of privacy, language, culture and religion.

Report 2: Care of Children. Parental responsibility; view of children; family support; services for disabled children; discrimination and racism; placements; leaving care; complaints; adoption.

Report 3: Physical and personal integrity. Available information on protection of physical and personal integrity; upholding children's rights to physical and personal integrity; child abuse and child protection procedures; educational measures; traditional practices threatening physical or personal integrity; rehabilitation of victims.

Report 4: An adequate standard of living. Does poverty exist? ability to afford the basic necessities; access to adequate housing, health care and the best possible health, education and family life; opportunities to play in a safe environment and participate in society; freedom from discrimination.

Report 5: Health and health care services. The right to health; preventative health services; children and young people affected by medical conditions; care and treatment of illness.

---

47   *UK Agenda for Children*, Children's Rights Development Unit, London, 1994.

Report 6: Environment. Children's involvement in environmental issues; adequate housing; the accessibility and safety of public places; transport and transport policy; environmental pollution and child health.

Report 7: Education. Exclusions; racism; children with special needs; poverty; truancy; children looked after by local authorities; consultation, participation and respect for the child; curriculum; protection and safety in schools.

Report 8: Play and Leisure. The right to rest and leisure; promoting and encouraging facilities for play and leisure activities; providing 'appropriate' services and facilities; safety and standards; information and the mass media.

Report 9: Youth Justice. Treatment of young people in custody; imprisonment; separation of children and adults; protection from violence; criminal responsibility; alternatives to judicial proceedings; alternatives to institutional care; non-discrimination; best interests; standards; review of placement.

Report 10: Child labour. Regulation of employment; health and safety; ignorance of the law; hours of work; terms and conditions of employment; rest periods and paid leave; welfare of children and young people; training opportunities for 16 to 17-year-olds.

Report 11: Immigration and nationality. Rights for all children without discrimination; the best interests of the child; the right to be consulted, to a nationality and identity, to family life and family reunion and the right to privacy; the rights of young refugees and of child victims.

Report 12: Children and violent conflict. Northern Ireland; impact of the violent conflict on children; emergency legislation; the right to life; harassment by security forces; paramilitary abuse; non-discrimination; juvenile justice; separation from parents; rehabilitative care; creating an environment for change.

Report 13: Abduction. Current procedures; age limits; family life; protection from abduction; prevention of abduction; abduction to other jurisdictions within the UK.

Report 14: International obligations to promote children's rights. International co-operation over information, inter-country adoption, disability, health, recovery of maintenance, education and prevention of sexual exploitation; protection of children affected by armed conflict; recovery and rehabilitation.

The Report draws on a broad range of expertise and experience and was prepared in collaboration with a wide range of organisations, individuals and young people. It has been endorsed by over 180 national organisations and associations and has been sent to the UN Committee on the Rights of the Child to provide an independent overview of what is happening to children in the UK.

The action required for compliance with the Articles of the UN Convention are clearly identified.

Article 12, the involvement of the child in decision making

It is worth looking in detail at some of the proposals for compliance with Article 12, in relation to the policies and practices necessary to enable children to participate in decision making.The Report rightly recognises that listening to children must start long before they reach a court room. Rights of direct representation must go hand in hand with an acceptance on the part of the parents and the rest of society that there is a need, firstly to ascertain the wishes and feelings of children when decisions are being made, and secondly, to give due consideration to them. The responsibility to involve children in decision making could be linked to the concept of parental responsibility generally. The suggestion in the Agenda is that the Scottish Law Commission's Report on Family Law proposal, namely that there should be in law a requirement that:

> before a person reaches a major decision which involves fulfilling parental responsibility, or exercising a parental right, the person shall, so far as is practicable, ascertain the views of the child concerned regarding the decision and shall give due consideration to those views, taking account of the child's age and maturity

should be incorporated into UK legislation.[48]

There was widespread support for such a provision, which already exists in a number of other countries, including Germany, Sweden, Norway and Finland. If such a requirement were introduced into legislation, it would provide a more explicit definition in law of the responsibilities associated with parenthood, and would impose a clear duty on parents to consider their child's wishes and feelings, in a manner consistent with the requirements embodied in Article 12 and Article 5 (concerning the state's duty to respect the rights and responsibilities of parents and the wider family, to provide guidance appropriate to the child's evolving capacities).

Compliance with Article 12, therefore, requires that the relevant family law in each jurisdiction in the UK is amended, to introduce a duty on those with parental responsibility, in reaching any major decision relating to the child, to ascertain the child's wishes and give them due consideration, subject to age and understanding.

The Agenda stresses the need for the effective involvement of young people, not only in decisions that affect them as individuals, but also in broader matters of policy and social planning. It is a positive step forward that the Social Services Inspectorate now include young people who have experienced a residential care system as members of their inspection teams looking at residential establishments. However, as the Report points out:

> effective involvement of young people will not happen until there is a major shift in the training of social work practitioners and in the culture of social services departments towards recognition of the civil rights of young people being looked after, and the fundamental importance of respecting those rights.[49]

In particular, the action required by compliance with Article 12, in respect of children looked after by local authorities and voluntary organisations, requires that:

---

48 See Report on Family Law, Scottish Law Commission, HMSO, 1992.
49 *UK Agenda for Children*, *op.cit.*, p.41. para. 4.7.9.

- local authorities and voluntary organisations produce guidelines on procedures for consulting with young people, both in relation to decisions that affect them as individuals, and in relation to broader service planning and development;
- the guidelines should be drawn up in consultation with young people;
- guidelines should be backed up by staff training and monitoring, and
- the government should make clear through guidance, or preferably legislation,that, where children's views conflict with other considerations, local authorities must take into account that the child's views should take precedence.

Children involved in divorce

The Report highlights the fact that, in uncontested cases, there is no opportunity for children to express a view on what they wish to happen and no opportunity for them to challenge a decision if they are unhappy once it has been made. This situation contravenes the provisions of Article 12 in terms of affording children direct representation in proceedings which affect their welfare. Compliance with Article 12, and the right to be heard in all relevant proceedings, would require that children were made automatic parties. Children in public law proceedings have this right,so such a change would also be consistent with the requirements in Article 2, that all the rights of the Convention may apply equally to all children. Accordingly, in order to comply with the requirements of Article 12, the following actions are required:

- in cases being heard by the courts, which affect children, they should be entitled to automatic party status;
- the child should be entitled to separate legal representation in all proceedings;
- a review of Scottish court and mediation processes should be undertaken, leading to a revised strategy and new court rules on children raising actions;
- research is undertaken into the operation of the No Order Principle, under the Children Act, in respect of its impact of children in divorce proceedings (see Chapter 9, The Representation Of Children in Private Law Proceedings).

Complaints procedures

The Report rightly emphasises that rights are meaningless if there are no means of redress when they are not properly respected, and highlights complaints procedures as central to a commitment to respecting children and young people's rights to have their views heard. Complaints procedures must be accessible to both children and parents and other adults who wish to facilitate and support the child in making a complaint. Procedures should also be accessible to children with disabilities, who have the same rights as other children.

In order to comply with Article 12, the provision of effective means of redress necessary for its implementation requires that:

- complaints procedures are established, promoted and monitored in full consultation with young children. Particular attention needs to be given to the access of disabled children to the complaints procedure.
- children in care should have the same access as other children to the courts to seek redress (for example, Children Act S. 8, Orders and Wardship) where complaints procedures do not provide satisfaction.

The UK Agenda for Children is impressive in its scope and in providing a systematic approach of the extent to which law, policy and practice in the UK complies with the principles and standards contained in the UN Convention on the Rights of the Child. Its most positive contribution is its clear and practical signposting of the way ahead, thus providing a bridge between policy and practice which will be of benefit to all practitioners involved in child care law and practice.

European Convention on the Exercise of Children's Rights

On November 10, 1994, the Council of Europe produced a draft Convention on the Exercise of Children's Rights for consultation with a view to publication in 1996. The object of the Convention is, in the best interests of children, to promote their rights, to grant them procedural rights and to facilitate the exercise of these rights by ensuring that children are, themselves or through other persons or bodies, informed and allowed to participate in the proceedings before a judicial authority affecting them. The draft convention emphasises the right of the child to exercise their rights in respect of consultation, participation and representation in all family proceedings that affect them.

Appendix 1

The UN Convention on the Rights of the Child

Recognizing that, in all countries in the world, there are children living in exceptionally difficult conditions, and that such children need special consideration,

Taking due account of the importance of the traditions and cultural values of each people for the protection and harmonious development of the child,

Recognizing the importance of international co-operation for improving the living conditions of children in every country, in particular in the developing countries,

Have agreed as follows:

PART I

Article 1

[Definition of a child: All persons under 18, unless by law majority is attained at an earlier age]

For the purposes of the present Convention, a child means every human being below the age of eighteen years unless, under the law applicable to the child, majority is attained earlier.

Article 2

[Non-discrimination: The principle that all rights apply to all children without exception, and the State's obligation to protect children from any form of discrimination. The State must not violate any right, and must take positive action to promote them all]

1.   States Parties shall respect and ensure the rights set forth in the present Convention to each child within their jurisdiction without discrimination of any kind, irrespective of the child's or his or her parent's or legal guardian's race, colour, sex, language, religion, political or other opinion, national, ethnic or social origin, property, disability, birth or other status.

2.   States Parties shall take all appropriate measures to ensure that the child is protected against all forms of discrimination or punishment on the basis of the status, activities, expressed opinions, or beliefs of the child's parents, legal guardians, or family members.

Article 3

[Best interests of the child: All actions concerning the child should take full account of his or her best interests. The State is to provide adequate care when parents or others responsible fail to do so]

1.   In all actions concerning children, whether undertaken by public or private social welfare institutions, courts of law, administrative authorities or legislative bodies, the best interests of the child shall be a primary consideration.

2.   States Parties undertake to ensure the child such protection and care as is necessary for his or her well-being, taking into account the rights and duties of his or her parents, legal guardians, or other individuals legally responsible for him or her, and, to this end, shall take all appropriate legislative and administrative measures.

3.   States Parties shall ensure that the institutions, services and facilities responsible for the care or protection of children shall conform with the standards established by competent authorities, particularly in the areas of safety, health, in the number and suitability of their staff as well as competent supervision.

Article 4

[Implementation of rights: The State's obligation to translate the rights in the Convention into reality]

States Parties shall undertake all appropriate legislative, administrative, and other measures, for the implementation of the rights recognized in the present Convention. With regard to economic, social and cultural rights, States Parties shall undertake such measures to the maximum extent of their available resources and, where needed, within the framework of international co-operation.

Article 5

[Parental guidance and the child's evolving capacities: The State's duty to respect the rights and responsibilities of parents and the wider family to provide guidance appropriate to the child's evolving capacities]

States Parties shall respect the responsibilities, rights and duties of parents or, where applicable, the members of the extended family or community as provided for by local custom, legal guardians or other persons legally responsible for the child, to provide, in a manner consistent with the evolving capacities of the child, appropriate direction and guidance in the exercise by the child of the rights recognized in the present Convention.

Article 6

[Survival and development: The inherent right to life, and the State's obligation to ensure the child's survival and development]

1.   States Parties recognize that every child has the inherent right to life.

2.   States Parties shall ensure to the maximum extent possible the survival and development of the child.

Article 7

[Name and nationality: The right to have a name from birth and to be granted a nationality]

1.   The child shall be registered immediately after birth and shall have the right from birth to a name, the right to acquire a nationality and, as far as possible, the right to know and be cared for by his or her parents.

2.   States Parties shall ensure the implementation of these rights in accordance with their national law and their obligations under the relevant international instruments in this field, in particular where the child would otherwise be stateless.

Article 8

[Preservation of identity: The State's obligation to protect and, if necessary, re-establish the basic aspects of a child's identity (name, nationality and family ties)]

1.   States Parties undertake to respect the right of the child to preserve his or her identity, including nationality, name and family relations as recognized by law without unlawful interference.

2.   Where a child is illegally deprived of some or all of the elements of his or her identity, States Parties shall provide appropriate assistance and protection, with a view to speedily re-establishing his or her identity.

Article 9

[Separation from parents: The child's right to live with his/her parents unless this is deemed incompatible with his/her best interests; the right to maintain contact with both parents if separated from one or both; the duties of States in cases where such separation results from State action]

1. States Parties shall ensure that a child shall not be separated from his or her parents against their will, except when competent authorities subject to judicial review determine, in accordance with applicable law and procedures, that such separation is necessary for the best interests of the child. Such determination may be necessary in a particular case such as one involving abuse or neglect of the child by the parents, or one where the parents are living separately and a decision must be made as to the child's place of residence.

2. In any proceedings pursuant to paragraph 1 of the present article, all interested parties shall be given an opportunity to participate in the proceedings and make their views known.

3. States Parties shall respect the right of the child who is separated from one or both parents to maintain personal relations and direct contact with both parents on a regular basis, except if it is contrary to the child's best interests.

4. Where such separation results from any action initiated by a State Party, such as the detention, imprisonment, exile, deportation or death (including death arising from any cause while the person is in the custody of the State) of one or both parents or of the child, that State Party shall, upon request, provide the parents, the child or, if appropriate, another member of the family with the essential information concerning the whereabouts of the absent member(s) of the family unless the provision of the information would be detrimental to the well-being of the child. States Parties shall further ensure that the submission of such a request shall of itself entail no adverse consequences for the person(s) concerned.

Article 10

[Family reunification: The right of children and their parents to leave any country and to enter their own in order to be reunited or to maintain the child-parent relationship]

1. In accordance with the obligation of States Parties under article 9, paragraph 1, applications by a child or his or her parents to enter or leave a State Party for the purpose of family reunification shall be dealt with by States Parties in a positive, humane and expeditious manner. States Parties shall further ensure that the submission of such a request shall entail no adverse consequences for the applicants and for the members of their family.

2. A child whose parents reside in different States shall have the right to maintain on a regular basis, save in exceptional circumstances, personal relations and direct contacts with both parents. Towards that end and in accordance with the obligation of States Parties under article 9, paragraph 2, States Parties shall respect the right of the child and his or her parents to leave any country, including their own, and to enter their own country. The right to leave any country shall be subject only to such restrictions as are prescribed by law and which are necessary to protect the national security, public order (*ordre public*), public health or morals or the rights and freedoms of others and are consistent with the other rights recognized in the present Convention.

Article 11

[Illicit transfer and non-return: The State's obligation to try to prevent and remedy the kidnapping or retention of children abroad by a parent or third party]

1. States Parties shall take measures to combat the illicit transfer and non-return of children abroad.

2.   To this end, States Parties shall promote the conclusion of bilateral or multilateral agreements or accession to existing agreements.

Article 12

[**The child's opinion:** *The child's right to express an opinion, and to have that opinion taken into account, in any matter or procedure affecting the child*]

1.   States Parties shall assure to the child who is capable of forming his or her own views the right to express those views freely in all matters affecting the child, the views of the child being given due weight in accordance with the age and maturity of the child.

2.   For this purpose, the child shall in particular be provided the opportunity to be heard in any judicial and administrative proceedings affecting the child, either directly, or through a representative or an appropriate body, in a manner consistent with the procedural rules of national law.

Article 13

[**Freedom of expression:** *The child's right to obtain and make known information, and to express his or her views, unless this would violate the rights of others*]

1.   The child shall have the right to freedom of expression; this right shall include freedom to seek, receive and impart information and ideas of all kinds, regardless of frontiers, either orally, in writing or in print, in the form of art, or through any other media of the child's choice.

2.   The exercise of this right may be subject to certain restrictions, but these shall only be such as are provided by law and are necessary:

(a) For respect of the rights or reputations of others; or

(b) For the protection of national security or of public order (*ordre public*), or of public health or morals.

Article 14

[**Freedom of thought, conscience and religion:** *The child's right to freedom of thought, conscience and religion, subject to appropriate parental guidance and national law*]

1.   States Parties shall respect the right of the child to freedom of thought, conscience and religion.

2.   States Parties shall respect the rights and duties of the parents and, when applicable, legal guardians, to provide direction to the child in the exercise of his or her right in a manner consistent with the evolving capacities of the child.

3.   Freedom to manifest one's religion or beliefs may be subject only to such limitations as are prescribed by law and are necessary to protect public safety, order, health or morals, or the fundamental rights and freedoms of others.

Article 15

[**Freedom of association:** *The right of children to meet with others and to join or set up associations, unless the fact of doing so violates the rights of others*]

1.   States Parties recognize the rights of the child to freedom of association and to freedom of peaceful assembly.

2.   No restrictions may be placed on the exercise of these rights other than those imposed in conformity with the law and which are necessary in a democratic society in the interests of national security or public safety, public order (*ordre public*), the protection of public health or morals or the protection of the rights and freedoms of others.

Article 16

[**Protection of privacy:** *The right to protection from interference with privacy, family, home and correspondence, and from libel/slander*]

1.   No child shall be subjected to arbitrary or unlawful interference with his or her privacy, family, home or correspondence, nor to unlawful attacks on his or her honour and reputation.

2.   The child has the right to the protection of the law against such interference or attacks.

Article 17

[**Access to appropriate information:** *The role of the media in disseminating information to children that is consistent with moral well-being and knowledge and understanding among peoples, and respects the child's cultural background. The State is to take measures to encourage this and to protect children from harmful materials*]

States Parties recognize the important function performed by the mass media and shall ensure that the child has access to information and material from a diversity of national and international sources, especially those aimed at the promotion of his or her social, spiritual and moral well-being and physical and mental health. To this end, States Parties shall:

(a)   Encourage the mass media to disseminate information and material of social and cultural benefit to the child and in accordance with the spirit of article 29;

(b)   Encourage international co-operation in the production, exchange and dissemination of such information and material from a diversity of cultural, national and international sources;

(c)   Encourage the production and dissemination of children's books;

(d)   Encourage the mass media to have particular regard to the linguistic needs of the child who belongs to a minority group or who is indigenous;

(e)   Encourage the development of appropriate guidelines for the protection of the child from information and material injurious to his or her well-being, bearing in mind the provisions of articles 13 and 18.

Article 18

[**Parental responsibilities:** *The principle that both parents have joint primary responsibility for bringing up their children, and that the State should support them in this task*]

1.   States Parties shall use their best efforts to ensure recognition of the principle that both parents have common responsibilities for the upbringing and development of the child. Parents or, as the case may be, legal guardians, have the primary responsibility for the upbringing and development of the child. The best interests of the child will be their basic concern.

2.   For the purpose of guaranteeing and promoting the rights set forth in the present Convention, States Parties shall render appropriate assistance to parents and legal guardians in the performance of their child-rearing responsibilities and shall ensure the development of institutions, facilities and services for the care of children.

3.   States Parties shall take all appropriate measures to ensure that children of working parents have the right to benefit from child-care services and facilities for which they are eligible.

Article 19

[Protection from abuse and neglect: The State's obligation to protect children from all forms of maltreatment perpetrated by parents or others responsible for their care, and to undertake preventive and treatment programmes in this regard]

1.   States Parties shall take all appropriate legislative, administrative, social and educational measures to protect the child from all forms of physical or mental violence, injury or abuse, neglect or negligent treatment, maltreatment or exploitation, including sexual abuse, while in the care of parent(s), legal guardian(s) or any other person who has the care of the child.

2.   Such protective measures should, as appropriate, include effective procedures for the establishment of social programmes to provide necessary support for the child and for those who have the care of the child, as well as for other forms of prevention and for identification, reporting, referral, investigation, treatment and follow-up of instances of child maltreatment described heretofore, and, as appropriate, for judicial involvement.

Article 20

[Protection of children without families: The State's obligation to provide special protection for children deprived of their family environment and to ensure that appropriate alternative family care or institutional placement is made available to them, taking into account the child's cultural background]

1.   A child temporarily or permanently deprived of his or her family environment, or in whose own best interests cannot be allowed to remain in that environment, shall be entitled to special protection and assistance provided by the State.

2.   States Parties shall in accordance with their national laws ensure alternative care for such a child.

3.   Such care could include, *inter alia*, foster placement, *kafalah* of Islamic law, adoption or if necessary placement in suitable institutions for the care of children. When considering solutions, due regard shall be paid to the desirability of continuity in a child's upbringing and to the child's ethnic, religious, cultural and linguistic background.

Article 21

[Adoption: In countries where adoption is recognized and/or allowed, it shall only be carried out in the best interests of the child, with all necessary safeguards for a given child and authorization by the competent authorities]

States Parties which recognize and/or permit the system of adoption shall ensure that the best interests of the child shall be the paramount consideration and they shall:

(a)   Ensure that the adoption of a child is authorized only by competent authorities who determine, in accordance with applicable law and procedures and on the basis of all pertinent and reliable information, that the adoption is permissible in view of the child's status concerning parents, relatives and legal guardians and that, if required, the persons concerned have given their informed consent to the adoption on the basis of such counselling as may be necessary;

(b)   Recognize that inter-country adoption may be considered as an alternative means of child's care, if the child cannot be placed in a foster or an adoptive family or cannot in any suitable manner be cared for in the child's country of origin;

(c)   Ensure that the child concerned by inter-country adoption enjoys safeguards and standards equivalent to those existing in the case of national adoption;

(d)   Take all appropriate measures to ensure that, in inter-country adoption, the placement does not result in improper financial gain for those involved in it;

(e) Promote, where appropriate, the objectives of the present article by concluding bilateral or multilateral arrangements or agreements, and endeavour, within this framework, to ensure that the placement of the child in another country is carried out by competent authorities or organs.

Article 22

*[**Refugee children:** Special protection to be granted to children who are refugees or seeking refugee status, and the State's obligation to co-operate with competent organizations providing such protection and assistance]*

1.   States Parties shall take appropriate measures to ensure that a child who is seeking refugee status or who is considered a refugee in accordance with applicable international or domestic law and procedures shall, whether unaccompanied or accompanied by his or her parents or by any other person, receive appropriate protection and humanitarian assistance in the enjoyment of applicable rights set forth in the present Convention and in other international human rights or humanitarian instruments to which the said States are Parties.

2.   For this purpose, States Parties shall provide, as they consider appropriate, co-operation in any efforts by the United Nations and other competent intergovernmental organizations or non-governmental organizations co-operating with the United Nations to protect and assist such a child and to trace the parents or other members of the family of any refugee child in order to obtain information necessary for reunification with his or her family. In cases where no parents or other members of the family can be found, the child shall be accorded the same protection as any other child permanently or temporarily deprived of his or her family environment for any reason, as set forth in the present Convention.

Article 23

*[**Handicapped children:** The right of handicapped children to special care, education and training designed to help them to achieve greatest possible self-reliance and to lead a full and active life in society]*

1.   States Parties recognize that a mentally or physically disabled child should enjoy a full and decent life, in conditions which ensure dignity, promote self-reliance, and facilitate the child's active participation in the community.

2.   States Parties recognize the right of the disabled child to special care and shall encourage and ensure the extension, subject to available resources, to the eligible child and those responsible for his or her care, of assistance for which application is made and which is appropriate to the child's condition and to the circumstances of the parents or others caring for the child.

3.   Recognizing the special needs of a disabled child, assistance extended in accordance with paragraph 2 of the present article shall be provided free of charge, whenever possible, taking into account the financial resources of the parents or others caring for the child, and shall be designed to ensure that the disabled child has effective access to and receives education, training, health care services, rehabilitation services, preparation for employment and recreation opportunities in a manner conducive to the child's achieving the fullest possible social integration and individual development, including his or her cultural and spiritual development.

4.   States Parties shall promote, in the spirit of international co-operation, the exchange of appropriate information in the field of preventive health care and of medical, psychological and functional treatment of disabled children, including dissemination of and access to information concerning methods of rehabilitation, education and vocational services, with the aim of enabling States Parties to improve their capabilities and skills and to widen their experience in these areas. In this regard, particular account shall be taken of the needs of developing countries.

Article 24

[Health and health services: The right to the highest level of health possible and to access to health and medical services, with special emphasis on primary and preventive health care, public health education and the diminution of infant mortality. The State's obligation to work towards the abolition of harmful traditional practices. Emphasis is laid on the need for international co-operation to ensure this right]

1.   States Parties recognize the right of the child to the enjoyment of the highest attainable standard of health and to facilities for the treatment of illness and rehabilitation of health. States Parties shall strive to ensure that no child is deprived of his or her right of access to such health care services.

2.   States Parties shall pursue full implementation of this right and, in particular, shall take appropriate measures:

(a)   To diminish infant and child mortality;

(b)   To ensure the provision of necessary medical assistance and health care to all children with emphasis on the development of primary health care;

(c)   To combat disease and malnutrition, including within the framework of primary health care, through, *inter alia*, the application of readily available technology and through the provision of adequate nutritious foods and clean drinking-water, taking into consideration the dangers and risks of environmental pollution;

(d)   To ensure appropriate pre-natal and post-natal health care for mothers;

(e)   To ensure that all segments of society, in particular parents and children, are informed, have access to education and are supported in the use of basic knowledge of child health and nutrition, the advantages of breast-feeding, hygiene and environmental sanitation and the prevention of accidents;

(f)   To develop preventive health care, guidance for parents, and family planning education and services.

3.   States Parties shall take all effective and appropriate measures with a view to abolishing traditional practices prejudicial to the health of children.

4.   States Parties undertake to promote and encourage international co-operation with a view to achieving progressively the full realization of the right recognized in the present article. In this regard, particular account shall be taken of the needs of developing countries.

Article 25

[Periodic review of placement: The right of children placed by the State for reasons of care, protection or treatment to have all aspects of that placement evaluated regularly]

States Parties recognize the right of a child who has been placed by the competent authorities for the purposes of care, protection, or treatment of his or her physical or mental health, to a periodic review of the treatment provided to the child and all other circumstances relevant to his or her placement.

Article 26

[Social security: The right of children to benefit from social security]

1.   States Parties shall recognize for every child the right to benefit from social security, including social insurance, and shall take the necessary measures to achieve the full realization of this right in accordance with their national law.

2.   The benefits should, where appropriate, be granted, taking into account the resources and the circumstances of the child and persons having responsibility for the

maintenance of the child, as well as any other consideration relevant to an application for benefits made by or on behalf of the child.

Article 27

[**Standard of living:** *The right of children to benefit from an adequate standard of living, the primary responsibility of parents to provide this, and the State's duty to ensure that this responsibility is first fulfillable and then fulfilled, where necessary through the recovery of maintenance*]

1. States Parties recognize the right of every child to a standard of living adequate for the child's physical, mental, spiritual, moral and social development.

2. The parent(s) or others responsible for the child have the primary responsibility to secure, within their abilities and financial capabilities, the conditions of living necessary for the child's development.

3. States Parties, in accordance with national conditions and within their means, shall take appropriate measures to assist parents and others responsible for the child to implement this right and shall in case of need provide material assistance and support programmes, particularly with regard to nutrition, clothing and housing.

4. States Parties shall take all appropriate measures to secure the recovery of maintenance for the child from the parents or other persons having financial responsibility for the child, both within the State Party and from abroad. In particular, where the person having financial responsibility for the child lives in a State different from that of the child, States Parties shall promote the accession to international agreements or the conclusion of such agreements, as well as the making of other appropriate arrangements.

Article 28

[**Education:** *The child's right to education, and the State's duty to ensure that primary education at least is made free and compulsory. Administration of school discipline is to reflect the child's human dignity. Emphasis is laid on the need for international co-operation to ensure this right*]

1. States Parties recognize the right of the child to education, and with a view to achieving this right progressively and on the basis of equal opportunity, they shall, in particular:

(*a*) Make primary education compulsory and available free to all;

(*b*) Encourage the development of different forms of secondary education, including general and vocational education, make them available and accessible to every child, and take appropriate measures such as the introduction of free education and offering financial assistance in case of need;

(*c*) Make higher education accessible to all on the basis of capacity by every appropriate means;

(*d*) Make educational and vocational information and guidance available and accessible to all children;

(*e*) Take measures to encourage regular attendance at schools and the reduction of drop-out rates.

2. States Parties shall take all appropriate measures to ensure that school discipline is administered in a manner consistent with the child's human dignity and in conformity with the present Convention.

3. States Parties shall promote and encourage international co-operation in matters relating to education, in particular with a view to contributing to the elimination of ignorance and illiteracy throughout the world and facilitating access to scientific and

technical knowledge and modern teaching methods. In this regard, particular account shall be taken of the needs of developing countries.

Article 29

[Aims of education: The State's recognition that education should be directed at developing the child's personality and talents, preparing the child for active life as an adult, fostering respect for basic human rights and developing respect for the child's own cultural and national values and those of others]

1.   States Parties agree that the education of the child shall be directed to:

(a)   The development of the child's personality, talents and mental and physical abilities to their fullest potential;

(b)   The development of respect for human rights and fundamental freedoms, and for the principles enshrined in the Charter of the United Nations;

(c)   The development of respect for the child's parents, his or her own cultural identity, language and values, for the national values of the country in which the child is living, the country from which he or she may originate, and for civilizations different from his or her own;

(d)   The preparation of the child for responsible life in a free society, in the spirit of understanding, peace, tolerance, equality of sexes, and friendship among all peoples, ethnic, national and religious groups and persons of indigenous origin;

(e)   The development of respect for the natural environment.

2.   No part of the present article or article 28 shall be construed so as to interfere with the liberty of individuals and bodies to establish and direct educational institutions, subject always to the observance of the principles set forth in paragraph 1 of the present article and to the requirements that the education given in such institutions shall conform to such minimum standards as may be laid down by the State.

Article 30

[Children of minorities or of indigenous peoples: The right of children of minority communities and indigenous peoples to enjoy their own culture and to practise their own religion and language]

In those States in which ethnic, religious or linguistic minorities or persons of indigenous origins exist, a child belonging to such a minority or who is indigenous shall not be denied the right, in community with other members of his or her group, to enjoy his or her own culture, to profess and practise his or her own religion, or to use his or her own language.

Article 31

[Leisure, recreation and cultural activities: The right of children to leisure, play and participation in cultural and artistic activities]

1.   States Parties recognize the right of the child to rest and leisure, to engage in play and recreational activities appropriate to the age of the child and to participate freely in cultural life and the arts.

2.   States Parties shall respect and promote the right of the child to participate fully in cultural and artistic life and shall encourage the provision of appropriate and equal opportunities for cultural, artistic, recreational and leisure activity.

Article 32

[**Child labour:** *The State's obligation to protect children from engaging in work that constitutes a threat to their health, education or development, to set minimum ages for employment, and to regulate conditions of employment*]

1.   States Parties recognize the right of the child to be protected from economic exploitation and from performing any work that is likely to be hazardous or to interfere with the child's education, or to be harmful to the child's health or physical, mental, spiritual, moral or social development.

2.   States Parties shall take legislative, administrative, social and educational measures to ensure the implementation of the present article. To this end, and having regard to the relevant provisions of other international instruments, States Parties shall in particular:

(a)   Provide for a minimum age or minimum ages for admissions to employment;

(b)   Provide for appropriate regulation of the hours and conditions of employment;

(c)   Provide for appropriate penalties or other sanctions to ensure the effective enforcement of the present article.

Article 33

[**Drug abuse:** *The child's right to protection from the use of narcotic and psychotropic drugs and from being involved in their production or distribution*]

States Parties shall take all appropriate measures, including legislative, administrative, social and educational measures, to protect children from the illicit use of narcotic drugs and psychotropic substances as defined in the relevant international treaties, and to prevent the use of children in the illicit production and trafficking of such substances.

Article 34

[**Sexual exploitation:** *The child's right to protection from sexual exploitation and abuse, including prostitution and involvement in pornography*]

States Parties undertake to protect the child from all forms of sexual exploitation and sexual abuse. For these purposes, States Parties shall in particular take all appropriate national, bilateral and multilateral measures to prevent:

(a)   The inducement or coercion of a child to engage in any unlawful sexual activity;

(b)   The exploitative use of children in prostitution or other unlawful sexual practices;

(c)   The exploitative use of children in pornographic performances and materials.

Article 35

[**Sale, trafficking and abduction:** *The State's obligation to make every effort to prevent the sale, trafficking and abduction of children*]

States Parties shall take all appropriate national, bilateral and multilateral measures to prevent the abduction of, the sale of or traffic in children for any purpose or in any form.

Article 36

[**Other forms of exploitation:** *The child's right to protection from all other forms of exploitation not covered in articles 32, 33, 34 and 35*]

States Parties shall protect the child against all other forms of exploitation prejudicial to any aspects of the child's welfare.

Article 37

[Torture and deprivation of liberty: The prohibition of torture, cruel treatment or punishment, capital punishment, life imprisonment, and unlawful arrest or deprivation of liberty. The principles of appropriate treatment, separation from detained adults, contact with family and access to legal and other assistance]

States Parties shall ensure that:

(a) No child shall be subjected to torture or other cruel, inhuman or degrading treatment or punishment. Neither capital punishment nor life imprisonment without possibility of release shall be imposed for offences committed by persons below eighteen years of age;

(b) No child shall be deprived of his or her liberty unlawfully or arbitrarily. The arrest, detention or imprisonment of a child shall be in conformity with the law and shall be used only as a measure of last resort and for the shortest appropriate period of time;

(c) Every child deprived of liberty shall be treated with humanity and respect for the inherent dignity of the human person, and in a manner which takes into account the needs of persons of his or her age. In particular, every child deprived of liberty shall be separated from adults unless it is considered in the child's best interest not to do so and shall have the right to maintain contact with his or her family through correspondence and visits, save in exceptional circumstances;

(d) Every child deprived of his or her liberty shall have the right to prompt access to legal and other appropriate assistance, as well as the right to challenge the legality of the deprivation of his or her liberty before a court or other competent, independent and impartial authority, and to a prompt decision on any such action.

Article 38

[Armed conflicts: The obligation of States to respect and ensure respect for humanitarian law as it applies to children. The principle that no child under 15 take a direct part in hostilities or be recruited into the armed forces, and that all children affected by armed conflict benefit from protection and care]

1. States Parties undertake to respect and to ensure respect for rules of international humanitarian law applicable to them in armed conflicts which are relevant to the child.

2. States Parties shall take all feasible measures to ensure that persons who have not attained the age of fifteen years do not take a direct part in hostilities.

3. States Parties shall refrain from recruiting any person who has not attained the age of fifteen years into their armed forces. In recruiting among those persons who have attained the age of fifteen years but who have not attained the age of eighteen years, States Parties shall endeavour to give priority to those who are oldest.

4. In accordance with their obligations under international humanitarian law to protect the civilian population in armed conflicts, States Parties shall take all feasible measures to ensure protection and care of children who are affected by an armed conflict.

Article 39

[Rehabilitative care: The State's obligation to ensure that child victims of armed conflicts, torture, neglect, maltreatment or exploitation receive appropriate treatment for their recovery and social reintegration]

States Parties shall take all appropriate measures to promote physical and psychological recovery and social reintegration of a child victim of: any form of neglect, exploitation, or abuse; torture or any other form of cruel, inhuman or degrading treatment or punishment; or armed conflicts. Such recovery and reintegration shall take place in an environment which fosters the health, self-respect and dignity of the child.

Article 40

[Administration of juvenile justice: The right of children alleged or recognized as having committed an offence to respect for their human rights and, in particular, to benefit from all aspects of the due process of law, including legal or other assistance in preparing and presenting their defence. The principle that recourse to judicial proceedings and institutional placements should be avoided wherever possible and appropriate]

1.   States Parties recognize the right of every child alleged as, accused of, or recognized as having infringed the penal law to be treated in a manner consistent with the promotion of the child's sense of dignity and worth, which reinforces the child's respect for the human rights and fundamental freedoms of others and which takes into account the child's age and the desirability of promoting the child's reintegration and the child's assuming a constructive role in society.

2.   To this end, and having regard to the relevant provisions of international instruments, States Parties shall, in particular, ensure that:

(a)   No child shall be alleged as, be accused of, or recognized as having infringed the penal law by reason of acts or omissions that were not prohibited by national or international law at the time they were committed;

(b)   Every child alleged as or accused of having infringed the penal law has at least the following guarantees:

   (i)   To be presumed innocent until proven guilty according to law;

   (ii)   To be informed promptly and directly of the charges against him or her, and, if appropriate through his or her parents or legal guardian, and to have legal or other appropriate assistance in the preparation and presentation of his or her defence;

   (iii) To have the matter determined without delay by a competent, independent and impartial authority or judicial body in a fair hearing according to law, in the presence of legal or other appropriate assistance and, unless it is considered not to be in the best interest of the child, in particular, taking into account his or her age or situation, his or her parents or legal guardians;

   (iv)   Not to be compelled to give testimony or to confess guilt; to examine or have examined adverse witnesses and to obtain the participation and examination of witnesses on his or her behalf under conditions of equality;

   (v)   If considered to have infringed the penal law, to have this decision and any measures imposed in consequence thereof reviewed by a higher competent, independent and impartial authority or judicial body according to law;

   (vi)   To have the free assistance of an interpreter if the child cannot understand or speak the language used;

   (vii) To have his or her privacy fully respected at all stages of the proceedings.

3.   States Parties shall seek to promote the establishment of laws, procedures, authorities and institutions specifically applicable to children alleged as, accused of, or recognized as having infringed the penal law, and in particular:

(a)   The establishment of a minimum age below which children shall be presumed not to have the capacity to infringe the penal law;

(b)   Whenever appropriate and desirable, measures for dealing with such children without resorting to judicial proceedings, providing that human rights and legal safeguards are fully respected.

4.   A variety of dispositions, such as care, guidance and supervision orders; counselling; probation; foster care; education and vocational training programmes and

other alternatives to institutional care shall be available to ensure that children are dealt with in a manner appropriate to their well-being and proportionate both to their circumstances and the offence.

Article 41

[Respect for existing standards: The principle that, if any standards set in national law or other applicable international instruments are higher than those of this Convention, it is the higher standard that applies]

Nothing in the present Convention shall affect any provisions which are more conducive to the realization of the rights of the child and which may be contained in:

(a) The law of a State Party; or

(b) International law in force for that State.

PART II

Article 42

[Implementation and entry into force: The provisions of articles 42 – 54 notably foresee:

(i)   the State's obligation to make the rights contained in this Convention widely known to both adults and children.

(ii)   the setting up of a Committee on the Rights of the child composed of ten experts, which will consider reports that States Parties to the Convention are to submit two years after ratification and every five years thereafter. The Convention enters into force — and the Committee would therefore be set up — once 20 countries have ratified it.

(iii)   States Parties are to make their reports widely available to the general public.

(iv)   The Committee may propose that special studies be undertaken on specific issues relating to the rights of the child, and may make its evaluations known to each State Party concerned as well as to the UN General Assembly.

(v)   In order to 'foster the effective implementation of the Convention and to encourage international co-operation', the specialized agencies of the UN (such as the ILO, WHO and UNESCO) and UNICEF would be able to attend the meetings of the Committee. Together with any other body recognized as 'competent', including NGOs in consultative status with the UN and UN organs such as the UNHCR, they can submit pertinent information to the Committee and be asked to advise on the optimal implementation of the Convention]

States Parties undertake to make the principles and provisions of the Convention widely known, by appropriate and active means, to adults and children alike.

Article 43

1.   For the purpose of examining the progress made by States Parties in achieving the realization of the obligations undertaken in the present Convention, there shall be established a Committee on the Rights of the Child, which shall carry out the functions hereinafter provided.

2.   The Committee shall consist of ten experts of high moral standing and recognized competence in the field covered by this Convention. The members of the Committee shall be elected by States Parties from among their nationals and shall serve in their personal capacity, consideration being given to equitable geographical distribution, as well as to the principal legal systems.

3. The members of the Committee shall be elected by secret ballot from a list of persons nominated by States Parties. Each State Party may nominate one person from among its own nationals.

4. The initial election to the Committee shall be held no later than six months after the date of the entry into force of the present Convention and thereafter every second year. At least four months before the date of each election, the Secretary-General of the United Nations shall address a letter to States Parties inviting them to submit their nominations within two months. The Secretary-General shall subsequently prepare a list in alphabetical order of all persons thus nominated, indicating States Parties which have nominated them, and shall submit it to the States Parties to the present Convention.

5. The elections shall be held at meetings of States Parties convened by the Secretary-General at United Nations Headquarters. At those meetings, for which two-thirds of States Parties shall constitute a quorum, the persons elected to the Committee shall be those who obtain the largest number of votes and an absolute majority of the votes of the representatives of States Parties present and voting.

6. The members of the Committee shall be elected for a term of four years. They shall be eligible for re-election if renominated. The term of five of the members elected at the first election shall expire at the end of two years; immediately after the first election, the names of these five members shall be chosen by lot by the Chairman of the meeting.

7. If a member of the Committee dies or resigns or declares that for any other cause he or she can no longer perform the duties of the Committee, the State Party which nominated the member shall appoint another expert from among its nationals to serve for the remainder of the term, subject to the approval of the Committee.

8. The Committee shall establish its own rules of procedure.

9. The Committee shall elect its officers for a period of two years.

10. The meetings of the Committee shall normally be held at the United Nations Headquarters or at any other convenient place as determined by the Committee. The Committee shall normally meet annually. The duration of the meetings of the Committee shall be determined, and reviewed, if necessary, by a meeting of the States Parties to the present Convention, subject to the approval of the General Assembly.

11. The Secretary-General of the United Nations shall provide the necessary staff and facilities for the effective performance of the functions of the Committee under the present Convention.

12. With the approval of the General Assembly, the members of the Committee established under the present Convention shall receive emoluments from United Nations resources on such terms and conditions as the Assembly may decide.

Article 44

1. States Parties undertake to submit to the Committee, through the Secretary-General of the United Nations, reports on the measures they have adopted which give effect to the rights recognized herein and on the progress made on the enjoyment of those rights:

(a) Within two years of the entry into force of the Convention for the State Party concerned;

(b) Thereafter every five years.

2. Reports made under the present article shall indicate factors and difficulties, if any, affecting the degree of fulfilment of the obligations under the present Convention. Reports shall also contain sufficient information to provide the Committee with a comprehensive understanding of the implementation of the Convention in the country concerned.

3.   A State Party which has submitted a comprehensive initial report to the Committee need not in its subsequent reports submitted in accordance with paragraph 1(b) of the present article, repeat basic information previously provided.

4.   The Committee may request from States Parties further information relevant to the implementation of the Convention.

5.   The Committee shall submit to the General Assembly, through the Economic and Social Council, every two years, reports on its activities.

6.   States Parties shall make their reports widely available to the public in their own countries.

Article 45

In order to foster the effective implementation of the Convention and to encourage international co-operation in the field covered by the Convention:

(a)   The specialized agencies, the United Nations Children's Fund and other United Nations organs shall be entitled to be represented at the consideration of the implemention of such provisions of the present Convention as fall within the scope of their mandate. The Committee may invite the specialized agencies, the United Nations Children's Fund and other competent bodies as it may consider appropriate to provide expert advice on the implementation of the Convention in areas falling within the scope of their respective mandates. The Committee may invite the specialized agencies, the United Nations Children's Fund and other United Nations organs to submit reports on the implementation of the Convention in areas falling within the scope of their activities;

(b)   The Committee shall transmit, as it may consider appropriate, to the specialized agencies, the United Nations Children's Fund and other competent bodies, any reports from States Parties that contain a request, or indicate a need, for technical advice or assistance along with the Committee's observations and suggestions, if any, on these requests or indications;

(c)   The Committee may recommend to the General Assembly to request the Secretary-General to undertake on its behalf studies on specific issues relating to the rights of the child;

(d)   The Committee may make suggestions and general recommendations based on information received pursuant to articles 44 and 45 of the present Convention. Such suggestions and general recommendations shall be transmitted to any State Party concerned and reported to the General Assembly, together with comments, if any, from States Parties.

PART III

Article 46

The present Convention shall be open for signature by all States.

Article 47

The present Convention is subject to ratification. Instruments of ratification shall be deposited with the Secretary-General of the United Nations.

Article 48

The present Convention shall remain open for accession by any State. The instruments of accession shall be deposited with the Secretary-General of the United Nations.

Article 49

1.   The present Convention shall enter into force on the thirtieth day following the date of deposit with the Secretary-General of the United Nations of the twentieth instrument of ratification or accession.

2.   For each State ratifying or acceding to the Convention after the deposit of the twentieth instrument of ratification or accession, the Convention shall enter into force on the thirtieth day after the deposit by such State of its instrument of ratification or accession.

Article 50

1.   Any State Party may propose an amendment and file it with the Secretary-General of the United Nations. The Secretary-General shall thereupon communicate the proposed amendment to States Parties, with a request that they indicate whether they favour a conference of States Parties for the purpose of considering and voting upon the proposals. In the event that, within four months from the date of such communication, at least one-third of the States Parties favour such a conference, the Secretary-General shall convene the conference under the auspices of the United Nations. Any amendment adopted by a majority of States Parties present and voting at the conference shall be submitted to the General Assembly for approval.

2.   An amendment adopted in accordance with paragraph (1) of the present article shall enter into force when it has been approved by the General Assembly of the United Nations and accepted by a two-thirds majority of States Parties.

3.   When an amendment enters into force, it shall be binding on those States Parties which have accepted it, other States Parties still being bound by the provisions of the present Convention and any earlier amendments which they have accepted.

Article 51

1.   The Secretary-General of the United Nations shall receive and circulate to all States the text of reservations made by States at the time of ratification or accession.

2.   A reservation incompatible with the object and purpose of the present Convention shall not be permitted.

3.   Reservations may be withdrawn at any time by notification to that effect addressed to the Secretary-General of the United Nations, who shall then inform all States. Such notification shall take effect on the date on which it is received by the Secretary-General.

Article 52

A State Party may denounce the present Convention by written notification to the Secretary-General of the United Nations. Denunciation becomes effective one year after the date of receipt of the notification by the Secretary-General.

Article 53

The Secretary-General of the United Nations is designated as the depositary of the present Convention.

Article 54

The original of the present Convention, of which the Arabic, Chinese, English, French, Russian and Spanish texts are equally authentic, shall be deposited with the Secretary-General of the United Nations.

In witness thereof the undersigned plenipotentiaries, being duly authorized thereto by their respective Governments, have signed the present Convention.

UK Declaration and Reservations

UN Convention on the Rights of the Child — UK Ratification

The instrument of ratification contained the following reservations and declarations:

(a) The United Kingdom interprets the Convention as applicable only following a live birth.

(b) The United Kingdom interprets the reference in the Convention to 'parents' to mean only those persons who, as a matter of national law, are treated as parents. This includes cases where the law regards a child as having only one parent, for example where a child has been adopted by one person only and in certain cases where a child is conceived other than as a result of sexual intercourse by the woman who gives birth to it and she is treated as the only parent.

(c) The United Kingdom reserves the right to apply such legislation, in so far as it relates to the entry into, stay in and departure from the United Kingdom of those who do not have the right under the law of the United Kingdom to enter and remain in the United Kingdom, and to the acquisition and possession of citizenship, as it may deem necessary from time to time.

(d) Employment legislation in the United Kingdom does not treat persons under 18, but under the school-leaving age as children, but as 'young people'. Accordingly, the United Kingdom reserves the right to continue to apply Article 32 subject to such employment legislation.

(e) Where at any time there is a lack of suitable accommodation or adequate facilities for a particular individual in any institution in which young offenders are detained, or where the mixing of adults and children is deemed to be mutually beneficial, the United Kingdom reserves the right not to apply Article 37(c) in so far as those provisions require children who are detained to be accommodated separately from adults.

(f) In Scotland there are tribunals (known as 'children's hearings') which consider the welfare of the child and deal with the majority of offences which a child is alleged to have committed. In some cases, mainly of a welfare nature, the child is temporarily deprived of its liberty for up to seven days prior to attending the hearing. The child and its family are, however, allowed access to a lawyer during this period. Although the decisions of the hearings are subject to appeal to the courts, legal representation is not permitted at the proceedings of the children's hearings themselves. Children's hearings have proved over the years to be a very effective way of dealing with the problems of children in a less formal, non-adversarial manner. Accordingly, the United Kingdom, in respect of Article 37(d), reserves its right to continue the present operation of children's hearings.

Part II
Representation

Chapter 3

The Representation of Children in Public Law Proceedings

The Guardian *ad Litem*/Reporting Officer (GAL/RO) service is central to the representation of children in public law proceedings, and stands as organisational testimony to the principle of having a special and independent professional who is there solely to guard the interests of an individual child in a particular situation, at a critical stage of their life.

The Development of the Guardian *ad Litem* and Reporting Officer Service

Considering the comparatively recent history of the representation of children in public law proceedings, it could be claimed that the present system incorporating the improvements introduced by the Children Act 1989, is one of the most comprehensive and sophisticated systems in any country. Children's cases now generally receive more court time and more expert attention than would have been thought possible even 15 years ago, when it was not uncommon for a contested care case to occupy only 10 or 20 minutes. Now, it is not unusual for hearings to be listed for one, two or even ten days. Designated family judges receive special training in children's cases and children's panel solicitors are required to acquire additional skills and expertise, before they are allowed to represent children. The right of children to instruct their own solicitor is a considerable advance for children's rights generally. The existence of guardians as an additional safeguard to the welfare of the child provides a neat and effective working synthesis of rights and welfare, which ensures that courts are given maximum information and opportunity to make proper and wise decisions in respect of children. Children have moved from a position in which scant consideration was given to their wishes and feelings. to one in which they may be bombarded by experts, interested in every aspect of their growth, thought and development. How have these changes come about in such a comparatively short time?

The representational anomaly and the call for 'independence'

In 1974, the committee of enquiry into the care and supervision in relation to Maria Colwell stated that 'had the views of an independent social worker been available to the court, they would have had the assistance of a second opinion which might, or might not, have endorsed the conclusions and recommendations contained in their (the social workers') report'.[1]

The need for an independent representative in care proceedings was recognised by the 1975 Children Act and, after November 1976, it was possible to appoint a guardian *ad litem* in cases in which local authorities were not opposing the application of a parent to revoke an existing care order (this was seen as a priority and would have covered Maria Colwell's situation). S.64 of the 1975 Children Act dealt with the appointment of a guardian *ad litem* in cases where the local authorities were opposing parents' applications to revoke care orders, but this section was not implemented until May 27, 1984 — nine years after it first appeared on the statute book. In the vacuum created by the lack of implementation, solicitors began to seek independent evidence and to instruct independent social workers. This practice was encouraged by a Law Society Memorandum, circulated in November 1980.[2]

Before May 27, 1984, the crux of the problem for solicitors was the representation anomaly, which made the child and the local authority parties to the care proceedings, leaving the parents unrepresented. In parental rights resolutions, the situation was reversed, in that it was the parents and the local authority who were represented, leaving the child without separate representation. In certain cases, solicitors had been taking instructions from parents who were the initiators of the proceedings and whose interests were clearly in conflict with those of the child. In addition, it often seemed unjust that the majority of the evidence on one party to the proceedings (the child) was supplied by the other party to the proceedings (the local authority). The conflicts inherent in such arrangements were explored by Hilgendorf in 1981.[3]

---

1 The Field Fisher Report, *Report on the Committee of Enquiry into the care and supervision provided in relation to Maria Colwell* (1974) HMSO, para. 227.
2 Reprinted in *The Law Society Gazette*, Vol. 77, No.41.
3 Hilgendorf, *Social Workers and Solicitors in Child Care Cases* (1981).

In response to the increasing demand for independent reports generated by solicitors representing children, the National Association of Mental Health (MIND), the Register of Independent Advisers (TRIAL), the National Council of One Parent Families (NCOPF), Family Rights Group (FRG), Justice for Children, the South Bank Group and Independent Representation for Children in Need (IRCHIN) all established panels of experienced social workers willing to prepare independent reports. In 1981, there were moves to establish a National Independent Social Work Advisory Service (NISAS). Those plans never came to fruition; however, between 1980 and 1984, there was a proliferation of networks around the country, with wide variations in policy and practice.

While there appeared to be a general acceptance of the principle of independent representation, controversy surrounded independent representatives. Key objections were the lack of a national system of accreditation and accountability and the fear that independent social work constituted the thin end of the wedge that would open the door to private practice in social work.

More pragmatic objections were the fact that the reports were commissioned by solicitors, who were not bound to produce them in full to the court, or indeed to produce them at all. The solicitors were potentially very much in control of the independent social workers, who depended on them to negotiate their fees through the legal aid fund. However, many independent social workers, such as IRCHIN accredited social workers, would only accept cases from solicitors representing children on condition that their report was produced in full to the court. This position has now been endorsed by the decision in *Essex County Council v. R.*,[4] in which Thorpe J established that the court in wardship had the power to order a party to disclose a report to which legal professional privilege attached, if it contained material relevant to the determination of the case, even if that material was adverse to the party's cause. Where the court was considering the welfare of the child, its power and responsibility enabled it to override legal professional privilege. Parties to proceedings owed a duty to the court to make full and frank disclosure of any material in their possession relevant to the determination of the future of the child.

Independent social workers were, however, at a disadvantage in obtaining access to the evidence, in particular information in local authority files. In contrast, guardians *ad litem*, although having no statutory right of access to social services department files (other than adoption agency records) until after the implementation of the Children Act 1989, were nevertheless in a much stronger position when requesting sight of files and access to key people, including the child.

The legal status of children in care

There had been a marked change in the status of children in care, with an increase in the proportion being subject to statutory rather than voluntary care

---

4 [1993] 2 F.L.R. 826.

November 1976

Guardian ad litem may be appointed in:

- **Unopposed revocation of care cases** s. 32 Children and Young Persons Act 1969

May 1984

Guardian ad litem may be appointed in:

- **Care proceedings** s. 32B Children and Young Persons Act 1969; s. 64 Children Act 1975
- **Adoption and freeing for adoption** s. 20 Children Act 1975
- **Access Proceedings** s. 12F Child Care Act 1980
  Note: Parents may initiate proceedings after written notice of cessation of access
- **Parental Rights Resolutions** ss. 7(1), 7(2) Child Care Act 1980
  Note: The child may be separately represented

October 1991

Case Management Role s. 41(10) Children Act 1989 (applies to proceedings under the Children Act 1989)

> *Includes:* timetabling and allocation of cases
> considering whether an order applied for or any other is appropriate
> accepting service documents on behalf of the children

Guardian ad litem should be appointed in:

- **Care and supervision proceedings** Part IV Children Act 1989
- **Protection of Children** Part V Children Act 1989
- **Specified Proceedings** s. 41(6)(i) Children Act 1989
- **Adoption and freeing for adoption** s. 65 Adoption Act 1976

November 1994

Case Management Role s. 41(10) Children Act 1989 (applies to proceedings under the Children Act 1989)

Guardian ad litem should be appointed in:

- **Care and supervision proceedings** Part IV Children Act 1989
- **Protection of Children** Part V Children Act 1989
- **Specified Proceedings** s. 41(6)(i) Children Act 1989 (includes s. 25 Surrogacy Arrangements Applications)
- **Adoption and freeing for adoption** s. 65 Adoption Act 1976
- **Surrogacy Arrangements** s. 30 Human Fertilisation and Embryology Act 1990

Figure 2   **The Development of GAL/RO Panels**

rising from 50 per cent in the 1960s to 70 percent in 1981. Courts had been reluctant to challenge the local authorities in the management of child care cases. Three important decisions — *Lewisham London Borough Council v. Lewisham Juvenile Court Justices and another*,[5] *A. v. Liverpool City Council*[6] and *W. v. Hertfordshire County Council*[7] — had contributed to the imbalance between the powers of local authorities and parents who, at that stage, were still not full parties to care proceedings and had no right of appeal. The imbalance allowed local authorities to seek the help of the courts though wardship, but denied parents similar access to the court, in order to challenge local authority decision making.

An increasing awareness of the need to safeguard the rights of children and their families had led, in the late 1970s, to the establishment of numerous pressure groups — the Family Rights Group, the Children's Legal Centre, Justice for Children, Independent Representation for Children in Need and the Voice for the Child in Care amongst others. Concern centred around the level of state intervention into family life and the administrative, rather than judicial, procedures for the assumption of parental rights and the termination of access to children in care. The combined pressure from these organisations and others paved the way for S.12 of the Child Care Act 1980 which gave parents the chance to seek review by the courts when access was terminated. Parents and children were now entitled to separate legal representation at the hearing and a guardian *ad litem* could be appointed to represent the child's best interests. At the same time, the Department of Health and Social Security published a Code of Practice on Access, which contained specific guidelines for facilitating parental contact with children in care and governing rehabilitative work with families.[8] Social services departments were also issued with a circular, setting out guidelines for the assumption of parental rights.[9] These measures were the first formal recognition that the balance of power had swung too far away from natural parents and needed to be redressed. Clearly, one way of re-establishing the balance, and breaking up the increasingly dichotomised local authority/parent dyad, was to provide children with effective and separate independent legal and social work representation through the implementation of Ss.64 and 65 of the Children Act 1975. This took place on May 27, 1984 and marked the second stage of the development of the panels (the first being the partial implementation, resulting in the appointment of guardians, in non-opposed cases, implemented in November 1976).

Implementation of the Children Act 1989, in October 1991, saw the beginning of the third, and most significant, phase of panel development, with a considerable extension both in the range of proceedings in which guardians *ad litem* were appointed, and their powers in relation to the court and the children they represented.

5 [1980] A.C. 273.
6 [1982] A.C. 363.
7 [1985] 2 All E.R. 301.
8 LAC (83)19, *Code of Practice: Access to Children in Care* (December 1983) HMSO.
9 LAC (84)5 *Parental Rights Resolutions*, 1984 DHSS.

The Establishment of Panels

On May 27, 1984 a co-ordination of existing, but piecemeal, child care legislation was achieved, which laid a duty on local authorities to establish panels of guardians *ad litem* and reporting officers, to act in four types of proceedings:

- care proceedings, S.32(b) of the Children and Young Persons Act 1969, S.64 of the Children Act 1975;
- access proceedings, S.12(f) of the Child Care Act 1980;
- parental rights resolution, S.7(1) and S.7(2) of the Child Care Act 1980;
- adoption and freeing for adoption, S.20 of the Children Act 1975.

Practice was guided by the 'Blue Book', produced in 1984 in recognition of the fact that the newly appointed guardians *ad litem* and reporting officers would be undertaking a new function within a substantially changed procedural framework.[10]

During the consultation period, prior to the implementation of the new legislation, doubts were expressed by both lawyers and social workers around two main areas. Firstly, the confusion about the parameters of the guardian *ad litem*'s role in relation to that of the child's legal representative: given that the guardian had originally been intended to act as the child's advocate, as well as social worker, investigator, substitute parent, expert witness and court officer, guardians were apparently to be social work and legal wizards.[11] Secondly, there were doubts about the ability of panel members to act independently, unfettered by conflicts of interest, when panels were to be administered and funded by local authorities, in a situation in which they were accountable directly to the court.

The Short Report, published less than two months before the implementation of the new provisions, counselled caution on the establishment of panels and recommended that the Department of Health ensure that they had sufficient information on the operation of guardians *ad litem* in care proceedings, to enable them to assess the impact of the new provisions.[12]

The original proposal was for guardians *ad litem* to act as advocates, as well as investigators and expert witnesses. This would have meant panel members representing children directly, without a solicitor being appointed to represent the child. In the event, the critics of the proposals carried the day and the children were given the benefit of both a legal advocate to represent their wishes and feelings and a guardian *ad litem* to put a view about their welfare before the court.

Information on the establishment of the panels was provided by four major reports:

---

10 *Guide for Guardians ad Litem in the Juvenile Court* (1984), Department of Health and Social Security.
11 Murch and Bader, *Separate Representation for Parents and Children, An Examination of the Initial Phase* (December 1984), University of Bristol, Family Law Research Unit.
12 Second Report from the Social Services Committee, *Children in Care*, (1984) para. 108 recommendation 33.

(a) *Separate Representation for Parents and Children: An Examination of the Initial Phase*, Mervyn Murch with Kay Bader, University of Bristol, Family Law Research Unit, Commissioned by the DHSS and published in December 1984;
(b) *Panels of Guardians ad Litem and Reporting Officers*, a Report of the Joint Working Party of the Association of Directors of Social Services, the Association of County Councils and the Association of Metropolitan Authorities, published in February 1986;
(c) The British Association of Social Workers Report on Guardians and Curators *ad Litem* and Reporting Officers, published in July 1986;
(d) *The Practitioner's View of the Role and Tasks of the Guardian ad Litem and Reporting Officer*, George Coyle for Barnardos, published in 1987.

The British Association of Social Workers (BASW) Report showed that, in 1985, there were 72 panels in England and Wales, with a probable total panel membership of approximately 3,500 guardians *ad litem* and reporting officers. Panel sizes varied from eight to nearly two hundred. From the evidence received, there appeared to be remarkably little relationship between panel size, the population served and the actual or potential workload.

A major point to emerge from the reports was the diversity in the various local arrangements, giving rise to potentially inconsistent standards of service delivery. Local authorities had been given less than five months to liaise with the courts, set up the scheme, recruit, appoint and train panel members and establish complicated administrative arrangements. Shortages of resources undoubtedly influenced the composition of the panels, because administering authorities, with no additional central funding, had been placed under considerable pressure to fulfil their statutory obligations, with the minimum possible outlay.

Mervyn Murch's study revealed that three types of panel had emerged:

(a) *reciprocators* — those using solely reciprocal arrangements with other local authorities, in which no money changed hands;
(b) *solos* — those using only freelance or non-statutory agency staff (fee-attracting) as panel members;
(c) *hybrids* — those using a mixture of fee-attracting members, staff from non-statutory agencies and neighbouring local authority personnel.

Initially, many local authorities opted for panels based on reciprocal arrangements, with staff from one local authority undertaking work from neighbouring local authorities and vice versa. A key determinant was the apparent economy of such arrangements, but it quickly became clear that the new provisions were bearing down most heavily on local authority panel members, who were being asked to undertake guardian *ad litem* work, in addition to their already onerous workloads, for no extra remuneration. As one guardian said: 'I can visualise the situation where I am interviewed by a guardian *ad litem* about work I have neglected while I was away being a guardian *ad litem*.'

Two years into the new arrangements, a fourth type of panel had appeared:

(d) *the consortium* — in which a group of local authorities appointed full time staff specifically for panel work.

The joint Association of Directors of Social Services/Association of County Councils/Association of Metropolitan Authorities Report noted that 'severe resource pressures on local authority panel members had led to their withdrawal from RO/GAL work and a major shift towards using fee-attracting RO/GALs.'

Independence of the guardian

Early fears about the independence of panels which were administered and funded by local authorities gathered momentum. In 1986, the local government organisations concluded that:

> almost all sources doubted whether true independence of RO/GALs could be compatible with the local authorities' responsibility to set up, administer, train and finance the panels. The panel members are accountable to one body (the court) and administered by another (the local authority). Local authorities alone control the input into the process. The courts are responsible for checking the output. The extent to which a panel could be really independent, if it is appointed by a group of local authority staff who have an involvement in perpetuating the child care practices of that local authority, is doubted.[13]

The core recommendation of a British Association of Social Workers Report, published in 1986, was that there should be an independently funded administrative structure for panels: 'we say this, firstly and most importantly, because we feel that the present arrangements invite erosion of the independent functioning which is crucial if panel members are to safeguard children's interests before the court.'[14] The Bristol Family Law Research Unit agreed. They also found themselves 'seriously questioning whether the local authority structure, upon which the panels were established, was the appropriate way of ensuring that courts around the country achieved a reasonable standard of practice.'

George Coyle's research (see above) recommended the establishment of a national or regional system of administration for panels, funded centrally and accountable to the Lord Chancellor's Department. His report identified lack of resources and the lack of an independent administrative base as major weaknesses in the developing system.

The crux of the problem was, and continues to be, the fact that, in order to have credibility, panels must be administered not just to the satisfaction of local authorities, but to the satisfaction of other parties to the proceedings, in whose eyes they must be seen to be functioning independently. Local authorities are, after all, one party to the proceedings and a structure which

---

13 Association of Directors of Social Services/Association of County Councils/Association of Metropolitan Authorities, *Panels of Guardians ad Litem and Reporting Officers* (February 1986), p. 4.
14 British Association of Social Workers Report on Guardians and Curators *ad Litem* and Reporting Officers (July 1986), p. 56.

invites conflict of interest must always lay itself open to criticism. The Report of the Inquiry into Child Abuse in Cleveland, in 1987, expressed concern that the independence of the guardian *ad litem* panels should be clearly demonstrated and, in the absence of other arrangements for the administration of the panels, the contracting out of the service to a voluntary organisation, such as the Children's Society, was commended. Undeniably, events in Cleveland served to highlight the importance of the Guardian's independent voice.[15]

The concerns of the Department of Health, however, focused not on independence, but on the difficulties of managing and co-ordinating what was perceived as the somewhat disparate workforce hastily assembled in 1984. Accordingly, in 1988, the Department of Health published a guide to the administration of the panels. The guide introduced the role of panel co-ordinator as the precursor of the present panel manager.[16] A Social Services Inspectorate inspection of the service before implementation of the Children Act 1989 signposted the move towards the smaller 'dedicated' workforce now existing.[17]

The implementation of the 1989 Act on October 14, 1991, with the attendant expansion of the guardian *ad litem* service, was seen as an opportunity to make different arrangements for the administration and funding of the service. An amendment to the Children Bill, proposed by the British Association of Social Workers, would have provided for the regional administration and central funding of guardian *ad litem* panels through the Lord Chancellor's Department and was backed not only by an impressive array of voluntary child care organisations, including the National Society for the Prevention of Cruelty to Children, National Children's Homes, The Children's Society and Barnardos, but was also supported by all the local government organisations, the Association of Directors of Social Services, the Association of Metropolitan Authorities and the Association of County Councils. The amendment attracted a greater degree of consensus than any other amendment, apart from the proposed revision of the leaving care provisions. Sadly, the opportunity was lost, although the Lord Chancellor did give undertakings that the administration and funding of panels would continue to be examined as part of the Department's rolling programme of reform of the family jurisdiction. However, guardians have striven to fulfil their function with a high level of professionalism, despite the fundamentally flawed arrangements for the administration of the service.

In July 1988 the Lord Chancellor's Department produced a consultation document, which considered improvements in the arrangements for care proceedings. Its most significant proposal was for the establishment of an Office of Child Protection — a regional office under the direction of an experienced family lawyer, which could combine the functions of independent

---

15 See *Evidence submitted to the Cleveland Inquiry: Guardians ad Litem and Reporting Officers* (1988), British Association of Social Workers, p. 18.

16 *Panel Administration: A Guide to the Administration of Panels of Guardians ad Litem and Reporting Officers* ('The Green Guide'), (1988) Department of Health and Social Security, para. 2.6. p. 8.

17 *In the Interests of Children: An Inspection of the GALRO Service*, (1990) SSI.

initial assessment,allocation, case management and protection within a single organisation, working closely with the courts. In the event, this suggestion was dropped, although with hindsight it should perhaps have been examined more closely, as it would have provided a regional, rather than a local authority, base for the developing service.[18]

Concerns about the independence of panels continued to be expressed and still feature in the Children Act Advisory Committee Annual Reports as an issue arousing concern:

> Examples of problems were brought to the committee's notice, where the independence of the GAL/RO service of individual guardians was felt to be threatened. These ranged from concerns about the adequacy of budgets to the sharing of note-paper with the local authority. ··· The committee acknowledged that the independent status of the guardian ad litem in carrying out his duties for the court on behalf of the child has to be ensured and perceived by all parties.[19]

Following the implementation of the Children Act 1989 in October 1991, local authorities made renewed efforts to distance themselves from the day to day workings of the panel by placing panels and their managers in the newly formed, arms-length inspection units. One fundamental problem is the difficulty of proving, beyond all reasonable doubt, that a constraint on independence has occurred, as constraint is, by its nature, invisible. However in a one notable action, guardians *ad litem* from Cornwall and the Isles of Scilly successfully challenged the right of the administering authority to set a prescriptive limit on the time that a guardian could spend on any one case. An application for judicial review was brought and upheld.[20] The President of the Family Division, Sir Stephen Brown, found that the Director of Social Services, in imposing the time limit, had exceeded the proper exercise of his authority, which, in that case, amounted to an abuse of power. The decision to impose a bench-mark scheme sought to restrict the discretion of the guardian to undertake work that might be considered necessary. Further, the Director of Social Services imposed this in an arbitrary manner.

One less publicised aspect of this case was that, in order to initiate the proceedings and meet the attendant legal costs, the Cornish guardians had (with considerable ingenuity) set up a Judicial Review Fund and invited colleagues round the country to contribute. The strength of feeling which attached to the case could be judged by the fact that sufficient funds were raised to enable the Cornish guardians to bring their case to a satisfactory conclusion. If the action had failed, there were many guardians in England and Wales who would have been substantially out of pocket! The case does, however, effectively illustrate both the theoretical and practical difficulties of proving 'conflict of interest', and the high priority panel members give to the need to function independently.

---

18 *Improvements in the Arrangements for Care Proceedings* (July 1988), Lord Chancellor's Department, Consultation Paper.
19 The Children Act Advisory Committee Annual Report (1992/93), Chapter 7, The Voice of the Child, p.65.
20 *R. v. Cornwall County Council, ex p. Cornwall and Isles of Scilly Guardians ad Litem and Reporting Officers Panel* [1992] 1 W.L.R. 427.

Protocol for the reduction of disputes between a GAL/RO panel and the responsible local authority

Concerns about the absence of a mechanism for dealing with problems between individual guardians, panels and local authorities led, in 1993, to the introduction of a protocol for the resolution of disputes between a GAL/RO panel and the responsible local authority. The protocol deals with disputes about both independence and panel budgets. The focus of the protocol, certainly in relation to disputes regarding independence, does seem to revolve firmly around the panel manager and the local authority, rather than addressing the issue from the point of view of the appropriate exercise of the guardian's independent, professional discretion. It does not address, for example, how the role of the full-time, employed guardian differs from that of other employees of the local authority social services department, particularly in relation to their direct professional accountability to the court, rather than to the panel manager.

The National Association of Guardians ad Litem and Reporting Officers (NAGALRO) have produced their own statement of principles relating to complaints procedure. This was done in response to the many enquiries about difficulties or potential difficulties with the many different complaints procedures which exist within local authorities. In particular, it provides for appeals to an independent person or body (not the Director of Social Services Department.) There is no provision for appeals within the Regulations.[21]

The Organisation and Management of the GAL/RO Service

In March 1993, there were 56 GAL/RO panels[22] covering England. These consisted of 37 single non-metropolitan counties, 7 single metropolitan districts, 10 consortia of metropolitan districts and counties and 2 consortia of London Boroughs.

Five panels were operated by voluntary child care organisations, on a contracted out basis. By October 1994, the total numbers of GAL/ROs in England and Wales had fallen from 3,500 in 1984 to just under 1,000. A breakdown of the figures shows an increasing reliance on fee-attracting panel members and a withdrawal from the service of probation officers, voluntary organisations' secondees and local authority employees. Thus, increasing numbers of increasingly complex cases are being carried out by an apparently diminishing workforce.[23]

Local authority duties

The 1991 GAL/RO Panel Regulations placed on local authorities the following duties:

---

21 *Principles Relating to Complaints Procedures*, (1994) National Association of Guardians ad Litem and Reporting Officers.
22 The establishment of the Black Country Consortium in June 1993 reduced the number of panels to 54.
23 *GAL/RO Service Annual Reports 1992–93: An Overview* (1993) Department of Health, p.6; Annual Report 1994.

- to establish a panel;
- to ensure sufficient numbers of GAL/ROs;
- to establish a complaints board;
- to establish a panel committee;
- to appoint persons as panel members;
- to decide on the suitability of persons for appointment as panel members and comply with other specified duties regarding such appointments;
- to have regard, in such appointment, to the number of children in the area from different racial groups;
- to follow a specified procedure before terminating a person's membership of the panel;
- to establish a complaints procedure, including a complaints board, with membership specified in Schedule 1;
- to appoint a panel manager;
- to ensure that specified records are maintained in respect of the operation of the panel;
- to make arrangements for the functioning of panel committees, ensuring that their membership complies with Schedule 2;
- to monitor the work of panel members at intervals specified;
- to identify and make reasonable provision for the training of panel members.

Role of the panel manager

The evolution of a dedicated panel manager is a crucial element in the development and organisation of the GAL/RO service, reflecting the concern of the Department of Health that guardians should be demonstrably accountable for the work they carry out, bearing in mind their position of enormous power in relation to vulnerable children.

The guidance summarises the responsibilities of the panel manager in the following terms:

- ensuring an adequate supply of GAL/ROs to the courts at all times and promoting the professional quality of the service;
- making arrangements for appropriate training and professional support for GAL/ROs;
- arranging for administrative support to panel members in their tasks;
- making appropriate arrangements for the approval and payment of expenses, fees and allowances;
- arranging reviews in respect of individual panel members;
- establishing and maintaining an effective management information system;
- preparing and managing the panel budget;
- receiving complaints about the service and, where necessary, activating agreed procedures in respect of complaints against GAL/ROs, in accordance with the regulations;
- activating the agreed procedures in respect of the termination and non-renewal of panel membership;
- servicing the panel committee;

- attending the Family Court Business Committee;
- preparing the annual report on the panel's activities;
- establishing appropriate written procedures for the above.

Each panel member must appoint a manager. In order to maintain the distance between the panel manager and other local authority employees, a number of restrictions are imposed:

- the panel manager must not be involved with the authority's services in respect of children and their families, except in respect of the panel and its functions;
- where the panel manager is a part-time appointment, it is essential that any other responsibilities carried by the panel manager should not be in respect of the local authority's services for children and their families;
- so far as is practicable, the panel manager's line manager should be located within the management structure of the social services department, or in the local authority's legal services department, but avoiding locations which deal predominantly with the provision of child care services or child care legal advice.[24]

The panel manager is employed by the local authority, or on their behalf. The manager is responsible for the delivery of an independent guardian *ad litem*/reporting officer service, adequate to meet the needs of the court in the areas served by the panel. The panel manager should be a key link in the chain of communication between different individuals and bodies, who are responsible for securing the welfare of children in court proceedings. Key areas of responsibility for panel managers include:

- ensuring an adequate supply of guardians *ad litem* for the courts, at all times, and promoting the professional quality of the service;
- making arrangements for appropriate training and professional support for guardians *ad litem* and reporting officers;
- arranging for administrative support to panel members in their tasks;
- making appropriate arrangements for the approval and payment of expenses, fees and allowances;
- arranging reviews in respect of individual panel members;
- establishing and maintaining an effective management information system;
- preparing and managing the panel budget;
- receiving complaints about the service and, where necessary, activating agreed procedures in respect of complaints against guardians *ad litem* and reporting officers, in accordance with the regulations;
- activating the agreed procedures in respect of the termination and non-renewal of panel membership;
- servicing the panel committee;
- attending the Family Court Business Committee;
- preparing the annual report on the panel's activities;

---

24 Children Act 1989 Guidance and Regulations Volume 7: *Guardians ad Litem and other Court Related Issues*, paras. 2.17 to 2.20.

● establishing appropriate written procedures for the above.[25]

The remit of the panel manager, vis-à-vis that of the panel member, is clarified in the Manual of Management of GAL/RO Panel Managers. The distinction between the professional remit of the panel members and the managerial remit of the panel manager requires emphasis. Panel members stand in direct relationship with the child and the court. On appointment to individual cases, they become officers of the court, charged with providing an independent professional evaluation of an individual case, in the light of the principles and provisions of the 1989 Act and other relevant legislation. It is the duty of a panel member to determine what is in the best interests of the child and to report on this to the court:

> The panel manager has a different, but not conflicting, role. His responsibility is to enable the panel members to carry out their professional tasks efficiently and effectively, for the benefit of the child in the individual case and in the light of the overall demands upon the service.[26]

It should be emphasised that the panel manager's role is not to supervise the guardian professionally, and the panel manager 'must at all times take great care to ensure that any information or advice given does not relate to a guardian's independent judgement about the child's welfare. This must be the particular responsibility of the guardian.'[27]

The panel manager, therefore, is in a slightly ambiguous position, being responsible, on the one hand, for providing a high quality service to the courts, but, on the other hand, having no line management control over any aspect of the guardians' exercise of their professional discretion. It is a difficult and contradictory role, imposed by the requirement for panels to continue to be funded and administered by local authorities, yet limited by the constraints imposed by the fact that the panel manager is an employee of the local authority, who may be a party to the proceedings. It is a 'hands on — hands off' situation, which requires a certain amount of intellectual dexterity. It is arguable, also, that such a complex structure is less cost effective than a regional alternative, in which panel managers could provide professional, as well as administrative, support. Clearly, panel members do need professional consultation and appraisal and, under the present arrangements, this has to be separately provided from limited panel budgets. Guardians have management; they do not have professional supervision and consultation. This makes re-appointment and appraisal of their professional practice enormously complicated. Their accountability is to the court for their practice, but to the administering local authority for all the 'pay and rations' aspects of the service. The difficulties of arm's length management are a matter of concern to the National Association of Panel Managers, which held its first meeting in London on December 8, 1994.

---

25 Children Act 1989 Guidance and Regulations, Vol.7 para. 2.23.
26 *Manual of Management for GAL/RO Panel Managers*, (1992) Department of Health, pp. 10 and 11.
27 *Manual of Management for GAL/RO Panel Managers*, ibid, p.20.

The role of the panel committee

Each local authority is required to establish a panel committee. The functions of the committee are derived from the responsibility of the local authority, set out in regulation 8 of the Guardians *ad Litem* and Reporting Officers (Panels) Regulations 1991.[28] The membership of the panel committee will be drawn from four categories:

- a representative of the local authority;
- a Justices' Clerk or a Magistrates' Clerk in the local authority's area;
- a person who has relevant experience of child care, who is neither an officer nor a member of a local authority;
- a representative of the panel, established under regulation 2(1).[29]

The panel committee must be chaired by a person who is not a representative of the local authority.

The terms of reference for the panel committee are:

- the standards of practice of guardians *ad litem* and reporting officers in relevant proceedings in their area;
- the appointment and reappointment of guardians *ad litem* and reporting officers to the panel, termination of their appointment and review of their work;
- the training of guardians *ad litem* and reporting officers; and
- matters arising from complaints concerning guardians *ad litem* and reporting officers and the administration of the panel (but not the investigation of particular complaints).[30]

This is a minimum list of tasks. Clearly it could be argued that the panel committee has a responsibility for all areas of responsibility undertaken by panel managers. The panel committee, in conjunction with the panel manager, will deal with appointments, termination of appointments, reappointments and complaints and may potentially be involved in the appraisal and reappraisal of panel members' work. Members of the panel committee, for example, will share responsibility for ensuring that an annual report is provided by each panel. This should include a summary of the activities of the panel members, a breakdown of financial expenditure, details of the membership of the panel committee and of the panel, including information on guardians *ad litem* and reporting officers and the work undertaken by each, summaries of training activities, of key policy and practice developments (for example meetings with the Family Court Business Committee) and of priorities to be addressed in the period to be covered by the next report. Copies of the annual report should be made available to the local authority's Social Services

---

28 S.I. 1991 No. 2051.
29 Guardians *ad Litem* and Reporting Officers (Panels) Regulations 1991, Sched. 2, para. 1(a)–(d).
30 Reg. 8.

Committee, the Family Court Business Committee and the Department of Health.[31]

Complaints about the operation of the guardian ad litem and reporting officer service

For the purpose of monitoring the administration and procedures of the panel and the work of guardians *ad litem* and reporting officers in relevant proceedings, each local authority shall establish a procedure for considering complaints about the operation of the panel in respect of their area, and about any member of that panel, including the refusal to reappoint a person to be a panel member.[32]

The local authority is required to investigate any such complaint and , if it cannot be resolved to the satisfaction of the person making the complaint, it shall be referred to the complaints board, which will make a recommendation to the authority in writing.[33] Complaints boards are established in relation to each individual complaint and do not have a fixed membership, in consideration of the fact that, for each complaint, the principle of independence must be observed and a constant complaints panel membership may prejudice that independence in relation to one panel member or another. Any person, in respect of whom a complaint is made, shall be notified by the local authority of the complaint, in writing, and shall be given an opportunity to make representations to the local authority. If the matter is referred to the complaints board, the local authority shall provide him with an opportunity to make representations to the complaints board.[34]

The local authority shall only make a decision on a complaint, referred to the complaints board, after having taken into account the recommendation of the complaints board and shall notify their decision, in writing, to the person who made the complaint and any person in respect of whom the complaint was made.[35]

It is a matter for each local authority to write their own complaints procedure, although this may give rise to some confusion in two main areas. Firstly, a timetable must be drawn up for the hearing, investigation and resolution of the complaint. Secondly, the right of the guardian *ad litem* to be represented and by whom must be considered. If that representation includes legal representation, there is the question of how that is to be financed. Many guardians *ad litem* are covered by professional indemnity insurance through the National Association of Guardians *ad Litem* and Reporting Officers, the British Association of Social Workers or UNISON (a merger of the National and Local Government Officers' Association (NALGO), National Union of Public Employees (NUPE) and Confederation of Health Service Employees (COHSE)). However some guardians are not covered, so it can by no means be taken for granted that all panel members will have professional indemnity

---

31 Children Act 1989 Guidance and Regulations Vol. 7, para. 2.85.
32 Guardians *ad Litem* and Reporting Officers (Panels) Regulations 1991, reg. 6(1).
33 Reg. 6(2).
34 Reg. 6(3).
35 Reg. 6(4).

insurance. The question of complaints about a guardian's practice is a very serious one. The resolution of the complaint may well drag on for over a year, during which time the individual guardian's practice is under a cloud. The format of the procedure is often imprecise and confusing. It is not clear, for example, at which stage a complaint passes from an informal investigation to a formal complaint, which will become part of the guardian *ad litem*'s professional record. Clearly, panel members must be accountable for the work they do, but the situation is complicated by the fact that they are statutorily responsible to the court for the work they carry out and, historically, courts have little involvement in the consideration of complaints in relation to an individual guardian's practice. A Protocol for the Resolution of Disputes between a GAL/RO panel and the responsible local authority, produced by the Social Services Inspectorate, emphasises the importance of the Panel Manager (and, indirectly, the local authority), rather than the courts in the settling of disputes (see the Appendix to this chapter.)

Expenses, fees and allowances of members of panels

Each local authority shall defray the reasonable expenses incurred in respect of relevant proceedings by members of the panel established in respect of their area, and pay fees and allowances for members of such panels. However, no expenses, fees or allowances shall be defrayed or paid by local authorities in respect of a member of a panel who is employed under a contract of service by a local authority or probation committee for 30 hours or more a week.[36]

The level of a guardian *ad litem*'s fee is a long-standing area of contention. There is no national scale of fees payable to guardians *ad litem* and reporting officers and this has led to regional variations in the rates paid for the same service. The Department of Health have made it clear that it is a matter for each local authority to fix panel fees.[37] The guardian *ad litem* service has to compete for priority in relation to all other local authority services. A survey carried out by the National Association of Guardians *ad Litem* and Reporting Officers, in 1990, found that fees varied by more than £11 per hour (ranging from £7.57 per hour in Leeds/Bradford/Calderdale to £19.14 per hour in Manchester). The fact that these two panels adjoin geographically must predispose prospective panels members to apply to Manchester rather than Leeds/Bradford/Calderdale. Such discrepancies skew the deployment of the work force and create the potential for the development of waiting lists in low paying areas. Many guardians are on more than one panel and local authorities may compete for the services of the same panel member. Traditionally, the rate for guardian *ad litem* work has been loosely based on the Law Society rate for independent reporting. That may have been the appropriate yard-stick in the past, but is no longer an appropriate guideline to use. The question of guardian *ad litem*'s fees was the subject of an application for judicial review by the Inner and North London Panel in July 1993. In the event the action was dropped.

---

36 Regs. 9(1) and (2).
37 Children Act 1989 Guidance and Regulations Vol. 7, para. 2.35.

Keeping records of the service

Each local authority shall ensure that records are kept in relation to the operation of the panel, which shall include:

- the name of each child in respect of whom a guardian *ad litem* or reporting officer is selected from the panel;
- a description of the relevant proceedings in respect of which the selection is made;
- the name and level of the court (whether High Court, County Court or the Family Proceedings Court);
- the name of any person selected from the panel, including whether he has been appointed in specific proceedings or in proceedings under the Adoption Act 1976, either as a guardian *ad litem* or as a reporting officer;
- the date of each appointment;
- the date on which work started in respect of that appointment and the date on which it finished;
- details of fees, expenses and allowances in each case in which there has been such an appointment; and
- the result of the proceedings in which there has been such an appointment.[38]

Retention and destruction of records

A Consultation Paper on the retention and destruction of guardian *ad litem* records was circulated to panel members and panel managers in April 1993 by the Social Services Inspectorate (SSI), after concerns had been expressed about the security and confidentiality of the storage of panel members' records.[39] The SSI survey found that guardians' records and copies of court reports proliferated in many different locations. In social work agencies, records were often stored without sufficient consideration of the need for separation from the agencies' own records. Fee-attracting guardians *ad litem* usually stored their records at home and often they were not kept securely. Courts were not generally prepared to keep guardians *ad litem* and reporting officer records, because of lack of space, but they kept copies of court reports. The SSI report recommended that confidential and secure record storage and secretarial services must be provided for guardians *ad litem* and reporting officers.[40] Volume 7 of Children Act 1989 Regulations and Guidance particularly discourages the long term storage of records at the guardian *ad litem*'s home address. The Guidance made it clear that the need for records to be returned to safe storage, on a long term basis, relates to further possible court cases, including, for example, claims for compensation or proceedings under the European Convention of Human Rights.[41]

---

38 GAL/RO (Panels) Regulations 1991, reg. 7(1) and 7(2)(a)–(g).
39 *In the Interests of Children*, (1990) SSI Inspection of the GAL/RO Service, Department of Health.
40 The GAL/RO Service, *Retention and Destruction of Records* (April 1993) Consultation Paper.
41 Children Act 1989 Guidance and Regulations Vol. 7, para. 2.76.

The SSI survey found that, in general, the collection and collation of information relating to the service had been carried out in a fairly *ad hoc* fashion.

The annual report for 1991/92 raised the question of whether or not the data collected by the GAL/RO panels provided the most informative basis for understanding how the service functioned nationally. There were wide discrepancies in the data collected, which led to a patchy picture of service provision. Accordingly, the Working Party Report on Data Collection for the GAL/RO Service was circulated by the SSI in 1993.

Termination of panel membership

The local authority may terminate a person's membership of a panel at any time, when they consider that he is unable or unfit to carry out the functions of the guardian *ad litem* or reporting officer. Before terminating a person's membership of the panel, the local authority shall:

● notify him in writing of the reasons why it is proposed that his membership of the panel shall be terminated;
● give him an opportunity of making representations to the local authority.

Where the local authority, having considered representation made under para. 2(b) of the Regulations, still propose to terminate a person's membership, they shall refer the matter to a complaints board. The complaints board shall make a recommendation to the authority, after taking account of any representation of the person whose membership the local authority propose to terminate. The local authority shall consider the recommendation of the complaints board as to the termination of a person's membership, and decide whether or not to terminate membership. They shall give notice to that person in writing of their decision, together with their reasons for the decision.[42]

The Regulations make it clear that the termination of panel membership is a matter for the local authority to determine. However, again the demarcation lines of independence are difficult to draw. The panel manager is in an unenviable situation, as he is restricted in his ability to comment on the guardian *ad litem*'s professional performance, but must confine himself to carrying out the procedures for termination of panel membership. It is likely that the reason to terminate the panel member's employment arises out of a perceived failure in his professional practice, over which the panel manager has no control. Nevertheless, the panel manager is in an advantageous position to observe an individual panel member's performance and, as a local authority employee, may have very definite views about areas of individual practice. Panel members must be accountable for their professional practice and the enormous responsibilities and powers they hold in relation to children and families mean that they must be subject to regular and consistent professional scrutiny. The problem is to establish an administrative structure which combines maximum professional autonomy and independence with the need

42 GAL/RO (Panels) Regulations 1991, reg. 5(1)(5).

to be professionally accountable. The continuing arrangements, whereby guardians *ad litem* and reporting officers are accountable to the court, but are reviewed, appraised and administered by local authorities, are unsatisfactory on this and a number of other counts.

Data collection

The Working Party Report identified the principal reasons for having reliable data:

- monitoring overall performance;
- demonstrating financial accountability and efficiency;
- improving professional knowledge and practice;
- informing policy developments;
- comparing service delivery between panels; and
- contributing to national statements about the service.[43]

There is an increasing pressure in the GAL/RO service to attempt to quantify the particular contribution it makes to the representation of children in public proceedings and to evaluate its standards of service delivery and efficiency.

Standards, Qualifications and training

'It is a matter for each local authority to decide whether the qualifications and experience of any person, who they propose to appoint to the panel, are suitable for the purpose of that person's appointment, as a guardian *ad litem* or a reporting officer.'[44] However the guidance makes it clear that most GAL/ROs should be qualified in social work and have several years of relevant expertise working with children:

> Exceptionally the local authority may decide that a particular applicant, who may not have a formal social work qualification, has, nevertheless, relevant experience and qualifications which make them suitable, bearing in mind that GAL/ROs are expected to have, not only experience with children and families, but knowledge of, and skills in, planning for children in care and adoption work.[45]

In Scotland, curators *ad litem* are not exclusively social workers. They may be teachers or educational psychologists and there was some debate in the House of Commons about whether or not social work was an exclusive qualification for the job.

In the event, panels have appointed a workforce which includes some of the most experienced and well-qualified practitioners in the child care field. One in five members has more than 20 years post qualifying experience and one in four between 15 and 19 years. More than 65 per cent of guardians presently employed have been on panels for more than four years. Furthermore, panel members appear to take a high degree of responsibility for their own further training and developmental needs.

---

43 *The GAL/RO Service, Data Collection* (1993) Report of Working Party, SSI, Department of Health.
44 GAL/RO (Panels) Regulations 1991, reg. 4(2).
45 Children Act 1989 Guidance and Regulations Vol. 7, para. 2.51.

According to a Training Report, carried out by the Social Services Inspectorate in 1993:

> guardians were actively involved in an impressive amount of post-qualifying training — including largely self-funded, post-graduate studies and attendance at a wide range of national, regional and local conferences, seminars and training events. Systematic approaches to panel training are, however, rather ad hoc; some guardians who may be on more than one panel are very well provided with training opportunities funded by the panel, others may be offered very little.[46]

The question of standards and quality control of the service are matters which continue to preoccupy the Department of Health. Accordingly, in June 1994, the Social Services Inspectorate circulated a consultation paper on standards and the guardian service.

> Agreement about standards is intended to have several practical outcomes. It will help ensure that within panel areas and across the country, children, families and courts can be assured of a consistent minimum but good standard of service. It will also help clarify standards where complaints procedures in respect of the GALRO Service are initiated. Standards will also have a key part in reviews of panel members (Appraisals). It will help promote professional discussion about quality and the ability of the service to achieve standards effectively and in an efficient way.[47]

Typically, standards will be derived from a range of sources including:

● legislation, regulation and case law;
● moral and ethical values;
● organisational (including governmental) policy, rules and guidelines;
● professional sources expressed through common practices, professional associations and codes of practice;
● research and academic texts.

The guardian's role as an autonomous professional, who is not part of a local government line management structure, ensures a high level of qualification in many panel members, but also means that there is no career structure for guardians and no clearly visible and accessible inducement to take their considerable knowledge and experience back into social services departments.

Comment

The Children Act Report 1992 emphasised that the right of the child to separate and independent representation in public law proceedings is a central principle of the 1989 Act. It recognised that there could be potential for conflict of interest, where the authority responsible for the provision of the guardian service is a party to the proceedings in which a guardian has been appointed to act for the child. It further noted that, in spite of the range of safeguards that had been built into the Regulations and Guidance and Rules of

---

46 *The GAL/RO Service Training Report* (February 1994), Department of Health, Social Services Inspectorate.
47 *The Guardian ad Litem and Reporting Officer Service Consultation Paper: Standards and the Guardian Service* (June 1994) Department of Health and Social Services Inspectorate, p.3, paras 2.3, 2.5.

Courts to underpin the independence of the guardian in the exercise of his or her professional judgment, nonetheless concerns continued to be expressed about the independence of the service, despite the existence of safeguards:[48]

> All of this underlines the crucial role of the guardian ad litem acting as a backstop, amidst swings of social work practice, and as a balancing agent between children's rights, children's rescue, and family and state autonomy, representing the child whose interest may well have become submerged in the welter of administrative, financial, political and bureaucratic considerations, which can quickly turn *best* into *vested* interest.[49]

The Role of the Solicitor

Central to the improvements in the representation of children in public law proceedings is the right of children to their own legal representation. A child who is the subject of care proceedings under the 1989 Act is a party to those proceedings.[50] In care proceedings, under Parts IV and V of the 1989 Act, a solicitor for the child can be appointed in three ways:

- by the child directly
- by the guardian *ad litem*;[51]
- by the court.

Following criticism of the level of skills available in children's cases,[52] the Law Society established a panel of child care law solicitors, who are deemed to have particular expertise in representing children. All members of the children's panel undergo specific training in the conduct of children's cases. The children's panel covers all proceedings under the Children Act 1989, where there is provision to represent children. The emphasis, however, is on representing children in public law proceedings, as the vast majority of children requiring representation will be in child protection and care proceedings. This is in spite of the fact that in terms of total numbers, there are many more children involved in private rather than public law proceedings. Solicitors on the children's panel are not restricted to representing children, but may represent other parties such as parents or grandparents. The panel cover all proceedings where children will be parties in terms of private and public law Orders and it is therefore necessary for all child care practitioners to be familiar with the full range of Orders.[53]

However, the children's panel does not cover adoption or wardship cases. The reason given is that adoption is a relatively small area of work, while wardship is available in such restricted range of circumstances that the

---

48 *Children Act Report 1992*, HMSO, para. 8.13.

49 Timms, 'The Guardian ad Litem: A Practitioner's Perspective', (1986) *Fam. Law* 339.

50 Rule 7, Family Proceedings Courts (Children Act 1989) Rules 1991, (S.I. 1991 No. 1395 (L.17)) and rule 4.7, Family Proceedings Rules 1991 (S.I. 1991 No. 1247 (L.20)).

51 S.41 of the 1989 Act, rule 11 of the Family Proceedings Courts (Children Act 1989) Rules 1991 and rule 4.11, Family Proceedings Rules 1991.

52 See the Short Report: *House of Commons Second Report from the Social Services Committee — Children in Care*, (1984) HMSO.

53 See 'The Child as Client — A Handbook for Solicitors who Represent Children'. Published Family Law 1992.

workload would be very small also. Of course, the reason why adoption is a relatively small area of work is because children have no separate legal representation in adoption proceedings. Further, although it is perfectly possible for other parties to proceedings, for example parents and grandparents, to instruct solicitors on the children's panel, this continues to be a comparatively rare occurrence. Since 1989, practice has revealed the comparatively poor quality of representation of other parties to the proceedings, in comparison with that now available to children through the provision of children's panel solicitors. Adults tend to instruct solicitors who have helped them to buy their houses, make their wills or represented them in criminal proceedings. None of these areas of expertise is calculated to improve the standard of parents' representation in proceedings under the Children Act 1989.

Children's panel members' undertaking

All solicitors who are members of the children's panel are bound by the following undertaking:

> I undertake that, when representing children in proceedings covered by the children Act 1989:
> (a) subject to paragraph 2, I will not normally delegate the preparation, supervision, conduct or presentation of the case, but will deal with it personally;
> (b) in each case, I will consider whether it is in the best interests of the child to instruct another advocate in relation to the presentation or preparation of the case;
> (c) if it is in the best interests of the client or necessary to instruct another advocate:
> (i) I will consider and advise the guardian ad litem (and the child, if of appropriate age and understanding), who should be instructed in the best interests of the child;
> (ii) I will obtain an undertaking from that advocate to:
> (a)   attend and conduct the matter personally, unless an unavoidable professional engagement arises; and
> (b)   take all reasonable steps to ensure that, so far as reasonably practicable, a conflicting professional engagement does not arise.[54]

The undertaking makes it clear that children's panel solicitors will be competent to conduct children's cases themselves. However, if for some reason they do not feel competent or are unavailable to give the matter their full attention, they should refer the matter to another member of the children's panel or, if appropriate, instruct a member of the Family Law Bar Association. Ironically, members of the Family Law Bar Association have not had the specialist training in child care matters which their colleagues on the children's panel have received. There is, sometimes, a delicate decision to be made about whether, in the best interests of the child, the case is best conducted by someone with finely tuned advocacy skills or by someone who has the experience and day to day knowledge of working closely with children and families. It is advisable, when a barrister has been instructed, that the

---

54 *The Children Panel Newsletter* (November 1991), The Law Society. The Law Society has produced specific guidance for children in private law proceedings. See chapter 9.

children's solicitor should also be available at court and at the pre-hearing briefings with the client. The fact that post-Children Act cases are generally more protracted and may involve a series of applications works against the consistency of involvement of one solicitor or barrister and it is important that solicitors are honest with guardians and with their clients about how much time they have available.

The quality of representation of children in public law proceedings rests on the effective partnership which has been built up between solicitors and guardians *ad litem*. Best results may be achieved where both are clear about their roles and are able to respect each other's opinions. It cannot be sufficiently emphasised that it is the role of the child's solicitor to act as an advocate for the child. His advocacy should be based upon the child's stated wishes and feelings. It is the role of the guardian *ad litem* to ascertain the wishes and feelings of the child and to take those views fully into consideration in putting a view to the court about what is in the best interests of the child. The conflict arises from the fact that what the child wants may not be what the child needs. In a situation of divergence between the views of the child and the guardian *ad litem*, the solicitor is placed in a difficult position, but it should be made clear that his role is to stand firmly alongside his client, the child, and continue to put the views of that child to the court as forcibly as would be the case if the guardian *ad litem* were in agreement with the views expressed. The appropriate balance between rights and welfare can only be achieved if the solicitor stands his ground on behalf of the child, even in the face of opposition from the guardian *ad litem*. Sometimes, solicitors have watered down the strength of their advocacy, in the knowledge that what the child wants is neither desirable nor possible. Nevertheless, powerful advocacy will ensure that the right of children to be consulted and to have their wishes and feelings considered is a central plank of the proceedings and should not be marginalised by the power of the guardian *ad litem*'s case. This is a delicate balance to achieve. Clearly one of the key questions for solicitors representing children is 'Is this child competent to give me instructions?'.

The competent child

It is the duty of the solicitor to act on the instructions of either the guardian *ad litem* or the child, but a solicitor should only accept instructions from the child if that child is of sufficient understanding to give instructions. A solicitor's professional training is not well designed to equip him or her to make such an assessment unaided, although solicitors who are members of the children's panel will probably have undergone some training in child development or will have gained a certain amount of knowledge through experience. The solicitor should take account of the emotional and psychological state of the child and consider whether or not the child is functioning at his or her chronological age although, as is implicit in the word 'understanding', a child's age is only one factor in determining whether or not the child should give instructions.[55]

---

55 See the Law Society's Family Law Committee's Guidance for Solicitors Working with Guardians *ad litem*.

The primary component in assessing a child's competence is the solicitor's own view of that competence, based on his meetings with the child. The views of the guardian *ad litem*, the child's carers, parents and teachers should also be taken into consideration.

Central to the debate about the competent child is the requirement in S.1(3), reinforced in S.22(5), that the wishes and feelings of the child should be considered in direct relationship to his age and understanding. This leaves it very much as a matter for the individual court or legal practitioner to take a view about how much weight to place on the child's stated wishes and feelings, bearing in mind that the welfare of the child is paramount.[56]

Article 12 of the UN Convention on the Rights of the Child requires that parties 'shall assure to the child, who is capable of forming his, or her, own views, the right to express those views freely in all matters affecting the child. The views of the child being given due weight, in accordance with the age, and maturity, of the child.' This direct right of participation in decision making has to be weighed against the requirements of Article 3 that, in all actions concerning children , whether undertaken by public or private social welfare institutions, courts of law, administrative authorities or legislative bodies, the best interests of the child shall be a primary consideration. Much discussion then hinges on the concept of the competent child, as a determining factor in reconciling rights and welfare.

The case of *Gillick v. West Norfolk and Wisbech Area Health Authority and the DHSS*[57] was influential in establishing the principle of the competent child, and in establishing the right of a 15-year-old girl to obtain contraceptive advice without the knowledge, or permission, of her parents. The history of the case was that Victoria Gillick, the mother of five young daughters, objected to guidance issued in a Department of Health and Social Security circular to the effect that, in exceptional circumstances, a doctor could give contraceptive advice to girls under 16 without their parents' knowledge. Mrs Gillick challenged the circular on the grounds that such guidance was unlawful.

The case created national, as well as judicial, controversy and focused public attention on the rights and responsibilities of parents in respect of their children. In defining competence, Lord Scarman said:

> It is not enough that she should understand the nature of the advice which she is being given:she must have sufficient maturity to understand what is involved. Further, parental rights are derived from parental duty, and exist only so long as they are needed for the protection of the person and the property of the child.[58]

In the absence of any clear, and generally accepted, guidelines about the age or stage of development at which children may be judged to be Gillick competent, there has been a paternalistic backlash, which has led to the imposing of bench-marks on competence, both in and out of court. In general, competence is thought to occur around the age of 11 or 12, in other words at the onset of adolescence.[59] This yardstick is endorsed by the government's

---

56 S.1(1).
57 [1986] A.C. 112.
58 *Ibid.*, at 189.
59 See Re. S.(A Minor) (Independent Representation) [1993] 2 F.L.R. 437.

proposal, contained in the White Paper on Reform of Adoption Legislation, to give children aged 12 or more the right to participate in their own adoption cases, by requiring their agreement before an adoption order is made, unless they are incapable of giving such agreement.[60] There is a basic inconsistency in establishing the age of criminal responsibility at 10, and finding children of that age guilty of murder, while at the same time assuming that they will not be capable of dealing competently with the question of their own proposed adoption before the age of 12. Experience shows that some children may be competent at seven, or even as young as three, and others not at 17.[61] The youngest chid to have approached IRCHIN for help directly was 10. He articulated his problems clearly over the telephone and followed up his referral by using his father's fax machine to send further details. Competence is not a function of chronological age, for children of different ages, like adults, have vastly different levels of intellectual and emotional maturity. In particular, between the ages of six and ten, children are particularly seized with the concept of fairness and, during that period, develop a very good grasp of what is reasonable, and unreasonable, behaviour.[62]

Case law, as it has developed since the implementation of the Children Act 1989, reflects the ambivalence of all adults, whether they be members of the judiciary, members of the public, or child care law professionals, about the circumstances in which children might be allowed to exercise their rights under the Act. This ambivalence arises from both psychological and intellectual barriers, existing in the minds of adults, which have to be overcome before it is possible for them to feel comfortable with the concept of what Eekelaar has described as 'dynamic self-determination'. Bainham identifies the elements to be reconciled as 'adolescent capacity, parental responsibility and medical paternalism.'[63]

The idea of children participating in, or having a right of veto about, decisions relating to their care, arouses anxiety in adults who fear this can only serve to complicate already complex and onerous problems associated with determining matters of children's welfare. In addition, there appears to be a fantasy that allowing children to have any influence on outcomes will somehow entail a loss of control by adults. The majority of those currently in authority over children have few personal experiences of being allowed to participate in key decisions made about their lives as children, as it was not until the 1960s that more permissive attitudes replaced a traditional 'seen and not heard' approach to child rearing. Many of those adults, if pressed, have only a passing intellectual commitment to the concept of children's rights and participation. Deep down, their emotional reality is that children benefit from more control (in this context 'control' is synonymous with security) and that adults generally, and genuinely, know best. It is easier to engage in intellectual discussions about the competence of the child than to embrace a philosophy

---

60 White Paper on *Adoption: The Future* (November 1993), CM. 2288, para. 4.3.
61 See further Spencer and Flin, *The Evidence of Children: The Psychology and the Law* (1990). See also Bainham, *Children: The Modern Law* (1993), Chapter 8, The Family and Medical Decisions.
62 See further Fahlberg, *Child Development*, (1982).
63 *Op. cit.*, p. 285.

and model of service provision which may necessitate a searching reappraisal of one's own childhood and child rearing practices.

It is hardly surprising, therefore, that post-Children Act case law is largely illustrative of attempts to reaffirm the right of the court to exercise its duty of welfare in relation to children. This has been particularly apparent in cases in which children have attempted to exercise their rights under S.38(6), S.43(8), and S.44(7), to refuse medical, psychiatric, or other, assessments. In the cases of *Re R.*(Medical Treatment)[64] in which the High Court in Wardship overrode the decision of a mature minor to refuse medical treatment, and *Re W.*,[65] the case of an anorexic girl who was refusing treatment, it is arguably both appropriate and desirable that the High Court overrode the child's refusal to receive treatment in life-threatening situations. These decisions were confirmed by Thorpe J in *Re K. W. and H.*[66] in which emergency treatment was administered to a Gillick competent child refusing medication. However it is clear, following the decision of Douglas Brown J in *South Glamorgan County Council v. W. and B.*,[67] that the courts are also prepared to intervene through the exercise of the inherent jurisdiction in non-life-threatening situations. In this case a severely depressed 15-year-old girl had refused to attend a psychiatric unit for assessment and treatment. Local authorities sought the intervention of the High Court, who overrode the girl's competent refusal and ordered her to be removed from home and examined in her best interests. This seems an inappropriate way of assuring a compulsory admission to a psychiatric hospital, if that was the objective.

In commenting on his decision, the President of the Family Division took the view that:

> In an appropriate case, where other remedies within the Children Act 1989 have been exhausted and found not to bring about the desired result, there was jurisdiction to resort to other remedies and the particular remedy presently was the remedy of providing authority for Doctors to treat the child and authority, if it was needed, for the local authority to take all the necessary steps to bring the child to the Doctors, so that she could be assessed and treated properly.[68]

In the light of the decision in this case, it may well be that only in exceptional circumstances will children be allowed to exercise their rights to refuse medical, or other, assessment. In *Re R.*, Lord Donaldson took the view that Gillick competent children only shared the right to give or withhold consent with their parents. A refusal by all three was needed to constitute a veto on treatment.[69]

Legal aid

The child will be entitled to legal aid in his or her own name and all applications for legal aid under the 1989 Act will be administered by the Legal Aid Board.

---

64 [1991] 3 All E.R. 177.
65 [1992] New L.J. 1124.
66 [1993] 1 F.L.R. 854.
67 [1993] 1 F.L.R. 574.
68 *Ibid.*, at 584.
69 [1992] 1 F.L.R. 190, C.A.

There are three routes for obtaining legal aid under the 1989 Act:

(1) in the normal way, subject to the means and merits test;
(2) pursuant to an emergency application;
(3) if care and emergency proceedings are commenced under S.31, S.43 or S.44 or an application is made under S.25, legal aid will be available for the child (and others — parents and those with parental responsibility) as of right, irrespective of means and merits, save that in the case of applications under S.25, legal aid will only be available to the child on this basis.

The following regulations govern legal aid arrangements under the 1989 Act:

(1) the Legal Aid Act 1988 (Children Act 1989), Order 1991 (S.I. 1991 No. 1924);
(2) the Civil Legal Aid (General) (Amendment) (No. 2) Regulations 1991 (S.I. 1991 No. 2036);
(3) the Legal Aid in Criminal and Care Proceedings (General) (Amendment) (No. 2) Regulations 1991 (S.I. 1991 No. 1925).

The Role of the Official Solicitor in Representing Children

Traditionally, the Official Solicitor has acted to represent children in wardship proceedings. S.41(8) gives the Official Solicitor the duty to act as guardian *ad litem* in certain High Court proceedings. The proceedings where the Official Solicitor will be appointed are those which commence, and are completed, in the High Court or which are allocated to the High Court from a lower court. In neither case will a guardian *ad litem* have been appointed and exceptional circumstances will call for Official Solicitor involvement rather than a panel guardian. When acting as a guardian *ad litem*, the Official Solicitor's duties will be those required of all guardians *ad litem*, as set out in Rule 11 of the Rules of Court.[70] The Official Solicitor will not be in membership of any panel of guardians *ad litem*.

The reason for the retention of the Official Solicitor's Department, in representing children, is that the Department has accumulated considerable expertise in regard to High Court procedures and child care cases, where wider issues of public policy and complexity are present. The frequent use of experts, such as paediatricians and child psychiatrists, in High Court proceedings has also afforded the Official Solicitor an opportunity to have access to such specialists nation-wide and the collective national knowledge of the Official Solicitor is deemed to be of value to the guardians *ad litem*, whose knowledge is normally regionally based. Panel managers are recommended to establish liaison links between their panel and the Official Solicitor, so that panel guardians *ad litem* may have access to such specialists, if the need arises in particular cases.[71] The duties and function of the Official Solicitor under the 1989 Act are laid down in the Lord Chancellor's Best Practice Direction

70 S.I. 1991 No. 1395.
71 Children Act 1989 Guidance and Regulations Vol. 7, paras. 272–274.

(Duties and Functions of Official Solicitor) of October 7, 1991. (This Direction does, of course, apply to all family proceedings and includes both public and private law proceedings.)

Appointment as guardian ad litem for a child who is the subject of proceedings

In specified ('public law') proceedings under the Children Act 1989, the Official Solicitor may only be appointed to act as a child's guardian *ad litem* in the High Court. In private law proceedings under the 1989 Act, he may act as the child's guardian *ad litem* in the High Court and the County Court, but not the Family Proceedings Court.

The criteria for the appointment of the Official Solicitor as the guardian *ad litem* of the subject child include cases in which there is disputed medical evidence or medical opinion is at variance, where there is a substantial foreign element, where there are special or exceptional points of law, or where he is already acting for the child in other proceedings. Subject to rule 9.2A of the Family Proceedings Rules 1991[72] the Official Solicitor may also act as the next friend of a child seeking leave to make an application under the 1989 Act or making an application in other family proceedings.

The Official Solicitor can also be appointed to act as the child's guardian *ad litem* in adoption and freeing proceedings in the High Court[73] and as the guardian *ad litem* of a child who is the subject of wardship proceedings under the inherent jurisdiction of the High Court.

Appointment as guardian ad litem for an adult party who is under mental disability or for a minor party other than the child who is the subject of proceedings

In the absence of any other suitable or willing person, the Official Solicitor is available to be appointed in the High Court (pursuant to R.S.C. Ord. 82, r. 2) or the County Court (pursuant to C.C.R. 1981, Ord. 10, r. 1) as guardian *ad litem* (or next friend) of:

- an adult party who is suffering from mental disorder within the meaning of the Mental Health Act 1983 to an extent that renders him/her incapable of managing his or her own property or affairs (medical evidence confirming this must be obtained by the Official Solicitor before he can accept the appointment); or
- (subject to Family Proceedings Rules 1991, r. 9.2A) a minor party, other than the child, who is the subject of proceedings.

Orders appointing the Official Solicitor should be expressed as being made subject to his consent. To ensure that he is allowed sufficient time to undertake the investigations he considers necessary in any particular matters, a

---

72 S.I. 1991 No. 2113 (L.34).
73 Adoption Rules 1984 (S.I. 1984 No. 265), r. 6(4) and r. 19(4).

substantive hearing date should not be fixed without prior consultation between the court listing officer and the Official Solicitor's caseworker.

Where the circumstances of the case justify seeking the involvement of the Official Solicitor, a questionnaire and a copy of the order appointing him, subject to his consent, should be sent with the court file to The Official Solicitor, 81 Chancery Lane, London WC2A 1DD. DX0012 Chancery Lane. Fax (0171) 911 7105. The Official Solicitor operates a help line on (0171) 911 7127, on which general advice can be obtained.

On November 27, 1992, the Official Solicitor wrote to all guardians *ad litem* panel managers, outlining the envisaged co-operation and interface between guardians and the Official Solicitor's Department. The letter stressed that the Official Solicitor would only be appointed in exceptional cases, where a panel member had not already been appointed and the court considered that special circumstances justified the involvement of the Official Solicitor, and continued:

> During the past two or three years, my staff have been assisted by panel members who have acted on my behalf, particularly in those cases at a distance from London, which have benefited from local involvement. With the decline in wardships, these cases are now more likely to be private law proceedings, but I should still like, from time to time, to approach panel managers to invite the assistance of a panel member in an appropriate case. In such appointments, I remain the guardian ad litem of the child and the report to the court contains my recommendations. In practical terms, that will normally mean that I adopt the panel member's recommendations and the panel member will, of course, be my expert witness. Legal advice and representation will usually be provided from this office (the Official Solicitor's office) and a nominated case manager on my staff will expect to discuss the case's progression . . . These are cases on which will be heard in either the High Court or County Court. I have no standing in the Family Proceedings Court.
>
> Occasionally I am also invited by the court to act as the guardian ad litem (or Next Friend) of an under-age or mentally disabled parent in family proceedings, where there is no other suitable person to provide representation. In these cases, my role is, of course, to advocate the interests of my incapacitated client.
>
> Finally, I would remind you that paragraph 4 of the Lord Chancellor's Direction provides that I may give advice and assistance to any guardian ad litem in any specified proceedings. For this purpose, a telephone 'helpline' was set up a year ago and my staff are always willing to assist, wherever possible, with legal or procedural guidance in High Court cases, or with the names of expert witnesses or in any appropriate way. It is helpful if any such calls are made, in the first instance, to my general office number — 071 911 7131. If the caller explains that it is a guardian ad litem enquiry, the call will then be routed to a senior member of staff. Enquiries from panel managers are equally welcome.

The letter goes on to request confirmation that members of guardian *ad litem* panels would be willing to accept occasional appointment on behalf of the Official Solicitor and also to point out that, on the vexed question of fees, the guardian would not, if appointed by the Official Solicitor, be acting as a panel guardian and that the Official Solicitor's office would be directly responsible for the payment of the guardian's fees at the current Law Society rates.

Guidance from the Lord Chancellor's Department, published in the Children Act Advisory Committee Report 1992/93, confirms the terms of the letter:

Cases where the Official Solicitor will consider acting as guardian *ad litem*:

In exceptional cases in the county courts or the High Court the Official Solicitor may be requested by the court to intervene on behalf of the child. The Official Solicitor has agreed that the following categories of cases indicate those in which he will consider acting for the child:

- where there is disputed medical evidence, or several variations in expert medical opinion (including psychiatric evidence);
- where the case involves a substantial foreign element;
- cases involving special or exceptional points of law;
- where the Official Solicitor is already representing the child in other current proceedings.

Staff should also note especially that the Official Solicitor cannot act for the child in adoption proceedings in the county courts, but can be available in these cases where the parents themselves are minors, or suffer mental disability.

Where courts encounter a free-standing Section 8 application connected to an existing adoption or freeing application, the existing guardian ad litem in the adoption or freeing proceedings is available to make any additional enquiries that may be requested by the court (Rules 6(9) and 18(6) and (7) Adoption Rules 1984). Another example of where an existing guardian may be called upon in a similar way is where current private proceedings for a Section 8 application are connected to an existing application for a secure accommodation order (Rule 4.11(10) Family Proceedings Rules 1991).

Contact with the Official Solicitor's office should normally be made in writing, and include the reasons given by the judge or district judge for wishing to appoint the Official Solicitor. These should be noted by the associate or clerk at the time, together with any special directions for enquiries or investigations to be made.[74]

It is worth emphasising that the Official Solicitor's Department is a corporate body and that its case workers are civil servants, seconded from other government departments. Representatives of the Official Solicitor's Department are not trained social workers or children's panel solicitors, although their considerable experience in the High Court does mean they have built up a substantial reservoir of knowledge, on which it would be helpful for panel members to draw, particularly when considering appropriate medical, psychiatric or psychological expert witness evidence on behalf of the child. Additionally, the Official Solicitor may be appointed as next friend or *amicus curiae* and, although the number of *amicus curiae* cases is still small, it tripled in 1994/95.

The Role of the Guardian *ad Litem* in Representing Children

The Children Act 1989 aims to strike a balance between the rights of children to express their views on decisions made about their lives, the rights of parents to exercise their responsibilities towards the child and the duty of the state to intervene, where the child's welfare requires it.[75] The guardian *ad litem* acts as the balancing agent in that particularly difficult equation. Speaking at the annual social services conference in London in September 1990, Lord Justice Butler Sloss described the guardian *ad litem* as 'the linchpin to the successful implementation of the Children Act 1989'.

Under the provisions of the 1989 Act, guardians *ad litem* are appointed earlier and more often in a wider range of proceedings in the Magistrates,

---

74 *The Children Act Advisory Committee Annual Report 1992/93*, Annex 3.
75 The Children Act 1989 Guidance and Regulations, Vol. 1: Court Orders.

Family Proceedings, County and High Courts. In addition to their role as independent expert on behalf of the child, they have a significant case management function under S.41.10 in assisting the courts to take a pro-active stance, in order to avoid unnecessary delays, expedite proceedings and explore the full range of possible orders and powers which the 1989 Act requires. Guardians are seen as the oil that greases the machinery of the Act, and their new responsibilities were underpinned with significant powers in respect of rights of access to local authority files, and the power to initiate directions hearings on issues bearing on the manegement rather than the determination of cases. It is significant that the Lord Chancellor visualised the role of the guardian under the 1989 Act as both the child's representative and an officer of the court:

> The crucial importance of the guardian ad litem's role is that it stands at the interface between the conflicting rights and powers of courts, local authorities and natural and substitute parents, in relation to the child. The guardian has to safeguard the child's interests, to ensure the most positive outcome possible for that child. The guardian also has to make a judgement between the potentially conflicting demands of children's rights, children's rescue, the autonomy of the family and the duty of the state.[76]

The Guidance stresses that the right of children to separate and independent representation in public law proceedings is a central tenet of the 1989 Act. It is essential that guardians *ad litem*, in reaching their judgments about the welfare of each child, should continue to be independent of the local authority or other organisation providing the service.[77]

The Role of Independent Social Workers

Since the establishment of panels of guardians *ad litem* and reporting officers, the practice of appointing independent social workers in care and related proceedings has virtually ceased. Clearly, if panels of independent experts are readily available, then the need for solicitors to instruct additional independent social work evidence disappears. Solicitors taking instructions from guardians *ad litem* should not find it necessary to ask an independent social worker for assistance. Only in a divergence situation, that is where a child and a guardian *ad litem* are giving conflicting instructions to the child's solicitor, should the solicitor (acting on the child's instructions) consider obtaining assistance from an independent social worker. In practice it seems excessive to have two independent social workers involved on behalf of one child, so long as the panels of guardians *ad litem* and reporting officers are to be credible as independent expert witnesses, and solicitors and other parties to the proceedings are satisfied as to the objectivity of their evidence. This is one of the main objections to panels of guardians *ad litem* and reporting officers being administered and funded by local authorities, as it undermines the

---

76 Timms, *Manual of Practice Guidance for Guardians ad Litem and Reporting Officers*, (1992) HMSO, Introduction.

77 The Children Act 1989 Guidance and Regulations Vol. 7: Guardians *ad Litem* and Other Court Related Issues, para. 2.4.

credibility of the service generally. However, independent social workers are now little used in proceedings in which guardians are appointed, although the possibility is not ruled out. There has, however, been an increase in the use of independent social workers investigating complaints about local authority social services departments.[78]

Appointment of the Guardian *ad Litem* and Reporting Officer

For the purpose of any specified proceedings, the court shall appoint a guardian *ad litem* for the child concerned, unless satisfied that it is not necessary to do so, in order to safeguard his interests.[79] This is a stronger directive to the courts to appoint guardians than was the case in previous provisions. In practice, it means that a guardian is appointed in the majority of public law cases, unless there are very strong contrary reasons. David Mellor, then Minister of Health, speaking during the passage of the Children Bill through the House of Commons in 1989, anticipated that guardians would be appointed in 90 per cent of cases, including High Court cases and the 'overspill' from wardship. This figure represented a considerable increase in panel workloads, bearing in mind that the Social Services Inspectorate report *In the Interests of Children* indicated that previously there had been an overall appointment rate of 56 per cent (66 per cent if education cases are excluded).[80] However the earlier figures masked enormous local variations, from 4 per cent to 88 per cent. The SSI Report also indicated that, although there were approximately 2,550 guardians *ad litem* available for work (as compared with 3,500 in 1986[81]), most of them were working sessionally or part time, so the figure represented only the equivalent of 180 full-time workers for the whole of England and Wales. The fact that guardians were to be appointed earlier, in a wide range of proceedings, and that the overall numbers of guardians appeared to be dropping, gave rise to fears that a shortage of resources in the service would result in delays in children's hearings. It is ironic that in some areas guardians may be direct contributors to the delays they are appointed to prevent.

Guardians to be appointed as soon as possible

As soon as practicable after the commencement of specified proceedings, or the transfer of such proceedings to the court, the Justices' Clerk or the court shall appoint a guardian *ad litem* unless:

● such an appointment has already been made by the court which made the transfer and is subsisting; or

---

78 See the *GAL/RO Service Annual Report 1992/93: An Overview* (1993), published Department of Health.
79 S.41(1).
80 *In the Interests of Children: An Inspection of the Guardian ad Litem and Reporting Officer Service* (1990) Social Service Inspectorate, Department of Health, paras. 1.3 and 1.5.
81 British Association of Social Workers, Working Party Report, *Guardians and Curators ad Litem and Reporting Officers*, (1986).

● the Justices' Clerk or the court decides that such an appointment is not
   necessary to safeguard the interests of the child.[82]

Any party may apply for the appointment of a guardian ad litem

At any stage in specified proceedings, a party may apply, without notice to the
other parties unless the Justices' Clerk or the court otherwise directs, for the
appointment of a guardian *ad litem*.[83]

Reasons for non-appointment should be made in writing

The Justices' Clerk or the court shall grant an application under rule 2 (above)
unless it is considered that such an appointment is not necessary to safeguard
the interests of the child, in which case reasons shall be given and a note of
such reasons shall be taken by the Justices' Clerk.[84]

The court may appoint a guardian ad litem at any time during the proceedings

At any stage in specified proceedings the Justices' Clerk or the court may
appoint a guardian *ad litem*, even though no application is made for such an
appointment.[85]

Parties to be notified of guardians's appointment

The Justices' Clerk shall, as soon as possible, notify the parties and any welfare
officer of an appointment under this rule or, as the case may be, of a decision
not to make such an appointment.[86]

Guardian to be notified of appointment and served with relevant documents

Upon the appointment of a guardian *ad litem*, the Justices' Clerk shall, as soon
as possible, notify him of the appointment and serve him copies of the
application and of documents filed under rule 17(1).

Eligibility of a guardian for appointment to a specific case

A guardian *ad litem* appointed from a panel established under S.41(7) shall
not:

---

82 Family Proceedings Courts (Children Act 1989) Rules 1991 (S.I. 1991 No. 1395), r. 10(1).
83 R. 10(2).
84 R. 10(3).
85 R. 10(4).
86 R. 10(5).

- be a member, officer or servant of a local authority which, or an authorised person (within the meaning of S.31(9)) who, is party to the proceedings, unless he is employed by such an authority solely as a member of a panel of guardians *ad litem* and reporting officers;
- be, or have been, a member, officer or servant of a local authority or voluntary organisation (within the meaning of S.105(1)), who has been directly concerned in that capacity in arrangements relating to the care, accommodation or welfare of the child during the five years prior to the commencement of the proceedings;
- be a serving probation officer (except that a probation officer who has not in that capacity been previously concerned with the child or his family and who is employed part time may, when not engaged in his duties as a probation officer, act as a guardian *ad litem*.[87]

Guardians are appointed from panels established, administered and funded by local authorities under S.41 CA Act 1989 and the Guardians *ad Litem* and Reporting Officers (Panels) Regulations 1991 (S.I. No. 2051), Appointment to Panels of Guardians *ad Litem*. It is the responsibility of the local authority, in respect of whose area the panel is established, to appoint persons to be members of the panel. It is a matter for the local authority to decide whether the qualifications and experience of any person whom they propose to appoint to the panel are suitable for the purposes of that person's appointment.[88] The local authority shall, in respect of any person whom they propose to appoint to the panel, interview each such person, consult the panel committee and obtain names of at least two persons who can provide a reference in writing for the persons whom they propose to appoint and take up those references.[89] The local authority shall notify in writing any person who is appointed to a panel of the appointment, which shall, subject to regulation 5 of these Regulations (Termination of Panel Membership), be for such a period not exceeding three years at any one time as the local authority shall specify on making the appointment.[90] Each local authority shall maintain a record of those persons whom they have appointed to be a member of the panel established in respect of their area.[91] Every local authority shall have regard to the number of children in their area who may become the subject of specified proceedings and the different racial groups to which they belong in making appointments.[92]

Guardians *ad litem* and reporting officers appointed under S.41 of the Children Act 1989 for the purposes of relevant proceedings, or under Rules made under S.65 of the Adoption Act 1976, must be selected from the panel established in respect of the local authority's area in which the court is situated (unless selected from another local authority's panel established under these Regulations).[93] Local authorities have a responsibility to ensure that the numbers of guardians *ad litem* on the panels are sufficient to meet local need

---

87 R. 10(7).
88 Reg. 4(2).
89 Reg. 4(3)(a)−(c).
90 Reg. 4(4).
91 Reg. 4(5).
92 Reg. 4(6).
93 Reg. 2(2).

without incurring delays. Each local authority shall ensure that, as far as possible, the number of persons appointed to the panel established in respect of their area is sufficient to provide guardians *ad litem* and reporting officers for all relevant proceedings in which guardians *ad litem* and reporting officers may be appointed and which may be heard in their area.[94]

Family Proceedings Courts (Children Act 1989) Rules 1991 (S.I. 1991 No. 1395), rule 10(7)(b) specifically excludes the appointment, in particular proceedings, of a guardian *ad litem* or reporting officer who was formerly a member, officer or servant of a local authority or voluntary organisation and who had a direct involvement with a particular child during the five years prior to the commencement of the proceedings. However a former local authority employee is not excluded from becoming a member of a panel established by that same authority. This has been a subject of criticism by many guardians and solicitors, who feel that close association with the policies and practices of that local authority cannot add to parents' confidence in the independence of the panels, and does not contribute to the ethos of independence which guardians are anxious to achieve, and which is endorsed by para. 2.4. of the Guidance:

> the right of children to separate and independent representation in public law proceedings is a central tenet of the Children Act. It is essential that guardians ad litem and reporting officers, in reaching their judgements about the welfare of the child, should continue to be independent of the local authority or other organisation providing the service. Arrangements for the management of the panel and the day to day work of the guardian ad litem and reporting officer must take full account of this requirement, within the existing framework of ultimate responsibility residing with the local authority.[95]

Repositioning panel managers in 'arms-length' inspection units within local authorities may seem to maintain only a theoretical commitment to the independence of the panels. The regulations leave the onus firmly on the individual guardian *ad litem* to declare their interest or knowledge of a particular child. It may well be that guardians will have had knowledge of a family over a number of years, while working for a local authority, even though they were not directly responsible for a particular child. A guardian who wishes to be seen to be independent should declare a conflict of interest. In practice the precise boundaries of conflict of interest may be difficult to draw, especially in a situation where a refusal to accept the case may result in additional pressures of work on panel colleagues or a delay in the proceedings being heard, neither of which would be in the interests of the child. On the other hand, the value of the eventual report would be diminished if the objectivity of its content is questionable. The safeguard for the child depends on the ability of the individual guardian to take a clear and fresh view of events, unfettered by any other consideration than the welfare of the child.

The National Association of Guardians ad Litem and Reporting Officers (NAGALRO) have given guidance on this matter in their code of practice, under the heading 'Previous employment':

---

94 Reg. 2(3).
95 Children Act 1989, Guidance and Regulations Volume 7, *Guardians ad Litem and Other Court Related Issues*, para. 2.4.

a GAL/RO must be seen to be independent of any other party in court proceedings; in some areas of the country, many panel members are ex-employees of the local authority, for whose panel they now work. For reasons of geography, this may be unavoidable, but it is not generally good practice for a GAL/RO to act in cases where she/he has been recently employed by one of the parties.[96]

Any guardian *ad litem* or reporting officer employed under rule 10(7) needs to be particularly aware of the need to work in ways that try to overcome perceived lack of independence.

In granting an Order of Certiorari, quashing the decision of the Cornwall Director of Social Services, who had sought to set a limit on the number of hours to be spent by guardians *ad litem* on cases, Sir Stephen Browne commented that, having read the letters of the Director of Cornwall Social Services to the guardians *ad litem*, he could understand that the guardians felt as though they were being treated as employees of the authority.[97] In fact, rule 10(7)(a) does allow guardians *ad litem* to be employed as full time panel members by a local authority. Addressing the newly formed National Association of Guardians *ad Litem* and Reporting Officers on November 8, 1991, the Lord Chancellor, Lord McKay, claimed that the provisions of rule 10(7)(a) and (b) were a necessary expediency in a situation where it was feared that there simply would not be enough guardians to meet the demands of the courts, following the implementation of the Children Act 1989.

Reappointment of a previous guardian

When appointing a guardian *ad litem*, the Justices' Clerk or the court shall consider the appointment of anyone who has previously acted as guardian *ad litem* of the same child.[98]

Termination of appointment

The appointment of a guardian *ad litem* shall continue for such a time as is specified in the appointment, or until terminated by the court.[99]

Giving reasons for termination of appointment

When terminating an appointment, the court shall give reasons in writing for so doing, a note of which should be taken to the Justices' Clerk.[100]

---

96 National Association of Guardians ad Litem and Reporting Officers' Code of Practice for Guardians ad Litem and Reporting Officers, p.4, para. 1.1–1.3.
97 *R. v. Cornwall County Council, ex p. Cornwall and Isles of Scilly GAL/RO Panel* [1992] 2 All E.R. 471.
98 R. 10(8).
99 R. 10(9).
100 R. 10(10).

Giving reasons for appointment or refusal to appoint

Where the Justices' Clerk or the courts appoint a guardian or refuse to make such an appointment, the Justices' Clerk shall record the appointment or refusal in the appropriate form in Schedule 1 of the Rules.[101]

Appointment of Solicitor

Rule 12 makes it clear that solicitors, appointed under S.41(3) or in accordance with rule 11(2)(a), shall act in accordance with instructions received from the guardian *ad litem*[102] unless the solicitor considers, having taken into account the views of the guardian *ad litem* and any direction of the court under rule 11(3), that the child wishes to give instructions which conflict with those of the guardian *ad litem* and that he is able, having regard to his understanding, to give such instructions on his own behalf. In this case, the solicitor should conduct the proceedings in accordance with instructions received from the child.[103]

Where no guardian *ad litem* has been appointed for the child and the condition in S.41(4)(b) is satisfied (the child has sufficient understanding to instruct a solicitor and wishes to do so), in accordance with instructions received from the child or in default from either guardian *ad litem* or the child, then the solicitor is to act in furtherance of the best interests of the child.[104] It is the responsibility of the solicitor to serve and accept service of documents on behalf of the child and, where the child has not himself been served and has sufficient understanding, he should advise the child of the contents of any document so served.[105] The child has the right, under rule 12(3), to terminate the appointment of any solicitor appointed under S.41(3) or in accordance with rule 11(2)(a). He may apply to the court for an order, terminating the appointment, and the solicitor and the guardian *ad litem* will then be given an opportunity to make representations.[106] The guardian *ad litem* may also ask for the appointment of a solicitor to be terminated, by applying to the court for an order terminating the appointment. In that event, both the solicitor and the child, if he is of sufficient understanding, should be given an opportunity to make representations.[107] If the appointment is terminated, the court must give reasons for so doing and these reasons must be noted by the Justices' Clerk.[108] Where the Justices' Clerk or the court appoints a solicitor under S.41(3), or refuses to make such an appointment, the Justices' Clerk shall record the appointment or refusal in the appropriate form in Schedule 1 of the Family Proceedings Courts (Children Act 1989) Rules 1991 and serve a copy on the parties and, where appointed, on the solicitor.[109] The solicitor

---

101 R. 10(11).
102 R. 12(1)(a).
103 R. 12(1)(a).
104 R. 12(1)(c).
105 R. 12(2).
106 R. 12(3).
107 R. 12 (4).
108 R. 12(5).
109 R. 12(6).

appointed for the child will normally be a member of the children's panel, but this is not specifically required in the rules.

The child's solicitor must act in accordance with the instructions of the guardian *ad litem* and should consult the guardian if in any doubt on any matters arising during the conduct of the case.[110] There is no specific guidance in the Rules about how solicitors should embark on their direct work with children. Clearly this is a matter for discussion between the guardian *ad litem* and the solicitor. Communicating with children requires skill and experience. The Manual of Practice Guidance for Guardians *ad Litem* and Reporting Officers recommends guardians do not appoint solicitors who are reluctant to see the child:

> guardians should be wary of a solicitor, who is not keen to meet the child, even if the child is only a few months old. Seeing the child will serve to bring him alive in the mind of his legal representative and help to focus his representation of the child's interests in court.[111]

Proceedings in which Guardians *ad Litem* and Reporting Officers may be Appointed

The range of proceedings in which a guardian *ad litem* may be appointed was considerably extended by the 1989 Act (see Figure 3, p.120). S.41(6) specifies the proceedings.

Part IV of the 1989 Act: care and supervision

Guardians *ad litem* may be appointed:

- in an application for Care Order or Supervision Order;[112]
- in family proceedings, where the court has directed the local authority to undertake an investigation of the child's circumstances and has made, or is considering whether to make, an interim Care Order;[113]
- in an application for the discharge of a Care Order or the variation or discharge of a Supervision Order under S.39;
- in an application to substitute a Supervision Order for a Care Order;[114]
- where the court is considering whether to make a Residence Order with respect to a child who is the subject of a Care Order;[115]
- in respect of contact between a child who is the subject of a Care Order and any other person;[116]
- in appeals arising from the making, or the refusal to make, a Care Order, Supervision Order, Contact Order or Residence Order (with respect to the child who is the subject of the Care Order);

---

110 Masson and Morris, *Children Act Manual* 1992, Sweet and Maxwell.
111 Timms, *Manual of Practice Guidance for Guardians ad Litem and Reporting Officers* (1992), HMSO, p. 93.
112 S. 31.
113 Ss 37(1) and 38(1)(a).
114 S. 39(4).
115 S. 8.
116 S. 34.

Proceedings	Separate legal representation	Independent social work representation	
Children Act 1989			
Public law cases	✔	✔	In proceedings under Part IV Care and Protection and Part V Emergency Proceedings, s. 25 Secure Accommodation applications and proceedings specified under s. 41(6)(i), the child has both independent legal and social work representation
Private law cases	X	X	Children involved in disputed s. 8 residence and contact applications have no right to be separately represented. However, they may: (1) apply for leave to initiate any s. 8 order; or (2) the Official Solicitor may be asked to represent their interests in certain situations; or (3) in a minority of cases, the Family Court Welfare Officer may be asked to prepare a report (s. 7).
Non-judicial proceedings arising from s. 26: Complaints and Representatives Procedure	X	X	There is an independent element in both stages of the complaints procedure ('the independent person') but that person is neither a legal nor a social work representative and is not involved in the investigation of the complaint. In hearings arising from s. 26 there is no provision for the child to have either separate legal or social work representation.
Adoption Act 1976			
Adoption and freeing for adoption s. 65	X[a]	✔	A guardian *ad litem* is appointed in contested adoptions. Separate legal representations for children is available only in the High Court.
Human Fertilisation and Embryology Act 1990			
Parental responsibility orders s. 30	X	✔	A guardian *ad litem* is appointed in applications for parental responsibility orders. There is no separate legal representation.

a Except in the High Court.

Figure 3 **Independent Representation of Children in Family Proceedings**

- in appeals arising from the variation or discharge (or refusal of an application to vary or discharge) the Orders listed above;
- in appeals arising from the refusal to substitute a Supervision Order for a Care Order.

Part V of the 1989 Act: emergency protection

Guardians may be appointed in:

- applications for an Emergency Protection Order;[117]
- applications for a Child Assessment Order;[118]
- applications for the extension of an Emergency Protection Order;[119]
- variation and discharge of an Emergency Protection Order;[120]
- variation and discharge of a Child Assessment Order;[121]
- appeals arising from the making, or refusal to make, an Order under Part V.

Proceedings specified under S.41(6)(i)

Under the provisions of this section, four additional categories of cases are named as 'specified' proceedings in the Family Proceedings Rules 1991 and Family Proceedings Courts (Children Act 1989) Rules 1991. These are:

- applications for a Secure Accommodation Order (in the Family Proceedings Court);[122]
- applications for the leave of the court to the proposed change of surname for a child who is the subject of a Care Order or the proposed removal of such a child from the United Kingdom;[123]
- applications for the arranging or assistance in arranging for a child in the care of the local authority to live outside England and Wales;[124]
- applications for the extension, or further extension, of a Supervision Order, originally made under S.31;[125]
- appeals arising from these proceedings.

Adoption and freeing for adoption proceedings

Guardians *ad litem* and reporting officers may be appointed in adoption proceedings and freeing proceedings, as set out in the Rules made under S.65 of the Adoption Act 1976 (the Children Act 1989 did not affect the provisions

---

117 S. 44.
118 S. 43.
119 S. 45.
120 S. 43.
121 S. 43.
122 S. 25.
123 S. 33(7).
124 Sched. 2, para. 19(1).
125 Sched. 2, para. 6(3).

in the Adoption Act 1976, which provide the framework for the appointment of guardians *ad litem* and reporting officers in adoption).

Surrogacy proceedings: Parental Orders

S.30 of the Human Fertilisation and Embryology Act 1990 makes provision for the court to make an Order in respect of a child who is born as a result of surrogacy arrangements, to be treated in law as the child of the surrogate parents' marriage, provided that artificial methods of conception with the gametes of one or both parents were used in the arrangements.[126] The draft Parental Orders for gamete donors provide for a guardian *ad litem* to be appointed, to safeguard the child's welfare and to advise the court on whether or not procedures have been correctly carried out.

Appeals

One of the guardian *ad litem*'s final tasks, in any case, is to consider an appeal on behalf of the child. In general, courts pay great attention to the guardian's recommendation, but in the case of a decision being made by the court not in accordance with the guardian's view about was in the best interests of the child, then an appeal should always be considered.

In an unreported case, a local authority sought a Supervision Order in the case of a young child who had been injured. The parents were willing to assent, the guardian recommended a Care Order, but the magistrates granted a Supervision Order in May 1992. The guardian decided to appeal. There were several grounds, the first, which was upheld, being that the magistrates had not given reasons for disagreeing with the guardian's recommendation. The appeal was heard in the High Court in July 1992, when the judge made an interim Care Order and limited the contact between the parents and the child. He also stated that the case should, on grounds of complexity, have been transferred from the Magistrates to the County Court. At the re-hearing of the case in the High Court, in December 1992, the guardian again argued for a Care Order while the local authority proposed a Supervision Order, to which, once again, the parents were willing to assent. The judge, Sir Stephen Brown, made a Care Order and noted that 'Guardians involved in complicated cases, on appeal, may be called upon to make lengthy and detailed investigations.'

Re M. (Minors)[127] was a case in point, and was unusual in several ways. Firstly, since the family feared that everyone in the county was biased against them, the judge decided to appoint a guardian from another panel. Secondly, as a result of the allegations being made by one parent against the other, the case raised exceptional concerns and anxieties. In consequence, the guardian conducted extensive interviews, observations and investigations and was directed by the judge to visit the United States. The hearing took 20 days and

---

126 S. 30(1).
127 [1993] 1 F.C.R. 256.

there were five parties — the mother, the father, the maternal grandparents, the local authority and the guardian.

Cases on appeal can also be extremely expensive. In one case, the guardian's bill reached almost £10,000. Appeals can help to delineate the boundaries of the guardian's role. There have been cases in which courts have attempted to appoint guardians in unspecified proceedings, not covered by the court rules.

In the case of *Essex County Council v. B.*, January 1993, there was an appeal from the magistrates to the High Court, involving an Essex panel member. One aspect of the case was whether there was power to appoint a guardian *ad litem* in non-specified proceedings. The decision of the Justices' Clerks, in the lower court, to revoke the Order appointing a guardian *ad litem* was upheld on appeal. The application in this case had been for an Education Supervision Order and the judgment established that guardians *ad litem* can not be appointed in such cases.[128]

In summary, S.41(9) makes provision for the constitution, administration and procedures of panels by local authorities, who are responsible for recruiting, training, paying, monitoring and deploying guardians. The panels are funded and administered by one party to the proceedings, but criticism of this structure is based not only on theoretical and professional arguments, but also in consideration of the very practical difficulties which the present structure imposes, in terms of the effective and efficient administration of panels. The administrative hoops which are necessary to maintain independence are time-consuming and complicated, particularly in relation to management, appraisal and reappointment procedures and the conduct of complaints arising from panel members' work. Nevertheless, in the ten years since their formal establishment GAL/ROs have earned the respect of courts and fellow childcare professionals, and their advice is accorded considerable weight.

---

128 These cases are reported in the *GAL/RO Service Annual Report 1992/93: An Overview* (1993), published Department of Health.

Appendix 1

Protocol for the Resolution of Disputes between a GAL/RO Panel and the Responsible Local Authority[129]

(a) Independence

● Where a dispute arises between the panel and the local authority on issues concerning the independence of the panel, the matter should be taken up by the panel manager. The first course of action for the panel manager should be to set out in writing to his line manager the actions being complained of and his suggested solution for resolving the situation. He should, at the same time, acquaint the GAL/RO panel chair with what he has done, so that the committee may, if they deem appropriate, add their representations to that of the panel manager.

● If the panel manager and his line manager are unable to reach a satisfactory resolution the panel manager should write to the Director of Social Services, explaining the situation and asking the Director to intervene and ensure that challenges to the panel's independence are removed. This correspondence should be copied to the panel committee chair, who may also wish to write to the Director.

● If the Director declines to act, or the panel manager believes his response is inadequate, he should raise the matter in the Family Court Business Committee, having first advised the Director of his intentions. In general it would be appropriate to write to the chair of the Family Court Business Committee, setting out the position, and copying the correspondence to the Director. If the panel manager considers the issues involved to be of sufficient importance, he should also, at the same time, copy the correspondence to the designated inspector in the Policy and Business Region of the Social Services Inspectorate.

● Should these actions still fail to bring about a solution satisfactory to the panel manager, he should write to the chair of the Children Act Advisory Committee, setting out the complete history of the dispute and asking the committee to become involved in the resolution. Such correspondence should be copied to the Director of Social services and the Social Services Inspectorate.

(b) GAL/RO Budgets

● A potential area of difficulty between a panel and a local authority is in the area of the GAL/RO budget. The panel manager may find himself in the position of having to request additional funding from the local authority where, for some reason, the panel budget looks like being exceeded. If this request were refused, the procedure under which the panel manager may explore this decision is set out below.

● As with disputes about independence, the local solution is obviously preferable. The importance of good communications between panel and local authority, in respect of budget issues, cannot be over-stressed. An early warning system needs to be in place, so the earliest possible notice can be given by the panel manager to the authority, where the budget is likely to come under severe pressure.

● The budget itself needs to have identified sub-headings, because this is helpful in preventing important areas, such as training, from not receiving enough funds, owing to the demands of other areas of expenditure. Monitoring the expenditure of a GAL/RO panel is obviously essential to the early warning system mentioned above, and the lines of communication about budget issues need to be understood. The management of the panel budget is a responsible task and any breach of the budget limit should be exceptional, due to unforeseen circumstances.

● In general, as with independent issues, the first course of action for the panel manager, where there is a dispute about securing adequate funding for the GAL/RO service, should be to set out in writing to his line manager the budget issue being complained of, and his suggested solution for resolving the situation. He should, at the same time, acquaint the GAL/RO panel chair with what he has done, so that

---

129 *The Children Act Advisory Committee Annual Report 1992/93*, Annex 2, p. 75.

the committee may, if they deem appropriate, add their representations to that of the panel manager.

● If the panel manager and his line manager are unable to reach a satisfactory resolution, the panel manager should write to the Director of Social Services explaining the situation, and asking the Director to intervene. The case to the Director needs to set out the full circumstances of the overspend of the budget and, in requesting additional funding, the possibility of identifying savings in subsequent years needs to be addressed by the panel manager. The panel manager should also appoint out, in the submission to the Director, that the GAL/RO service is a statutory one and that adequate funding to ensure the service can operate must be secured. This correspondence should be copied to the panel committee chair, who may wish to write to the Director.

Chapter 4

The Investigative Role of the Guardian ad Litem in Public Law Proceedings

Panels of guardians *ad litem* and reporting officers are established under S. 41(7) of the 1989 Act and governed by the Guardians *ad litem* and Reporting Officers (Panels) Regulations 1991 (S.I. 1991 No. 2051). The Guidance and Regulations relating to panels are contained in Volume 7 of the Children Act 1989 Guidance (Guardians *ad Litem* and Other Court Related Issues). In addition, the Department of Health produced two Manuals of Guidance — one for panel members and one for guardian *ad litem* panel managers.[1]

Following implementation of the Children Act 1989, guardians are appointed more often, at an earlier stage, and in a wider range of proceedings. They have an additional case management role in avoiding delay, expediting proceedings and effecting appropriate transfer. The role is one of comparative professional isolation, but potentially one of great rewards in being in a position to have a positive impact on the life of a vulnerable child.

The *Manual of Practice Guidance* emphasises the investigative role of the guardian and the necessary qualities of critical analysis and appraisal, based on

---

1 Timms, *Manual of Practice Guidance for Guardians ad Litem and Reporting Officers*, HMSO (1992) and *Manual of Management for GAL/RO Panel Managers*, HMSO (1992).

Care and Related Proceedings

Care and supervision Part IV Children Act 1989

- Applications **for** and **to discharge Care Orders** and **Supervision Orders** (s. 31)
- Where the Court is considering **contact** for children in care (s. 34)
- Where the Court is considering a s. 8 **Residence Order** for children in care
- Where a **Care Order** is being considered in proceedings arising from s. 37(1)
- Substituting a **Supervision Order** for a Care Order (s. 39(4))
- Related **Appeals**

Protection of Children Part V Children Act 1989

Applications for and to discharge:

- **Emergency Protection Orders** (s. 44)
- **Child Assessment Orders** (s. 43)
- Advice to Court on child's ability to make an informed decision re medical or other assessment (s. 43)
- Related **Appeals**

Specified Proceedings s. 41(6)(i) Children Act 1989 (includes s. 25 Surrogacy Arrangements Applications)

Applications for:

- **Secure Accommodation Orders** (s. 25)
- Children in care to live outside England and Wales (Sched.2, para. 19(1))
- Changing a child's surname or removing them from the UK while a care order is in force (s. 33(7))
- Extending or further extending a **Supervision Order** (Sched. 3, para. 6(3))
- Related **Appeals**

Case Management Role

S. 41(10) Children Act 1989 (applies to proceedings under the Children Act 1989)

Includes:
- timetabling and allocation of cases
- expediting proceedings and avoiding delay
- considering whether Order applied for or any other is appropriate
- accepting service documents on behalf of the children

Adoption and freeing for adoption

S. 65 Adoption Act 1976

- Adoption
- Freeing for adoption
- Appointment of Reporting Officers — witnessing agreements for adoption

Surrogacy Arrangements

S. 30 Human Fertilisation and Embryology Act 1990

- Applications for parental orders

Figure 4   Proceedings in which a Guardian *ad Litem* or Reporting Officer may be Appointed

the persistent teasing out of the relevant facts and options available to the court, taking a balanced view of potential negative and positive outcomes.

The role requires both the skills of a private investigator and an assertive representative, combined with a patient capacity for warmth and wisdom in dealing with hurt and bewildered children. All this has to be accomplished within a framework which attempts to reconcile the court's timetable with that of the child.[2]

Powers and Duties of the Guardian ad Litem

The responsibilities of the guardian are very closely linked to those of the court and emphasise the fact that, in all their decision making, the courts will be looking to the guardian for assessment and recommendations. Guardians *ad litem* and the court have the same overriding duties — to consider the need to reduce delay, to have regard for matters set out in the welfare check-list, and to consider all available options.[3] It is the responsibility of the guardian *ad litem*, as it is of the court, to give paramount consideration to the child's welfare.[4] In addition, guardians, like the courts, must consider — in recommending an Order — whether doing so would be better for the child than making no Order at all.[5]

The guardian *ad litem* shall:

- be appointed in accordance with rules of court;[6] and
- be under a duty to safeguard the interest of the child, in the manner prescribed by such rules.[7]

Separate representation for the guardian and the child

Having appointed a solicitor for the child, where it appears to the guardian *ad litem* that the child is instructing the solicitor direct or intends to, and is capable to conduct the proceedings on his own behalf, he shall so inform the court and thereafter:

- shall perform all his duties set out in the rules, other than duties under Family Proceedings Courts (Children Act 1989) Rules 1991 (S.I. 1991 No. 1395 (l.17)), para. (2)(a) (which relate to appointing a solicitor) and such other duties as the court may direct;
- shall take such part in the proceedings as the Justices' Clerks or the court may direct and may, with the leave of the Justices' Clerk or the court, have legal representation in his conduct of those duties.[8]

---

2 See further Timms, *op. cit.* p.35.
3 S. 1(2); S.1(3)(a)–(f).
4 S. 1(1).
5 S. 1(5).
6 The Family Proceedings Rules 1991 (S.I. 1991 No. 1247) Part IV and The Family Proceedings Courts (Children Act 1989) Rules 1991 (S.I. 1991 No. 1395).
7 S. 41(2).
8 R. 11(3)(a).

Attending and advising court

The guardian *ad litem* shall, unless excused by the Justices' Clerks or the court, attend all directions, appointments in, and hearings of, the proceedings and shall advise the Justices' Clerk or the court on the following matters:

- whether the child is of sufficient understanding for any purpose, including the child's refusal to submit to a medical or psychiatric examination or other assessment that the court has power to require, direct or order;
- the wishes of the child in respect of any matter relevant to the proceedings, including his attendance at court;
- the appropriate forum for the proceedings;
- the appropriate timing of the proceedings or any part of them;
- the options available to the court in respect of the child and the suitability of each option, including what orders should be made in determining the application;
- any other matter concerning which the Justices' Clerk or the court seeks his advice or concerning which he considers that the court should be informed.[9]

In advising the court on the appropriate forum for the proceedings, the guardian will base his advice on the criteria for transfer of cases:

- exceptional complexity, importance or gravity;
- the need to consolidate with other proceedings, for example adoption and contact applications; and
- urgency.

In looking at the timetabling of the proceedings, guardians will be particularly aware of the need to avoid delay. Advice to the court may be given either orally or in writing. If the advice is given orally, a note of it shall be taken by the Justices' Clerk or the court.[10]

In consideration of the demands on panel members' time, imposed by the demands of frequent directions hearings, the Children Act Advisory Committee have recommended that 'in appropriate cases, courts may indicate to guardians that they may be released from court after giving evidence, so that their time may be more effectively used.'[11] This is an option which should be used sparingly, given the guardian's central role in all proceedings.

Child's attendance at court

Courts have been cautious in encouraging, or even permitting, the child's attendance at court, even when guardians have recommended that they be present.

---

9 R. 11(4)(a)−(f).
10 R. 11(5).
11 The *Children Act Advisory Committee Annual Report 1992/93*, Chapter 7, The Voice of the Child: Guardians ad Litem, p. 66.

The guardian and the solicitor together will consider the question of the child's attendance or non-attendance at court. Gone are the days when children, regardless of age, were required to be produced in court. In many cases their presence served very little purpose and contributed to the distress of the occasion. Now however opinion is divided regarding practice and policy in relation to attendance of children at court. There was considerable debate before the implementation of the 1989 Act about whether magistrates should have the right to see children alone, just as judges do in chambers. Providing children are properly briefed it can be helpful to them, and oddly comforting, to see the place and the people who are involved in making decisions about their life. Clearly the child's attendance at court must be properly managed. For example if the child is to attend court he should have an opportunity to familiarise himself with the surroundings and be fully briefed about the procedure to be followed. The practical arrangements will need to be carefully managed too, to ensure that the child is not left waiting in a room with other parties, whom he may rather not see, for example if an abusing parent is present. The decision about whether or not a child may attend court is not one that can be based purely on chronological age but must be geared to the particular child in the particular case at a particular level of intellectual and emotional development. These are matters on which the guardian and the child's solicitor will be able to advise the court, in the same way as they will be considering the child's ability to make an informed decision regarding consent to medical or other examination, although perhaps in the light of recent case law it may be prudent to warn the child that the court may make a final decision.[12]

S.95(1) allows the magistrates to exercise their discretion in allowing the child to be present at a hearing. Rule 11(4)(b) of the Family Proceedings Courts (Children Act 1989) Rules 1991 deals with the attendance of the child at court and the duty of the guardian *ad litem* to advise the Justices' Clerk or the court on the wishes of the child in respect of any matter relevant to the proceedings, including his attendance at court. However, guardians should be aware that judges may not always agree with guardians about the presence of children in court. In *Re G. (A Minor)* (Care Order),[13] Mr Justice Waite warned that 'the presence of children should not be encouraged to develop into settled practice', even though the girl in question was 13 and her wish to be present in court had been supported by the guardian. He went on to say that 'guardians *ad litem* should think carefully before arranging for children to be present at hearings and should be prepared to consider their reasons for thinking that the child should be present and justify them before the court if necessary.'

In *J. v. Lancashire County Council*, May 25, 1993,[14] a 15-year-old girl, who had been present throughout the hearing in the Family Proceedings Court, was ordered to leave the court during the hearing of the appeal, on the grounds that there would have to be some exceptional circumstances to justify her presence, having regard to 'welfare considerations'. In giving guidance on

---

12 See Child Attendance at Court, Chapter 5 below.
13 *The Times*, November 19, 1992.
14 Reported in the *Children Act Advisory Committee Annual Report 1992/93*, p. 72.

the procedure to be followed in similar cases, the judge stated that the court should be informed, in advance, of any application, which would be ruled upon by the bench before the substantive hearing commenced, in order to prevent the child being exposed to painful discussions. It would also enable the court to consider representations, with the welfare of the child as the paramount consideration. This provides an interesting subsuming of the right of the child to be present within questionable definitions of the child's welfare. The lower courts appear to be taking a more forward looking view, by allowing justices to see the child in private, contrary to views expressed in pre-Children Act debates.[15]

Notifying interested parties of the proceedings

The guardian *ad litem* shall, where practicable, notify any person whose joinder as a party to those proceedings would be likely, in the guardian *ad litem*'s opinion, to safeguard the interests of the child, of that person's right to apply to be joined under rule 7(2) of the Family Proceedings Courts (Children Act 1989) Rules 1991 and shall inform the Justices' Clerk or the court:

● of any such notification given;
● of anyone whom he attempted to notify under this paragraph, but was unable to contact; and
● of anyone who, he believes, may wish to be joined to the proceedings.[16]

The guardian *ad litem* should, for example, ensure that all those with parental responsibility or all those who have a right to parental responsibility have been notified. The net must be cast widely in order to bring in anybody who may have an interest in or a contribution to make to the child's welfare. It would be important to involve grandparents, for example, at the earliest possible opportunity. Equally, an overproliferation of parties can sometimes unnecessarily confuse matters.

Preparing a written report

The guardian *ad litem* shall, unless the Justices' Clerk or the court otherwise directs, not less than seven days before the date fixed for the final hearing of the proceedings, file a written report advising on the interests of the child; and the Justices' Clerk shall, as soon as practicable, serve a copy of the report on the parties.[17] The rules clearly state that it is the responsibility of the Justices' Clerk to serve copies of the reports on the parties. In some areas courts have been asking guardians *ad litem* to perform this duty themselves. Most guardians provide two or three copies of their report to the court in order to facilitate its circulation as soon as possible.

---

15 *Re M. (Minors)*, January 21, 1993, reported in the *Children Act Advisory Committee Annual Report 1992/93*, p. 72.
16 R. 11(6).
17 R. 11(7).

Serving and accepting service of documents on behalf of the child

The guardian *ad litem* shall serve and accept service of documents on behalf of the child, in accordance with the Family Proceedings Courts (Children Act 1989) Rules 1991, r. 8(3)(b) and (4)(b) and, where the child has not himself been served and has sufficient understanding, advise the child on the contents of any documents so served[18] (both the solicitor and the guardian *ad litem* have this duty).

The position regarding the right of the child to have sight of evidence is not clear. In *Re M. (Minors)* (Disclosure of Evidence)[19] it was held, by Butler-Sloss LJ, that the power to withhold confidential evidence from a party to proceedings concerning children should only be used in exceptional cases, where real harm would otherwise ensue to the child. In this case, the potentially damaging evidence was contained in an Addendum to the Court Welfare Officer's Report. Presumably the same ruling would apply to the guardian's report, but it is not clear that the injunction not to withhold evidence from parties would always include the child.

The guardian ad litem's investigations

The guardian *ad litem* shall make such investigations as may be necessary for him to carry out his duties and shall, in particular:

- contact or seek to interview such persons as he thinks appropriate or as the court directs;
- if he inspects records of the kinds referred to in S.42, bring to the attention of the court (through the Justices' Clerk and such other persons as the Justices' Clerk or the court may direct) all such records and documents which may, in his opinion, assist in the proper determination of the proceedings; and
- obtain such professional assistance as is available to him, which he thinks appropriate, or which the Justices' Clerk or the court directs him to obtain.[20]

Right of the guardian ad litem to have access to local authority records

1. Guardians ad litem have the right, at all reasonable times, to examine and take copies of:

    (a) any records of, or held by, a local authority which were compiled in connection with the making or proposed making by any person of any application under this Act with respect to the child concerned; or

    (b) any other records of, or held by, a local authority which were compiled in connection with any functions which stand referred to their social services committee under the Local Authority Social Services Act 1970 as far as those records relate to that child.

---

18 R. 11(8).
19 [1993] 2 W.L.R. 20.
20 R. 11(9)(a)−(c).

2. Where a guardian ad litem takes a copy of any record which he is entitled to examine under this section, that copy, or any part of it, shall be admissible as evidence of any matter referred to in any:

(a)   report which he makes to the court in the proceedings in question; or
(b)   evidence which he gives in those proceedings.

3. Sub section 2 has effect regardless of any enactment or rule of law which would otherwise prevent the record in question being admissible in evidence.[21]

S.42 gives guardians, for the first time, a statutory right of access to, and the right to copy, local authority records and to use them in evidence. A separate right of access to National Society for the Prevention of Cruelty to Children (NSPCC) records is provided for in an amendment to S.42 contained in para.18 of Schedule 16 to the Courts and Legal Services Act 1990.

In addition, access to the records of voluntary organisations and registered children's homes is provided for in the regulations: each voluntary organisation, where they are acting as an authorised person, and every person carrying on a registered children's home shall provide a guardian *ad litem* of the child:

(a) such access as may be required to:
(i)   case records and registers maintained in accordance with these regulations; and
(ii) the information from such records or registers held in whatever form (such as by means of computer);

(b) such copies of the records and entries as he may require.[22]

Each voluntary organisation, where they are not acting as an authorised person, and every person carrying on a registered children's home shall provide a guardian *ad litem* of a child:

(a) such access as may be required to:
(i)   records in so far as they relate to the child maintained in accordance with these regulations; and
(ii) the information from such records held in whatever form (such as by means of computer);

(b) such copies of the records and entries as he may require.[23]

Guardians have no statutory right of access to medical records, except where they form part of the social services file documents.[24]

In order to expedite proceedings, if guardians *ad litem* intend to adduce part of the local authority file as evidence, they should notify the local authority in advance, indicating the part of the file which they wish to use. This gives the local authority the opportunity to make representations to the court if they feel

---

21 S. 42.
22 Regulation 11 of the Arrangements for Placement of Children (General) Regulations 1991 No. 890.
23 Regulation 16, of the Children's Homes Regulations 1991 (S.I. 1991 No. 1506).
24 There has been a debate about whether or not guardians appointed in care proceedings have a right of access to the Adoption Agencies Form F which gives information about the prospective adopters. Bracewell J took the view that they did not. However, on appeal, it was confirmed that guardians *ad litem*, acting in care proceedings, do have access to Form F — *Manchester City Council v. T.*, [1994] 1 FLR 632 CA.

it would not be in the child's interests to disclose such information, or if they wish to claim that a particular part of the file is privileged.

Assisting the court

In addition to his duties under other paragraphs of this rule, the guardian *ad litem* shall provide to the Justices' Clerk and the court such other assistance as it may require.[25]

The right of other parties to question the guardian ad litem about oral or written evidence

A party may question the guardian *ad litem* about oral or written advice tendered by him to the Justices' Clerk or the court under this rule.[26]

The rules stress the centrality of the role of the guardian *ad litem* throughout the proceedings. The guardian is pivotal in all decision making — not just in relation to the recommendations which he makes to the court, but also in advising on the conduct and management of the case.

Case management role: the pro-active guardian

Rules of court may make provision as to:

● the assistance which any guardian *ad litem* may be required by the court to give to it;
● the consideration to be given by any guardian *ad litem*, where an order of a specified kind has been made in the proceedings in question, as to whether to apply for the variation or discharge of the order;
● the participation of guardians *ad litem* in reviews of a kind specified in the rules, which are conducted by the court.[27]

Arising from this section, guardians are given a very significant case management role, in particular in assisting the court with the timetabling of cases and the avoidance of delay. Guardians are encouraged to be pro-active in investigating the creative new menu of S.8 Orders and in diverting proceedings away from Parts IV and V of the 1989 Act if necessary. They are also encouraged to engage in a certain amount of 'forum shopping' in order to expedite proceedings. In previous legislation, the key task for the guardian had been the investigation and the preparation of a report recommending whether or not the Order applied for should be made in the best interests of the child. Now guardians are able to recommend a completely different policy in relation to the child, if they feel it is appropriate. They may recommend not the Order applied for, but an alternative Order, for example a S.8 Residence Order.

---

25 R. 11(10).
26 R. 11(11).
27 Children Act 1989, S. 41(10)(a)−(b). In relation to the GAL/RO's case management role see further *Practice in Progress: The A−Z of Case Management*, IRCHIN/Department of Health, 1994.

They are no longer limited to the consideration of the Order before the court. They may recommend that no Order is made at all. All of this puts the guardian very clearly in the driving seat, both in conducting, and managing and controlling the allocation and timetabling of the case and in reviewing the options for the child in relation to the whole range of both private and public law Orders. To this extent, guardians have assumed a new role as gatekeepers to care. They are certainly required to scrutinise local authority applications very closely. This is in part a legacy of public concern regarding the level and exercise of local authorities' powers of intervention into family life and the removal of children following events in Cleveland, Rochdale and the Orkneys.[28]

Effective case management necessarily brings GAL/ROs closer to the court, but it need not, and should not, take the guardian further away from the child. All of the guardian's additional duties are aimed at underpinning and enhancing their powers as independent representatives of the child. The guiding principle should be, therefore, 'How will this timetable, this form or this delay affect the child?' The case management responsibilities offer the guardians increased scope for keeping the child centre stage in all proceedings, and give them the power to be pro-active rather than reactive in controlling events on behalf of the child.

Even if magistrates refuse to transfer cases, guardians (and other parties) have the right to request transfer to the nearest care centre, if that is judged to be in the child's best interests. This view was endorsed by Bracewell J in *Essex C.C. v L*:[29] the system should be used to avoid delay such as that which occurred in *B v B*,[30] where it was stressed that directions hearings were not formalities, but were to ensure that cases were as tightly timetabled as possible.

Guardians should be aware that, if circumstances require it, cases may be transferred downwards as well as horizontally. This is provided for under the Children (Allocation of Proceedings) Order 1991.

Additional Powers

In order to assist guardians *ad litem* in carrying out their substantial duties, they are given considerable extra powers which emphasise their role as court adviser as well as court reporter.

The guardian's report   The court is directed to take account of any statement or evidence contained in the guardian's report, regardless of any enactment or rule of law which would otherwise prevent it from doing so.[31] This provision is important since it allows for the inclusion of hearsay evidence in the guardian's report. This is underpinned by S.96(3) which allows for the admissibility of evidence which would otherwise be inadmissible under any

---

28 For a picture of the strong feelings aroused by the Cleveland enquiry see Bell, *When Salem came to the Boro': the True Story of the Cleveland Child Abuse Crisis* (1988).
29 *The Times*, December 18, 1992.
30 [1994] 1 FCR 811.
31 S. 41(11).

rule of law relating to hearsay in, amongst others 'Evidence in connection with the upbringing, maintenance or welfare of a child'.[32]

In addition, the Children (Admissibility of Hearsay Evidence) Order 1991 (S.I. 1991 No. 1115) abolished the hearsay rule in all children's proceedings from October 14, 1991. In civil proceedings before the High Court or County Court and in family proceedings in a Magistrates' Court, evidence given in connection with the upbringing, maintenance or welfare of a child shall be admissible notwithstanding any rule of law relating to hearsay.

Right of access to records   Guardians are given a statutory right of access to, and right to copy, local authority as well as adoption agency records.[33]

Separate representation for the guardian   Where it appears to the guardian *ad litem* that the child:

- is instructing the solicitor direct;
- intends to, and is capable of, conducting the proceedings on his own behalf;

he shall so inform the court through the Justices' Clerk and thereafter:

- shall perform all of his duties under the Family Proceedings Courts (Children Act 1989) Rules 1991 para. (2)(a) (appointing a solicitor to represent the child) and such other duties as the Justices' Clerk or the court may direct;
- shall take such part in the proceedings as the Justices' Clerk or the court may direct; and
- may, with the leave of the Justices' Clerk or the court, have legal representation in his conduct of those duties.[34]

This is a neat theoretical synthesis of rights and welfare, ensuring that the child's right to legal advocacy is balanced by the guardian's duty to safeguard the child's welfare. The theoretical position is weakened by the practical omission in the rules of any provision for the separate representation for the guardian to be legally aided. The Civil Legal Aid (General) (Amendment) (No. 2) Regulations 1991,[35] regs. 3 and 5, Legal Aid Advice, Annex K, England and Wales, specifically exclude guardians *ad litem* and anybody acting in a representative fiduciary or official capacity from representation for the purposes of the Children Act 1989. Some panels have negotiated arrangements with the administering authority, whereby the authority undertake to pay any costs involved. However, in view of the financial considerations involved, some administering authorities have offered guardians legal advice from their own legal department, thus placing guardians in a difficult position of either accepting legal advice from another party to the proceedings or being left without funding for separate legal representation. The *Manual of Practice*

---

32 S. 96(3) and (4)(a)−(b).
33 S.42(1)−(3).
34 R. 11(3).
35 S.I. 1991 No. 2036.

Guidance for Guardians ad Litem and Reporting Officers states clearly that the reasonable expenses of such appointments will fall to local authorities to meet,[36] but this remains a matter for debate in some areas. The Children Act Advisory Committee have recommended that guardians should be eligible for legal aid in cases of divergence and have urged local authorities to make arrangement for the payment of guardians in such cases.[37]

In the meantime local authorities are urged to make 'proper provision in this area' and act in accordance with Department of Health guidance, although this is a little vague, stipulating that in such a situation the local authority may be 'liable' not 'obliged' to meet the costs.[38]

Withdrawal of applications If any of the parties seek to withdraw an application, the guardian *ad litem* must be consulted and have an opportunity to make representations.

An application may be withdrawn only with the leave of the court. Requests to withdraw applications may be made orally, in which case the guardian must be present, or in writing, in which case the guardian must be heard before the court considers the request. Seven days' notice of the hearing of the request to withdraw applications must be given to all parties, including the guardian *ad litem*. (These provisions apply equally to any welfare officer appointed, except that, unlike the guardian *ad litem*, the welfare officer is not granted an opportunity to make representations.)[39] This rule emphasises the findings in *R. v. Birmingham Juvenile Court, ex p. G.*[40] that it is the court, not the parties, who have the prerogative to decide on whether or not applications shall be withdrawn. In the Birmingham case, a guardian successfully prevented the local authority withdrawing their application for a Care Order, on the grounds that it was in the interests of the child that all the evidence should be heard before the court made a decision.

Guardian's right to terminate the appointment of a solicitor Where the guardian *ad litem* wishes an appointment of a solicitor under S.41(3) to be terminated he may apply to the court for an order terminating the appointment. The solicitor and, if he is of sufficient understanding, the child, shall be given an opportunity to make representations. The reasons for the termination shall be noted by the Justices' Clerk.[41]

Additional parties to the proceedings The guardian has considerable power to promote the right of interested parties to be joined in the proceedings. It is part of his responsibility to contact such people and to draw the attention of

---

36 Timms, *op.cit.*, p. 26.
37 *The Children Act Advisory Committee Annual Report 1992/93*, Chapter 7, p. 66; *Annual Report 1993/94*, Chapter 6, p. 56.
38 Children Act 1989 Regulations and Guidance Vol. 7, para. 2.36. See also *Re M. (Minors) (Care Proceedings: Child's Wishes)* [1994] 1 FLR 749: guardians have a responsibility to bring conflicts of view between themselves and the child to the attention of the court as soon as possible.
39 R. 5.
40 [1990] 2 Q.B. 573.
41 R. 12(4) and (5).

the court to the contribution they have to make to the case and to the child's welfare.[42]

Advice to the court about the child's ability to make an informed decision regarding medical or other assessment   Where the court makes an interim Care Order or interim Supervision Order it may give such directions (if any) as it considers appropriate with regard to the medical or psychiatric examination or other assessment of the child; but if the child is of sufficient understanding to make an informed decision, he may refuse to submit to the examination or other assessment.[43]

A Child Assessment Order authorises any person carrying out the assessment, or any part of the assessment, to do so in accordance with the terms of the Order. However, regardless of this, if the child is of sufficient understanding to make an informed decision, he may refuse to submit to a medical or psychiatric examination or other assessment.[44]

Where the court makes an Emergency Protection Order it may give such directions (if any) as it considers appropriate with respect to the medical or psychiatric examination or other assessment of the child.[45]

It is the responsibility of the guardian *ad litem* to advise the Justices' Clerk or the court on whether the child is of sufficient understanding for any purpose, including the child's attendance at court or refusal to submit to a medical or psychiatric examination, or other assessment that the court has power to require, direct or order.[46] The key word here is 'advise' not persuade. It is not a matter for the guardian *ad litem* to attempt to change the child's mind but to advise the court on the competence of the child to make an informed decision. It could be argued that part of the guardian's responsibilities is to ensure that the child has sufficient and accurate information on which to make an informed decision. The duty of the guardian in this matter is consistent with the duty throughout the rules, to advise the court on the welfare of the child while protecting the child's right to have his wishes and feelings in the matter incorporated as part of the decision making process. In practice this is a confusing area. The *Gillick* case produced the concept of the 'competent child'[47] by establishing that if children were of sufficient understanding and intelligence to enable them to understand fully what was proposed and to be capable of making up their own mind on the matter, then the parental right and the court's right to give or to refuse consent yielded to the child's right to make his own decisions, whether or not the child was consenting or refusing consent. However, *Re R.* seemed to indicate that, even if a child was competent to refuse consent to treatment, the court could — exercising its wardship jurisdiction — override that refusal if it were in the child's best interests to do so.[48] Doctors are loath to treat children without their consent. However, in specified cases, the lack of consent will not prevent the treatment

---

42 R. 11(6).
43 S. 38(6).
44 S. 43(7) and (8).
45 S. 44(6).
46 R. 11(4)(a).
47 *Gillick v. West Norfolk and Wisbech Area Health Authority and the DHSS* [1986] A.C. 112.
48 *Re. R. (A Minor)* (Wardship: Consent to Treatment), [1991] 3 W.L.R. 592.

being carried out, after consent has been obtained from another competent source, for example the parents or the court. Doctors who treat 'Gillick competent' children without their consent in an emergency would not be liable, provided they had the consent of a holder of parental responsibility, nor would there be a need to apply for a Specific Issue Order.[49]

Although much hangs on the judgment which must be made by the guardian *ad litem* about the status of the child's refusal or otherwise, nevertheless courts will pay careful attention to the views of parents and medical practitioners. The decision in *Re. R.* appears to undermine the commitment in the statute to respecting the child's right to refuse to consent to treatment. Respecting a child's views does not mean allowing him to die. In *Re W. (A Minor)* (Medical Treatment: Courts' Jurisdiction)[50] the court overrode the right of a young girl suffering from anorexia nervosa to refuse medical treatment.

A person with parental responsibility may also be allowed to override the child's views.[51] The issue of whether parents, or those with responsibility, may have the power to override the express views of a competent child in non-life-threatening situations is worrying, as was the case in *South Glamorgan C.C. and W and B.* However, reassuringly a court cannot order a doctor to treat a child in a manner inconsistent with his clinical judgment.[52]

The *Children Act Advisory Committee Annual Report 1992/93* reminds practitioners that the Ministry of Health Circular dated April 14, 1967 is still effective and that there is no need to obtain a Court Order in order to carry out life saving blood transfusions and operations on children, provided firstly that the procedure is considered necessary and is carried out after full discussion with the parents and secondly, that a supportive second opinion has been obtained. However, in the case of older children who may be expressing a view themselves, local authorities may still choose to obtain a Court Order.

The sterilisation of a minor is always a matter for the High Court to determine, and the Official Solicitor must be involved.[53]

In general, the court is protective of children's rights to be spared unnecessary examinations. No person may, without leave of the Justices' Clerk or the court, cause the child to be medically or psychiatrically examined or otherwise assessed for the purpose of preparation of expert evidence for the use of proceedings. An application for leave to do so shall, unless the Justices' Clerk or the court directs otherwise, be served on all parties to the proceedings and on the guardian *ad litem*. Where the leave of the Justices' Clerk or the court has not been given no evidence arising out of an examination or assessment to which that paragraph applies may be adduced without leave of the court.[54]

The court then is mindful of the risk of secondary abuse, identified so clearly in the Cleveland Inquiry Report. It seeks to protect children from unnecessary

---

49 *Re K.W. v. H. (Minors)* (Consent to Treatment) [1993] 1 F.L.R. 854 [1993] Fam. Law. 280 (Family Division).
50 [1993] Fam.64, C.A.
51 See *Re K., W. and H. (Minors)* (Consent to Treatment) [1993] 1 F.C.R. 240, F.D.
52 *Re J. (A Minor)* (Medical Treatment) [1992] 2 F.L.R. 165; *South Glamorgan C.C. and W and B* [1993] 1 F.L.R 574.
53 *Re H.G.* Specific Issue Order: Sterilisation [1993] 1 F.L.R. 857, F.D.
54 R. 18.

examinations and provides an effective sanction against this situation arising by refusing to consider evidence from expert witnesses which has been prepared without the leave of the court. This presents another facet of the guardian *ad litem*'s role in this matter, as they are in a strong position to alert the court to excessive or unnecessary examinations and, by facilitating effective communication and liaison about the quality and quantity of expert witness reports to be adduced, may keep the distress and disruption for the child to a minimum.

An interesting question arises in relation to rule 18, Family Proceedings Courts (Children Act 1989) Rules 1991 and definitions of examination and assessment. It would be unnecessarily restrictive if rule 18 was interpreted to cover evidence put before the court as a result of ascertaining, rather than assessing, the wishes and feelings of the child. The guardian *ad litem*, therefore, is centrally involved in an essentially contentious and emotive area of the law. His judgment about whether or not a child is competent to give or refuse consent to medical treatment will be relied on very heavily by courts in this, as in other matters. Some guardians have felt apprehensive about becoming involved in such a delicate area of practice. However, medical practitioners, those with parental responsibility and the courts will all have a view about the child's competence.

The guardian's access to confidential documents   No document, other than the record of an order held by the court and relating to relevant proceedings, shall be disclosed other than to:

- a party;
- the legal representative of a party;
- the guardian *ad litem*;
- the legal aid board; or
- a welfare officer

without leave of the Justices' Clerk or the court.[55]

The guardian is one of a privileged group who have access to most confidential documents.[56] They are not, however, licensed to have access to records kept by the Human Fertilization and Embryology Authority (see further Chapter 8 below).

Advance disclosure of guardian's report   Documents to be filed and served under Family Proceedings Rules 1991[57] r. 4(22) should include the statements which formed the basis of the evidence of witnesses, together with any reports including the report of the guardian *ad litem*.[58]

The indirect role of the guardian *ad litem* in representation and complaints procedures   Guardians *ad litem* may play an indirect role under S.26 which requires every local authority to establish a procedure for considering any

---

55 R. 23.
56 S 42.(1) and (2).
57 S.I. 1991 No. 1247.
58 *Knowsley Metropolitan Borough Council v. U.* January 25, 1993, F.D.

representations (including any complaint) made to them by any child who is being looked after by them or who is not being looked after by them but is in need.

S.26(3) lists those who may make such representations and includes such other person as the authority considers has a sufficient interest in the child's welfare to warrant his representations being made by them.[59] It is arguable that under this section, guardians *ad litem* will be in a position to initiate representation and complaints to local authorities on behalf of children whom they represent. This view is endorsed by the *Manual of Practice Guidance for Guardians ad Litem and Reporting Officers* (at 23). The Manual identifies complaints procedures as a key element in quality control and highlights the important role of the guardian in acting as a bridge to enable children and young people to use complaints procedures effectively. The involvement of guardians in proceedings arising out of S.26 complaints procedures does not fall within the role of the guardian *ad litem* as set out in the court rules. It is not one of the specified proceedings and therefore local authorities are under no obligation to fund such work. However, in the course of their work with children, it will be appropriate for guardians to ensure that they have the necessary information about complaints and representations procedures and about where to obtain skilled advocacy and support in pursuing such complaints.[60]

If the guardian *ad litem* is involved with the solicitor in establishing whether or not there are grounds for the child to apply to the Criminal Injuries Compensation Board, the court's permission must be obtained before sending the guardian *ad litem*'s report, as one of the documents cited in support of the claim.

The Role of the Guardian ad Litem in Care and Supervision Proceedings under Part IV of the 1989 Act

Proceedings in which guardians may be appointed

Guardians may be appointed in:

- all applications for Care and Supervision Orders;[61] where the court has directed the local authority to undertake an investigation of the child's circumstances and has made, or is considering whether to make, an interim Care Order;[62]
- an application for the discharge of a Care Order or the variation or discharge of a Supervision Order;[63]
- an application to substitute a Supervision Order for a Care Order;[64]

---

59 S. 26(3)(e).
60 See Representations Procedure (Children) Regulations 1991 (S.I. 1991 No. 894).
61 S. 31.
62 S. 37(1) and S. 38(1)(a).
63 S. 39.
64 S 39(4).

- in which the court is considering whether to make a Residence Order with respect to a child who is the subject of a Care Order;[65]
- with respect to contact between a child who is the subject of a Care Order and any other person;[66]
- in applications for the making of interim Orders.[67]

Care and Supervision Orders

On the application of any local authority or authorised person, the court may make an Order:

- placing a child with respect to whom the application is made in the care of a designated local authority; or
- putting him under the supervision of a designated local authority or a probation officer.[68]

The criteria for the making of either a Care Order or a Supervision Order are that the court, and the guardian, must be satisfied:

- that the child concerned is suffering, or is likely to suffer, significant harm; and
- that the harm, or likelihood of harm, is attributable to:
  - the care given to the child, or likely to be given to him if the Order were not made, not being what it would be reasonable to expect a parent to give him; or
  - the child being beyond parental control.[69]

The condition of a Care and Supervision Order is that the child must be under the age of 17 (or under 16 if married). The Order ceases when the child reaches the age of 18 and no extension is possible.

The 1989 Act establishes one route into care, through the application of one set of criteria. Only a local authority or authorised person may apply for a Care or Supervision Order. It is no longer possible for local education authorities and the police to initiate proceedings. The local authority alone has the statutory responsibility for investigating when a child is thought to be suffering harm, for promoting the upbringing of children in need by their families and for reducing the need to bring care proceedings at all.

Police Powers

The police have an emergency power not available to other agencies, to detain a child in a place of protection without prior application to the court. Other powers are:

---

65 S.8.
66 S. 34.
67 S. 38.
68 S. 31(1).
69 S. 31(2).

- the right to enter premises in order to save life and limb;[70] and
- the right, having first obtained a warrant, to enter premises and search for children in an emergency.[71]

A Care or Supervision Order will be sought only where there appears to be no better way of safeguarding and promoting the welfare of the child suffering, or likely to suffer, significant harm. The local authority has a general duty to promote the upbringing of children in need by their families, so far as this is consistent with its duty to promote the children's welfare and to avoid the need for proceedings where possible; it should have regard to the court's duty to consider the positive advantages of making an order while, at the same time, giving paramount consideration to the child's welfare. This means that voluntary arrangements through the provision of services to the child and his family should always be fully explored. Where a Care or Supervision Order is the appropriate remedy, because control of the child's circumstances is necessary to promote his welfare, applications in such proceedings should be part of a carefully planned process.[72]

Where a guardian *ad litem* is to be appointed, the appointment should be made as soon as the application is received by the court, or as appropriate, and should help the court prevent any unnecessary delay in dealing with the case. Where an application for a Care or Supervision Order follows on from the making of an Emergency Protection Order or a Child Assessment Order, a guardian *ad litem* will usually already have been appointed.[73]

Interim Orders S.38

Where in any proceedings on an application for a Care Order or Supervision Order the proceedings are adjourned or the court gives a direction under S.37(1), the court may make an interim Care Order or an interim Supervision Order with respect to the child concerned.

A court shall not make an interim Care Order, or interim Supervision Order under this section, unless it is satisfied that there are reasonable grounds for believing that the circumstances with respect to the child are as mentioned in S.31(2).[74] The criteria are not the same as those for a full time Care Order; the court is required to believe that there are reasonable grounds that the criteria set out in S.31(2) are satisfied. This is in consideration of the fact that it would not be realistic to require proof of the condition at the interim stage, when the guardian *ad litem*'s final report will not have been received nor the evidence heard. The child's version of events may form an integral part of 'reasonable grounds for believing', as could, for example, medical evidence that certain symptoms were consistent with abuse. After further assessment, this may be rejected at the full hearing. Court findings of fact leading to the making of interim Orders should, therefore, not be binding on the court (or

---

70 Police and Criminal Evidence Act 1984, S. 17(1)(e).
71 Children Act 1989, S. 102.
72 Children Act 1989 Guidance and Regulations Vol. 1, Chap. 3, para. 3.2.
73 *Ibid.*, para. 3.4.
74 S. 38(1)(a)−(b) and S. 38(2).

the guardian *ad litem*) at the final hearing and should not be regarded as prejudicial to any of the parties to the proceedings. As when making full Orders, the court must also have regard to the child welfare principles and check- list in S.1(1) to (3) and to the presumption against making an Order in S.1(5).[75]

The court has specific power to give directions on medical or psychiatric examination or other assessment of the child when it makes an interim Care or Supervision Order.[76] However, care proceedings should not be used simply to obtain an examination or assessment of the child. If the applicant's main concern at this stage is to secure such an examination or assessment and the parents cannot be persuaded to co-operate on a voluntary basis, a Child Assessment Order should be sufficient. If the authority believes an interim Order is likely to be necessary, even though the child does not need to be removed, an interim Supervision Order is to be preferred. Medical and other assessment directions may only be necessary where a Child Assessment Order reveals only a partial picture of harm or failure to thrive, or the authority's concerns are not dispelled and further investigation is called for.[77] Interim Care and Supervision Orders, with or without directions, offer considerable flexibility to the guardian in considering what is best for the child at this stage in the proceedings.

Schedule 3 of the Act goes into considerable detail about the powers of the supervisor to give directions to the supervised child, including the power to live in specified places for a specified length of time; to require the child to present himself to specified people at a specified time of day or days; and to require the child to participate in specified activities on a specified day.[78]

Applications to discharge Care Orders or to vary or discharge Supervision Orders[79]

A Care Order may be discharged by the court on the application of:

- any person who has parental responsibility for the child;
- the child himself; or
- the local authority designated by the Order.

A Supervision Order may be varied or discharged by the court on the application of:

- any person who has parental responsibility for the child;
- the child himself; or
- the supervisor.[80]

---

75 Children Act 1989 Guidance and Regulations Vol. 1, para. 3.37.
76 S. 38(6).
77 Children Act 1989 Guidance and Regulations Vol. 1, para. 3.4.3.
78 Sched. 3, para. 2(1)(a), (b) and (c).
79 S. 39.
80 S. 39(1) and (2).

On the application of a person who is not entitled to apply for the Order to be discharged, but who is the person with whom the child is living, a Supervision Order may be varied by the courts in so far as it imposes a requirement which affects that person.[81]

Where a Care Order is in force with respect to a child, the court may, on the application of any person entitled to apply for the Order to be discharged, substitute a Supervision Order for the Care Order.[82] When a court is considering whether to substitute one Order for another, any provision of the 1989 Act which would otherwise require S.31(2) to be satisfied at the time when the propose Order is substituted or made, shall be disregarded.[83]

It is interesting to reflect that it was the situation in which the local authority were applying to discharge a Care Order, with the agreement of the parents, which was seen as a priority when guardians *ad litem* were first introduced to the courts in November 1976. The point at which a child was discharged from care with the agreement of the local authority was seen to be a time of acute vulnerability for the child. In comparison with the time and attention spent on care proceedings, very little social work time is spent in planning for the discharge of children from care, bearing in mind that the majority of children in care do eventually return home.

Local authorities are required by the Review of Children's Cases Regulations 1991,[84] made under S.26(2), to consider at least at every statutory review of a case of a child in local authority care, whether to apply for discharge of the Care Order. In deciding whether or not to discharge or vary Orders the courts and the guardian *ad litem* must have regard to the welfare check-list and the principles in S.1. The court's concern will focus on what, if any, alternative provisions can be made to safeguard and promote the welfare of the child.

Applications with respect to contact between the child who is the subject of a Care Order and any other person[85]

Where a child is in the care of a local authority, the authority shall (subject to the provisions of this section) allow the child reasonable contact with:

- his parents;
- any guardian of his;
- where there was a Residence Order in force with respect to the child immediately before the Care Order was made, the person in whose favour the Order was made; and
- where immediately before the Care Order was made, a person had care of the child by virtue of an Order made in the exercise of the High Court's inherent jurisdiction with respect to children, that person.

On an application made by the authority or the child, the court may make such Order as it considers appropriate with respect to the contact which is to

---

81 S. 39(3).
82 S. 39(4).
83 S. 39(5).
84 S.I. 1991 No. 895.
85 S. 34.

be allowed between the child and any named person.[86] S.34 is arguably one of the most significant sections in the Act, in that it establishes the assumption of reasonable contact between parents and children in care. It establishes that a local authority must allow reasonable contact with the child's parents and certain other people, unless directed otherwise by a Court Order, or a local authority temporarily suspends contact in urgent circumstances.[87] It requires the court to consider contact arrangements before making a Care Order and gives it wide powers to deal with problems. The underlying principle is that the authority, the child and other persons concerned should, as far as possible, agree reasonable arrangements before the Care Order is made, but should be able to seek the court's assistance if agreement cannot be reached or the authority want to deny contact to a person who is entitled to it under the 1989 Act. These provisions substantially improve the position of parents and others seeking contact, compared with the previous legislation, and limit the authorities' power to control and deny contact.

It should be recognised that there will be situations where contact will be detrimental to the child's welfare. This possibility should be considered at the pre-court proceedings stage, when plans for contact have been drawn up.[88] The provisions in S.34 recognise that contact is too important an issue to be regarded as simply a matter of management within the sole control of the local authority. S.34 contact is quite separate from the contact provisions in Part II of the 1989 Act. An S.8 contact Order cannot be made when a child is in local authority care[89] and any existing S.8 Order is automatically discharged on the making of a Care Order.[90]

In order to protect children from repeated applications for a Contact (or any other) Order, if this is deemed not to be in their interests, S.91(17) stipulates that if an application for an Order has been refused the person concerned may not reapply for the same Order in respect of the same child within six months, without the leave of the court. Clearly, guardians *ad litem* have a part to play in considering the effect of repeated applications on the child's peace of mind and welfare.

The Contact with Children Regulations 1991 (S.I. 1991 No. 891) set out the responsibilities of local authorities who seek to refuse contact under S.34.

Proceedings in which the court is considering whether to make a Residence Order with respect to a child who is the subject of a Care Order[91]

The making of a S.8 Residence Order to replace a S.31 Care Order would signal the passing of the child from the public to the private sphere of law. The implications of making the Order are very similar to those involved in deciding whether or not to discharge a Care Order. Effectively the making of the S.8

---

86 S. 34(1)(a)−(d).
87 S. 34(6).
88 Children Act 1989 Guidance and Regulations Vol. 1, para. 3.76.
89 S. 9(1).
90 S. 91(2).
91 S. 8.

Residence Order removes a child from the local authority's sphere of influence and effectively discharges him from care. The guardian *ad litem*'s central role in these proceedings is to fully investigate the capacity and motivation of those who are applying for the S.8 Residence Order in respect of the child. The guardian *ad litem* would need to be assured that the future arrangements for the child are clear and understood by all parties to the proceedings. The guardian must be satisfied particularly about any elements of risk or uncertainty surrounding the application.

The Role of the Guardian ad Litem in Proceedings Under Part V of the 1989 Act: The Protection of Children

Applications for Emergency Protection Orders and the extension of Emergency Protection Orders

Where any person (the applicant) applies to the court for an Order to be made under this section with respect to a child, the court may make the Order if, but only if, it is satisfied that:

(a) there is reasonable cause to believe that the child is likely to suffer significant harm if:

    (i) he is not removed to accommodation provided by, or on behalf of the applicant; or

    (ii) he does not remain in the place in which he is then being accommodated;

(b) in the case of an application made by a local authority:

    (i) enquiries are being made with respect to the child under S.47(1)(b);

    (ii) those enquiries are being frustrated by access to the child being unreasonably refused to a person authorised to seek access and the applicant has reasonable cause to believe that access to the child is required as a matter of urgency; or

(c) in the case of an application made by an authorised person:

    (i) the applicant has reasonable cause to suspect that a child is suffering, or is likely to suffer, significant harm;

    (ii) the applicant is making enquiries with respect to the child's welfare; and

    (iii) those enquiries are being frustrated by access to the child being unreasonably refused to a person authorised to seek access and the applicant has reasonable cause to believe that access to the child is required as a matter of urgency.[92]

The Emergency Protection Order is open to much earlier challenge than the Place of Safety Order that it replaced. Parents wishing to challenge the Order may do so after 72 hours. The Emergency Protection Order lasts for only 8 days, with one possible extension of seven more, making a total of 15 days. Orders may be made on application to a single justice, they may be made *ex parte* and, with the leave of the clerk to the court, they may be made orally. Guardians *ad litem* are appointed as soon as possible after the making of the Emergency Protection Order. If the making of the Order is challenged

---

92 S. 44(1).

guardians must be ready, at very short notice, to form a view about whether or not the challenge should be upheld.

Before implementation of the 1989 Act, many panels established duty systems in order to be prepared for the influx of cases at short notice. In the event comparatively few challenges have been made after 72 hours.

In many cases children are removed from home on Emergency Protection Orders, to prevent further contact with an alleged abuser. Although there is no Ouster Order in the 1989 Act, the guardian *ad litem* will want to investigate the possibility of removing the alleged abuser, rather than the child, at a very early stage. This may be done if the non-abusing parent agrees to apply to the County Court for a short term Ouster Injunction under S.1 of the Domestic Violence and Matrimonial Proceedings Act 1976, or to the Magistrates' Court for an Exclusion Order under S.16 of the Domestic Proceedings and Magistrates' Courts Act 1978. In practice, there is a limited use of Ouster Orders arising from public law proceedings, compared with their frequent use in private law proceedings where *ex parte* Ouster Orders have been granted for what may be perceived as comparatively minor reasons. District judges have been criticised for 'being rather too eager to protect the wife'. In one case the only injuries sustained by the wife, on her own admission, were 'the sort of bruises which you get when you bump into furniture'.[93]

Contrast this situation with the difficulty of ousting the alleged abuser in public law proceedings where, in the vast majority of cases, the child is removed, with all the trauma that entails, while the alleged abuser stays comfortably at home. If it is indeed that easy to obtain ex parte Ouster Orders, there is considerable scope to investigate their increased use in the interests of children, as well as mothers.

If the local authority apply for the extension of an Emergency Protection Order it is usually because they are considering whether or not they have grounds for care proceedings. If they consider that they have enough evidence to proceed, it is likely that they will apply for an interim Care Order. It is often the case, therefore, that guardians appointed after the making of an Emergency Protection Order go on to act in the application to extend the Emergency Protection Order and then in the subsequent care proceedings, beginning with an application for an interim Care Order. However, if after the making of the Emergency Protection Order, the local authority decide not to proceed, but to allow the Order to lapse, the guardian *ad litem*, who may have great concerns following his preliminary investigations, may need to be pro-active in initiating proceedings on behalf of the child and in ensuring that the court hears all the available evidence.

Applications for a Child Assessment Order and the variation and discharge of a Child Assessment Order and Emergency Protection Order

The court may make a Child Assessment Order in respect of a child only if satisfied that:

---

93 (1993) 23 Fam.Law, Letters, p. 565.

- the applicant has reasonable cause to suspect that the child is suffering, or is likely to suffer, significant harm;
- an assessment of the state of the child's health or development or the way in which he has been treated is required to enable the applicant to determine whether or not the child is suffering, or is likely to suffer, significant harm;
- it is unlikely that such an assessment will be made or be satisfactory in the absence of an Order under this section.[94]

A Child Assessment Order is not an emergency procedure and no court may make a Child Assessment Order if it is satisfied that there are grounds for making an Emergency Protection Order with respect to the child.[95]

A Child Assessment Order has effect for a period not exceeding seven days beginning from a specified date. It may be possible for the seven days not to run concurrently — in fact this would be a much more practical way of dealing with the Order as it would enable guardians *ad litem* and others to set up appointments with appropriate experts who are to be part of the child's assessment process. The likelihood of having paediatricians and child psychiatrists or psychologists all available in the same week is very slim, so the process of assessment must be carefully and methodically planned in order to cause the minimum disruption for the child. It must be stressed that the Child Assessment Order is a planned Order. It is not something that can be applied for and carried out in an *ad hoc* way. Guardians will want to know:

- what form the assessment will take;
- who will be carrying it out;
- where it will be carried out; and
- when it will be carried out

before agreeing to such a Order. In practice, perhaps because of some of these difficulties, there has been very little use made of the Order, although it does have a positive contribution to make as one of a range of Orders available to protect children. Its advantages are that it deals with the single issue of enabling an assessment of the child to be made where significant harm is suspected, but when the child is not thought to be at immediate risk. It also allows the local authority, or authorised person, to find out more about the state of the child's health or development in a less interventionist way than that involved in the making of an Emergency Protection Order. One key determinant in the decision whether or not to support the making of a Child Assessment Order will be the attitude of the child to the proposed assessment. The guardian must advise the court on the child's competence to refuse to co-operate with the necessary arrangements, whether on physical, intellectual or emotional grounds. Guardians are understandably reluctant to coerce children into agreeing to assessments of uncertain outcome or benefit, in the face of that child's distress. They will, however, want, to ensure that children have accurate information about what is entailed in any proposed assessments. Refusal may be based on ignorance or apprehension about the procedures to be used. Allowances must be made for the child's anxiety or even outright

---

94 S. 43(1)(a)–(c).
95 S. 43(3).

distrust of the court's capacity to understand what is involved — here the guardian can be of great benefit to the child.

Involvement of the Guardian ad Litem in Certain Family Proceedings (S.37 Applications)

S.37 is where private and public law proceedings meet. In any family proceedings in which a question arises with respect to the welfare of a child, the court may judge it appropriate for a Care or Supervision Order to be made and may direct the appropriate authority to undertake an investigation of the child's circumstances.

Where the court gives a direction under this section, the local authority concerned shall, when undertaking the investigation consider whether they should:

- apply for a Care Order or for a Supervision Order with respect to the child;
- provide services or assistance for the child or his family; or
- take any other action with respect to the child.

The information shall be given to the court before the end of the period of eight weeks beginning with the date of direction, unless the court states otherwise.[96]

If the local authority decide to apply for a Care or Supervision Order, then a guardian *ad litem* is appointed to represent the child in the normal way. S.37 therefore provides a bridge or cross-over point between public and private proceedings. In practice, it has given rise to some confusion, not least to the families involved who may find that they have been blessed with the attentions of a family court welfare officer, a local authority social worker and a guardian *ad litem* — all within the space of a few weeks. Consider a situation where a couple are in the process of divorce. The court is concerned about the residence and contact arrangements for the children and requests a S.7 report from a family court welfare officer. The family court welfare officer is also concerned and, on the basis of that concern, the court gives a direction under S.37 asking the local authority to undertake an investigation. Having completed their investigation the local authority decide to apply for an interim Care Order, at which point a guardian *ad litem* is appointed. This is a confusing scenario for parents and children, in three main areas. Firstly, the stage at which the guardian *ad litem* is appointed, and the extent of his involvement. Some courts have appointed a guardian at the same time as they have given directions for the local authority to begin an investigation, but some have waited and only appointed in exceptional circumstances, for example where there were fears that the child was being seriously abused. Secondly, whether S.37 can be used to appoint guardians *ad litem* in private law proceedings, generally, as a way of obtaining a report and a representative for the child. This would be a highly desirable state of affairs, but unfortunately does not fall within the proceedings specified in the Children Act 1989 and guardians *ad litem* who have been appointed by hopeful judges via

---

96 S. 37(1), (2) and (4).

the provisions of S.37 have been told that such appointments were inappropriate and furthermore would not be funded by local authority panels. Thirdly, some courts have appointed guardians rather than family court welfare officers in S.37 cases, apparently as an alternative reporting procedure.

The *Children Act Advisory Committee Annual Report 1992/93* expresses concern about the apparent misuse of this section, which appears wide and varied. In particular the committee was made aware of circumstances in which a S.37 report had revealed serious parental deficiencies, but nevertheless the local authority had declined to apply for a Care or Supervision Order, thereby placing the court in difficulty.[97] Reference is made to this situation in a *Best Practice Guide* produced by the Sheffield Family Court Business and Services Committee's orders for investigation by local authority made under S.7(1) or S.37(1) of the Children Act 1989.[98]

> Child protection can be achieved in some instances, in particular where the carer of the child is not in question, but the child is at risk from interference by a person other than the carer, by a directive or an injunctive order, a prohibited steps order, a 'no contact' order, a direction or a condition under S.11(7) of the Children Act 1989. An injunction may be appropriate where there are family proceedings already before the court. The court may make an order under S.8 of the 1989 Act of its own motion. However, where the carer is not protecting a child from significant harm, the local authority should apply for a care order or a supervision order.[99]

In April 1993 the Social Services Inspectorate, in response to concerns expressed by panel managers and others, carried out research on all S.37 directions made in the preceding 12 months. The survey was carried out by means of a questionnaire. The general information related to the number of S.37 directions which resulted in a guardian being appointed under S.41(6)(b) in the period April 1, 1992 to March 31, 1993, in the area served by the guardian *ad litem*/reporting officer panel.

The survey findings, drawing on panel members' and panel managers' experience of 80 cases, confirmed the picture of confusion on a number of legal, policy and practice issues surrounding S.37 appointments. The following extracts illustrate the points at issue:

> At the Family Court Services Committee in March 1992, I expressed some concern about S.37 directions where divorce court welfare officers had already reported, where local authority and guardian ad litem both had to submit reports by the same date, following the S.37 directions, which meant parallel investigations. Our suggestion was that the local authority report first, and the guardian ad litem report subsequently, therefore commenting on the local authority's assessment. Alternatively the guardian ad litem should not be appointed until the local authority had reported, and an application under S.31 had been made.
> The local authority would report, on application under S.31, but the guardian ad litem would then continue to report, in effect, in private law proceedings. This can be costly, and time consuming, and guardians ad litem have to resist involvement in subsequent reviews. In one case, the guardian ad litem sought to be discharged at the

---

97 Section 37 directions made in private law rose from 1,205 between January and June 1992 to 1,890 between January and June 1993: The Children Act Advisory Committee, *Annual Report 1992/93*, p.32.

98 *Best Practice Guide*, June 22, 1993.

99 *Nottinghamshire County Council v. P.* [1993], 3 W.L.R. 637, C.A.

time of the 'final' disposal of the private law matters in September 1992. A visiting judge agreed to do so — but the guardian ad litem continued to receive notices of hearings and subsequent directions up to March 1993.

In one case, a guardian ad litem challenged a judge's view that, despite the local authorities recommendation, no application under S.31 need be made. The guardian wished to appeal the decision. Initially the Legal Aid application was accepted, but subsequently a decision was made that the appeal did not involve the child's welfare and was an inappropriate use of legal aid funds. The Legal Aid Board contacted the panel manager and expressed the view that, despite the local authority having reported, they remained unspecified proceedings and it was acceptable for the guardian ad litem to continue.[100]

Out of 80 cases studied in the GAL/RO Services Survey Report, 42 detailed concerns about S.37 enquiries, including the local authority's refusal to pay the guardian *ad litem* fees; unclear demarcation of role between the guardian, the court welfare officer, the local authority social worker and the Official Solicitor; difficulties in explaining the role to the child's family and the child; pressures on the guardian *ad litem* to become drawn into a mediation role between the parties and the precise nature, scope and duration of the guardian's enquiries. In the absence of more precise guidelines, individual guardians *ad litem* have, to some extent, developed the role according to the facts and requirements of a particular case.

Involvement in S.37 applications can become a protracted commitment for guardians *ad litem*. In one case the guardian *ad litem* was appointed for a hearing scheduled for four days at the end of August 1993, by which time the guardian had been appointed for nine months. The basis for the continuing involvement was 'tentative, unclear and unsatisfactory, both from a practice and a professional stance.'[101]

In an effort to clarify the situation the following Best Practice Guidance on S.37(1) directions has been adopted by the Children Act Advisory Committee, and is set out as Annex 1 to Chapter 4 of the *Children Act Advisory Committee Report 1992/93*:

1. A direction under S.37(1) is appropriate where the court desires an investigation because 'it appears to the court that it may be appropriate for a care or supervision order to be made' (S.37(1)).
2. A direction under S.37(1) is NOT lawful unless it appears to the court that a care or supervision order may be appropriate. Thus, in private law proceedings, a direction under S.37(1) should not be used as a device for the purpose of enabling the court to appoint a guardian ad litem. Unless 'it appears to the court that it may be appropriate for a care or supervision order to be made', any referral for a welfare investigation should be made under S.7.
3. The purpose of a S.37(1) direction is to enable the court to cause the local authority to assess whether a care or supervision order is needed. It is not to obtain a general welfare report. However, the making of a S.37(1) direction will also cause the local authority to consider whether and which child welfare support services should be provided by local authority, or other action taken, as well as or instead of a care or supervision order: S.37(2), and note the details of the duty of the local authority to report to the court under S.37(3).

---

100 The Children Act 1989, Section 37 Directions, The GAL/RO Services Survey Report (November 1993), Department of Health and Social Services Inspectorate, paras. 2.12., 2.13 and 2.14.
101 Hardy, *Guardian ad Litem, Practice in Progress Regional Report* (1993), published IRCHIN with the Department of Health.

4. Upon a direction under S.37, the local authority must report back within eight weeks, unless the court otherwise directs: S.37(4). The date for the next hearing must be fixed: Family Proceedings Rules 1991 (S.I. 1991 No.1247 (L.20)) rule 4.15(2)(ii), Family Proceedings Courts (Children Act 1989) Rules 1991 (S.I. 1991 No.1395 (L.17)) rule 15(5)(ii). The date for the report should also be specified under Family Proceedings Rules 1991, rule 4.14(2) or Family Proceedings Courts (Children Act 1989) Rules 1991, r. 14(2).

5. When a county court which is not a care centre makes a direction under S.37(1), it will facilitate expedition of any proceedings begun by the local authority if the court makes a direction under the Children (Allocation of Proceedings) Order 1991 (SI 1991 No.1677), Art 3(2)(b) for the application to be made to the appropriate care centre.

Appointment of a panel guardian ad litem
6. When a court has made a direction under S.37(1), and 'has made, or is considering whether to make, an interim care order', (S.41(6)(b)), 'the court shall appoint a guardian ad litem for the child concerned, unless satisfied that it is not necessary to do so in order to safeguard his interests': S.4(1).

7. The court cannot appoint a panel guardian unless the proceedings are 'specified' within S.41(6). Section 41 does not authorise the court to appoint a guardian ad litem, upon making a S.37(1) direction, if the court has not made, and is not considering whether to make, an interim care order: S.41(6)(b).

Section 7(1) Referrals
8. Section 7(1) is for cases where the court desires a welfare investigation and report. This might include a child protection issue, e.g. abusive interference with a child by a parent or another person who does not have care of the child: in such a case an injunction may be the appropriate remedy.

9. The reporter under a S.7(1) order is the eyes and ears of the court and is required to investigate and to report to the court on the welfare of the child. The reporter is an independent agent of the court, is not a party to the proceedings, and is not legally represented.

10. Whether an order under S.7(1) should be directed to the Court Welfare Service or the local authority may be affected by:
   (i) previous involvement with, and knowledge of, the family by the local authority, in which case the local authority is likely to be appropriate, particularly if the involvement is recent or continuing;
   (ii) local arrangements between the Court Welfare Service and the local authority for distribution or sharing of investigation work.

11. When considering whether to make a S.7(1) referral or a S.37(1) direction, the court should, as far as practicable, obtain the available relevant information from any social worker or court welfare officer who is currently involved with the child, or a duty court welfare officer.

12. Upon making a S.7(1) referral, the date for the next hearing must be fixed: Family Proceedings Rules 1991 (S.I. 1991 No. 1247), r. 4.15(2)(ii), Family Proceedings Courts (Children Act 1989) Rules 1991 (S.I. 1991 No. 1395 (l.17)), r.14(2) or Family Proceedings Courts (Children Act 1989) Rules 1991, r.14(2).

Communication to local authority of S.37(1) direction or S.7(1) referral
13. It is important that, whenever a court makes a S.7(1) direction or a S.7(1) referral to a local authority, the authority should be informed as quickly as possible. An immediate telephone notification should be confirmed in writing. Family Proceeding Courts (Children Act 1989) Rules 1991, r.4.26(3) and Family Proceedings Courts (Children Act 1989) Rules 1991 r.27(3) require that a copy of a S.37(1) direction shall be served on the local authority as soon as practicable. Family Proceedings Rules 1991, r.4.26(4) and Family Proceedings

Courts (Children Act 1989) Rules 1991 r.27(4) provide for the court to direct which parts of the documentary evidence should be served on the local authority where a S37(1) direction has been made.[102]

Comment

Since implementation of the Children Act 1989, guardians have not only been involved in a wider range of proceedings, but have also experienced a substantial growth in numbers of cases which are of greater complexity and longer duration than was the case before October 1991. Typically, the guardian's investigations have become more extensive, involving more extended family members over a protracted period of involvement, punctuated by frequent directions hearings. The slower turnover of cases has meant that guardians have become closer to acquiring a case load, and, in some cases, may be the professional with the longest involvement in the child. This, in turn, has implications both for the boundaries of the role and for the effective use of guardian's time and professional expertise.

The Role of the Guardian ad Litem in Other Specified Proceedings

S.41(6) and Family Proceedings Courts (Children Act 1989) Rules 1991,[103] r.2(2) specify four additional types of proceedings in which the guardian *ad litem* may be appointed. These are:

- applications for Secure Accommodation Orders,[104] (S.25) (see below Chapter 6);
- applications for children in care to live outside England and Wales;[105]
- applications to change a child's surname or to remove him from the UK while a Care Order is in force;[106] and
- applications to extend or further extend a Supervision Order.[107]

Applications for children in care to live outside England and Wales[108]

The appointment of the guardian *ad litem* in such cases is a general safeguarding mechanism. It is anticipated that the guardian *ad litem* will advise the court on whether or not the application is in the interests of the child and alert the court to any risks that may be involved. In particular they will be concerned with the impact of such an application on the child's existing

---

102 *Children Act Advisory Committee Annual Report 1992/93*, Annex 1, Chapter 4, Best Practice Guidance on S. 37(1) Directions.
103 S.I. 1991 No. 1395 (L.17).
104 S.25.
105 Sched. 2, para. 19(1).
106 S. 33(7).
107 Sched. 3, para. 6(3).
108 Sched. 2, para. 19.(1).

attachments, peer group relationships, activities, education, contact with siblings and other members of the extended family. They will be particularly concerned to listen to the child's wishes and feelings in the matter.

Applications to change a child's surname or remove him from the UK while a Care Order is in force[109]

Change of name   The guardian will particularly focus on the impact of any change of name on the child's sense of identity and what the likely reaction to any change could be, on the child and on other members of the family. Is the change of surname contributing positively or negatively to the child's long term welfare? Clearly the child's own wishes and feelings, if he is of a sufficient age and understanding, will weigh heavily in the matter.

Removal from the UK while the Care Order is in force   Key considerations here are:

- the impact of removal on the child;
- whether or not the child wishes to be removed, if old enough to give a view;
- considerations of the long term implications for the maintenance of existing attachments and relationships;
- the viability of the arrangements for the child's care outside the UK, including the assessment of any potential risk to the child and the need to set up adequate and appropriate supervision of the child abroad. Again the criteria must be whether or not the welfare of the child can be adequately protected and his welfare assured under the new arrangements.

---

109 S. 33(7).

Appendix 1
Skills Profile for GAL/ROs
Practice

Ability to:

- present a balanced and independent view of the child's situation to the court;
- be a competent and effective representative of the child;
- command credibility as an expert witness on general child care matters;
- communicate with children and young people;
- read and assimilate available documentation files and witness statements;
- organise and pursue a disciplined and targeted investigation of all the available facts of the case, including a willingness to initiate new lines of enquiry if necessary, and to demonstrate a rigorousness of approach in checking out old ones;
- interpret accurately the material gathered through the process of investigation;
- assess risk, and the capacity for change within the child's birth and extended family;
- understand and demonstrate a knowledge and understanding of human growth and development, issues, race, culture, religion, disability, disadvantage, psychiatric and psychological disorders and psychodynamic theories of personality;
- work in partnership with the child's solicitor, including an appropriate apportionment of work;
- write succinct and logical reports containing a structured analysis of the facts, a clear representation of the options available to the court, and a reasoned and clear recommendation;
- practice in an anti-discriminatory manner;
- demonstrate and incorporate within the work a sound understanding of the principles of participation and involvement of the child in decision making;
- integrate and understand both children's rights and children's welfare.

Case Management

Ability to:

- understand the judicial, legal, social, political and local government systems which surround the child;
- operate within those systems, to achieve the best possible outcome for the child;
- be effective in managing the timetabling of the case to streamline proceedings and avoid delay;
- facilitate and initiate liaison and communication between all parties and organisations concerned with the child;
- ensure that the case is heard in the appropriate court, by facilitating necessary transfer;
- assess the impact of the proceedings on the child and to act quickly to protect the child from further stress and distress;
- make a judgment, with the solicitor, about the amount of expert witness evidence (if any) that is necessary, bearing in mind the negative indications of delay and confusion for the child;
- evaluate, and exercise judgment about the level, timing and manner of state intervention into lives of children.
- ensure that relevant issues are placed on the agenda of the Family Court Business and Services Committees;
- liaise with the panel manager to expedite the efficient and effective running of the panel.

Appendix 2

Report Outline

The following report format is reproduced from the *Manual of Practice Guidance for Guardians ad litem and Reporting Officers*.[110] It is not intended to be prescriptive, and should take account of both the need to avoid undue repetition (bearing in mind that all evidence will be disclosed in advance and some will be agreed before the hearing), and the need to provide a report which can be free-standing and give as complete a picture of the child's situation at the time of the proceedings as possible. In every case there should be a section on the child's wishes and feelings which should be quite separate from the guardian's assessment of the implications of those wishes and feelings. In every report, guardians should seek to identify evidence which is in dispute and should provide the court with a clear statement of the options available to the child, together with a clear and reasoned analysis of those options and their likely outcomes.

It should, above all, be closely linked to providing information linked to the welfare checklist in S.1(3). The trial recommendation should be clearly stated and clear reasons for it given. The front sheet should be marked 'Confidential' and the paragraphs numbered.

Section 1: Front Page

Name of child/children (if there are siblings then there should be a separate section in respect of each child named in the application)

Case Number (to be used in applications)

Birth date and age of child/children

Type of proceedings (relevant sections and sub-sections of the Act)

Court

Statement of Order sought

Date of Hearing

Guardian ad litem report prepared by: Name
                                         Date of appointment

Section 2

(i)   In preparing this report I have interviewed the following people (list everyone interviewed, with dates, number of occasions seen, relationship to the child/children)

(ii) I have read the following documents

(iii) I have spoken to the following on the telephone (name, relationship, date)

(iv) I have attempted to interview the following, but have not done so for the following reasons (if relevant)

(v)   Make a statement of any special matter you wish to bring to the attention of the court. If you have a particular concern about this child, or about any particular aspect of the case, it is helpful to the court to have early warning of this. For example, there may have been a breakdown of communication between the police and the social services department, or some adverse policy or practice which may work to the detriment of the case (for example, timetabling or allocation), which could be notified under this section.

---

110 Timms, (1992).

Section 3: Suggested outline

(1) STATEMENT OF THE ORDER BEING SOUGHT, AND BY WHOM,
    including:
- a summary of the nature and outcome of any previous orders or applications,
  including a consideration of any avoidable delay (section 1(2));
- a statement of any particular matters arising or omitted from the information on the
  application form;
- a statement of existing directions given, either to the court or the guardian.

(2) CHRONOLOGICAL HISTORY OF THE CASE, including:
- the structure of the family, including siblings, the wider extended family and
  individuals of central importance in the child's life;
- statement of the sequence of events which either precipitated or informed the
  application and the decisions made in relation to the child.

— This should not be an open-ended section, but should focus on the aspects of the
  history of direct relevance to the case.

(3) INFORMATION ABOUT THE CHILD (if not included on the Application form),
    including:
- a list of those who have parental responsibility; (if this is fully listed on the
  application form it may not be necessary to duplicate)
- section 1(3)(d) — his age, sex, background and any other relevant characteristics
- — in particular this section should include information about the child's race,
  culture, religion and list the languages spoken and understood by the child. It
  should also examine any issues of disability and gender relevant to the case; (none of
  this information is required on the application form, so guardians should always
  include it)
- section 1(3)(b) — a statement of the child's physical, emotional and educational
  needs, including any special needs or requirements. The guardian should be
  satisfied that there is full medical information available, and that the parents'
  knowledge of the child's history is recorded. Steps should be taken to ensure that,
  wherever possible, there is no disruption to the child's education and that, where
  there has been a change of school, full information is transferred.

(4) THE LOCAL AUTHORITY (OR OTHER APPLICANT'S) PLAN FOR THE
    CHILD, including:
- a critical appraisal of the local authority's policy and practice in relation to this
  particular child, including any harm the child has suffered, or is likely to suffer;
- a statement of the proposed arrangements for the child: the guardian should receive
  a copy of the care plan in plenty of time to include an assessment of what is
  proposed;
- an appraisal of the services provided to the child, and his family, under Part III of
  the Act — services to Children and their Families. What positive steps have the local
  authority taken to keep the family together?
- if the application is for the discharge, or variation, of a care or supervision order,
  the guardian should consider the requirements of local authorities under the Review
  of Children's Cases Regulations 1991.

(5) ARRANGEMENTS FOR REASONABLE CONTACT, including:
- a clear statement of who the child is seeing, and in what circumstances, with
  particular reference to contact with siblings;
- how these arrangements are working out in practice;
- any views the other parties, or those with parental responsibility, may have about
  the existing, or proposed, arrangements;
- are they 'reasonable'?

(6) THE CAPACITY OF THE CHILD'S PARENTS/CARERS TO MEET THE
    CHILD'S PRESENT NEEDS (section 1(3)(f)), including:
- an assessment of risk factors;

- section 1(3)(e) — a statement of any harm the child has suffered, or is likely to suffer;
- section 1(3)(f) — how capable each of his parents, and any other person in relation to whom the court considers the question to be relevant, is of meeting his needs.

(7) THE WISHES AND FEELINGS OF THE CHILD, including:
- section 1(3)(a) — a clear statement of the child's ascertainable wishes and feelings;
- any written or drawn material prepared by the child (this section should not include the guardian's own views about any of the child's statements).

(8) THE GUARDIAN'S SUMMARY AND ASSESSMENT OF THE CHILD'S SITUATION, including:
- giving a clear picture of the child's present situation;
- highlighting any areas of special needs or concern, including any disadvantage or discrimination the child may have suffered.

(9) OPTIONS AVAILABLE TO THE COURT
- section 1(3)(g)—'the range of powers available to the court under this Act in the proceedings in question', including:
- a clear statement of the options, making full use of the menu of section 8 orders and a range of other orders available under the Act, with a reasoned analysis of the likely effects of the different courses of action. This should include consideration of the merits of an interim supervision order, with a section 8 residence order as a way of avoiding removal from home.

(10) Section 1(5) — WILL MAKING AN ORDER BE BETTER THAN MAKING NO ORDER AT ALL, including:
- a statement of why the order is, or is not, justified, e.g. have the threshold criteria been met?
- a statement of whether making an order will be better than making no order at all, even if the conditions for the making of an order have been satisfied. In making this judgement, guardians should be aware of the likely outcome for the child, e.g. is there a suitable placement available which will meet the needs of this particular child?

(11) RECOMMENDATION
The guardian's recommendation should:
(a) be clearly stated;
(b) be logically reasoned and related to the evidence;
(c) make full use of the menu of orders available under the Act;
(d) incorporate positive features of the child's life, while attempting to offset the effects of the negative;
(e) consider the powers available to the local authority under Part III of the Act, as an alternative to the making of a court order;
(f) allow the child's participation in the decision making, if of appropriate age and understanding;
(g) include the guardian's recommendations for contact. The recommendation should include advice to the court regarding arrangements for contact under section 34(5). It may include short, or extended, visits involving overnight stays, or it may be limited to indirect contact through letters or telephone calls. The guardian must define the purpose of the contact:
- in meeting the child's needs; and
- in forming part of the plan for this particular child.
Contact may be:
(i)   part of a plan for reuniting the child with his family;
(ii) to maintain constructive and consistent links with people who are important in the child's life;
(iii) increasing the child's sense of security and comfort through a particularly difficult time, e.g. while awaiting the outcome of court proceedings.

(h)   allow the development of the child's unique identity, taking into account issues of race, culture and religion;
(i)   offer minimum disruption;
(j)   allow the child hope of a positive future;
(k)   include any conditions to be attached to any order made. Section 11(7) provides the power to attach conditions and directions to a section 8 order.

Section 4: After the Hearing

After the hearing there are some matters which the guardian will need to consider:

- does the child understand the outcome of the proceedings and the implications for their future?
- is it appropriate to consider lodging an appeal on behalf of the child?
- are there matters of policy or practice on which the guardian ad litem wishes to comment formally to the local authority?
- are there matters about the conduct or procedure of the case which the guardian would like to be conveyed to the panel manager for discussion at the Family Court Business Committee?
- has the guardian arranged for the confidential and secure storage of one report and return, or shredded confidential case material and reports?
- is the child eligible for compensation through the Criminal Injuries Compensation Scheme?
- is the child aware of his right to make applications to the court on his own account, to vary, discharge or apply for orders under the Act? This includes applying for leave to make an application for a section 8 order, where appropriate.
- is the child aware of his rights to make representations and complaints under section 26 if he is distressed or worried by some aspect of his care, and of his rights to have access to an independent person, and to services of advice and advocacy, to assist him in making his representations?

Chapter 5
Representation in Action in Care and Related Proceedings

Panel Facts and Figures

The Annual Report presenting an overview of the Guardian *ad Litem* and Reporting Officer service, published in September 1993, identified 1,190 guardians *ad Litem* employed on 54 panels. This figure refers to 1,190 appointments rather than 1,190 different people, as some panel members are employed on two or even more panels. Bearing in mind that, in 1984, there were approximately 3,500 guardians, the current figures indicate the establishment of the smaller, dedicated workforce envisaged by the Department of Health. Of the 1,190 panel members, 318 (26.7 per cent) were local authority employees, 669 (56.2 per cent) were sessional fee-attracting panel members, 59 (5 per cent) were seconded to panels from voluntary organisations and 104 (8.7 per cent) were probation officers. These figures indicate clearly that the contribution of probation and voluntary child care organisations is diminishing, while the number of sessional, fee-attracting and local authority employed guardians continue to increase. The 1994 overview showed that the total number of GAL/ROs in England and Wales had dropped to just under 1000. Overall panel membership dropped by 53 per cent between 1989 and 1994, by which time 26 out of 54 panels were composed entirely out of fee-attracting members. Panels vary in size from 119 guardians (Inner and North London Panel), to 7 (Solihull) and 8 (Buckinghamshire and Cambridgeshire). Some panels are composed, almost exclusively, of local authority employees. Interestingly these panels are in the north of England (North of the Tyne, Wigan/Bolton/Salford, Rochdale/Bury/Oldham and Merseyside).

Compared with 1991/92 the demand for guardians had increased significantly in most areas. On some panels the number of appointments had increased by more than 40 per cent (Nottinghamshire), 50 per cent (Cleveland), 85 per cent (Wigan/Bolton/Salford) and 65 per cent (North of the Tyne). Decreases in number of appointments had occurred in more rural areas, for example −2 per cent (Hampshire), −32 per cent (Isle of Wight).

A large number of panels indicated that actual expenditure had risen since 1991/92 and was set to rise again in 1993/94. The annual cost of the service is £16 million. Case complexity in Children Act 1989 proceedings, including multiple applications, increase in directions hearings and transfer of hearings to higher courts are adding to the costs and the number of hours spent on individual cases. The average case now takes 23.2 weeks to complete, as compared with the 12 week timetable aspired to before the implementation of the Children Act 1989.

Matters to be Considered by the Guardian ad Litem

Significant harm

Crucially the guardians must address themselves to the issue of whether the harm suffered, or likely to suffer, by the child is significant in the terms of the 1989 Act. 'Harm' may be taken to mean ill-treatment or impairment of health or development. Ill-treatment may include physical, sexual or emotional abuse. 'Development' may mean physical, intellectual, emotional, social or behaviourial. The significance of harm is not necessarily in direct proportion to the severity of the injuries. A parent can look the other way and a child can fall and sustain fractures and concussion. A cigarette burn, on the other hand, may appear comparatively minor, but may be the result of a premeditated holding of a burning cigarette against the child's limb for a considerable length of time. Such an action requires premeditated cruelty, and is of much more serious significance than casual negligence. Children may be outwardly well clothed and well fed, but exhibit the frozen watchfulness that speaks of years of emotional abuse. Where the question of whether harm suffered by a child is significant turns on the child's health or development, his health or development shall be compared with that which could be reasonably expected of a similar child.[1] In *Re O. (A Minor)*(Care Proceedings: Education)[2] Ewbank J suggests that guardians will ask the following questions:

- have services provided by the local authority under Part III of the Act on a voluntary/partnership basis with the family been tried? If so have they failed?
- is the degree of risk or actual abuse so serious that the child's removal from harm is necessary to protect his safety and welfare?
- are the statutory criteria for the making of a Care Order or Supervision Order likely to be satisfied by the available evidence?[3]
- if the statutory criteria are met is it better for the child that the court makes an Order rather than no Order?[4]

---

1   S.31(9) and (10).
2   [1992] 4 All E.R. 905.
3   S.31.
4   S.1(5).

The fact that the court, the local authorities and the guardians may now look to the future harm of the child, as well as harm that it is too late to prevent, is a very positive step forward. In a Court of Appeal decision, Sir Stephen Brown, the President of the Family Division, held that: 'the words 'likely to suffer' required a weaker burden of proof than the 'balance of probability' required in civil proceedings. Courts must take a realistic view about a 'real significant likelihood' of harm and not be unduly restricted by the precise wording of the statute.'[5] Post-Children Act practice has contributed significantly to working definitions of significant harm.

In the case of *Humberside County Council v. B.*[6] Booth J helpfully clarified the two steps of the process. First, the court must be satisfied that the child is suffering or is likely to suffer significant harm as a matter of factual proof; the welfare of the child is irrelevant to this issue. A finding that there is actual or likely significant harm does not of itself justify an Order. Instead, and as a function of the second stage of the process, the court must have regard to the welfare check-list set out in S.1 of the Act before making a decision of whether or not to make an Order. Finally, the court must consider whether the making of an Order will be better than making no Order at all.[7]

'Significant harm' is harm that the court should consider was either considerable or noteworthy or important and as 'harm which the court should take into account in considering the child's future'. The concept of 'reasonable care' refers to the care likely to be given by the person or people who may have caused the significant harm. It is not a measure to be applied when considering the merits of other carers, for example grandparents.[8] In *Re M.*[9] however, the Court of Appeal suggested that local authorities should not only rely on past significant harm, but should also be able to prove the likelihood of future harm, if the Order is not made. *Re M.* was a particulary sad and dramatic case, in which the father murdered the mother of the four-month-old baby, who was the subject of the care proceedings. By the time the case reached the High Court the child's father was in prison for murder, and the local authority withdrew its application, in favour of supporting a maternal cousin's application for a S.8 Residence Order. This was opposed by the guardian *ad litem* (and the father) on the grounds that the maternal cousin was unlikely to meet the emotional needs of a child whose mother had died in such tragic circumstances. Bracewell J took the same view, and made a Care Order. This decision was reversed by the Court of Appeal, on the grounds that the matter swung on the issue of risk of significant harm, not that of who could provide a better home for the child, the maternal cousin or unknown adoptive parents.

The judgment in *Re M.* appears somewhat at odds with the President's approach in the *Newham* case (see note 5), in which he stated that he 'did not believe that parliament intended them to be widely restrictive when evidence clearly indicated that a certain course should be taken in order to protect the child.'

---

5   *Newham London Borough Council v A.G.* [1993] 1 F.L.R. 281.
6   [1993] 1 F.L.R. 257.
7   S.1(5).
8   *Northamptonshire County Council v S.* [1992] 3 W.L.R. 1010.
9   [1994] 2 W.L.R. 200.

However, the House of Lords subsequently overturned the decision of the Court of Appeal. Lord Mackay held that the words 'is suffering' relate to the date at which the local authority initiated procedures to protect the child:

> It is true that an important change has been made in the statutory provisions in respect that it is now permissible under the second branch of S.31(2)(a) to look to the future even if no harm has already occurred in the past. This is an important difference from the previous legislation but in my opinion to read the present legislation as the Court of Appeal has done is substantially to deprive the first branch of S.31(2)(a) of effect, as in the argument before your Lordships became very apparent. It is also clear that while Parliament added the new provisions looking to the future without any necessary connection with harm already suffered, it wished to retain the first branch in respect of harm which the child is suffering.[10]

Parents and risk

In making their assessment of the child's situation and the likelihood of future harm guardians *ad litem* will be looking at:

- the risk to the child within the family of physical, sexual or emotional abuse or neglect;
- the capacity of the non-abusing partner and the wider extended family to protect the child from an alleged abuser;
- the degree of responsibility accepted by the parents and wider family for the child's current situation;
- evidence of the parents' determination, capacity and opportunity to change;
- the family's recognition of the need for help and a willingness to co-operate with professionals in receiving it;
- the degree of the parents' warmth and affection towards the child, and their ability to put the needs of the child before their own;
- the parents' capacity to stick to any agreed arrangements, for example contact arrangements;
- the parents' ability to put themselves in the child's situation and identify with the child's pain;
- the use parents have made of support services provided by the local authority under Part III of the 1989 Act;
- evidence of parents working in partnership with the local authority, and honouring agreements and contracts made with them;
- the availability of resources to provide the necessary services to children and families to provide the necessary protection, and the provision of social work services that is both appropriate and adequate;
- any evidence of previous injuries or multiple forms of abuse;
- whether the child is too weak, young or vulnerable to be in a position to protect himself and whether there is an adult or older sibling within the family who is willing or able to protect him;
- evidence of long-term serious personality problems or pathological patterns of behaviour within the family;

---

10   Lord Mackay, *Re. M (A Minor)*, House of Lords, July 21, 1994; *The Times*, July 22, 1994; *Practitioners' Guide to Child Law Newsletter*, Vol. 8, No. 3, July–August 1994, p. 26.

- parents' stated wishes do not accord with their recorded actions, i.e. they say they want the child home, but make no attempt to avail themselves of all the opportunities for contact.[11]

The question of whether or not the non-abusing adult will be able to protect the child from the abusing adult is critical. The abuser may have worked hard to present the child in the most negative terms, for example, the child is always crying, irritable, disobedient, always in the way, causing trouble between the two adults. If the non-abusing partner colludes with the alleged abuser and deludes himself, or herself, into agreeing that the child deserves the 'punishment' that is meted out, then the prospects for the child are bleak indeed. If, on the other hand, the mother loves and identifies with the child, is mature enough emotionally herself not to be dependent on the relationship with the abuser, then she may interpose herself between the abuser and the child and be able to stand her ground, thereby offering effective protection. In general terms abusing families tend to be predominantly patriarchal, whereas families who foster are predominantly matriarchal. It is important for guardians to establish where the power and control lie within a particular family constellation.

It would, however, be naive for guardians to focus on family pathology alone as an adequate explanation or predictor of abuse. They must also be fully aware of the social, political and economic environment in which abuse occurs. It is no accident that children in care are predominantly the children of the poor and the disadvantaged. An over-emphasis on 'the disease model of child abuse can, by concentrating on dangerous people, ignore dangerous conditions'.[12]

Prediction of abuse

Guardians, like child protection social workers, have to accept that there are no foolproof indicators of high-risk cases. Families in which tragedies occur may be in no way remarkably different from dozens of others in similar surroundings. A study of child abuse enquiry reports 1980 to 1989 did, however, identify a number of recurring scenes or indicators:

- *history of unstable, damaging or violent adult relationships* (see the Heidi Koseda enquiry);
- *violence outside the family* (see the Kimberley Carlisle enquiry);
- *signs in children* — particularly appropriate language development, height, weight and age appropriate growth and development (see the Beckford and Carlisle enquiries);
- *behaviour change* — clinging, rocking, sleep disturbance, thumb-sucking, unkempt appearance, bumps, scratches, pallor, poor health (see Liam Johnson, Lucy Gates and Kimberley Carlisle enquiries — Kimberley was described as withdrawn, sallow, pasty and still);
- *warnings of abuse from neighbours, friends, extended families and parents*;

11 Timms, *Manual of Practice for Guardians ad Litem and Reporting Officers* (1992).
12 Parton, *The Politics of Child Abuse* (1985).

- *statements from children* — these require time, understanding and accurate interpretation;
- *clusters of signs* — a combination of signs may be a significant indicator, for example, non-attendance at nursery, disharmony between the parents, deterioration of conditions in the home and inadequately clothed children (see the Jasmine Beckford,the Heidi Koseda and the Liam Johnson enquiries);
- *critical patterns* — these are common themes, as opposed to warning signs, for example, the passivity of the family waiting for help, the need for child protection agencies to consider (and understand) the process of their relationship with children and families, as well as the content, and finally, the long-term stress, fear and confusion carried by child protection workers, especially when they may be inexperienced or inadequately trained and supported;
- *recurrent incidents and concerns* — this will entail a careful recording and sharing of information;
- *resistance to professional intervention* — examples of non-cooperation with helping agencies (see Charlene Salt and the Liam Johnson enquiries which particularly noted the difficulty of working with families with a high level of social skills, who may be adept at dealing with social workers);
- *lying and deceitfulness* — enquiries stress the need for social workers to verify facts and guard against seeing what they want to believe;
- *failure to attend day nursery, or school* (see the Jasmine Beckford enquiry — two months before Jasmine died she was removed from the day nursery);
- *non-access* — a history of abortive or aborted visits to the home, and attempts by families to shut out the outside world (see the Kimberley Carlisle enquiry);
- *whereabouts unknown* — difficulties in determining the whereabouts of the child and parents;
- *violent behaviour* — a history of incidents of violent behaviour on the part of the parents, either towards themselves or others;
- *pressure within the family not to disclose* — the Cleveland enquiry identified the pressure put on children by perpetrators of sexual abuse, not to tell;
- *a period of silence* — this is a characteristic of the last few weeks of a child's life, during which time, for whatever reason, effective contact does not take place;
- *the deaths of children* — there is no particular pattern of the way in which deaths are reported.

The lessons learned through the retrospective judgments of the enquiries underline the minute and careful attention to detail required in the course of the guardian's investigation.[13]

---

13   *Child Abuse: A Study of [19] Enquiry Reports 1980–1989* (1991), Department of Health, HMSO, pp. 63–73. See also *Lessons of Child Abuse Enquiries from 1973–1981* (18 reports). See further Lyon and de Cruz *Child Abuse* (2nd. ed., 1993) and also Adcock, Hollows and White, *Child Protection Training Pack* (1991) and *Child Protection Update (February* 1994), published National Children's Bureau.

The nature of the emergency

Social workers have been greatly criticised for removing children precipitously, without adequate planning or consideration for the traumatic effect on both the child and its family.[14] The guardian *ad litem*, who is involved in emergency proceedings will be looking extremely closely at what happened on the day or the night of the child's removal from home. It is often possible to pinpoint the manner of the child's removal as the point at which the relationship between parents and the social services department began to deteriorate. Partnership with parents does not mean collusion with parents. It means identifying the point at which the child has suffered, or runs the risk of suffering, significant harm. If the messages to the parents have been clearly articulated, and any existing agreements clearly defined, then the family should understand, even if they do not agree with the reasons for the child's removal. It is sometimes difficult to achieve an exact and appropriate balance between the concepts of partnership and intervention and control. At what point does a child in need become a child at risk of significant harm? Parents can sometimes feel personally betrayed by social workers whom they have considered as friends and allies, also being the person who physically removes the child from the house. In all but the most dire emergencies it is essential that the removal of the child is effected in a planned and co-ordinated way which protects the child from any additional unnecessary trauma and fear, as well as avoiding undue provocation of the parents at a time when they are acutely distressed and shocked. Criticisms of the way that children were precipitately removed in Orkney, Rochdale and Cleveland in the early hours of the morning gave rise to a great deal of public and professional concern. The need for a planned removal is stressed by the guidance given in *Working Together*:

> except when a child is in acute physical danger it is essential that the timing of the removal of children from their homes should be agreed, following consultation with all appropriate professionals. They should weigh up the likely, immediate and long-term effects of removing the child against the possibility of harm if they leave the child at home and balance this with the need to secure evidence of criminal offences and, in some cases, to arrest the suspects. In many cases there will be no need to remove the child and simultaneously arrest the suspect living in the same house. In other cases however, particularly those involving several children and adults in different households, it may be important to prevent suspects from communicating with each other or destroying evidence. In those cases it may be necessary for co-ordinated police action, distressing though this may be, at a time of day when the whole family is at home. In other cases, although early morning police action might secure better forensic evidence, such action may not be crucial to the overall welfare of the children and should not therefore be part of the plan for investigation. In all cases the long term protection of, and well-being of, the child will be the over-riding concerns. The likelihood of securing the child's well-being through the courts will be an important consideration.[15]

The guidance stresses that any action should be taken in collaboration with other agencies involved, for example, the police or the National Society for the

---

14 See Inquiries into the removal of children in Cleveland and Orkney: *Report of the Inquiry into Child Abuse in Cleveland 1987* (1988) CM 412, HMSO; *Report of the Inquiry into the Removal of Children from Orkney in February 1991* (1992), HMSO.

15 *Working Together: A Guide to Arrangements for Inter-Agency Co-operation for the Protection of Children from Abuse* (1991) HMSO, para. 3.8.

Prevention of Cruelty to Children (NSPCC). Because the functions of each agency are different in the investigation of an allegation of child abuse, it is essential that methods of joint working are established, agreed and promulgated in the local area child protection committee procedural handbook. This should cover consultation, how enquiries will be pursued and the arrangements for obtaining court orders and removing the child if necessary.[16] The prime social work duty is to protect the child from harm, not to provide evidence for criminal proceedings for which the burden of proof is different, and for which responsibility lies directly with the police. In criminal proceedings it must be proved beyond reasonable doubt that the alleged offence took place. In care proceedings the court must be satisfied that, on the balance of probability, the child requires protection. This is a weaker burden of proof than beyond reasonable doubt, therefore, although there may be a finding of not guilty in the criminal court, the civil court may still find the threshold criteria for care proceedings met. This is often a source of confusion to alleged abusers who, having been found 'not guilty' on the criminal charges, expect to have their child returned home.

Once the child has been removed, parents commonly suffer a shock and distress akin to that following a death in the family. The psychological processes are the same: shock, denial, anger and mourning. The anger, which is part of the process of loss, is often directed at the agents of the removal—the social workers, who may from that point be denied entrance to or be reluctant to enter the home. It is at this point that all hope of working in partnership with parents may be lost, as the social worker retreats into the protective cover of the case conference, leaving parents alienated on the outside. Social work attention now focuses on the child, who becomes the primary client, to the exclusion of the parents.

Summary of the role of the guardian in challenges to the making of Emergency Protection Orders

These are proceedings which are heard at short notice 72 hours after the Order has been made. The guardian will have a very limited time in which to:

- examine the circumstances which lead to the Order being made;
- form an opinion about whether the emergency is continuing, i.e. would the court consider that there is 'reasonable cause to believe the child concerned is likely to suffer significant harm if the order is not extended'?[17]
- provide information to the court on the position of the child and the child's wishes and feelings;
- be in a position to ask questions of local authority witnesses. If, exceptionally, no solicitor has been appointed, the guardian should be in a position to ask questions directly of local authority witnesses;
- check that the possibility of reducing the risk by removing the person believed to pose that risk to the child has been considered;

16   *Ibid.*, para. 3.7.
17   S.45(5).

- provide the court with an assessment of the extended family's capacity to protect the child if the Order is discharged and the situation at home is still in doubt;
- provide a clear recommendation to the court, bearing in mind that the first priority is the safety of the child;
- advise the court about the child's contacts. These are not the arrangements that must stand for all time, but are those which will best meet the needs of the child at a time of extreme insecurity, confusion and distress. The guardian should also pay particular attention to maintaining contact with siblings and grandparents;
- advise the court as to whether there is a need for any directions or assessment.

The impact of local authority policy and planning on the welfare of the child

One major disadvantage which local authorities have *in loco parentis* is the fragmented nature of their care in relation to particular children. The *Manual of Practice Guidance for Guardians ad Litem and Reporting Officers* stresses the fact that a major part of a guardian *ad litem*'s role in relation to the local authority is to provide for the court a critical appraisal and examination of the local authority's policy, practice and planning concerning the particular child or children.[18] In particular the guardian *ad litem* should:

- ascertain the stated policy procedures and practice of the local authority; then
- examine how those policies, procedures and practices are working out in reality and in planning for the future of this particular child. Particular attention should be paid to the existence of any blanket policies which may be skewing the planning in relation to an individual child. The guidance on family placements enlarges on this point:

> all factors relevant to the welfare of the individual child must be taken into account in assessing the child's needs and making decisions about the child's welfare. None of the separate factors involved should be abstracted and converted into a general pre-condition which over-rides the others or causes any of them to be less than fully considered. The only general policy that is acceptable in making decisions about placing children is that all relevant factors should be considered. Different factors will obviously vary in importance in relation to different children or in relation to the same child at different times. It will be right, in those circumstances, to weigh different factors differently but it is not right to define any factor as of such general significance or primacy that it over-rides or qualifies the duty to consider together all factors varying on the welfare of the child as an individual.[19]

The first duty of local authorities is to seek to maintain children in their family home.[20] In this context guardians will be aware that the provision of services to children and families comes before consideration of care

18   Timms, (1992), p. 83.
19   Children Act 1989 Guidance and Regulations Vol. 3, para. 2.22.
20   Children Act 1989, Sched. 2.

proceedings or emergency proceedings. The fact that many local authorities have written their own 'children in need' documents, according to the resources available rather than the needs identified, does not alter the statutory responsibility of local authorities to provide the full range of services required by legislation. In this context guardians *ad litem* will be looking at the creative opportunities (often unexplored) offered by S.27 which provide for the possibility of social services seeking help from other local authority departments, for example housing, health and social security. It is however encouraging to see that some members of the judiciary are pushing the boundaries. One judge required a local housing manager to attend court during care proceedings to explain why the mother in the case had not been adequately housed.

Partnership with parents: care plans and written agreements

Central to the guardian's appraisal will be an examination of the local authority plan for the child. Local authorities have a statutory duty to draw up a plan in writing to a child whom they are proposing to look after or accommodate, in consultation with the child, his parents and other important individuals and agencies in the child's life.[21] Planning for the child should begin prior to the placement. After placement the plan should be scrutinised and adjusted (if necessary) at the first review four weeks after the date the child was first looked after and at subsequent reviews.[22]

In some cases, such as an emergency or immediate placement, it may not be possible to draw up a long term plan prior to placement. However a provisional outline plan should always exist. The firm plan should then be drawn up as soon as possible after the child has been looked after or accommodated. Once a plan has been drawn up it should be notified to the child and his parents. Persons who have been consulted, and other relevant individuals, should be notified on a 'need to know' basis (this would presumably include the guardian *ad litem*). This notification should normally take place prior to placement. Where this is not possible, notification should be given as soon as possible after placement. Any amendments made to the plan at the first or subsequent reviews should be recorded in writing and notified to those consulted, or involved in the reviews, as required by the review regulations.[23]

Where a child is looked after subject to a Court Order, the local authority should still seek to work in partnership, and reach agreements with the parents wherever possible. The arrangements made must be recorded in writing and a copy given to the parents.[24]

Regulation 5(3) requires the responsible authority to produce a written copy of the agreement which incorporates the detail of the plan and the

---

21   Arrangements for the Placement of Children (General) Regulations 1991 (S.I. 1991 No. 890) reg. 3.
22   Children Act 1989 Guidance and Regulations Vol. 3, para. 2.17.
23   *Ibid.*, para. 2.18.
24   *Ibid.*, para. 2.19.

arrangements made. There is no requirement for the agreement to be signed, but in cases where the parent, though consenting to the plan, does not wish to sign the agreement, the responsible authority will wish to sign the document to indicate their commitment to the plan for the child. A copy of the agreement should be sent to the person with whom it is made. The child should also receive a copy in a form appropriate to his understanding. The older child of 16 or over should be encouraged to sign the agreement when he has referred himself to the local authority.[25]

The key part of the guardian's responsibility therefore is to check the terms and conditions, and indeed the existence of a care plan. The critical appraisal of the care plan will be an essential element in assisting the guardian's deliberations about whether it will be better to make an Order than to make no Order at all.[26] Guardians will wish to ascertain the minimum level of intervention needed to safeguard the welfare of the child, and also the benefits or positive advantages involved in making the Order.

Although some local authorities were already making contracts with parents before the implementation of the 1989 Act, post-Children Act practice has involved much work on the construction of written agreements in child protection.

In relation to written agreements two key areas of concern arise:

Written agreements should be a blueprint for working in partnership, not a document for coercion Furthermore they are the products of bureaucratic rather than judicial decision making, in that it is possible for local authorities to impose more stringent requirements on parents through written agreements than those which would be required by the court. Guardians will want to look at the spirit as well as the content of the partnership agreements. To this end the Family Rights Group have listed 10 conditions which should be met in writing agreements:

- the motivation of the social worker/agency must be pro-client;
- agreements should be negotiated, not imposed;
- all participants can take advice inside or outside the agreement meetings;
- the family's view must be genuinely respected;
- the local authority tasks must be clearly defined;
- the agreement will be both followed and reviewed;
- the agency is willing to reconsider whether the terms and the implementation of the agreement were fair;
- the final document is agreed by all;
- it is written in clear and unambiguous language; and
- the contents can be appealed against.

In general these are helpful conditions although the guardian *ad litem* may wish to impose a caveat on the first condition that the motivation of the social worker or agency must be pro-client. Clearly parents' rights have to be balanced against those of their children. It is a matter of professional judgment

---

25 Arrangements for Placement of Children (General) Regulations, reg. 5(3).
26 S.1(5).

as to the precise point at which the interests of parents and child diverge and partnership must give way to protection.

Care plans may be too generalised and unspecific There is a regrettable tendency for local authority social workers to take refuge in carrying out a full orange book assessment as a primary plan for the child.[27] The orange guide attempts to set out a clear practice framework for assessment. The purpose of undertaking such an assessment is for the social worker, in consultation with management and with professionals in other agencies, to understand the child's and family's situation well enough to enable longer term plans designed to protect the child and help the family to be soundly based. This is a perfectly reasonable aim. Unfortunately monitoring and evaluation are sometimes given a higher profile than the accurate interpretation of the material collected, or the formulation of positive proposals for change. Monitoring the situation is not an end in itself, but the means to ends which must be clearly identified in the care plan at the outset. In the last three years Family Group Conferences, based on the New Zealand model, have been increasingly used by agencies seeking to achieve real partnership with families when meeting children's needs.[28]

Summary of the elements of critical appraisal

The guardian will wish to:

● *Examine the local authority file* in order to:
   ● establish an accurate and chronological view of the events;
   ● check for factual inaccuracies and confusion of act and opinion. In particular check that hearsay evidence has not acquired the status of truth through frequent repetition;
   ● examine how the process of decision making has evolved; and
   ● check the appropriateness of the local authority plan in the context of evidence.
● *Advise the court as to whether the Order sought by the local authority is appropriate* and suggest alternatives where necessary, bearing in mind that if guardians do suggest an alternative, such as a S.8 Order, local authorities cannot be compelled to provide the resources to make the Order work or be forced to work in certain directions.
● *Check whether parents/carers and children have attended reviews and case conferences.* Local authorities should involve the child and his parents in review meetings where they consider it appropriate.[29]
● *Check whether the responsible authority has made arrangements for the child to be examined by a registered medical practitioner,* and

---

27 See *Protecting Children: A Guide for Social Workers Undertaking a Comprehensive Assessment* (1988) HMSO ('The Orange Book').
28 Constructing written agreements see also Aldgate (ed), *Using Written Agreements with Children and Families,* (1989), Family Rights Group; Dale, Davies, Morrison and Waters, *Dangerous Families* (1986); Family Rights Group written agreement forms for work with children and families (1990); and Thoburn, Lewis and Shemmings, *Family Involvement in Child Protection* (1991) Conference Discussion Paper 1, University of East Anglia Social Work Development Unit.
29 Review of Children's Cases Regulations 1991 (S.I. 1991 No.895) reg. 7(2).

obtained a written assessment on the state of health of the child and his need for health care to be made.[30] This should happen:

- at least once in every period of six months before the child's second birthday; and
- at least once in every period of 12 months after the child's second birthday unless the child is of sufficient understanding and he refuses to submit to the examination. Reviews are also held under the provisions of the 1981 Education Act for children with special needs.[31]

- *Scrutinise the local authority's efforts* to maintain the child in his family home, working partnership with parents and facilitate reasonable contact between parent and child;
- *Scrutinise and comment on local authority's evidence and applications* at an early stage in the proceedings.

Critical appraisal is an aspect of their role which must be handled sensitively by panel members, however it is essential for two main reasons — firstly because the child may have become 'lost' in a bureaucratic morass in which many people know about one aspect of his health and development, but nobody is fully informed about the whole child. The child may have become compartmentalised into oblivion. Furthermore collective responsibility for a child is part of a tenuous chain of accountability, which is hard to identify at any particular point. Indeed it is very difficult to ascertain precisely who in a local authority is responsible for a particular child at a particular time as collective responsibility peters out at the elected member's level. Secondly guardians' critical appraisals play a positive role in improving policies and practices in relation to children generally by acting as an early warning system of where the bureaucratic care of children is falling down. This is an aspect emphasised by the *Manual of Practice Guidance for Guardians ad Litem and Reporting Officers*:

> guardians are often loath to criticise colleagues in social services departments who may be extremely hard pressed and demoralised. Accepting and colluding with things that are wrong within the system is however not a constructive way of helping to improve matters for either children or social workers. Guardians' reports will now be subjected to much more effective systems of central collation and monitoring which will include the production of an annual panel report. They therefore provide a bird's eye view of local authorities' practices and policies and will be a valuable source of statistical evidence about how the 1989 Act is being implemented and what improvements may be required. In this way guardians will inform as well as critically appraise practice ...[32]

Positive handling of a sensitive role and an avoidance of gratuitous criticism can ensure that local authorities seek the critical appraisal of guardians both as a safeguard for the child, and as a positive aid to the development of practice. Equally guardians must be even-handed in their treatment of both parents and

---

30 *Ibid.*, reg. 6.
31 See also Regulation 7 and Schedule 2 of the Arrangements for Placements of Children (General) Regulations 1991 and Schedule 3 of the Review of Children's Cases Regulations 1991.
32 Timms, *op. cit.*, p.88.

local authorities in order to achieve the appropriate balance of family and state autonomy required by the 1989 Act. They are in a position of considerable power and should take care to be sensitive to the pressures and limitations of local authority practice without being diverted from their key role in appraising the local authority *in loco parentis*.

The wishes and feelings of the child

The guardian *ad litem* is the child's representative and central to that task is the representation of the child's wishes and feelings to the court. The welfare checklist places a high priority on the ascertainable wishes and feelings of the child concerned (considered in the light of his age and understanding).[33] The guardian *ad litem* is expected to advise the Justices' Clerk or the court on the wishes of the child in respect of any matter relevant to the proceedings, including that child's attendance in court,[34] and to advise the court about the ability of the child to make an informed decision regarding the child's consent to medical or other examination.[35]

However, where the court determines any question with respect to the upbringing of a child the child's welfare shall be the court's paramount consideration and it is under a duty to safeguard the interests of the child in the manner prescribed by the court rules.[36] In the event of the child's stated wishes being in conflict with the guardian's judgment about what is necessary for the child's welfare then the guardian will continue to represent a view about the child's interests while the child's solicitor will ensure that the court is fully informed about the child's wishes in the matter, hopefully without detracting from the power of his advocacy by making it clear in his submissions that he does not agree.

However, in any event, even in a divergent situation the guardian has a responsibility to endeavour to incorporate the child's stated wishes and feelings as one very important component in the decision making process. This is not to say that the child's stated wishes should override all the other considerations in the determination of welfare, but that the child's wishes and feelings should have been fully taken into account in arriving at the final recommendation. This means that the guardian's written report should contain a separate and clear statement of the child's ascertainable wishes and feelings, uncluttered by the guardian's or any other person's assessment of those wishes and feelings,

---

33 S.1(3)(a).
34 Family Proceedings Courts (Children Act 1989) Rules 1991, r. 11(4). See *Re G (A Minor) (Care Order) The Times*, November 19, 1992. A thirteen year old girl had been present throughout the proceedings in court, and the guardian had felt that this was in her best interests. Waite J, however, warned that the presence of children should not be encouraged to develop into 'settled practice' and that guardians should be prepared to give the court their reasons for thinking it was advisable. This case seems to illustrate the difficulty some members of the judiciary have in acknowledging children's rights as well as protecting their welfare.
35 *Ibid.*, r. 11(4)(a). See also *Re R (Medical Treatment)* [1991] 4 All E.R. 177; *Re W* [1992] NLJ 1124; *South Glamorgan and W and B* [1993] 1 F.L.R. 574.
36 S.41(2)(b).

which should come in a separate part of the report. This statement should stand alone so it may be clearly identified to the court, and taken into consideration when a decision is reached. To this end it is desirable that panel members are people who have experience and expertise in communicating with children and appreciate that communicating with children is not an end in itself, but the means to an end—the appropriate incorporation of the child's wishes into the decision making. It is important that guardians employ techniques for communicating with children which are appropriate to both the age and ability of the child concerned. This presupposes that they will have some knowledge and expertise in identifying general development factors, for example age, developmental maturity and the understanding of short and long-term memory and the consequences of one action as opposed to another. It will be important to assess other relevant factors, such as the child's own ability to communicate, and external factors which may have a bearing on the child's wishes and feelings, for example pressures from any of the other parties and an awareness of the circumstances surrounding, and choices available in the case. Guardians should be clear that they are involved in a task-centred, time-limited involvement with the child, with a specific purpose in view— ascertaining that child's wishes and feelings about the proceedings in which they are involved, and being sure that the child is aware of the options available, and has the necessary information on which to make a decision, according to their competence, age and understanding. The objective is to obtain a clear view of the child's wishes and feelings, not to delve deep into the child's psyche to elicit material which may be very interesting but is of no direct relevance to the questions at issue. The merits of plain speech should not be despised. One can sympathise with one 10-year-old who asked 'why does my guardian keep asking me to draw pictures when I can speak?'

Listening to what children have to say is not the same as agreeing with children about what they need. The right of the child to have their wishes and feelings taken into consideration should not be seen as placing a limitation on the court to give paramount consideration to the best interests of that particular child; rather the participation of the child in the decision making, through the identification of the child's wishes and feelings, should facilitate and inform the making of an appropriate decisions in each case. A key concern for the guardian is the process of enabling the child to express his wishes and feelings without burdening them with the responsibility for the final outcome. The key to successful participation is trust and confidence between the guardian and the child.

Practical approaches to involving children in decision making

- Explore and reinforce the child's sense of identity at each stage in the discussion.
- Be aware of, and be sensitive to, the child's existing emotional attachments, even if these are to 'unworthy objects'.
- Be particularly sensitive to preserving positive links with the wider extended family and, in particular, grandparents and siblings.

- Help the child to incorporate as many positive aspects of his past life in future planning as possible, while seeking to offset the effects of the negative.
- In order to participate effectively in decision making, children need accurate and truthful information. Information empowers children to make meaningful choices and sometimes adults and professional have difficulty in allowing the child the right to information.
- Ensure that the child knows what options are available, realistic and desirable.
- Try to determine whose timetable is driving the decision making. Is it the courts', the social workers', the foster carers', the parents', or the child's? Try to allow matters to progress at the child's pace, giving time to challenge decisions if necessary.
- Consult the child at each stage of decision making.
- Keep the child's choices as open and flexible as possible, for as long as possible.
- Be aware of the impact of the child's past experience of separation, loss, guilt and rejection on the ability of the particular child to make free decisions. Children are very sensitive to their parents' pain, and will go to considerable lengths to spare them additional distress, even if that means additional stress for the child. Who will be upset or hurt by the child's decision? Is the child making a reactive or proactive choice?
- Bear in mind that the ability of individual children to make decisions will depend on their stage of conceptual, intellectual and emotional development and the circumstances in which they are asked to make choices.
- Make a clear plan of work with the child and stick to it. Be reliable and, above all, honest about what is possible and what is not.

A discussion paper produced by the National Council of Voluntary Child Care Organisations lays out four preconditions which are necessary before children are able to effectively participate in decision making:

- information about services, and access to personal records, so that views are informed;
- support and advocacy so that views are effectively communicated;
- the choice to be present when decisions are made, and to have views represented in some other way if they do not wish to attend decision making meetings;
- the right to challenge decisions or to make a complaint and to have someone independent involved.[37]

Some particular considerations for the guardian will be:

- *The need to fit their piece of work with the child around the requirements of a court driven timetable.* Children have their own sense of time and urgency which is unlikely to correspond with that of other parties to the proceedings. In particular, relationships cannot be hurried. If the guardian pushes the case too fast the child may not be able to keep up, or may

---

37 *Developing Children's Rights Services in Voluntary Child Care Organisations* (1993) A Discussion Paper, The National Council of Voluntary Child Care Organisations.

disassociate himself with the whole process. If the guardian does not go fast enough the court proceedings may be upon them before the piece of work with the child is finished constructively.

- *The need for planning.* Because of the constraints on time guardians should be clear about what they are hoping to achieve with the child within what time span. What questions have to be answered?
- *Contact.* Guardians will be particulary required to advise the court about contact arrangements and will therefore be required to have precise and detailed information at an early stage about the child's key relationships. Do the particular facts of the case merit a closer examination with the child of the attachment to any of the key family members? What is the child's attitude and relationship with siblings and the wider extended family— cousins, uncles and aunts, grandparents etc? Guardians should be open-minded about this. The child's key relationships may not always be on the list of those with parental responsibility. One guardian was very pleased to re-establish contact between the child and his dog.
- *Is what the child wants what the child needs?* Are these two mutually exclusive or is a balance achievable and/or desirable?
- *The guardian will be aware of the need to keep the choices for the child as open and flexible as possible for as long as possible.*
- *The guardian will want to ensure that the child knows what options are available, realistic and desirable in the present circumstance.*
- *Ascertaining what involvement the child wishes to have in the proceedings.* The guardian will want to know the child's views about attendance at court or about any proposed medical or other examinations.

In general, child care professionals have interpreted the stated wishes and feelings of children through a paternalistic umbrella of welfare. It is now being much more widely recognised that a more constructive model is one which incorporates concepts of client self-determinism within definitions of welfare. The right of the child to participate in the decision making and to be consulted is accepted as a central tenet of welfare, and in this model the child's wishes and feelings assume a central importance in an upward thrust of participation which informs and underpins interpretations of the child's best interest. Thus the wishes and feelings of the child are central, rather than peripheral, and are given appropriate weight in welfare deliberations. Moreover plans have a greatly increased chance of success when the child understands and owns them:

> sometimes the wishes and feelings of a child are so powerful that they make it impossible for the system to promote its particular view of the child's welfare. With children as with adults there is actually very little that you can do in the absence of the child's co-operation. This is not a problem with very young children, but I think it is safe to say that the older the child, the more notice has to be taken of this difficulty. It is not simply that there is a notional conflict between wishes and feelings. It is that a practicable care plan must have, at its heart, a notion of the welfare of the child that is 'doable' in the light of, among other things, the wishes of the child.[38]

---

38 Mitchell, 'Key Practice Issues' in *Practice in Progress* Northwest Report (September 1993), GAL/RO Regional Conferences IRCHIN with the Department of Health, p. 23.

Options available to the court

One major change brought about by the 1989 Act is the much increased range of options available to the court in making decisions concerning children. The court does not have to make the Order applied for—it can make any one of a whole range of Orders available under the 1989 Act, if it believes that making an alternative Order, or indeed making no Order, would be better for the child than making the Order applied for. The corollary of this is that guardians *ad litem* are much less restricted in the choices available to an individual child: instead of a S.31 Care Order applied for, for example, they may recommend a S.8 Residence Order with or without a S.8 Contact Order. This presupposes that guardians are fully conversant with the menu of Orders available and confident in using the potential they offer to mix and match Orders to meet the needs of an individual child. The 1989 Act provides scope for considerable initiative and ingenuity in this direction. The Act prohibits the court from making an Order unless it is satisfied that the Order will positively contribute to the child's welfare. Guardians will wish to bear this in mind when making their recommendations:

> There are two main aims — *the first* is to discourage unnecessary court orders being made, for example as part of a standard package of orders. If orders are restricted to those cases where they are necessary to resolve a specific problem this should reduce conflict and promote parental agreement and co-operation. *The second* aim is to ensure that the order is granted only where it will positively improve the child's welfare and not simply because the grounds for making the order are made out as, for example, in care proceedings where the court may decide that it would be better for a particular child not to be in local authority care.[39]

The assumption of reasonable contact

Starting from the point that the child comes into care the local authority has a responsibility to allow the child reasonable contact with his parents or guardian or any other person who has had care of the child and who is named in a current S.8 Residence Order or a High Court Order. If authorities wish to terminate contact between any of these people and a child they may only do so if:

● they are satisfied that it is necessary to do so in order to safeguard or promote the child's welfare; and
● the refusal is decided upon as a matter of urgency and does not last for more than seven days.

Under the provisions of the 1989 Act therefore there are two types of contact, S.34 Contact and S.8 Contact Orders. S.34 applications are specified proceedings, S.8 are not.

As regards S.34, guardians have two main areas of responsibility. Firstly to check the arrangements for reasonable contact at all stages of all applications. Contact arrangements are an ongoing part of all proceedings, and the court

---

39 Children Act 1989 Guidance and Regulations Vol. 1, paras. 1.11 and 1.12.

will want to be fully appraised of the reasonable and current arrangements which are in operation at all stages from the time the Emergency Protection Order is made, right through the interim hearings through to the final hearing. Secondly, guardians will be specifically involved in looking at local authority applications to terminate contact under S.34(6)(a) and (b).

The assumption of reasonable contact therefore permeates all public law proceedings under the 1989 Act. The re-designation of adoption as family proceedings, and the availability of S.8 Contact Orders in those proceedings have brought about a considerable shift in both practice and policy in relation to contact issues. Until 1980 it was possible for local authorities to terminate contact through a purely internal bureaucratic procedure. The access legislation in 1980, coupled with the publication of the Code of Practice on Access, brought local authority practices in relation to contact under judicial scrutiny. With the implementation of the Children Act 1989, the all pervasive assumption of reasonable contact puts the court in an even stronger position in relation to scrutinising local authority policies and practices in this area. In many ways it is the aspect of pro-Children Act practice which has required the most adjustment and reorientation from local authorities. Local authority social workers were rather taken aback by the contact provisions. One of the questions most commonly heard at pre-Children Act 1989 training sessions was, 'Yes, but how do we terminate contact?' In some cases the assumption of reasonable contact is seen as a barrier to achieving permanence for the child. This in turn may be based on a dual misunderstanding of the purposes of contact as well as the precise meaning of permanence which, in its true sense, encompasses both the permanent return of the child to the birth family as well as the permanent placement with substitute carers. It is unfortunately the case that contact is sometimes seen as a barrier to permanence, rather than an essential part of achieving it. The assumption of reasonable contact has important knock on effects and implications for the recruitment and training of prospective foster parents, of whom much is required in terms of facilitating and enabling contact. Clearly it is better for a mother and baby who have been separated to see each other in the warm and comfortable surroundings of a foster home rather than the sterile and somewhat bleak accommodation offered by a local authority social services department office or other more neutral environments. This does however impose considerable stresses on foster families. Take the case of foster parents who take in a six-week-old baby who is the subject of an Emergency Protection Order. For such a young baby it is essential that contact is both regular, frequent and of sufficient duration to enable the mother to continue to be involved in the everyday care of the baby, thus establishing a mutual attachment. Accordingly contact is fixed six days of the week for up to four hours each day. The placement continues through a series of interim and care proceedings. Ten months later the baby is still there, and so is the mother — six days a week for a considerable part of the day in the foster mother's home. The foster mother is spending at least as much time with the baby's mother as with her own husband and family. Her own social life is also severely restricted, because of the need to be there each day to facilitate the contact. Clearly this requires considerable dedication and commitment from the foster family. Such people may be an increasingly rare commodity.

In practice local authority policies in relation to contact vary enormously, and have emerged as one of the most anxiety provoking areas of work for guardians. The main areas of difficulty identified by guardians are:

- local authorities recommend pragmatic contact arrangements which are resource, rather than child, led;
- local authorities frequently use contact as a bargaining counter, that is 'You agree to our application for a Care Order and we'll give you three days' contact instead of two';
- guardians have noted that local authorities are sometimes explicit in their details for contact arrangements when they intend to reduce it;
- the general lack of resources is seen as a barrier to contact, for example the lack of contact centres, lack of availability of staff to supervise contact and restricted mileage allowances which limits social workers' ability to promote contact;
- lack of training for social workers, foster parents and members of adoption panels;
- when contact is mentioned, usually by the guardian *ad litem* at the first hearing, local authorities are sometimes unprepared and have not formulated adequate plans for contact;
- guardians have found that there is sometimes too much contact with 'significant others' who may appear in the child's life only at court proceedings. Judgments may be made early on of a relative's importance or otherwise, and may not be considered or reconsidered appropriately as the case progresses. Clearly this is a role for the guardian *ad litem* to consider the continuing contact needs of the child;
- guardians have found that care plans do not always cover the question of contacts, particularly in cases where the local authority are applying for a Care Order with a permanent alternative placement in mind. Care plans themselves are often seen as a last resort, usually produced in time for the final hearing. However, good care plans produced at early hearings and addressing the how, why and when of contact, greatly facilitate the timetabling of cases;
- in general the purpose of contact is often not thought through in advance so there is a confusion about whose needs are being met — the child's or the parents. Guardians find that social workers sometimes do not ask for children's views on contact in advance of the initial proceedings;
- the purpose of contact is often very confused. Sometimes it may be used as a test of the parents' commitment and motivation, rather than as a means of meeting the child's needs.

In practice guardians can have a considerable impact on contact arrangements. They may:

- make suggestions aimed at focusing attention on the contact provisions and the imaginative use of resources in terms of the finances available;
- arrange directions hearings when arrangements are not kept and take a proactive role in court in raising the issues in relation to contact;

- look at alternatives to direct contact, for example, photographs, letters, use of videos and tapes where the child prefers there should be no direct contact;
- reinforce the positive aspects of contact and encourage ambivalent local authorities to review contact arrangements;
- critically appraise the purposes of contact in relation to the needs of the child;
- question the logistics of complicated contact arrangements. While quality contact can facilitate long term planning there is a concern about children attempting to live a normal existence within complex contact arrangements. The logistics of these arrangements, for example in relation to six children in four placements with contact with separated parents plus grandparents and aunts, are very confused and complex;
- guardians are in a powerful position to identify blanket policies relating to contact which may not be working in the interests of individual children. For example one local authority had issued a draft policy on contact which said that contact in long term placements would only be considered where it would be of no cost to the authority.

Guardians stand at the interface between child care philosophy, policy and practice and nowhere is this more evident than in their involvement in arrangements for reasonable contact. The clear messages are that philosophies need to be more closely related to well validated and relevant research. Policies should be flexible enough to meet the needs of individual children and practice should be child-led, not resource-limited.[40]

Reasons for contact
- contact may help a child to feel less rejected by his family;
- contact may promote the child's adaptation to and feeling of security within the placement;
- contact may promote the child's intellectual and emotional development;
- contact may enable the child to develop a stable sense of self-identity and positive role models from members of his own race, culture or religion (this will be particularly important for children who are trans-racially placed);
- contact may enable the child to develop a realistic picture of his family.

Reasons for termination or refusal of contact
- where chronic and serious harm or distress may reasonably be attributed to existing contact arrangements;
- where a child or young person persistently refuses to see his family;
- where the parent or guardian concerned wilfully or persistently seeks to undermine the long-term planning for the child.[41]

---

40 For a further discussion on this and other matters see *Practice in Progress*, four reports from the GAL/RO Regional Conferences, June to September 1993, IRCHIN with the Department of Health.
41 Mitchell, 'From Access to Contact' *Panel News* Vol. 4, No. 1, March 1991. See also 'The Children Act 1989 Contact Orders Study: A study of local authority decision making around contact applications under S.34' (1994) Department of Health and Social Services Inspectorate.

Termination of contact

Under S.34(6) the local authority may temporarily refuse reasonable contact if:

● they are satisfied that it is necessary to do so in order to safeguard or promote the child's welfare; and
● the refusal is decided upon as matter of urgency or does not last for more than seven days.

Under S.34(4), contact may be terminated by an application to the court, either by the local authority or the child. The success or failure of contact arrangements may well prove an accurate indicator of the state of the local authority's partnership with parents.

A. v. M and Walsall Metropolitan Borough Council established that local authorities should not pre-empt the final hearing by terminating contact except in exceptional circumstances.[42]

Re M (A Minor) (Contact: Conditions)[43] helpfully clarified the courts' powers in relation to contact, and what conditions it is impossible to impose. It was established that:

(a) the court does not have coercive powers over the parent with whom the child lives, for example to require the writing of progress reports;
(b) if the court has power to require a parent to read written communications from the other parent to a child, it should only so order
  (i) with the consent of that parent; and
  (ii) giving that parent a right of reasonable censorship.[44]

It is in the interests of both parents and child to have mutual contact,[45] and courts may use their powers to make a S.8 Order of their own even if the person named in the order (in this case the paternal grandmother) has not applied for contact.[46]

Re F (Minors) (Denial of Contact)[47] was a particularly interesting case which gave guidance on the weight to be given to the child's wishes regarding contact in a situation where those wishes might be in conflict with the child's welfare. The judge in *Re F* saw the two boys involved (aged 9 and 12) and on the basis of his conversation with them recognized the extra significance of the child's own views — even bearing in mind the paramountcy principle in S.1(1).

The court has the power under S.34(4) to make an interim order refusing contact, but should bear in mind the local authority's long term plan for the child in deciding whether or not to make such an order.

Section 1(5), the No Order or Positive Advantage Principle

In recommending any Order both the court and the guardian *ad litem* must consider whether or not making the Order will be better for the child than

---

42 [1993] 2 F.L.R. 244.
43 [1994] 1 F.L.R. 272.
44 *Children Act Case Notes* Part 2. Fam. Law 24 [1994] 393.
45 *Re R (A Minor) (Contact)* [1993] 2 F.L.R. 762.
46 *Re H (A Minor) (Contact)* CA, June 21, 1993.
47 [1993] 2 F.L.R. 677.

making no Order at all. In practice this has led to some confusions and misunderstandings. In the months immediately following implementation, local authorities appeared to be almost paralysed by the complexities of the new legislation, among them the confusions about the apparent injunction to make as few Orders as possible. It has been argued that the no Order principle is a misnomer and that it would be more appropriate to refer to S.1(5) as the minimum intervention principle or the principle of 'positive advantage'. Much of the misapprehension has arisen because some local authorities have apparently been under the impression that Orders will not be granted by the courts unless they can show that they have been working in partnership with the family and have exhausted all the possibilities of non-statutory intervention. In an attempt to clarify the situation the Children Act Advisory Committee issued draft guidance on the subject in the summer of 1993. It is worth looking at this in some detail as courts rely heavily on the recommendations of the guardians *ad litem* in this, as in other, matters:

> It has been reported to the committee that some local authorities may feel inhibited from applying for care orders (and some courts from granting such orders) if the possibility of working co-operatively in partnership with the family has not been exhausted. While interpretation of the Act rests with the courts the committee thought that an expression of their views, pending any judgement on these matters, might be helpful.
>
> The notion of partnership derives from the provision on parental responsibility which remains, whether or not a care order has been made. The care order adds parental responsibility to the applicant (usually the local authority) and gives the authority to kerb the parents' use of theirs under S.33(3). The issue is therefore not whether further working in partnership is possible, but whether S.1(1) is satisfied, and whether it would be better for the child for the local authority to have the parental responsibility (Ss. 31 and 33).
>
> Prima facie if 'reasonable parental care' is lacking, and the child is beyond control leading to a risk of significant harm to the child *either* someone else must be shown as being able to supply it *or* the local authority should have the task. If the latter, the authority will still need to satisfy the court that they can deliver in this particular case. The plan proposed by them is the best indication to the court of what the future of the child may be.
>
> At the time when they believe that the threshold criteria in S.31 are met, the local authority should then decide whether they do not need an order because there are other ways of making up the parental deficit, or whether to apply to the court for a care order. The court will determine the application in the light of the reality of the situation at the relevant time, not of what might have been if other steps had been taken, nor of what might be if the local authority were to try other measures. A delayed application is not likely to be in the interests of the child. If in genuine doubt whether an application should be made the authority should proceed to enable the court to reach a view under S.1(5).[48]

The Guidance stresses that partnership with parents and statutory Orders are not mutually exclusive. Clearly it is in the interests of children that local authorities work in partnership with parents on a voluntary basis for as long as possible but there are some cases in which, even when parents are fully co-operative, they are simply unable for a variety of reasons to afford the child the

---

48   'Draft Guidance from the Children Act Advisory Committee' *Seen and Heard*, the Journal of NAGALRO (National Association of Guardians ad Litem and Reporting Officers), Vol. 3, September 1993, at 17.

protection he needs. The obligation for local authorities to work in partnership does not cease once the Order is made. S.1(5) therefore does not signal the breakdown of partnership with parents, but rather provides a check and balance against which both the guardians and the court can weigh the relative advantages and disadvantages of making a particular Order. Orders should not be applied for as the direct function of the stage that local authorities have reached in their negotiations, agreements or partnership with parents. Rather it is a matter for the court to decide on the basis of the evidence before it whether the criteria are met and which Orders are appropriate. This was the view taken in *Re D. (A Minor)* (Care or Supervision Order).[49]

The Guardian *ad Litem* and the Court
Avoiding delay

Post-Children Act practice has clearly established the guardian *ad litem* as an officer of the court, as well as a representative of the child. The guardian carries onerous responsibilities, not only for making a recommendation to the court which will be in the child's best interests but also for ensuring that the court-driven machinery keeps moving. The guardian's case management role, which arises from S.41(10), is considerable given that both the court and the guardian have a responsibility to avoid delay, which may be prejudicial to the welfare of the child.[50] S.32(1) requires the court to draw up a timetable for the case and to ensure that the timetable is adhered to. The guardian is required to advise the court on the feasibility of the proposed timetable and the adequate timing of the proceedings.[51] The guardian is also required to expedite the transfer of appropriate cases, both vertically and laterally. They advise the court on the possibilities of concurrent jurisdiction for the prompt and expeditious hearing of the proceedings. Because of their recent and on going investigations guardians are in a key position to pinpoint the part of the system or the person causing the delay.

In this context it is helpful to look at Joyce Plotnikoff's work on the timetabling of case proceedings before the implementation of the Children Act 1989. In particular, Plotnikoff's research showed that timetabling should not merely focus on each individual case, but identify elements of good and bad practice which may either alleviate or exacerbate delays in the system generally.[52] There is a message here for guardians in their wider role of case management. They should be looking at the big picture and relating not only to the parties but to the judicial bureaucratic systems operating around the child. Swift and effective avenues of communication to the Family Court Business and Users Committee are vital elements in expediting proceedings.

---

49 [1993] 2 F.L.R. 423.
50 S.1(2).
51 R.11(4)(d).
52 Plotnikoff, *The Timetabling of Care Proceedings before the Implementation of the Children Act 1989: Evaluation of a Pilot Project in a Magistrates' Court* (1992), HMSO, for the Department of Health.

All of this assumes that, in their case management role, guardians will be essentially proactive and it was this aspect of the role that was considerably emphasised at a series of four regional conferences for guardians *ad litem* and reporting officers held in 1993.[53] To some extent the guardian *ad litem* is required to act as the court's watchdog in identifying problems at an early stage and initiating directions hearings to deal with them promptly. No other child care professional has such comprehensive powers, both in relation to the child and the court. The new case management role requires new skills and it also requires time for both guardians and other court users to accustom themselves to the enhanced scope of the guardian's powers and duties. Guardians may need to act promptly and innovatively in particular cases. If, for example, a Justices' Clerk to the court refuses to transfer a case it is open to the parties to apply for reconsideration to the appropriate County Court Care Centre. If guardians think that their application to have a case transferred has been inappropriately refused, they should refer the matter swiftly to the Care Centre using application form CHA58 'Application for reconsideration of refusal to transfer'. One reason for making such an application for transfer may be that the court has failed to discharge its responsibilities to set a strict timetable. Each court has a duty to fix a date for the next hearing or directions appointment at the end of each directions appointment, interim hearing or adjournment or as soon as is practicable thereafter. Parties and their representatives must be able to state their availability for future hearings. Once established the timetable cannot be changed without the leave of the court.[54] In practice there are still some magistrates and judges who attempt to leave the court without fixing a return date. Braver guardians are learning to block their path, bearing diaries and a placatory smile.

Courts anticipate an early involvement of the guardian, especially in applications to discharge Emergency Protection Orders after 72 hours and in cases where the court is being asked to consider making a Secure Accommodation Order.[55]

In order to be available to act promptly many panels established duty rotas to coincide with the implementation of the 1989 Act in October 1991. Since that time many of the duty systems have been disbanded as there were not sufficient urgent applications to justify the cost of maintaining them. Many panels have found the use of electronic pagers provides both flexibility and cost effectiveness.

The Practice In Progress conferences looked at how effective guardians had been in achieving transfer within the concurrent jurisdiction. Some interesting points were made. In most areas vertical transfer was automatic if the case looked as though it would take more than two days. However some Magistrates' Courts were holding onto cases regardless of the time involved. Lateral transfers were fewer, although one case in Macclesfield was laterally transferred to Anglesey! It was reported that one case had been transferred up, then back down because the Higher Court was unable to hear it in time and

53   *Practice in Progress*, op.cit.
54   *The Children Act Court User Guide* (September 1991), Lord Chancellor's Department and the Home Office.
55   S.25.

further delay was judged to be prejudicial. The whole issue of guardians' time management was complex when trying to timetable cases with courts who were sometimes booking more than one final hearing to the same judge on the same day.

Guardians felt it was questionable whether or not they had sufficient knowledge to make an early decision about transfer unless the situation was clear cut. Usually extensive early enquiries had to be made in a very short time and guardians were concerned that sometimes the decision they might make at that stage would not necessarily be as sound as they would like. Early transfers were usually by agreement, as the criteria were apparent. Late transfers were occurring because of disagreement between parties or additional applications arising during the course of the original proceedings. Guardians felt that it was a judicial responsibility to decide on case priority, therefore it was the guardian's task to apply pressure to urge the judiciary to list urgent cases.[56]

Summary of matters on which guardians might be called upon to advise the court

- *Setting a reasonable timetable* within which the case can be heard, taking into account the time within which appropriate assessments, if necessary, can be made and reports prepared.
- *Identification of parties* — identification of persons whom it would be appropriate for the court to join as parties.
- *Identification of things that are not being done*, for example, timetables not being adhered to, orders not being complied with or reports not being prepared, submitted or circulated in adequate time.
- *Alerting the court promptly to any new information* that may become available in the course of the case.
- *Expediting the transfer of cases should this be necessary.*
- *Exploring the full range of options* available to the court in relation to the best interests of a particular child.
- *Assessing advantages of making a particular Order*, rather than any other Order, over making no Order at all.[57]
- *Attendance of the child at court.*
- *Avoiding delay*, which might be harmful to the child.
- *The competence of the child to exercise his/her right to refuse medical, or other, examination.*

In terms of longer term strategies for avoiding delay in the system, it would be ironic if a shortage of suitable, trained and experienced guardians was allowed to become a significant factor in delaying proceedings. An enormous burden of work is being carried by a comparatively small workforce, and now is the time for constructive thought to be given to the future recruitment, training and employment of panel members.

---

56   Mitchell, 'Practice Issues' in *Practice in Progress*.
57   S.1(5).

The guardian ad litem and the solicitor

An essential and central feature of the representation of children in public law proceedings is the representational partnership between the guardian *ad litem* and the child's solicitor. If that partnership is working well a constructive balance of rights and welfare is achieved which will ensure that the child is protected while being enabled to participate in decisions being made about his life within an environmental framework which offers him the opportunity to achieve his maximum potential, educationally, emotionally and physically. Early fears that solicitors would treat guardians *ad litem* like glorified articled clerks working as assistants, not equal partners in the relationship were, in the event, unjustified. From the start both members of the partnership have worked together constructively and indirectly the very strong relationships that guardians have established with members of the children's panels have strengthened their position in relation to the courts, by giving them access to first hand legal knowledge and advice, a situation many local authority social workers would envy.

The guardian's first task on appointment is to appoint a solicitor for the child. The choice of solicitor will depend on the guardian's initial assessment of the demands of this particular case. Does the case demand particularly strong advocacy skills, for example, or is it a case which requires a particularly sensitive handling of the solicitor/child relationship? Many guardians have built up extremely effective working relationships with a small group of solicitors. It is, however, advisable for guardians to spread their net reasonably widely so as to bring in as wide a range of experience and expertise as possible for the children that they represent; and this is a practice encouraged by the Family Law Committee, which has expressed concern that the formation of 'collusive relationships' could be detrimental to the interests of the system in general and of children in particular. One of the key determinants in appointing a solicitor is ascertaining that they have sufficient time available to give to the case. Guardians must attend each directions hearing, and it is essential that they have the benefit of the child's solicitor to advise them at those hearings. Guardians should be satisfied that the solicitors they appoint are willing and able to make a commitment to see the case through. The more experienced and successful the solicitor is in his practice the less time he is likely to have available. More inexperienced solicitors may be able to make up for their lack of experience with increased time and undivided attention that they are able to spend on the case. This is the equation which the guardians must balance in relation to the representational needs of each child. Guardians must also be satisfied that the solicitor they choose will be robust in their representation of the child's wishes and feelings. The judge in *Re H.*[58] found that the solicitor was in error in failing to take exclusive instructions from that child; and the guardian *ad litem* was in error in failing to make this clear.

Once appointed, the guardian will arrange a meeting with the solicitor as soon as possible. The work with the solicitor will fall into three main areas:

---

58   [1993] 1 F.L.R. 440.

Apportioning the work and discussing the case management aspects of the case
This will include:

- checking the papers received from the court to ensure that the guardian and the solicitor are in possession of all relevant information;
- checking that the legal aid for the child has been applied for;
- checking the date for the court hearing, including the amount of time that will need to be put aside for the hearing;
- discussing whether or not the case satisfies the transfer criteria to another court or whether the court in which the case is listed is the appropriate one;
- checking the timetable for the case, keeping a sharp eye on the need to avoid delay and expedite proceedings;
- receiving and acting on relevant documents received on behalf of the child;
- making a plan for the work with the child concerned, deciding when and where the solicitor will meet the child and whether or not the guardian *ad litem* should be present. Part of the work with the child will involve ensuring that the child, if of a sufficient age and understanding (and this is particularly relevant to S.25 secure accommodation applications), is fully aware of the timetable for the case, the likely conduct of the case, the scope of the investigation and the evidence that is likely to be adduced at the hearing. Involving the child in the process as far as is appropriate can help to reduce the anxiety and enhance the child's sense of security and confidence in the power of the solicitor and the guardian *ad litem* to represent his case effectively before the court;
- listing possible witnesses or expert witnesses;
- obtaining any additional relevant documentation, for example details of criminal records or transcripts of previous hearings if they are available.

Analysing the available information and planning the presentation of the case in court
Once the major part of the investigation is complete the guardian will want to review the case with the solicitor. At this stage they will be able to draw up a complete list of outstanding issues and tasks to be completed before the presentation of the case. These will include:

- discussing the guardian's recommendation on the basis of the available information, including any expert witness evidence;
- discussing the available Orders and options and arrangements for contact;
- chasing up any expert witness evidence which is still not available;
- deciding which witnesses are to be called and reviewing the evidence they will give, including the presentation of any affidavits necessary;
- comparing the local authority's care plan, if appropriate, with the needs of the child;
- identifying evidence that is agreed and evidence that is in dispute and reviewing the guardian's evidence in light of any discrepancies;
- scrutinising the local authority case and the Order applied for, deciding whether or not the criteria for the making of the particular order being applied for are met;
- if it is intended that documents from the local authority file should be adduced in evidence, the child's solicitor should notify the local authority's legal department of the part of the file to be produced;

- by this time it should be clear whether or not the child wishes to give separate instructions and if a divergent situation does occur then the child's solicitor and the guardian should formalise the arrangements for separate representation—the solicitor for example will need to decide whether or not the child is competent to give instructions. The guardian may need to obtain separate legal representation. This will almost certainly involve giving notice to the panel manager of the need for the guardian to have separately funded legal representation as this is not covered by the legal aid scheme.

Reporting and representing

The court rules require that the guardian *ad litem* shall file a written report advising on the interests of the child, not less than seven days before the date fixed for the final hearing of the proceedings unless the Justices' Clerk or the court otherwise directs.[59] At least two weeks before the hearing, therefore, the child's solicitor and guardian should be in a position to go through the guardian's report together and with the child, if appropriate. At that stage they should be in a position to review all the evidence which they are adducing on behalf of the child, including reports and statements from expert and other witnesses. If any gaps emerge it will be for the solicitor to organise witnesses, reports and statements while the guardian pursues any outstanding point arising during the course of the investigation so that both feel competent to cover any aspect of the child's case which might arise in the course of the hearing. Discussion on the presentation of the case should take place at this point and hopefully not be left until half an hour before the case is due to be heard, at which stage it is too late to avert delay or chase up witnesses.

If, during the course of the investigation, new information has emerged, the guardian *ad litem* and the child's solicitor should decide on the best way to bring that information before the court. This may entail requesting a directions hearing.

Similarly, if the guardian *ad litem* and the child's solicitor become concerned about any one aspect of the case, for example slippage in timetabling resulting in unacceptable delay, difficulties attached to the obtaining of a particular expert witness's report, or concerns about the contact arrangements for the child while the case is waiting to be heard, all of these things should be brought to the attention of the court before the final hearing.

A key feature of the present arrangements is the advance disclosure of all reports. It is particularly important that the guardian *ad litem* and the child's solicitor receive a copy of the local authority care plan before submitting the guardian's final report, as the plan proposed for the child will have a direct bearing on whether or not the guardian *ad litem* will be in a position to advise about whether or not the Order applied for is appropriate and whether making the Order will be better than making no Order at all. Guardians and children's solicitors should be forceful in insisting that they have sight of the care plan in sufficient time to study it in some detail.[60]

---

59 R.11(7).
60 S.1(5).

Once the report has been lodged with the court the guardian *ad litem* should:

- check with the court that the report has been circulated to the other parties in good time to avoid any unnecessary delay;
- prepare the final details of the child's case, making sure that witnesses have been notified about the time and place of the hearing and that they have the means and directions to get there.

On the day of the hearing the guardian should arrange to arrive with the child's solicitor at least one hour before the hearing in order to iron out any last minute hitches and confusions, and to be available to check that the witnesses have arrives. They will also want to be there in good time to see the child, if the child is attending court, and to provide support and reassurance while waiting to go into court.

After the hearing
After the case has been heard the guardian *ad litem* and the solicitor will want to ensure that the child, if present, understands exactly what has been decided and what is to happen to them next. In the event of an adjournment the guardian and the child's solicitor will want to ensure that the court does not rise before identifying a return date.[61]

After the hearing the guardian *ad litem* and the solicitor will want to:

- check that the child is aware of the outcome and the decision made;
- discuss whether or not an appeal is appropriate. Appeals should be lodged within 21 days of the hearing;[62]
- discuss whether the child is eligible to claim compensation for pain, suffering, shock arising out of acts of rape and sexual offences or other type of abuse or attack under the Criminal Injuries Compensation Scheme;
- if parental responsibility has been assumed by the local authority, ensure that the child knows of the existence and purpose of the S.26 representation and complaints procedures, the availability of independent visitors if the child has no family or friends to visit him, and that the child also understands (if of sufficient age and understanding) that he may contact a children's panel solicitor himself in order to initiate further proceedings.

Issues of Policy and Practice
Separate legal representation

The GAL/RO Service Annual Report 1992/93 and the Regional Practice In Progress Reports both illustrate some of the difficulties the guardians encounter in seeking to obtain separate legal representation.

---

61   See further Liddle, *Acting for Children, The Law Society's Handbook for Solicitors and Guardians ad Litem* (1992).
62   *C. v Solihull M.B.C.* [1993] 1 F.L.R. 290 and *S. v South Oxfordshire C.C.* [1993] 1 F.L.R. 452 are both examples of cases in which the guardian appealed on behalf of the child.

A number of reports comment directly on the difficulty that may be posed where the older child instructs the solicitor directly and the guardian is left without legal representation. On one panel the cost of separate legal representation for guardians in the year 1992/93 amounted to £16,051 for eight appointments and in another panel the projected overspend on the 1992/93 budget was almost wholly attributable to the appointment of a barrister and solicitor to represent a guardian in a very complex case. Some local authorities remain unconvinced about the need for guardians to have separate legal representation:

> local authority representatives are less convinced of the necessity of legal representation for guardians, arguing that guardians have a unique authority as officers of the court. They also have to take into account their overall responsibility to make the best use possible of the fund available to them to promote the interests of all children in need in their respective area.[63]

Divergence often occurs in S.25 Secure Accommodation Orders and Care Orders which are contested by teenagers. Clearly the 1989 Act and the Court Rules envisaged that guardians could be represented in divergent situations; however it seems curiously half-hearted to provide such a contingency in the Court Rules without also securing the funding to pay for it and it can put guardians in a difficult position in terms of attempting to negotiate with their administering authority for funds to secure separate legal representation at a time when all their energies should be devoted to an examination of the child's situation.

Independence

The Manual of Practice Guidance for Guardians ad Litem and Reporting Officers identifies four separate aspects of independence:

● independence of professional opinion;
● personal independence;
● perceived independence; and
● an administratively independent structure from which to operate.

All four aspects are necessary components of an independent service.

Independence of professional opinion This refers to the ability of the guardians to exercise their professional judgment, based on their experience and expertise in working with children and families. In carrying out their work they are not part of a line management structure and the decisions they make are autonomous rather than arrived at as part of a collective decision making process. It is essential that they be free to exercise that professional discretion untrammelled by any other consideration, save that of the welfare of the child which provides the independent voice which was so lacking in the case of Maria Colwell in 1973.

---

63 The Guardian ad Litem and Reporting Officer Service, *Annual Reports 1992–93 — An Overview*, p. 50, para. 5.20.

Personal independence   There are two aspects of this. Firstly, as the *Manual of Practice Guidance* points out, there may exceptionally be times when guardians *ad litem* feel that they cannot offer an objective view about a case because of some raw or unresolved experience in their own lives. If, for example, panel members are themselves going through a process of divorce and separation involving disputes about contact, it may be that they will feel that they cannot be entirely objective about contact issues at that time. Any factor which is likely to skew the judgment of the guardian *ad litem* should be recognised as a feature of the guardian's own professionalism, and should be stated at the outset so that the work can be undertaken by another member of the panel. The second aspect of personal independence bears on the question of personal eligibility and arises from the fact that local authorities may re-employ their own ex-employees as panel members who may carry with them considerable knowledge about particular children and their families. The Court Rules stipulate that a panel member should not have been concerned with a particular child in five years before their appointment to the panel,[64] while the Guidance in Volume 7 makes it clear that guardians should be their own watchdogs in this matter:

> Where panels have consortia or reciprocal arrangements the possibility of a GAL/RO employed by a local authority having knowledge of a particular case will be reduced but not removed. It will also be easier for alternative GAL/ROs to be found. Single authority panels will need to ensure that flexibility to provide suitable guardians is not restricted by drawing a large proportion of their membership from the category of employee of the local authority, particularly if those persons formerly were employed as social workers with a child care remit in that local authority · · ·[65]

Perceived independence   The fact that panel members may be re-employed by their own local authority clearly has a bearing on the perceived independence of panels although in practice there have been few challenges to the appointment of individual guardians on that basis. The interests of natural justice dictate that the guardian must be, and must be seen to be, independent of all other parties. That is sometimes difficult in situations where local authorities have been known to send their guardians out with identity cards stamped with the local authority logo. It is important that members of the public and all parties to the proceeding can see clearly that the guardian is operating independently. This is sometimes a difficult concept to explain to parents. The National Association of Guardians *ad Litem* and Reporting Officers devoted their annual general meeting seminar to the subject of the independence of the guardian. Speaking at that seminar, Mark Hinchliffe questioned 'How well would a guardian *ad litem* be able to demonstrate independence in the face of questioning from a parent who knew all the facts?'[66] One area in which perceived independence is most at risk is in relation to the attendance of the guardian at child protection conferences.

---

64   R.10(7).
65   Children Act 1989 Guidance and Regulations Vol. 7, para. 2.48.
66   Mark Hinchliffe, 'Is she owt to do with the Council?' Address to the National Association of Guardians *ad Litem* and Reporting Officers, March 29, 1993, also in *Seen and Heard*, Vol. 3, June 1993, p. 9.

Many guardians are now attending on a routine basis. While this may well be convenient and time-saving, there is a danger that with the best of intentions they may be drawn into the decision-making process and their credibility in the eyes of the other parties will be effectively undermined.

Administrative independence   Local authorities have the freedom to choose whatever arrangements best suit their local circumstances. This freedom however is not absolute. The service has to be provided in accordance with the panels regulations and accompanying guidance, together with the Rules of Court. The right of a child to separate and independent representation in public law proceedings is a central principle of the 1989 Act. There clearly could be potential for conflict where the authority responsible for the provision of the guardian service is a party to proceedings in which a guardian has been appointed to act for the child. This was recognised in a range of safeguards that built into the regulations, guidance and Rules of Court[67] to underpin the independence of the guardian in the exercise of his or her professional judgment. These include the appointment of a panel manager who is independent of the child care services management, establishment of a panel committee with independent representation and the setting up of a complaints procedure—again with an independent element.

Nonetheless concerns continue to be expressed about the independence of the service, despite the existence of these safeguards. Clearly if there is any suggestion that a guardian in reaching his or her professional judgment as to what is in the best interests of the child is not able, for any reason, to exercise independence then this is a matter to be brought to the attention of the court.[68]

In spite of consistent criticism, post-Children Act panels have continued to be administered and funded by local authorities. The Department of Health has made it clear that, while acknowledging the difficulties, there are no current plans to make any changes:

> Many have argued that the service, which still at times is unflatteringly described as 'that cottage industry' cannot really develop while it remains a local authority responsibility. Frankly I have to say that that is not the view of the Department—the present system is here for the foreseeable future. It is no good thinking that just round the corner is some ideal structure for the GAL/RO service which will magically cause anxieties—about accountability, professional independence and cash limits—to disappear. It is within the current legal framework that continuing improvements must take place. Developments since October 1991 clearly demonstrate that this is possible ···[69]

Meanwhile local authorities must ensure the independence of panels in accordance with the Regulations. In pursuit of this objective there is a requirement for a number of safeguards to be built into the administrative arrangements:

---

67   Rules of Court, r. 4.11 (The Family Proceedings Rules 1991 S.I. 1991 No. 1247, Part IV) and r. 11 (The Family Proceedings Courts (Children Act 1989) Rules 1991, S.I. 1991 No. 1395).
68   The *Children Act Report 1992*, HMSO, paras. 8.13 and 8.14.
69   Poyser, 'Update on National Scene' in *Practice in Progress*, p.5.

- the employment of a panel manager who is at 'arm's length' from the administering local authority and who carries no other responsibilities for that local authority's child care policies and practices;
- the setting up of a panel committee with an independent chair and membership;
- arranging, but not personally providing, 'appropriate training, consultation and support';
- the provision of a direct telephone line, separate postal address and appropriate note-paper for panels.

In spite of these strategies the present arrangements for the administration of panels do not satisfy the criteria for independence, and the proper development of the service is being hampered by the constraining hand of local authority administration which courts conflict of interests and often fails to take sufficient account of the local authority's position as a party to the proceedings.

This is a view endorsed by the National Association of Guardians *ad litem* and Reporting Officers in their introduction to a paper on the role and function of the panel manager:

- The National Association acknowledges that the present system of panel management is flawed, and that it will remain so until panels cease to be administered (and guardians cease to be paid for) by local authorities. Until this situation changes, we believe it is essential for the credibility of the service that everything is done to ensure that the independence of guardians is not diminished. We believe that there is no inherent conflict between this goal, and that of maintaining and even improving the effectiveness of the service. However, we are aware that independence will be more under threat as local authorities examine their budgets and seek savings to meet financial limits set by central government.
- The role of the panel manager is to manage the service, but not the GAL/ROs themselves who are, regardless of their employment status, independent professionals. This is a difficult role, governed by the conflicting demands of ensuring there is a high quality and efficient service, whilst not interfering with the GAL/ROs independence. It involves setting up and monitoring systems, but not directly supervising workers.
- The Association considers a possible viable future arrangement would be for panels to be administered from County Court Care Centres, with professional matters the responsibility of a separate Management Committee, made up of a wide and well informed range of people.[70]

The establishment of an independent, nationally funded and regionally administered service which included the independent representation of children in private as well as public law proceedings is the logical next step. Such a structure would satisfy criteria of both independence and accountability.

---

70   See also 'Is she owt to do with the Council?', cited in Note 66. The view taken was that the distinction drawn by the Lord Chancellor, between 'independent judgment' on the one hand and 'separate or independent organisational arrangements for the delivery of that judgment' on the other, is artificial. Hinchliffe took the view that 'soon guardians may well have to demonstrate to the court that they deserve to be regarded as independent in the same way as other experts called in civil proceedings'.

Boundaries of the role

The 1989 Act significantly extends the powers and duties of the guardian in relation to both the child and the court, by extending the scope of the proceedings in which guardians can become involved, and by giving them significant powers in relation to the court in the management of the case. A question still remains, however, about at what point the guardian's involvement ceases, and this debate is of particular relevance in relation to S.37 applications. Does the guardian *ad litem* consider the best interests of the child, focusing solely on the proceedings before the court, or is there a need to take a longer term view and consider the options, with a view to safeguarding the interests of the child until he or she reaches adulthood? Pre-Children Act Court Rules directed the guardians *ad litem* to 'regard as the first and paramount consideration the need to safeguard and promote the infant's best interests until he achieves adulthood.'[71]

In contrast, S.41(2)(b) establishes that the guardian is under a duty to safeguard the interests of the child in the manner prescribed by the rules. The words 'until he achieves adulthood' do not appear. Their omission in current legislation may relate, in part, to a debate which occurred at the time of the Cleveland Inquiry. At that time guardians had attempted to use wardship to challenge the local authority's decision making. The judicial response suggested that the role of the guardian was limited to the facts before the court at a certain time, rather than a longer term interest in the child's welfare. A guardian, who instigated judicial review on the issue of how far a local authority must consult the guardian *ad litem* before reaching decisions relating to the child's care, was suspended from her panel duties by the local authority, for exceeding her authority.[72]

Historically, therefore, courts have been protective of local authorities' decision making and have generally upheld the principles established in *A. v. Liverpool City Council*,[73] in which parents were sharply discouraged from attempting to use the inherent jurisdiction to question local authority discretion.

Paradoxically, since the implementation of the Children Act 1989, although the words 'until the child achieves adulthood' have been omitted from the statute, guardians *ad litem* are now specifically required to consider the menu of Orders available and, if appropriate, recommend options to the court, other than the Order applied for. However, the debate about the boundary of the role is still applicable in two main areas:

● *In situations where the local authority is failing to comply with its statutory duties towards the child.* Could, for example, a guardian *ad litem* initiate an action for breach of statutory duty on behalf of the children they have represented, in the same way as the Official Solicitor acted in such a capacity in the case of *X. (Minors) v. Bedfordshire County Council*?[74] The

---

71 Magistrates' Courts (Children and Young Persons) Rules 1970 as amended in Appendix 1. Guide for Guardians *ad Litem* in the Juvenile Court DHSS 1984 (S.I. 1970 No. 1792), r.6(b).
72 *R. v. North Yorkshire County Council, ex. p. M.* [1989] Q.B. 411.
73 [1982] A.C. 363.
74 [1993] *The Times*, November 24, 1993, D.C.

outcome of this case, however, was not encouraging, in that it was held that no private law action lay in the respect of breach of statutory duty. The decision in *A. v. Liverpool City Council*[75] was resuscitated by Turner J who asserted that the Children Act 1989, far from superseding the effect of the Liverpool decision, had, in fact, reinforced it and that it was contrary to the public interest to permit an action for negligence to be brought against this (or presumably any other) local authority.[76]

● *Complaints procedures under S.26 of the Children Act 1989.* If, as appears to be the case from the above, children have no recourse in private law proceedings, even with the help of a next friend, to challenge local authority decision making, then this endorses the view expressed in the Manual of Practice Guidance that guardians do have a role to play in initiating complaints procedures under S.26 of the Children Act 1989, as this appears to be the only avenue open. This again underlines the question of how effective and robust, and independent, internally administered complaints procedures can be.[77] The ultimate deterrent, as far as guardians are concerned, is the local authority's ability to refuse payment for any work panel members carry out in non-specified proceedings. No doubt the debate will continue. Surely, however, guardians acting in good faith should have regard to the long term outcomes of the decisions being taken, taking into account the adult the child will become, as well as the shorter term impact on the child today. This is a view endorsed by the National Association of Guardians ad Litem and Reporting Officers, who state in their Code of Ethics that 'although the roles are time limited and proceedings based, when considering the child's interests a long term view should be taken.'[78]

The guardian as expert witness

Independent social workers representing children before the formal establishment of panels appeared in court as expert witnesses, and after 1984 panel members were generally regarded as having expertise in general child care matters. Since implementation of the Children Act 1989, attention has been focused on the precise nature of that expertise, and there has been an increasing trend towards instructing child psychiatrists and psychologists and paediatricians. In *Re G.*, Wall J suggested helpful guidelines for the instruction of experts — including asking the guardian to advise on the choice of expert.[79]

Courts have become concerned about the plethora of sometimes conflicting expert witness evidence, and guardians have become a little less sure of their status in the eyes of the court—particularly after *B v B*,[80] in which a guardian was directed to restrict their views to matters which came within their expertise as social workers rather than volunteering views on whether sexual

---

75 [1982] A.C. 363.
76 See also *Nottinghamshire County Council v. P.* [1993] 3 All E.R. 815, C.A.
77 See further Chapter 10 below.
78 NAGALRO Code of Ethics, para 4,2.
79 *Re G.* (Children's Cases: Introduction of Experts) [1994] 2 F.C.R. 106; see also *Re C.*, *The Times*, December 7, 1994.
80 [1994] 1 F.L.R. 811.

abuse had or had not taken place.

In spite of this, presenting expert witness evidence is an imprecise science, as the Cleveland Enquiry demonstrated, and guardians should have confidence in their general child care knowledge and expertise—especially in respect of evaluating possible outcomes and options for a particular child in relation to the care system and general local authority care policy and practice.

The guardian as an agent of change

Although guardians may have a limited role in judicial challenges of local authority decision making, nevertheless they are significant agents of change in terms of the process of decision making generally. Current debates about the specific contribution of the guardian *ad litem* in public law proceedings, bearing in mind the high percentage of cases in which guardians' recommendations echo those of the local authority, fail to take into account the impact that the guardian's involvement in the case can have in acting as a catalyst for local authorities to review and rethink cases. Guardians can initiate change merely through their involvement in the proceedings. Guardians have to strike a delicate balance between observing and critically appraising the decisions being made in respect of children and, on the other hand, asking questions which may prompt a subtle change of emphasis on the part of the care authority. The advance disclosure of witness statements and the proposed care plan give ample opportunity for an exchange of views, which, in some cases, may border on negotiation. In every case, the focus of the guardian is to achieve the best possible outcome for the child. That includes all aspects of the case from the transfer of cases to the appropriate court to the hearing, to the direct challenging of the care plan for the child, if that should be necessary.

The involvement of the guardian *ad litem* in case conferences, for example, illustrates the difficulty in balancing observation without involvement. The *Manual of Practice Guidance* stresses the fact that guardians should always avoid becoming part of the collective decision making process. Attendance at case conferences offers an opportunity to be drawn in. As one guardian put it: 'guardians have significant status and any information given by them may have a greater impact than that of others (sometimes which is already observable amongst the different professions, or just individuals attending case conferences).' The guardian's very presence, therefore, may have the potential to skew the proceedings. 'Guardians have drawn attention to the inherent contradiction in trying not to be part of the decision making process while, by one's very involvement, one has influence, especially given the guardian's knowledge and expertise.'[81]

In September 1991 the Department of Health published guidance which confirmed the fact that guardians would be present at case conferences as observers, not participants, and emphasised the guardian's position as an officer of the court, not a member of the case conference. Following that, it appeared that, although guardians sometimes attended case conferences, they

---

81   Bourton, *Seen and Heard* Vol. 3, June 1993, p.35.

attended as silent observers. Accordingly, on March 29, 1993, a letter was
sent from the Department of Health to panel managers in the following terms:

> It seems that some people are now interpreting 'observer' as silent observer, i.e.
> attendance is conditional on the GAL not saying anything. The Department wishes
> to stress that if the GAL has factual information, apparently not known to the other
> agencies, which is clearly relevant to the planning for the child's welfare, they should
> speak up.[82]

This accords with the advice given in the *Manual of Practice Guidance* that the
exceptions to the rule of non-attendance at case conferences would be
specifically, firstly, a situation where the court directs that the guardian should
attend and, secondly where the guardian needs to ensure that members of the
case conference are in possession of a particular piece of information which
has a direct relevance to the welfare of the child and which the timetable
dictates should be passed on to those making decisions in relation to the child,
with the least possible delay, for example at a case conference following an
application for an Emergency Protection Order, when all the professionals
concerned are working to a very tight timetable. In such a situation the
guardian may attend the meeting to impart the relevant piece of information
and then leave, having ensured that the Minutes noted that the guardian had
attended in an observational role only, and not as part of the collective decision
making process. To do otherwise would jeopardise the independent status of
the panel member. Some panel members feel that even attending a case
conference to pass on information presents them to the conference in a
participant light, and this is a concern which has been expressed by
NAGALRO. The guiding principle must always be what is necessary or
expedient to secure the best interests of the child. Clearly the guardian cannot
comment on and appraise objectively the local authority's plan for the child if
he has been a party to the discussions which have gone on, in any forum,
whether a case conference or otherwise, about the formulation of a plan for
the child.

All of this emphasises that the power of the guardian's capacity to bring
about change is now considerable, as they have an extensive remit, under
S.41(10) and the court rules, to advise the court in virtually every aspect of the
case. In scrutinising local authority applications, guardians have the power to
recommend that proceedings be diverted away from Parts IV and V of the Act
to Part III, Support for Children and Families. In this way, guardians can have
a powerful impact on the way in which the Act is implemented.

Officer of the court or representative of the child?

Inevitably, with the addition of the substantial case management roles now
allocated to the guardian, panel members are increasingly seen as officers of
the court, in that they have the power to initiate transfer of cases, act to avoid
delay, and generally expedite proceedings. At one level, guardians are being
used to oil the wheels of the new unified jurisdiction, and courts have come to

---

82   Department of Health, letter to panel managers of March 29, 1993, quoted in *Seen and
      Heard* Vol. 3, June 1993, p.35.

rely on their advice and direction, not just in relation to the final recommendation, but in the process and conduct of the case. A decade has passed since the introduction of guardians in all care and related proceedings, and it is important at this point that guardians do not lose touch with their origins. The overwhelming case for the introduction of the guardian *ad litem* was not so that the courts had an officer on whom they could rely and depend in public law proceedings, as they do on the family welfare officers in private law proceedings. It was that there should be an independent representative of the child to instruct the solicitor on the child's behalf, and safeguard the welfare of particular children in the face of other bureaucratic, political and organisational pressures. The history of the GAL service is quite different from that of the family court welfare officer. The guardian is not merely a reporter but a representative, and this is an important distinction to maintain.

In practice, guardians have become adept at incorporating new roles and new responsibilities. In particular, they have embraced a partnership with Justices' Clerks in the same way as they successfully established strong working partnerships with solicitors. Guardians are beginning to flex the muscles of their case management role, while clinging fiercely to their role as independent expert. The roles are not mutually exclusive, but they do need vigilance, wisdom and balance to maintain. Effective case management necessarily brings guardians closer to the court, but it should not distance them from the child. Guardians involved in increasingly long and complex cases will be relieved to hear that Wall J has issued some useful guidance on the preparation of court bundles.[83] Material should be presented chronologically, properly paginated and indexed. Where video interviews of children are to be used, it should either be discussed at a directions appointment or there should be agreement about how they should be used between the solicitors. Where there is to be a challenge to the interview techniques used, transcripts should be obtained and placed in a separate bundle. If the judge is to be asked to view the videos in private, the agreement of all parties should be obtained and they should try to agree which parts should be shown.

The interface of criminal and civil proceedings

Although it is now generally accepted that civil proceedings should not await the outcome of criminal cases, delay is still being caused in some areas by the criminal proceedings taking priority. There are also problems involved in guardians gaining access to criminal evidence in order to inform their recommendations in care proceedings. Sometimes the Crown Prosecution Service allows guardians access to files but makes conditions, for example 'we will allow you to see the files but don't use any of the evidence'. It would be helpful if there was more liaison and dialogue between the child protection panel, the police and social services and the areas of co-operation should be considered at the outset of the case. Possibly the Family Court Business

---

83   *B v B* [1994] 1 F.L.R. 323. See also in relation to the timetabling of cases, Plotnikoff and Woolfson, 'Timetabling of Interim Care Orders Study' (1994), Department of Health — Social Services Inspectorate.

Committees could be instrumental in resolving some of these problems. There are areas of conflict between lawyers representing alleged abusers and social workers attempting to protect children, for example on occasions the Crown Prosecution Service have been reluctant to allow social workers to commence therapeutic work with sexually abused children in case it affected their recollection of events and distorted their subsequent evidence. Guardians have been concerned about children being prepared to give evidence in court, and have felt that they would like to have an influence on such situations, in particular that they needed access to the Crown Prosecution Service's files, plus a code of practice regarding the use of evidence. There have been occasions where guardians have been requested to give evidence in criminal proceedings, on the basis of the information they have gained in the course of investigating the civil proceedings. The confusions call for a clearer understanding of the role of the guardian on the part of all those who participate in child protection work.

The position of the child who is a witness in criminal proceedings as well as the subject of care proceedings deserves closer attention. There may be a case for the guardian's role to be extended to support child witnesses in these situations.

The criminal injuries compensation scheme

Children represented by guardians *ad litem* may qualify for compensation under the criminal injuries compensation scheme if they were victims of crimes of violence. Applications should be made to the Criminal Injuries Compensation Board within three years of the relevant incident taking place.

The child as witness

Until the implementation of the Criminal Justice Act 1991, young children were assumed to be incompetent witnesses, unless it was proved to the contrary. However, following the recommendations of the Home Office Advisory Group (the Pigot Committee), which reported in December 1989, the Home Office, in conjunction with the Department of Health, produced a *Memorandum of Good Practice on Video Recorded Interviews with Child Witnesses for Criminal Proceedings*:

> The main purpose of the Memorandum is to help those making a video recording of an interview with a child witness where it is intended that the results should be acceptable in criminal proceedings. Such a recording can spare the child from having to recount evidence to the court in person and provide a highly valuable, early record of the child's account. If handled properly, the video recorder interview will be in the interests of the child and in the interests of justice.[84]

---

84 *Memorandum of Good Practice on Video Recorded Interviews with Child Witnesses for Criminal Proceedings* (1992) Home Office with the Department of Health, HMSO, Introduction.

The Memorandum addresses the concerns which emerged as a result of the Butler Sloss report,[85] following the enquiry into abuse of children in Cleveland, by laying down guidelines for interviews with children. The Butler Sloss report expressed particular concern about the numbers of interviews (and examinations) that children were being subjected to in the course of the child abuse enquiry, not to mention subsequent criminal proceedings. The Memorandum identifies that one important reason for video recorded interviews with children is to reduce the number of times that they are called upon to repeat their accounts during the investigation of the case. The Memorandum stresses that the interviews described within it are not, and should never be, referred to as 'therapeutic interviews', nor should the term 'disclosure interview' ever be used to describe them. The Memorandum stresses that video recordings may also be admissible in civil proceedings, thus sparing the child repetitious interviews by both police and social services. Video recorded interviews with children are admitted as evidence in criminal trials under S.32(a) of the Criminal Justice Act 1988. The Criminal Justice Act 1991 goes further in protecting the child from cross-examination on their evidence in chief, provided that the recorded interview covers the matters which would otherwise be dealt with, so that the video recording takes the place of the first stage of the child's evidence. Further, the accused is barred from cross-examining the child in person, through the use of live television links, so that the child may be seen and heard in the court on television monitors, without appearing in the court room. The court may reject the video recording, or any part of it, in the interests of justice. This has important implications for the child care professionals carrying out interviews with children, as they must be fully cognisant of the rules of evidence and the law relating to interviewing children. This applies equally to the guardian *ad litem*, who should have access to any video recorded material, rather than themselves indulging in repetitious interviews. The Memorandum makes the point that all practitioners (both legal and social work) will need to prepare carefully in order to make the best of the reforms, both in the interests of the child and of justice.

S.96 of the Children Act 1989 brings civil proceedings in line with criminal proceedings in allowing the unsworn evidence of children to be heard, provided that they understand that it is their duty to speak the truth and they have sufficient understanding to justify their evidence being heard.[86] In addition, this section relaxes the hearsay evidence rules in connection with the upbringing, maintenance or welfare of a child.[87] This would allow a guardian, for example, to relay to the court the information given to them by the child. It also means that children themselves can give unsworn evidence and this provision is covered by the Children (Admissibility of Hearsay Evidence) Order 1991.[88] The hearsay rule is not only relaxed in favour of the child, it is relaxed in favour of the guardian *ad litem*. S.41(11) of the Children Act 1989 provides that:

---

85   Report of the Inquiry into Child Abuse in Cleveland 1987, CM. 412 (1988).
86   S.96(2).
87   S.96(4)(b).
88   S.I. 1991 No. 1115.

regardless of any enactment or rule of law which would otherwise prevent it from doing so, the court may take account of:

(a) any statement contained in a report by a guardian ad litem who is appointed under this section for the purposes of the proceedings in question; and

(b) any evidence given in respect of the matters referred to in the report, in so far as the statement of evidence is, in the opinion of the court, relevant to the question which the court is considering.

The present situation, in relation to child witnesses, represents a considerable advance on the historic position in which children have to prove their competence to give evidence, based on an evaluation of their ability to differentiate between the truth and lies or make-believe. Spencer and Flin reveal that 'there is actually very little systematic research into the frequency with which children or adult witnesses tell lies.' The Pigot Committee (1989), discussing this issue concluded: 'we understand, however, that, contrary to the traditional view, recent research shows that untruthful child witnesses are comparatively uncommon and that, like their adult counterparts, they act out of identifiable motives.'[89]

The assumption of incompetence appeared to be based on five main assumptions:

- children's memories are unreliable;
- children are egocentric;
- children are highly suggestible;
- children have difficulty distinguishing fact from fantasy;
- children make false allegations, particularly of sexual abuse.

However, in a comprehensive review of the evidence, Spencer and Flin concluded that:

> Today the reasoning behind the restriction placed on children's evidence is out of line with modern scientific knowledge of children's intellectual capabilities and the typical behaviour patterns of child victims ··· This traditional assumption of childhood incompetence may have stemmed from a historical pre-disposition to regard infancy and childhood as a general period of weakness and incapacity and to treat children almost as if they were a different species.[90]

Children as young as three may be competent witnesses.[91] The evidence is very helpfully reviewed in a section on the child as witness in a Child Witness Pack produced by the NSPCC and ChildLine, in conjunction with a number of other children's charities in consultation with The Home Office, The Lord Chancellor's Department, The Department of Health and the Crown Prosecution Service. The pack contains a booklet of information and advice for parents of children who are to be witnesses and a book for young witnesses, 'Tell me More About Court', as well as an activity book, 'Lets get ready for Court'. This will be useful for children who are attending court. The pack is an important source of information and advice for solicitors and

---

89   Spencer and Flin *The Evidence of Children, the Law and the Psychology* (1990), p. 271.
90   *Ibid*. See Ch. 4 'The Competency Requirement', p.44, for a full examination of children's competence as witnesses.
91   See 'The Evidence of a Three Year Old Child' [1987] *Criminal Law Review* 677.

guardians working with children, as well as for children and their families.[92]
The pack incorporates the changes produced by the Criminal Justice Act 1991
and advises children on 'going live' via the video links.

Although the principles and progress of the law relating to the evidence of
children is now much improved and clarified, the precise charting of the
territory which lies somewhere between the criminal[93] and civil proceedings
is less clear and is an area in which guardians continue to experience some
difficulty.

Shortage of guardians from black and ethnic minorities

In general, the composition of GAL/RO panels should reflect the communities
that they serve and in this context there is still a considerable way to go in
recruiting guardians *ad litem* and reporting officers from black and ethnic
minorities. Panel managers are attempting to address this problem through
positive recruitment procedures. There is also a lack of competent interpreters.[94] Guardians should consider approaching black lawyers to represent
black children. The Society of Black Lawyers was founded in 1973 and some
of the lawyers are on the Children's Panel. There is also a Society of Asian
Lawyers founded in 1990; the Association of Black Social Workers and Allied
Professions (ABSWAP) can also provide professional advice and
publications.[95]

Practice directions

Since implementation of the Children Act in October 1991 there have been
four directions by the President of the Family Division:

- Appeals for Magistrates' Courts, January 31, 1992;
- Distribution and transfer between the High Court and County Courts of
  Family Business and Family Proceedings, June 5, 1992;
- Applications by children, February 22, 1993;[96] and
- Hearings before the High Court Judges—time estimates, November 22,
  1993.[97]

---

92 *The Child Witness Pack* (1993) NSPCC/ChildLine. Available from NSPCC, 67 Saffron Hill,
    London, EC1N 8RS. See also 'The Child, the Court and the Video: A study of the
    implementation of the Memorandum of Good Practice on video interviewing of child
    witnesses' (1994), Department of Health and Social Services Inspectorate.
93 See further Morgan and Williams, 'A Role for a Support Person for Child Witnesses in
    Criminal Proceedings' *British Journal of Social Work*, Vol 23, No. 2, pp. 113–121.
94 See Baker, Hussain and Saunders, *Interpreters in Public Services* (1991).
95 See further Sumpton, 'The Particular Needs of Black Children' *Seen and Heard*, December
    1992.
96 See further Chapter 9 below.
97 These practice directions are listed in Annex 1 at p. 85 of the Children Act Advisory
    Committee Annual Report 1992/93.

The National Association of Guardians ad Litem and Reporting Officers: A Code of Ethics and a Code of Practice for Guardians *ad Litem* and Reporting Officers

The National Association of Guardians *ad Litem* and Reporting Officers held its inaugural meeting on April 2, 1990. They have produced a Code of Ethics and a Code of Practice for their members. The Code of Ethics contains the following statement of principles:

- the guardian ad litem shall maintain independence in all aspects of his/her work;
- the GAL/RO shall act in the child's best interests;
- the GAL/RO shall be committed to bring to court the best evidential base on which decisions must be made;
- the GAL/RO shall accord value to the child's individuality and shall be concerned to enhance her well-being without prejudice;
- the GAL/RO shall approach every individual without prejudice;
- the GAL/RO shall be willing to communicate fully about his/her role, function and value base;
- the GAL shall search for the means of providing the best realistic outcome for the child;
- the GAL/RO shall conduct his/her work expeditiously.[98]

---

98   NAGALRO, *Code of Ethics for Guardians ad Litem and Reporting Officers* (1991); see also their *Code of Practice for Guardians ad Litem and Reporting Officers*, and *The Role and Function of Panel Managers*, (1991). In June 1994, the Department of Health and Social Services Inspectorate circulated a consultation paper, *Standards and the Guardian Service*, introducing 20 standards for good quality service. It is anticipated that these standards will be incorporated into appraisal systems.

Chapter 6
The Role of the Guardian ad Litem in Secure Accommodation

In 1987/88 there were 1,800 admissions into secure units, 57 per cent of which concerned children in care who were either being accommodated or were subject to Care Orders. Twenty-five per cent of the children were on remand awaiting a court hearing, 3 per cent were children convicted of serious offences under S.53 of the Children and Young Persons Act 1933.[1]

S.25 of the 1989 Act deals with applications to place children in secure accommodation. Such applications are Family Proceedings and the Children (Admissibility of Hearsay Evidence) Order 1991.[2] Secure accommodation is dealt with in the Children (Secure Accommodation) Regulations,[3] 1991, the Children (Secure Accommodation) (No.2) Regulations 1991,[4] in Volume 1 of the Children Act 1989 Guidance and Regulations Vol. 1, Chapter 5 and Vol. 4, Chapter 8. Before implementation of the Children Act 1989 guardians ad litem were not directly involved in secure accommodation applications and the involvement of panel members has presented a new and challenging area of work straddling both the care and juvenile justice systems in a potentially confusing combination.

---

1   Alan and Hill, 'Placements of Last Resort' Community Care, November 15, 1990.
2   S.I. 1991 No. 1115.
3   S.I. 1991 No. 1505.
4   S.I. 1991 No. 2034.

The Introduction of Secure Accommodation

Secure accommodation is accommodation provided for the purpose of restricting liberty.[5] Although society has always locked up difficult children it was not until the early 1960s that secure accommodation specifically for children emerged as a separate category of provision. The first unit was opened at Kingswood in Bristol in 1964, followed by two others — Redhill in Surrey in 1965 and Redbank in Cheshire in 1966. Before that the former approved schools and children's homes had informal arrangements for separating difficult children from the rest of the group. The Children and Young Persons Act 1969 institutionalised the confusion between justice, punishment and welfare. The Act was a compromise which attempted to decriminalise the young offender while retaining an adversarial court as a forum for the case to be heard.

A justice model incorporates notions of free will, as opposed to determinism, and the concept of *mens rea*. The child is believed to be in control of his own behaviour, and thus carries responsibility, providing his guilt can be proved. The welfare model sees delinquency as one manifestation of disturbance, or deprivation, carrying with it a notion of diminished responsibility, maintaining care and treatment rather than punishment. If the second model is adopted then offenders may be said to merit the same treatment as those who have committed no offence but are victims of abuse or neglect. This is a theoretical dilemma which has never been adequately resolved, and the resulting ambivalence permeates the system. In recent years, public opinion on young offenders has hardened and produced some regressive social policy in relation to them. Tougher measures include proposals to build 'secure training centres' for persistent 12 to 15 year old offenders. In March 1994 the principle of *doli incapax*, which had previously been a safeguard for 10 to 14 year olds by requiring that the prosecution must show that they knew that what they were doing was seriously wrong, was effectively overruled by the judgment of Mann LJ in *C. v D.P.P.*[6]

Philosophical confusions have resulted in structural confusions also, and secure accommodation provides a physical environment in which definitions become increasingly blurred, with absconding often emerging as the vehicle by which young people travel from the care to the criminal system.

Children were dealt with in the same courts by the same magistrates as children who were entering care through civil proceedings. In order to support the new legislation the government introduced a new grant aid programme in 1975 which provided local authorities with 100 per cent funding to meet the capital costs of providing new secure units. Accordingly the late 1970s and early 1980s saw a rapid expansion in the numbers of secure accommodation units. Publicity surrounding the case of Mary Bell, a 12-year-old girl convicted of murder, highlighted a perceived need for even more specialist units to accommodate the most difficult children, for whom no suitable facility was available. Accordingly two youth treatment centres, St Charles in Essex — which opened in 1971 — and Glenthorne in Birmingham — opened in 1979 —

---

5   S.25.
6   *The Times*, March 30, 1994.

were established. Originally designed for troublesome, rather than troubled, children[7] the additional capacity created after 1975 saw a rapid increase in numbers of children entering secure units from local authority care without regulation or authority from the court, who had ostensibly become too difficult to manage in open conditions. The Criminal Justice Act 1991 established separate Youth Courts and fuelled the debate about the precise interface between the juvenile justice and welfare systems, and created two separate routes into secure accommodation — the criminal and the civil. Once in the secure unit children who were being locked up to protect society mingled freely with those who were being locked up for their own protection. The contradictions, inherent in such a system, are illustrated by a case in 1993 in which a teenage girl who, having been sent to a secure unit for 'treatment' after suffering long-term sexual abuse, discovered that the boy with whom she had struck up a relationship in the unit was there because he had raped a young girl. The upsurge in numbers of children entering secure units through the care system was, to some extent, regulated by the Criminal Justice Act 1982, which introduced statutory safeguards governing admission to secure accommodation. Before that there was no formal guidance, or criteria, about the circumstances in which restriction of liberty might, or might not, be appropriate. Paradoxically, Howard Parker's research made it apparent that the welfare model could be producing a more punitive form of juvenile justice than a straight justice model based on a tariff system.[8]

There was a growing awareness that concentration on the best interests of the child could be producing a more punitive form of care than had been ideologically envisaged.[9] A key concern was that children were entering secure accommodation through purely administrative procedures set up by local authorities and other bodies 'who were able to restrict the liberty of children indefinitely without recourse to a court of law and without any specific right of appeal against that continued incarceration.'[10]

The introduction of the Secure Accommodation (No.2) Regulations 1983[11] meant that, for the first time, children were protected from unnecessary and inappropriate restrictions of liberty. The regulations required that local authorities must seek the authority of the court to keep a child in security for more than 72 hours in any 28 day period. They also required that a child be legally represented, and introduced an appeals procedure. The influx of children from care into the secure system had been largely predicted by a study of the three original secure units, Redbank, Redhill and Kingswood.[12] The study concluded that many entrants were casualties of the child care system and that, if this was the case, there was a danger that the new units would quickly be filled. The subsequent offending and re-entry to security of the boys

---

7   See further Hoghughi, *Troubled and Troublesome: Coping with Severely Disordered Children* (1978).
8   See Parker, *Receiving Juvenile Justice* (1981).
9   See Morris, Giller, Szwed and Geach, *Justice for Children* (1981) p. 1.
10 Stephens and Hopper, 'The New Role of The Guardian in Secure Accommodation Applications' in *Applications for Secure Accommodation Orders; The Views of Selected Speakers at Eight Regional Conferences* (1992),p. 21.
11 S.I. 1983 No. 1808.
12 Millam, Bullock and Hoyes, *Locking Up Children* (1978).

from the three units was high, both directly from the units and after leaving. For example, 26 per cent of the boys went directly into prison custody and of those released to the community, 62 per cent entered custody within two years. Thus the study clearly illustrated the overlap between the child care system and subsequent entry into youth custody.

In surveying secure accommodation in 1988, Roger Bullock concluded that:

> all the evidence suggests that young people with similar problems, are still drifting around different welfare systems whether special education, health, social services or penal establishment. Where problematic people end up seems largely a matter of local policies, and of the resolve of some settings and agencies to hang on to difficult adolescents rather than transfer them. What is also clear is that young people's difficulties cannot be met by the efforts of a single agency and that their problems are deep-seated and long-standing.[13]

There are also extraordinarily wide geographical variations in the use of secure accommodation, with the north and northwest of the country having admission rates 50 per cent higher than for the south and southeast of England.[14]

Between 1982 and 1985 the Dartington Research Unit looked at 104 young people leaving two youth treatment centres, St Charles and Glenthorne. They found that, apart from the S.53 cases who had entered secure accommodation through the criminal route, young people there on Care Orders fell into four groups. A sixth were long-term child guidance and special education cases, well known to a variety of centres and residential schools. Their behaviour deteriorated until, in early adolescence, they were transferred for control reasons to the care of social services. A quarter of the Care Order cases in contrast were long term social services clients taken into care when young people, because of family breakdown or abuse, and fostered until such placements broke down, then they quickly moved through a series of residential establishments as their behaviour became more disturbed. Half the Care Order admissions to the youth treatment centres, however, had been in care for a short time and their behaviour had come to the attention of welfare agencies in early adolescence. Then there was a sudden and rapid deterioration in their behaviour, which caused them to pass quickly via residential care to secure accommodation — thus 28 per cent of the Care Order boys and 33 per cent of the Care Order girls had been in care for less than a year before entering the centres. It seems that their difficulties had been hidden and protected until they suddenly erupted to the wider notice of the welfare authorities. A final small group of Care Order children, probably one in ten, displayed bizarre behaviour and caused great anxiety to social workers by their mercurial and unpredictable behaviour.[15]

In spite of the Secure Accommodation (No.2) Regulations 1983, a research study of secure accommodation carried out by the University of Leicester revealed a somewhat dismal picture. It identified:

---

13   Bullock, 'Secure Provision Ten Years On' in *Secure Units: The Way Ahead* (1988) Conference Papers, Orchard Lodge Regional Resource Centre.
14   Stewart and Tutt, *Children in Custody* (1987).
15   Bullock, *op. cit.*

- widespread use of the 72 hour provision by local authorities. In other words, children were being locked up for the maximum period allowed without the need to obtain the authority of the court, enabling neither the child nor his representative to challenge the appropriateness of the placement;
- that court proceedings themselves were frequently cursory — an average hearing lasted 13 minutes, the shortest three minutes;
- legal representation of children was variable, but predominantly passive. Solicitors were observed:
  - to take instructions from their client at the very last moment, to side with the social worker rather than their client;
  - not to cross examine witnesses; and
  - not to contest Orders, but to proceed in the best interests of the child, or what the solicitors perceived to be in their best interests.

Magistrates had little difficulty in reaching their decisions — most applications and particularly renewal applications, were rubber stamped by the court, and in nearly every case Secure Orders were made for the length requested by the local authority. The report's conclusion stated: 'it will be clear that the idea that judicial hearings protect the liberty of individuals against excessive state intervention is, so far as secure accommodation is concerned, little more than libertarian rhetoric.' The Report specifically recommended the extension of the guardian *ad litem* system to cover children in secure accommodation:

> no independent assessment of the children's needs, rights and interests was provided [to the courts] and it was assumed that the care authority's social worker would, without conflict, be both dispassionate expert and prosecution witness. This seemed to us a point where ambiguity was both unnecessary, and unhelpful, and it is to be hoped that the extension of the guardian system will go some way towards resolving this problem · · ·[16]

In 1988 the government carried out a review of secure accommodation provision and issued a consultation document in November 1989. The results of this consultation were incorporated into the Children's (Secure Accommodation) Regulations 1991 and the Guidance in Volume 4, Chapter 8 of the Children Act 1989 Guidance and Regulations, which took effect on October 14, 1991, with the implementation of the Children Act 1989. The main conclusions were:

- there is need for secure accommodation and it should have Secretary of State approval;
- provision and use varies between local authorities (local authorities with comparable levels of demography, geography, levels of crime and social deprivation produced vastly different rates of use of secure accommodation);
- providers are users;
- court scrutiny is poor;

---

16 Harris and Noel Timms, *Between Hospital and Prison — Or Thereabouts, Secure Accommodation in the Child Care System* (1993). See also Harris and Timms, 'Children in Secure Accommodation' *British Journal of Social Work*, Vol. 23, No. 6, December 1993, p. 597.

- there are too many small units;
- there is poor gate-keeping;
- there is no need for increased provision;
- there is inefficient use of secure accommodation and there should be a duty to provide alternatives.[17]

Concerns about children and young people entering secure accommodation via the civil route resulted from October 1991 in the inclusion of S.25 secure accommodation applications in the list of specified proceedings in which guardians *ad litem* are appointed. This constituted a completely new area of work for guardians, and the prospect of the new role generated some confusion and anxiety. For the first time guardians were becoming involved on the perimeter of the juvenile justice system, and were being asked to collude in a rather contradictory process involving locking up children for their own good, thus posing a series of complicated ideological, moral and ethical problems for individual panel members. However, once guardians became involved in the S.25 applications they became largely convinced of the need for their involvement, not as agents of social control, but as representatives of children and young people, who, at a young age, can find themselves totally isolated at the bottom of what can be a fairly rapid downward spiral through care into secure accommodation. The guardian *ad litem* can act as the safeguard at the point of their entry into the secure unit, and can either resist the making of the order or endeavour to ensure that the Secure Orders are made for valid and appropriate reasons, according to the stated criteria rather than in the pursuance of negative policies of disposal.

Routes into Secure Accommodation

There are three main routes into secure accommodation — the criminal route, the civil route and, for a very small number of exceptional cases, the psychiatric route. Guardians are only involved in the civil route in which S.25 applications are heard in the Family Proceedings Court, unless the criminal remand is from the Crown Court, in which case any secure accommodation will be remitted to the Family Proceedings Court. The civil route is however the route through which most children enter secure accommodation.

Children taking the civil route have the benefit of a guardian *ad litem*, those entering secure units via the criminal or psychiatric routes do not have a guardian appointed, although it is fair to say that, in the case of mental health legislation, fairly stringent criteria are applied before children enter specialist secure units.

Secure units are the physical interface between the juvenile justice and the care systems. Here confusions, anxieties and contradictions abound. Because of the lack of a coherent unifying philosophy secure units tend to develop their own regimes and treatment programmes. If one judges by outcomes then the predominating ethos is one of criminality rather than care; the majority of children who enter secure units enter via the civil route, the majority of those

---

17   Stephens and Hopper, *op. cit.*

Criminal Route
No GAL appointed

- Children and Young Persons Act 1993, s. 53(1) and (2): child convicted of serious offences, e.g. murder, arson and rape.

- Children and Young Persons Act 1969, s. 23 as substituted by Criminal Justice Act 1991, s. 60 Remand to Secure Accommodation.

- Police and Criminal Evidence Act 1984, s. 38(6).

Psychiatric Route
No GAL appointed

- Mental Health Act 1983, s. 118, para. 30 and Mental Health Act 1983, Code of Practice *re* children and young people under the age of 18.

Civil Route
GALs appointed

- Children Act 1989, s. 25(1)(a) and/or (b)
  Young people have both a legal representative and a guardian *ad litem*.

Note: No child under 13 may be put in secure accommodation without the permission of the Secretary of State.

These routes lead into the secure accommodation shown in Figure 6, p. 222.

Figure 5 **Principal Routes into Secure Accommodation**

who leave continue through the criminal system. This renders the job of the guardian *ad litem* as gatekeeper, safeguarder and representative of the best interests of the child at the point of entry into secure accommodation one of the most critical areas of panel members' work.

Children to whom S.25 of the 1989 Act does not apply

S.25 of the 1989 Act shall not apply to a child:

- who is detained under any provision of the Mental Health Act 1983; or
- in respect of whom an Order has been made under S.53 of the Children and Young Persons Act 1933 (punishment of certain grave crimes); or
- to whom S.20(5) of the 1989 Act (accommodation of persons over 16 but under 21) applies and who is being accommodated under that Section; or
- in respect of whom an Order has been made under S.43 of the 1989 Act (Child Assessment Order) and who is kept away from home pursuant to that Order.[18]

In addition a child under the age of 13 years shall not be placed in secure accommodation in a community home without the prior approval of the Secretary of State to the placement of that child.[19]

The criminal route

This broadly divides into those who are remanded to secure accommodation, and those who have committed grave crimes.

- children convicted of grave crime at Crown Court, such as murder, arson and rape;[20]
- children detained under S.38(6) of the Police and Criminal Evidence Act 1984 (detained children);
- children remanded to local authority accommodation under S.23 of the Children and Young Persons Act 1969, as substituted by S.60 of the Criminal Justice Act 1991 (remand to local authority accommodation) but only:
  - where the child is charged with, or convicted of, a violent or sexual offence, or an offence punishable, in the case of an adult, with imprisonment for 14 years or more; or
  - where the child has a recent history of absconding whilst remanded in local authority accommodation, and is charged with, or has been convicted of, an imprisonable offence, alleged or found to have been committed while so remanded and (in either case) the court is of the opinion that only such a requirement would be adequate to protect the public from serious harm from the child.

---

18   Children (Secure Accommodation) Regulations 1991, reg. 5(1) and (2).
19   *Ibid.*, reg. 4.
20   Children and Young Persons Act 1933, S.53(a) and (b).

Initially, there was some confusion about whether or not guardians were ever to be appointed in criminal proceedings. The matter was however clarified by the Guidance and Regulations which states that: 'the opportunity has been taken in the Criminal Justice Act 1991 to correct a small anomaly in S.92(2) of the Children Act 1989.'[21] That section specifies that proceedings under the 1989 Act shall be treated as family proceedings in relation to the Magistrates' Court.

As such, all applications for authority to restrict liberty under S.25 of the 1989 Act would fall to be dealt with as civil proceedings. However this would not normally be appropriate where an application to restrict liberty was connected with the appearance of a child before a court in criminal proceedings. The intention was that the latter court should also have power to authorise restriction of liberty. The position has now been amended by S.60(3) of the Criminal Justice Act 1991. This says that:

> in the case of a child or young person who has been remanded or committed to local authority accommodation by a youth court or a magistrates court other than a youth court any application under Section 25 of the Children Act 1989 shall, notwithstanding anything in Section 92(2) of the Act or Section 65 of the 1980 Magistrates' Court Act be made to that court.

It should be noted that the power to consider applications under S.25 does not extend to the Crown Court. When a juvenile is remanded to appear before the Crown Court for trial, or sentence, it will be necessary for applications for Orders under S.25 to continue to be made to a Youth Court or a Magistrates' Court other than a Youth Court. Guidance about the maximum duration of a court authority to restrict liberty in remand cases is given in para. 8.46 of Volume 4 (Residential Care) of the Children Act 1989 Guidance and Regulations. S.63 of the Criminal Justice Act 1991 was brought into force on the same day as the implementation of the Children Act 1989. A letter from the Department of Health which accompanied circulation of Volume 7 of the Guidance and Regulations made the matter even clearer: 'guardians ad litem will not be appointed in applications for secure accommodation in remand and committal proceedings heard in the adult magistrates court or juvenile court.'

The criteria for placement in secure accommodation via the criminal route are set out in Children (Secure Accommodation) Regulations 1991, reg. 6(2):

> no child shall be placed in secure accommodation unless it appears that any accommodation other than that provided for the purpose of restricting liberty is inappropriate because:
> ● the child is likely to abscond from such other accommodation or
> ● the child is likely to injure himself or other people if he is kept in any other such accommodation.

The above criteria apply to children who are detained under S.38(6) of the Police and Criminal Evidence Act 1984, and those who have ben remanded to local authority accommodation, according to the provision of S.23 of the Children and Young Persons Act 1969, as substituted by S.60 of the Criminal Justice Act 1991, if they are either charged with, or convicted of, an offence

---

21   Children Act 1989 Guidance and Regulations Vol. 7, para. 5.5.

imprisonable, in the case of a person aged 21 or over, for 14 years or more, or charged with or convicted of an offence of violence or have been previously so convicted.

The maximum length of time that a child on a S.23 remand may be detained in secure accommodation is the length of the remand itself.[22] No such child may be detained for more than 28 days without further authorisation from the court.[23]

Children who have been convicted of certain crimes are detained according to the provision of S.53 of the Children and Young Persons Act 1969. Their detention is subject to the discretion of the Home Office.

The psychiatric route

This applies only to a very small number of children. However, S.118 of the Mental Health Act 1983 applies equally to children as to adults. S.118 refers to the responsibilities of the Secretary of State to prepare, and from time to time revise a Code of Practice which covers, amongst other things, the committal of children and young people to secure units in order to receive specified forms of medical treatment. Para. 30 of the Code of Practice deals with the position of children and young people under the mental health legislation.[24]

The general principles of the Code of Practice, which applies to children and young people under the age of 18, are:

- young people should be kept as fully informed as possible about their care and treatment. Their views and wishes must always be taken into account;
- unless statute specifically overrides, young people should generally be regarded as having the right to make their own decisions (and in particular, treatment decisions), when they have sufficient 'understanding and intelligence';
- any intervention into the life of a young person considered necessary, by any reason of their mental disorder, should be the least restrictive possible and result in the least possible segregation from family, friends, community and school;
- all children and young people in hospital should receive appropriate education.

There is no minimum age limit for children to be treated under the Mental Health Act 1983, and the Code of Practice acknowledges the complexity of dealing with the care and treatment, particularly of those under 16, stressing that it is essential for those responsible for the child or young person's care to request copies of any Court Orders in relation to the child, and check who has parental responsibility in order to inform decisions about examination, assessment or treatment.

---

22 Reg. 13(1).
23 Reg. 13(2).
24 Code of Practice, Mental Health Act 1983, 'Children and Young People', Revised August
    1993, Department of Health.

The section on consent to medical treatment is extremely useful, as it helpfully summarises the position, and applies equally to young people who are not detained under the Mental Health Act 1983. It is, therefore, of direct relevance to guardians *ad litem* appointed, not only in S.25 applications, but in all specified proceedings.

If a child under 16 has 'sufficient understanding and intelligence' he can take decisions about his own medical treatment in the same way as an adult. Otherwise the permission of parents/guardians must be sought (save in emergencies where only the treatment necessary to end the emergency should be given). If parents/guardians do not consent to treatment, consideration should be given to both the use of the child care legislation and the Mental Health Act 1983 before coming to a final conclusion as to what action should be taken. Under S.100 of the Children Act 1989 a local authority may also seek leave to ask the High Court to exercise its inherent jurisdiction to make orders with respect to children, if the conditions set out in S.100(4) are met.

The same principles concerning consent apply where the under 16-year-old is in the care of the local authority. Where such a child does not have sufficient 'understanding and intelligence' to take his own treatment decisions, treatment can be authorised by any person or body with parental responsibility. A local authority has parental responsibility for a child in its care, i.e. under a Care Order. Wherever possible, parents should be consulted. However local authorities can, in the exercise of their powers under S.33(3)(b) of the Children Act 1989, limit the extent to which parents exercise their parental responsibility. In certain pre-Children Act wardships, although the children are deemed to be in care within the meaning of S.31 of the Children Act 1989, court directions may still require treatment decisions to be agreed by the court. Where the children are wards of court (and also not deemed to be subject to a Care Order under S.31 of the Children Act 1989) the consent of the High Court must be sought. In an emergency, consent may be obtained retrospectively (but this should be regarded as wholly exceptional).

Young people aged 16 and 17 who have the capacity to make their own treatment decisions, can do so in the same way as adults.[25] Where such a young person does not have this capacity, the authorisation of either parent, guardian, or care authority (whichever has the lawful authority in relation to the particular young person) must be obtained. The consent of the High Court must be obtained in the case of wards of court,

No minor of whatever age has power by refusing consent to treatment to override a consent to treatment by anyone who has parental responsibility for the minor, including a local authority, with the benefit of a Care Order or consent by the court. Nevertheless, such a refusal is a very important consideration in making clinical judgments and for parents and the court in deciding whether themselves to give consent. The importance increases with the age and maturity of the minor.[26]

In cases involving Emergency Protection Orders, Child Assessment Orders, interim Care Orders and full Supervision Orders under the Children Act 1989,

---

25 Family Law Reform Act 1969, S.8.
26 See *Re W. (A Minor)* (Medical Treatment: Court's Jurisdiction) [1992] 3 W.L.R. 758 at 772 — also known as *Re J. (A Minor)* (Consent to Medical Treatment).

a competent child has a statutory right to refuse to consent to examination, assessment and, in certain circumstances, treatment. Such refusal is not capable of being overriden.[27]

Nevertheless, this does not look so clear in the light of the decision in the case of *South Glamorgan County Council v. W. and B.* Douglas Brown J overruled the refusal of a severely depressed 15-year-old girl to enter a psychiatric unit for assessment and treatment. The girl was fully competent, but the court overrode her refusal and caused her to be removed for treatment. The view was taken that:

> In an appropriate case where other remedies within the Children Act 1989 had been exhausted and found not to bring about the desired result, there was jurisdiction to resort to other remedies and the particular remedy presently was the remedy of providing authority for Doctors to treat the child, and authority, if it was needed, for the local authority to take all necessary steps to bring the child to the Doctors, so that she could be assessed and treated properly.[28]

Guardians should also refer to the Children Act 1989, Sched. 3, paras. 4 and 5, which refer respectively to psychiatric and medical examination and treatment, and bear in mind that courts may make a Supervision Order under S.31, including a specific direction that the child undergo medical or psychiatric examination or treatment. However, no court shall include such a requirement in an Order unless it is satisfied that:

● the child has sufficient understanding to make an informed decision;
● he consents to its inclusion; and
● satisfactory arrangements have been made, or can be made, for the treatment or examination.

Much, however, depends on the opinion of the medical practitioner concerned, who may refuse to treat the child if he is of the opinion that the treatment should be changed or cease, or that the child is not susceptible to treatment. The practitioner then makes a report in writing to the supervisor, who notifies the court, or may cancel or vary the Order.[29] Children themselves, as parties, have the right to a second medical opinion.

Where a child is looked after by a local authority and placed in accommodation where liberty is restricted (for example National Health Service secure units or a registered mental nursing home), application must be made to the Family Proceedings Court within 72 hours, if the restriction is to last beyond that period.

Expensive small specialist units, such as the Gardener Unit attached to Prestwich Hospital Manchester and the Special Unit at St Andrew's Hospital in the Midlands, are a diminishing resource and may become casualties of the contract culture in welfare provision. They do not offer purchasers enough beds to be a significant part of a purchasing budget, and so are likely to be overlooked, in spite of the fact that their specialist facilities are sorely needed by many young people. Specialist units seek to involve young people in

---

27   Code of Practice, Mental Health Act, *op. cit.*, para. 30. p. E5/91.
28   [1993] 1 F.L.R. 574 at 584.
29   Sched. 3, paras. 4 to 7.

therapeutic programmes to help with a variety of problems, for example, persistently suicidal behaviour or drug abuse.

Many severely aggressive or psychiatrically disturbed adolescents are contained under S.53 of the Children and Young Persons Act 1933, however the reasons for their offending behaviour may well be psychiatric illness, or disturbance. In general the more passive, suicidal adolescent is likely to enter secure accommodation through the psychiatric route while the violent, aggressive, uncontrollable adolescents enters via the criminal route. Those children who are detained under the provisions of the Mental Health Act 1983 are not covered by the secure accommodation regulations but are covered by the Code of Practice. As an additional safeguard, Mental Health Act Commissioners regularly visit children in secure accommodation operating within National Health Service facilities.

It appears contradictory that children who are categorised so clearly in the differential routes into secure accommodation appear undifferentiated on arrival, in that children, once absorbed into the population of a particular secure unit, mix freely. It is hard to sustain the philosophies of care, justice, containment and treatment within one system, and it is certainly a bewildering system for the children who are a part of it.

Civil Route

The criteria for the use of accommodation for restricting liberty are that a child who is being looked after by a local authority may not be placed and, if placed, may not be kept in accommodation provided for the purpose of restricting liberty (secure accommodation) unless it appears that:

- he has a history of absconding and is likely to abscond from any other description of accommodation and if he absconds he is likely to suffer significant harm; or
- if he is kept in any other description of accommodation he is likely to injure himself or other persons.[30]

The criteria apply therefore not just to the initial placement but to the power to keep children in secure accommodation. The criteria must be met and must continue to be met while the child remains in the secure unit.

The guidance stresses that secure accommodation is a serious step to take. It must be a last resort, only taken when there is no appropriate alternative and when all other options have been comprehensively considered and rejected:

> never because no other placement was available at the relevant time, because of inadequacies in staffing, because the child is simply being a nuisance or runs away from his accommodation and is not likely to suffer significant harm in doing so, and never as a form of punishment. It is important, in considering the possibility of a secure placement, that there is a clear view of the aims and objectives of such a placement and that those providing the accommodation can fully meet those aims and objectives, Secure placements, once made, should be only for as long as is necessary and unavoidable. Care should be taken, to ensure that children are not retained in security, simply to complete a predetermined assessment of 'treatment'

---

30 S.25.

programme. It is important that plans are made for continuity of care, education and, where appropriate, access to professionals (e.g. psychiatric support) when the child leaves secure accommodation.[31]

Local authorities have a duty under the 1989 Act to take reasonable steps designed to avoid the need for children within their area to be placed in secure accommodation.[32] Careful consideration should be given to the existing range of alternative facilities and services available locally, identifying any gaps or inadequacies in such provisions, and how these might best be met, either by the local authority itself or in co-operation with other agencies. In addition steps should be taken to ensure that all decisions to seek a placement for a child in secure accommodation are taken at a senior level within the authority. This should be not less than an Assistant Director level, and such a person should be accountable to the Director of Social Services for that decision. The decision itself should also give authority for the duration of the order sought. Local authorities managing secure units have a particular responsibility to ensure that children accommodated in the non-secure part of the home are not unnecessarily placed in the associated secure facility, and that the criteria for restricting liberty are applied equally rigorously to such children as those being considered for admission from outside the home.[33]

The placement of a child it is looking after in secure accommodation should, wherever practicable, arise as part of the local authority's plan for the child's welfare. In planning such a placement, and in considering any decision with respect to a child looked after in such accommodation, a local authority must have regard to its general duties under S.22 of the 1989 Act including the duty to safeguard and promote the child's welfare[34] and so far as is reasonably practicable ascertain the wishes and feelings regarding the matter of the child, his parents, any other person who has parental responsibility for him and any person whose wishes and feelings they consider relevant.[35] For children who are provided with accommodation on a voluntary basis under S.20(1) of the Act, a person with parental responsibility for a child may at any time remove him from the accommodation which has been provided[36] unless the exceptions in S.20(9) apply. This includes removal from placements in secure accommodation whether or not the authority of the court to restrict the liberty of the child has been obtained. However in line with the requirements of the Guidance and Regulations covering voluntary arrangements, a written agreement about the placement made between the local authority and parents should include the expected duration of the placement, and the arrangements for bringing the placement to an end.[37]

The Guidance makes it clear that those children entering secure accommodation via the civil route, do so under an umbrella of welfare. This has particular significance for guardians *ad litem* who may be exploring other options available to the child. It is particularly important to discuss the child's

---

31   Children Act 1989 Guidance and Regulations, Vol. 4, para. 8.5.
32   Sched. 2, para. 7(c).
33   Children Act 1989 Guidance and Regulations Vol. 4, para. 8.6.
34   S.22(3)(a).
35   S.22(4).
36   S.20(8).
37   Children Act 1989 Guidance and Regulations Vol. 4, para. 8.7.

situation and future with all those who have parental responsibility, as they may be in a position to remove the child from secure accommodation.

S.25 of the 1989 Act is also subject to the provisions of S.1., in that the court must be satisfied that giving paramount consideration to the child's welfare requires the making of a Secure Order[38] and that it will be better for the child to make an Order rather than making no Order at all.[39] If at any stage the criteria for keeping the child in secure accommodation do not apply he should be released and put in alternative accommodation as the court's authorisation is merely that — an authorisation.[40] Again the Guidance emphasises that the criteria must not only apply at the point of entry, but must apply at all times throughout the period of the child's accommodation in a secure unit.

Definition of Restriction of Liberty

The accommodation of children in secure conditions is not something that happens only in secure units. The interpretation of the term 'accommodation' provided for the purpose of restricting liberty in S.25(1) of the 1989 Act is ultimately a matter for determination by the court; however it is important to recognise that any practice or measures which prevents a child from leaving a room or building of his own free will may be deemed by the court to constitute 'restriction of liberty'. For example while it is clear that the locking of a child in a room or part of a building to prevent him leaving voluntarily is caught by the statutory definition, other practices which place restrictions on freedom of mobility are not so clearly defined — the electronic surveillance of children is one example, the use of drugs is another.

A child meeting the criteria may be placed in secure accommodation for a maximum period of 72 hours without court authority.[41] A local authority or other body wishing to keep the child in secure accommodation beyond that period, must make application to the relevant court for authority to keep the child in secure accommodation. Such applications may only be made by the local authority looking after the child or, as the case may be, the local education authority person carrying on the residential care home, nursing home or mental nursing home.[42]

The maximum period for which a court may authorise a child to whom S.25 of the 1989 Act applies to be kept in secure accommodation is three months.[43] A court may from time to time authorise a child to whom S.25 of the Act applies to be kept in secure accommodation for a further period not exceeding six months at any one time.[44] It was established in *Re B. (A Minor) (Secure Accommodation Order)*[45] that detention in secure accommodation dates from

---

38   S.1(1).
39   S.1(5).
40   Children Act 1989 Guidance and Regulations Vol. 4, para. 8.9.
41   Children (Secure Accommodation) Regulations 1991, reg. 10(1).
42   Reg. 8 and Children Act 1989 Guidance and Regulations Vol. 1, para. 5.6.
43   Reg. 11.
44   Reg. 12.
45   *The Times*, May 27, 1994; see Fam. Law September 1994, 519.

Youth Treatment Centres

- Glenthorne

- St. Charles special provision for dangerous adolescents. *Average stay 2 years*

Health and Education Authorities Specialist Units

- St. Andrews Hospital
- The Gardener Unit
- Prestwich Hospital

Short Term
29 units

- Short stays
- Remands
- Emergencies

Long Term

- Aycliffe, Co. Durham
- Eastmoor, Leeds
- Kingswood, Avon
- Red Bank, Lancashire
Average stay 4 months

Note: See Criminal Justice and Public Order Act 1994:
Clauses 1 to 15 introduce new Secure Training Order for 12 to 14-year-olds;
Clause 16 extends the powers of courts to order custodial sentences of up to 14 years for 10 to 13-year-olds

Figure 6   **Secure Units**
Having satisfied the criteria, children may go to any of these units

the date of the court order, and not from the date when the child is placed in secure accommodation.

Each local authority looking after the child in secure accommodation in a community home shall appoint at least three persons, at least one of whom must not be employed by the local authority by or on behalf of which the child is being looked after, who shall review the keeping of the child in such accommodation for the purposes of securing his welfare within one month of the inception of the placement and then at intervals not exceeding three months where the child continues to be kept in such accommodation.[46]

The persons appointed under Regulation 15 to review the keeping of a child in secure accommodation shall satisfy themselves as to whether or not:

- the criteria for keeping the child in secure accommodation continued to apply;
- the placement in such accommodation in a community home continues to be necessary; and
- any other description of accommodation would be appropriate for him

and in so doing shall have regard to the welfare of the child whose case is being reviewed.

Those undertaking the review have a duty if practicable to ascertain and take into account the wishes and feelings of the child, his parents, any person with parental responsibility, any other person who has had the care of the child whose views the persons appointed consider should be taken into account, the child's independent visitor if one has been appointed, and the local authority managing the secure accommodation in which the child is placed — if that authority are not the authority who are looking after the child.[47]

The local authority shall, if practicable, inform all those whose views are required to be taken into account under para 2 of the outcome of the review and the reasons for such an outcome.[48]

The Role of the Court

It is the role of the court to safeguard the child's welfare, from inappropriate or unnecessary use of secure accommodation by both satisfying itself that those making the application have demonstrated that the statutory criteria, in S.25(1) or Regulation 6 as appropriate, have been met. Following the judgment of Butler Sloss LJ in Re M. in the Court of Appeal on November 10, 1994, it appears that the welfare of the child is relevant to a S.25 application, but is not a paramount consideration and that all the S.1 requirements (including the welfare checklist) do not apply to it. In specified proceedings, within the meaning of S.41, the court is required to appoint a guardian ad litem for the child, unless it is satisfied that it is not necessary to do so in the interests of the child.[49]

---

46   Reg. 15.
47   Reg. 16(2).
48   Reg. 16(3).
49   Children Act 1989 Guidance and Regulations Vol. 1, para. 5.7.

Courts must also consider carefully, as a separate issue, the length of time that the Order should cover, and listen to the recommendations of the guardian on this matter, as any other.

In Re W.[50] the local authority applied for an Order to last for three months. The 15-year-old girl, who was the subject of the application, opposed this, supported by her guardian *ad litem*, who suggested that five weeks was the appropriate length of time. The justices made an order for three months, but the case was successfully appealed on the grounds that, firstly, the bench had not considered the length of the Order as a separate issue, and secondly, had failed to listen to the guardian's recommendation. The Court of Appeal stressed that, where the justices failed to follow the recommendation of the guardian (or a court welfare officer) then they must give a full explanation of their reasons.[51]

Legal Representation

The court must not make a Secure Accommodation Order under S.25 unless the child is legally represented. The only exception is where a child, having been informed of his right to apply for Legal Aid and having had the opportunity to do so, has refused or failed to apply.[52]

If, as may well be the case, given that Secure Accommodation Orders involve children over the age of 13 the guardian *ad litem* and the child have a divergence of opinion about the recommendation to be put to the court then, as in proceedings under Parts IV and V, the legal representation stays with the child, and the guardian, although entitled to separate legal representation, is still not entitled to Legal Aid. In practice this means that guardians *ad litem* may find themselves in court at very short notice, having already identified the divergence of opinion between themselves and the young person, but not having had time to negotiate with the administering local authority in order to secure separate legal representation for themselves. As far as the child's own legal representation is concerned it may be that, by the time the guardian is appointed, the child is already represented by a solicitor who may or may not be a member of the children's panel. One of the guardian's first tasks therefore will be to ensure that the child receives adequate and satisfactory legal representation, preferably by someone who has experience and expertise in dealing with cases within the civil jurisdiction.

The Welfare of the Child

The question of the precise weight that the court and the guardian should give to the welfare of the child has proved both confusing and problematic. In

---

50   [1993] 1 F.L.R. 692.
51   See further Lyon, 'Current Legal Issues — The Guardian ad Litem and the Children Act 1989 in Practice', in *Practice in Progress*, (1993), GAL/RO Regional Conferences, IRCHIN with the Department of Health; Timms, 'The Guardian ad Litem and S.25 Applications — Re M: Do Thorough Little Menaces have a right to have their welfare considered?' *Panel News*, Vol. 7, No. 4, December 1994, 34.
52   S.25(6).

Hereford and Worcester County Council v S[53] it was held that S.1 applies to
S.25 applications and that the court must make the welfare of the child its
paramount consideration. Also, that S.1(2) and (5) apply, but that the criteria
in the welfare checklist (S.1(3)) were not of particular relevance, but were not
irrelevant; for instance the ascertainable wishes and feelings of the child would
be considered. Subsequent case law has moved steadily towards the view taken
by Butler Sloss LJ in *Re M.* that S.1 was not designed to apply to Part III of the
Act, and that the welfare of the child, although of great importance, must take
its place among other relevant criteria — among them the provision of
S.25(1)(b) that if he is kept in any other description of accommodation, he is
likely to injure himself or other persons.

Accommodated Children

Any child who is being provided with accommodation by a local authority, a
local education authority, a health authority, a NHS Trust, a residential care
home, a nursing home or a mental nursing home might find himself the subject
of secure accommodation proceedings, subject to the relevant criteria and
subject to the secure accommodation regulations. However they may be
removed from secure accommodation by someone with parental
responsibility, subject to the provisions of S.20(8). It is well worth guardians
considering this provision when looking at the alternatives available to the
child.

The Role of the Guardian ad Litem in S.25 Applications

Before implementation of the Children Act 1989 it was anticipated that it
might be necessary to establish a system of duty guardians who could be
available to act quickly in challenges to Emergency Protection Orders, and in
secure accommodation applications. Pre-implementation, it was thought that
the appointment of guardians in emergency proceedings would provide the
bulk of the work to be carried out at short notice. In the event guardians found
themselves precipitated into S.25 applications at short notice, and with very
little initial preparation. If the Order is a re-application, the guardian will have
more time to carry out investigations. The powers and duties of the guardian
ad litem in S.25 applications are the same as in all other proceedings under the
1989 Act, however there are some distinctive features of the guardian's role in
relation to S.25 applications under the 1989 Act.

Key considerations for the guardian will be:

- The existence and quality of the child's legal representation.
- The need to ascertain the child's wishes and feelings as a matter of urgency.
- The need to identify a divergence of opinion between the guardian and the
  child at an early stage. Guardians can insist on knowing where the child is
  to be placed. They need to know where the child will sleep that night. It is
  not good enough for an Order to be made for any available bed.
- Guardians should be particularly aware of the requirements of S.1(5), that
  is the Order should be a positive advantage to the child. The relative

53 [1993] 2 F.L.R. 360.

impact on the child should receive consideration in terms of long term welfare not short term disposal.

- The guardian will want to examine the suitability of the placement in terms of the child's race, culture and religion.[54]
- Guardians should be aware of the particular impact of secure accommodation on girls. Research indicates that it is the child care system, rather than the criminal system, which generates the female population of secure units. Possibly for this reason girls appear to stay in secure units far longer than boys. In London two thirds of boys referred to secure units are physically waiting in courts, police stations or in penal custody at the time of referral, whereas girls are twice as likely as boys to be in children's homes or foster homes at the time of referral (half of the girls and less than a quarter of the boys). Girls are more likely to be referred to secure provision because they are violent to the staff in residential homes, they are suicidal or engaging in self-injuring behaviour, or their sexual habits or activity are causing anxiety. They are not necessarily committing these acts more frequently, it is possible that they are simply more likely to be seen as needing security when they do commit them.[55]
- Guardians should check that all those with parental responsibility are aware of their right to remove the child from secure accommodation. It is only possible to prevent a person with parental responsibility from removing a child from secure accommodation by initiating proceedings under Part V of the 1989 Act.
- The guardian should consider the local authority's application in the light of their responsibility to consider placing the child with parents or others with parental responsibility, or other members of the extended network of family and friends as an alternative to secure accommodation.[56]
- The local authority also has a responsibility to place the child near their own home and with their siblings.[57]
- The guardian *ad litem* should be assured that the local authority has taken into account the child's wishes and feelings and allowed them to participate in the decision about possible placement.
- The weight to be given to the welfare of the child, particularly in relation to asking for an adjournment in order to investigate matters relevant to the child's welfare rather than the establishment of the criteria in S.25. Theoretically the provisions of S.1(3), the welfare check list, do not apply as S.25 is in Part III not Part IV of the Act. Case law has been confusing on this matter.[58]

---

54   S.22(6).
55   Cawson, 'Provision for Young Women' in *Secure Units: The Way Ahead* (1988), Conference Papers, Orchard Lodge Regional Resource Centre; *Gender and the Criminal Justice System* (1992), Home Office.
56   S.23(4) and (6).
57   S.23(7).
58   See *Oxfordshire County Council v. R.* [1992] 3 All E.R. 660. Children in voluntary children's homes and registered children's homes may not be kept in secure accommodation nor are such agencies allowed to administer secure accommodation units. See now *Re M. (A Minor) (Secure Accommodation)*, CA, November 10, 1994, unreported; *M v Birmingham Council* [1994] 2 F.L.R. 141.

- The guardian *ad litem* should discuss the local authority's care plan for the child in terms of the child's wishes and feelings and their own assessment of what is necessary for the child's welfare. Secure accommodation should not be a back door to treatment or assessment or indeed part of a short term holding operation. It should form part of a positive plan for the welfare of the child.

- Guardians *ad litem* dealing with S.25 applications should pay particular attention to the child's educational needs at what is often a critical time in the child's life. Because of the shortage of secure accommodation in some areas children are often sent some distance away from their homes and schools. The likely impact of a disruption in their education, as well as in every other aspect of their life, should be carefully considered against the possible advantages, Indeed education may be a key indicator of whether making the Order would be better than making no Order at all.[59]

- What is the particular population of the secure unit in which it is proposed to place the child? Is it predominantly composed of children who are there under the provisions of S.53 of the Children and Young Persons Act 1933? Are most of them on remand under S.23 of them Children and Young Persons Act 1969? What is the ethos of the establishment — is it punishment, treatment or care orientated?[60]

- The guardian will wish to examine the options available to the court which, in the case of S.25 applications, are more limited than in other proceedings in that S.8 Orders are not available as S.25 applications are not family proceedings[61] so the court's only options are to either make or refuse to make the Order. In addition it should be noted that the Order is permissive, it enables but does not oblige the authority or the person making the application to continue the placement for the duration of the Order, neither does it empower the authority or person to continue the placement once the criteria under which the Order was made cease to apply.[62]

- Guardians must be particularly aware of the impact of delay because of the serious issue of restriction of liberty involved.[63]

---

59 S.1(5).
60 The general shortage of appropriate provision for children who are the subject of S.25 applications is a continuing and recurring problem. The National Association of Guardians *ad Litem* and Reporting Officers are looking at the feasibility of a national resource centre that will create a database of alternatives to secure accommodation, and the availability of beds nationally.
61 S.8(3).
62 Children Act 1989 Guidance and Regulations Vol. 4, para. 8.42. See *R. v. Northampton Juvenile Court, ex. p. Hammersmith and Fulham London Borough* (1985) 15 Fam. Law 125 — secure accommodation was held to include a behaviour modification unit at a hospital where the regime was intended to restrict liberty. See also Pindown Enquiry (*The Pindown Experience and the Protection of Children* (1991), Report of the Staffordshire Child Care Inquiry 1990) in relation to unlawful restriction of liberty. See also Children Act 1989 Guidance and Regulations Vol. 4, paras. 8.10 and 8.14 regarding the use of time out facilities, i.e. they must comply with secure accommodation provisions. See also the Report of the Social Services Inspectorate — Inquiry into Aycliffe Centre for Children (1993), Department of Health.
63 See *Oxfordshire County Council v. R.* [1992] 3 All E.R. 660. This case also established that magistrates should give full reasons for their decisions in S.25 applications.

- Guardians should consider and make a recommendation about the appropriate length of time for the Order to run.
- Guardians should check the arrangements for the child's appearance at court. Some children who are the subject of S.25 applications have been kept in police cells while awaiting the court appearance.

Interim Orders

Because of the haste with which many children and guardians *ad litem* are precipitated into S.25 applications — often having less than 72 hours notice — many guardians *ad litem* have felt tempted to recommend the making of interim Secure Accommodation Orders, as means of remaining involved and buying time. However, a word of caution: in some cases it has appeared that the child has spent longer in secure accommodation on interim Orders than would have been possible if full Orders had been made. The guardian *ad litem* should take care that interim Orders should not be made unless they are satisfied that the criteria for the making of the full Order are likely to be met. Some applications for interim Orders are a function of the guardian *ad litem*'s anxiety about what will happen to the child in what may appear to be a very unsure situation, especially, as is sometimes the case, if no particular unit has been identified for the child by the time the court case ends. In such situations the guardian *ad litem* should ensure that the child going into secure accommodation is aware of the following:

- The possibility of appeal. If there is a need to appeal written evidence will be necessary.
- The right to a statutory review one month after placement. The child should be aware that the review panel will consist of three people including one person independent of the local authority.
- That they may have access to an independent representative who can visit them in the secure unit. Many units now have independent representatives attached to them. (For a further examination of the role of the independent representative in secure units see Chapter 10.)
- If the child has no regular visits from friends or members of his family the guardian *ad litem* should ensure that the child is aware of his right to have an independent visitor to visit, advise and befriend him.
- Children and young people in secure accommodation have the right to make representations and complaints under the provisions of S.26. In particular they should be aware of the regulations governing the restriction of liberty and should be fully aware of the content and provisions of the relevant complaints procedure.
- All children and young people going into secure accommodation should be aware of the provisions of the Children Act 1989 which enable them to seek leave to make application to initiate S.8 applications on their own account. They should also be aware of their right to see a solicitor, and guardians should ensure that they go into secure accommodation knowing how to get in touch with a member of the local children's panel.

• Guardians should ensure that children are aware of the guidelines covering their secure accommodation, and should be familiar with the guidelines for the management, control and discipline of children in secure accommodation in *Safe and Sound*[64] — the social services inspectorate's practice guide on the running of secure accommodation.

In particular, as *Safe and Sound* stresses, children should be prepared for admission to secure accommodation by being given information about the unit, perhaps by means of a video. The practice guide also warns against admission procedures, like routine searches, compulsory bathing and changing clothing, and recommends these do not constitute a threat to other children or staff. Children should not be sent to bed early (in most units children are locked into their bedrooms at night, partly to relieve staffing pressures). Visits from friends and family should be encouraged, and should be subjected to minimum restrictions and surveillance. Guardians, therefore, are in a position to clarify with the child what is expected of the unit. They should pay particular attention to the practical needs of children from black and ethnic minorities.

Commentary

Many guardians feel that they do not know enough about the longer term effects of locking up children. Society needs to be protected but are guardians locking up young people to protect society as an indirect punishment or genuinely in their best interests? Why should young people who are sent to secure accommodation under S.53 not have guardians and S.25 young people have them? Locking up children in secure accommodation exposes them to risks and those risks have to be balanced against the risks they are exposed to elsewhere or indeed the risks that their continued liberty poses to society. Research indicates the S.25 admissions to secure accommodation may well open the way to criminal activity. How does a child leave secure accommodation? What are the exit routes once the three months is up? Where are the checks to ensure that the child is helped back into the community and receives the advice and support that they clearly require? Sometimes there is no route within the secure placement to a non-secure unit.

However, the involvement of guardians in safeguarding the interests of children who are the subject of S.25 applications and entering secure accommodation via the civil route is an important advance. Panel members have a distinctive contribution to make, in that there is somebody there to challenge the grounds for the Secure Accommodation Order. The number of appeals has already risen. Before the Act was implemented in 1991 appeals against the secure accommodation applications were virtually non-existent. The former process, in which the local authority made the application, proved the grounds, and the child's solicitor (chosen by the local authority) was reluctant to oppose, is now substantially improved. There is a much greater

---

64 *Safe and Sound* (1994), Department of Health, Social Services Inspectorate. See also *Guidance on Permissible Forms of Control in Children's Residential Care* (1993), Department of Health.

emphasis on safeguarding and promoting the longer term interests of the child or young person, and the fact that a guardian is involved serves to focus the attention on this particularly disturbing and disturbed group of young people. The question of the precise weight to be given to the welfare of the child in S.25 applications remains an issue of concern and debate. Case law is now in potential conflict with guidance in Volumes 1 and 4 of the Children Act 1989 Regulations and Guidance.

Chapter 7

The Role of the Guardian ad Litem and Reporting Officer in Adoption and Freeing for Adoption Proceedings

Adoption law and practice is in a repositioning phase, awaiting the new legislation required to take account of significant changes — demographic, social and familial — which have taken place in the two decades which have elapsed since the passing of the Adoption Act 1976. The Children Act 1989 made a number of amendments to the existing adoption legislation (see Chapter 1 above), but there is a need for substantial overhaul and review of present day law and practice, in relation to the adoption of children in the 1990s and beyond.

The Review of Adoption Law[1]

Background

An inter-departmental working group was set up in July 1989 to review the law relating to adoption. Four consultation papers were issued by the Department of Health:

- The Nature and Effect of Adoption (September 1990);
- Agreement and Freeing (September 1991);
- The Adoption Process (November 1991); and

---

1 *Review of Adoption Law* (October 1992), Report to Ministers of an Interdepartmental Working Group — A Consultation Document, Department of Health and Welsh Office.

● Inter-Country Adoption (January 1992).

The consultation papers were accompanied by three background papers on:

● International Perspectives of Adoption (Ellen France, Background Paper No. 1);
● Review of Research Relating to Adoption (June Thoburn, Background Paper No. 2); and
● Inter-Country Adoption (A Review of Research) (June Thoburn and Marilyn Charles, Background Paper No. 3).

Wide consultation followed the publication of the seven papers, and led in October 1992 to the publication by the Department of Health of a consultative document reviewing Adoption Law. The Department of Health also commissioned a review of research (published in the Review of Adoption Law as Appendix C) and drew on the final report of the Pathways to Adoption Research Project, which had been commissioned by the Department of Health.[2]

The Adoption Act 1976, as amended by the Children Act 1989, provides the legislative framework for adoption. The 1976 Act incorporated the recommendations of the Houghton Committee, who undertook a review of adoption law between 1969 and 1971 and recommended the facilitation of adoption for children 'drifting' in public care.[3] The Adoption Act 1976 restricted the power to arrange adoptions to local authorities and approved adoption societies, placed local authorities under a duty to provide a comprehensive adoption service, and gave adults who had been adopted the right to obtain a copy of their original entry in the Register of Births at the age of 18. Key provisions of the Children Act 1975 also had a profound influence on subsequent child care practice in relation to adoption and fostering, as it acknowledged a potential conflict of interest between parent and child, thereby diminishing the importance of the blood tie philosophy. It established a legal mechanism by which parents could lose their parental rights through passage of time (three years), rather than as a function of any parental offence. The recommendations of the Houghton Committee had far more impact on subsequent legislation than the recommendations of the Finer Committee which, having looked at the needs of one parent families, recommended the establishment of a specialist, preventive service to support those facing family breakdown.[4]

The Children Act 1975 and the Adoption Act 1976 together provided a powerful springboard for major changes to take place, both in facilitating the adoption of older children in care and in the recruitment of adoptive parents, willing to adopt both older children and those who had special needs.[5]

---

2 Lowe and Murch, *Final Report of the Pathways to Adoption Research Project* (1992), University of Bristol Centre for Socio-Legal Studies.
3 The Houghton Report on the Adoption of Children, Cmnd. 5107 (1972).
4 Finer Report, Report of the Committee on One-Parent families, Cmnd. 5629 (1974).
5 See the work of Parents and Children in finding adoptive parents for hard to place children in *Finding Families for 'Hard to Place' Children: Evidence from Research* (Wedge and Thoburn, ed. 1986).

By 1990, however, there had been major social changes affecting adoption. In 1977, the year after the Adoption Act 1976, nearly 13,000 children were adopted, of which about 3,000 (23 per cent) were babies of less than one year old. Nearly 10,000 (74 per cent) were aged between one and 14 and just under 500 (3 per cent) were aged 15 to 17.

By 1991 the total number of adoptions had nearly halved to just over 7,000. The most significant decline was in the number of healthy babies available for adoption, with the numbers falling from nearly 3,000 to under 900 (from 23 per cent to 12 per cent of the total). The number of children adopted in the higher age groups had fallen to under 6,300 but the proportion to the whole had increased from 77 per cent to 88 per cent.[6] However, the decline in the number of children available for adoption[7] has not been matched by the decline in the number of couples wishing to adopt.

The most significant factor which emerges from these figures is that the availability of children, particularly babies of under one year old, has declined significantly in relation to the demand to adopt children by prospective adoptive parents. Now, more than ever, it is important to keep firmly in mind that adoption is a service for children, not for adopters.

The Review's main recommendations

The welfare of the child. Agencies and courts should give paramount consideration to the child's welfare, in any decision relating to adoption, except where determining whether to make an Adoption Order without the agreement of a parent. The welfare test should refer not only to the welfare of the children throughout childhood, but to his or her welfare in adult life as well.

Inter vivos guardianship. The Review introduces the concept of an *inter vivios* guardian, to replace of custodianship. Where a court makes a Residence Order in favour of a person other than a parent or step-parent, and considers that that person will be responsible for the child's upbringing until he or she grows up, the court should have a further power to appoint, where appropriate, that person as the child's *inter vivos* guardian, who should have parental responsibility until the child reaches the age of 18. The *inter vivos* guardian would have all the attendant rights, duties and powers of a guardian under S.5 of the Children Act 1989, except for the right to agree or withhold agreement to the adoption of the child and the power to change the child's surname (except with the leave of the court). *Inter vivos* guardianship must be sufficiently attractive to rival the attractions of an Adoption Order, which entails a permanent transfer of parental responsibility. The fact that the guardianship ceases at 18 may be seen as a relative disadvantage, as it was in custodianship.

The representation of children in adoption proceedings. Children aged 12 or over should automatically have party status. In cases concerning children

---

6 *Adoption: The Future* (November 1993), Department of Health, HMSO, paras. 3.2 and 3.3.
7 *Ibid.*, para. 3.10.

under 12, all courts should have the power to add the child as a party, in appropriate cases. This is a considerable improvement on the present situation, in which children are only parties to the proceedings in the High Court. On the other hand, the proposed legislation falls short of granting the full party status, and an entitlement to legal representation for all children, of any age, that is required to comply with Article 12 of the UN Convention on the Rights of the Child (see Chapter 2 above). A guardian *ad litem* should be appointed for the child in every adoption application, not just those which are contested.

Abolition of freeing for adoption and introduction of a Placement Order. Where an agency is planning to place a child with prospective adopters, a Placement Order must be granted by the court, before a placement is allowed to proceed. A Placement Order must not be made, without a prior hearing, if the adoption (or any related matter such as the level of contact) is contested by the child, anyone with parental responsibility, or any member of the child's family. A Placement Order would have the effect of giving parental responsibility to the prospective adoptive parents. It would not take away any other person's parental responsibility.

Where a pregnant woman, or the mother of a child under six weeks of age, requests an adoption agency to place her child for adoption, it should be lawful for the agency to place the child, without first obtaining a Placement Order. The proposal to introduce Placement Orders to replace freeing provoked considerable debate and led to a further consultation document.[8] The new proposals sought to ensure appropriately early court consideration of the adoption plan and the introduction of children to their prospective new parents, while also seeking to reduce the *fait accompli* aspects of adoption commented on by many practitioners.[9] It would also eliminate the possibility of unnecessary delay. The relative merits of the Placement Order continued to be widely debated, and led in April 1994 to the publication of a consultative document, 'Placement for Adoption'.

The wishes and feelings of the child. Agencies should have a duty to ascertain the wishes and feelings of the child, his or her parents, any person who is not a parent but who has parental responsibility for the child, and any other person whose wishes and feelings the agency considers to be relevant; courts should give due consideration to such wishes and feelings. Children should have access to a complaints procedure. The child's race, culture and religion should be taken into consideration in decision making.

The right of the child to know their origins. The legislative framework should underline an adopted child's right to know that he or she is adopted. In addition, the agency or guardian *ad litem* should have a duty to compile a package of information for the child about his or her background. (Contrast

---

8 Placement for Adoption: A Consultation Document (April 1994), Department of Health Welsh Office and Lord Chancellor's Department.
9 See Comments of guardians *ad litem* on adoption proceedings in the *Practice in Progress* Regional Reports (1993), GAL/RO Regional Conferences, IRCHIN with the Department of Health.

this with the position of the child born as a result of surrogacy arrangements, see Chapter 8 below.)

New adoption legislation should incorporate key provisions of the Children Act 1989, for example:

- in making any decisions relating to adoption, agencies and courts should have regard to the principle that delay is likely to be prejudicial to the welfare of the child;
- adoption legislation should contain a list of key factors, similar to S.1(3) of the Children Act 1989 (the welfare checklist), which the court must consider when deciding whether to make a Placement or Adoption Order, including giving a view on the impact of adoption throughout the adopted person's life, and not just their childhood;
- the court should not make an Adoption Order unless it considers that to do so would be better for the child than to make no Order at all.[10]

The right of the child to agree to the adoption. The court should not be allowed to grant an Adoption Order in respect of a child of 12 years or over, unless the child has agreed to the adoption by particular adopters or the court has dispensed with the child's agreement. This has proved a controversial recommendation, over which there is considerable difference of opinion within the child care world. Some take the view that the measure imposes too much responsibility on a child, of any age, while others feel that all children who are 'Gillick competent' should have the right to be consulted and to agree to the adoption, regardless of their age. The court should be allowed to dispense with the child's agreement only if the child is incapable of giving agreement. The agreement would be to a particular placement, whereas the parent's agreement is to adoption in general.

Grounds for dispensing with parental agreement. Of the existing grounds for dispensing with parental agreement, only the first (that the parent cannot be found or is incapable of giving agreement) should be retained. The remaining grounds should be replaced by a single test which should apply in all situations where a parent, who is capable of giving agreement, can be found, and is withholding agreement. This test should require the court to be satisfied that the advantages to the child of becoming part of a new family are so significantly greater than the advantages to the child of any alternative option, as to justify overriding the wishes of the parent or guardian. The only other ground for dispensing with parental agreement should be that a parent, who agreed to adoption when a Placement Order was made, has withdrawn that agreement, and the court considers that there have not been any significant changes since then, such as would justify a different outcome. A parent should have the option of agreeing to a particular adoption placement, but should be able to review any subsequent adoption placement which the agency may make.

Step-parent adoption. There should be a new type of Adoption Order, available only to step-parents, which does not make the birth parent an

---

10 S.1(5), the principle of minimum intervention or positive advantage.

adoptive parent, but in all other respects resembles a normal Adoption Order. There should be provision for a step-parent Adoption Order to be undone, where the marriage is ended by divorce or death. A step-parent should be able to acquire parental responsibility if he and the child's parents make an agreement to share the parental responsibility. The desire for the parent and the step-parent to have Adoption Orders made in their favour is understandable, but it must be balanced against the increased incidence of divorce in second and subsequent marriage and the right of the child to maintain his right to a primary identity. There should be a mandatory period of 12 months between the application and the making of an Adoption Order in all non-agency applications.[11]

Other non-agency applications. A person with whom a child is living should be allowed to apply for an Adoption Order at any time, with the agreement of those with parental responsibility. Where the necessary agreement has not been given, a person should be allowed to apply if the child has lived with him or her for a cumulative period of three years (within the previous five years).

Complaints procedures. Adoption legislation should make clear that users of local authority adoption services have access to complaints procedures under the Children Act 1989. Approved adoption societies should have a duty to operate similar complaints procedures.

Inter-country adoption. The Review makes a number of recommendations in relation to inter-country adoption, aimed at streamlining and regularising the process. Inter-country adoption procedures should be restricted to non-relatives. Children should be permitted to join relatives in the United Kingdom, where the child cannot be cared for in any suitable manner in the country of origin, and admission to the United Kingdom to join a relative would be the best way of safeguarding the child's welfare. The present discretionary arrangements for the admission of children into the United Kingdom for adoption should be brought within the immigration rules. Criteria relating to adoption requirements should be dealt with separately in adoption legislation, so that entry clearance is no longer the vehicle for the whole process. Children should be admitted to the United Kingdom for adoption only where authorisation has been granted by the responsible authority in the United Kingdom that the adoption should proceed, subject to immigration requirements being met. The recommendations seek to facilitate inter-country adoption, where this is in the interests of the particular child, but also seek to protect the welfare of the child and to eliminate corrupt and criminal practices. Local authorities should have a duty to provide services, in connection with inter-country adoption, or arrange for them to be provided by appropriate adoption societies. Where a child is brought into the United Kingdom without authorisation (leading to the possibility of criminal proceedings) and temporary admission has been granted, local authorities should have the power to apply to a court for an Order authorising them to remove the child from the prospective adopters, so that an investigation can be made into the child's welfare. These measures are designed to separate the

---

11 *Adoption: The Future, op. cit.,* para. 3.9.

issues of immigration from those of adoption and avoid *fait accompli* situations, in which the court's only realistic alternative is to ratify an existing situation.[12]

Recommendations regarding the role of the guardian ad litem and reporting officer

Interestingly, there is no mention of the role of the reporting officer in any of the consultative documents or in the Review. The Review makes the surprising proposal (now apparently dropped) that guardians *ad litem* would be well placed to take over responsibility for the investigation of non-agency applications, on the basis that 'local authorities are not generally able to accord high priority to these duties and do not always allocate them to specialist adoption workers.'

The Review recommends that guardians *ad litem* should be appointed in every case, not just in those that are contested. There may be a clue, here, about the future role of the reporting officer. If guardians are to be appointed automatically in non-contested adoptions, then presumably they may well also witness agreements, thus removing the need for a separate role of reporting officer.

The Review envisages that a guardian *ad litem*, appointed at the time of the application for a Placement Order, would retain involvement with the case throughout the placement and assume three main areas of responsibility:

● representing the child's interests;
● informing the court, if a parent decides to withdraw agreement or the adoption plan is contested in some other way;
● monitoring the progress of the application and advising the court on the appropriate timing of proceedings.

These recommendations substantially increase the guardian's responsibilities to the period before, as well as during, the adoption proceedings. They also introduce a case management aspect of the role which corresponds to similar duties under the Children Act 1989.[13] The guardian may be involved with the child for a considerable period of time and the recommendations were criticised for confusing the role of the guardian, who has an investigative rather than an ongoing social work role, with that of local authority social worker. It would constitute a major departure from the role as presently understood to transfer the task of preparing reports which are required under Schedule 2 of the Adoption Rules 1984 in non-agency cases to guardians *ad litem*, although this would put them in a very advantageous position, firstly, to hurry up the process, and secondly, to comment on the recommendation. Some sources have doubted the availability and expertise of guardians to

---

12 Thoburn and Charles, 'Inter-Country Adoption (A Review of Research)', Interdepartmental Review of Adoption Law, Background Paper No.3.
13 S.41(10).

perform these roles.[14] Both the National Association of Guardians *ad Litem* and Reporting Officers (NAGALRO) and Independent Representation for Children in Need (IRCHIN) expressed major concerns relating to the proposed changes to the role of the guardian *ad litem* in step-parent adoptions. In particular, they felt those guardians would no longer be in an position to effect an objective appraisal and provide a second opinion. Additionally, it would be very difficult for a guardian to be seen as the advocate and voice for the child, in a situation where he or she was working closely with the parents. The proposals could be seen to compromise the perceived independence of guardians, who are anxious to retain as much distance from the local authority as possible.[15]

The idea that guardians will undertake direct work with children in step-parent adoptions[16] 'by compiling a package of information' would inevitably change the guardian's existing role to one in which he or she takes on the function of an adoption social worker. There would also be considerable resource implications. This task could take several weeks or months to complete, and, as step-parent and relative adoptions now account for about half the total adoptions, guardians *ad litem* would be responsible for half the total adoption work.

While acknowledging that it would be inappropriate for guardians *ad litem* to have responsibility for the direct counselling of applicants and other parents, the Review suggests that guardians should inform the local authority that a non-agency application has been made. The local authority would have no substantial duties in respect of that child, other than to provide advice and counselling on the request of any of the parties concerned. This would mean, effectively, that the guardian would be the only social worker having a direct input into the procedure, yet they would be preparing the Schedule 2 report, advising the local authority of the application, preparing the subsequent report for the court, and then commenting on the placement in relation to the best interests of the child.

The proposals in the Review would constitute a considerable departure from the role of the guardian as child's representative, and critical appraiser of local authority policies. Guardians *ad litem* are there to form an independent view of local authority policy and practice, in relation to individual children. They are not there to form a part of it. In particular, they are not there to bolster up and make good local authority services. The proposal attracted considerable criticism[17] on the basis that the new duty, as envisaged, would constitute a distortion of the guardian's role and, in carrying out what was essentially a local authority responsibility, direct accountability to the courts may well become skewed. The proposal might be convenient , but it would be contrary to the philosophy and primary function of the guardian *ad litem* service. In addition, in terms of resources, the role of the guardian *ad litem* has already been considerably extended under the Children Act 1989, and to impose

---

14 *The BAAF (British Agencies for Adoption and Fostering) Response to the Review of Adoption Law* (1993), para. 38.2.
15 *Ibid.*
16 *Ibid.*, para. 27.5.
17 NAGALRO, BAAF, IRCHIN and others.

additional duties of this nature would constitute a additional burden on what is already a scant resource.

Adoption: The Future — the White Paper

Considering the extent of consultation, and the depth of the examination of the issues involved in the consultation documents and the Review, the resulting White Paper *Adoption: The Future*[18] presented to parliament in November 1993 was disappointing in its brevity and generalisation. Some of the Review's recommendations, including those concerning the role of the guardian *ad litem*, were conspicuous by their absence. There was no timetable for implementation, and it begs many issues. In particular, it appears to view adoption primarily from the point of view of the prospective adopters rather than the child. However, the presentation was generally welcomed as a statement of intent to reform adoption law.

The role of the guardian ad litem and reporting officer

Comment on the role of the guardian *ad litem* in the White Paper was restricted to the following: 'a guardian ad litem (GAL) will be appointed in many adoption cases, to watch over the interests of the child. Their function will be modelled on their role in care cases under the Children Act.'[19] The indicators are that the Review proposals in relation to the role of the guardian will not be carried forward into new legislation. Significantly, the role of the reporting officer is not mentioned at all.

Children's rights in adoption proceedings

The White Paper endorses the recommendations in the Review and states its intention that all children aged 12 or more must agree before an Adoption Order is made, unless they are incapable of giving such agreement; and that they and other children in suitable cases should be eligible for party status in adoption proceedings. They would participate in their own adoption cases and be able, directly, to inform the court of their own preferences. They would have the right to apply for legal representation.

A right to full party status, therefore, is restricted to young people of 12 or over. Arguably, it is children under 12 who are the most in need of the double security of a solicitor of their own and a guardian *ad litem*, as they are the group who are the most vulnerable and whose future will be most affected by adoption. They will also, of course, be much the largest group of children coming before the courts, as the majority of adoption applications are made in respect of children under the age of 10.

---

18 *Adoption: The Future* (November 1993) Department of Health, HMSO.
19 *Ibid.*, para. 4.4.

Summary of the main provisions of the White Paper

The White Paper appears to hedge its bets on a number of issues, in particular the pros and cons of having a Placement Order, open adoption and the complexities of inter-country adoption. In all decisions there is a need for 'skilled, professional assessment' alongside 'common-sense human judgements'. There is, however, a clear statement of intent that whatever changes are made will create no extra costs.

Specific commitments are given to:

- a new and simpler alternative to step-parent adoption, giving rise to a new parental responsibility agreement to be entered into by the birth parent with her new spouse;[20]
- for those who will prefer adoption, the form of the Adoption Order is being altered, so that the birth parent is not obliged to adopt her own child;[21]
- there will be a new Guardianship Order, intended to allow relatives or others caring for a child, including long term foster parents, to obtain legal recognition of their role and, without going so far as adoption, to put their relationship with the child onto a clearer and permanent basis.[22]

No application could be made to dissolve the Order, except with the prior leave of the court. It will, however, still end at 18. This new foster plus status will be known as *inter vivos* guardianship.[23] Both of these new Orders are intended as alternatives to adoption.

Adoption must be likely to offer a significantly better advantage to the child than any other option. If the court is satisfied that this is indeed the case, it will be able to override a refusal of consent by the birth parents.[24]

Contact and open adoption

The White Paper recognises the increasing tendency to maintain some contact between an adopted child and his birth family, particularly in the case of older children. However, 'the government considers that once an adoption order is made, the most important objective is to support the new family relationship'.[25]

Where the birth parents wish to maintain direct contact, provided there is free consent by the child and the new family, this should generally be allowed. If the adoptive parents oppose the prospect, their views should have the greater weight, though where older children are adopted out of families with whom they have formed a bond, the issues need particularly careful judgment and the child's view will be correspondingly significant.[26] Again, the White Paper

---

20 *Ibid.*, para. 5.21.
21 *Ibid.*, para. 5.22.
22 *Ibid.*, para. 5.23.
23 *Ibid.*, para. 5.24.
24 *Ibid.*, para. 5.5.
25 *Ibid.*, para. 4.14.
26 *Ibid.*, para. 4.15.

appears to be hedging its bets on the issue of continuing contact between a child and its natural parents.

The White Paper stresses that each case must be considered on its merits and there can be no central blueprint. By regulation, the government intends to ensure that the courts and the adoption agencies will assess the most suitable arrangements for contact between the birth family and the child after his adoption.[27]

There is a commitment to the right of children to know their origins and to obtain information about their birth parents, provided those birth parents themselves agree.[28] An open approach to adoption is sensible and humane, provided always that the prospects for a secure and successful adoption are not jeopardised.[29] This rather suggests that adoptive parents will have a great deal of power in relation to deciding whether or not contact will continue. If a children's rights approach to this matter had been adopted, for example, endorsement of the rights of children to their origins and to maintain links with their past, if they so wished, might have constituted a more positive approach to the future development of contact arrangements.

The adoption contact register

The White Paper expands the use of the adoption contact register, by providing for the possibility that birth parents and other relatives might wish to record a desire not to be contacted.[30] The White Paper is silent on whether the charge for so recording will also be £35 in line with the fee charged to those who wish to lodge information on the register. The fee may, in part, account for the contact register's relative under-use. Adopted children will continue to have a right to apply to the Registrar General, once they reach the age of 18, to seek the information they need in order to obtain a copy of their Birth Certificate. Full Birth Certificates normally contain the names and addresses of parents at the time of the birth.[31]

The role of adoption agencies

The White Paper envisages three main functions concerning contact:

● making arrangements to keep open the possibility of voluntary contact between adopted children and their birth family, which many already regard as good practice;
● consulting and counselling birth parents in cases where there is no contact about whether they wish to be kept informed about their child's progress;
● counselling prospective adoptive parents about the advisability, or otherwise, of contact between the child and the birth parents and ascertaining their wishes, and those of the child, in the matter.

27 *Ibid.*, para. 4.16.
28 *Ibid.*, para. 4.18.
29 *Ibid.*, para. 4.20.
30 *Ibid.*, para. 4.22.
31 *Ibid.*, para. 4.24.

Adoption panels

The Adoption Agencies Regulations 1983 provide the current framework for the establishment of adoption panels, the appointment of their members and the scope of their responsibilities. The White Paper commits itself to issuing consultation on new regulations concerning the functions and membership of the adoption panels, which are seen as central in implementing policies and practice in relation to adoption and fostering. Adoption panels should help authorities and agencies to apply common sense, as well as human and professional values.[32]

The White Paper envisaged more independent membership of the panels, in order to extend the range of interests from which they operate.[33] The future of Adoption Panels was the subject of a consultation paper circulated by the Department of Health in June 1994.

Complaints procedures

The government intends to introduce a new complaints procedure, both for authorities and voluntary agencies, modelled on the procedures introduced in the Children Act 1989, S.26. The White Paper says that there should be at least one person amongst those *investigating* the complaint wholly independent of the authority, who will the right to express an opinion on the report. If it is indeed the case that future legislation introduces an independent person to investigate complaints, rather than simply being involved in their consideration, this will be a considerable improvement on the procedures available under the Children Act 1989. However, this may well be a drafting error in the statement, rather than a statement of commitment.

Inter-country adoption and the Hague Convention (1993)

Before 1990 there were fewer than 50 adoptions a year of children from overseas in England and Wales. In recent years, however, there has been a considerable increase in the numbers of couples in the United Kingdom wishing to adopt children from countries whose Adoption Orders the UK does not recognise. This has occurred for two reasons. *Firstly*, because of the lack of availability for adoption of babies and very young children in this country and *secondly*, because of the increased interest in, and compassion for, children who have been displaced and disadvantaged by political upheaval, particularly in central and south American and eastern European countries.

In general the government wishes to see the same principles and safeguards and, so far as is realistic, the same clarity of procedure introduced for overseas adoption as for domestic adoption. Ideally there should be an international mutual recognition of Adoption Orders. To this end the UK government has ratified the Hague Convention on private international law on inter-country adoption. The UK became a signatory to the Convention on January 20,

---

32 *Ibid.*, para. 4.44.
33 *Ibid.*, para. 4.45.

1994. The Convention is consistent with the UN Convention on the Rights of the Child and the 1986 UN Declaration of Social and Legal Principles relating to the protection and welfare of children with special reference to foster placement and adoption nationally and internationally. The principles underlying the Hague Convention, as set out in the White Paper on Adoption include:

- inter-country adoption should only take place after the best interests of the child have been properly assessed and in circumstances which protect his fundamental rights;
- birth parents or others responsible for consenting to adoptions should understand what they are consenting to, and its implications. They should be objectively counselled and should not be offered financial or other inducements;
- agencies acting in inter-country adoptions should be suitably staffed and supervised;
- no-one should derive improper financial gain from adoption;
- adoptive parents should be carefully and objectively assessed for their suitability.

Adoptions carried out between ratifying states, according to the Articles of the Hague Convention, will be known as 'Convention Adoptions' and in each state there will be established a 'central authority' and 'accredited bodies'. The central authority should normally be part of this country's central government and would, for example, be responsible for transmitting information required to the comparable body of another convention country. This role should be discharged by the Department of Health in England and the Welsh Office in Wales.[34]

Future adoption legislation

There is as yet no timetable for the introduction of a Bill for reform of adoption legislation. However, the considerable detail about the intention of the government in respect of adoption law and practice, particularly with regard to its intent to introduce provisions which mirror many of those in the Children Act 1989, mean that practitioners will be looking to the Review and the White Paper to inform their decision making, even before the introduction of the Bill.

The Role of the Guardian *ad Litem* in Adoption and Freeing Proceedings

The statutory framework

The role of the guardian *ad litem* in adoption and freeing proceedings is covered by the:

---

34 *Ibid.*, paras. 6.18 to 6.22.

- Adoption Act 1976 (as amended by Schedule 10 and Schedule 15 of the Children Act 1989); S65 of the Adoption Act 1976 deals with guardians *ad litem* and reporting officers;
- the Adoption Agency Regulations 1983 (S.I. 1983 No. 1964);
- The Adoption Rules 1984 (S.I. 1984 No. 265) as amended by the Adoption (Amendment) Rules 1991 (S.I. 1991 No.1880);
- Adoption Court Rules — Local Authority Circular (LAC) (84) 10;
- the Magistrates' Courts (Adoption) Rules 1984 (S.I. 1984 No.611);
- Access by Adopted People to Birth Records, Children Act 1975, implementation of S.26 Circular LAC (76)21;
- Freeing and Protecting Children Circular LAC(84)2;
- The Children Act 1989 Guidance and Regulations Vol. 9, 'Adoption Issues', Vol. 3, 'Family Placements' and Vol.4, 'Residential Care';
- Arrangements for Placement of Children (General) Regulations 1991 (S.I. 1991 No.890)
- Adopted Persons (Contact Register) (Fees) Rules 1991 (S.I. 1991 No. 952);
- Adoption Allowance Regulations 1991 (S.I. 1991 No. 2030).

Legal representation of the child in adoption proceedings

Unlike proceedings under the Children Act 1989, a child is not a party in adoption and freeing proceedings, except in the High Court, where he is automatically a party. This means that guardians *ad litem*, except when they are appearing in the High Court, do not normally have the benefit of legal advice, nor do the children that they represent. The lack of direct legal representation means that children do not have a right of appeal if the case is decided in a way which is contrary to recommendations which the guardian believes are in the child's best interests.

Under the Adoption Rules 1984, the guardian may theoretically apply to be joined as a respondent to the proceedings under the court's general power to direct that persons may be made respondents.[35] The guardian will have to ask the judge or Justices' Clerk to do this, and the court will have to be satisfied that this is an appropriate course of action. Theoretically, the move entitles the guardian to legal aid. In practice, the Legal Aid Board may still refuse payment. The guardian should ensure that he is not personally assessed on his own income. This can be avoided if, in making the application, the guardian makes it clear that he is applying for legal aid for the child in a representative, rather than a personal capacity. Regulation 6 of the Civil Legal Aid (Assessment of Resources) Regulations 1989[36] covers this situation:

> where an application for legal aid is made by a person only in a representative, fiduciary or official capacity, the assessment officer shall, in computing the income and capital of that person and the amount of any contribution to be made, disregard the personal resources of that person.

---

35 Rr. 4(3) and 15(3).
36 S.I. 1989 No.338.

Some administering authorities have been willing to pay for legal representation for the child. However, this is a matter to be negotiated by the guardian on behalf of the child and it is a far from satisfactory situation. Some administering authorities have been less than enthusiastic about financing a legal representative to oppose their own case. In effect one party to the proceedings is dependent on the goodwill of another (opposing) party to the proceedings for the adequate legal representation which should be a matter of right, not gift. The White Paper proposals provide for full party status for children over 12. Although this falls far short of what is required, it is still a small step in the right direction. Meanwhile, guardians continue to have a significant responsibility for ensuring that children have adequate legal representation in adoption proceedings.

The child's welfare

Guardians *ad litem* in adoption and freeing for adoption proceedings are bound by S.6 of the Adoption Act 1976:

> in reaching any decision relating to the adoption of a child a court or adoption agency shall have regard to all the circumstances, first consideration being given to the need to safeguard and promote the welfare of the child throughout his childhood; and shall, so far as practicable, ascertain the wishes and feelings of the child regarding the decision and give due consideration to them, having regard to his age and understanding.

The statutory duty of welfare in adoption proceedings gives first, but not paramount, consideration to the welfare of the child. However, if the White Paper proposals are followed through into new legislation, adoption would be brought into line with other family proceedings, in giving paramount consideration to the child's welfare.[37]

The implication of the present law is that the welfare of the child must be the first consideration, outweigh any one other factor, but not all factors. The judgment of Hollings J in *Re H*. (Adoption: Non-Patrial), although dealing with an unusual immigration situation, is relevant:

> if the court considers, on the evidence and information it has before it, that the true motive of the application is based upon the desire to achieve nationality and the right of abode rather than the general welfare of the minor, then an adoption order should not be made. If, on the other hand, part of the motive— or it may be at least as much— is to achieve the real emotional or psychological, social and legal benefits of adoption, then an adoption order may be proper, notwithstanding that this has the effect of overriding an immigration decision or even an immigration rule.[38]

The court must take account of the following factors in determining the welfare of children:

---

37 The duty to give paramount consideration to the welfare of the child does not apply to children born as a result of surrogacy arrangements, although applications under S.30 of the Human Fertilisation and Embryology Act 1990 are designated family proceedings. See further Chapter 8 below.
38 [1982] 3 All E.R. 84, C.A. See also *Re W. (A Minor)* (Adoption: Non-Patrial) [1986] Fam. 54 [1985] 3 All E.R. 449, C.A.

- *The wishes and feelings of the child*, having regard to his age and understanding (presumably both under and over the age of 12).[39]
- *The child's future*, as well as present, welfare.[40] This would include consideration of the benefits of the proposed adoption.
- *The views of the child about prospective placement*. Authorities are required, in making any decision, to have regard to the wishes and feelings of the child, subject to the child's understanding. The more mature the child, the more fully he will be able to enter into discussion about plans and proposals. Children need information and explanations, so that they are in a position to develop views and make choices.[41]

The court should take account of:

- *Race and culture*. In making placement decisions in respect of any child, a local authority has a duty to take account of the child's racial origin and cultural and linguistic background.[42] However, the need for a same race placement should not be an overriding factor in decision making,[43] and the court could decide that the advantages of moving a mixed race child outweigh the advantages of maintaining the status quo.[44]
- *Religion*. 'An adoption agency shall, in placing a child for adoption, have regard (so far as is practicable) to any wishes of a child's parents and guardians as to the religious upbringing of the child.'[45] In placing children for adoption, local authorities have a duty to consider their religious persuasion.[46]
- *Foster parents*. Foster parents can often become adoptive parents, so it is important to bear in mind that, before placing a child with foster parents, local authorities are required to satisfy themselves that the child's needs, arising from his racial origin and cultural and linguistic background, will be met so far as is practicable, placing a child, where possible, with a foster parent of the same religious persuasion, or who will undertake to bring the child up in that religious persuasion.[47]

The appointment of the guardian ad litem

The appointment and duties of the guardian *ad litem* in adoption and freeing for adoption are dealt with respectively in rules 18 and 6 of the Adoption Rules 1984.

---

39 S.6 Adoption Act 1976. See *Re G.* (T.J.)(*An Infant*) [1963] 1 All E.R. 20, C.A. and *Re B. (A Minor)* (Adoption) [1988] 18 Fam. Law 172.
40 S.6 Adoption Act 1976. See *Re D. (A Minor)* (Adoption Order: Validity) [1991] Fam. 137, C.A.
41 S.6 Adoption Act 1976. Children Act 1989 Guidance and Regulations Vol. 3, para. 4.5.
42 Children Act 1989, S.22(5)(c).
43 See *Re J.K.* (Adoption: Trans-Racial Placement) [1991] 2 F.L.R. 340.
44 See *Re P. (A Minor)* (Adoption) [1990] 1 F.L.R. 96.
45 S.7 Adoption Act 1976. See also the Department of Health's Guidance on Issues of Race and Culture in the Family Placement of Children (1990).
46 Children Act 1989, S.22(5)(c).
47 Arrangements for Placement of Children (General) Regulations 1991 (S.I. 1991 No. 890) and The Children Act 1989 Guidance and Regulations Vol. 3, paras. 4.3 and 4.4.

As soon as practicable after the originating process has been filed, or after receipt of the statement of facts supplied under Rule 19, if the child is not free for adoption and it appears that a parent or guardian of the child is unwilling to agree to the making of the adoption order, the proper officer shall appoint a guardian ad litem of the child and shall send him a copy of the originating process, together with any documents attached thereto.[48]

The conditions for appointing the guardian *ad litem*, therefore, are that the child is not free for adoption and that the adoption is contested.

The guardian *ad litem* may be a social worker, a probation officer, or in the High Court, the Official Solicitor.[49] Appointments to panels are dealt with in the Guardians *ad Litem* and Reporting Officers (Panels) Regulations 1991.[50] Probation Officers are limited to acting as guardians *ad litem* in adoption, which means that, in practice, they have had a progressively smaller involvement with the service since 1984.

Where there are special circumstances, and it appears to the court that the welfare of the child requires it, the court may, at any time, appoint a guardian *ad litem* of the child, and where such an appointment is made, the court shall indicate any particular matters which it requires the guardian *ad litem* to investigate. For example, see Adoption Rule 47(8) which deals with the procedure to be adopted in the event of a child's removal from placement. The proper officer shall send the guardian *ad litem* a copy of the originating process, together with any documents attached thereto.[51]

The same person may be appointed as reporting officer under Rule 17(1), in respect of a parent or guardian who appears to be willing to agree to the making of the Adoption Order, and as the guardian *ad litem* of the child under the same rule, whether or not appointed as reporting officer. The guardian *ad litem* may be appointed as reporting officer in respect of a parent or guardian of the child who originally was unwilling to agree to the making of an Adoption Order, but who has later signified his or her agreement.[52]

There is provision in the rules for guardians *ad litem* and reporting officers to be interchangeable. For example, a reporting officer, who finds that a parent is not willing to agree to the adoption of a child, may report back to the court and be reappointed as a guardian *ad litem*, to carry out a full investigation. This may happen at any time during the proceedings. It is most important, therefore, that reporting officers are not seen as people who need lesser qualifications than guardians *ad litem*, as the rules clearly require that reporting officers should have the necessary qualifications to carry out the whole range of guardian *ad litem* duties. In the early days, following the establishment of panels in 1984, some local authorities were appointing level 2 social workers as reporting officers and level 3 social workers as guardians *ad litem*. This does not seem to be a prevalent practice now. It is certainly not desirable, as the court rules clearly envisage that the roles will be interchangeable.

---

48 Rule 18 of the Magistrates Courts' (Adoption) Rules 1984 as amended by the Family Proceedings Courts (Matrimonial Proceedings etc.) Rules 1991.
49 R. 18(4).
50 S.I. 1991 No. 2051.
51 Rr. 18(2) and 6(2).
52 Rr. 18(3) and 6(3).

Guardians *ad litem* must be appointed from panels established by regulations under S.41(7) of the Children Act 1989.[53] They must be independent and shall not be a member, or employee, of any respondent body (except where a local authority is made a respondent only under Rule 15(2)(d)) nor have been involved in the making of any arrangements for the adoption of the child.[54]

The duties of the guardian ad litem in adoption and freeing for adoption

The prime responsibility of the guardian *ad litem* is to safeguard the interests of the child before the court. In order to do this, the guardian shall, as far as is reasonably practicable:

(a) investigate:
   (i) so far as he considers necessary the matters alleged in the originating process, the report supplied by the applicant, and, where appropriate, the statement of facts supplied under rule 7; and
   (ii) any other matters which appear to him to be relevant to the making of an Adoption Order or the making of an Order freeing the child for adoption.
(b) advise whether in his opinion the child should be present at the hearing of the process; and
(c) perform such other duties as appear to him to be necessary or as the court may direct.[55]

Having completed his investigations, the guardian *ad litem* shall make a report in writing to the court drawing attention to any matters which, in his opinion, may be of assistance to the court in considering the application.[56] Guardians may, at any time, make an interim report to the court and thereby seek directions if it appears necessary.[57] Guardians *ad litem* must attend any hearing of the application unless the court otherwise orders.[58] The guardian's report is confidential,[59] subject to the right of a party to inspect that part of the guardian's report that refers to them.[60]

Local authority circular LAC(84)10 amplifies the Adoption Court rules in relation to the appointment and duties of the guardian *ad litem*. The court will appoint a guardian *ad litem* for the child in every contested case, but there may exceptionally be special circumstances in uncontested cases where the child's welfare makes a guardian *ad litem* necessary. If the court thinks this is so, a guardian *ad litem* will be appointed under rule 6(2) and the court will indicate

---

53 Rr. 18(5) and 6(5).
54 Rr. 18(5) and 6(5).
55 Rr. 18(6) and 6(6).
56 Rr. 18(7) and 6(7).
57 Rr. 18(8) and 6(8).
58 Rr. 18(7) and 6(10).
59 Rr. 18(7) and 6(11).
60 R. 53(2).

what particular matters it wants him to investigate. He must be sent copies of the same documents as the guardian *ad litem* appointed in a contested case, except that there will be no statement of facts.[61] Applications by an agency to free a child for adoption, or by applicants to adopt a child, indicate whether or not each parent is willing to agree and the guardian *ad litem* will normally be appointed as soon as the application has been lodged. If, however, the application does not enclose the statement of facts supporting the agency's request for the parent's agreement to be dispensed with (perhaps because the parent was originally willing to agree but changes his mind after the application is lodged) then the proper officer of the court will appoint the guardian *ad litem* once the statement of facts is received. When a guardian *ad litem* is appointed he must be sent a copy of the adoption agency's application form, of the required enclosures (such as the child's birth certificate), of the statement of facts and of the agency's background report for the court.[62]

Guardians should be particularly aware of conflict of interest, even if the person appointed has not been connected with the adoption agency applying for the Order, or with any other body involved with the care of the child, and not been personally involved with the adoption arrangements. Nevertheless there 'might be reasons of professional ethics for declining the appointment because of previous work with the child or his parents, or the prospective adopters.'[63]

Once appointed it is not the guardian's task to gather background information on behalf of the court, as the adoption agency applying for the Freeing Order or placing the child for adoption will have supplied this in its own report to the court under Schedule 2 of the Adoption Rules 1984. The guardian *ad litem* must look into what is said in the agency's application forms, and the Schedule 2 report and, in a contested case, in the statement of facts. He is only required to do this to the extent that he considers necessary, because it is not intended that he should cover all the same ground again as a matter of course. There is no point in his repeating enquiries which have already been satisfactorily concluded by the adoption agency. On the other hand, he cannot be fettered if he is to fulfil his function of safeguarding the child's interest, and so he must bear in mind the possible need to check and verify any aspect of the application.[64]

The guardian *ad litem* will therefore need to read the documents carefully and critically, and he should always interview the agency's worker and inspect the relevant case records. This may identify gaps in the information, conflicting professional judgments, or statements which appear to be questionable. It may provide leads to necessary matters for further or direct enquiry, and enable the guardian *ad litem* to decide which particular aspects he should investigate further. The overall approach of the guardian *ad litem* to his duties should be that he is satisfying himself that matters are as stated, on the basis of being reasonably assured rather than certain, and that where he has occasion for doubt he will take active steps to enquire into any relevant matter.

---

61 LAC(84)10, para. 18.
62 LAC(84)10, para. 17.
63 LAC(84)10, para. 23.
64 LAC(84)10, para. 24.

It may be more practicable for some of the enquiries to be made through an agent.[65]

In a contested case, there is a conflict of views between the adoption agency and the parent about whether adoption is in the child's best interests, and the court will look to the guardian *ad litem*'s report to help it to reach a decision. The guardian *ad litem* should not have preconceived notions about what might be best for the child, and he would need to test the agency's case for adoption, as well as examining the unwilling parent's views. He should check that the parent has sought legal advice, and then discuss fully with him why he is objecting to adoption, and what alternative way of providing for the child's future care he can offer. The adoption agency which is applying for the Freeing Order or has placed a child for adoption should have explored these issues thoroughly in counselling the parent, and should have given him written information about the legal implications of adoption and freeing, and about the relevant procedures. It is not the guardian *ad litem*'s task to explain these matters again, but he may be able to clarify points which the parent has misunderstood and may find easier to accept from an independent person; some natural parents, for example, mistakenly believe that if the application is refused in a case where the prospective adopters have asked for their identity to be kept confidential, then their identity will be made known, and a parent may even have a right to meet them.[66]

The guardian *ad litem* should lodge his written report with the court at least a month before the hearing date, so that it is available for the court's scrutiny of all the case documents under rule 9(3). The guardian *ad litem* may also, under rule 6(8) make an interim report if he wishes to have the court's directions on a particular point. The guardian *ad litem*'s report is confidential, although a parent (or the child in High Court cases) may be able to inspect references to himself in the report under rule 53(2). It is helpful if the report deals, as far as possible, with individual parties in separate sections.[67]

Access to records

Section 42(1) of the Children Act 1989 gives a guardian *ad litem* the right to examine and take copies of any records of, or held by, a local authority or the NSPCC relating to the application before the court. The guardian therefore has (and has had since 1984) access to the adoption agency records in relation to the child. This includes access to Form F, the adoption agency's form, which records information in relation to prospective adopters. In the case of *Manchester City Council v. T.*[68] it was held that guardians *ad litem* appointed in care proceedings also have a right of access to Form F. At the initial hearing, it was the view of Bracewell J that there was a difference between the role of the guardian *ad litem* appointed in care proceedings and in adoption, which meant that the guardian *ad litem* was not entitled to see Form F. It was in fact

---

65 LAC(84)10, para. 25.
66 LAC(84)10, para. 26.
67 LAC(84)10, para. 28.
68 [1994] 1 F.L.R. 632 C.A.

on the basis of the information gleaned from Form F that the guardian *ad litem* took the view that the proposed placement would not be in the child's best interests. The Court of Appeal reversed this decision and took the view that where a local authority sought a Care Order with a view to placing a child with specific prospective adopters, S.42(1)(b) of The Children Act entitled the guardian *ad litem* to examine and take copies of the Form F. S.42(2)(a) also gave the guardian *ad litem* the right to include the relevant information from Form F in the report to the court.

Form F is a confidential document under regulation 14 of the Adoption Agencies Regulations 1983. Regulation 15 of the Adoption Agencies Regulations specifically says that an adoption agency shall provide access to its case records, and the indexes to them, and disclose such information in its possession as may be required to, amongst others, a guardian *ad litem* or reporting officer appointed under rules made pursuant to S.20 of the 1975 Act, for the purposes of the discharge of his duties on that behalf.[69] Under these regulations the duty to disclose information does not extend to the guardian *ad litem* appointed in care proceedings. However, the judgment in *Manchester County Council v. T.* overrides the position as set out in the Adoption Agencies Regulations, and confirms the right of the guardian *ad litem* appointed in both adoption and care proceedings to have access to all the adoption agency's records, including Form F.

Checklist of the guardian's duties in relation to the child, the court, the applicants, the birth parents and the adoption agency

Guardians should not start their investigations until they have received the Schedule 2 report, and other documentation. However, exceptionally in *Re G.D. (Adoption Application)*[70] where the passage of time is likely to be a major determinant of the case, guardians may consider commencing enquiries before the arrival of the report, but this should be the exception rather than the rule.

The child:

● will the Adoption or Freeing Order be in the best interests of this particular child?
● what are the needs of this particular child, including needs in relation to race, culture, religion, language and education?
● what are the wishes and feelings of the child (if of sufficient age and understanding) regarding the application?
● what are the present and proposed contact arrangements, if any, and how does the child feel about them?
● are there any lapsed contacts still of importance to the child?
● is the child aware of the application and the circumstances surrounding it (if of sufficient age and understanding) and has any necessary counselling been carried out by the adoption agency?

---

69 Reg. 15(c).
70 Unreported, October 24, 1991, F.D.

- the guardian will be expected to advise the court as to whether or not the court needs to direct that the child should not attend the hearing, and this should be decided in consultation with the child;[71]
- if it appears to the guardian that the child should be a party to the proceedings, the court should be asked to consider transferring the case to the High Court.

The court (remember there will normally be no solicitor):

- investigate the circumstances surrounding the application;
- investigate any particular matters, as directed by the court,
- receive and check any relevant documents;
- bring to the attention of the court, at an early stage, any material matters which have a bearing on the case;
- interview relevant people, including the child, the applicants, the birth parents and other extended family members, if appropriate;
- make an early decision about the need for expert evidence, and inform the court;
- be prepared to inform and advise the court on existing contact arrangement;
- request a hearing for directions if necessary;
- inspect all relevant records;
- prepare a report and lodge it with the court one month before the final hearing;
- think through how to represent the child, bearing in mind your ability to address the court on the question of whether an Adoption Order should be made.[72] The assumption is that the child will attend, unless there are special circumstances.

The applicants:

- will they meet the needs of this particular child and provide a permanent home for him? This should include consideration of race, culture, religion, language and educational needs;
- have they received appropriate counselling and support from the adoption agency making the application?
- are they aware of the existence and purpose of the adoption contact register? What is their attitude towards contact (if appropriate) by the birth family, including siblings and other extended family, in view of the fact that many more children will arrive at this point with continuing links with their families?

The birth parents:

- why are they withholding their agreement to the making of the Adoption or Freeing Order?
- what is their plan for the child?

---

71 R. 23(4).
72 R. 23(1).

- are they (or any other person with parental responsibility) likely to make an application for any of the other Orders available under the Children Act 1989, either in private or public law proceedings?
- have the birth parents received appropriate counselling from the adoption agency and are they aware of the existence and purpose of the adoption contact register?
- what are the existing contact arrangements, if any? is there any problem either in frequency, type or arrangements for contact? if contact exists, is it reasonable? remember that contact may include indirect contacts via birthday cards, letters and telephone calls, and that the court can make a Contact Order of its own motion.

The adoption agency:

- has the agency fulfilled its duties under the Adoption Agencies Regulations 1983?
- is the Schedule 2 report available, accurate and complete? does it tally with the information on the file, and that given to the adoption panel?
- has the adoption agency counselled:
  — the child;
  — the birth parents;
  — the applicants
  (as required by regulations 7 and 8 of the Adoption Agencies Regulations 1983)?
- has the agency carried out its other specific duties in relation to them, i.e. obtaining medical reports and references for the applicants? has the agency provided information to the applicants, as required by regulation 12?
- is an Adoption or Freeing for Adoption Order the best Order for this child at this stage in its life?
- are the particular adoptive parents suitable for this child? do they meet the child's racial, cultural, religious and linguistic needs?
- has the adoption agency considered the question of contact? if so, what is their view? are they going to act as intermediaries for the provision of information?
- would the Order mean that the child lost touch with siblings, grandparents or other extended family particularly those with whom there has been contact?
- has information been provided to the child, the birth parents and the applicants about the adoption contact register?

Additional points in relation to freeing applications:

- have the birth parents made a declaration under S.18(6) of the Adoption Act 1976, i.e. do they wish to be informed of the child's situation and any proposed adoption?
- does the child (if it is of sufficient age and understanding) wish the Order to be made?
- what are the longer term implications of making the Freeing Order? for example, what are the realistic expectations of making a suitable placement if the child is freed? what are the agency's proposals? have

prospective adopters been identified? if not, does this child have any special needs which may make adoption more or less likely? A court cannot dispense with the agreement of a parent unless the child is placed or likely to be placed.[73]

● what are the arrangements for contact with siblings (if any) and the wider extended family?

● if prospective adopters have been identified the guardian should interview them, even though they are not parties to the proceedings;

● if the birth parents are not married, where is the putative father, and what are his views about the freeing adoption? does he know what is happening and is he likely to apply either for a Parental Responsibility Order or a S.8 Residence or Contact Order? He will be a party to the proceedings if he is liable to contribute to the maintenance of the child if there is an agreement or a Court Order.[74]

● finally, would being freed weaken or strengthen the likelihood of the child achieving permanence of placement?[75]

Although theoretically the case management role under S.41(10) of the Children Act 1989 does not apply in adoption proceedings, nevertheless guardians will wish to expedite proceedings and avoid delay as far as possible.

The Role and Duties of the Reporting Officer in Adoption and Freeing for Adoption Procedures

The role of the reporting officer is to protect the rights of the relinquishing parents and the child by ensuring that the agreement to the Adoption or Freeing Order is given unconditionally, freely and with a full understanding of the nature and effect of the Order. The role of the reporting officer in freeing for adoption applications is dealt with at rule 5 of the Adoption Rules 1984 and the role of the reporting officer in adoption proceedings is dealt with at rule 17. Although the role of the reporting officer in witnessing the agreement to the adoption or freeing for adoption is limited it is, nevertheless, of critical importance in ascertaining the status of the agreement, as well as witnessing the signature.

Appointment of the reporting officer in adoption (rule 17) and freeing for adoption (rule 5)

As soon as practicable after the originating process has been filed, or at any other stage thereafter if it appears that a parent or guardian of the child is willing to agree to the making of an adoption Order and is in England or

---

73 S. 18(3) Adoption Act 1976.
74 Adoption Rules 1984, r. 4(2)(f).
75 See further Lambert, Buist, Triseliotis and Hill, *Freeing Children for Adoption* (1990) British Agencies for Adoption and Fostering, Research Series 7.

Wales, the proper officer shall appoint a reporting officer in respect of that parent or guardian and shall send to him a copy of the originating process and any other documents attached thereto, and of the reports supplied by the applicant.[76] The same person may be appointed as reporting officer in respect of two or more parents or guardians of the child.[77] It is not possible to appoint a reporting officer when the parent is outside England or Wales.

The reporting officer must be appointed from a panel established by regulations under S.41(7) of the Children Act 1989 but shall not be a member or employee of the applicant or any respondent body, nor have been involved in the making of any arrangements for the adoption of the child.[78] The duty of the reporting officer is to:

- ensure, so far as is reasonably practicable, that any agreement to the making of an Adoption Order is given freely and unconditionally and with full understanding of what is involved;
- confirm that the parent or guardian has been given an opportunity of making a declaration under rule 18(6) of the Act, (that he prefers not to be involved in future questions concerning the adoption of the child);
- witness a signature by the parent or guardian of the written agreement to the making of the Adoption Order;
- investigate all circumstances relevant to that agreement and any such declarations;
- where it is proposed to free for adoption a child whose parents were not married to each other at the time of his birth and whose father is not his guardian, interview any person claiming to be the father in order to be able to advise the court on matters listed in S.18(7) of the Act (that he has no intention of applying for either a Parental Responsibility Order, or for a S.8 Residence or Contact Order). The question of to what lengths guardians or reporting officers should go to ascertain the whereabouts and intentions of a putative father is a difficult one. Putative fathers, particularly those being assessed by the Child Support Agency, may feel that contributing to the child's maintenance should entitle them to some say in their upbringing, and it is important to attempt to clear the ground on these matters in advance of the hearing. The rules provide for the possibility of more than one reporting officer being appointed, for example, a reporting officer in another part of the country can be nominated to conduct an interview with the putative father.

On completing his investigations, the reporting officer should make a report in writing to the court, drawing attention to any matters which, in his opinion, may be of assistance to the court in considering the application.[79] The reporting officer may go back to the court to obtain directions on any matters at any time. He may also make an interim report to the court, if it appears necessary. In particular, the reporting officer shall make a report if a parent or

---

76 Rr. 17(1) and 5(1).
77 R. 2.
78 R. 3.
79 Rr. 17 and 5(4)(a)−(f).

guardian of the child is unwilling to agree to the making of an Adoption Order, and in such a case the reporting officer shall notify the applicant.[80] The court may, at any time before the final determination of the application, require the reporting officer to perform such further duties as the court considers necessary.[81] The reporting officer shall attend any hearing of the application, if so required by the court.[82] The report made to the court by the reporting officer is confidential.[83]

Rule 17 corresponds to rule 5 for freeing proceedings with the following differences:

- parents are not asked in Adoption Order proceedings whether they want to be involved in future questions about the child's adoption (because if an Adoption Order is made they cannot subsequently resume the parental rights and duties) and the reporting officer is therefore required to deal with this in Adoption Order proceedings;
- no special enquiries are necessary in Adoption Order proceedings about the putative father's intentions regarding parental responsibility or contact.[84]

The prohibition on appointing as reporting officer anyone concerned with a respondent body does not apply in Adoption Order proceedings, if that body is a local authority whose connection with the case is that it was notified of the proposed adoption (where the child was not placed for adoption by an adoption agency). This means that local authorities can use their own social workers to act as reporting officers in step-parent adoptions. Most local authorities maintain a certain number of panel members who are in fact their own staff acting in 'mother's own adoptions'. This is far from ideal, as the reporting officer could be put in a position of criticising a fellow worker from their own local authority.

Guardians *ad litem* have considerable power, once appointed, and this imposes a 'reciprocal' duty on the part of the local authority, not only to disclose proposals for change in relation to the child, but also to listen to the views of the guardian *ad litem*. Thus Ewbank J in the case of *R. v. North Yorkshire County Council, ex p. M.*[85] In this case, the parents sought judicial review of the local authority's decision to place their child for adoption six weeks before their application for discharge of the Care Order was due to be heard. The guardian *ad litem* argued that the decision was improper, because the local authority had not consulted her. The court upheld her view.

The freed child

It should be noted that, if the child is free for adoption, there will be no automatic appointment of a reporting officer (or guardian *ad litem*) since the

---

80 R. 5(5).
81 R. 5(6).
82 R. 5(7).
83 R. 5(8).
84 LAC(84)10, para. 49.
85 [1989] Q.B. 411.

question of parental agreement will have been settled in the freeing procedures; however, the court, nevertheless:

> has a discretionary power in adoption order proceedings to appoint a guardian ad litem for a freed child if, exceptionally, there are special circumstances where the child's welfare makes a guardian ad litem necessary (and in such a case the guardian ad litem may wish to ask the court for sight of the case documents from the freeing proceedings).[86]

The position of the freed child has given rise to concern as, once the child is freed, there is no external oversight of the child's situation, and the onus rests with the natural parents to apply to the court if the child has not been placed within one year of being freed provided that they have not made a declaration to the effect that they wish to have no further involvement. However, it is not clear what mechanisms exist to ensure that parents will know what is happening to their child, and no direct responsibility lies with the local authority to inform the court of children who have been freed and placed. Consequently it is hard to know how the court would be in a position to know that there were special circumstances which require the appointment of a guardian *ad litem*. However, the court should have a new Schedule 2 report or an addendum to it. Under the White Paper proposals there will no longer be 'freed' children who may languish in a legal limbo after being freed and before being placed. The introduction of the Placement Order would mean that the court would be involved earlier in the process, and would have the power to review the proposed arrangements for the placement of the child at an earlier stage. However, the very question of whether rehabilitation with the birth family is to be ruled out before the child is permanently placed remains.

Counselling relinquishing parents

It is the responsibility of the adoption agency to provide support and counselling to parents relinquishing their children for adoption. However, where the child was not placed for adoption by an adoption agency, the local authority which was notified of the proposed adoption will have interviewed the parent in the course of its investigation, and will have explored relevant issues with him, including his understanding of what adoption involves and the possible need for legal advice. If it seems to the reporting officer that the parent needs any further counselling he should draw this to the local authority's attention.[87] Clearly reporting officers will have to be satisfied that the necessary counselling has been carried out. This is an area of practice which is most likely to have been neglected. Social work attention is focused on the child and, once the child is removed, social work attention to the relinquishing families wanes fairly rapidly. The guilt and grief felt by many birth mothers is something which may stay with them, unresolved, for the rest of their lives. The decision to part with a child is a particularly raw and lonely form of grief which can cast long shadows over future health and

---

86 LAC(84)10, para. 51.
87 LAC(84)10, para. 50.

relationships.[88] Sensitive counselling at the point of relinquishment can pay substantial dividends for future healthy relationships, not just in freeing the child to settle in a new family, but in increasing the chances of future happiness for the birth mother and any other children she may have.

Checklist of the duties of the reporting officer in adoption and freeing for adoption proceedings

- *Receive documentation.* The reporting officer should receive from the court the completed application form, one or two blank copies of agreement Form 7, the child's birth certificate, the Schedule 2 report (this very often arrives separately some weeks, or even months, after the other documentation), the notice of the hearing, health reports (where applicable) and a notice of the appointment of the reporting officer and a copy of Form 16 (which should be completed and returned to the court immediately by the reporting officer to acknowledge receipt of all the documents).

- *Receive and read the Schedule 2 report,* which is the key document for guardians *ad litem* and reporting officers. The Schedule 2 report will explain the circumstances leading to the proposed application and should contain a full history of the case. If there is continuing and unacceptable delay in the arrival of the Schedule 2 report the reporting officer should seek directions from the court. Except in very exceptional circumstances, for example, the imminent emigration of one of the parties to the proceedings, the reporting officer should not see the relinquishing parent before they have had an opportunity to read an assimilate all the matters in the Schedule 2 report.

- *See the relinquishing parent* with a view to ascertaining whether or not the agreement to adoption or freeing for adoption is given freely and with a full understanding of what is involved.

- *Investigate all the circumstances* relevant to the giving of the agreement, including whether or not adequate counselling has been made available by the adoption agency or the local authority, if they are not the same.

- *Additional information.* The reporting officer may want to request information from the Schedule 2 report writer, particularly if it appears that more work is needed in the light of any circumstances revealed by the interview with the relinquishing parent.

- *The adoption contact register.* Check that the parent understands the existence and function of the adoption contact register, including the fact that there is a minimum fee of £35 for lodging information.

- *Witness the signature of the willing parent.* If the reporting officer is satisfied on all these aspects of the matter, he or she should witness the signature of the willing parent to the child's adoption or freeing for adoption.

---

88 See Bouchier, Lambert and Triseliotis, *Parting with a Child for Adoption: the Mother's Perspective* (1991).

- *Write a report for the court.* The reporting officer should then write a report for the court enclosing the completed Form 7 (Adoption Proceedings) or Form 2 (Freeing Case).
- *Any other duties.* In addition, the reporting officer shall carry out any other duties which the court may direct.
- *Identify the child's birth certificate.* The reporting officer should ask the parent to identify the child's birth certificate, by signing the back of it.
- *Check on contact issues.* If there are contact issues which are not fully resolved, in the opinion of the reporting officer, he or she should notify the court or request the appointment of a guardian *ad litem*.
- *Implications of adoption.* The reporting officer should ensure that the birth parents understand the implications of adoption or freeing for adoption and should inform them that, although they have signed the agreement form, they may withdraw their agreement up to the time the Adoption Order is made. It should, however, be made clear that if parents do this, their position may be prejudiced if a long period has elapsed and the child has had the opportunity to settle with the prospective adopters. Once informal agreement has been given to the making of an Adoption Order (not formal agreement as witnessed by a reporting officer[89]) and an application for adoption has been made (or an application for a Freeing Order has been made without agreement), the child cannot be removed without the leave of the court.
- *The child's right of access to birth records.* Reporting officers should also explain the implications of the adoptive child's right to have access to their birth record and to the contents of the adoption contact register at the age of 18. It is important for relinquishing parents to understand the full implications in terms of the child's right to initiate contact with them once they are grown up. However, reporting officers should be aware of giving the impression that this will be the likely outcome, as it is important for parents to understand the full significance of the Adoption Order in terms of severing legal links between them and their children.

Witnessing agreements

A reporting officer must carry out personally his duty of witnessing parental agreement to adoption. He can neither delegate this duty nor arrange for an agent to undertake it on his behalf. The court will, therefore, normally appoint as reporting officer someone from the parent's area of residence in England and Wales.[90] If agreement is required from a person outside England or Wales, one of the following people must instead witness the parent's written agreement to the child's adoption:

- in Scotland, a Justice of the Peace or a Sheriff;
- in Northern Ireland, a Justice of the Peace;
- outside the United Kingdom, one of the following persons:

---

89 See *Re T. (A Minor)* (Adoption Parental Consent) [1986] All E.R. 817 C.A.
90 LAC(84)10, para. 11.

- any person for the time being authorised by law in the place where the document is executed to administer an oath for any judicial or other legal purposes;
- a British Consular Officer;
- a notary public; or
- if the person executing the document is serving in any of the regular armed forces of the Crown, an Officer holding a Commission in any of those forces.

Additional duties of the reporting officer in freeing for adoption proceedings

In addition to the other duties, the reporting officer in freeing proceedings shall 'confirm that the parent or guardian has been given an opportunity of making a declaration under S.18(6) of the Adoption Act 1976 that he prefers not to be involved in future questions concerning the adoption of the child.'[91] The written agreement in freeing for adoption (Form 2) allows the parent either to make this declaration or to state that he does not wish to do so.[92]

Where it is proposed to free a non-marital child for adoption, and his father is not his guardian, then the reporting officer should interview any person claiming to be the father in order to be able to advise the court regarding the father's intention or non-intention of applying for any of the Orders available to him under the Children Act 1989.

The reporting officer's report to the court

The reporting officer's report will be concise, outlining the actions of the reporting officer, and any areas of concern he may have about the contents of the Schedule 2 report. There should also be:

- a brief statement of the circumstances in which the agreement has been given;
- confirmation of the parents' understanding of the implications of adoption;
- confirmation that information about the existence and function of the adoption contact register has been given;
- a statement of any other matters which the reporting officer feels it is appropriate to bring to the attention of the court, for example in freeing applications, whether or not the relinquishing parent has made a declaration.[93]

---

91 R. 5(4)(b).
92 LAC(84)10, para. 13.
93 Timms, *Manual of Practice Guidance for Guardians ad Litem and Reporting Officers* (1992) HMSO, p. 140. See also Hazell and Richards, *The Guardian ad litem and Reporting Officer in Adoption Proceedings* (1986).

The Adoption Process

Courts and applications

Applications for both Adoption and Freeing for Adoption Orders may be made to all levels of court:

- the Family Proceedings Court, where the child is, or in the case of a freeing application, where the parent or guardian is;[94]
- any divorce County Court where they may be heard by a district judge, if uncontested;
- contested applications must be transferred to the family centre;[95]
- the High Court, in the Principal Registry of the Family Division.[96]

Transfer to the High Court carries with it the advantage of automatic legal representation for the child.

The adoption agency's duties

Adoption agencies have substantial duties in relation to the children they place, their parents or guardians and the prospective adopter. These duties are dealt with in the Adoption Agencies Regulations 1983.[97] In particular, they must provide counselling services for the child, his natural parents and the prospective adopters and they must explain the legal implications of, and procedures in relation to, adoption and freeing for adoption and provide them with written information about adoption services and the legal process.[98] The responsibility to provide these services and information extend to the father of an illegitimate child where his identity is known to the agency.[99] They also have a duty to ascertain what his intentions are as regards the child, for example, does he intend to apply for parental responsibility or to initiate any S.10 proceedings? Putative fathers should also be notified, if their whereabouts are known to the agency, of the decision to make an application to free the child for adoption.[100]

Adoption agencies are in a very powerful position to steer adoption policies. Guardians *ad litem*, however, are in an equally powerful position to monitor placement practices, particularly in relation to those children who are being adopted from care. It is extremely important for guardians *ad litem* to check, with both relinquishing and adoptive parents, that the agency has carried out all its responsibilities in respect of both relinquishing and prospective adoptive parents.

---

94 Magistrates Court (Adoption) Rules 1984 (S.I. 1984 No.611), rr. 4 and 15.
95 Children (Allocation of Proceedings) Order 1991 (S.I. 1991 No. 1677 (L.21), Art. 14 and Family Proceedings (Allocation to Judiciary) Direction 1991.
96 Adoption Rules 1984 (S.I. 1984 No. 265), rr. 4 and 15.
97 S.I. 1983 No. 1964.
98 Rr. 7 and 8.
99 R. 7(3)(a).
100 Adoption Act 1976, S.14.

The Schedule 2 report

The Schedule 2 report is the report prepared by the adoption agency which explains the background to the adoption application. In considering the application for adoption the court will rely heavily on both the Schedule 2 report and the report of the guardian *ad litem* or the reporting officer. The Schedule 2 report will be the main source of information for guardians and they should examine it carefully and with great attention to its detail. It is assumed that the Schedule 2 report will be prepared by somebody experienced in adoption work.[101]

Matters to be covered in Schedule 2 reports are listed in Schedule 2 of the Adoption Rules 1984. It is worth guardians checking this list against any Schedule report they receive, as the requirements to the report are extremely detailed and comprehensive, covering all aspects of the child's physical, social, emotional and educational development, including any special needs in relation to the child's health, whether the child has any rights or interest in property, and in particular, the child's wishes in respect of religious and cultural upbringing.[102]

The report should contain comprehensive information about each natural parent, including their parents and brothers and sisters with their ages. The physical description, personality, religion, educational attainments, past and present occupations and interests of the natural parents should all be listed. If, for any reason, this information is not available, the reasons for the omissions should also be detailed.[103]

Details of the prospective adopters should include their hopes and expectations for the child's future.[104]

The adoption agency should also include in their report a brief account of their own action in the case, and details of any alternatives to adoption considered. There should be a resumé of the reasons for considering that adoption would be in the child's best interest, including a date of the relevant decision,[105] and a report by the agencies' medical adviser of the health history of the parties.[106]

The availability of S.8 Orders, as alternatives to adoption, mean that the guardian *ad litem* will be particularly aware of the prospective adopters' attitudes to any possibility of contact between the child and the relinquishing parents.[107] The Schedule 2 report is the guardians' main source of information and, as a general rule, they should not commence their enquiries without it. The wait that this often entails led the judge in one case to say that he saw:

> no reason why the guardian should wait for the Schedule 2 report, especially when this will mean that the passage of time between the guardian ad litem's appointment

---

101 LAC(84)10, para. 59.
102 Adoption Rules 1984, Sched. 2, para. 1(0).
103 Sched. 2, para. 2.
104 Sched. 2, para. 4.
105 Sched. 2, para. 5(a).
106 Sched. 2, para. 7(a).
107 See also Hazell and Richards, *Schedule 2 Reports: A Guide for Report Writers and Their Supervisors* (1993), published by the Cardiff Institute of Higher Education and the Catholic Children's Society (Westminster).

and the final hearing will be a major determinant of the case. In the case of GD, by the time the case was heard, nothing short of adoption would be sufficient to meet the child's needs for security.[108]

In fact, the unacceptable aspect of delays involving Schedule 2 reports is the delay in the adoption agency preparing them and sending them to the guardian.

The adoption panel

Under the Adoption Agencies Regulations 1983 an adoption agency must establish at least one adoption panel, to which all proposed placements must be referred for consideration. The panel must be given a written report of the agency's views on the proposed placement, which should include the agency's reasons for considering that the prospective adopters might be able to meet that particular child's needs, and might therefore be suitable adoptive parents for him. The report must not, however, prejudice the issues which are for the panel to consider.[109]

The panel must consist of no more than 10 members of which at least one must be a man and one a woman. The chairman should have experience in adoption work. In addition, the panel should include the following:

● two of the social workers in the employment of the adoption agency;
● at least one member of the adoption agency's management committee, where the agency is an approved adoption society, or where the agency is a local authority, at least one member of that authority's social services committee;
● the person nominated as the medical adviser to the adoption agency under regulation 6(4) or one of them, if more than one are appointed; and
● at least two other persons not being members or employees of the adoption agency or elected members, where the agency is a local authority.

The White Paper proposals seek to include more independent membership of adoption panels.[110]

Although each panel has the same task, reviewing the proposed adoption of the child, approving the applicants as prospective adoptive parents and taking a view about whether or not a particular family will meet the needs of a particular child, each panel operates in its own individual way. The panel should apply checks and balances to adoption agency policy and practice, and should not be a rubber-stamping mechanism. However, inevitably, individual panel members' own life experiences, value judgments and, in particular, their views about family life, are bound to have an impact on decision making. The panel should be in a position to question the assumptions on which placement policies are based, and, in particular, should ensure that the needs of a particular child are not in conflict with the agency's own stated child care

---

108 *Re G.D. (Adoption Application)* unreported, October 24, 1991, F.D., reported in the *Local Government Review*, August 1, 1992.
109 Regs. 5 and 9 of the Adoption Agencies Regulations 1983 and LAC(84)10, para. 66.
110 Adoption Agencies Regulations 1983, reg. 5.

policies. In particular, adoption panels should be looking at what attempts have been made to rehabilitate the child with their birth family, before accepting the recommendation that a child be placed for adoption. Panels have been criticised as arenas where power struggles between senior management, counsellors and others can impose their own agendas:

> all too often panels spent little or no time exploring each others' attitudes and values and, as a consequence, the panel can be or appear to be inconsistent because which case gets through depends on which panel members attend particular meetings · · · I do believe in panels as I think it is vital that the practice of workers is scrutinised by others outside their work section and from a more independent position, but I am not convinced that the present system works as well as it could, in the interests of children and their families.[111]

The impact of the adoption panel on placement policies is a subject which could benefit from examination under a rather stronger light than has been the case hitherto. Hopefully this will happen as part of the review of adoption legislation. However, the indications are that adoption panels will assume more, rather than less, importance within the system and it is therefore important that they function in a sufficiently child-centred and independent manner. Meanwhile, guardians *ad litem* should not be afraid to engage in critical appraisals of both the recommendations of the adoption panel, and the decisions made by adoption agencies.

Dispensing with parental agreement to adoption

An Adoption Order shall not be made unless the child is free for adoption by virtue of an Order made in England and Wales (or the equivalent provision in Scotland) or, in the case of each parent or guardian of the child, the court is satisfied that:

- he freely, and with full understanding of what is involved, agrees unconditionally to the making of an Adoption Order (whether or not he knows the identity of the applicants); or
- his agreement to the making of the Adoption Order should be dispensed with on a ground specified in the Adoption Act 1976, S.16(2).

The grounds are that the parent, or guardian:

- cannot be found or is incapable of giving agreement;
- is withholding his agreement unreasonably;
- has persistently failed, without reasonable cause, to discharge the parental duties in relation to the child;
- has abandoned or neglected the child;
- has persistently ill-treated the child;
- has seriously ill-treated the child (this does not apply unless 'because of the ill-treatment or for other reasons' the rehabilitation of the child within the household of the parent or guardian is unlikely).

---

111 Pennie Pennie, 'Adoption Panels: Room for Improvement' *Adoption and Fostering*, British Agencies for Adoption and Fostering quarterly journal, Vol. 17, No. 2, summer 1993, at 44.

The Adoption Law Review expressed concern at the insufficient weight given to a parent's lack of agreement. Where it is decided that adoption is in a child's interest there is, in practice, very little room left for the court to give any weight to parental views. This cannot be regarded as satisfactory in relation to an Order which irrevocably terminates a parent's legal relationship with his or her child.

The Review attributed this problem to the comparatively late stage at which courts are normally asked to resolve the question of parental agreement. This means that the:

> parents' right to argue, say, that the court should grant a residence or that further work should be undertaken to enable the child to return home or to be cared for by relatives, has effectively been overridden by the passage of time. We propose that, where parental agreement is withheld or is likely to be withheld, a placement should not be allowed to proceed until the court has decided whether or not to dispense with parental agreement.[112]

Many of the difficulties in this area stem from the difference between pre- and post-Children Act practice. Theoretically, the difference should not be immediately apparent, as in many respects the Children Act 1989 confirmed what should already have been good practice, in terms of making an assumption of reasonable contact between parents and children. However, the ability of the local authority to assume parental rights and terminate parental contact through purely internal administrative procedures before 1984, and the lack of constraint on local authority use of wardship before 1991, taken with a lack of availability of resources for preventative services to children and families, all contributed to a legacy of practice which sometimes sits uneasily with current requirements for contact to be considered at every, and at an early, stage in planning for the child. The Review proposes that, in addition to the existing ground that the parent cannot be found or is incapable of giving agreement, there should be one other test which should:

- address the question of the advantages of becoming part of a new family and having a new legal status (rather than the question of where the child should reside);
- focus on the needs of the child rather than any parental shortcomings;
- require the court to be satisfied that adoption is significantly better than other available options and that parental wishes should therefore be overridden.

It might be expressed in terms of the court being satisfied that the advantages to a child of becoming part of a new family and having a new legal status are so significantly greater than the advantages to the child of any alternative option as to justify overriding the wishes of a parent or guardian.[113]

Inevitably, the question of whether the parent is being reasonable in withholding agreement, is inextricably linked with questions concerning the welfare of the child. The test of reasonableness is an objective one, taking account of all the facts. Those facts will include the need of the child for security and existing contacts with the birth family. The decision cannot be

---

112 Review of Adoption Law, paras. 12.1 and 2.2.
113 *Ibid.*, para. 12.6.

based solely on the issue of natural justice[114] or the view of professional social workers about the course of action which will be in the best interests of the child as that attributes to welfare an overriding importance.[115] In *Re W*. Lord Hailsham endorsed the decision in *Re L. (An Infant)*[116] in the following terms:

> it does not follow from the fact that the test is reasonableness that any court is entitled simply to substitute its own view for that of the parent. In my opinion it should be extremely careful to guard against this error. Two reasonable parents can perfectly reasonably come to opposite conclusions on the same set of facts without forfeiting their title to be regarded as reasonable. The question in any given case is whether a parental veto comes within the band of possible reasonable decisions and not whether it is right or mistaken. Not every reasonable exercise of judgement is right, and not every mistaken exercise of judgement is unreasonable. There is a band of decisions within which no court should seek to replace the individual's judgment with his own.[117]

It is the business of the court to make the legal decision to whether or not the parent is being reasonable in withholding agreement. It is the business of the guardian *ad litem* to make a recommendation on the basis of the course of action which will be in the best interests of the child.

Step-parent adoption

Of the 7,000 children adopted every year in England and Wales, step-parent and relative adoptions now account for about half the total. They are the largest group of protected children.

A child who is not placed for adoption by an adoption agency becomes a protected child when notice is given to a local authority of intention to apply for an Adoption Order.[118]

The Children Act 1975 introduced custodianship, and at that time it was anticipated custodianship might to some extent replace adoption as a preferred adoption for step-parents attempting to legalise their relationship with step-children. In fact, custodianship has not been nearly as widely used as was anticipated 20 years ago. To introduce a new type of Order available only to step-parents is to be welcomed.

It has been estimated that there are between 1 million and 1.5 million children living in step-families. The vast majority of those do not apply to adopt. However, in 1984 over 4,000 children were adopted by a couple of whom one was a natural parent. In her review of research relating to adoption June Thoburn identifies professional tensions between the clean break notion of adoption, as if the child was born to you, as compared with the acceptance of difference and the desirability of keeping some contact with the past. All the debates which apply to adoption generally are brought into much sharper focus in relation to step-parent or in family adoptions.[119]

---

114 *Re B.A.* [1985] F.L.R. 1008.
115 *Re C.R. v. North Yorkshire County Council, ex. p. M.* [1988] 3 W.L.R. 1344.
116 *The Times*, July 19, 1962.
117 *Re W.* [1971] A.C. 682 at 700.
118 Adoption Act 1976, S.32.
119 Review of Adoption Law, Appendix C, Review of Research Relating to Adoption, by June Thoburn.

In other areas the law is very much in favour of continuing links between biological parents and children, not least because of the issue of maintenance. The Law Commission's Working Paper on Custody and the Children Act 1989 emphasised the importance of continuing parental responsibility after marital breakdown. However, given the prevalence of second marriages and step-parent adoptions, it is surprising that there are few systematic studies of the effects on children of adoption by a parent and step-parent. Ninety-five per cent of families applying for adoption consist of a birth mother and step-father.[120] The motivation for step-parent adoption is complex. It has been suggested that the mother is usually the moving force because she wants to provide the children with greater security and remove complications from their lives.[121] There may also be the desire to exclude the birth father and sever his relationship with the children.[122] The step-father might want status in the family.[123] The application may be a practical solution to problems of name difference, inheritance or the position on the death of the birth parent.[124]

Step-parent adoption is seen as something that is of benefit to the reconstituted family as a whole, rather than something that is seen as of direct benefit to the child concerned, apart from the indirect benefit of being like an ordinary family. As far as the guardian *ad litem* is concerned, the advantages of ratifying a *de facto* relationship between a step-father and his children must be balanced against the risk of legalising a situation which may exclude a birth father from his child's life. In view of the present complexity of both the emotional and the legal situation regarding the desirability of step-parent adoption, guardians *ad litem* should look carefully at these applications.[125]

Thoburn found that what little evidence is available suggests that many Schedule 2 writers lack the skills and specialist knowledge to ascertain the wishes and feelings of a child who is dependent on the approval of the parent and step-parent who are applying to adopt. The more knowledgeable and skilled GAL/ROs will only interview the child in the minority of cases where a parent is opposing the application, unless the court instructs them to do so, or the reporting officer seeks directions with a view to being appointed as guardian *ad litem*. It appears to be uncommon for non-custodial parents to contest adoption by a parent and step-parent, and there are consequently few applications to dispense with agreement.[126]

Inter-country adoption

As a result of the ratification of the Hague Convention (see chapter 2), UK practices in relation to inter-country adoption will be generally tightened up. It

120 Masson and Norbury (1981) and Chatterton (1989), quoted by Masson, 'Step-parent Adoptions' in *Adoption: Essays in Social Policy, Law and Sociology* (Bean ed. 1984), p. 147. See also *Mine, Yours or Ours? A Study of Step-parent Adoption*, HMSO.
121 Thompson (1967) in Masson, *op. cit.*, p. 147.
122 Bisset Johnson (1978) in *ibid.*, p. 147.
123 Bisset Johnson, *op. cit.*
124 See Masson, *op. cit.*
125 See further Masson, *op. cit.*, and *Step-families: What do we know? What do we need to know?* De'Ath ed. 1992.
126 Thoburn, Review of Adoption Law, Appendix C, Review of Research Relating to Adoption, para. 133.

is intended that it will become a criminal offence to bring a child to the United Kingdom for adoption without having obtained authorisation to proceed from the relevant health department or agency to which the responsibility is delegated. The role of the local authorities in undertaking or arranging an assessment of parents wishing to adopt children from overseas will be strengthened. In general, the Hague Convention is seen as acting as a catalyst for the improvement of standards and the streamlining of the process of inter-country adoption generally. Once it has become an established system of co-operation, the provisions of the Convention should increase safeguards against child trafficking.[127] At the moment, children who are brought to the UK for adoption fall into two groups — those who enter the country with prior entry clearance and those who do not. Particular problems hinge on the status of the natural parents' agreement or lack of agreement to the proposed adoption and the difficulties in ascertaining the views, and even the whereabouts, of the birth parents. Background information about inter-country adoption and the policy and procedure which apply when UK nationals wish to adopt a child from overseas are contained in the Department of Health Chief Inspector Guidance CI(90)2, CI(90)17 and CI(91)14, as well as Home Office leaflet RON117. Guardians are advised to be alert for developments and changes in relation to inter-country adoption and to keep up to date with guidance issued to local authorities and other adoption agencies.[128]

Trans-racial adoption

In recent years there has been increasing emphasis on the right of a child to grow up in a family of his or her own racial origin. Same race placements are thought to provide pride in one's own race and culture which is necessary for healthy emotional growth. The 1976 Act was silent on the question of ethnicity or culture, although there has been an increasing awareness of the problems faced by children of mixed parentage in particular.[129] The problem can be summed up in one staff member's statement: 'our black children leave here feeling they are white.'[130]

---

127 *Adoption: The Future*, CM. 2288 (1993), para. 6.28.
128 For a further discussion of inter-country adoption see Timms, *Manual of Practice Guidance for Guardians ad Litem and Reporting Officers, op. cit.*, Part 4, p. 128; the Review of Adoption Law, Part X, Inter-Country Adoption; and Thoburn and Charles, 'Inter-Country Adoption', Inter-Departmental Review of Adoption Law, Background Paper No. 3, including a review of research which is relevant to inter-country adoption. See also *Inter-Country Adoption: Practical Experiences* (Humphrey and Humphrey ed. 1993).
129 Bebbington and Miles, 'The Background of Children who Enter Local Authority Care' *British Journal of Social Work*, Vol. 19, No. 5, October 1989; and Fratter *at al.*, *Outcomes of Family Placement* (1991). See also *Patterns and Outcomes in Child Placement—Messages from Current Research and their Implications* (1991), HMSO, p. 15.
130 Partridge, *Young People Leaving Care in Oxford* (May 1989), Oxfordshire County Council, quoted in Patterns and Outcomes in Child Placement: Messages from Current Research and their Implications (1991) HMSO. See also Bavn, *Black Children in the Public Care System* (1983) and Smith and Berridge, *Ethnicity and Childcare Placements* (1994). See also the following Social Work Monographs published by the University of East Anglia: White, *Black Children: White Adopters*; Weise, *Transracial Adoption*; Yaya, *Transracial Fostering — A Black Perspective*.

THE ADOPTION PROCESS

269

The White Paper tries to draw a balance line between inflexible policies and a realistic acknowledgement and assessment of what remains to be done in the field of trans-racial adoption. In particular in terms of the recognition of a need for much more vigorous policies of recruitment of foster and adoptive parents from a wide range of ethnic and cultural origins. The White Paper acknowledges the importance of questions of ethnicity and culture, and believes it right to consider these factors alongside others in matching children and parents and will introduce a broad requirement to this effect in line with what is now in the Children Act:

> However, in some cases it is clear that those assessing parents may have given these factors an unjustifiably decisive influence and failed to make a balanced overall judgement of the parents' suitability. The Chief Social Services Inspector has emphasised that ethnicity and culture are among the issues to be considered but they should not necessarily be more influential than any other. There is no conclusive research which justifies isolating such questions from other matters needing assessment or which supports the proposition that children adopted by people of a different ethnic group will necessarily encounter problems of identity or prejudice later in life.[131]

There will be many groups and professionals who would debate this last assertion. Children adopted by people of a different ethnic group may not necessarily encounter problems of identity or prejudice later in life, but the fact remains that the possibility that they are very likely to do so should be faced honestly. The White Paper favours an awareness of the need for ethnic matching, as just one factor to be taken into account in assessing prospective parents:

> On these, as in all other matters, any preferences expressed by the birth parents or ascertainable from the child should be given weight alongside others in an assessment that covers all his characteristics, circumstances and needs. In assessing the prospective parents, what should weigh most heavily is the judgement made of their capacity to help and support the child through all the challenges he or she will face in life, and not just any risk of difficulty attributable to ethnic background. The government will reinforce this approach in guidance.[132]

What is clear is that the unique needs and right of each child to have their feelings respected, and their rights to both an individual and a racial identity recognised should be paramount considerations in placement decisions.

Refusal to make an Adoption Order

If the court decide not to make an Adoption Order the status quo is maintained, and the child stays in the current placement, unless the court makes an alternative Order, which it is empowered to do under the provisions of the Children Act 1989. However, if so required, the unsuccessful applicants must return the child to the adoption agency within seven days.[133]

---

131 *Adoption: The Future, op. cit.*, paras. 4.3.1. to 4.3.3.
132 *Ibid.*, para. 4.3.4.
133 Adoption Act 1976, S. 30(3).

After adoption

Adoption is not the end, but the beginning of a new family and a new relationship. Adoptive parents are encouraged to tell their children about adoption from an early age, so that they will never remember a time when they didn't know they were adopted.

Adoptive parents should receive a written note from the adoption agency, containing background information about the child and his family. Children should be encouraged to talk about their natural family and questions should be answered in an honest and straightforward manner. At 18 adopted children are legally entitled on application to a copy of their original birth certificate.[134]

Adoption: Practice Issues

Permanence

Academic debates about the tensions inherent in attempting to reconcile notions of children's rights and children's welfare are mirrored in the continuing and long running debate on the precise meaning of 'permanence' in child care social work. 'Permanence', like 'best interests', is an umbrella term which is open to a wide variety of interpretation, including both a permanent return home and a placement in a permanent substitute home. The term requires a determined dissection of its various components, and an examination of its impact on adoption agency practice and policy, particularly in relation to contact and the possibility of achieving more open adoptions.

Permanence philosophies were rooted in the early 1970s, when the publication of *Children Who Wait*[135] and *Beyond the Best Interests of the Child*[136] were to form the basis of the permanence philosophy and lead to many innovative and welcome developments in the fields of adoption and fostering. These two publications highlighted the plight of children who drift in long term foster or residential care respectively, and emphasised the importance of the psychological parent as the substitute carer, who is the centre of the child's emotional well-being. Permanency planning 'aims to refocus the child welfare services in a way which accepts the primacy of the needs of children over the claim for inherent advantages of the relationship between the biological parent and child.[137]

Great stress was laid on the importance of permanent homes for children as a developmental need and, in consequence, as a right. Long term fostering, with its high breakdown rates, fell into disrepute and the plight of nearly 7,000 children, who were found to be 'drifting' in care,[138] may have led to the

---

134 See 'Telling your child about his adoption', Annex C (LAC(84)3 and HC(84)1).
135 Rowe (1973).
136 Freud, Solnit and Holstein (1973).
137 Morris, *The Permanency Principle in Child Care Social Work* (1984), Social Work Monographs, published by the University of East Anglia in Association with Social Work Today, p. 4. See also Maluccio, Fein and Olmstead, *Permanency Planning for Children — Concepts and Methods* (1986), Tanstock Publications.
138 Rowe, *op. cit.*

erroneous impression that permanence could only be achieved through the development of robust policies in relation to terminating parental contact and freeing children for placement in new adoptive homes.[139]

The concept and practice of terminating parental contact gained great ascendancy through the 1980s. Many child care social workers, some of whom still occupy senior positions in local authority departments, had more training on terminating parental contact than on any other aspect of child care practice. In order for a child to have the advantage of a permanent placement, links with the parents had to be sacrificed, and were sometimes systematically destroyed by social workers, who believed they were acting in the best interests of the child who needed re-parenting. Emphasis was placed on the importance of healthy bonds of attachment[140] either to their own or to 'psychological' parents,[141] but there was a failure to consider fully the negative effects of cutting off the child from his former identity. Some children as old as seven were renamed, as well as reparented. The social work profession became polarised, increasingly, between what Fox called 'kinship defenders and society as parent protagonists',[142] and lost sight of the fact that rehabilitation and rescue were not mutually exclusive, but were different sequential points along the same continuum.

It was unfortunate that the thrust towards permanence coincided with substantial cuts in social services budgets, and made adoption a seductively cheaper option than committing slender resources to preventive services, under what was then S.1 of the Child Care Act 1980.

> The strenuous efforts put into the establishment of children in substitute homes threw into sad relief the lack of any organisation or commitment to prevention, to parallel that of fostering and adoption. If half the funds and intellectual effort which has gone towards developing strategies for finding alternative families had been put into what we can only lamely call 'preventative work', there would be unquestionable advantage to all concerned.[143]

By 1982, it began to appear that interpretations of permanence had become unacceptably skewed towards substitute care, rather than being preceded by constructive efforts to ensure the child's permanent return home.[144] This point was emphasised by Hussell and Monaghan:

> let us be clear firstly what the approach is and is not about. Primarily and crucially, it is about stopping children slipping into long term care. It is as much to do with good quality, imaginative, preventative and rehabilitation work as with permanent separation. It is not the operation of an adoption mafia, nor is it a management tool for saving money.[145]

---

139 See *Terminating Contact: An Exploration of the Issues Relating to Children in Care* (Adcock and White ed. 1979).
140 See further Sluckin, Herbert and Sluckin, *Maternal Bonding* (1983).
141 Freud, Solnit and Holstein, *op. cit.*
142 See Fox, 'Two Value Positions in Recent Child Care Law and Practice' *British Journal of Social Work* (BJSW) Vol. 12, No. 3, June 1982, at 265; and Fox-Harding, *Perspectives in Child Care Policy* (1991), Longman.
143 House of Commons Second Report from the Social Services Committee, *Children In Care* (1984) HMSO (The Short Report), para. 31.
144 See Maluccio, Fein, Hamilton, Klier and Wand, 'Beyond Permanency Planning' (1980) *Child Welfare* 59.
145 Hussell and Monaghan, 'Going for Good' *Social Work Today*, Vol. 13, No. 47, August 17, 1982.

Meanwhile, social workers were being encouraged to circumvent the courts' decision making, by presenting them with *fait accompli* situations: 'since placement is a matter for social work, as well as legal expertise, there may be good arguments for delaying proceedings, until the child is in his new family. Evidence can then be brought of his new attachments and the court asked to ratify an existing situation.[146]

This somewhat Machiavellian advice was characteristic of a strong section of social work opinion and may account for the fact that, 15 years later, courts are struggling to impose their control over local authority placement policies, by reviewing decisions at an earlier stage, with the express purpose of avoiding the scenario proposed above.

The emphasis on permanent substitute care has had a considerable impact on the termination of contact between children and their natural families. This is, unfortunately, an attitude which still persists and which serves to undermine the philosophies of partnership with parents and the assumption of reasonable contact, which underpin the Children Act 1989. If contact is still continuing, children are sometimes seen as less marketable in terms of permanent placement. The strength of the legacy of deeply entrenched and misunderstood interpretations of permanence philosophies should not be under-estimated as a key factor in inhibiting the changes of culture, which are necessary within social services philosophy and practice, if the principles of the Children Act 1989 are to be successfully absorbed into current practice. It is unfortunate that this persistent ambivalence is reflected, rather than examined, in the White Paper:

> there is, however, some concern that local authorities may sometimes work to keep a child with an unsatisfactory family for too long, when it would be better to apply to the court for an order authorising an alternative family placement with perhaps a view to adoption. There is also some feeling that planning for a child who needs a permanent new family can be more difficult because of the emphasis in the Act on maintaining contact with birth families.[147]

Contact

The assumption of reasonable contact, which permeates all proceedings under the Children Act 1989, means that many more children will reach the point of adoption with existing and continuing arrangements for contact with their family of origin. In addition, with the increase in numbers of adoptions from care, children are likely to be older and to have clear memories of their own parents. It may well be easier for all the adults concerned to go for a clean break approach and justify this on the basis that it is less complicated and less confusing for the child. However, at the end of the day, existing relationships must be incorporated into positive planning for the child's future. This is a very difficult area and one on which guardians are increasingly being called upon to advise courts. The White Paper identifies the most important objective as supporting the new family relationship, and sees free consent by the child

146 Adcock, 'Social Work Dilemmas' in *Terminating Parental Contact* (1980) Published by ABAFA — The Association of British Adoption and Fostering Agencies. Discussion Series 2.
147 *Adoption: The Future, op. cit.*, para. 3.16.

and the new family as critical in the decision as to whether birth parents should be allowed to maintain direct contact with their children after adoption.

In the past, the breaking of old ties has been seen as a preliminary requisite for the establishment of new affectional bonds within the adoptive family. The idea that there is, somehow, a limit to the number of people who can have a place in the child's affections is not supported by research findings. Regular access to parents is associated with fewer fostering breakdowns.[148]

Adoption in the 1990s must increasingly take into account the right of older children to maintain any positive advantages which are likely to accrue from maintaining contact with the birth parents, and also the need to maximise the potential for healthy emotional and psychological growth and development by reinforcing positive aspects of the child's identity. It is, perhaps, one of life's injustices that adoptive families have to work so hard to establish and sustain affectional bonds with children, particularly older children, while natural parents, however inadequate and unreasonable, may, by their very existence, reinforce the child's sense of identity and belonging.

In spite of the wealth of excellent research material relating to many aspects of care, contact and foster care practitioners still remain confused.[149] However, practices in relation to access have always been remarkable for flying in the face of the available evidence.[150] The problems are both ideological and practical. Ideologically, the research findings generally point to the overall advantages of children, particularly older children, maintaining either direct or indirect links with their family of origin. The advantages for the children, in these arrangements, are clearly indicated. The disadvantages for adults, particularly those fostering and adopting children, are less clearly articulated and deserve closer analysis. In spite of the movement towards more open adoption practices, there is a strong undertow pulling practitioners back towards the narrower definition of permanence, as promulgated in the late 1970s and early 1980s.

Ideological ambivalence is reflected in practice. Some social workers are still not entirely convinced that contact is a good thing. Moreover, the shortage of time and resources to devote to establishing successful contact arrangements mitigate against the development of constructive approaches to the maintenance of links. Consequently, outcomes may be less successful than would have been hoped, and the self-fulfilling prophecies are perpetuated.

---

148 Berridge and Cleaver, *Foster Home Breakdown* (1987); Thoburn and Rowe, 'Research: A Snapshot of Permanent Family Placement' (1988) *Adoption and Fostering*, Vol. 12 No. 3. See also Triseliotis and Russell *Hard to Place: The Outcome of Adoption and Residential Care* (1984).

149 See The Review of Adoption Law, Appendix 6, Review of Research Relating to Adoption by June Thoburn, and in particular, Fratter, Rowe, Sapsford and Thoburn, *Permanent Family Placement: A Decade of Experience* (1991); *Adoption Essays in Social Policy, Law and Sociology* (Bean, ed. 1984); Lambert, Buist, Triseliotis and Hill, *Freeing Children for Adoption* (1990); *Social Work Decisions in Child Care* (1985) HMSO; *Patterns and Outcomes in Child Placement: Messages from Current Research and their Implications* (1991) Department of Health, HMSO; Rowe, Caine, Hundleby and Keene *Long-term Foster Care* (1984); Milham, Bullock, Hosie and Haak, *Lost in Care: The Problems of Maintaining Links Between Children in Care and their Families* (1986); Thoburn, Murdoch and O'Brien, *Permanence in Child Care* (1986); Berridge and Cleaver *Foster Home Breakdown* (1987).

150 Parsloe and Gibson, 'What Stops Parental Access to Children?' (1984) *Adoption and Fostering* Vol. 8 No.1.

Guardians have expressed concern about changes in fashion regarding ideas about contact, and the feeling that these can change from office to office, even from social worker to social worker. There is an institutional culture about contact, permanence and other issues and social workers have a distressing propensity to swallow theories whole. Often, guardians have felt that it was their task to point this out, tactfully, and especially to identify situations where blanket policies might be affecting outcomes for individual children. The net result of this is that the new contact provisions are not meeting children's needs appropriately. A large part of the problem is the shortage of foster or adoptive parents who are willing or able to take on the complicated 'best contact packages'. There is a lack of consistent and coherent thought about the purposes of contact for a particular child. Is it a prelude to rehabilitation, or part of a linking exercise to reinforce the child's sense of identity and security? In particular, there is a lack of clarity and continuity in thinking about the purpose of particular contacts in terms of the range of relationships which children need and want to sustain throughout their childhood and indeed the rest of their lives.[151]

It is not the shortage of research which is the major problem, (although there is, as yet, little research on the long term outcomes for children in 'open' adoptions),[152] it is the shortage of time and training to integrate research into current practice and to recruit and train social workers with the requisite knowledge and expertise to deal with one of the most complex areas of human relationships. Here, guardians *ad litem* in adoption have a key role to play in critically appraising adoption agencies' plans for children.

Fears that the Children Act 1989 may be interpreted in ways that impede planning for children in need of new families were examined in a study which asked 'Are children still waiting?'[153] The study lends only limited support of this view. It is clear that greater weight is being given to the expressed wishes of children and parents and that, on occasion, this may be seen to conflict with the long term interests of those children.

It is, unfortunately, difficult to provide the element of fine tuning often needed. In relation to these and other matters, courts will be relying heavily on the advice of guardians *ad litem* in adoption proceedings.

Pros and cons of contact   Guardians will be particularly concerned about the following matters:

● whether or not the birth family have accepted that there is no question of rehabilitation, and that adoption entails a permanent transfer of legal responsibility for the child;
● the extent and quality of pre-existing contacts and their contribution or otherwise to the child's welfare;

---

151 The Views of Guardians expressed in the Reports of the 'Practice in Progress' conferences. IRCHIN with the Department of Health 1993.
152 See Mullender, 'The Spread of Openness in New Zealand: The Two Ends of the Process, Meeting in the Middle' in *Open Adoption: The Philosophy and the Practice* (1991); and Adcock, Karuik and White (eds.), *Exploring Openness in Adoption* (1993), pub. Significant Publications.
153 Thomas and Beckett, 'Are children still waiting? Recent Developments and the Impact of the Children Act 1989' *Adoption and Fostering*, Vol. 18, No. 1, Spring 1994.

- the wishes and feelings of the child, not just in relation to whom he wants to see, but how often in what circumstances, with whom and for how long?
- what indirect contacts are necessary or desirable, in particular, the exchange of birthday cards, telephone calls, photographs and school reports?
- what is the view of (a) the child;
                      (b) the adopters; and
                      (c) the natural parents
  about the proposed form of contact?
- how will that contact undermine or support the relationship of the child and the adopters?
- are all the adults in the situation likely to agree about the arrangements? If there is agreement, the arrangements will have a much better chance of working.
- is there enough flexibility in the proposed arrangements to accommodate the developing child's needs?
- is there a risk that the relinquishing parents may seek to persistently undermine the security of the adoptive placement?
- are the proposed arrangements in the long term best interests of the child and how will they contribute to the child's total well-being?
- are the attitudes of both the adoptive parents and the relinquishing birth parents 'reasonable' and likely to be sustained, in terms of consistency of messages and actions concerning contact?
- are the arrangements sufficiently child-centred? Has the child been fully informed and consulted about what is to happen (provided he is of sufficient age and understanding)?

Contact: a child-centred approach The prospect of accepting children's original families as any permanent parts of their lives can be deeply threatening to prospective adopters, on a number of different levels. They feel fearful of the effects of possible intrusion, by people who may be unpredictable, potentially abusive and generally undermining of their best efforts to create a safe environment for children. They may feel that children will be pulled by conflicts of loyalties and disturbed by the prospect of visits. At the most basic level, they may fear that they will eventually lose a child to his family of origin and they fear the potential loss of the exclusive and central relationship, which may be perceived as the right of every parent.

Equally, relinquishing parents may feel that it is their duty to attempt to maintain links with their child, to ensure, even from a distance, that the child is safe and well. At the very least, relinquishing parents find it hard to accept the pain of not knowing whether their child is alive or dead. Some families have their own ways of reassuring themselves about the child's welfare. One grandfather got a job with the local taxi company, and managed to create a situation in which he drove his seven-year-old grandchild, who had been adopted, to school every day. He never told her who he was, but the child's original family had the enormous comfort of knowing that the child was well and happy. In a sense, that knowledge allowed them to feel much more positive about the painful decision that had been made in giving up the child. It reinforced their sense of self-worth and allowed them to feel that they had made a positive choice, enabling the child to be part of new family.

One young mother of 19 freed her baby daughter to adoption after recognising that the child's violent and disturbed putative father would never allow her to live in peace with the child. While she was taking care of his child, he would not leave her alone. In relinquishing her baby, she made a brave choice to sacrifice her relationship with the child, in order to protect her from a potentially abusive and insecure future. The mother opened a building society account, planning to put away a small sum every week, so that if her daughter chose to try and find her once she was grown up, her mother would have something to give her as evidence of her constant love and concern.

Dilemmas about the pros and cons of contact are only a manifestation of what is a much more profound problem of incorporating the child's past into the future. The older the child, the more the memories, the more delicate a task this will be. There can be no hard and fast rules, because each child is individual and has a unique experience. Part of the skill is in recognising the child's special experience and incorporating it into positive planning for the future. Much depends on his age and understanding. He may never have understood why his parents, apparently, didn't want him, or actively rejected him. He may not know where they are, or if they are alive or dead. The process of separation, for older children, may have been protracted and intensely painful. Nevertheless, these memories are a powerful part of his emotional life, even if he doesn't speak about them. If the adoptive parents cannot accept the reality of the child's existing relationships, they will be rejecting a core part of him and, ultimately, risk creating a psychological no-go area which, itself, may undermine their longer term relationship with the child. In this sense, in the right circumstances, contact may contribute to the security of the placement, by creating an environment in which there is honesty and acceptance of the child's whole identity.

Open adoption

S.12(6) of the Adoption Act 1976 allows courts to attach such terms and conditions to an Adoption Order as they think fit. Although such terms and conditions may include contact, it was not until implementation of the Children Act 1989, bringing with it substantial amendments to adoption law, that the question of open adoption, or adoption with contact, became a live issue for courts, children, their representatives and their social workers. The availability of S.8 Orders in any proceedings under the Adoption Act 1976 has opened the door to the possibility of continuing links between relinquishing parents and children, which would have been unthinkable only a few years ago. It should be stressed that the possibility of open adoption should not be regarded as a volte face, in terms of existing placement policies. It does, however, increase the range of options available to the court, in meeting the needs of the particular child. Courts will be cautious and sparing in their use of such Orders.

In normal circumstances, it may be desirable that there should be a complete break, but each case has to be considered on its own merits. The court is unlikely, except in the most exceptional circumstances, to impose terms or conditions as to access to the child's natural family, to which the adopting family will not agree.[154] This approach is reflected in the White Paper, which lays emphasis on supporting the new family relationships, as the most important objective, once an Adoption Order is made.[155] The White Paper does, however, acknowledge the need for less secrecy and for adopted children to have more information about their birth parents and original wider extended family. Open adoption, therefore, is being approached with a cautious optimism.

Competing contact and adoption applications concerning a child, even now that they can be hear concurrently, pose one of the most difficult areas of practice for child care social workers and guardians *ad litem*. Fears that there would be a spate of applications for S.8 Orders, in respect of children already adopted, have been effectively quashed by courts taking a fairly strong line that, once an Adoption Order has been made, the question of contact is effectively closed, barring a dramatic change of circumstances.[156] Applications for S.8 Contact Orders made by birth parents, following the making of an Adoption Order, should be transferred to the High Court, where the Official Solicitor will be appointed to represent the child.

Contact may take all forms, ranging from indirect contact, an annual Christmas and birthday card, the occasional telephone call or the sending of photographs or school reports, through the occasional visit, to regular contact visits, which maintain birth parents as a regular and routine part of the child's everyday life. There is likely to be a greater emphasis on indirect contacts, which may safeguard the child's security and placement, but also afford them the advantages of knowing about their birth family and having access to very basic facts about themselves.[157] Adopters should at the very least be encouraged to keep up-to-date the child's life story book, with for example any photographs and school reports they receive. In practice, the child's needs for contact with his family of origin may not be constant. He may be curious about the different aspects of his birth and background, at different ages and stages of development. The quality of the adoptive placement and the state of the child's relationship with his legal parents will also be other variables which will have a bearing on each particular case.[158]

The available research evidence suggests that there are a number of benefits which accrue from greater openness in adoption and the ability of all children to maintain meaningful links with birth parents. There is also room for a

---

154 The House of Lords in *Re C. (A Minor)* (Adoption: Access) [1989] A.C. 1.
155 *Adoption: The Future, op. cit.*, para. 4.14.
156 Re C. (A Minor) (Adopted Child: Contact) [1993] 2 F.L.R. 431.
157 The research of Rowe *et al.* has shown, not only how little information children themselves had about their birth family, but how ignorant foster and adoptive parents can be of significant facts about their children and events in their lives. See Rowe, Caine, Hundleby and Keene, *Long Term Foster Care* (1984).
158 Cooper, 'Paediatric Aspects', Ch.4, and Bentovim, 'Psychiatric Issues', Ch.5, both in *Terminating Parental Contact* (1980), Association of British Adoption and Fostering Agencies, Discussion Paper 2.

variety of different arrangements.[159] There are indications that many birth parents would be happy with semi-open adoption and would be happy to receive regular news about the child's general health and welfare.[160]

The question of contact needs to be addressed, before placing the child for adoption. Since October 1991, it has been possible to hear contact and adoption applications concurrently and this is a considerable advance. A local authority's wish to facilitate an adoptive placement is not sufficient reason for them to terminate contact.

In *Re B.* (Children in Care: Contact)[161] Care Orders were made on February 4, 1992 in respect of two girls. On December 3, 1990, the girls were placed with foster parents, where they remained for two years. In May 1991, the local authority made plans for the girls' adoption. From March 1992, the mother started seeing her daughters regularly. In September 1992, there was a hearing at Birmingham County Court where, *inter alia*, the local authority applied for an Order under S.34(4), authorising them to refuse contact between the girls and their mother, in order to facilitate placing the children with prospective adopters. The mother opposed this application, because she sought rehabilitation with the daughters. The County Court judge made the Order under S.34(4) principally because he considered that, in accordance with *Re S.* (Child in Care: Access)[162] he could not interfere with local authority's plans for the child. The guardian *ad litem*, supported by the mother, appealed, and, in overturning the County Court decision and reinstating contact between mother and child, Lord Justice Butler Sloss took the view that *A. v. Liverpool City Council* and *Re. W.* do not prevent courts from investigating the local authority's plans.

> My understanding of the Children Act is that it aims to incorporate the best of the wardship jurisdiction within the statutory framework without any of the perceived disadvantages of judicial monitoring of administrative plans. It provides for the court a wide range of options and the possibility of its own motion to set in train a line of investigation not contemplated or asked for by the parties. Like wardship, however, these wide powers are to be sparingly used.[163]

Consequently, pre-Children Act authorities, such as *Re S.* and the *West Glamorgan* case, must be approached with caution. These cases concluded that contact should not be awarded to a parent, where this may frustrate the local authority's long term plans for the child, unless it could be shown that the local authority disregarded cogent evidence suggesting that parental contact is required in the interest of the child.

There is now a presumption that contact will always be of benefit unless it is proved otherwise and, notwithstanding the local authority's plans for the child's adoption, the court may require the local authority to justify those long term plans, to the extent that they exclude contact. However, if rehabilitation has been previously ruled out and the parent is applying for contact, but not

---

159 See Triseliotis, 'Open Adoption' in *Open Adoption: The Philosophy and the Practice* (Mullenden ed. 1991), p.32.
160 Sawbridge, 'On behalf of Birth Parents' in *Open Adoption, ibid.*, p. 117.
161 [1993] 1 F.C.R. 363. C.A.
162 [1991] F.C.R. 82.
163 [1993] 1 F.C.R. 379.

for discharge of the Care Order, the onus is on the parent to point out changes in circumstances which merit further investigation and justify reconsideration of the local authority's plans. If the court decides that the parent should be given a chance, it can make an interim Order for contact, with a direction for review at a later date.[164]

The arguments rehearsed by the President of the Family Division in *Re E.*, clearly indicate that local authorities are under a duty to investigate, not just consider, the possibility of open adoption and that if they have not done this, this may be a reason for courts to refuse their applications to terminate contact under S.34. In the end, however, it is a matter for the court to decide which Order to make, on the basis of the respective merits of long term placements. The ultimate responsibility rests with the court, not with the local authority.

Re E. concerned two boys, aged five and a half and nearly four. They were children with varying particular needs and suffering particular disadvantages in their circumstances. The parents had their own difficulties, which prevented them from exercising the appropriate level of care for their children. The local authority applied for a Care Order under S.31 and prepared a care plan. At the subsequent hearing, there was no dispute about the fact that the circumstances of the children and their parents required that a Care Order should be made. However, the question of contact took six days to resolve. The local authority wanted to 'be in a position to terminate contact when the children were placed with long term foster parents', in pursuance of their adoption plan. It was proposed that contact should be reduced progressively during the succeeding months and finally terminated when children were placed with the proposed adoptive parents.

The parents and the guardian *ad litem* opposed this application, which the local authority had justified on the basis that continued face to face contact between the children and their parents would conflict with their care plan, which provided for the closed adoption of the children. The local authority's case rested on the decision made in *West Glamorgan County Council v. P (No.2).*[165] In turn, the *West Glamorgan* case had established that the principles set out in *Re S. (Child in Care: Access)*[166] applied equally to a case brought under the Children Act 1989. In essence, this would mean that the court should not exercise its powers to allow contact when it was aware that this would be incompatible with the decision of the local authority in relation to the child's long term care, unless satisfied on cogent evidence that the welfare of the child required such a decision and the local authority had disregarded relevant evidence, or was acting capriciously.

The fact that the judge adopted this test in the *West Glamorgan* case proved to be grounds for appeal in *Re E.*,[167] where it was submitted that test had been discredited in the subsequent case of *Re B. (Children in Care: Contact).*[168]

---

164 *Cheshire County Council v. B.* [1992] 2 F.C.R. 572.
165 [1992] 2 F.C.R. 406.
166 [1991] F.C.R. 82.
167 [1994] 1 F.C.R. 584, C.A.
168 [1993] 1 F.C.R. 363.

In *Re B.* Butler Sloss LJ identified the two types of contact applications, those which ask for contact as such and those which are attempts to set aside the Care Order itself. In the first category, there is no suggestion that the applicant wishes to take over the care of the child and the issue of contact often depends upon whether contact would frustrate long term plans for the child in the substitute home where continuing contact may not be for the long term welfare of the child. The presumption of contact, which has to be for the benefit of the child, has always to be balanced against their long term welfare, particularly in decisions about where they will live in the future. Contact must not be allowed to de-stabilise or endanger the arrangements for the child and, in many cases, the plans for the child will be decisive of the contact application. There may also be cases where the parent is having satisfactory contact with the child and there are no long term plans, or those plans do not appear to the court to preclude some future contact. The proposals of the local authority, based on their appreciation of the best interests of the child, must command the greatest respect and consideration from the court, but parliament has given to the court, not to the local authority, the duty to decide on contact between the child and those named in S.34(1). Consequently, the court may have the task of requiring the local authority to justify their long term plans, to the extent only that those plans exclude contact between parent and child. In *Re E.* it was submitted that the decision in the *West Glamorgan* case did not give due weight to the provisions of the Children Act, which require the local authority to give due consideration to the wishes and feelings of the child and the parents.

The assumption that the local authority shall allow a child in care reasonable contact with, amongst others, his parents is fundamental to the provisions of not only S.34 but of the whole of the Children Act. This contrasts with pre-Children Act legislation and the position under the Child Care Act 1980.

In *Re E.* it was clear from the evidence of the guardian *ad litem*, amongst others, that there was no real likelihood of the discovery or identification of proposed adoptive parents who would countenance continuing contact after adoption. Indeed the local authority had made no specific investigations to find out what the situation might be.

The local authority's case was, firstly that there was no prospect of actual rehabilitation with the parents and secondly, that the level and quality of contact with the children and parents which did exist was of a 'relatively low quality'. The view of the guardian *ad litem*, supported by expert witness evidence from a clinical psychologist, was that the parents would have a stabilising effect on the children's life and that they were in no way likely to undermine a permanent placement. On appeal, the court refused the local authority's application to terminate contact under S.34 and upheld the position of the guardian *ad litem* and the solicitor acting for the children. In allowing the appeal, Simon Brown LJ said:

> in short, even when the S.31 criteria are satisfied, contact may well be of singular importance to the long term welfare of the child, firstly, in giving the child the security of knowing that his parents love him and are interested in his welfare, secondly, by avoiding any damaging sense of loss to the child in seeing himself

abandoned by his parents, thirdly, by enabling the child to commit himself to the substitute family, with the seal of approval of the natural parents, and, fourthly, by giving the child the necessary sense of family and personal identity. Contact, if maintained, is capable of reinforcing and increasing the chances of success for permanent placement whether on a long term fostering basis or by adoption.[169]

The fact that the local authority had made no efforts to find prospective open adopters, as opposed to closed adopters, was a significant factor in the case and is indicative of the way that current law and practice have moved since implementation of the Children Act. The fact that there were no prospective applicants on the existing register willing to consider open adoption was not considered by the court to be sufficient reason to justify the local authority's proposals for closed adoption.[170] The judgment in Re E. is a powerful incentive to guardians *ad litem* and local authority social workers to consider the advantages of open adoption. It also has implications for the responsibility of the local authority to recruit and train prospective adoptive parents, to ensure that registers include applicants who are prepared to work with natural parents and local authorities in maintaining links with relinquishing families, in appropriate cases.

Summary

Open adoption may provide the best outcome for the older child, by providing a permanent placement, reinforced by and incorporating the child's existing identity and relationships. It is suggested, here, that the welfare of the child should be the determining factor in these matters, not the wishes of the adoptive parents, who may effectively hold the court to ransom by vetoing contact arrangements. If this were to happen, courts would be likely to take a fairly dim view. However, because of the complex and emotionally charged issues involved, not to mention the conflicts of interests inherent in the wide range of differential views about contact, now more that ever, the child, or children, in adoption proceedings require both separate legal and social work representation in all courts hearing adoption applications, not just those in the High Court. This would ensure a voice for children in the discussion about the own lives. Secrecy in adoption law and practice is a feature of the last seventy years, since the first Adoption Act in 1926. The need for secrecy arose primarily out of the stigma of illegitimacy and the need to 'hide the shame' of unmarried mothers.[171] The protection of the newly formed adoptive family was another factor.

Totally closed adoption can be about negative feelings, secrecy, guilt, grief, loneliness and loss. More open adoption practice offers an opportunity for more positive feelings for everybody concerned, providing the relinquishing parents with support for their continuing concern and interest in the child and allowing adoptive parents the opportunity for an honest and open relationship

---

169 *Re E.* (Children in Care: Contact) 1 F.C.R. 594. C.A.
170 *Re E.* (Children in Care: Contact) [1994] 1 F.C.R. 584. C.A.
171 See Howe, Sawbridge and Hinings, *Half a Million Women: Mothers who Lose their Children by Adoption* (1992) and Toynbee, *Lost Children* (1985), the story of adopted children searching for their mothers.

with their adopted child, including the information which will enable them to reassure the child about his origins. This honesty is likely to diminish the chances of losing their child to the birth parents at 18 and the advantages to the older child are more likely to be considerable. They find themselves accepted by both birth parents and adoptive parents. The relinquishing parents' involvement in future arrangements allows the child the freedom to attach to the adoptive parents, with the relinquishing parents' permission and without a conflict of loyalty, which is so important in terms of healthy psychological development. The child is not split by conflicts of interest between the key people in his life. His sense of identity is not only preserved, but reinforced and augmented by access to both families. The birth parents can help the child to settle in the adoptive placement, provided that the work on relinquishing has been concluded successfully. These are all positive aspects of open adoption. Equally, there will be negative indications for a significant number of children and these should be identified clearly. The criteria must be based on the right of the child concerned to have the benefit of any positive contribution that the birth parents may be able to make to their well-being either, in terms of physical contact or positive messages, to provide reinforcement of the child's sense of self-worth and security. The detail of the contact 'package' requires careful thought, with consideration of the degree and type of contact which is necessary to achieve the required outcomes, in terms of ensuring emotional and physical growth, both through the establishment of secure attachments and the recognition of the child's unique identity. This requires considerable diagnostic skill and expertise, as well as sound legal decision-making.

A change in the law cannot be sufficient to bring about appropriate changes in practice overnight, but a review of adoption legislation offers the possibility of an increased range of options for children and is an opportunity that guardians *ad litem* should not be afraid to explore, on behalf of the children they represent.[172]

---

172 See further *Open Adoption, the Philosophy and the Practice* (Mullender, ed. 1991).

Chapter 8

The Role of the Guardian ad Litem in Surrogacy Arrangements

Applications under S.30 of the Human Fertilisation and Embryology Act 1990

The role of the guardian *ad litem* in surrogacy arrangements is introduced by S.30 of the Human Fertilisation and Embryology Act 1990 (Parental Orders), and is as set out in:

The Children (Allocation of Proceedings) (Amendment) Order 1994 S.I. No. 2164 (L.12)

The Family Proceedings (Amendment) (No. 2) Rules 1994 Supreme Court of England and Wales County Courts S.I. 2165 (L.13)

The Family Proceedings Courts (Children Act 1989) (Amendment) Rules 1994. Magistrates Courts S.I. 2166 (L.14)

The Parental Orders (Human Fertilisation and Embryology) Regulations 1994 S.I. 2767

LAC (94)25 Human Fertilisation and Embryology Act 1990

Parental Orders (Human Fertilisation and Embryology) Regulations 1994: Powers and Duties of Local Authorities, Health Authorities and Guardians *ad Litem*.

Section 30 of the Human Fertilisation and Embryology Act 1990 was implemented on 1 November 1994.

All appeals arising from the refusal to make a Parental Order will be heard in the High Court.

Surrogacy

As the numbers of babies available for adoption has dwindled significantly, so the increasing problem of involuntary childlessness has increased and become more apparent. It has been suggested that as many as one in six couples in Britain and America were infertile in 1986 — twice as many as 10 years earlier.[1] Adoption, surrogacy and donor insemination are all ways of counteracting childlessness and, in the area of assisted reproduction, medical science has led the way, with the law being called upon to review and legitimise existing technical realities, rather than first laying down a philosophical and ethical framework for their development. Following the birth of the first test-tube baby, Louise Brown, in 1978, medical science made a series of very rapid technological advances in pioneering new techniques of assisted reproduction, and the long-term storage of donated genetic material.

Surrogacy is the practice whereby one woman carries a child for another with the intention that the child should be handed over after birth. Surrogacy arrangements may involve either:

● Full surrogacy — both artificial insemination and egg donation by the commissioning parents so that the child has no genetic relationship with the host mother who gives birth to him or her;

or more commonly:

● Partial surrogacy — the surrogate mother is artificially inseminated with the sperm of the commissioning father. In this case the child is genetically related to both the commissioning father and the surrogate mother.

Partial surrogacy requires no complicated medical procedures and it is therefore hard to assess how often informal arrangements are made. It will be important for guardians to establish exactly what the arrangements were in the case of a particular child, as the psychological imperatives involved in the relinquishing of a child genetically related to the surrogate mother will be different from those involved in the case of a mother giving birth to a child with whom she has no genetic link.

Informal surrogacy arrangements are as old as time, and are mentioned in the Old Testament. Surrogacy occurs most commonly where a couple's childlessness is the result of female infertility whilst the male partner is fertile. A surrogate mother is then found who is willing to be impregnated with the male partner's sperm and, having given birth, gives the child back to the father and his partner. The mother who carried the child is deemed to be its legal mother in the absence of any other Order. It was, however, the advances in medical science which allowed for the gestation of an embryo, provided by both commissioning parents, following the implantation in the host mother by

---

1   Bellina and Wilson, *The Fertility Handbook: A Positive and Practical Guide* (1986)

means of assisted reproduction programmes and, in particular, the commercial surrogacy agencies established in the USA in the early 1980s, which led to the establishment of a Committee of Enquiry into Human Fertilisation and Embryology (the Warnock Committee) in 1982. The remit of the Committee, chaired by Dame Mary Warnock, was to examine the social, ethical and legal implication of developments in the field of assisted reproduction. In general, there was an acceptance of the inevitability of continuing embryo research. Pandora's Box had been opened, and it was too late to close it again. However, there were many who shared the concern of BAAF (British Association for Adoption and Fostering) that: 'we cannot believe that it is right to create children with a deliberate intention of separating them from their birth mother.'[2]

Following the publicity surrounding the Kim Cotton case in January 1985[3] which aroused widespread public concern about commercial surrogacy arrangements, the Surrogacy Arrangements Act 1985 made it illegal for third parties to negotiate or facilitate any surrogacy for payment. It also banned advertisements for or of surrogacy services. The law, therefore, did not ban surrogacy, but it banned surrogacy as a commercial enterprise. In fact, it is difficult to monitor and regulate surrogacy.

Numbers of surrogate births are not high, but they are growing. It has been estimated that there was one surrogate birth in 1987, as against 29 in 1992. According to Kim Cotton, the Chairperson of Childlessness Overcome Through Surrogacy (COTS) 'surrogacy is more widely available than we were led to believe, as some hospitals act very quietly.'

COTS estimated that between 1987 and 1993 there were 89 surrogate births.[4] The Department of Health estimates that there may now be nearly 200 children who have been born as a result of surrogacy arrangements, some of whom are reaching school age. Until implementation of S.30 of the Human Fertilisation and Embryology Act 1990 the only way for the commissioning couple to legitimise the legal arrangements between themselves and the child born as a result of surrogacy arrangements was through adoption. If one of the applicants is a parent, the application can be treated as a step-parent adoption. This had obvious disadvantages. Adoption is a very cumbersome process for those seeking to adopt a child, who may well be their own genetic offspring. Prospective adoptive parents are assessed with a view to adopting any child, rather than a particular child, whereas commissioning parents wish to be the parents to a particular, rather than any, child. There was, therefore, a perceived need for a different procedure capable of dealing with complex surrogacy arrangements. The point is highlighted in the case of *Re W. (Minors) (Surrogacy)*.[5] Twins born as a result of surrogacy arrangements were allowed to stay in the care of their genetic (commissioning) parents, provided that they gave an undertaking to the court that they would make an

---

2   BAAF Policy Statement, July 1987, quoted by Walby in Walby and Symons *Who am I? Identity, Adoption and Human Fertilisation* (1990).
3   *Re C. (A Minor)* (Ward Surrogacy) [1985] F.L.R. 846.
4   Blythe, *Infertility and Assisted Reproduction: Practice Issues for Counsellors* (1991), PROGAR (British Association of Social Workers Project Group on Assisted Reproduction).
5   [1991] 1 F.L.R. 385.

application for a parental order within 28 days of the implementation of S.30 of the Human Fertilisation and Embryology Act 1990. The complexity revolves around three main areas:

- the opportunities for commercial exploitation of all parties concerned, but particularly the child and the birth mother;
- the need to examine and regulate the ingenuity of medical technology; and
- the right opportunities for the development of complex and convoluted conflicts of interest between the child, and its surrogate and commissioning parents.

The Human Fertilisation and Embryology Act 1990

The provisions of the Human Fertilisation and Embryology Act 1990 were based upon responses to a Consultation Paper in 1986 and a White Paper published in 1987, both issued following the publication of the Warnock Report in 1984.[6]

The provisions of the 1990 Act regulate services in connection with embryo research, infertility treatments, which involve the creation of an embryo outside the body, and artificial insemination by donor (AID). It established the Human Fertilisation and Embryology Authority (HFEA) which was set up to control and license centres providing treatment under the 1990 Act. The Authority maintains a Code of Practice, giving guidance on the proper conduct of licensed activities.

The main provisions of the 1990 Act came into force between November 1990 and August 1991. Under the 1990 Act the Surrogacy Arrangements Act 1985 remains in force, but a new S.1(A) was introduced by S.36(1) of the 1990 Act which states that no surrogacy arrangement is enforceable by law. The position remains that a local authority has a duty to make enquiries, when it knows that a baby has been, or is about to be, born as a result of surrogacy, in order to be satisfied that the baby is not, or will not be, at risk as a result of the arrangement. However, local authorities can be assured that when the treatment has been undertaken by a licensed clinic, it will have been undertaken in accordance with the Code of Practice published under S.25 of the 1990 Act, and with regard to S.13(5) (a late addition to the Bill), which requires account to be taken of the welfare of any child who may be born as the result of the treatment. Where the circumstances of the birth, or subsequent arrangements for the baby, are not clear, hospital or social work staff may be alerted. Since the Children Act 1989, an Emergency Protection Order will not be available unless the criteria laid down in S.44(1)(a) are satisfied. In other situations where the local authority has been unable to

---

6   See Department of Health and Social Security, Report of the Committee of Enquiry into Human Fertilisation and Embryology (The Warnock Report), Cmnd. 9414 (1984) and see also Department of Health and Social Security, (1987) *Human Fertilisation and Embryology: A Framework for Legislation*, Cm. 259 (1987) and Department of Health and Social Security, (1986) *Legislation on Human Infertility Services and Embryo Research*, Cm. 46 (1986).

satisfy itself that the child is not at risk, the local authority responsibility for checking the well-being of the child remains. This may arise where no licensed treatment centre has been involved. The Act has five main aims. These are:

- to make provision in connection with human embryos and any subsequent development of such embryos;
- to prohibit certain practices in connection with embryos and gametes;
- to establish a Human Fertilisation and Embryology Authority;
- to make provision about the persons who, in certain circumstances, are to be treated in law as the parents of a child; and
- to amend the Surrogacy Arrangements Act 1985.

The Human Fertilisation and Embryology Authority

The Authority was established in April 1991 in response to deep public concern about the implications which the new techniques might have for the perception and valuing of human life and human relationships. Under S.7 of the 1990 Act the Authority has to prepare an arrival report, which the Secretary of State is required to lay before parliament. Its general functions are set out in S.8 of the 1990 Act, which states:

The Authority shall:

- keep under review information about embryos and any subsequent development of embryos and about the provision of treatment services and activities governed by this Act, and advise the Secretary of State, if he asks it to do so, about those matters;
- publicise the services provided to the public by the Authority or provided in pursuance of licences;
- provide, to such an extent as it considers appropriate, advice and information for persons to whom licences apply or who are receiving treatment services or providing gametes or embryos for use for the purposes of activities governed by this Act, or may wish to do so, and
- perform such other functions as may be specified in regulations.

The Authority's principal task is to regulate, by means of a licensing system, any research or treatment which involves the creation, keeping and using of human embryos outside the body, or the storage or donation of human eggs and sperm. It must also maintain a Code of Practice giving guidance about the proper conduct of licensed activities. The object of the Code is wider than to secure the safety or efficacy of particular clinical or scientific practices, it is concerned with areas of practice which raise fundamental ethical and social questions.

The Code of Practice is guided by four main principles:

- the respect which is due to human life at all stages in its development;
- the right of people who are, or may be, infertile to the proper consideration of their request for treatment;
- a concern for the welfare of children which cannot always be adequately protected by concern for the interests of adults involved; and
- a recognition of the benefits, both to individuals and to society, which can flow from the responsible pursuit of medical and scientific knowledge.

The Code of Practice recognises that these considerations might sometimes conflict.[7] The Code of Practice covers the responsibilities of staff engaged in both clinical and scientific services, the facilities including counselling facilities available for those using the services of the Human Fertilisation and Embryology Authority, arrangements for assessing both clients and donors, and also covers issues of consent, information, counselling and storage and handling of gametes and embryos. Guardians will be particularly concerned with the parts of the Code of Practice which deal with the welfare of the child and the arrangements for storage of records, including access to records and confidentiality.[8]

People seeking licensed treatment from the Human Fertilisation and Embryology Authority must be offered three types of counselling:

- *Implications counselling.* This aims to enable the person concerned to understand the implications of the proposed course of action for himself or herself, for his or her family, and for any children born as a result.
- *Support counselling.* This aims to give emotional support at times of particular stress, e.g. when there is a failure to achieve pregnancy.
- *Therapeutic counselling.* This aims to help people to cope with the consequences of infertility and treatment and to help them to resolve the problems which these may cause. It includes helping people to adjust their expectations and to accept their situation.

The welfare of the child

One of the conditions of a treatment licence for a human fertilisation and embryology clinic is that: 'a woman shall not be provided with treatment services unless account has been taken of the welfare of any child who may be born as a result of the treatment (including the need of that child for a father) and of any other child who may be affected by the birth.' This applies to every woman, whether or not she is resident in, or a citizen of, the United Kingdom. 'Any other child' includes children who already exist within the client's household or family.

The condition applies only to centres with a treatment licence but it covers any of the services they offer to assist conception or pregnancy, whether or not these require a licence. However, the degree of consideration necessary will be greater if the treatment is required to be licensed under the Act, and particularly if it involves the use of donated gametes.[9]

Licensed clinics are directed to consider the following factors under the Code of Practice:

- Centres should take all reasonable steps to ascertain who would be the legal parent (or parents) of any child born as a result of the procedure and

---

7   See Introduction, Human Fertilisation and Embryology Authority Code of Practice established under S.26 of the Human Fertilisation and Embryology Act 1990.

8   It is recommended that all guardians who are involved in S.30 applications should have a copy of the Code of Practice, which may be obtained from the Human Fertilisation and Embryology Authority, Paxton House, 30 Artillery Lane, London E1 7LS.

9   The HFEA Code of Practice, paras. 3.12 to 3.20.

who it is intended will be bringing him or her up. When clients come from abroad, centres should not assume that the law of that country relating to the parentage of a child born as a result of donated gametes is the same as that of the United Kingdom.

- People seeking treatment are entitled to a fair and unprejudiced assessment of their situations and needs, which should be conducted with the skill and sensitivity appropriate to the delicacy of the case and the wishes and feelings of those involved.
- Centres should seek to satisfy themselves that the client's GP knows of no reason why the client might not be suitable to be offered treatment, including anything that might adversely affect the welfare of any resulting child.
- Centres should obtain the client's consent before contacting the GP, however, failure to give consent should be taken into account in considering whether or not to offer treatment.
- If any of these particulars or enquiries give rise for concern, for example, evidence that prospective parents have had children removed from their care or evidence of a previous relevant conviction, the centre should make such further enquiries of any relevant individual authority or agency as it can.
- Centres should obtain the client's consent before approaching any individual authority or agent for information, however, failure to give consent should be taken into account when deciding whether or not to offer treatment.

Specific factors to be taken into account are:

- commitment of the person seeking treatment and that of their husband or partner, if any, to having and bringing up a child or children;
- their ages and medical histories and the medical histories of their families;
- the needs of any child, or children, who may be born as a result of treatment, including the implications of any possible multiple birth and the ability of the prospective parents (or parent) to meet those needs;
- any risk of harm to the child or children who may be born, including the risk of inherited disorders, problems during pregnancies and of neglect or abuse; and
- the effect of a new baby or babies upon any existing child of the family.[10]

Where people seek treatment using donated gametes, centres should also take the following factors into account:

- the child's potential need to know about his or her origins and whether or not the prospective parents are prepared for the questions which may arise while the child is growing up;
- the possible attitude of other members of the family towards the child and towards his or her status in the family;

---

10   *Ibid.*, paras. 3.14, 3.15, 3.16, 3.22, 3.23, 3.24 and 3.25.

- the implications for the welfare of the child if the donor is personally known within the child's family and social circle; and
- any possibility known to the centre of a dispute about the legal fatherhood of the child.[11]

This is satisfactory as far as it goes, however, there is concern about the potential conflict between the rights of adults to have children and the right of those children to have their welfare considered as a matter of paramount importance.

The Child's Right to Information about his Identity

Article 8 of the UN Convention on the Rights of the Child deals with the preservation of the child's identity, and Article 7 deals with name and nationality. The Convention makes it clear that children should have access to information which will enable them to know their origins. Similarly, both the Review of Adoption Law and the White Paper *Adoption: The Future*[12] stress the responsibility of adoptive parents to tell their children the truth about their birth and family history and seek to move away from the culture of secrecy which has shrouded adoption proceedings. If, as anticipated, future adoption legislation echoes the principle already established in the Children Act 1989 that the welfare of the child is of paramount consideration, then children who are the subject of S.30 applications will be a disadvantaged group in having account taken of their welfare but not paramount consideration. The question arises as to why these children should have few rights to the details of their identity as individuals human beings, as required by Article 8 of the UN Convention on the Rights of the Child:

> States Parties undertake to respect the right of the child to preserve his or her identity, including nationality, name and family relations, as recognised by law, without unlawful interference; where a child is illegally deprived of some, or all of the elements of his or her identity, States Parties shall provide assistance and protection, with a view to speedily re-establishing his or her identity.[13]

However, it has been argued that Articles 8 and 12 of the European Convention on Human Rights, which guarantee a respect for family and the right to found a family, create, in the words of the Warnock Report, 'a *right* to take full advantage of the techniques which are available to alleviate infertility.'[14] Presumably it is for national governments to attempt to achieve a legislative compromise between these potentially conflicting Articles.

The current law in Britain, therefore, generally upholds the principle of donor anonymity although the provisions of the Human Fertilisation and Embryology (Disclosure of Information) Act 1992 did to some extent relax the restrictions on the disclosure of information imposed by S.33(5) of the 1990

---

11   *Ibid.*, paras. 3.16 and 3.17.
12   (November 1993) Department of Health, HMSO.
13   Article 8.1 and 2.
14   Snowden and Snowden, *The Gift of a Child*, (1984) quoted in Walby and Symons, *Who am I? Identity, Adoption and Human Fertilisation* (1990).

Act. Those born as a result of surrogacy arrangements will be entitled to seek information from the Registrar General, enabling them to establish who their surrogate parents are, once they achieve the age of 18.[15] At that time they may make an application for non-identifying information about the donors and the applicant must be given an opportunity to receive counselling. In addition, the child at 18 has a right to obtain information as to whether or not he or she might be genetically related to a proposed spouse. Young people between 16 and 18 contemplating marriage will only be able to check whether they are genetically related to the proposed spouse. This is of course dependent on the commissioning parents giving the child the relevant information relating to the circumstances of his birth.

Children who are born with a congenital disability, following the use of donated gametes, may, under existing legislation, obtain information about the donor identity of their parents. This highlights the potentially vulnerable situation of many children born as a result of surrogacy arrangements, who will have no knowledge of their medical, as well as their physical and genetic inheritance.

If commissioning parents have no obligation to tell their children the facts of their birth, then it follows that those children will not be aware that they have a right to know the facts about their surrogate parents. Justification for this lack of openness generally lies in consideration for the problems that it would present for adults, rather than the children, involved, particularly the emotional problems for the infertile parent and the complexities which may arise from the ramification of the relationship between the child and for potential parents, the birth mother and her partner, who may or may not be the genetic parents, and the commissioning parents, one or both of whom may be the genetic parent. The child has, in effect, two sets of parents and will need information about both to answer the question 'Who am I?' The potential complications which may arise from this intricate pattern of relationships are daunting but, nevertheless, have to be addressed if the child is to emerge at the end of the day as a whole person confident in himself and his relationships. Safeguarding the interests of donors may be important, but safeguarding the rights of children must be paramount.

> Background knowledge of one's family is like baby food — it is literally fed to a person as part of a normal nourishment that builds up his (or her) mental and emotional structure, and helps the person to become acquainted with what he (or she) is, so that he can seize his inheritance of himself.[16]

Many guardians *ad litem* embarking on this work will be conscious of the British Association of Social Workers' Code of Ethics, and its assertion that:

> basic to the profession of social work is the recognition of the value and dignity of every human being, irrespective of origin, race, status, sex, sexual orientation, age, disability, belief or contribution to society. The profession accepts responsibility to

---

15   See Human Fertilisation and Embryology Act 1990 LAC (94)25 para. 6. Parental Orders (Human Fertilisation and Embryology) Regulations 1994, Access to birth records — Counselling.

16   Kornitzer, 'The Adopted Adolescent and the Sense of Identity', quoted in *Who am I?, op. cit.*, p. 39.

encourage and facilitate the self-realisation of each individual person, with due regard for the interests of others.

The National Association of Guardians *ad Litem* and Reporting Officers' Code of Ethics commits its members to acting in the best interests of children, and to accord value to the child's individuality.[17] They are also directed to take a longer term view of the child's interests than that dictated by the time-limited court proceedings.[18]

The child born as a result of surrogacy arrangements does not have the same right as an adopted child to obtain a copy of the original birth certificate when he or she is grown up. After a Parental Order is made, a record will be kept in a separate register but the Human Fertilisation and Embryology Act permits donors of gametes to preserve their anonymity, and there is no provision on the court rules for the granting of a Parental Order to commissioning parents to be dependent upon their undertaking to reveal information about their genetic origin to the children concerned. The Parental Order procedure is based on amended adoption provisions as the most convenient legal, not philosophical, or even ethical, approach. There is a question about at what stage confidentiality becomes secrecy, and in this sense it is necessary to distinguish those children who are the subject of parental applications under S.30 from children generally who are born as a result of donor insemination:

> it has been alleged that anonymity is essential to ensure a continuing supply of donated genetic material. Deceit concerning the child's true genetic origins is said to be justified on several grounds. There is some evidence that assisted reproduction services themselves still enjoy equivocal social acceptance, acknowledgement of recourse to them also reveals a stigmatising condition of infertility, while children born following donor insemination no longer suffer the legally imposed indignity of illegitimacy. Public knowledge about the truth of the conception might still expose them to public scorn or stigma. Within the family it has been argued that openness may cause emotional problems for the infertile parent (usually the father, so the real reason may be the reluctance to face up to the issue of male infertility), relationship problems between the child and the non-genetic parent, and conflicts concerning the absent, unknown genetic parent ... Recipients of assisted reproduction have become pawns in the face of conflicting attitudes and advice concerning secrecy and openness in assisted reproduction. Broadly speaking, clinical practitioners tend to advocate secrecy, and occasionally outright deception, while social workers and social scientists tend to advocate openness.[19]

There is also a question as to how feasible it will be to keep the child's true parentage a secret for what will effectively be a lifetime. This means, not only the commissioning parents keeping the secret, but also the wider network of family and friends. It is not hard to visualise a situation in which the child may be confronted with this information during a family row, or during the course of acrimonious divorce proceedings, which have a one in three chance of taking place. There is a case for the establishment of a surrogacy contact

17   Principles 2.2 and 2.4.
18   Principle 4.2.
19   Blythe, *Infertility and Assisted Reproduction: Practice Issues for Counsellors* (1991), British Association of Social Workers 54.

register, to parallel the functions of the adoption contact register for those children whose legal parentage has been conferred by the making of a S.30 Parental Order. This seems unlikely in view of the fact that the law, as it stands, endorses a situation in which young people have no right to know who they are.

S.30 The Human Fertilisation and Embryology Act 1990

Commissioning parents, who wish to be treated in law as the parents of a child born as the result of surrogacy arrangements, may apply to the court under S.30 of the Human Fertilisation and Embryology Act 1990 for a Parental Order. The Order has the same legal effect as adoption, and confers wider parental powers than a Parental Responsibility Order. The holders of the Order are parents for all purposes.

The court may make an Order providing for a child to be treated in law as the child of the parties to a marriage (referred to in this section as 'the husband' and 'the wife') if:

(a) the child has been carried by a woman other than the wife as the result of the placing in her of an embryo or sperm and eggs or her own artificial insemination;

(b) the gametes of the husband or the wife or both are used to bring about the creation of the embryo[20]

provided that the following conditions are satisfied:

● The husband and the wife must apply for the Order within six months of the birth of the child or, in the case of a child being born before the coming into force of the Act, within six months of the said Act coming into force.
● At the time of the application and of the making of the Order:
  (a) the child's home must be with the husband and the wife; and
  (b) the husband or the wife or both of them must be domiciled in a part of the United Kingdom or in the Channel Islands or in the Isle of Man.
● At the time of the making of the Order both the husband and wife must have attained the age of 18.
● The court must be satisfied that both the father of the child (including a person who is the father by virtue of S.28 of the Act) where he is not the husband, and the woman who carried the child, have freely and with full understanding of what is involved, agreed unconditionally to the making of the Order. This condition does not require the agreement of a person who cannot be found, or who is incapable of giving agreement and the agreement of the woman who carried the child is ineffective for the purposes of that sub-section if given by her less than six weeks after the child's birth.

---

20   S.30(1)(a)−(c).

● The court must be satisfied that no money (other than for expenses reasonably incurred) has been given or received by the husband or the wife for, or in consideration of:

(a) the making of the order;
(b) any agreement required by sub-section (5);
(c) the handing over of the child to the husband or wife; or
(d) the making of any arrangements with a view to the making of the Order, unless authorised by the court.[21]

The proceedings under S.30 are family proceedings, within the meaning of S.8(3) of the Children Act 1989.[22]

Treatment services will not be provided to a woman unless: 'account has been taken of the welfare of any child who may be born as a result of the treatment (including the need of that child for a father) and of any other child who may be affected by the birth.'[23] This section was a late addition to the Bill which, as first presented, did not contain any reference to the welfare of children born as a result of surrogacy arrangements.

The amended Family Proceedings (Children Act 1989) (Amendment Rules) 1994 (Magistrates' Courts)[24] and the Family Proceedings (Amendment) (No.2) Rules 1994[25] (County Courts) provide for the appointment of a guardian *ad litem* in all Parental Order applications to investigate the matter set out in S.30(1) to (7)of the 1990 Act and to investigate any matter contained in the application form or other matter which appears to be relevant to the making of a Parental Order and advise the court on whether there is any reason, under S.1 of the Children Act 1989, to refuse the Parental Order.

Courts and applications

The applicants are required to complete an application form CHA74 and lodge it at the Family Proceedings Court in their home area. They should attach to the application form a copy of the child's birth certificate and a copy of the applicants' marriage certificate. All cases will commence at the Family Proceedings Court and most will be completed there. Exceptionally, cases may be transferred to the County Court or to the High Court. Transfer will be governed, as in other family proceedings, by the Children (Allocation of Proceedings) Order 1991[26] as amended by the Children (Allocation of Proceedings) (Amendment) Order 1993.[27] The Legal Aid (Scope) Regulations 1994 amend the Legal Aid Act 1988 to include applications under S.30 of the 1990 Act.

Those proposing to apply to the court for a Parental Order, who wish their identity to be kept confidential, may apply to the proper officer for a serial

21 S.30(2)–(7).
22 S.30(8).
23 Human Fertilisation and Embryology Act 1990, S.13(5).
24 S.I. 1994 No. 2166 (L.14).
25 S.I. 1994 No. 2165 (L.13).
26 S.I. 1994 No. 1677 (L.21).
27 S.I. 1993 No. 624.

number to be assigned to them for the purposes of identifying them in the proposed proceedings.[28]

The appointment of the guardian ad litem

From November 1, 1994, it has been possible to appoint a guardian *ad litem* in S.30 (Parental Order) applications. The appointment and duties of the guardian *ad litem* are dealt with in the Family Proceedings (Amendment) (No. 2) Rules 1994 and in the Magistrates Court, The Family Proceedings Courts (Children Act 1989) (Amendment) Rules 1994[29] which amend the Family Proceedings Courts (Children Act 1989) Rules 1991.[30]

As soon as practicable after the application has been filed, the Justices Clerk shall appoint a guardian *ad litem*.[31] The guardian *ad litem* shall be appointed from a panel established in accordance with the Guardians *ad litem* and Reporting Officers (Panels) Regulations 1991.[32] Applications under S.30 of the 1990 Act are specified proceedings for the purposes of section 41 of the Children Act 1989(a) in accordance with S.41.6(i) of that Act.

A guardian *ad litem* will be appointed under S.65(1) of the Adoption Act 1976, as applied by the 1994 Regulations. As with all other appointments of guardians *ad litem* and reporting officers, the appointment of the guardian in Parental Order applications is a judicial function carried out by the court.

Guardians are to be appointed as soon as the application for the Parental Order has been filled in by the commissioning couple. The Human Fertilisation and Embryology Act 1990 seeks to regularise and resolve the position of children born as a result of surrogacy arrangements. The Surrogacy Arrangements Act 1985 made it an offence to be involved in the making of surrogacy arrangements in which money changed hands. There is, however, the problem of enforcing the making of proper arrangements, and the question of the status of the child born as a result of arrangements which are in breach of the requirements of the Surrogacy Arrangements Act 1985, and the Code of Practice established by the National Fertilisation and Embryology Authority. S.30 seeks to provide a way of legitimising the position of children born as a result of surrogacy arrangements, through the granting of a Parental Order to the commissioning parents.

The child is not a party to the proceedings and therefore the guardian *ad litem* will not be able to appoint a solicitor to represent the child. This applies even if the case is heard in the High Court and differs from the position of the child in adoption proceedings in this respect. The guardian *ad litem* is therefore taking on an extremely onerous and complex task without the benefit of legal advice for the child and without the option of an appeal on behalf of the child at the end of proceedings. In the High Court the official solicitor shall, if he consents, be appointed as the guardian *ad litem* of the child, although in a County and High Court where the official solicitor does

---

28 Family Proceedings (Amendment) (No.2) Rules 1992 (S.I. 1992 No. 2067 (L.14)), r. 4(a)(3).
29 S.I. 1994 No. 2165 (L.13) and S.I. No. 2166 (L.14).
30 S.I. 1991 No. 1395 (l.17).
31 Rule 4A.5 and Rule 21E.
32 S.I. 1991 No. 2051. R. 21E(2).

not consent to act as guardian *ad litem*, the guardian *ad litem* shall be appointed from a panel in the normal way.

Duties of the guardian ad litem

In carrying out their duties guardians *ad litem* will be bound by S.6 of the Adoption Act 1976 as modified by the Parental Orders Regulations:

> in reaching any decision relating to the application for a parental order a court shall have regard to all the circumstances, first consideration being given to the need to safeguard and promote the welfare of the child throughout his childhood and shall, so far as practicable, ascertain the wishes and feelings of the child regarding the decision and give due consideration to them, having regard to his age and understanding.

In addition to such of the matters set out in the Family Proceedings Courts (Children Act 1989) Rules 1991, r.11 (except r.11(4)(e)), as are appropriate, the guardian *ad litem* shall:

- investigate the matters set out in S.30(1) to (7) of the 1990 Act[33]
- so far as he considers necessary, investigate any matters contained in the application form, or other matter which appears relevant to the making of a Parental Order; and
- advise the court on whether there is any reason under section 6 of the Adoption Act 1976(a) as applied with modifications by the Parental

---

33 (1) The court may make an order providing for a child to be treated in law as the child of the parties to a marriage (referred to in this section as 'the husband' and 'the wife') if
   (a) the child has been carried by a woman other than the wife as the result of the placing in her of an embryo or sperm and eggs or her artificial insemination,
   (b) the gametes of the husband or wife, or both, were used to bring about the creation of the embryo, and
   (c) the conditions in subsection (2) to (7) below are satisfied.
(2) The husband and the wife must apply for the order within six months of the birth of the child or, in the case of a child born before the coming into force of this Act, within six months of such coming into force.
(3) At the time of the application and of the making of the order
   (a) the child's home must be with the husband and the wife, and
   (b) the husband or the wife, or both of them, must be domiciled in a part of the United Kingdom or in the Channel Islands or the Isle of Man.
(4) At the time of the making of the order both the husband and the wife must have attained the age of 18.
(5) The court must be satisfied that both the father of the child (including a person who is the father by virtue of section 28 of this Act), where he is not the husband, and the woman who carried the child have freely, and with full understanding of what is involved, agreed unconditionally to the making of the order.
(6) Subsection (5) above does not require the agreement of a person who cannot be found or is incapable of giving such agreement and the agreement of the woman who carried the child is ineffective for the purposes of the subsection if given by her less than six weeks after the child's birth.
(7) The court must be satisfied that no money or other benefit (other than for expenses reasonably incurred) has been given or received by the husband or wife for or in consideration of
   (a) the making of the order,
   (b) any agreement required by subsection (5) above,
   (c) the handing over of the child to the husband and the wife, or
   (d) the making of any arrangements with a view to the making of the order,
   unless authorised by the court.

Orders (Human Fertilisation and Embryology) Regulations 1994(b) to refuse the parental order.[34]

The amended Magistrates court rules establish that Rules 7(1), 9, 10(1)(b), 10(11), 11(2), 11(3) and 12 of S.I. 1991 No. 1395 shall not apply in S.30 proceedings. This means in effect that children will not be parties to the proceedings. Guardians will be appointed in all cases, and guardians will not be able to instruct solicitors for the children they represent. Earlier draft rules also specifically excluded Rule 4.11(e) — 'the options available to it in respect of the child, and the suitability of each such option including what order should be made in determining the application'. The final court rules give guardians the power to consider other options apart from the possibility of making a S.30 Parental Order. One of those options will be the possibility of the guardian asking the court to consider making a direction under S.37 to initiate a local authority investigation if they had concerns about the position of the child who was the subject of the application.

The court rules also make provision for the removal or return of the child on application to the court. In the event of such an application being made under S.27(1), 29(1) or 29(2) of Adoption Act 1976 as applied with modifications by the Parental Orders (Human Fertilisation and Embryology) Regulations 1994, the guardian *ad litem* must be served with a copy of the complaint, attend court, and be heard on the subject of whether the application should be granted (S.I. 1994 No. 2166(L.14) Rule 21J(3) and S.I. 1994 No. 2165 (L.13) 4.A.10).

The court rules and regulations do not make it clear whether the rights of the parents or the rights of the child are to predominate. In particular, it will be a matter of great concern to guardians that very basic police and health checks will not have been carried out when they are appointed. There will be no check to ensure that commissioning couples are not Schedule 1 offenders, although this was cited as a matter of concern in the Warnock Report.[35] Furthermore, the guardians have no right of access to HFEA files, in fact, as a non-licensed person, they are specifically prohibited from having such access. They have no rights to initiate police or health checks, and those who have undergone fertility treatment have a right to veto the disclosure of specific information to another person who is not covered by a licence, that is, to a guardian *ad litem*.[36]

The circular requires guardians to carry out child protection checks with the local social services department, and to check on the health and welfare of existing children in the family of the commissioning couple. It therefore seems illogical that they do not have the power to seek out other information which has a direct bearing on the case, and on the welfare of the child.

---

34 S.I. 1994 No. 2166 (L.14) R. 21E(3).

35 *Op. cit.* Chapter 2 of the Warnock Report expressed concern that infertility treatment could be provided without 'due regard' for the interests of any child that may be born as a result, and cited the possibility of Schedule 1 offenders seeking treatment as one of the risks.

36 See Annex A, Consent to disclosure of identifying information about my/our fertility treatment to another person who is not covered by a licence: Human Fertilisation and Embryology Authority Code of Practice.

Another point of concern is that the welfare checklist, S.1(3), does not legally apply in S.30 applications. This seems doubly illogical given the guidance in paragraph 35 of the circular that, in exceptional circumstances, the court will be able to make a S.8 Order rather than a Parental Order, and that if they are considering whether to make a S.8 Order, they will have to take into account the provisions of the welfare checklist and the principle of minimum intervention or positive advantage in S.1(5). It seems logical in that case that they should have had the benefit of the guidance of the guardian's report in respect of the matters covered by the welfare checklist before this situation arises. The circular suggests that in reporting to the court about the welfare of the child, the guardian *ad litem* and the child may find it helpful for the information to be presented within the 'framework' of the welfare checklist.

S.38 of the Act states that anyone who can show conscientious objection to any of the activities governed by the Act is not allowed to participate in them. This section, however, does not apply to guardians *ad litem*, whose appointment and enquiries fall outside this provision.

The guardian's task in S.30 surrogacy applications

The focus of the guardian's enquiries should be aimed at establishing for the court:

● whether or not the requirements set out in S.30 are satisfied;
● whether there is any reason why the Court should not make a Parental Order in the light of the child's welfare principle set out in section 6 of the Adoption Act 1976, as modified by the Parental Orders Regulations.

Although guardians need to appreciate that their role with families in Parental Order applications has differences from other types of guardian appointment, their duty to report to court is broadly similar to other proceedings in which they may be involved.[37]

In carrying out their duties guardians should note that as these are family proceedings and because the court is determining a question with respect to the child's upbringing, sections 1(1)(a) and 1(2) of the Children Act 1989 apply to the extent that they are not covered by the modified wording of section 6 of the Adoption Act. However, section 1(3) to 1(5) (including the welfare checklist) are not legally applicable to parental order applications.

In considering the welfare of the child the guardian *ad litem* will need to bear in mind whether the applicants have been treated at a licensed centre, in which case any concerns may be in relation to changes in circumstances since treatment ended, and whether there is any cause to believe significant harm to the child might arise if the parental order is made. In other circumstances (where no licensed treatment centre was involved) the guardian *ad litem* will need to address the S.6 principle bearing in mind that no assurances have been taken of the welfare of the child in accordance with the code and S.13(5). The wording of S.6 as modified by the Parental Orders Regulations is:

---

37   LAC (94)25 paragraph 19.

in reaching any decision relating to the application for a Parental Order, a court shall have regard to all the circumstances, first consideration being given to the need to safeguard and promote the welfare of the child throughout his childhood; and shall so far as practicable ascertain the wishes and feelings of the child regarding the decision and give due consideration to them, having regard to his age and understanding.

Nevertheless, in reporting to the court about the welfare of the child, the circular suggests (at paragraph 32 and 33) guardian *ad litem* and the court may find it helpful for the information to be presented within the framework of the 'welfare checklist' in S.I. 3(a)−(f) of the Children Act 1989. Presenting the information about the welfare of the child within the framework of the welfare checklist is subtly different from being given a duty to consider the matters in the checklist in making a recommendation to the court, and guardians may feel uneasy about the somewhat ambiguous nature of their powers in relation to the child's welfare.

Having received a copy of Form CHA74 (the application form) the guardian *ad litem* should:

- interview the birth parents — bearing in mind that there is no official consent form for relinquishing the child as in adoption. There is no minimum age for a surrogate mother.
- interview the applicants to check the accuracy of the information on the form; be aware that in the absence of an agency report, approximating to a Schedule 2 report in adoption, the information which he or she receives will have been supplied by the applicants (one of the parties to the proceedings) and not by an 'independent' source;
- see the child.

The name and address of the licensed treatment centre is included in the application form.

Guardians will have to think through the content of the direct work with children. Commissioning couples may feel extremely threatened by the guardian's appearance, especially if the child (as presumably will be the case) will have no knowledge of the proceedings in which they and the guardian will be involved. It may be helpful to think of some form of explanatory letter being sent to applicants from the guardian and maybe this is something that should be dealt with in the guidance, rather than being left to the discretion of each individual guardian, as these will be extremely sensitive situations. In early drafts of the court rules, the guardian had no duty to see the child. As matters stand now, the guardian will see the child, and may ascertain his wishes and feelings with regard to the proposed Order. (In the normal course of events it will, of course, be young infants who are the subject of Parental Order applications, but there is the question of the existing backlog of older children.)

There are three groups of children who may be born as a result of surrogacy arrangements:

- those who have been born as a result of services provided by a licensed clinic;

- those who have not; and
- those children who may be the subject of transitional arrangements (S.30(2) of the Act allows applications to be made in respect of children born before the coming into force of the Act). There will be a number of children, possibly aged up to seven, who may be the subject of these transitional arrangements and in respect of whom Parental Order applications may be lodged.

The guidance differentiates between the third group and the first two.

Applications in respect of these children in the transitional period are still subject to the same conditions in S.30 as other applications, however, the length of time that some of these children may have lived with the applicants may require the guardian *ad litem* to pay particular attention to certain issues which may have arisen. For example other persons may have gained parental responsibility, a local authority or voluntary organisation may have provided accommodation for the child, or there may be other relevant information known to the local authorities. With the older child, guardians *ad litem* are reminded that in the modified wording of S.6 of the Adoption Act 1976, there is a need to ascertain, as far as practicable, the wishes and feelings of the child regarding the decision. This will be difficult if children have no knowledge of the circumstances of their birth and conception.

In the case of the first group, the application will contain written confirmation of the child's genetic relationship with the applicants from the licensed clinic. In the second case, those children who have been born through arrangements made outside clinics, the guardian should request proof of the relationship between the child and the commissioning couple from the licensed clinician who carried out the medical procedures.

The guardian should then be in a position to report to the court on the circumstances of the child's conception and birth. Were the surrogacy arrangements legal? Has the licensed clinic proceeded according to the Code of Practice?

The guardian should check the status of the agreement to the transfer of parental responsibility from the birth mother to the commissioning couple. This may present difficulties as the surrogate mother may not be resident in the UK and, incidentally, the child may not even have had a right of entry, as the question of the nationality of the child born as a result of surrogacy arrangements is not addressed in the Human Fertilisation and Embryology Act 1990.

The guardian should check the date of the agreement against the date of the birth of the child, bearing in mind that the agreement is invalid if given by the birth mother less than six weeks after the baby's birth. If no agreement has been forthcoming, the guardian should clarify the reasons for this. If the mother is said to be incapable of giving agreement, then a medical note is necessary and the applicant should bear the cost of obtaining this. If the mother cannot be found the guardian should discuss with the court what steps, if any, are to be taken. If at all possible, the guardian *ad litem* should interview the birth mother and father and partner, if appropriate, to establish the terms of the agreement.

The guardian must check that any expenses declared by the applicants, as arising from their application, are as stated, and this should form part of the guardian's written report. If the guardian concludes that the expenses were (or were not) reasonably incurred, the supporting reasons will need to be set out in the report. However, if the guardian *ad litem* feels unable to make this judgment, then this too should be explained in the report. Notwithstanding the evidence given by the guardian *ad litem*, it is for the court to determine in relation to S.30(7) whether any expenses have been reasonably incurred. All of this must bear in mind the requirement in the Act that children born as part of surrogacy arrangements should not be part of a commercial transaction. There is a considerable grey area here as regards reasonable expenses and those who are in a position to incur them. Infertility treatment is expensive and not always available on the National Health Service. As far as it is possible to ascertain, commissioning couples may need in the region of £20,000 to cover the expenses involved in the acquisition of a child through surrogacy arrangements. Guardians, therefore, will be anxious to ensure that there is no question of exploitation of poor birth mothers by more affluent commissioning couples. Realistically, however, it will be very difficult for guardians to be absolutely sure about the precise nature of the financial arrangements. Will they, for example, be required to see receipts, check invoices or otherwise follow up the expense claims?

The guardian *ad litem* should contact the social services department in whose area the applicants reside in order to ascertain whether they have relevant knowledge of the applicants and family. In pursuit of their enquiries, the guardian *ad litem* may wish to initiate police or health checks and to inspect the files of the clinic carrying out the surrogacy arrangements, however, as unlicensed people, they have no statutory right of access to such information (beyond their rights of access to records under S.42 of the Children Act 1989) and there are no procedures laid down for acquiring it. Guardians are, therefore, in a somewhat unenviable situation of being charged with a statutory duty to carry out an investigation with limited statutory powers to help them in their task. Their role is undoubtedly more constricted than in other proceedings under the Children Act 1989 and the Adoption Act 1976. Many guardians feel extremely concerned about lending the credibility of their role to proceedings which pose profound moral and ethical problems, as well as very practical constraints in carrying out the task as appointed.

Refusal to make an Order under S.30

The guidance visualises that there may be quite exceptional circumstances in which the guardian feels that, notwithstanding the possibility of other court proceedings which may be initiated to secure the child's future, a Parental Order is not in the child's best interest. Possible reasons for such a conclusion might be clear evidence that the applicants were rejecting the child or that their own marriage was under great strain and likely to break up. Where difficulties have arisen, each individual situation must be assessed on its particular merits. Guardians should explore possible options, and should note that there is no provision for the court to make an interim Parental Order, so that a situation might be further assessed. Under the Court Rule 11(7) the report of the guardian *ad litem* will be given to the court and served on the parties. However, if, exceptionally, the guardian *ad litem* recommends that the parental order application should not be granted, the guidance suggests that the guardian *ad litem* may wish to ensure that the court is aware of the recommendation in advance of the hearing. The guardian's role cannot be extended to undertake other duties (such as counselling the parties) should the court not decide to make a Parental Order. The guardian's appointment ends with the court deciding to make, or not to make, the Order. However, under the provision of S.10(1)(b) of the Children Act 1989 the court may make an S.8 Order (including an interim S.8 Order) in respect of the child if it considers that the Order should be made, even though no such application has been made. This is only likely to happen in rare cases. Guardians *ad litem* should also note that a Parental Order may not include such terms and conditions as the court thinks fit.[38] However, the court does have the discretion, not only to make the Parental Order, but also an Order under S.8 of the Children Act 1989 by virtue of S.10(1)(b) of the 1989 Act. Where the court is considering whether to make a S.8 order, it will have to take account of the provisions in S.1(3) and 1(5). The court can also exercise its powers under S.37.

The concern which arises about the *fait accompli* nature of some adoption applications must also exist in relation to the children who may be subject to transitional arrangements under S.30 and who may now be six or even seven years old. Will the court really have any choice about ratifying existing arrangements in relation to these children, and are there any other realistic choices open to the guardian and the court, other than to make a Parental Responsibility Order and end the legal limbo in which the child is stranded? However, one of the problems for the guardian in considering such applications will be the knowledge that if the parents were applying for and Adoption Order rather than a Parental Responsibility Order, the criteria for making the Order, and the attention to the child's welfare, would be greater than is the case in applications for a Parental Responsibility Order. Refusal to tell the child the true facts about his birth will presumably not be considered sufficient grounds for the refusal to make an Order.

The guardian ad litem's report

Rule 11(2) is intended to ensure that the guardian *ad litem*'s report is primarily for the court. The court may decide, with appropriate advice from the guardian *ad item*, whether all or some of the report should be shown to the applicant and, if present, the birth mother and other respondents. However, if, exceptionally, the guardian *ad litem* recommends that the Parental Order application should not be granted, the guardian *ad litem* may wish to ensure that the court is aware of the recommendation in advance of the hearing. The court will therefore be able to exercise its discretion as to whether to withhold some or all of the report from any of the parties. The guidance at annex F

---

38   See Adoption Act 1976, S.12.

includes a proposed pro forma for guardian *ad litem* reports which suggests that these reports are expected to be exceptionally brief and limited in their scope. A fuller format might include the following information:

- the nature of the application;
- list of who has been seen and who has not been seen;
- statement of documents seen;
- brief history of the child's birth and the circumstances surrounding it, including a full explanation of the nature of the surrogacy arrangements and the source of the child's gametes. This brief history should include an explanation of terms;
- statement of what facts are agreed and what are not;
- details of the status of the agreement to the application, including the date on which the agreement was signed, the circumstances in which it was given and the guardian's own view of whether or not the agreement is satisfactory for the purposes of S.30;
- a statement of agreed and disputed evidence;
- statement of financial arrangements, what has been paid and to whom, and a list of the payments for in vitro treatment prior to surrogacy. What treatment was provided by which clinic, was the clinic licensed, who were the registered clinicians and what information has it been possible to obtain about the procedures in relation to this application? The guardian should attempt to make some assessment of what is a normal payment in surrogacy arrangements and what is acceptable and unacceptable, for example, were there any exploitative aspects of the arrangements?;
- statement of health factors in relation to the child, for example, any relevant facts concerning the gestation period and relevant information about the host mother's health including a note of smoking and drinking habits. This should also apply to the commissioning parents;
- there should be a separate section in the report dealing with the child's welfare, general care, medical history and genetic inheritance;
- knowledge of origins — the guardian *ad litem* should explore some of the issues around the commissioning couple's attitudes and intentions in relation to telling the child the facts about his birth;
- the commissioning couple — this section should cover facts about the commissioning family, the circumstances which led to them making the application and should also include details of other children within the family and any relevant factors about their health and welfare which might have a bearing on the willingness or otherwise of the court to make an Order;
- there should be a section in the report for the guardian to identify any special considerations which he or she wishes to bring to the attention of the court in this case. For example, if there are immigration issues relating to the child's status in the UK or significant factors about the child's health or present development.
- options available to the court — as a result of their investigations, the guardian would wish to ask the court to consider making a S.8 Order or to initiate a S.37 investigation by the local authority. In such a situation, the

court has a responsibility to consider the requirements of the welfare checklist, S.1(3) and S.1(5), whether making an Order would be better than making no Order at all, and therefore the guardian *ad litem* may also consider these matters in advising the court of any other matter which they think should be brought to its attention;[39]

● the guardian should make a clear recommendation to the court about whether or not the application for a Parental Responsibility Order should be made.

The report should be submitted at least 7 days before the date of the hearing. Records made by the guardian should be treated as confidential according to normal practice.

Professional Concerns about the Role of the Guardian in Surrogacy Proceedings

Surrogacy: a service for adults

S.30 could be said to provide a thin veneer of welfare to what is essentially medically driven legislation governing the procedures by which infertile parents may be assisted to have children. Its primary focus is to provide services to adults, rather than to protect the rights of children whose welfare must be measured alongside the right of each person to reproduce.

Weight to be given to the long term welfare of the child

The key problem for guardians will be the potential for conflict of interest between the right of the adult to have children and the right of the child born as a result of that procreation to have his or her welfare considered by the court as a matter of paramount importance. The dilemma is summed up by Mary Warnock:

> it is plausible to talk about the good of the child when the child exists and there are alternative futures before it between which someone must choose. To choose whether or not a baby should be born in the first place is a different kind of choice altogether. The whole undertaking is in fact for the sake of the infertile, would-be parents. It is they who want the baby.[40]

Limited powers of investigation

A large proportion of surrogacy arrangements, perhaps as many as half of them, are made on an informal basis without any intervention of a clinic. Even where a licensed clinic has been involved in the arrangements, much of the Code of Practice is permissive. Clearly it is better that guardians be involved to

---

39   R.11(4)(f).
40   Warnock, 'The Good of the Child, (1987) *Bioethics* 141 at 144, quoted in Bainham and Cretney, *Children: The Modern Law*, Jordan Publishing Ltd 1993 p. 211.

safeguard the interests of children than they not be involved, but they must be resistant to the suggestions in the draft guidance, which indicate that the scope of their investigations may be more limited, and will be underpinned by fewer powers than in other proceedings. The circular states that Parental Order applications are different from other types of guardian *ad litem* appointments. All specified proceedings are different, but the role of the guardian should be consistent and their powers and duties should be the same in all proceedings in which they are appointed.

Lack of party status for the child

It seems wrong that in surrogacy cases, where it is glaringly apparent that the interests of the child may be in conflict with those of the surrogate and commissioning parents, there is no right of legal representation. The guardian is, therefore, acting without the benefit of legal advice for the child, in an extraordinarily complicated and sensitive area. Although the applicants (the commissioning couple) have a right of appeal if an application for a parental order is not granted, presumably the guardian has no right of appeal on behalf of the child.

Lack of knowledge of long term outcomes

There is, as yet, no firm empirical evidence to demonstrate the lifetime consequences for children born as a result of surrogacy arrangements. All the evidence in relation to adopted children points to their strong need to know the facts about their parentage.[41] It is only possible to imagine the potentially shattering effect of inadvertent discovery of the facts of their birth on the children concerned.

Summary

The Human Fertilisation and Embryology Act 1990 provides a legal framework for children born as a result of assisted reproduction techniques, but there are profound moral and ethical concerns which cannot be circumscribed by a law which is essentially pragmatic. The Act recognises the existence of medically assisted reproduction, it does not address the matter of whether such practices are consistent with any agreed ethical framework. Guardians are exempt from the conscientious objection clause in the Act, but they may be faced with situations which may cause them profound unease, but which, nevertheless, provide children who are the subject of S.30 applications with their only opportunity to achieve any separate representation before the court.

---

41 See Triseliotis, *In Search of Origins* (1973), McWhinnie, *Adopted Children: How they grow up* (1967), 'The case for greater openness concerning AID', in *AID and After* (1984), BAAF AGM Paper and Blythe, 'Children's Welfare, Surrogacy and Social Work', *British Journal of Social Work* (1993) Vol. 23 p. 259.

The argument is that all children are born as a result of their parents' wish to reproduce. In that way, children born as a result of surrogacy arrangements are no different from any other child. Other parents do not receive a licence to have children. However, in the specification of S.30 applications as family proceedings, with the corollaries of the application of the welfare checklist and the principle of the paramountcy of the child, then matters become rather more complicated. Unlike adoption proceedings, there is apparently no responsibility on the guardian *ad litem* to comment on the suitability or otherwise of the commissioning parents. There are no official consent forms for guardians to witness as in adoption. There will be no Schedule 2 report and no placing agency, nor is it envisaged that the child will have a solicitor to represent his or her interests. It could be said that children born as a result of surrogacy arrangements should have the same rights to know their origin as adopted children. A statement of facts filed when the S.30 order is made would be a safeguard for them. However, the case is different, in that the supply of donors of genetic material may well rapidly dwindle if their anonymity cannot be guaranteed, and without them assisted reproduction would not be possible at all. This brings the debate back to the question of whether the legislation is medically driven or welfare orientated. If the welfare of the child is to be given first consideration, then there is clearly a case for carrying out basic police and medical checks on commissioning parents and the donors of genetic material. At the very least, guardians should have the right to check that commissioning parents are not Schedule 1 offenders, as well as carrying out their discretionary duty to make the relevant enquiries of the Social Services department.

There is a backlog of children who have already been born as a result of surrogacy arrangements. It is important that guardians become involved, not just as part of a rubber stamping mechanism to regularise *de facto* situations, but as part of a genuine attempt to safeguard the rights and interests of children who are the subject of such applications, and to ensure that these children are entitled to the same consideration of their rights and welfare as all other children whose welfare is covered by the provisions of the Children Act 1989.[42]

---

42   See further the Human Fertilisation and Embryology Act 1990; the Surrogacy Arrangements Act 1985; the Report of the Committee of Enquiry into Human Fertilisation and Embryology (Warnock Report) Cmnd. 9314 (1984); the Human Fertilisation and Embryology Authority Code of Practice, revised June 1993; Blythe, *Infertility Reproduction Issues for Counsellors* (1991); Walby and Symons, *Who am I? Identity, Adoption and Human Fertilisation* (1990); and *Truth and the Child: A Contribution to the debate on the Warnock Report* (Bruce, Mitchell and Priestley ed.) (1988). See also Bruce, 'AID and Identity: The Child's Right to Know' (1986) *International Children's Rights Monitor*, Vol. 3, No. 1; Snowdon and Mitchell, *The Artificial Family* (1981).

Appendix 1

Glossary of Terms

(As defined in the Draft Regulations and Guidance, issued by the Department of Health)

birth parents   the woman who gives birth to a child (the surrogate mother) and her husband, also known as surrogate parents.

commissioning couple   the husband and wife for whom a surrogate mother carries a child.

gametes   sperm and eggs.

genetically related   the child is said to be genetically related to a person if the child was conceived using that person's gametes.

legal father

- the husband of a surrogate mother, unless it can be shown that he did not consent to her treatment; or
- if the surrogate mother is single, or if married and her husband did not consent to the treatment, the father is the man with whom she received treatment as long as he is not the genetic father; or
- there will be no legal father when:
  - a surrogate mother is treated alone, either if she is single or if she is married in cases where her husband has not consented to her treatment;
  - a surrogate mother who is single or, if married, whose husband did not consent to her treatment, is treated with a man who is the genetic father of the child.

surrogate mother   a woman who carries the child for a commissioning couple as a result of the placing in her of an embryo or sperm and eggs or through her artificial insemination.

Parental Order   an Order which provides for a child to be treated in law as a child of the commissioning couple.

Appendix 2

Case Example

Commissioning parents (Applicants).   Michael and Carol Smith are aged 40 and 39 respectively. They have been married for 12 years. They have been trying to have a child for 10 of those 12 years, and have undergone a series of unsuccessful fertility treatments. It was eventually established that Carol is infertile. They have rejected the possibility of adoption, as the chances of being able to adopt a very young baby are limited, and anyway there is a long waiting list. In addition, they would like to have a genetic link with their child, and this will be possible if a surrogate mother can be found. Mr Smith is a civil engineer and his wife is a teacher.

Surrogate mother.   Susan Brown is 28. She is divorced with three little girls, aged seven, five and four. She met Carol at an aerobics class, sympathised with her problems of infertility and offered to have a baby for her. She had easy pregnancies and the money she received during the pregnancy would allow her to stay at home and look after her own three children, and she was anxious to have an opportunity to do this.

   Susan Brown attended the licensed clinic for counselling, and subsequently conceived a child with Michael Smith. The Smith's paid her £200 a week during the pregnancy, and for a six-week period afterwards. This sum was roughly based on Susan Brown's salary as a secretary. Susan Brown subsequently gave birth to a healthy baby boy, who is now living with the Smiths.

The application.   The Smiths have applied for a Parental Order, under S.30 of the Human Fertilisation and Embryology Act 1990. A guardian has been appointed.

The guardian ad litem*'s investigation.*   As a result of her enquiries, the guardian discovers that, although she has given verbal agreement to the Order, Susan Brown is very depressed. During the pregnancy she and her ex-husband were reconciled. Her financial position has changed, and her husband is pressing her to keep the baby, as they have both always wanted a boy. She sees the baby regularly, as she and the Smiths live in the same town, and she says she completely under-estimated the impact of giving him up. The Smiths are aware of her distress, and are planning to move again as soon as the Parental Order has been made, to avoid the possibility of any further contact between the two families. They have no intention of ever telling the child who his genetic mother really is. Mrs Brown is also concerned that if she withdraws agreement, there will be pressure to repay approximately £10,000 received as weekly payments during he pregnancy, and she and her husband do not have that amount of money.

Questions for the guardian
- What is the status of Susan Brown's agreement?
- Are the financial arrangements satisfactory?

Chapter 9
Representation of Children in Private Law Proceedings

Children whose Parents are Separated or Divorced

By the year 2000 it has been estimated that 3.7 million children will have experienced at least one parental divorce. Britain has one of the highest divorce rates in western Europe, and divorce rates have doubled since 1971, when the Divorce Reform Act 1969 was implemented. Denmark is now the only country which has a higher number of divorces per head of the population. If the present trends continue, 37 per cent of all marriages now taking place will end in divorce.[1]

Two thirds of divorcing couples have dependent children under 16 years old. Each year, approximately 150,000 children go through divorce with their parents, of whom approximately 25,000 are going through the process for the second or even the third time. Children involved in private law proceedings have no independent legal or social work representation and very little opportunity to participate in arrangements for their own future. Provided their parents agree about the residence and contact arrangements, the court need never be involved. Some of these arrangements may be made with a view to the parents' convenience rather than the child's wishes and there are increasing numbers of children and young people who alternate between one home and another, never being quite sure where they or their belongings will be on any given weekend.

There are, too, increasing numbers of children who are born outside marriage:

> one of the most remarkable demographic trends that emerged in the 1980s was the doubling of the numbers of children born outside marriage from 77,000 in 1980 to 177,000 in 1988. These figures represent a rise in the proportion of births which are extra-marital from 12 per cent in 1980 to 25 per cent in 1988, the majority born to

---

1   Murch and Hooper, 'The Family Justice System' (1992) *Family Law* 9.

women under the age of 25 years . . . Two out of five co-habiting couples in Britain have dependent children.[2]

Where the relationship fails, 90 per cent of children stay with their birth mothers.[3]

This statistic should be looked at in conjunction with the fact that 70 per cent of lone mothers are claiming income support.[4]

In November 1992 the Family Budget Unit, University of York, estimated that: 'the income of families on income support is below what is necessary to maintain minimum standards of living. A family of four children on income support would receive £105 a week, while the cost of maintaining a minimum standard of living is about £141.40 a week'.[5]

The long term implications of these quite dramatic changes in demographic trends have yet to be fully explored and integrated into social policy. Many children can expect to form part of what may be a series of reconstituted family groups through the course of their childhood and adolescence. Consequently it is hard to maintain the fiction that the rights of children in private law proceedings can continue to be safely delegated to parents, who often have partisan and vested interests in the outcome. This is especially so in situations where there are clear conflicts between the rights of parents to their own personal autonomy and freedom to make new relationships and the rights of children to have their needs met and their wishes consulted.[6]

The Need for Separate Representation

The Children Act 1989 brings together public and private law in one statute, but it does not provide an equitable and rationalised approach to the representation of all children. Children involved in public law proceedings are comparatively well served, having both the benefit of the solicitor and a guardian *ad litem* in a relatively sophisticated synthesis of rights and welfare. The arrangements for children in private law proceedings are much less satisfactory, in that there is no direct social work representation and children have to seek the leave of the court to be granted party status in any S.8 application. Although the right of the child to initiate proceedings under the Act has been widely heralded as a new dawn for children's rights, the reality of post-Children Act practice has been that those rights remain more theoretical then real. Courts have been reluctant to open the floodgates of children's litigation in private law proceedings, aware perhaps that the numbers involved are very much more substantial than those involved in public law proceedings. One only has to scratch the veneer of a few of the thousands of contact and residence applications to discover children who have become casualties in the acrimonious battle-ground of divorce and separation. The annual costs of divorce and family breakdown are approximately £180 million a year and

---

2   *Ibid.*, at 12.
3   Kierman and Wickes, *Family Change in Future Policy* (1990).
4   *National Children's Homes Fact File*, 'Children in Britain 1992', page 8.
5   'Children Now' p.48.
6   See *Looking to the Future: Mediation and the Grounds for Divorce* (December 1993), a consultation paper, the Lord Chancellor's Department.

there are associated costs to the National Health Service in terms of stress related illness. Relate has estimated that the cost of marital breakdown in 1987/88 was £1.3 billion in welfare benefits, legal aid, court and NHS costs.[7]

While the provisions for children involved in public law proceedings are built around a recognition that the interests of parents and children may well be in conflict, there is no such acknowledgment of the possibility of conflict of interest in private law proceedings. Indeed the philosophy of the Act is rooted in Lord MacKay's assertion that:

> the bedrock of a free society lies in the independence and integrity of the family. That view is founded on the belief that, save where there is a demonstrable and recognised neglect or abuse, it is for parents to decide how to bring up their children, not the organs of the state, be they legislative, executive or judicial.[8]

Unfortunately, the legislators took for granted that the best interests of children would be served by the facilitation of agreement between their parents. The notion of agreement is, in turn, based on the concept of the reasonable parent. Reasonable parents will wish to come to an agreement about the residence and contact arrangements for their children and they will, as responsible parents, take into account (the Act assumes) the best interests of their children. The underlying assumption, that parents involved in private law proceedings are reasonable and those involved in public law proceedings are not, is an obvious over-simplification. Paradoxically, the child whose parents agree about the arrangements for residence and contact may be the child who suffers the most devastating distress and trauma in attempting to comply with those arrangements, which may suit the interests of the parent, but may impose grave restrictions on the developing child. The provisions of the Child Support Act 1991 provide a further complication, in that there may now be pressing financial, as well as emotional, reasons for parents to wish to retain custody of their children, and the welfare of the child is not a dominant feature of the Act.

A more positive approach to the rights of children and young people involved in divorce and separation could provide the key to the ongoing debate about the central role of reconciliation in the Lord Chancellor's rolling programme of divorce law reform. In New Zealand, in all proceedings as to guardianship, custody and access to children, the court must appoint a lawyer to represent the child's interests. The Australian courts have a similar discretion to order separate representation. The system of Family Courts established in Australia and New Zealand demonstrates that adversarial litigation, which can be so damaging to children, does not have to be an inevitable feature of divorce proceedings. The Family Court is far more sensitive to the child's wishes and feelings than other, more conventional, judicial settings. In 1981, the Norwegian government created the office of Children's Ombudsperson, on the grounds that children constitute a weak and vulnerable group within society. The Ombudsperson's duties are defined by statute and include promoting the interests of children both in the private and

---

7   *Ibid.*, para.2.18.
8   The Lord Chancellor's address to the President of the Family Division's Conference, October 27, 1989.

public sectors and continually assessing the conditions under which Norwegian children are growing up.

In the UK children are largely powerless to influence events during the dissolution of their parents' marriage. It has been suggested that divorce is one of the areas of life that most exemplifies the treatment of children as property rather than persons.[9] They can become the objects of negotiation between conflicting parties, their futures being decided without their consultation, and their best interests either overlooked or ignored.[10]

The position of children in divorce

The following case examples illustrate, not only the problems experienced by children caught in the crossfire of divorce, but their relative powerlessness in the face of articulate and determined adults and a court-driven machinery for the regulation of arrangements concerning residence and contact.

Gemma   Gemma is seven and an only child. Her parents divorced a year ago. The arrangements for residence and contact were agreed through a process of conciliation. The resulting Orders were not contested and both Gemma's parents are happy about them. Gemma stays with her mother from Monday to Friday. At 6.00 p.m. on a Friday evening she is taken to her father's house 60 miles away. She spends Friday night, Saturday night and Sunday with her father. On Monday morning, at 8.00 a.m., he drives her back to her school, leaving her there in time for her 9 o'clock lessons. At 3.30 p.m. on Monday her mother collects her. Gemma has had a very pretty room at both her mother's and her father's houses. However, her father's new partner has recently given birth to a baby son and Gemma has been moved to a smaller room, to make room for the new nursery — after all she is only there for part of the week. She is conscious that her father is very pleased to have a son and she is beginning to feel less central, both in his affections and in his new household. Gemma's new step-mother is affectionate to Gemma, but is younger than her own mother and sees a seven-year-old as quite self-sufficient. With her own baby to look after she assumes that Gemma can fend for herself as she is a 'big girl'.

Meanwhile, Gemma's mother has been depressed following the divorce and separation. She gave up work when she had Gemma and has now had difficulty in finding a job. She works as a secretary in a busy office and does not get home until 5.45 p.m. Between 3.30 p.m. and 5.45 p.m. Gemma is looked after by a child minder. She likes the child minder, but her house is always very noisy and busy as there are four children under five being cared for there, as well as Gemma. By the time Gemma and her mother arrive home and have their supper, both are very tired. Because Gemma spends each weekend

9   Freeman, *The Rights and Wrongs of Children* (1983), Frances Pinter.
10   See *Child Right*, June 1985, No. 18, at 12–13, the case of three children sexually and physically abused by their father who tried to fight his application for access. In the words of one of the children: 'in our case, which started over two years ago, six different people closely involved with us and the divorce case did not attempt to find out what our wishes or points of view were, or totally disregarded them and us. They were our Doctor, two different solicitors, a local court welfare officer, a senior court welfare officer and the Official Solicitor. You will see how badly young people are treated by people they should be able to trust and get help from.'

with her father, she feels she sees very little of her mother and is feeling increasingly confused about where she belongs. Most out-of-school activities take place at the weekend, when Gemma is 60 miles away. She cannot go to Brownies on a Friday night and frequently misses parties. This means that she feels she is losing some of her friends at school because she is never able to go to their houses at the weekend, or to invite them to hers. Recently she asked her mother if she could go to her father on alternate weekends. Her mother became quite agitated, saying that the arrangements had been made and any change would mean going back to court. She did not want to upset the now amicable arrangements with her ex-husband, as this might affect his attitude to the financial support which she and Gemma were receiving. On her last visit Gemma asked her father and step-mother if they would mind if she came to see them less often. Her step-mother immediately became very upset and angry. She said that Gemma's mother had always tried to undermine Gemma's relationship with her father and was jealous of his new relationship. Gemma had heard her father and step-mother talking, later on that evening. Their view had been that Gemma had been manipulated into making this request by her mother, who was using Gemma rather than confronting them openly herself. From this, Gemma has concluded that any expression of her own wishes and feelings in the matter will cause more trouble between her parents and she feels worried and anxious about being the instrument of further dispute. Consequently, she has decided to keep her feelings to herself. Recently her school teacher has contacted her mother to say that she is worried about Gemma, who has become withdrawn and isolated.

In legal terms Gemma's case is a success. Her father and mother agreed the Residence and Contact Orders through a process of negotiation and conciliation. As the Orders were not contested, no Family Court welfare officer was appointed and there was no independent assessment of the impact of the proposed arrangements on Gemma. Following the implementation of the Children Act 1989 in October 1991, the satisfaction hearings, formerly held under S.41 of the Matrimonial Causes Act 1973, requiring the parties to appear in court and satisfy the judge about the arrangements for the children, have been abolished and the satisfaction or otherwise of the arrangements judged purely on the basis of a paper exercise. Gemma's parents agreed about the arrangements for their daughter, so there was nothing to indicate to the judge that there was cause to investigate further, and the divorce was made absolute. Nor do the courts have any powers of review over arrangements relating to children. The only way to change the arrangements would for either one of Gemma's parents to initiate new proceedings to review the S.8 Residence or Contact Orders. In this instance, neither parent has any desire to do so, as the arrangements suit each of them individually. Theoretically, Gemma may seek leave to initiate a review of the S.8 contact arrangements herself. This will depend on her finding a children's panel solicitor willing to represent her. Clearly Gemma is not in a position to do this and is effectively trapped within the existing arrangements.

William William is aged 11. His parents are in the middle of an extremely bitter battle over residence and contact. Both want him to live with them. Both wish to stay with William in the matrimonial home. William is in an agonising dilemma — not only does he have to choose between his parents, but he is aware that whichever parent is not chosen will be evicted from the family home. The court appointed a Family Court welfare officer to make a report. He saw William alone for an hour, during which time William felt completely unable to express the distress and anxiety he was feeling. He tried to give the impression that he did not mind which parent he lived with, as he did not want to carry the burden of guilt for rejecting either parent and being the cause of them losing their home. He is aware that whichever parent 'wins', he will be left feeling miserable and guilty about the other.

In William's case the court accurately identified the conflict between his parents and appointed a Family Court welfare office to prepare a report under S.7 of the 1989 Act. The Family Court welfare officer will see both William's parents and will attempt to conciliate between them so that they can agree an arrangement which will meet both their stated needs. The Family Court welfare officer has a general duty to ascertain William's wishes and feelings under S.1(3) of the 1989 Act and the court has a corresponding duty to take those wishes and feelings into consideration. However, William will not be a party to the residence and contact proceedings. He will have no direct representation in court and, unlike the guardian *ad litem* in public law proceedings, the Family Court welfare officer will be there as an officer of the court, not as a representative of the child. William has, therefore, no direct avenue of representation to the court other than through the conciliation based process.

Gemma and William are children caught up in divorce and are not particularly unusual. There is nothing in their cases that will ever hit the headlines, for there are thousands like them. The lack of independent representation means that they are effectively subsumed by, and dependent upon, their parents' wishes. If their parents are reasonable and understanding, they may incorporate the wishes and feelings of the child into their agreements. However, experience shows that there is no more unreasonable area of dispute than that involving children in divorce proceedings. Normally balanced and conscientious people can become unrealistic, unreasonable, and at worst, vindictive, when faced with the prospect of losing their child. In such raw and painful situations, it cannot be assumed that the interests of the child will always be accurately represented and properly considered by the divorcing parents. In addition, there are, of course, many thousands more children in respect of whom arrangements are never open to court scrutiny, because their parents were never married.

Purposes of divorce

In 1966, the Law Commission published its Report *The Field of Choice*. It analysed the purposes of divorce as follows:

> First, the law should make it possible to dissolve the legal tie, once that has become
> irretrievably broken in fact. If the marriage is dead, the object of the law should be

to afford it a decent burial. Secondly, it should achieve this in a way that is just to all concerned, including the children as well as the spouses, and which causes them the minimum of embarrassment and humiliation. Above all, it should seek to take the heat out of the disputes between husband and wife and certainly not further embitter the relationships between them or between them and their children. It should not merely bury the marriage, but do so with decency and dignity and in a way which will encourage harmonious relationships between the parties and their children in the future.[11]

The Commission identified the need to protect the interests of children involved in divorce as a primary objective of any reformed divorce law.

The Divorce Reform Act 1969 established the principle that the breakdown of the marriage should be the sole ground for divorce. Although there had been a steady upward trend in the divorce rate since 1858, when divorce first became available, there was a substantial increase in the number of divorce petitions as opposed to those for judicial separation, once the Divorce Reform Act 1969 was implemented. By the year 2010, the Policies Studies Institute predicts that divorce and re-marriage will be the norm. Around half of all divorced parents remarry or form new relationships. Half of those new relationships end in divorce.

What we are seeing amounts to new expressions of the age old problem of family breakdown and restructuring. Social policy in many areas, such as financial benefits, housing or contact with separated children, will have to acknowledge the implications of these new expressions.[12]

There is the question of the purpose of the court proceedings and the role of the courts. The inter-departmental review of family and domestic jurisdiction stressed that:

Firstly, the courts are judicial institutions, whose purpose is to dispense justice according to law. Secondly, the courts are required by the law, particularly in relation to children, to have regard to the welfare of those directly affected. Thirdly, the welfare of those affected is usually more likely to be achieved through agreement between them than judicial decision. Fourthly, even where the court is not required to have regard to the welfare of the parties, seeking solutions by agreement is to be preferred to the pursuit of contested litigation.[13]

The review saw 'no reason' to suppose that justice and welfare cannot march together but 'we endorse the Finer Committee's views that: "the individual in the family court must, in the last resort, remain the subject of rights, not the object of assistance." '[14]

There are echoes here of Dame Butler Sloss's statement in the Cleveland Enquiry Report that children are people, not objects of concern. Children should be the subject of rights and not the object of assistance. The question arises, therefore, whether the primary objective of the court, the dispensing of justice, can be achieved in a situation in which a significant proportion of those

---

11 The Law Commission, *Field of Choice* (1966), para. 17.
12 Bullock, 'Stepfamilies: What do we know, what do we need to know?' in *Agenda for Future Action* (De'Ath, ed. 1993).
13 Interdepartmental Review of Family and Domestic Jurisdiction (1986), Lord Chancellor's Department, para. 7.6.
14 *Ibid.*, para. 7.8.

most directly affected by the decisions have no right of independent representation in the proceedings.

Law must be viewed within the social and economic context in which it operates. The Divorce Law Reform Act 1969, which was incorporated into the provisions of the Matrimonial Causes Act 1973, reflects society's ambivalence about the reasons for divorce and the apportionment of blame. Although the concept of fault still exists, the principle of irretrievable breakdown receives considerably more emphasis. One corollary of this is the enhanced importance of conciliation and of negotiated settlements between the two parties. Underlying the concept of irretrievable breakdown is the contemporary view that parties within a marriage retain their rights as individuals — rights to fulfil their own potential, rights to retain control over their own lives and to make compromises as a matter of choice rather than necessity. Paradoxically, at the point where individuals in marriage become parents, the rights of their children to have their best interests considered first may impose considerable strain on comparatively immature relationships. Many of today's parents have been brought up to have high expectations of life, education, employment and personal happiness. The economic stringencies of the 1990s place additional pressures on family life. In situations where mortgages are based on joint incomes, both men and women are faced with a contracting number of choices and daily problems of child care. The present law does not acknowledge the considerable potential for conflict of interest between the right of the parent to fulfil their own potential and the right of the child to have their welfare put first.

The Child Support Act 1991, implemented in April 1993, tacitly accepted the enormous problems involved in the maintenance of children of divorced parents by setting up the Child Support Agency to ensure that absent parents (particularly fathers) did not evade financial responsibility for their children. What the Child Support Act 1991 or any other Act does not address is the problem of how to involve the non-custodial parent in a continuing emotional, as well as financial, investment in the child's future. Half of all divorced fathers lose contact with their children under the current system. As yet there is no agency or system which has a specific responsibility to provide ongoing assessment, support and protection to the one in eight children who have experienced parental divorce by the time they are 10 and one in five by the age of 16.[15] In considering the problems involved, the Law Commission produced a draft checklist which courts might take into account in attempting to operate the welfare principle in relation to children involved in private law proceedings. This checklist was drafted in 1986 and predated the welfare checklist in the Children Act 1989. It suggested that the court should take account of the following factors:

1. the quality of the love, affection and other emotional ties existing between the child and each of the parties;
2. the nature of the emotional ties existing between the child and any person other than the parties;
3. the effect upon the child of separation from either party or from any other person with whom he has been living;

---

15   S.1(3).

4. the capacity and disposition of each of the parties to provide for the child's emotional needs in the future, including the recognition of his ties with other people;
5. the length of time the child has lived in his existing environment and the effect of any change, including changes of neighbourhood, school, local activities and access to relatives and friends;
6. the capacity (bearing in mind any financial provision or property adjustment which may be ordered) and disposition of each of the parties to provide properly for the child's accommodation, hygiene, food, medical care, appropriate supervision and companionship and otherwise for his physical needs and development;
7. the capacity (bearing in mind any financial provision which may be ordered) and disposition of each of the parties to provide properly for the child's education and intellectual development, both at home and at school;
8. the capacity and disposition of each of the parties to provide properly for the child's social and ethical development;
9. where relevant, the ethnic, cultural or religious background of the child and each of the parties;
10. the quality of the relationship existing or likely to exist between the child and any other member of each household and the likely effect of that member upon the capacities and disposition of each of the parties in paragraphs 4, 6, 7 and 8 above;
11. any risk of ill treatment by either party or by any present or likely member of that party's household;
12. any other special circumstances, including any particular aptitude or disability of the child;
13. the wishes and feelings of the child.

Although the wishes and feelings of the child is included as a last item in the list, there is some discussion in the consultation document about how the wishes and feelings of the child should be taken into account by the court.[16] The current situation would suggest that there has been little progress since 1986.

Effects of divorce

If children had any part in the decision making in separation and divorce, then the divorce rate would plummet overnight. Children who want their parents to separate are exceptional, and usually restricted to those who have been involved in situations where there has been extreme violence or years of mental cruelty. Generally, children want their parents to stay together. It is, however, the sad case that in the majority of cases, the wishes and feelings of the children are accorded only marginal significance. It is not that parents are deliberately selfish or ignorant of their child's wishes. Rather, it is that they identify their own best interests and those of their child as being one and the same thing, making the assumption that if they are happy, then the happiness of the child will follow. While it would be reassuring to be able to believe this, it is unfortunately not the case. The process of divorce is, for children, akin to a devastating bereavement. The child is suddenly adrift in a sea of separation and loss at a time when neither parent may be emotionally robust enough to

---

16   The Law Commission, *150,000 Children Divorced a Year: Who Cares? Law Reform and Invitation for Views* (1986).

deal effectively with both their own and the child's distress. Research findings on the effects of divorce on children indicate:

- children's development is greatly influenced by the relationship with, and between, the parents;
- conflict between parents has been linked to greater social and behaviourial problems among children;
- emotional stress on the part of parents and pre-occupation with matters concerned with the divorce lead to a decline in effective parenting. This manifests itself in little or no emotional support for the child, lack of discipline and supervision and breakdown in family communication;
- when parents separate, the loss often results in low self-esteem in children, who feel that they are the cause of the parent leaving;
- when conflict continues through a separation and divorce, the effects on the child can be very damaging;
- if conflict between the parents can be reduced, then the trauma for the child can be reduced in certain circumstances.[17]

Philip Graham's summary of the emotional problems facing children involved in divorce and separation is also informative:

1. They may be used as pawns in a continuing marital dispute by parents who, although physically separated, are emotionally linked by their dislike of each other;
2. Children may be used as message-bearers by parents who cannot bring themselves to communicate directly;
3. Children may be at risk of emotional upset, because the separate parent may not keep to contact times in a regular and predictable way;
4. Children may have to listen to parents denigrating each other, when they are fond of both of them;
5. Children have to be flexible enough to make relationships with new partners their parents might find, or be able to cope with the ambivalent feelings these new parental figures elicit in them.[18]

The rate of psychiatric disorders in the child of divorced parents is higher than that in the general population.[19] At the point at which the child needs extra emotional support, the parents are distracted and preoccupied with their own emotional needs and are frequently unaware of their child's emotional needs. In a study of 131 children involved in divorce, the majority were not consulted about visiting arrangements.[20]

The Booth Committee, set up in 1983 to examine divorce procedures in England and Wales, found that the statement of proposed arrangements for the children is frequently filled in with the minimum of information, including little detail about access arrangements. Two recommendations of the Booth Committee were that there should be more information requested from

---

17 *Looking to the Future: Mediation and the Ground for Divorce* (December 1993), paras. 4.4. and 4.5. — A consultation paper, the Lord Chancellor's Department.
18 Graham, *Child Psychiatry: A Developmental Approach* (2nd ed. 1991), p. 413.
19 Hetherington, Cox and Cox, *Effects of Divorce on Parents and Children* (1982).
20 Wallerstein and Kelly, *Surviving the Break-up* (1980).

parents about arrangements for the children and that parents should be referred to out of court conciliation services at the start of divorce proceedings.

There are significant differences between the perceptions of parents regarding separation and divorce and the perceptions of their children. In a study of 101 children involved in divorce, Anne Mitchell found that nearly two thirds of children had been upset by the separation (and many of the rest could not remember their feelings) but less than one third of their parents thought that their children had been upset in any way.[21]

'Nobody seems to be listening to me' is a common complaint from children involved in divorce. 'Your father/mother and I have just got it sorted out, don't start rocking the boat now' is a common reaction from parents to children questioning residence and contact arrangements, which are more often based on the convenience of the parents than the wishes of the children. Mervyn Murch's research highlighted parents' failure to give adequate explanations of their situation to children involved in separation and divorce.[22]

Research commissioned by the Joseph Rowntree Foundation into the effects of divorce and separation on children was heralded as challenging the common view that it is better for parents to divorce than for their children to continue to live in conflict. In a study carried out in Exeter, 152 children aged nine to ten and 13 to 14 were interviewed; half were from families who had stayed together, half from families which had separated. The study adopted a child-centred, rather than dispute resolution approach. It showed that children whose families had broken up were more likely to suffer a number of problems, ranging form psychosomatic illnesses, such as headaches and bedwetting, to difficulties in relationships with friends and at school and a generally low sense of self-esteem. A particularly vulnerable group were those who were going through the process of divorce and separation for the second, or even the third, time.[23]

As well as the emotional disadvantages of divorce for children, there are other, more tangible, drawbacks, although care must be taken in looking at research findings which link delinquency, lack of educational achievement and behaviourial problems with divorce.[24] There can be little doubt that children of divorced parents are likely to experience a drop in standards of living, attributable largely to the fact that 90 per cent of children stay with their mother after divorce, while the main earning capacity is likely to lie with the father, who withdraws himself and a substantial proportion of his income

---

21   Mitchell, *Children in the Middle: Living Through Divorce* (1984). See also Brynna Kroll, *Chasing Rainbows — Children, Divorce and Loss*, Russell House Publishing, 1994.
22   Murch, *Justice and Welfare in Divorce* (1980).
23   *Children living in re-ordered Families* (1994), Social Policy Findings, No. 45, Joseph Rowntree Foundation, with the Department of Child Health, Exeter University.
24   Martin, Fox and Murray, *Children Out of Court* (1981); Mitchell, *Children in the Middle* (1985). See also Surless, *Children in Divorce* (1984), a study of information available to the Scottish Courts on children involved in divorce actions, Edinburgh Scottish Office, Central Research Unit. See also Rutter, 'Parent/Child Separation: Psychological Effects on the Children' (1971), *Journal of Child Psychology and Psychiatry* 233; Ferry, *Growing up in a One Parent Family* (1976). See further The Report of the Committee on One Parent Families, The Finer Committee, Cmnd. 5629 (1974). The Finer Committee recommended the establishment of conciliation services for divorced and separating couples.

from the family home. The establishment of the Child Support Agency in 1991 purported to help remedy this unfortunate side effect of divorce. It is worth noting, however, that the Select Committee which examined the assessment criteria adopted by the Child Support Agency in the autumn in 1993 found that, of the additional £453 million targeted by the Child Support Agency, approximately £50 million went directly to the children of divorced parents while the rest went into the Treasury to provide a cushion against which other welfare benefits might be drawn.[25]

Representation of children in divorce proceedings

Legal Representation   Children are not parties in divorce proceedings. The ground for the divorce is that the court must be satisfied that the marriage has irretrievably broken down and must be satisfied that one of the following facts is the case:

● that the respondent has committed adultery and the petitioner finds it intolerable to live with the respondent;

● that the respondent has behaved in such a way that the petitioner cannot reasonably be expected to live with the respondent;

● that the respondent has deserted the petitioner for a continuous period of at least two years, immediately preceding the presentation of the petition;

● that the parties to the marriage have lived apart for a continuous period of at least two years immediately preceding the presentation of the petition and the respondent consents to a decree being granted;

● that the parties to the marriage have lived apart for a continuous period for at least five years, immediately preceding the presentation of the petition.[26]

Those seeking divorce are required to list their children and to provide particulars to the court about them. The general principle is that it is better for the children if parents can agree arrangements about residence and contact. Attempts to reach agreement may be facilitated by processes of conciliation and mediation.[27] Two points should be stressed in relation to mediation services generally. Firstly, it is an adult-centred service, focusing on the need for parents to agree about residence and contact as a primary objective. It is not child-centred in the sense of incorporating the wishes and feelings of the child as an essential element in the decision making. Secondly, it is not a state aided service. Conciliation and mediation services rely on voluntary funding and, as such, are available only in certain areas. *Looking to the Future* proposed a mediation service which could refer couples to conciliation or, in cases where the marriage could be saved, could help to settle custody and property divisions without recourse to the courts.

---

25   See Garnham and Knights, *Putting the Treasury First: The Truth about Child Support* (1994), Child Poverty Action Group.
26   Matrimonial Causes Act 1973, S. 1.
27   See Newcastle Conciliation Project Unit 1989, Report to the Lord Chancellor on the costs and effectiveness of conciliation in England and Wales, University of Newcastle-upon-Tyne.

The court has a general duty to consider the welfare of the couple's children under 16 and the proposed arrangements for the upbringing and welfare of any children must be set out by the parents and filed with the petition. Before implementation of the Children Act 1989, the judge would hold a satisfaction hearing at which the arrangements for the children were considered and reviewed before granting a decree nisi. The procedure of giving satisfaction was initiated in 1958, based on a concern that the independent interests of children should not be overlooked in what was seen as a contest between adults. Although it was subjected to severe criticism, on the grounds that the judge was being asked to perform a welfare, rather than judicatory, function, nevertheless it did lay a duty on the court to scrutinise the arrangements for children, which Schedule 12, para. 31 to the Children Act 1989 is said to have diluted radically.[28] The new arrangements are consistent with the philosophy of the 1989 Act, that parents are the best judges of their own children's interests and are capable of reaching agreement between themselves, if left alone to do so. The law thus clearly defines the arrangements for children as the responsibility of parents, makes an assumption about the capacity of the 'reasonable' parent to make appropriate arrangements and diminishes the responsibility of the state in relation to the nation's children. A large majority of divorces are uncontested and go through under the special procedure, whereby the district judge, if satisfied with the evidence submitted by the petitioners, may grant a decree nisi without the couple ever being present. Incidentally there is also an important cost-saving element in economising on the holding of hundreds of satisfaction hearings each year. As Andrew Bainham points out:

> parental wishes, especially where they are expressed as an agreement, will be likely to determine an increasing number of children matters. Clearly this is to the benefit of parents. Whether it will also further the interests of children is more questionable. What is certain is that this is not an easy question to answer, since it raises an endemic problem of determining when it is proper to recognise a convergence of children's interests with those of their parents and when a conflict of interests exists.[29]

Bainham's view is that, if too much weight is given to the parents' view, in the interests of non-intervention, this may well be at the expense of the child's welfare.

The question of the separation of children's rights from those of their parents is examined by Michael Freeman, who identifies four classifications of children's rights:

- rights to welfare;
- rights of protection;
- rights to be treated like adults; and
- rights against parents.

Freeman views the parent as the representative of the child. Where the interests of parents and child are in conflict, then parental representation ceases and

---

28   See Bainham and Cretney, *Children: The Modern Law* (1993).
29   *Ibid.*, p. 55.

some other person or body is justified in assuming the representational task in relation to the child, preferably by providing children with separate representation in court.[30] The second arm of Freeman's analysis of children's rights in relation to parents in conflict situations is that children should be able to act entirely independently. It could be argued that while the Children Act 1989 clearly delegated the determination of matters in relation to children to the good offices of the parents, it did, as a safeguard, allow children to initiate proceedings on their own account, acting independently. There is an agreed system within public law proceedings to deal with conflict between children and the state, or the local authority acting on the state's behalf, with separate legal and independent social work representation afforded to the child, but there is no parallel system for the child involved in divorce proceedings. Freeman supports Gerald Dworkin, who analyses the responsibility of parents in relation to their children in the following terms:

> parents ought to choose for [children] not as they might want but in terms of maximising those interests that will make it possible for them to develop life plans of their own. We ought to preserve their share of what Rolls calls 'primary goods', that is such goods as liberty, health and opportunity which any rational person would want to pursue, whatever particular life plan he chooses.[31]

There is considerable ambivalence on the part of parents, solicitors and members of the judiciary in the matter of children initiating their own applications. One concern is the involvement of the child in essentially adversarial procedures which lay the child open to the rigours of cross examination. Mrs Justice Booth summarised the matter in the following terms:

> The ability, which the Act gives to the child to make an application and to represent himself, does not lie easily with the adversarial procedures of the court. For example, may it always be desirable for a child even of 'sufficient understanding' to hear his parents give evidence and be cross examined? In some cases it may not be. But does the court have the jurisdiction to exclude a child from hearing the evidence if it is his application which is before the court? But does the court have the power to prevent it if he has filed a statement of evidence which is controversial? If the child is to give oral evidence should this be done by video link? It would be very easy to suggest that court procedures be modified in the best interests of a child, but it could also be very dangerous to move the goal posts to suit an individual case. There is a need for uniformity and while procedures must be adaptable they must also be certain.[32]

Whilst it is clearly not desirable to precipitate children into giving evidence in legal proceedings, nevertheless excluding them is not the answer and there is considerable experience to suggest that dangers and disadvantages arise from denying children full party status in proceedings which bear directly on their happiness and welfare.

'Looking to the Future' acknowledges that the Family Court Welfare Service offers 'more of a safety valve than a serious incentive to couples to mediate issues at the early stages, before opposing stances have been adopted by

---

30 Freeman, *The Rights and Wrongs of Children* (1983), pp. 48 – 52.
31 *Ibid.*, p. 51, quoting Dworkin.
32 'The Laws Relating to Children', the Honourable Mrs Justice Booth speaking at the closing address to the Lawyers for Children Conference, September 24, 1993, reported in *Family Law*, November 1993, at 653.

lawyers on behalf of one or both spouses.'[33] The welfare of individual children is therefore at the mercy of the adversarial system. Denying them direct representation within that system can only serve to exacerbate their powerlessness and vulnerability.

The Criminal Justice Act 1991, acting on the recommendations of the Pigot Committee,[34] establishes that a video can replace a child's evidence in a criminal court and lays down guidelines, including the use of video recordings, which can facilitate the taking of children's evidence. These guidelines are contained in a *Memorandum of Good Practice*. In the Foreword the point is made that the interests of justice and the interests of the child are not alternatives. Children have a right to justice and their evidence is essential if society is to protect their interests.[35] If this is true of children involved in criminal proceedings, surely it is also true of children whose futures are being decided in private law proceedings. Principles must apply to all children involved in proceedings, not only to some children involved in certain proceedings at certain times. It may be easier for adults to cope with children by excluding them from painful court proceedings, but by doing so they may be condemning them to years of protracted stress and anxiety. As Mrs Justice Booth says:

> It is the adversarial process that sometimes makes it difficult for the judge to see a child privately. Many children wish to see the judge who is to determine their futures, to tell him their views as to what should happen. They do not want to leave it to the welfare officer or guardian ad litem.

One can only concur with Mrs Justice Booth when she says, further, that 'Judges in general are thought to be acting over cautiously in the implementation of the Act and are not bringing to it that imagination and initiative which it deserves.'[36] Case law gives some inconsistent messages.

Re S.[37] deterred solicitors seeking leave for children under 12 or 13 years, by recommending that: 'the court and the child's solicitor should be shown to consider that a child of eleven has sufficient understanding to give coherent instructions in a matter calling for insight and imagination,, which only maturity and experience can bring.' *Re H. (A Minor)* (Role of Official Solicitor) ([1993] 2 F.C.R. 437) however upheld the right of a 15-year-old boy to dispense with the Official Solicitor as a representative of his best interests, and to give instructions on his wishes and feelings directly through his own solicitor. Courts are however suspicious of applications on behalf of children which are unsupported by an adult. Where the person applying for leave to make an application for a S.8 Order is not the child concerned the court shall, in deciding whether or not to grant leave, have particular regard to:

- the nature of the proposed application for the S.8 Order;
- the applicant's connection with the child;

33 *Op. cit.*, para. 6.8.
34 Report of the Advisory Group on Video Evidence (1989) Home Office.
35 *Memorandum of Good Practice on Video Recorded Interviews with Child Witnesses for Criminal Proceedings* (1992), Home Office in conjunction with the Department of Health.
36 Mrs Justice Booth, *op. cit.*, at 653.
37 *Re S (A Minor)* (Independent Representation) [1993] 2 F.L.R. 437.

- any risk there might be of that proposed application disrupting the child's life to such an extent that he would be harmed by it; and
- where the child is being looked after by a local authority, the authority's plans for the child's future and the wishes and feelings of the child's parents.[38]

The court may grant leave, either with or without a hearing, but if they intend to refuse an application there must be a hearing. The reason for the application being made by the child, rather than the person in whose favour the Order would be made, should also be a factor in determining whether or not leave will be granted.[39]

The only opportunity for the courts to obtain an objective view of the child's wishes and feelings is through the Family Court welfare officer's report. Under S.7 of the Children Act 1989, a court considering any question with respect to children under the Act may:

(a) ask a probation officer; or
(b) ask a local authority to arrange for:
   (i) an officer of the authority; or
   (ii) such other person, other than a probation officer, as the authority considers appropriate;

to report to the court on such matters relating to the welfare of that child as are required to be dealt with in the report.

It should be stressed that, unlike the guardian *ad litem* who is both an officer of the court and a representative of the child, the Family Court welfare officer is a reporting officer and has no specific responsibility to report to the court on the child's wishes and feelings, although he is encouraged to visit the child. The general responsibility of the Family Court welfare officer is governed by S.1(3) of the Children Act 1989 to have regard to the matters in the welfare checklist, in particular to the ascertainable wishes and feelings of the child concerned (considered in the light of his age and understanding).[40]

In 90 per cent of cases the court does not appoint a Family Court welfare officer to prepare a report. This happens only in contested cases, when parents cannot agree the arrangements for their children. However, the facts, as put before the judge, are submitted entirely by the parents and their legal representatives. Children have no independent input into that system. The Family Court welfare officers are generally held in high esteem by courts but they suffer from four significant drawbacks in attempting to act on behalf of children:

- they are officers of the court, not representatives of the child;
- their aim is to bring about agreement between the parents about the arrangements for the children. They are therefore part of a mediation or dispute resolution process. Once that agreement has been reached, their duty is to report to the court, not to question the basis on which that agreement is constructed. Their role as mediators may be in direct conflict

---

38   Children Act 1989, S.9(1)(a)−(d).
39   See *Re S.C. (A Minor)* (Leave to Seek Residence Order) *Family Law*, November 1993 at 618.
40   S. 1(3)(a).

with their responsibility to report to the court on the interests of the children;

● while some Family Court welfare officers undoubtedly have expertise in ascertaining the wishes and feelings of children and young people, others do not. Family Court welfare officers are generally seconded to civil sections directly from criminal work. Although many undertake civil work conscientiously and effectively, others suffer from the lack of a child-centred orientation and do not give a high enough priority in their report to the child's stated wishes and feelings;

● in the vast majority of cases, the Family Court welfare officers are not appointed at all and there is no chance of any outside objective involvement in relation to the child.

The role of the Family Court welfare officer

The duties of the court welfare officer are dealt with in the Family Proceedings (Amendment No.2) Rules 1992.[41] The welfare officer may be asked by the court 'to report on such matters relating to the welfare of that child, as are required to be dealt with in the report.'[42] The report may be made in writing, or orally, as the court requires.[43] The hearsay rule is relaxed to allow the court to take account of any statement or evidence given in relation to matters referred to in the report.[44]

The role of the court welfare officer has not been changed by the Children Act 1989. Theoretically, it is possible for courts to appoint both a court welfare officer and a guardian in the same proceedings but, in practice, this duplication of effort does not occur and it was held to be inappropriate to appoint a welfare officer where a guardian *ad litem* had already prepared a report. However, if the court welfare report was already in preparation and the children were separately represented by a solicitor, then the report should be completed. In this case (*L v L (Separate Representation)*) the court welfare officer acknowledged that in the face of the child's strongly held views, she was not able to represent the child satisfactorily.[45]

Courts rely heavily on the expertise of court welfare officers as welfare specialists. Case law confirms the high regard in which they are held by the courts.[46] Although they are not witnesses, but independent officers of the court, they may be called to give evidence and their evidence tested in the normal way.[47] Family Court welfare officers enjoy a certain amount of latitude in relation to the court, in that their reports must of necessity contain a certain amount of hearsay,[48] which the courts accept without hesitation. If

---

41 S.I. 1992 No. 2067. See also Annex to Chapter 6, Children Act Advisory Committee Report 1993/94, p. 59.
42 S. 7(1)(b).
43 S. 7(3).
44 S. 7(4)(a) and (b).
45 *Re S (A Minor) (Guardian ad Litem)* [1992] 2 F.C.R. 554, and *L v L* (Separate Representation) [1994] 1 F.L.R. 890.
46 *Cadman v. Cadman* (1982) 3 F.L.R. 275.
47 *Edwards v. Edwards* (1986) 1 F.L.R. 187.
48 *Thompson v. Thompson* (1986) 1 F.L.R. 212.

the court, unusually, does not accept the Family Court welfare officer's recommendations, then it must give its reasons.[49] There have, however, been various criticisms of some aspects of court welfare practice.[50]

Family Court welfare officers have been criticised by children, themselves, for failing to take account of their wishes and feelings, failing to spell out the reason for their visit and the options available to the child and taking refuge in encouraging the child to draw sad and happy faces or engaging in other games aimed at facilitating communication, rather than giving the child information and asking straightforward questions. Children, particularly younger children, may not be seen at all, or may not be seen alone in a situation in which they feel free to express their views. In a study of over 200 welfare reports, prepared by Family Court welfare officers working in six probation areas, representing a cross-section of areas in terms of size, service, population and geographical location, reference to the wishes of children was made in only 30 per cent of reports, although in 58 per cent of reports the oldest child was aged over five years and in 28 per cent over 10 years. In only 3 per cent of cases do reports indicate that enquiries were made expressly to determine the wishes and/or feelings of any of the children.

> Another major issue raised by the research, which is of central importance in the light of the provisions of the Children Act 1989, concerns variations between courts and areas in the amount and adequacy of information in reports, concerning issues such as standards of care, parental commitment, access arrangements, children and, in particular, their wishes and feelings. Such information would seem to be central to the court's deliberations concerning the welfare of the child and the apparent predominance of evaluative, as opposed to factual, statements about key areas of their welfare raises important questions about practice, not only in terms of the nature and extent of direct contact with children, but also in terms of what information is gleaned from such contacts and how this is presented in reports.[51]

A study of the impact of the implementation of the Children Act 1989 on Family Court welfare teams revealed the difficulties experienced by welfare officers in reconciling the need to ascertain the wishes and feelings of the child without burdening the child with decisions that should be made by adults. For this reason, some welfare officers never saw the child alone. The researchers were struck by how few respondents drew attention to the nature and intensity of the adult's conflict as a factor — both in directly causing a degree of 'regression' (due to high insecurity) in the child and as an indication of the appropriateness of putting the child 'on the spot' in the first place.[52]

There is a lack of clarity of the role in relation to the Civil Court Welfare Service and its position in relation to mainstream criminal work. It has been

---

49   *Stephenson v. Stephenson* (1985) F.L.R. 1140, *Re T.* (1981) F.L.R. 59, *Hutchinson v. Hutchinson* (1981) 2 F.L.R. 167, *W. v. W.*, *The Times*, June 14, 1988.

50   See *Scott v. Scott* (1986) 2 F.L.R. 320, *Re H.* [1986] 1 F.L.R. 476, *Maryman v. Hardy* [1987] 151 J.P.N. 526 and *Butler v. Butler* C.A. December 11, 1987. See further James, Hey, Greatbatch and Walker, 'The Welfare Officer as Expert: Reporting for the Courts' *Journal of Social Welfare and Family Law* (1992) No.5.

51   *Ibid.*, p. 408 from James and Hey with Greatbatch and Walker, *Court Welfare Work Research Practice and Development* (1992).

52   Cantwell and Truider, *For Better or Worse: Research into the Impact of the Children Act 1989 on the Work of Family Court Welfare Teams* (1993).

suggested that the change of title from Civil Court Welfare Service to Family Court Welfare Service has compounded this confusion.

> Is the primary role about investigating and reporting to the court, or helping families to resolve their disputes by means of mediation? The service suffers from a lack of direct responsibility to a commitment from a single department. The court welfare service is part of the probation service responsible to the Home Office, but welfare officers are accountable in their work to the civil courts under the control of the Lord Chancellor's Department.[53]

A strategy document for probation service Family Court welfare work identifies the statutory duties of probation officers undertaking Family Court welfare work as follows:

- the preparation of welfare reports;[54]
- dispute resolution, directed towards achieving agreement out of court;[55]
- supervision, in the rare circumstances specified in the Act, of a child who is subject to a supervision order;[56]
- providing advice and assistance to any person named in a Family Assistance Order;[57]
- attending court hearings if directed to do so;[58]
- acting as guardian *ad litem* or reporting officer in proceedings under the Adoption Act 1976.[59]

None of these six functions relates to any aspect of representing children in private law proceedings. The document confirms that the general principles in S.1 of the Children Act 1989 provide a framework for Family Court welfare work. They are:

- the welfare principle (that the child's welfare is the paramount consideration);
- parental responsibility;
- minimum intervention by the courts;
- minimum delay.

The strategy document further outlines priorities for the future development of the service and comments that, although these six functions are not exclusive, other activities previously undertaken under the umbrella of Family Court welfare work should be run down by the beginning of the 1994/95 financial year, to enable resources to be concentrated on core responsibilities.

---

53   Hall, 'Restructuring the Civil Court Welfare Service' (1994) 24 *Family Law* p 105.
54   Probation Rules 1984 (S.I. 1984 No. 647), r. 35(i), amended by the Probation (Amendment) Rules 1991 (S.I. 1991 No. 2035).
55   Probation Rules 1984, r. 35(i) amended by the Probation (Amendment) (No. 2) Rules 1992 (S.I. 1992 No. 2077).
56   Probation (Amendment) Rules 1984, r. 35(j) as amended by the Probation (Amendment) Rules 1991.
57   Probation Rules 1984, r. 35(k) as amended by the Probation (Amendment) Rules 1991.
58   Family Proceedings Courts (Children Act 1989) Rules 1991 (S.I. 1989 No. 1395 (L.17)), r. 13, as amended by the Family Proceedings Courts (Miscellaneous Amendment) Rules 1992 (S.I. 1992 No. 2068 (L.19)) and Family Proceedings Rules 1991 (S.I. 1991 No. 1247), r. 4.13 as amended by the Family Proceedings (Amendment No. 2) Rules 1992 (S.I. 1992 No. 2067 (L.14)).
59   Probation Rules 1984, r. 35(a) as amended by the Probation (Amendment) Rules 1991.

The Probation Rules specifically limit the involvement of probation officers in dispute resolution to those cases in which the court directs the service to become involved. Referrals from outside agencies, solicitors (or children) are precluded. The document recommends that 'local committees discuss with independent mediation and conciliation organisations how best to provide dispute resolution services in collaboration.'[60]

The only place where the needs of children feature in this document is in the title. There are no chapter or even paragraph headings which adopt what might be loosely termed a child centred approach, although the following goals are identified:

- To treat the welfare of the child as the paramount consideration in all questions about his or her upbringing.
- To promote the belief that children are generally best looked after within the family with both parents playing a full part and with legal proceedings used only in the last resort, to protect a child's welfare.
- To provide a service of quality, which makes the best use of public money, is properly targeted and is consistent with the achievement of equality and opportunity.

In October 1994, the Home Office published guidance on 'National Standards for Probation Service Family Court Welfare Work'. These standards are more explicit in directing family court welfare officers to see children with a view to ascertaining their wishes and feelings.

> All children should be seen by the court welfare officer unless there are strong grounds for not doing so. If a child is not seen the reasons for this must be given in the report. Wherever their age and maturity permit it children should be offered the opportunity to express their wishes and feelings. These must be reported to the court. Children should never be forced to express a view. Nor should they ever be made to feel as if they are taking responsibility for decisions about them which properly belong with adults.

('National Standards for Probation Service Family Court Welfare Work', Home Office, October 1994, para. 4.17.)

In addition, court welfare should ensure that children understand that their views will be reported to the court (para. 4.18, *ibid.*) This is welcome guidance, and hopefully the service will receive appropriate training on this aspect of their role, but it still does not solve the problem of the representational anomaly for children.

The publication of *'Looking to the future: Mediation and the Ground for Divorce'*[61] in December 1993, with its proposals for a 'process' divorce, may, if adopted, have a significant impact on the future development of the service and the provision of assistance in dispute resolution. However, the opportunity should not be lost to focus on the needs of the child involved in separation and divorce as direct clients with separate rights, rather than to continue to meet their needs obliquely through their parents.

---

60   *Helping the Court to Serve the Needs of Children Involved in Separation and Divorce: A Strategy Document for Probation Service Family Court Welfare Work* (1993) Home Office, pp. 2 and 3.
61   *Op. cit.*

Differences between advocacy and mediation

It is clear that Family Court welfare officers have a model of dispute resolution based on principles of conciliation and mediation. Family mediation is defined as a way of solving disputes without resorting to adjudication through the courts. The objectives are:

- to help couples reach agreements about the future;
- improve communications;
- to help couples co-operate in bringing up their children.

Family mediation services are a comparatively recent development and are still a relatively rare commodity. Mediation may be provided by the Family Court welfare officer at the request of the court or by local voluntary and private sector services affiliated to the National Association of Family Mediators and Conciliation Services or the Family Mediators Association. The indications are that less than a third of divorcing couples receive mediation services.[62] The mediation process is much better adapted to identifying those marriages which are capable of being saved than in the adversarial legal process.[63]

However, the consultation document rightly identifies the contradictory aspects of incorporating a process of non-adversarial mediation within the confines of the adversarial process, driven by courts and lawyers. Similarly, it is also acknowledges that it is too soon to assess the impact of the work of the Child Support Agency on mediation.

There are fundamental differences in approach between advocacy and mediation. Advocacy focuses on people, not processes. If the children involved in divorce had access to advocacy services, they would have a direct representative of their view, and someone who is clearly on their side. Conciliators, on the other hand, can only help by not taking sides and are therefore ineffective as representatives of the child's view. Present conciliation and dispute resolution services focus on the need to negotiate a settlement. They are court driven, rather than child orientated. They also cease to be operative once the relevant Court Orders are made. A child centred advocacy service can recognise that the welfare of the child is an ongoing concern, not something that dissipates as a function of the length of time that has elapsed since the court proceedings.

Remedies for children in private law proceedings

There are two key questions to be considered. One is 'In what circumstances is it a) desirable and b) possible to obtain separate legal representation for children in private law proceedings?' and the other, 'What are the mechanisms,

---

62   *Ibid.*, paras. 7.13 and 7.14. See also the report to the Lord Chancellor on the cost-effectiveness of conciliation in England and Wales, the Conciliation Project Unit, University of Newcastle-upon-Tyne, 1989. The report confirmed that mediation is effective in reducing the areas of dispute and in increasing the parents' well-being and satisfaction. The process was more effective if it was not court based.

63   *Looking to the Future, op. cit.*, para. 7.18.

if any, for ensuring that the wishes and feelings of the child are brought to the attention of the court?' Theoretically, children may become directly represented in one of two ways — either by being made a party to the proceedings or by initiating proceedings on their own behalf.

It is arguable that the position of children in private law proceedings is considerably strengthened by their power both to intervene in and to initiate S.8 applications under the provisions of the Children Act 1989. However there are three major stumbling blocks.

The child has to seek the leave of the court to intervene in proceedings Even supposing that a child is able to contact and instruct a suitable children's panel solicitor, all such applications for leave must be transferred to the high court under a Practice Direction issued by Sir Stephen Brown, President of the Family Division.[64] Under S.10 of the 1989 Act, the prior leave of the court is required in respect of applications by the child concerned for S.8 Orders (Contact, Prohibited Steps, Residence and Specific Issue Orders). Rule 4.3 of the Family Proceedings Rules 1991 and rule 3 of the Family Proceedings Courts (Children Act 1989) Rules 1991 set out the procedure to be followed when applying for leave. Such applications raise issues which are more appropriate for determination in the High Court and should be transferred there for hearing.

The child must be competent to apply Even if the child is able to negotiate the considerable hurdles involved in convincing a solicitor that he is competent to bring proceedings and survives the delays which may be inherent in the seeking of leave through the High Court, he still has to convince the court that he is of sufficient age and understanding to bring proceedings on their own account. In *Re T. (A Minor) (Child Representation)*[65] it was suggested that, by virtue of Rule 9.2A(10) the court, rather than the solicitor, has the ultimate right to decide whether a child who comes before it as a party without a next friend or guardian *ad litem* has the necessary ability, having regard to his understanding, to instruct his solicitor. *Re F. (A Minor)* concerned the rights of a 13-year-old girl who wished to initiate family proceedings against her parents without the intervention of a next friend. In the ordinary way, she would not have been able to pursue that application in her own right — it could only have been maintained by a next friend on her behalf. However Rules of Court enacted under the Children Act 1989, namely r.9.2A as amended, authorise a minor to bring or defend certain family proceedings without the intervention of a next friend or guardian *ad litem* in certain specified cases, one of which is that a solicitor should have obtained and accepted the child's instructions to act for him, after satisfying himself that the minor is capable of giving him instructions for that purpose. The issue, fiercely debated in *Re S. (A Minor) (Independent Representation)*[66] was the question

---

64 *Practice Direction (Fam. D.) (Children Act 1989: Applications by Children)*, February 22, 1993. See also *Re S.C. (A Minor)* [1994] 1 F.L.R. 96 which deals with the direction of the court in such applications.
65 [1993] 4 All E.R. 518.
66 [1993] 3 All E.R. 36.

of to what extent, if at all, the minor's understanding — in cases where the child is proposing to instruct his own solicitor — is a matter for consideration by the court or whether it is exclusively a matter for assessment by the solicitor who is deciding whether or not to accept instructions. In short, are solicitors competent to decide on the competence of children to give instructions? Although no definition of understanding is attempted by the 1989 Act or the Rules guidance, in *Re S.* the view was put that 'different children have differing levels of understanding at the same age, and that understanding is not an absolute. It has to be assessed relative to the issues in the proceedings. Where any sound judgment on these issues calls for insight and imagination, which only maturity and experience can bring, both the court and the solicitor will be slow to conclude that the child's understanding is sufficient.'

Both *Re T.* and *Re S.* emphasise that, while the Children Act 1989 may give a theoretical boost to the right of children to initiate proceedings on their own account, those rights are likely to be filtered through the benevolent paternalism of the court's view of their capacity to understand the matters before the court. It is not likely that courts will be guided exclusively by the solicitor's assessment of the child's competence to give instructions. To an extent, this retreat from the central acceptance of the child's right to initiate proceedings has been precipitated by publicity surrounding cases, both here and in America, in which children sought to 'divorce' their parents. It is almost as though the judiciary was overwhelmed by the spectre of the hundreds of children's cases which might result from allowing children separated party status in disputes against their parents. However, if children are not properly represented this is a legitimate ground for appeal. Thorpe J comments, in *Re H. (A Minor)* (Care Proceedings)[67] which dealt with a very disturbed 15-year-old boy, that it put the case a bit high to suggest that any child of 15 years had sufficient understanding to instruct a solicitor — a child had to have sufficient understanding within rationality. The later case of *Re H. (A Minor)* (Role of Official Solicitor) ([1993] 2 F.C.R. 437) does not however support this view.

There are many difficulties for children who seek to initiate proceedings. Some of these are highlighted by the Children's Legal Centre in their booklet for Children entitled '*Your Say in Court*'. The child must be in possession of accurate information about what Orders are possible under the Children Act 1989. Then he or she must have enough ingenuity to locate a suitable children's panel solicitor. This may involve making enquiries at the child's local Citizen's Advice Bureau or telephoning the Law Society. There is then the tricky business of making an appointment. While children have a right to see solicitors confidentially, it is a concept that many parents would find difficult to accept, if they knew about it, and the child would find extremely difficult to arrange if they didn't, even if the difficulties inherent in any conflict of interest between parents and child are disregarded. Parents may very well take the view that it is not in their child's best interests to see a solicitor and actively discourage such a venture. Even if the child successfully negotiates these hurdles, there is the question of obtaining Legal Aid and choosing a solicitor

---

67   [1992] 2 F.C.R. 330.

who is prepared to act on the child's instructions.[68] Family court welfare officers are under no duty to advise children of their rights in relation to the initiation of proceedings.

The right of the child to act without a next friend   The controversially amended rule 9.2A, authorising minors to bring or defend certain family proceedings without the intervention of a next friend, while attracting little comment at the time of its introduction, is now the subject of rather closer scrutiny. Rule 9.2A states that:

(i) where a person entitled to begin prosecute or defend any proceedings to which this Rule applies is a minor to whom this part applies he may, subject to para.4, begin prosecute or defend as the case may be such proceedings without a next friend or guardian *ad litem*:
(a) where he has obtained the leave of the court for that purpose; or
(b) where a solicitor:
   (i) considers that the minor is able, having regard to his understanding, to give instructions in relation to the proceedings; and
   (ii) has accepted instructions from the minor to act for him in the proceedings and, where the proceedings have begun, is so acting.
(ii) a minor shall be entitled to apply for the leave of the court under para. (1)(a) without a next friend or guardian *ad litem* either:
(a) by filing a written request for leave, setting out the reasons for the application; or
(b) by making an oral request for leave at any hearing in the proceedings.
(iii) on considering a request for leave, filed under para. (2)(a) the court shall either:
(a) grant the request, whereupon the proper officer shall communicate the decision to the minor and, where the leave relates to the prosecution or defence of existing proceedings, to the other parties to those proceedings, or:
(b) direct that the request be heard *ex parte* whereupon the proper officer shall fix a date for such a hearing and give to the minor making the request such notice of the date so fixed as the court may direct.
(iv) where a minor has a next friend or guardian *ad litem* in proceedings, and the minor wishes to prosecute, or defend the remaining stages to the proceedings without a next friend or a guardian *ad litem* the minor may apply to the court for leave for that purpose, and for the removal of the next friend or guardian *ad litem*; and para. (2) shall apply to the application as if it were an application under para. (1)(a).

Not only does the child have the right to act without a next friend, but if a next friend or guardian *ad litem* has been appointed by the court the child has the right, under para.(4) to apply for leave to remove such a guardian. In *Re H. (A Minor) (Independent Representation)* a 15-year-old boy applied successfully to retain the services of his own solicitor, and to dispense with the services of the Official Solicitor who had been appointed by the court as his guardian *ad litem*.[69] Such cases are, however, few and far between and in practical terms the obstacles facing children who attempt to initiate proceedings on their own account are, quite simply, overwhelming. Even if

---

68   *Your Say in Court: Taking your own Case to Court under the Children Act 1989* (1993), Children's Legal Centre. See also 'When Parents Separate', a handbook of law and practice — The Children's Legal Centre, 20 Compton Terrace, London N1 2UN (1994), and Hazel Houghton James, 'Children Divorcing their Parents', *The Journal of Social and Welfare Law* No. 2 1994 pp. 185–199.
69   [1993] 2 F.C.R. 437. (The Official Solicitor was re-appointed as *Amicus Curiae*.)

they do succeed in convincing a solicitor that they are competent to give instructions, solicitors have encountered grave difficulties in obtaining legal aid to act in the High Court on their behalf.[70] Given that there will be few children who have the personal means to pursue their own applications, the question of whether or not legal aid is available is crucial, if they are to be enabled to pursue any applications on their own behalf. Although legal aid is automatically available for children in public law proceedings, the same is not the same in private law proceedings. Children applying have to go through a complicated process of assessment even though, in 1989, the child's eligibility to legal aid is based solely upon his or her own means. The complicated procedure and the delay in obtaining legal aid for children provides yet another obstacle, and introduces more delay — both of which in effect act as deterrents to the initiation of children's own applications, and, incidentally, to solicitors considering them.

The danger for the court is in determining whether or not the child is pursuing somebody else's interests, rather than his or her own. The court must guard against the manipulative parent, or even a manipulative solicitor, and some judges see rule 9.2A, as amended, as a very mixed blessing, regarding the involvement of a next friend or guardian *ad litem* in children's applications as the best safeguard in ensuring that only the children's interests weigh in the final decision making. Thorpe J asks:

> Is there sufficient safeguard in the Court of Appeal's construction of rule 9.2A to allow anxieties and the need for reconsideration? To answer that, we must first consider danger areas. In my experience the greatest is the tendency and capacity of parents to exercise an influence over a child which is, in fact, harmful but which the child is perhaps the last to see as harmful. The facts that lay behind the appeal in *Re S* are an illustration of this type of case. If the child is defendant, the manipulative parent wishes to discard the guardian ad litem who he or she rightly perceives as a check upon his or her ability to influence the development of the child's evidence and submissions. Conversely a manipulating parent may wish to apply to the court for something which he or she cannot achieve by negotiation. However prospects may be unpromising, either as a result of an earlier application previously refused, or because of inability to obtain legal aid. To such a parent putting the subject child up to make the application seems very attractive. Then, if only the hurdle of the application for leave can be successfully cleared (admittedly much harder to achieve as a consequence of the President's Direction of 22 February 1993), the case will receive streamlined treatment as a result of its distinguishing novelty. Of course, against these dangers the guardian ad litem is the best possible safeguard for, as in the case of *Re S*, he or she will ensure that the child is not used as a cat's paw and the child's true interests and welfare are advocated. Another danger area is the solicitor whose ambition for success and acknowledgement is rampant. Of course such an individual is a rare bird and, as the judgments for the Court of Appeal emphasise, the vast majority of solicitors are highly responsible and far distant from such motivation. But to such an individual, a child client, unencumbered by next friend, offers the prospect of some local attention if not national publicity.[71]

---

70   Rule 9.2A(1) of the Family Proceedings Rules 1991 (as amended).
71   'A View from the Court', His Honour Mr Justice Thorpe speaking at the Southwestern Regional Conference for Guardians ad Litem and Reporting Officers, published as *Practice in Progress*, GAL/RO Regional Conference Reports, the Department of Health with IRCHIN (Independent Representation for Children in Need), September 24, 1993, also in (1994) 24 *Family Law* 20.

The question arises as to what is the correct test to apply to children seeking leave. Is the grounding principle the likely successful outcome of the application, or the welfare of the child as the paramount consideration?

In *Re C. (A Minor) (Leave to Seek a S.8 Order)*[72] Johnson J took the view that the matter to be determined in relation to the child must be of sufficient moment and importance to justify judicial intervention. Further, the grounding principle must be the welfare of the child as defined in S.1(1) — that the child's welfare is of paramount importance.

In *Re C* the application of a 15-year-old girl for a Residence Order to stay at a friend's house, and Specific Issue Order to allow her to take a holiday abroad against her parent's wishes, were turned down on the grounds that these were matters that could be resolved by discussion. In *Re S.C. (A Minor) (Leave to Seek Residence Order)*[73] Booth J refused a 14-year-old girl leave to apply for a Residence Order to live with a friend's family on the following grounds: 'that such an application should be made ex parte, even if S.10(8) is satisfied, the court is not bound to grant leave and, most interestingly, the child's welfare is not the paramount consideration of the court in exercising discretion.' This last followed the view expressed by Balcombe LJ in *Re A. (Minors) (Residence Order, Leave to Apply)*[74] that: 'in granting or refusing an application for leave to apply for a S.8 Order, the court is not determining a question with respect to the child concerned.'[75]

It seems difficult to sustain this view, given that S.10(8) is silent on the criteria to be applied for the granting of leave to children beyond requiring that the child be of sufficient understanding to make the proposed application for the S.8 Order. It does not address the question of whether adults should judge the proposed terms of the S.8 Order to be either reasonable or desirable, but what S.10 does do is establish the right of the child to apply. In that sense Booth J's interpretation may be nearer what was intended. However, these differential interpretations by senior members of the judiciary highlight the practical tensions inherent in philosophical confusions of rights and welfare.

Either the child has the right to initiate proceedings on their own account or a guardian *ad litem* acts in their best interest. What is clear, is that a healthy balance can only be achieved by combining the statutory right of the child to initiate proceedings on their own account, and to be party to the proceedings with full separate and independent legal representation, with a concomitant provision for the incorporation of the best interests of the child, through the introduction of a next friend or guardian *ad litem* to put a view to the court about the child's best interests, thus mirroring the situation in public law proceedings.

There are considerable confusions in this area, among the judiciary as well as amongst solicitors acting for children and children themselves. In *Re T (A Minor) (Child: Representation)*[76] a 13-year-old girl applied for a Residence

---

72 (1994) 1 F.L.R. 26.
73 (1994) 1 F.L.R. 96.
74 [1992] 3 W.L.R. 422.
75 See also *J.R. v. Merton London Borough* (1992) 2 F.C.R. 174, C.A. For a commentary on these cases see *Practitioner Guide to Child Law, Newsletter*, Vol. VII, No. 8, February 1994.
76 [1993] 2 F.C.R. 445.

Order so that she could go and live with her grandparents and her aunt. The solicitor decided that she was competent to give instructions under the Family Proceedings Rules 1991, r.9.2A(1)(b)(i). The child could therefore bring the proceedings without a guardian *ad litem*. The proceedings were transferred from the County Court to the High Court where T's adoptive parents opposing her application successfully applied for her to be made a ward of court and for the Official Solicitor to be appointed as her guardian *ad litem*. The wardship proceedings were then consolidated with T.'s application for a Residence Order. T. appealed on the grounds that she had satisfied her solicitor that she had the required level of understanding to give instructions. It was a matter for her to decide what those instructions should be. In allowing T.'s appeal Waite LJ took the view that rule 9.2A applies to all family proceedings, including proceedings under the High Court's inherent jurisdiction. Therefore wardship could not be used to override the right of the child to instruct a solicitor without a guardian *ad litem*, provided that the conditions under rule 9.2A(1)(b)(i) had been satisfied.

The Children Act 1989 is required to maintain a balance between the principle that children are entitled to have their views taken seriously and their interests protected. In *Re F (A Minor) (Independent Representation)*[77] the judge, in attempting to assess the individual child's understanding in the context of the proceedings gave the following guidelines:

1. Whereas a solicitor had to consider before accepting instructions that the child was able, having regard to his understanding, to give them, the court, before granting leave, had to consider that the child had sufficient understanding to participate as a party in the proceedings without a next friend or guardian *ad litem*.
2. The tests were framed with reference to the child's understanding not his age.
3. Rule 9.2A(8) made it clear that the court might revoke the leave where it considered the child's understanding was insufficient to testify the granted leave.
4. References in Rule 9.2A(4) and (6) to apply for leave and the removal of the guardian *ad litem* or next friend were to be read conjunctively so that if the court granted leave under sub-section (4) it had also to remove the next friend or guardian *ad litem*.
5. Where the child's request for leave was made in writing before a next friend or guardian *ad litem* was appointed rule 9.2A(3) did not expressly contemplate that the other parties would be heard. Where a hearing was to be fixed and although the rules did not confer any right on the parties to be heard on the child's application the judge always had the discretion to hear any parties thought to be necessary or desirable in the interests of justice.[78]

Role of the Official Solicitor in representing children in private proceedings[79]

In certain situations it is possible for the Official Solicitor to be appointed to act as guardian *ad litem* to children involved in private law proceedings. In

---

77 [1993] F.L.R. 427 C.A.
78 *Family Law* Vol. 23 September 1993 p. 542.
79 Any solicitors finding themselves in need of advice may contact the Association of Lawyers for Children c/o Mr Ian Robertson, Griffiths Robertson, 46 West Street, Reading, Berkshire RG1 1TX (telephone 01734 574018). In cases where solicitors wish to instruct Counsel it

private law proceedings under the 1989 Act, he may act as the child's guardian *ad litem* in the High Court and County Court, but not in the Family Proceedings Court. The criteria for the appointment of the Official Solicitor as the guardian *ad litem* of the subject child include cases in which:

- there is disputed medical evidence or medical opinion is at variance;
- there is a substantial foreign element;
- there are special or exceptional points of law; or
- he is already acting for the child in other proceedings.

The Official Solicitor may also act as *amicus curiae*, or next friend of the court, as well as directly representing the child. Consequently his role may be potentially confusing, as he may be an adviser as well as a representative of the child's best interests. Clearly courts rely on the Official Solicitor in complex cases, but his present role appears to be essentially reactive according to the requirements of each case, rather than as part of an integrated philosophical framework which acknowledges the tensions between rights and welfare.

Subject to rule 9.2A of the Family Proceedings Rules 1991 (as amended) the Official Solicitor may act as a next friend of a child seeking leave to make an application under the 1989 Act or making an application in other family proceedings. He may also act as the guardian *ad litem* of a child who is the subject of wardship proceedings, or proceedings under the inherent jurisdiction of the High Court (although the numbers of these cases have fallen dramatically following the implementation of the Children Act 1989 and the attendant restrictions on imposed on the powers of the local authority to invoke the inherent jurisdiction of the High Court).[80]

The practical mechanism for requesting the involvement of the Official Solicitor is the completion of a short questionnaire which should be sent, together with the court file, to the Official Solicitor's office. The questionnaire consists of nine questions covering the nature of the proceedings, the name of the person for whom the Official Solicitor is invited to act and a short statement of the special circumstances that are thought to make the Official Solicitor's involvement appropriate, having regard to the criteria for the Official Solicitor's involvement as set out in the relevant practice direction. Having received the questionnaire, the onus is on the Official Solicitor to decide whether or not it is appropriate for him to become involved. Clearly the cases in which this is possible, or desirable, are limited by the criteria and by resources available to the Official Solicitor's Department. In practice the majority of cases passing through the courts would not meet the Official Solicitor's criteria. In most cases there is no substantial foreign element, disputed medical evidence or exceptional points of law. They are normal children involved in what is coming to be increasingly normal experiences of

---

may be preferable to instruct a member of the Family Law Bar Association. Details of the membership of this Association can be obtained from the Bar Council Records Office, 11 South Square, Grays Inn, London WC1R 5EZ (Telephone 0171 242 0082).

80 'The Official Solicitor, Best Practice on His Appointment as Guardian ad Litem in Family Proceedings', Lord Chancellor's Direction of October 7, 1991 reported at (1991) 2 F.L.R. 471, Court Business January 1993 B2480, *Family Law*, February 1993, at 604.

separation and loss and, as such, they merit no special consideration in terms of separate representation.

The role of the Official Solicitor may give rise to confusion about whether he is acting in a welfare or representational capacity. This ambiguity was highlighted by the case of the 12-year-old boy who sought to sue the Official Solicitor in person for not accurately representing his wishes and feelings to the court and for acting in a way which was contrary to his explicit instructions.[81]

Representing the child's wishes and feelings in the court

It will be clear, from the above, that it is only a very small minority of children who will be able to achieve separate party status and the right to legal representation in private law proceedings. If one adopts a child centred approach to representational problems, the problem (as perceived by the children) is not simply their lack of party status, but the lack of any identifiable or effective path of communication between them and the courts, through which they can inform those who are making decisions about their wishes and feelings. It is this aspect of events which is experienced by children and young people as a basic unfairness. Children are realistic enough to realise that their wishes and feelings will not be paramount in adult decision making. They do, however, increasingly seek ways of communicating their wishes and feelings to the court. Some children see their needs in relation to the court in refreshingly simple and sensible terms. 'I want the court to listen to what I have to say, take account of what I want and then make the decision for me, so that I don't feel guilty about choosing one parent and rejecting the other.' In a minority of cases the Family Court welfare officer is involved, and has a duty to consider the wishes and feelings of the child when preparing a report for the court under S.7 of the Children Act 1989. Debates about whether or not the Family Court welfare officer is the appropriate person to convey the wishes and feelings of the child to the court are almost academic in view of the fact that Family Court welfare officers are appointed in such a small number of cases. Ideally, the provisions which pertain in public law proceedings, which allow for the appointment of both a solicitor and a guardian *ad litem* in every case involving children, would be extended to cover all children in private law proceedings. This would have very considerable cost implications for the legal aid budget, and is frankly unlikely in the prevailing economic climate of treasury-limited services. Although courts have responsibility to take into consideration the wishes and feelings of the child in making decisions, there appear to be no acceptable avenues (except through the Family Court welfare officer or the Official Solicitor, as already identified) through which children may make their wishes known to the court. In many cases courts have been reluctant to listen to the views of children if those views are not conveyed to them through the acceptable channels, i.e. through the Family Court welfare officer or the Official Solicitor. However, since the implementation of the Children Act 1989 and the wider publicity given to the UN Convention on the Rights of the

---

81   The *Mail on Sunday*, December 19, 1993. See also *Re A.D. (A Minor)* [1993] 1 F.C.R. 573.

Child, children and young people are more aware of their rights, and the fact that there is a new Act, and a new Convention which lays down guidelines which may help them. The right of the child to initiate proceedings on their own account was widely publicised, and is emphasised in many of the booklets and information leaflets that are circulating not only in social work departments, but in schools and colleges. Children and young people are becoming more aware of their rights, and are seeking ways to exercise them. In particular they want to exercise the right to have their wishes and feelings heard. IRCHIN (Independent Representation for Children in Need) have investigated the possibilities of putting the child's wishes and feelings before the court by providing qualified and experienced children's social work advocates to assist in the process. The most successful outcomes were those in which the advocate was able to take the pressure off the child by putting their view to the parents, while enabling the child to contact and instruct an appropriate children's panel solicitor in initiate proceedings on their behalf. The following case illustration shows how the involvement of an independent social work advocate can work effectively to put the child's wishes and feelings before the court, and can also act as a catalyst in helping to bring about negotiated, rather than disputed, settlements between parents.

Beth's case   Beth is 13. She rang ChildLine, who referred her to a children's advocacy service. Her parents are in the process of divorce, and Beth is the subject of disputed residence and contact applications. Her parents only communicated through her, and she was finding the situation very difficult to handle. Beth had been visited by a court welfare officer on one occasion, but she did not feel she was able to communicate her wishes and feelings to the officer — in fact she had not understood at the time that this was a person who was there to represent her views.

Following the referral the children's advocate (an experienced social worker and guardian *ad litem*) rang Beth, and had a preliminary conversation on the basis of which she instructed a children's panel solicitor to act on her behalf. The solicitor obtained emergency legal aid, and applied to intervene in the proceedings at the County Court on Beth's behalf. With Beth's agreement the children's advocate wrote to her parents to inform them of her involvement, and subsequently obtained their agreement to Beth's application. The advocate and the solicitor visited Beth together, and prepared a first statement of her case. Later the children's advocate and the solicitor attended court and filed the statements on Beth's behalf. The judge granted leave for Beth to intervene in the proceedings, and ruled that the matter would remain in the County Court as the delay that would occur if the matter were transferred to the High Court was judged not to be in Beth's best interests. At the final hearing Beth expressed clear wishes about the need for a Contact Order, as she did not think that she could rely on her parents to co-operate without an Order. However she wanted the court to make the decision about residence as she did not want to feel guilty about choosing one parent or the other. In the course of the advocate's involvement it became clear that Beth had come under considerable pressure from both her parents. The advocate was able to put Beth's views to the court, and to her father and mother who subsequently, following out of court negotiation, agreed Residence and Contact Orders which met the majority of Beth's wishes. Beth was effectively relieved of the pressures created by her parents' acrimony. The fact that she had an advocate and a solicitor to put her views to a judge who was willing to hear them, led to a speedy and satisfactory resolution.

What this case illustrates is the need for an agreed procedure or process to meet children's needs during the process of divorce and separation. Present procedures are adult- rather than child-centred, and the early involvement of children's representatives, who can stand beside the child, and support then through the whole process could provide a satisfactory outcome for the child, and could also be cost-effective in diverting proceedings away from an adversarial court setting, towards negotiated settlements which incorporate the wishes and feelings of the child as a key component in the decision making.

There is an urgent need for more child-centred research in this area of law and practice, but the work already carried out indicates the need for a child-centred dispute resolution service and support for the thousands of children involved in private law proceedings. Such a service could hopefully be incorporated as part of a support service for the family jurisdiction, which could encompass the representation of children in private, as well as public, law proceedings. It would also fulfil Britain's responsibility to implement in full its obligations under Article 12 of the UN Convention on the Rights of the Child, which deals with the right of the child to be consulted and to be represented in any judicial proceedings affecting the child.

Summary of issues arising

Courts appear to be setting benchmarks about the age at which a child may give instructions. Should the child be Gillick competent or 13 plus? In addressing children's panel solicitors at a Solicitors Family Law Association Conference in Manchester in September 1993 Mrs Justice Booth counselled caution in granting leave for children to become parties in the process of which they may be the subject of distressing cross-examination.

The child's voice. If children under the age of 12 or 13 are unable to give instructions, how can younger people, who are arguably the most vulnerable to the whims of the 'unreasonable' parent, put their views before the court? Is this function adequately covered by the Divorce Court welfare officer who is an officer of the court, not a representative of the child? Experience suggests that the answer to this is 'No'.

Cumbersome procedures. Following the President's Practice Direction on February 22, 1993 and having applied for leave for the child to intervene in proceedings in the High Court, do cases have to stay in the High Court with all the delay and formality that that entails or can they be transferred down to the County Court? The theoretical answer to this question must be 'yes' but in practice this is unlikely to happen.

Difficulties in obtaining Legal Aid. Even if children find a solicitor who is prepared to initiate proceedings on their behalf experience shows that legal aid for proceedings in the High Court is likely to be refused. This makes solicitors even more reluctant to act for children.

Do courts want to hear what children have to say? Is it really intended that children should be able to initiate proceedings and are courts really prepared to allow children's wishes and feelings to influence decision making or are we leading children up blind alleys?

Avenues for children. What is the appropriate procedure for ensuring that children's views are brought to the attention of the court, given that it is unlikely that the guardian *ad litem* service will be extended to children involved in private law proceedings in the foreseeable future.

Use of children's advocacy services. Can social work advocacy be used constructively to help children involved in private proceedings using the model established in Beth's case?

Lack of a child-centred service for children involved in divorce and separation. Present services focus on the child only at the point at which the case is before the court. There is no recognised service or procedure which helps children once the Orders are made and they are locked into the consequences of their parents' decisions. If the parents are not sensitive to the child's changing needs there is no review of the arrangements on behalf of the child.

Looking to the Future: Mediation and the Ground for Divorce

Looking to the Future[82] contains proposals for the reform of divorce law. The objectives of good divorce law should be:

- to support the institution of marriage;
- to provide practicable steps to prevent the irretrievable breakdown of marriages;
- to ensure that couples understand the practical consequences of divorce before making any irreversible decision;
- when divorce is unavoidable, to minimise the bitterness and hostility between the parents and to reduce the trauma for the children;
- to keep costs to a minimum.

The Law Commission proposes that, under the reformed law, the court should have the power to direct that the spouses attend a preliminary interview with a specified person or agency in order that they can be given an explanation of the nature and purpose of mediation, and an opportunity to participate, if they agree. That person or agency would be required to report back to the court within a given time limit. This power should be exercisable by the court of its own motion or on application by either spouse — only after a marital breakdown statement has been filed. The aim would be to give the couple maximum opportunity to resolve their disputes amicably. No later than 12 weeks after the statement had been filed the court would hold a preliminary assessment hearing, at which neither party would necessarily be present. The

---

82   *Op. cit.*

court would have a specific duty, as part of the assessment, to 'identify any "relevant" children of the family and consider whether or not to exercise any of its powers under the Children Act 1989 in respect of them.'[83]

There are two major flaws in this from the child's point of view. Firstly, the proposals still make the fairly large assumption that the agreement of the parents will lead to a satisfactory outcome for the child. There is no objective review of the impact of the arrangements on the life of the child. Secondly, the proposals contain no provision for a direct service to children involved in divorce and separation, but adopt an indirect and arguably unscientific and essentially scatter-gun approach to the issue of children's long term welfare, based on a flimsy faith in the reasonableness of parents. If one of the primary aims of a reformed divorce law is to reduce trauma for children then the process should focus on the child from the beginning, and afford them effective representation in the ongoing discussions, both in and out of court. Mediation is, after all, the means to an end, and not the end in itself. An early and direct focus on the child would, it is suggested, not only expedite proceedings, but would also provide a more streamlined and cost-effective path to the resolution of disputes and the breaking up of the adversarial parental dyad.

The Draft European Convention on the Exercise of Children's Rights produced by the European Council in November, 1994, may, by reinforcing and endorsing the right of the child to separate and independent representation in all family law proceedings including residence and contact disputes, add fuel to the mounting pressure for the guardian *ad litem* service to be extended to children in private law proceedings.

Article 6 of the European Convention on Human Rights in also helpful in protecting the child's right of access to Court in all cases where family law rights are affected.

There are encouraging signs that, although Britain has led the way in the representation of children in public law proceedings, it is Europe which will lead in correcting the representational imbalance which exists for the far greater numbers of children involved in private law proceedings.

---

83 *Looking to the Future*, op. cit., Appendix D, paras. 13, 14 and 15.

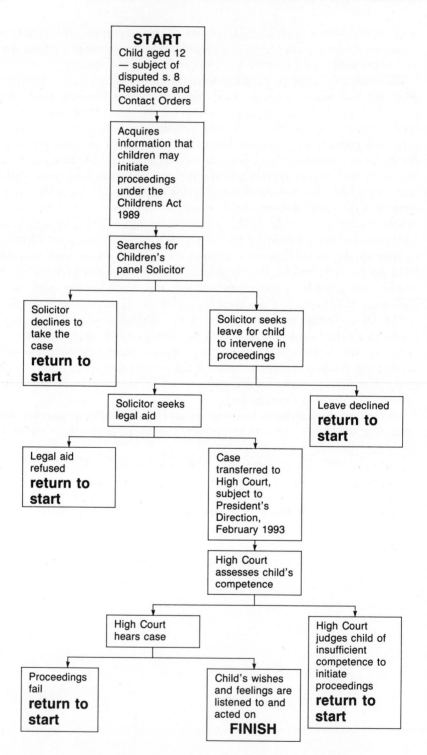

Figure 7 **Representation of Children in Private Law Proceedings:**
Obstacle Course for a 12-year-old

Appendix 1
Solicitors Family Law Association (SFLA) Code of Practice[84]
Introduction

An SFLA solicitor believes that, in resolving the problems arising at the end of family relationships or in family crises, it is preferable to promote a conciliatory atmosphere and to deal with matters in a sensitive, constructive and cost-effective way. To help put this into practice, SFLA members subscribe to a Code of Practice.

The Association was created in 1982 when there was widespread concern that too often solicitors and the court process were adding to the distress and anger that can arise on the breakdown of a family relationship. Our members believe that solicitors could, and should, deal with matters in a way designed to ensure that people's dignity is preserved, with every encouragement to reach agreement and avoid unnecessary litigation. The result will be to achieve the same or more satisfactory solutions but at less cost — in terms of emotion and money.

Most importantly, they will be solutions that do not destroy the possibility of former family members dealing with each other in a civilised way, for example in parents agreeing arrangements for the benefit of their children, notwithstanding their own differences. Experience shows that agreed solutions are more likely to be adhered to than those imposed by a court. Even when proceedings are inevitable so that a court has to decide matters, it is to the advantage of the whole family that proceedings are conducted in a constructive and realistic manner, rather than as if in the midst of a war zone.

What the Association is

(1) It is an association of solicitors and currently has over three thousand members, each of whom subscribes to a Code of Practice, Most members undertake legal aid work. The Law Society recommends that all solicitors practising family law should follow the Code of Practice. Members should inform their clients of the Code as it will form the basis of the approach that they adopt.

(2) Its administration has an office staffed by full-time personnel. Most areas of the UK have a regional group.

(3) It is also a representative body. It is actively involved in law reform, both initiating improvements and responding to proposals for change.

(4) It provides education for its members, to equip them to deal with both the legal and practical issues of family breakdown and the emotional consequences. It encourages the use of mediation where appropriate.

(5) Members vary in experience, from newly qualified to those qualified many years. Membership is not a guarantee of excellence or specialisation. Admission to the Association is on the basis of a commitment to the Code and confirmation that the solicitor will endeavour to ensure his work is carried out in accordance with the Code. Although members are proposed and seconded by fellow members, there is no test of ability.

What the Code is not

(1) Adherence to the Code is not a sign of weakness, nor does it expose the client to disadvantage. The approach adopted should be firm and fair. The solicitor is not

---

84   See also 'Guidance on Acting For Children in Private Law Proceedings under the Children Act 1989' (1994), The Law Society.

prevented from taking immediate and decisive action where this is required. Even where there are ongoing discussions, they may often proceed in parallel with court proceedings, in case negotiations do not produce a settlement.

(2) It is not a strait-jacket. The guidelines of the Code cannot be absolute rules inasmuch as the solicitor may have to depart from them if the law or professional rules or duties to the client so require.

Code of Practice

(1) General

(1.1) At an early stage the solicitor should inform the client of the approach he adopts in family law work.

(1.2) The solicitor should advise, negotiate and conduct matters so as to encourage and assist the parties to achieve a constructive settlement of their differences as quickly as may be reasonable, whilst recognising that the parties may need time to come to terms with their new situation.

(1.3) The solicitor should ensure that the client appreciates that the interests of the children should be the first concern. The solicitor should encourage the client to see the advantages to the family of a constructive and non-adversarial approach as a way of resolving their differences. The solicitor should explain to the client that in the cases where there are children, the attitude of the client to the other family members in any negotiations will affect the family as a whole and may affect the relationship of the children with the parents.

(1.4) The solicitor should encourage the attitude that a family dispute is not a contest in which there is one winner and one loser, but rather a search for fair solutions. He should avoid using words or phrases that imply a dispute when no serious dispute necessarily exists.

(1.5) Because of the involvement of personal emotions in family disputes, the solicitor should, where possible, avoid heightening such emotions in any way.

(1.6) The solicitor should have regard to the impact of correspondence on the other party when writing a letter of which a copy must be sent to that party. He should also consider carefully the impact of correspondence on his own client before sending copies of letters to the client. The solicitor should avoid expressing personal opinions as to the conduct of the other party.

(1.7) The solicitor should aim to avoid mistrust between parties by encouraging at an early stage full, frank and clear disclosure of information and openness in dealings.

(2) Relationship with client

(2.1) The solicitor should ensure that his relationship with his client is such that his objectivity is preserved and his own personal emotions do not cloud his judgment.

(2.2) Whilst recognising the need to advise firmly and guide the client, the solicitor should ensure that where the decision is properly that of the client, it is taken by the client and that its consequences are fully understood, both as to its effect on any children involved and financially.

(2.3) The solicitor should always ensure that the client is fully aware of the impact of costs on any chosen course of action. The solicitor should throughout have regard to the cost of negotiations and proceedings.

(2.4) The solicitor should ensure that the client is aware if the existence and range of all other services which may be of assistance in bringing about a resolution and helping members of the family through the process of family breakdown, such as mediation and counselling.

(3) Dealings with other solicitors

(3.1) In all dealings with other solicitors, the solicitor should show courtesy and endeavour to create and maintain a good working relationship.
(3.2) The solicitor should not denigrate the other solicitors involved in the case to the client.

(4) Dealings with the other party in person

(4.1) In dealings with another party who is not legally represented the solicitor should take particular care to be courteous and restrained. Special care should be taken to express letters and other communication clearly, avoiding technical language where it is not readily understandable to the layman or might be misunderstood.
(4.2) Wherever any party is not legally represented, that party should, in the interests of both parties and the family, be advised to consult a solicitor.

(5) Court proceedings

(5.1) The taking of any action or proceedings which is likely to cause or increase animosity between the parties must be balanced against the likely benefit to the client and the family.
(5.2) Where the purpose of taking a particular step in proceedings may be misunderstood or appear hostile, the solicitor should consider explaining it, at the first practical opportunity, to the other party or his solicitors.
(5.3) Before filing a petition, the solicitor should consider with the client whether the other party or his solicitor should be contacted in advance as to the intention to petition, the 'facts' on which the petition is to be based and/or the particulars to be alleged, with a view to proceeding by agreement. A client should be advised that filing a petition and/or statement of arrangements without first attempting to agree the contents is likely to increase feelings of contentiousness and hostility, making any settlement much more difficult to achieve. It may also earn the disapproval of the court and may have a bearing on the issue of costs.
(5.4) The solicitor should advise the client that on receipt for approval from the other spouse of a petition or statement of arrangements, and other than in exceptional circumstances, a client should not first file their own petition without giving their spouse at least five working days' written notice of the intention to do so.
(5.5) The solicitor should discourage a petitioner client from naming a co-respondent unless there is a compelling reason to do so.
(5.6) A solicitor should conduct family law proceedings, including the preparation, advocacy and implementation, in the most cost-effective manner and in such a way as not to increase hostility unnecessarily and as to allow reasonable opportunity for settlement.

(6) Children

(6.1) The solicitor should, in advising, negotiating and conducting proceedings, encourage both his client and other family members to regard the welfare of the child as the first and paramount consideration.
(6.2) The solicitor should aim to promote co-operation between parents in decisions concerning the child, and should consider encouraging arrangements to be reached direct or through mediation.
(6.3) Issues of arrangements for the children on the one hand and finance on the other must be kept separate. They should be referred to in separate letters.

(6.4) The solicitor should remember that the interests of the child may not coincide with those of the parent, and in exceptional cases it may be appropriate for the child to be separately represented: this may be by the Official Solicitor, a panel guardian (in specified proceedings) or in the case of a 'mature' child by a solicitor direct.

(7) The child as client

(7.1) A solicitor should only accept instructions from a child direct if the solicitor has the requisite training and expertise in this field. The solicitor should make a personal commitment to undertake all preparation and advocacy for the child and give the child the same respect afforded to an adult as client.

(7.2) A difficult and continuing duty for the solicitor is to assess the child's capacity to give instructions.

(7.3) The solicitor should ensure that the child has sufficient information throughout the proceedings to make informed decisions; advice and information should be presented in a clear and understandable form. The solicitor must be aware that certain information may be harmful to the child.

(7.4) The child's solicitor should maintain a neutral approach as between each parent, the local authority and other parties.

(7.5) Detailed guidelines have been drawn up by the SFLA for those members acting for children. Copies are available from the Secretary.

Copies of the Code can be ordered from Mary l'Anson, SFLA, PO Box 302, Orpington, BR6 8QX.

SFLA Guide To Good Practice For Solicitors Acting For Children

The SFLA endorses the UN Convention on the Rights of the Child, and in particular Article 12.

* **ARTICLE 12**
'1. States Parties shall assure to the child who is capable of forming his or her own views the right to express those views freely in all matters affecting the child, the views of the child being given due weight in accordance with the age and maturity of the child.'

'2. For this purpose, the child shall in particular be provided the opportunity to be heard in any judicial and administrative proceedings affecting the child, either directly or through a representative or an appropriate body, in a manner consistent with the procedural rules of national law.'

This guide is intended for solicitors acting for or contacted by children in:

(1) private law proceedings; and
(2) in public law proceedings when there is or may be a conflict between the Guardian ad Litem and the 'mature' child.

Acting for a child directly involves a high degree of personal commitment, expertise, knowledge and training. Each member of the Children Panel must give an undertaking as to the conduct of cases. This undertaking is in the following terms:

1. 'Subject to paragraph 2, I will not normally delegate the preparation, supervision, conduct or presentation of the case, but will deal with it personally.
2. In each case I will consider whether it is in the best interests of the Child to instruct another advocate in relation to the presentation of the case.
3. If it is in the best interests of the child or necessary to instruct another advocate:

3.1 I will consider and advise the Guardian ad litem (and the child if of appropriate age and understanding) who should be instructed in the best interests of the child;

3.2 I will obtain an undertaking from that advocate to:

(a) attend and conduct the matter personally unless an unavoidable professional engagement arises; and

(b) take all reasonable steps to ensure that so far as is reasonably practicable, a conflicting professional engagement does not arise.'

Any Solicitor contemplating acting for a child must be prepared to make such a commitment.

If it is necessary to instruct another advocate it would be advisable to use a solicitor on the Children Panel or Counsel experienced in dealing with children's cases. Although there is no specialist Children Panel at the Bar, it is important that Counsel (and their clerks) are prepared to make the commitment to the child that is required by the undertaking above. Ideally a conference (at an appropriate place and time for the child) prior to any Court hearing at which Cousel will appear should be arranged in order that the child will know and feel comfortable with his representative.

The term 'Guardian ad Litem' when applied in children's proceedings has a number of different meanings:

a) Guardian ad Litem appointed from the Panel in specified proceedings (most public law) under Section 41 of the Children Act 1989 will be referred to in this Code as 'Guardians ad Litem'.

b) 'Guardians ad Litem' and 'Next Friends' acting under either RSC Order 80, CCR Order 10, or FPR 1991 r. 9.2 and 9.5 for children taking or defending proceedings (subject to FPR 1991 r.9.2(A)) will be referred to as 'Guardians'.

c) Guardian ad Litem or reporting officer appointed in adoption proceedings;

d) The official solicitor may be appointed (subject to his consent) to act as Guardian ad Litem for a child in non-specified proceedings (FPR 1991 r.9.5) or in specified proceedings under s.41 (only in the High Court) and is referred to as 'the Official Solicitor'.

This guide should be read in conjunction with:

a) the SFLA Code of Practice;

b) the Law Society Family Law Committee's Guidance for Solicitors working with Guardians ad Litem (to be found in 'Acting for Children' by Christine Liddle, September 1992);

c) the Law Society's Guidance on Confidentiality and Privilege — Child Abuse and Abduction in the Guide to the Professional Conduct of Solicitors;

d) the Law Society's guidance Acting for Children in Private Proceedings under the Children Act 1989.

A. *General Principles*

1. A Solicitor should be sensitive to issues of gender, race, sexuality, culture and religion, both in dealing with the child as a client and the issues in any particular case.

2. A Solicitor must retain a professional and objective relationship with the Client and not allow his or her own emotional response to either the child or any issue in the case to interfere with that professional relationship.

3. It is important for practitioners to recognise the extent and limitations of their professional duty towards children as clients and how that duty differs from other professionals involved.

(a) In cases in which the Official Solicitor represents a child, he has a duty to communicate their wishes to the Court but is not obliged to follow 'instructions' if they do not coincide with what he perceives to be in the child's best interests. The role is therefore a hybrid one.

(b) A Guardian ad Litem appointed in specified proceedings (usually public law cases) has a duty to advise the Court what is in the child's best interests from their professional point of view, and again has a duty to communicate the child's wishes to the Court. The GAL will appoint a solicitor whose client is the *child*.

(c) The solicitor takes instructions from the GAL only if the child is not sufficiently mature to instruct direct or, when the child is sufficiently mature the child's instructions do not conflict with the GAL's views. The mature child who is in conflict with the GAL will give instructions to his solicitor and they must be followed (as with any other client) even if contrary to the client's interests as perceived by the solicitor. NB. As with any client the client must remember his duty to the Legal Aid Board in the case of wholly unreasonable instructions.

(d) In cases where the solicitor takes instructions from a child direct in private proceedings, he should follow the child's instructions and his view of what should be done in the child's best interests is only relevant for the purposes of advising the client of the likely approach and outcome of the Court and the proceedings. In practice this is sometimes difficult.

4. The manner in which the child's instructions are carried out should be in accordance with the SFLA Code of Practice having particular regard to the need to maintain the continuing relationships within the family and with other professionals who will remain involved (social workers, child psychiatrists etc).

5. A child as client should always be given the same respect afforded to an adult as client.

B. *Seeing the Child*

1. When acting for a child, the solicitor should always meet the child and due regard should be taken for the most appropriate setting and style for such a meeting. Interviews should be short and taken at the child's pace.

2. Although caution should be exercised, it may be appropriate to interview the child early on, in the absence of the case papers in order to establish a preliminary view as to the child's understanding (or 'maturity'). It may then be appropriate to proceed further to a more detailed assessment (see below — Section C).

3. When a child approaches a solicitor direct s/he ought to be seen immediately, if possible. It should be established whether the parents/carers know the child is at the office and discussion should take place with the child as to whether or not they should be told. If the child wishes simply to obtain independent advice on a particular issue, without the knowledge of his or her parents/carers, this wish should be respected (subject to the Law Society Guidelines on Confidentiality above). Subject to those instructions, if there are current proceedings in which solicitors are involved, consideration should be given to informing all the solicitors as soon as possible that you are seeing the child.

4. When receiving a referral from either a parent involved in proceedings or any other adult party or their solicitors, a solicitor should question why the referral is being made. This may involve contacting that party or speaking to that solicitor to establish whether the child is seen as a potential ally to buttress an existing claim. The solicitor should then consider whether it is a justifiable case in which the child needs and should have independent representation.

5. It should not be forgotten that leave is needed to see any case papers if you are seeing a child who is not yet a party.

C. *Assessing Understanding*

1. From the outset the solicitor will need to assess the child's understanding and capacity to give instructions. Maturity can be assessed on the child's ability to understand the nature of the proceedings and to have an appreciation of the possible consequences both in the long and short term of the applications to the Court.

2. The duty to assess a child's understanding is the solicitor's duty and it continues throughout the case. As the proceedings progress the child will need to understand (and the solicitor to explain) such factors as:
   — what parents and other parties want for the child.
   — what the Guardian ad Litem and other experts recommend for the child
   — an outline of the essential law relevant to the proceedings

3. In addition, in private law proceedings, the Court must consider the child's understanding when a child seeks leave to apply for a section 8 order. The Court is then the final arbiter as to whether or not the child has the understanding to pursue his application. In any such consideration by the Court it has been held that 'the solicitor's judgement is to be respected and to be given great weight.' It will be important that the child understands that his solicitor's judgement may be overruled by the court.

4. If a solicitor is acting on the direct instructions of a child in specified proceedings, he cannot then represent the Guardian before the Court if there is a conflict between them. If he is in doubt as to the child's capacity to give instructions, and what the child is saying is in conflict with the Guardian, the solicitor should seek the advice of one of the other professionals involved in the case such as a child psychiatrist, social worker or teacher or an independent expert may have to be approached (eg. child psychiatrist). When making these consultations the solicitor should remain sensitive to their duty of confidentiality to the child. Ultimately, an application can be made to the Court.

5. If it appears that a child's decision-making ability has become impaired, the solicitor should re-assess the child's capacity and consult with the Guardian ad Litem, the Official Solicitor (in private law proceedings in the County or High Court), or other professional involved (see para. 4 above), being careful not to breach the child's confidentiality or prejudice his case. If need be, applications should be made to the Court ex-parte for suitable directions, including the appointment of a Next Friend/ Guardian in private law proceedings.

D. *Taking Instructions*

1. A solicitor should ensure a mature child as client has sufficient information to be able to make informed decisions. However the solicitor should be aware that the client may feel under pressure to agree to a course of action in a wish to please and later regret such a decision. It is important to proceed at the child's pace and allow the child sufficient 'space' and 'permission' to change course or ultimately withdraw. It is easy for the solicitor effectively to take over the litigation and the solicitor should be sensitive to this risk.

2. Solicitors must be aware of the need to advise child clients of their statutory right to refuse consent to medical or psychiatric assessment or treatment. The child should be warned that in certain circumstances the Court may override their decision.

3. Under the professional rules solicitors are generally under a duty to allow clients unfettered access to any relevant documentary evidence which the solicitor holds, save where such evidence would adversely affect the client's physical or mental condition. However, as a matter of good practice, there may be exceptional cases such as serious child sexual abuse when the nature of the document is such that it would be inappropriate for clients to be sent a copy of the document for their

retention. When representing a child, solicitors should be particularly careful about showing documents to the child and, if in any doubt as to whether a document should be disclosed, should seek the opinion of the Guardian ad Litem (if any) or other professional involved in the case. Speaking to a senior colleague or another Children Panel solicitor may also be of help. Ultimately directions can be sought from the Court as to disclosure.

4. When acting for several children where the extent of access to the evidence afforded varies, the solicitor should warn children to whom documents are disclosed, not to disclose those documents to others who are not entitled to see them.

5. If it is necessary to file factual evidence on behalf of a child (as opposed to communicating wishes and feelings in submissions), and statement prepared must be in clear, concise language which the child can understand. The statement should be read and understood by the child before it is signed. The solicitor may need to read the statement to the child.

6. Legal professional privilege attached to medical reports obtained with the leave of the Court in the course of proceedings may be overriden by the Court. The child, like any other client should be warned of the risks involved in seeking reports which may contain unfavourable material before such reports are sought.

E. Correspondence

1. In relation to correspondence, the solicitor must keep the child informed by the means most appropriate to his or her level of understanding. If the case goes on over an extended period of time, regular contact with the child should be maintained either by visits or letters. The frequency of such contact will depend on the circumstances of the case and the age of the child.

2. The solicitor should be particularly vigilant when acting for children to maintain even-handedness in correspondence with adult parties and their solicitors.

3. If in public law proceedings, the child's solicitor finds himself in conflict with the Guardian ad Litem, the duty of confidentiality is owed to the client (the child) and unless the child consents to the disclosure of information to the Guardian ad Litem, or any other person, no such information should be disclosed (subject to the guidance on abduction and abuse referred to above).

F. Dealing with Conflict of Interests

1. Where a solicitor is representing more than one child in the proceedings, he must be aware of the possibility of a conflict arising. An initial question for determination is how many of the children are of sufficient understanding to instruct the solicitor direct.

2. If there is a conflict, either between one or more mature children, or between a mature child and the Guardian ad Litem in relation to other children, the solicitor must consider whether he can continue to act for any of the children involved in the light of information received at the time. If the solicitor takes the view that he must cease acting for all or some of the children, he should inform the children, the Guardian ad Litem and the Court of the position, so that separate representation can be arranged. The solicitor should help the children seek alternative representation.

G. Mediation

1. It is possible (although unlikely) that a solicitor taking instructions from a child direct will become involved in mediation in private proceedings. This may take the form of a conciliation appointment within the Court system or a series of appointments through a private service. Through representation the child obtains

an adult and powerful voice. It is essential that this voice is not used inappropriately and that the solicitor does not undermine or destroy trust between the child and the family, or interfere in the line of communication between them. The solicitor may assist in re-establishing trust and communication but this must be done in such a way as to enable the solicitor to dis-engage when appropriate to do so.

H. In Court

1. A child is entitled to attend Court hearings if he wishes to do so, subject to the overriding discretion of the Judge to bar any party from the hearing (Family Proceedings Rules 1991 Rule 4.16 and Family Proceedings Courts (Children Act 1989) Rules 1991 Rule 16 (and under s.95 in proceedings under Part IV and Part V Children Act 1989)). A child should be warned that he may be excluded. This issue may need to be dealt with at a directions hearing before the Judge who will hear the case. The solicitor should be sensitive to the fact a child may not wish to be in close physical proximity to certain parties in and outside the Court.

2. The solicitor should warn the child that they may hear evidence which may be upsetting and the solicitor should be sensitive to the child's emotional state throughout the hearing.

3. The solicitor should offer to show the client the Court room and make sure that there are arrangements for the child if the child asks to leave the hearing.

4. In any Court hearing, the solicitor should be extremely careful about their approach to other advocates and be even handed in their approach to them and their clients. It is important that the whole of the case and especially examination and cross-examination is conducted in language which is understood by the child (if present in Court) and that cross-examination is not aggressive.

5. Every effort should be made to keep the hearing strictly to the issues and as short as possible.

I. The Child as Witness

1. It is possible that a child who is instructing a solicitor direct will have to give live evidence at a Court hearing. The child may have filed a statement and if so, the statement will of course represent the child's evidence in chief. If relied upon, the child is open to be cross-examined on its contents. The protection of the hearsay rule (through which the child's evidence can often be effectively given by another party) is not likely to be as helpful when the child is separately represented.

2. It is important for the child that if giving evidence is likely, he is as well prepared as possible. A solicitor should consider the likelihood of the child testifying before the hearing itself and tell the child of his views. The child is likely to be worried about speaking in Court and needs to know if this is likely.

3. If the child is to give evidence he should be reassured about the privacy of the proceedings but told of the other people who will be in the Court room. This includes Court staff and in particular ushers who may be wearing black gowns and in respect of whom the child may have wholly unrealistic ideas! The solicitor should tell the child where he will be sitting and if possible shown in advance. It is the solicitor's duty to ensure arrangements are made for the child to give evidence behind a screen if it is appropriate in the circumstances of the case (with the leave of the Court). The solicitor should establish with other advocates whether or not they anticipate extensive cross-examination and encourage them to consider the child's natural anxiety about giving evidence, in the hope that they may limit their cross- examination to the pertinent issues.

4. In relation to the substantive evidence to be given by a child it is important not to coach a child but it would be acceptable to give the child an idea of the kind of

questions which will be asked, and that it is alright for them to say they cannot remember (if this is the case) or that they do not understand the question. Generally the more information the child can be given about what is likely to happen the easier it will be for him to give evidence in a relaxed manner, with the minimum of trauma. Opening evidence in chief should be by way of gentle questions dealing with non-contentious issues to enable the child to relax.

5. The solicitor should also do all he can to minimise the time the child has to wait outside the Court as this will naturally increase the child's anxiety. Arrangements should be made to use the care room or children's suite at the Court (if the Court is so equipped).

J. Ending the Relationship

1. A solicitor should ensure that he remains accessible to the child and is sympathetic yet professional. Over-dependence by either the child or the solicitor on the other should be discouraged.

2. It is important that the solicitor prepare the child for the end of the relationship and begin telling the child, before the end of the case, that the solicitor's role will shortly be over.

3. Rule 9.2a(9) Family Proceedings Rules 1991 provides that where a solicitor acts for a child direct under Rule 9.2A i.e. without a Guardian or next friend and the conditions provided for in that rule cease to apply the solicitor must inform the Court 'forthwith'. The conditions are:

    . . . the minor is able, having regard to his understanding, to give instructions in relation to the proceedings (R.9.2A(1)(b)(i)); or
    [the solicitor] has accepted instructions from the minor to act for him in the proceedings and, where the proceedings have begun, is so acting. (R.9.2A(1)(b)(ii)).

    This means that if the child loses capacity to instruct the Court should be informed (see above C.5); and where instructions are withdrawn by the child, the Court must be informed.

4. In specified proceedings the child may wish to terminate his solicitor's appointment under Rule 4.12(3). This rule only applies to solicitors appointed under the provisions of s.41(3) (appointment by the Court) or R.4.11(2)(a) (appointment by GAL). The child must apply to the Court for an order terminating the appointment and the solicitor must assist the child in doing so, by the provision of information as to the right to apply and assistance in relation to procedure etc. The solicitor and GAL have the right to make representations in their own right to the Court, but should consider whether to do so would be in the child's best interests.

5. Rule 4.12(4) FPR 1991 provides for the termination of a solicitor's appointment by a GAL. As above, an application must be made by the GAL to the Court and the solicitor (and the child if of sufficient understanding) has the right to make representations.

6. If either such an application is made every effort should be made to ensure the application does not interfere in the determination of the central issues in a case, and that such applications (under either Rule) are dealt with in as amicable a way as possible.

7. At the conclusion of proceedings the child should be advised of their right of appeal if appropriate and when the solicitor's role is over, the solicitor should ensure that the child has access to information both in terms of his care (if appropriate) (s.26 Children Act 89), and/or of his right to make further applications to the Court. This should be done orally and confirmed by letter to which the child could refer at a later stage. It is important however not to undermine the re-establishment of family relationships which may have been under pressure during the course of proceedings.

20th June 1994

Chapter 10
Representation of Children in Non-Judicial Proceedings

There are many decisions made about children and young people which do not involve them in court proceedings, but which are, nevertheless, crucial in influencing the pattern, outcomes and quality of their lives.

Participation and Consumer Choice: In the Contract Culture

The establishment of complaints and representations procedures under the Children Act 1989 may be seen as the second stage in the independent representation of children, the first stage being the establishment of panels of guardians *ad litem* and reporting officers to represent children in public law proceedings. Complaints and representations procedures should therefore not be viewed in isolation but within a wider conceptual framework, which encompasses a 20-year socio-legal debate about the appropriate balance to be struck between children's rights and welfare, and which seeks to establish the independent representation of children in all decision-making forums.

The introduction of the internal market for welfare provision has focused attention on the purchaser provider split, with less emphasis on the rights of service users to participate in decisions being made about services provided for them. Service users, particularly children, find it difficult to question different aspects and different outcomes of service delivery.

In the new contracted-out world, in which health and social services buy services from one another through the operation of an internal market, clients' rights, advocacy and complaints procedures assume an enhanced importance, as essential elements in quality control. Complaints procedures are not just a safety net or a deterrent against bad practice, existing at the margin of social welfare provision. They are, and should be, essential features of good practice.

The right of the consumer to question decisions, and to choose between different services, is an essential ingredient in a participatory model of service provision and has been stressed in a number of major reports.[1] However, in the field of social welfare provision, service users and service providers do not meet on equal terms, and this is particularly true in the case of children and young people. The change in culture and shifts in philosophy required in espousing, accepting and establishing services which incorporate children's rights as a central plank of their organisation is a much more complicated process than that involved in consumer feedback and quality assurance in the wider commercial world. Children, as consumers, have little choice about the brand of service they receive, or indeed, whether or not they want to buy into it at all. In such a situation, the provision of both independent procedures and independent representation in non-judicial decision-making forums assumes a central importance. This was an aspect of local authority provision stressed by the Wagner Committee in 1988. They recommended:

> Each local authority should have a clear and well-publicised complaints procedure and comparable measures should be taken by private and voluntary agencies . . . People who require assistance in presenting their complaints should have the services of an advocate or personal representative who is entirely independent of those providing the service.[2]

The Department of Health also encouraged the establishment of complaints procedures.[3]

Complaints Procedures

The responsibility for ensuring the quality of services to children and families rests firmly with each individual local authority. There is no one central body which regulates and promotes good practice in social work and social care in the United Kingdom, although a proposal to establish such a body, or a general social work council, has received widespread support from both professional and local government organisations.[4] In assessing the need for such a body, Roy Parker looked at whether or not existing complaints procedures provided sufficient and adequate mechanisms for looking at allegations of serious professional transgressions. It was found that virtually every recent report dealing with the field had called for improvements. Two studies in the 1980s were particularly depressing. In 1985, the National Consumer Council conducted a survey of complaints procedures in social services departments in England and Wales. This showed that the majority of

---

1   The National Institute of Social Work, *The Roles and Tasks of Social Work* (1982), p 193. The Second Report from the Social Services Committee, *Children in Care* (1984), para. 3.60, rec. 107 and BASW, *Clients are Fellow Citizens* (1980).

2   *Residential Care: A Positive Choice* (The Wagner Report), HMSO (1988), paras 3.21 and 3.23. On this theme, see further Biehal, 'Participation Rights and Community Care', *British Journal of Social Work*, Vol. 23, No. 5, October 1993.

3   Circular LAC(84)5, para. 9 and The Residential Care Homes Regulations 1984 (S.I. 1984 No. 1345), reg. 17.

4   See Parker, *Safeguarding Standards: A Report on the Desirability and Feasibility of Establishing a United Kingdom Independent Body to Regulate and Promote Good Practice in Social Work and Social Care* (1990).

authorities had no formal procedures that covered all aspects of the personal social services. Furthermore, many authorities had no formal or written procedures. A second study, undertaken by the Centre for Criminological and Socio-legal Studies at Sheffield University between 1984 and 1986, looked at complaints procedures in England and showed that only half of the responding authorities claimed to have a formal complaints procedure (that is, a written statement) that covered all aspects of the work of their social services department, and another 16 per cent had formal procedures for certain aspects (such as children in care or residential accommodation). Overall, two-thirds of the authorities that responded had some kind of formal procedure, although only half publicised them.[5]

In the absence of a central regulatory body, and in view of the increasing complexity of the purchaser/provider split in the provision of welfare and in responsibilities between Health and Social Services Departments, it was not surprising that both the National Health Service and Community Care Act 1990 and the Children Act 1989 placed a statutory requirement on local authorities to establish and publish complaints procedures. Services to children and families may be provided through primary health programmes provided by health authorities or through services to children in need and community care programmes provided by social services departments.

S.50 of the National Health Service and Community Care Act 1990 amends S.7 of the Local Authority Social Services Act 1970 in relation to complaints procedures:

(1) The Secretary of State may by order require local authorities to establish a procedure for considering any representations (including any complaints) which are made to him by a qualifying individual or anyone acting on his behalf in relation to the discharge of, or any failure to discharge, any of their social services functions in respect of that individual.

(2) In relation to a particular local authority, an individual is a qualifying individual for the purposes of sub-section (1) above if:
   (a) the authority have a power or duty to provide, or to secure the provision of a service for him; and
   (b) his need or possible need for such a service has (by whatever means) come to the attention of the authority.

(3) A local authority shall comply with any directions given by the Secretary of State as to the procedure to be adopted in considering representations made as mentioned in sub-section (1) above and as to the taking of such action as may be necessary in consequence of such representations.

(4) Local authorities shall give such publicity to any procedure established pursuant to this section as they consider appropriate.[6]

The National Health Service Management Executive emphasises that objectives for the handling of complaints should be seen as contributing to organisations under customer service goals. In producing a set of principles and a checklist for dealing with internal complaints, a Citizens Charter

---

5 National Consumer Council, *Complaints Procedures in Social Services Departments: A Survey Report* (1986), and Lewis, Seneviratne and Cracknell, *Complaints Procedures in Local Government*, Vol. 1, Centre for Criminological and Socio-legal Studies, University of Sheffield.

6 S. 50(7)(6).

Complaints Taskforce identified accessibility, simplicity, speedy handling, fairness, confidentiality, effectiveness and provision of feedback information to management as key principles to be achieved. An element of independence does not feature in the list.[7]

Health service managers are, however, encouraged to consider establishing supporting advocacy services:

> managers will need to consider the most appropriate mechanisms for enabling users to utilise that information to define their treatment in consultation with the specialists involved in their care. One particular method is by establishing advocacy services. Advocacy is about giving the individual user a voice and getting the NHS and SSDs to listen to that voice and to take account of its needs and preferences. In order to ensure that there is no conflict of interest in the representation of users' views, advocacy therefore needs to be independent of service provision. Purchasers can support advocacy projects by:
>
> - Commissioning the provision of independent advocacy via a third party within the service provider setting; or
> - Incorporating appropriate clauses within the contract with the provider unit to guarantee the advocate a voice.[8]

S.26 of the Children Act 1989 is more prescriptive in terms of a requirement to include an independent element in the procedure.

> (3) Every local authority shall establish a procedure for considering any representations (including any complaint) made to them by:
> (a) any child who is being looked after by them or who is not being looked after by them but is in need;
> (b) a parent of his;
> (c) any person who is not a parent of his but who has parental responsibility for him;
> (d) any local authority foster parent;
> (e) such other person as the authority considers has sufficient interest in the child's welfare to warrant his representations being considered by them
> about the discharge by the authority of any of their functions under this part in relation to the child.
>
> (4) The procedure shall ensure that at least one person who is not a member or officer of the authority takes part in:
> (a) the consideration; and
> (b) any discussions which are held by the authority about the action (if any) to be taken in relation to the child in the light of the consideration.
>
> . . .
>
> (7) Where any representation has been considered under the procedure established by the local authority under this section, the authority shall:
> (a) have due regard to the findings of those considering the representation; and
> (b) take such steps as are reasonably practicable to notify (in writing):
>   (i)   the person making the representation;
>   (ii) the child (if the authority considers that he has sufficient understanding); and
>   (iii) such other persons (if any) as appear to the authority to be likely to be affected

---

7 The Citizens Charter Complaints Task Force, *Effective Complaints Systems and Checklist* (November 1993), HMSO for the Cabinet Office.
8 *The Health of the Nation*, Key Area Handbook on Mental Illness (January 1993), Department of Health and the Social Services Inspectorate, paras 4.13, 4.14 and 4.15.

of the authority's decision in the matter and their reasons for taking that decision and of any action which they have taken or propose to take.

(8) Procedures must be written down and publicised, as the local authority thinks appropriate.

While S.26(4) requires that at least one person, who is not a member or officer of the authority, takes part in both stages of the consideration of the complaint or representation, it is a significant omission that there is no independent element in the investigation of the complaint.

The Representations Procedure (Children) Regulations 1991[9] set out the procedures to be adopted, including the requirement that local authorities keep records of each complaint made, the outcome and whether or not the complaint was resolved within the required time limits.

During the passage of the Children Bill through Parliament, MPs raised the question of independent investigation of complaints. In looking at the particular example of the Melanie Klein Home in Greenwich, in her own constituency, Mrs Rosie Barnes drew attention to the experience of children who had become victims of the social services rather than being supported by them:

> I have a particular example of that in a children's home in Greenwich where the key worker was disciplined for serious offences, and was ordered to be demoted and transferred, very much against the wishes of the Principal of the second children's home which was for severely disturbed teenage girls but, on the direct instruction of the Director of Social Services, the worker was placed in the second home. Within a short time, one of the girls in the Home alleged that she had been raped.
>
> There is a potential conflict of interest if that case is investigated by the Director of Social Services who has been responsible for the placement of that employee in that particular Home. I am asking for a provision in the Bill that would make it possible for a girl in such a case to ask for an independent investigation . . . I want such girls and boys to know that if they have a complaint and wish it to be investigated by people who are not responsible for their future maintenance and well-being, they will have someone to whom they can turn.[10]

Mrs Barnes went on to highlight the weakness of complaints procedures which were 'gradually sucked back into the heart of the social services department'. She cited the example of complaints procedures in Greenwich, where the final opportunity for the case review was within the local authority whose decision was binding. Mrs Barnes called for an independent investigation of complaints so that any children in care who have 'serious complaints can be sure that they are heard by people who will listen fairly, who will not disbelieve them, and who will have no motive for wishing their version of events not to be true. Children need such independent representation'.[11]

Unfortunately, there is no provision in the Act for the independent representation of children in the investigation of complaints, and this remains a major weakness. Another is that complaints procedures, as they have evolved, are internal administrative procedures operated through bureaucratic systems. It is ironic that now that the internal procedures which used to exist

---

9 S.I. 1991 No. 894.
10 Mrs Rosie Barnes, Children Bill, *Hansard*, H.L. Vol., col. 1156 (April 27, 1989).
11 *Ibid.*, col. 1158.

for the assuming of parental rights and termination of access have been abolished, because of widespread criticism about the lack of outside scrutiny, a complex new system of internal procedures have been established by the Children Act.

The Department of Health and the Social Services Inspectorate have together produced Practice Guidance on Complaints Procedures in Social Services Departments. The ministerial foreword makes it clear that the requirement to introduce effective complaints procedures is an important part of the government's wider community care policies, and underlines a commitment to ensure good quality services and to encourage a sympathetic and responsive attitude towards people who complain. The *Caring for People* White Paper describes complaints procedures as an 'essential safeguard for users, and [they] will also act as an important monitoring and management instrument for social services authorities and service providers alike'.[12]

The Right to Complain emphasises that those who are vulnerable in society, particularly children and families, are dependent on the good offices of the social services department and are likely to feel intimidated at the prospect of complaining about it. Complaints procedures 'are most likely to ensure quality and protect individuals when they stem from a recognition of users' needs and rights'.[13] This strong message emphasises the need not just for procedures, but for attitudes which accept and facilitate the use of those procedures.

The practice guidance highlights the need to resolve problems before they become complaints. In order to achieve this objective, the authority should demonstrate its commitment by appropriate changes in practice which acknowledge the unequal balance of power between users and providers of services.[14] In this sense, complaints about faulty goods are much easier to contemplate than complaints about faulty services, because the service users, as patients or clients are now called, are essentially dependent on the goodwill of service providers — doctors and social workers, for example — to relieve their suffering or provide very fundamental help to them, hence the imbalance and inequality of the relationship.

Local authorities, voluntary organisations and registered children's homes (responsible authorities) are also required to have a procedure for considering representations (including complaints about children's services). The procedure relates to Sections 24(15), 26(3) to 26(8), 59(4) para. 10(2)(1) of Schedule 6 and para. 6 of Schedule 7 to the Children Act 1989. It should cover all representations about local authorities' actions in meeting their responsibilities to any child in need under Part 3 of the Act. Voluntary organisations and registered children's homes are also required to set up representations procedures to consider representations — including complaints — made by or on behalf of children accommodated by them but not looked after by the local authority. The Representations Procedure (Children) Regulations 1991[15] set a minimum standard of provision that responsible

---

12   *Caring for People: Community Care in the Next Decade and Beyond* — *Policy Guidance* (1990), HMSO.
13   *The Right to Complain, op. cit.*, para. 6.6.
14   *Ibid.*, paras 1.6 and 1.7.
15   S.I. 1991 No. 894.

authorities should establish to meet the requirements of the Children Act 1989.[16]

The main difference between the procedures required for other local authority social services functions inserted by S.50 of the National Health Service and Community Care Act 1990 is that the Children Act requires the involvement of an independent person at both stages of the consideration of a representation or a complaint. It is clear that consideration, in this context, is not the same as investigation.

The Regulations require each local authority to appoint a designated officer to assist the authority in the co-ordination of all aspects of their consideration of the representations.[17] Often, this is a team manager from a neighbouring team, although some authorities are now using investigating officers from outside their own authority. This is a matter of choice, however, not a requirement. They are also required to establish a panel or group of three persons, at least one of whom should be independent. The panel is appointed by the authority, to consider complaints reviewed by the responsible authority under the complaints procedure, when the complainant remains dissatisfied. The panel then makes a recommendation about further action.[18]

The independent element in the complaints procedure is supplied by the appointment of an independent person, who must not be a member or officer of the authority handling the child's case. This person is required by S.26(4) to take part in the authority's consideration of a complaint made to them. The independent person shall take part in any discussions which are held by the local authority about the action (if any) to be taken in relation to the child in the light of the consideration of the representations.[19] The Guidance stresses that the independent person is not an advocate for the child, nor an investigator; his role is to provide an objective element in the authority's considerations.[20]

What is a complaint?

A complaint is a written or oral expression of dissatisfaction, or disquiet, in relation to an individual child about the local authority's exercise of its functions under Part 3 and para. 4 of Schedule 7 of the Children Act 1989, and matters in relation to children accommodated by voluntary organisations and registered children's homes. A complaint may arise as a result of an unwelcome or disputed decision, concern about the quality or appropriateness of services, delay in decision making about services or about their delivery or non-delivery. (The precise meaning of complaint is a matter for interpretation by the courts.)[21]

---

16 Children Act 1989 Guidance and Regulations Vol. 4, para. 5.1.
17 Reg. 3(1).
18 Regs 8 and 9.
19 Reg. 6(2).
20 Children Act 1989 Guidance and Regulations Vol. 4, para. 5.5(e).
21 Ibid., para. 5.5(e).

The Guidance and Regulations stress that it is envisaged that there will be a high degree of co-operation between parents and authorities in negotiating and agreeing what form of action will best meet a child's needs and promote his welfare. There is also emphasis on the informed participation of the child and his parents in decision making about services for the child. The procedure should ensure that the child, his parents and others significantly involved with the child have confidence in their ability to make their views known and to influence decisions made about the child's welfare.[22]

The Guidance is much clearer about the lengthy procedures to be established than about the sanctions available to complainants. Local authorities are only required to give due consideration to the findings and to notify those involved. There is no requirement to take any action or to provide specific redress.

What is a valid complaint?

A local authority's procedures must deal with complaints (from the people named in S.26(3)) about local authority support for families and their children under Part III of the Act. This will include complaints about day care, services to support children within their family home, accommodation of a child after care and decisions relating to the placement of a child or the handling of the child's case. The processes involved in decision making, or the denial of a service, must also be covered by the responsible authority's arrangements.[23]

Further, the responsible authority should allow representations to be made about matters which affect a group of children rather than an individual child, to be processed within their Children Act procedure; for example, inappropriate restrictions on the lives of children in residential care, such as preventing children's activities for the convenience of staff, fixing meal times to suit staff, rather than to fit in with the normal needs of children, or preventing children's normal activities outside the home.[24] The emphasis in the Guidance is on early problem solving in order to ensure that problems do not develop into complaints.

One weakness of the system, as it has developed, is the lack of centralised thinking about the establishment of complaints procedures. This has left each local authority to write its own procedures, according to its own system of priorities and according to the particular ethos of that local authority. A checklist for the development of complaints procedures in voluntary child care organisations was produced in 1993 as an aid to voluntary organisations involved in setting up their complaints procedures. It stressed the relationship between complaints procedures and quality assurance, but also identified the potential conflict of interest between a quality assurance and a children's rights approach.

Having a clear sense of purpose in developing complaints procedures is particularly important in a climate of competing ideas and philosophies. Organisations are being

---

22   Ibid., paras 5.1 and 5.3.
23   Ibid., para. 5.8.
24   Ibid., para. 5.9.

urged to strive for 'total quality assurance', with complaints procedures as a crucial element. Striving for quality is a perfectly legitimate aspiration, but it is quite distinctive and different from the goal of securing the rights of young people. Arguably, the primary focus of the quality assurance approach is on securing improvements in the organisation, rather than on promoting the rights of young people. This is not to deny that young people may benefit greatly from quality assurance, but simply to recognise that its aims and therefore some of its priorities will be different from those of a rights approach.[25]

The primary purpose of complaints procedures under the Children Act 1989 should be to safeguard the rights of children and young people. Procedures on their own are of limited utility. As Mike Lindsay, the first Children's Right Officer, has said: 'successful complaints procedures are more a matter of getting attitudes right, not procedures'.

The checklist poses three questions for agencies developing complaints procedures to ask themselves:

● How are young people made aware of, and encouraged to identify, their own needs and rights?
● What options are available to young people who are unhappy about some aspect of their treatment by others, particularly if they feel inhibited in sharing this with those providing the service?
● What effective action will be taken to rectify problems raised by young people?

The last part is particularly important. Procedures without sanctions are of limited use in protecting children. Crucially, any complaints or representations procedure must initially recognise that children and young people in particular, as one of the most vulnerable groups in society, have a very small number of free-standing rights under common and criminal law, and that these rights are not within the gift of any individual or organisation. Therefore, complaints procedures must incorporate those rights and not diminish or offer less to the child than remedies and procedures available through judicial channels. If children are to be genuinely empowered through complaints procedures, then other individuals or professional groups may have to relinquish some of their power in relation to them. At best, complaints procedures should offer children a speedy and readily available avenue for the resolution of problems and disputes. At worst, they may constitute second level quasi-judicial forums in which the rights of the children and the rights of employees may well be inadequately represented.

Representation at reviews and case conferences

S.26(1) and (2) deals with the responsibility of local authorities to require the case of each child who is being looked after by a local authority to be reviewed at four weeks, three months and then every six months subsequently. The

25 Hodgson, *A Checklist for the Development of Complaints Procedures in Voluntary Child Care Organisations* (April 13, 1993), National Council of Voluntary Child Care Organisations.

Review of Children's Cases Regulations 1990[26] establish provisions for the conduct of reviews. S.26(2)(d) requires the authority, before conducting any review, to seek the views of:

- the child;
- his parents;
- any person who is not a parent of his but who has parental responsibility for him; and
- any other person whose views the authority consider to be relevant, including in particular the views of those persons in relation to any particular matter which is to be considered in the course of the review.

S.26(2)(e) requires the authority to consider during the review whether an application should be made to discharge the Care Order and S.26(2)(g) requires the authority to inform the child, as far as is reasonably practicable, of any steps he may take under this Act. S.26(2)(i) requires the authority to notify details of the results of the review and of decisions taken by them in consequence of the reviews to:

- the child;
- his parents;
- any person who is not a parent of his but who has parental responsibility for him; and
- any other person whom they consider ought to be notified.

Children's advocates can have a key role to play in reviews; firstly, in ensuring that the child has sufficient information to participate fully and competently in the discussion if he or she is of sufficient age and understanding and, secondly, in ensuring that the local authority consider other options for the child, apart from the option of remaining in care. If the child has a view about a possible alternative, the advocate can make sure that that view is considered and that attention is focused on the child's perception of his situation. Once the review is over, the advocate can ensure that the child receives details of the result of the review and of the decision taken.

Arguably, both guardians *ad litem* and children's advocates would qualify as 'any other person whose views the authority consider to be relevant' in the same way as they would have a locus in complaints procedures to have their representations considered on the grounds that 'they are such other person as the authority consider has a sufficient interest in the child's welfare to warrant his representation being considered by them'.[27] In the case of guardians, however, there would be no requirement for panels to pay fees and expenses arising from such involvement.

Since implementation of the Children Act 1989, there has been much more emphasis on the right of children to represent their views to decision-making forums such as reviews and case conferences. The right of the child to have the support of a friend or social work advocate is now generally accepted. The right of the child to take along a legal adviser is more problematic. The

---

26   S.I. 1990 No. 895.
27   S. 26(3)(e).

presence of legal representatives is thought to have an inhibiting effect on the discussion.

General issues in relation to complaints

Interface between the arm's length inspection units, complaints procedures and minimum standards   The situation as it has developed appears to be as follows. Local authorities contract out specific services, and establish the minimum standard of service provision acceptable to them, according to local resources and competing priorities. Each authority's 'Children in Need' document will set out what services the local authority intend to provide. The minimum standard will vary from one authority to another. Designated complaints officers are situated in the 'arm's length' inspection units established to deal with the evaluation and monitoring of quality controls within local authorities. The designated complaints officer, therefore, will be an employee of the local authority who have set the minimum standard of service delivery. The responsibility for the service rests with the contracted out service provider or with the local authority directly and they will be 'inspected' by the local authority inspection unit at 'arm's length'. The question then arises as to what is a reasonable and an acceptable complaint. As one Director was heard to say: 'quality control is not about excellence, it is about a minimum standard. It is no good complaining about the lack of a Rolls Royce service when we only ever set out to provide a Mini'.

What, then, of the relationship between the adoption of minimum standards and complaints procedures, given that the Social Services Inspectorate view is that any judicial review of services provided will be carried out on the basis of 'best practice' rather than a minimum standard? It should also be borne in mind that local authorities have a statutory requirement to provide certain services to clients, including children, under the National Health Service and Community Care Act 1990 and the Children Act 1989, and that the statutory definition of children in need takes precedence over 'Children in Need' policy documents produced by social services departments.

Interface between disciplinary, child protection and complaints procedures   Confusion arises about the point at which the disciplinary procedures freeze the complaints procedures, and which procedure takes precedence in which situations and why. Some local authorities have produced complaints procedures for clients and a companion document for employees stating at the beginning that any complaints or representations will be aimed at the organisation and not at the individual member of staff. In practice, things are not quite so straightforward. Roy Parker, in *Safeguarding Standards*,[28] makes a clear differentiation between complaints about service provision and complaints about actions of individual service providers. There are times when the rights of the client will be in clear conflict with the rights of a member of staff and there are a great number of complex issues arising from the use of different procedures. For example, take the case of a child in residential care

---

28   *Op. cit.*

who alleges an assault by a member of the residential care staff. The child may be attempting to initiate the complaints procedure, the member of staff's position will be covered by disciplinary procedures and the local authority will be deciding whether to initiate the child protection procedures. The police may be considering criminal proceedings. It is generally the case that disciplinary procedures take precedence over complaints procedures. Here, the rights of the child may be in direct conflict with the rights of the employee. Internal disciplinary hearings are governed by employment legislation designed to protect employees and are quite different from the rights of the child to be heard under the Children Act 1989, or the Criminal Justice Act 1988, in that the child has no direct right of hearing. In internal disciplinary proceedings, the word of the child is not taken alone and, in some cases, employees' unions have stipulated that the child's word should not be accepted unless corroborated by a member of staff. This sits uneasily with the enhanced status of the child as witness in other proceedings. In disciplinary proceedings, the child may not have the right to attend the hearing and often there is no clear finding of culpability. In one case a member of staff who allegedly physically assaulted a child was told, at the end of the disciplinary proceedings, that his practice was being watched and that there would be an entry on his record to that effect. The young person concerned wished to know whether the person had been found guilty or not, that is, had he been believed? It is extremely hard to explain to a child that somebody's practice is being watched, but that does not mean that he was guilty. This rather ambiguous finding means that members of staff, once the disciplinary procedures have been completed, may go back on duty — in this particular case being in sole charge at night of the young person who had made the complaint. The child then made another complaint, which was that he was frightened to be alone with this member of staff during the night shift. He was told that a complaint could not be made on this basis, as he would be questioning the outcome of the disciplinary proceedings which had now been concluded to the satisfaction of the organisation.

Complaints procedures should be there to protect the rights of service users to question service providers. It is essential, therefore, that complaints procedures do not exist in isolation but are viewed alongside employment law, disciplinary procedures and the right of all client groups under different pieces of legislation. It may well be, in certain situations, that the rights of the child to be protected are potentially in conflict with the rights of employees or other adults. The Warner Report highlighted the need for the most stringent criteria to be applied to the recruitment and selection of staff in residential children's homes, and made proposals for 'far more rigorous and thorough procedures', some of which the writers of the report acknowledged would conflict with existing arrangements,[29] in particular, 'possibly because of their preoccupation with equal opportunities issues, local authorities explore few other specified areas, such as significant childhood events or the stability of the candidate's personal relationships'.[30]

---

29   *Choosing with Care*, Report of the Committee of Inquiry into the Selection, Development and Management of Staff in Children's Homes (1992), HMSO, para. 4.68.
30   *Ibid.*, para. 4.63.

Which is paramount — the right of the child to have stringent enquiries made on his behalf, or the rights of potential employees to personal privacy and equalities of opportunity?[31]

Lack of independent social work advocacy and representation Children attempting to make complaints are in an extremely vulnerable position. They fear that making a complaint may lead to the withdrawal of services or even to more active victimisation. While that threat may never be made, or may not materialise, the child's fear of some form of retaliation is often a deterrent to the making of complaints. Additionally, clients, particularly children, are reluctant to use procedures which they do not fully understand, and find forbidding and difficult. Experience shows that it is virtually impossible for a child or a young person to complain effectively without an independent advocate to stand beside them. Even with a social work advocate, it is a tortuous obstacle course which one often hesitates to encourage the child to negotiate. Very often, a child in care who complains has their complaint or problem interpreted as a function of their maladjustment or disturbance. Child care professionals fear the child's right to complain, thinking that it may be used frivolously or maliciously, and this underlying fear means that many residential establishments do not have the necessarily supportive ethos to enable children to feel that it is 'OK' to complain. Young people do not always recognise when experiences are inappropriate or unacceptable. Bullying may be so common that there is no awareness on the part of the young person that it is unacceptable or illegal. They have no knowledge of what constitutes a legitimate complaint. The first problem, therefore, is enabling children to complain at all. Out of 3,810 complaints made under S.26, 542 were made by children.[32] During the consultation stage, which preceded the implementation of the Children Act 1989, there was a strong feeling that children involved in complaints should have access to independent social work support and advocacy. The role of the independent person, as then conceived and as it is now, did not satisfy criteria, firstly, of the need for an independent person to be involved in the investigation of the complaint and, secondly, for that person to be an independent representative for the child appointed directly by the child rather than the local authority concerned in the complaint. Thirdly, the scope of the role of independent person is confined within the restricted parameters of the local authority's procedure. The role of the independent person was therefore seen as an essentially weak one in attempting to equate the imbalance of power between vulnerable children and powerful bureaucracies. In the event, advocacy did not achieve the positive profile that would have been desirable in the Guidance and Regulations; however, in a rather half-hearted way, it was not ruled out:

---

31 See also Howe, *The Quality of Care* (1992), Report of the Residential Staffs Inquiry, Local Government Management Board.

32 The Children Act Report 1992, Cm 2144 (1992). (The Children Act Reports are annual reports by the Secretaries of State and for Wales on the Children Act 1989 in pursuance of their duties under S.83(6) of the Act.)

Advocacy as a service to the child as part of child care service provision is not ruled out by these Regulations, nor is it ruled out if a responsible authority wishes to provide such a service to support the child in this, or other, procedures.[33]

Volume 3 of the Guidance and Regulations, dealing with family placements, is a little more encouraging:

> in some situations the position of the child may be an unhappy one. The child may be dissatisfied with the current arrangements for his care or the absence of progress in achieving a plan for the future. He may dislike and distrust his carers and those in authority who have responsibility for him. He may feel that his views are ignored or never sought, and that he has no realistic opportunity to complain or challenge the validity of the legal processes which affect him. He may then disclose that he is being abused by his carers. In such a bleak scenario, the child has an urgent need for skilled advocacy. This is not a role the independent visitor is expected to play. Instead, the independent visitor must be able to recognise the needs of the child in such serious situations and, with the child's agreement, draw their concerns to the attention of the child's social worker or, if necessary, a more senior officer in the social services department. In certain cases it may be appropriate to refer the matter to one of the voluntary organisations which specialises in advocacy.[34]

The independent visitor, as opposed to the independent person, is a voluntary visitor who befriends children in care who have no close family or friends to visit them. Thus, the Regulations make it clear that neither the independent visitor nor the independent person are children's representatives or advocates (see Figure 8).

Lack of Independent Legal Representation for the Child

Clearly, it is not intended or desirable that children and local authorities should always require legal representation in what are somewhat euphemistically described as 'internal problem solving procedures'. However, experience shows that the more likely it is that the complaint is justified, the closer will be the local authority's consultation with their legal department. As tension mounts, the child may be faced with an escalation of quasi-judicial procedures, which include daunting hearings in which the child is required to make oral representations. In such situations, the child is considerably disadvantaged in not having access to legal representation. In one case, on receiving notification of a hearing of the complaint to be held in the somewhat awesome surroundings of the local Town Hall, the young person received a letter to the effect that, although the local authority would be bringing a representative from their legal department, she was not entitled to legal representation on her own behalf. Procedures which fail to take into account the laws of natural justice cannot be seen as fair or balanced by recipients of local authority services. Used as they are to their lives being ordered by the local authority *in loco parentis*, the majority of children would not be in a position to question the involvement of the local authority's legal adviser while being deprived of one of their own. In this particular case, the child was fortunate to have an independent social work advocate who was able to find a children's panel

---

33 Children Act 1989 Guidance and Regulations Vol. 4, para. 5.17.
34 *Ibid.*, Vol. 3, paras 7.47 and 7.48.

Guardian *ad Litem* and Reporting Officers

Introduced November 1976 in unopposed care cases only. Extended to all care cases and adoption with the implementation of Children Act 1975, ss. 64 and 65 — May 1984. Considerably extended by the Children Act 1989 from October 1991 — GALs appointed in all care and related proceedings specified in s. 41(6)(i) including applications for Secure Accommodation Orders, s. 25.

Further extended to cover surrogacy arrangements under s. 30 of the Human Fertilization and Embryology Act 1990 — May 1994

Role To safeguard the best interests of children before the courts.
To ensure that agreements to adoption are freely given with a full understanding of the implications of adoption.

Independent Social Workers

Used extensively before 1984 to represent children in public law proceedings. Now may be used to represent children where a GAL/RO is not appointed and an independent social work expert is required. Not widely used since 1984.

Role To represent the best interests of the child before the court.

Independent Representatives or Visiting Advocates

A social work representative who represents the views of all young people in secure accommodation. Usually a volunteer with a social work background.

1. See Children Act 1989 Guidance and Regulations Vol. 4, Residential Care, Chapter 8, Secure Accommodation.
2. Children (Secure Accommodation) Regulations 1991 (S.I. 1991 No. 1505) regs. 15 and 16 refer to the involvement of an independent element in reviews.
3. Children (Secure Accommodation) (No.2) Regulations 1991, S.I. 1991 No. 2034.

Role To represent the wishes and feelings of the child, and ensure that the Secure Accommodation regulations are observed.

Independent Persons

Before 1982, this meant the independent member of the social services sub-committee, which reviews the placement of young people in Secure Accommodations.

As introduced in October 1991, following implementation of the Children Act 1989, the independent person is
(1) involved in the *consideration* but not the *investigation* of complaints or representations arising from s. 26 of the Children Act in 1989. Independent persons are appointed by local authorities in association with the complaints procedure.

See: 1. Children Act 1989 and Representations Procedure (Children) Regulations 1991, Reg. 2.1
2. Representation Procedures, Children Act 1989 Guidanace and Regulations, Vol. 4, Residential Care, Chapter 8, Secure Accommodation

(2) involved in reviews of secure accommodation

See: 3. Children (Secure Accommodation) Regulations 1991, Regs 15, 16.

Role To see fair play by providing an objective view of the facts of the complaint or review.

Independent Visitors

Introduced by the Children and Young Persons Act 1969 to provide visitors to isolated children in care.

Extended under the Children Act 1989 to cover all children not visited by a parent in the last 12 months.

See: 1. Sched. 2, para. 17(1–7) Children Act 1989 and Children Act 1989 Guidance and Regulations Vol. 4, Residential Care, Chapter 6 Independent Visitors
2. Definition of Independent Visitors (Children) Regulations 1991 (S.I. 1991 No. 892) (Reproduced as Annex F, Vol. 4) Children Act Guidance and Regulations — Residential Care

Role To befriend on a long term basis

Independent Advocates (multi-disciplinary)

May act in or out of court in public and private law, but mainly in quasi-judicial procedures arising from s. 26 representations and complaints procedures. This will also support children and young people in making representations and expressing their wishes and feelings at all decision making forums including case conferences and reviews.

See 1. Children Act 1989 Guidance and Regulations Vol. 3, Family Placements, para. 7.43.
2. Children Act 1989 Guidance and Regulations Vol. 4, Residential Care, Chapter 5, Representations Procedures.

Role To ascertain the wishes and feelings of children and young people and ensure that their voice is heard in all decision-making forums.

Figure 8 Independent What? The Independent Social Work Representation of Children

solicitor who was willing to do eight hours direct advocacy at that, and subsequent hearings, without payment in order to ensure that the child had effective representation. In this case, through effective advocacy, the complaint was substantiated and acted as a catalyst for major changes to be made in the regimes in the authority's residential establishments. Children also need accurate and accessible legal advice about the statutory responsibilities of their 'parent' local authorities. There is, at present, no mechanism for financing such legal representation in quasi-judicial proceedings. The legal aid scheme does not cover legal advocacy in complaints procedures, although some children's panel solicitors are willing to represent children in these proceedings. The only option is to stretch the boundaries of the Law Society's ABWOR (Advice by Way of Representation) scheme to cover some aspects of direct advocacy as well as advice. One desirable alternative would be to extend the legal aid scheme to cover such cases, but this seems unlikely in the foreseeable future.

What do Children in Care Complain about?

- Moving without consultation and without proper plans.
- Unjust punishments.
- Rough handling by care staff.
- Breaches of confidentiality (personal information left around).
- Educational problems, problems of re-entering the system after a move, lack of positive planning about education — sometimes there is not even a decision to dispute.
- Not being treated as a person of worth, including unfair or demeaning treatment and being held up to ridicule by other children or staff.
- Having their wishes and feelings ignored. Children complain that review meetings are sometimes used as a forum to criticise them.
- Many children are not aware of how to use the complaints procedure.[35]

Other complaints have indicated:

- The failure to hold statutory reviews. The lack of a channel of complaint or representation other than through the officer in charge.
- The use of block punishments, which were inconsistently or unfairly administered.
- Children being actively discouraged from joining organisations like the National Association for Young People in Care (NAYPIC) and fear of reprisals if they did.
- The routine reading of children's private mail.
- Regular room searches and 'tipping' of personal belongings.
- There was no assistance in obtaining legal help and advice.
- Young women being denied free access to sanitary wear.

---

35 'Breakdown of Complaints' compiled by the Advocacy, Advice and Representation Service for Children and Young People (ASC) (1993). See also Morris and Wheatley, 'Time to Listen: The experiences of young people in foster and residential care. A Childline Study' (1994).

- Inaccurate or inadequate information concerning contraception and sexually transmitted diseases.
- Lack of access to a telephone.

NAYPIC exposed some appalling practices in residential establishments, including controlling children through the withholding of food and drink and visits from family and friends. In some cases, children were forced to wear discriminating clothing to identify 'runners' or those likely to abscond — all practices now prohibited by the Children's Homes Regulations 1991.[36]

Case examples

The following examples illustrate how advocates may help young people in care.

John is 13. He is unhappy in his children's home because the other children bully him and hide his books and personal possessions. He has asked for a lock on his bedroom door, but has been told this is not allowed. He has had a quarrel with his key worker and doesn't know how to start resolving his problems. John's advocate listened to John's fears and helped to resolve the quarrel with the key worker. He also suggested that John should have a locked box in which to keep private and personal belongings, and helped staff look at bullying as a problem for everyone in the home, not just for John. He kept on visiting John until he [John] felt more secure.

Susan is nearly 16. She has been in care since she was three and has been in eight different children's homes. Recently, she has been placed in an Independence Unit where she is settled and happy. She has been told that she must leave shortly after her 16th birthday. She was not consulted before this decision was made. Susan is frightened of leaving the shelter of the Unit and wants to know her rights in the situation. In particular, she would like to stay in the Unit for a further six months. The advocate successfully negotiated with the care authority and, with Susan's agreement, drew up a phased plan for leaving care, involving a further period in the Independence Unit and help in finding a safe place to live.

Tom is 12. His sister, in the same home, is seven and has told Tom that she is being sexually abused by a member of staff. Tom told his key worker, who thought he was trying to cause trouble for the member of staff concerned, and did not believe him. Tom doesn't know what to do next, as he and his sister have no friends or family who visit. Tom's advocate listened to him and to his sister and ensured that a proper investigation was made. The local authority instigated disciplinary procedures.

Gemma is 10. She has been in care for a year and has gradually lost contact with her younger sister who went to a foster home. She is worried about her little sister, as she promised her mother that she would look after her. Gemma's advocate listened to Gemma and located her sister through the social

---

36   S.I. 1991 No. 1506.

services department. Gemma's right to see and be in contact with her sister was recognised and regular meetings were set up. As a result of the meetings, Gemma's sister's foster parents offered to have Gemma too, and so the sisters were reunited.

All of these cases show the isolation of children in care and their extreme vulnerability.

Home closure

Home closure is one area in particular in which young people need first-line legal advice and help in stating their case. In one case, a 16-year-old girl had been moved to eight different children's homes in 12 years. She had been moved from establishments where she was happy for purely financial reasons and with no consideration for her own wishes or educational continuity.[37] In the last 15 years, there have been a number of cases in which children have successfully sought injunctions to prevent local authorities closing their children's home.

The first of these cases was *Att.-Gen. v. Hammersmith and Fulham London Borough Council*.[38] The case was unsuccessful in that the judge took the view that the welfare principle did not apply to home closure decisions, as these were not about individual children.

In the case of *Liddle v. Sunderland Borough Council*,[39] this ruling was reversed by a judge who took the view that the closure of a children's home affected each individual child within it.

In *Re R. v. Solihull Metropolitan Borough Council, ex p. C.*[40] and *R. v. Avon*,[41] both found local authorities in breach of their duties under S.18(1) and S.22(1) of the Child Care Act 1980, with the courts ruling that the local authority did not have the powers to divest itself of its legal duty to ensure that it properly considered the effects of its decision on each individual child.

These cases successfully established the principle of consultation before the decision to close the home is taken.

In the first post-Children Act 1989 case involving home closure, one of a growing band of Children's Rights Officers assisted a group of young people in Leeds to challenge the local authority's decision to close their home without prior consultation or involvement of the children in the decision-making process. The young people sought judicial review and, assisted by the Children's Rights Officer, put together a powerful case. S.22(4) of the Children Act 1989 requires that a local authority shall, 'before making any decision with respect to a child whom they are looking after, ascertain the wishes and feelings of the child, the parents and any other person with parental

37 Advice, Advocacy and Representation Services for Children and Young People (ASC), First Annual Report, 1993.
38 *The Times*, December 18, 1979. See also *Tilley v. Wandsworth London Borough Council* [1981] 1 W.L.R. 854.
39 (1983) Fam. Law 250.
40 (1984) F.L.R. 363.
41 *R v. Avon County Council, ex parte K* (1986) 1 F.L.R. 443. See Cliffe and Betridge, *Closing Children's Homes: An End to Residential Childcare?* (1991), NCB.

responsibility'. The young people began legal action against the social services department, arguing that the closure decision had been made without consulting them and had breached S.22 of the Children Act 1989. As the solicitor representing the children said: 'the problem with being consulted after the event, is that you can't have any real faith that anything you say will make any difference'.

The Social Services Inspectorate, who were advising the social services department in Leeds, suggested that the Director rescind the decision, apologise for the way it was taken and start again. On this basis, the children's application for judicial review of the local authority was dropped. However, the fact that the High Court had decided to give the case a full hearing had a powerful effect on the children: 'at first they thought there was nothing they could do. When I said there was a case for judicial review, they were taken aback, but now they are different. They are outspoken and challenging, and they have given social services managers hell'.[42]

Advocacy Services

Independent advocates

Although the concept of advocacy received less than whole-hearted support in the Children Act 1989 Guidance and Regulations, nevertheless post-Children Act practice has seen a proliferation of advocacy services for children, both being offered as an additional service by existing child care organisations such as the Children's Society, National Children's Home and Barnardos, and as a specialist national service being developed by ASC (Advice, Advocacy and Representation Services for Children and Young People).

The Utting Report identified, and found persuasive, the argument that a child in care needs someone with whom he or she can talk through problems before a decision is made on how best they might be handled. It concluded that the Department of Health should, once the operation of the new complaints procedures under the Act has been evaluated, consider how best to meet this point.[43] The Report went on to consider whether there was scope for developing the role of the independent visitor in relation to children in residential care and in particular to children with disabilities.[44] There would be cogent arguments against such a course of action. The independent visitor is essentially a lay person who may have no particular knowledge or experience of either the law or local authority practices and procedures. Representation can only be effective if the children's advocate is perceived by those making the decision as someone sufficiently powerful and knowledgeable to equate the imbalance of power between the child and the whole panoply of bureaucratic decision making.

In May 1992, two voluntary organisations, IRCHIN (Independent Representation for Children in Need) and VCC (Voice for the Child in Care),

42 Shane Ellis, Children's Rights Officer, Leeds, reported in the *Northern Star*, October 15 to 22, 1992. See also 'At Home in the Grange', *Community Care*, September 24, 1992.
43 *Children in the Public Care: A Review of Residential Child Care* (1991), HMSO.
44 *Ibid.*, para. 3.48.

having respectively pioneered independent representation in complaints procedures, and services of independent representation for children in secure accommodation, worked together to establish ASC (Advice, Advocacy and Representation Services for Children and Young People). ASC places emphasis on the need for children to have a direct line out of the residential establishment to an independent service of advocacy, advice and support. Based in Manchester, ASC works in association with ChildLine, whose counsellors answer a freephone line specifically established for children in care who wish to make contact with either an advocate or an independent representative for children in secure accommodation. ASC's service is confidential and independent, and ASC's accredited advocates comprise an experienced multi-racial and professional multi-disciplinary team which includes experienced guardians *ad litem*, Family Court welfare officers, clinical psychologists, teachers, children's panel solicitors and youth workers. ASC provides both free-standing advocacy or services under contract to local authorities or voluntary organisations.

Advocates are expected to have a wide-ranging and detailed knowledge of the statute, regulations and guidance relating to the care and control of children in residential care, as well as experience of the processes of judicial and bureaucratic decision making.

In the first 15 months of operation, ASC advocates had direct contact with nearly 300 children seeking help with a wide range of problems, ranging from lack of private space to serious allegations of physical and sexual abuse. The prompt appearance of a competent children's advocate in a residential establishment can have a galvanising effect on proceedings. The stages of the process have been defined as follows:

1. Referral.
2. Defining the problem.
3. Reviewing the action.
4. Establishing the desired outcome.
5. Planning.
6. Action.[45]

ASC found that children rarely make frivolous complaints in order just to make trouble. Often the reverse is the case. Children will tolerate injustice for all sorts of reasons rather than make a complaint. Experience from work completed has confirmed the desperate need for children as a particularly vulnerable group to have access to independent advice and support when problems arise. The difficulties encountered in some cases by the advocates themselves illustrate the powerlessness of children in defending their rights against large and bureaucratic organisations.[46]

There are three common reactions when children make complaints:

- firstly — the problem may be denied on the basis that the child has misunderstood or over-reacted;

---

45   ASC Information Booklet (1993), ASC, 1 Sickle Street, Manchester, Freephone 0800-616101.
46   *Ibid.*

- secondly — the complaint may be explained away as a function of the child's disturbance; for example, he is attention seeking or he likes causing trouble;
- thirdly — attempts may be made to undermine the credibility of the advocates themselves. Listening to the child rather than the professionals, who have a statutory responsibility to pursue the courses of action which will be in the child's best interests, may be experienced as deeply threatening by the workers involved.

Advocates require specific skills in tact and diplomacy, patience and negotiation. Advocates may mediate but will not come to agreement about the child without the child's own permission. The advocate will, however, help to establish with the child what choices are available, and what the positive and negative outcomes of each course of action will be.

Children's Rights Officers

In the last few years an increasing number of local authorities and voluntary child care agencies throughout the UK have appointed Children's Rights Officers and the Children's Rights Officers Association was established in September 1992. The Association aims to enhance the rights of young people by encouraging its members and others to involve young people in their day-to-day care, in decisions and child care policies affecting them under current legislation and within the UN Convention on the Rights of the Child. Children's Rights Officers are in an invidious situation, as they are employed by local authorities but are committed to establishing and developing children's rights services which may potentially be in conflict with more generalised concepts of welfare. The first Children's Rights Officer in the UK was Mike Lindsay, who was appointed in Leicestershire in February 1987.

Local authorities have tended to see the provision of advocacy services and the appointment of Children's Rights Officers as either/or options. In fact, they are not mutually exclusive. Children's Rights Officers are employees of the local authority and are there to facilitate and develop its children's rights services. There is still a need for independent outside advocacy, and the situation works best for children where local authorities are sufficiently enlightened to have appointed Children's Rights Officers who can facilitate referral to independent social work and legal advocacy in appropriate cases. Children's Rights Officers are central in creating a culture that is sympathetic to the child's need to have access to agreed procedures and effective representatives within local authorities' own social services departments.

Independent What?

Independent person

Introduced in 1990, following implementation of the Children Act 1989 under the provisions of S.26(4), the independent person may be involved in two stages of the *consideration* but not the *investigation* of the complaint or representation arising from S.26. The responsible authority must appoint an independent person, both to consider complaints as individuals at the first stage and as part of a panel (of three people) at the second stage. The independent person must be neither a member nor an officer of the authority[47] and it is recommended that neither should they be a spouse of an officer or member of the responsible authority.[48] Independent people are chosen, and employed, by local authorities. They need not be people with any particular experience of child care law and practice. It is the responsibility of the local authority to be able to identify, at short notice, independent persons with particular skills or knowledge which may be required in a particular case. Independent people should be given a letter of appointment explaining the duties they will be required to carry out, drawing attention to important issues such as confidentiality and making clear the working arrangements involved in the consideration of the complaints. On receipt of a complaint, the local authority appoint an independent person to consider the complaint with the responsible authority and to respond within 28 days of its receipt.[49] If the complainant is unsatisfied with the first response and requests within 28 days that his complaint be reviewed, a panel is constituted by the responsible authority to meet within a further 28 days. The panel is required by regulation 8(3) to include at least one independent person. This is not necessarily, but may be, the same independent person who was involved in the first stage of the procedure. The recommendation of the panel is recorded in writing within 24 hours of the completion of their deliberations and a copy is sent to the responsible authority, to the complainant and to the first stage independent person (if different from the independent person on the panel). At no stage is the independent person involved in the investigation of the complaint, which is entirely a matter for the designated officer within the local authority (the complaints officer).

The Children Act Report 1992 endorses the view that the role of the independent person in the complaints process is not to act as an advocate for the child, nor as an investigator, but to provide an objective element in the responsible authority's consideration of the complaint. The majority of independent people come from the voluntary sector, with only 32 out of 107 local authorities providing independent people through specialist advocacy services. The Children Act Report 1992 records that between October 14, 1991 and June 30, 1992 there were 3,810 complaints in 108 authorities. There were very wide discrepancies in numbers of complaints in each local authority, varying from 2,347 from the Shire county authorities to only 129 and 347 complaints in Inner and Outer London respectively. The reasons for this variation are not clear. The Children Act Report suggests that different criteria apply and that systems for registration may not be comparable. This is one of the inevitable consequences of allowing each local authority to write its own complaints procedure and its own 'Children in Need' document. The

---

47 Representations Procedure (Children) Regulations 1991 (S.I. 1991 No. 894), reg. 2(1).
48 Children Act 1989 Guidance and Regulations Vol. 4, para. 5.35.
49 Representations Procedure (Children) Regulations 1991, regs 5 and 6, and paras 5.33, 5.35 and 5.41.

Children Act Report comments that further definition may be needed on what should be recorded as a complaint.

A series of Social Services Inspectorate national workshops on complaints revealed that support for complainants was being very widely interpreted, and also clearly demonstrated the different approaches to complaints and complaints procedures adopted by different local authorities — some of whom still have no dedicated complaints officer or procedure specific to child complaints. The workshops particularly identified the needs of young children to have the help of a suitable friendly and independent adult to help them. Children and young people with learning disabilities or sensory disabilities or those whose first language is not English will also need particular help in communicating their concerns.[50]

Independent visitor

Paragraph 17 of Schedule 2 of the Children Act 1989 places a duty on a local authority to appoint an independent visitor in respect of any child they are looking after if they believe that it would be in a child's best interests and certain conditions are satisfied. The need for such an appointment arises where communication between the child and his parent or a person who is not a parent but who has parental responsibility has been infrequent, or where he has not visited or been visited by his parents or a person who is not a parent but who has parental responsibility during the preceding 12 months. Under the old law, the appointment of visitors was restricted to children who were accommodated in community homes which provided education[51] and then only in respect of children in compulsory care. The Children Act 1989 extends the requirement to include all children who are being looked after by a local authority. A child is being looked after by a local authority if he is in care or if he is not in care but is provided with accommodation by the authority.[52] Independent visitors have a duty to visit, advise and befriend the child.

The person appointed must not be connected with the local authority, as laid down in the Definition of Independent Visitors (Children) Regulations 1991.[53] Appointed by local authorities they are essentially volunteers, although they may claim their reasonable expenses. The authority have the right to give the independent visitor notice in writing if they wish to terminate their appointment. Where a local authority proposes to appoint a visitor for a child, an appointment shall not be made if:

● the child objects to it; and
● the authority are satisfied that he has sufficient understanding to make an informed decision.

Further, the local authority shall terminate the appointment if:

● the child objects to its continuing; and

50   Children Act Report 1992, paras 3.50, 3.51 and 3.52, Tables 3.12 and 3.13.
51   Child Care Act 1980, s. 11.
52   S. 22(1) and Chlidren Act 1989 Guidance and Regulations Vol. 6, paras 6.2 and 6.3.
53   S.I. 1991 No. 892.

● the authority are satisfied that he has sufficient understanding to make an
informed decision.

The Secretary of State may make regulations as to the circumstances in
which a person appointed as a visitor under this paragraph is to be regarded as
independent of the local authority appointing him.[54] Hopefully, those
circumstances would not include the metamorphosis of the independent visitor
into an independent advocate, as this would not satisfy criteria either of
sufficient independence from the local authority or effective representation for
the child.

Independent person in reviews of secure accommodation

Regulations 15 and 16 of the Children (Secure Accommodation) Regulations
1991 deal with the review by local authorities looking after children of the
placement of such children in secure accommodation in community homes.
This review is additional to the review required by the Children Act 1989,
S.25.

Each local authority looking after a child in secure accommodation is
required to ensure that the child's case is reviewed within one month of the
start of the placement, and thereafter at intervals not exceeding three months.
The first review must be within one month of placement.[55] The local
authority must appoint three people to undertake reviews, one of whom must
be independent and not employed by the local authority looking after the
child, or by the local authority managing the secure accommodation.[56] Those
conducting the review must be satisfied that:

(a) the criteria for keeping the child in secure accommodation continue to
apply; and
(b) such a placement continues to be necessary and whether or not any
other description of accommodation would be appropriate for the
child;
and in doing so they must have regard to the welfare of the child.[57]

The views of the independent visitor and the child, among others, must be
taken into account in making any decision.[58]

Independent social work advocates

There is no specific requirement for independent social work advocates in the
Children Act 1989, although they are not ruled out by the Guidance and

---

54   Sched. 2, para. 17.7.
55   Children (Secure Accommodation) Regulations 1991, reg. 15.
56   Ibid.
57   Ibid., reg. 16(1).
58   Ibid., reg. 16(2) and (3); see Guidance and Regulations Vol. 4, paras 8.53–8.57.

Regulations,[59] and there is a recognition in the Guidance that there will be situations where children may need the help of an advocate, in which case they are recommended to approach one of the voluntary organisations offering such services.[60] A number of voluntary child care organisations, including ASC, offer independent advocacy services.

The advantage of independent advocacy is that the activities of the advocate are not confined within the limits of a particular complaints procedure established by a particular local authority. Advocates will be in a position to put a full range of options to the child including, if necessary, the possibility of judicial review. To that extent, advocates provide a safeguard, and fetter rampant local authority discretion in its decision making in relation to children.

Independent representatives

Independent representatives are social work representatives, usually volunteers, who visit and represent young people in secure accommodation. There is no statutory requirement for secure units to appoint independent representatives, but the role has been extensively pioneered by Voice for the Child in Care and now many units have independent representatives attached. The role of the independent representative is to visit any child or young person, with his or her agreement, as soon as possible after he or she is admitted to a secure unit and at regular intervals until he or she leaves the unit. The independent representative will establish a pattern of confidential discussions, will take up any matter which the child or young person wishes to be raised, helping to write letters or seeing the appropriate person, but not entering into discussions about his or her conduct, behaviour and progress with staff or other people unless expressly asked to do so by the young person. Independent representatives are needed because, when a young person is committed to secure care, even though the legal requirements have been observed and a three-monthly or six-monthly hearing has taken place in court (or at the tribunal if the young person is detained under mental health legislation), it is important that there should be another way to safeguard his or her rights to fair and appropriate care and treatment. The court provides authority for secure accommodation to be used. It does not review the exercise of that authority.

Guardians *ad litem* have been particularly aware of the isolation of children once they have entered the secure unit, and in some cases have asked for interim rather than full Orders so that they can continue to have an involvement in the case. The availability of an independent representative, particularly for young people who do not receive regular visits from family or friends, provides a contact with the outside world and an opportunity for the young people to make a problem or complaint known outside the unit. It is expected that children will receive appropriate medical and educational care, that they will have opportunities for regular exercise in the fresh air, that

---

59   See Children Act 1989 Guidance and Regulations Vol. 4, para. 5.14.
60   *Ibid.*, Vol. 3, para. 7.4.3 and Vol. 4, para. 6.47.

contact with families will be maintained if possible, and that mail will not be censored.[61]

It is expected that staff will refer to, and abide by, the guidance on permissible forms of control in children's residential care published by the Department of Health in April 1993. The guidance identifies two types of persuasive rather than coercive physical presence (e.g. standing in the doorway to prevent the child leaving and holding the child to prevent them harming themselves or others). The guidance stresses that the amount of control any individual member of staff has will depend on their personal authority and the respect in which they are held by the young people in their care. However, the guidance identifies seven guiding principles which provide a framework about whether an intervention is justified:

> It is imperative that staff exercise sound judgement and act with discretion in deciding how to react in a particular set of circumstances.
>
> (i) A distinction must be maintained between the use of a 'one-off' intervention which is appropriate in the particular circumstances and using it repeatedly as a regular feature of a regime.
>
> (ii) Staff must be able to show that the method of intervention was in keeping with the incident that gave rise to it.
>
> (iii) The degree and duration of any force applied must be proportional to the circumstances.
>
> (iv) The potential for damage to persons and property in applying any form of restraint must always be kept in mind.
>
> (v) The failure of a particular intervention to secure a child's compliance should not automatically signal the immediate use of another more forceful form of intervention. Escalation should be avoided if possible; especially if it would make the overall situation more destructive and/or unmanageable.
>
> (vi) The age and competence of the child should be taken into account in deciding what degree of intervention is necessary.
>
> (vii) In developing individual child care plans, consideration should be given to approaches to control that would be appropriate to that child's case.[62]

Independent social workers

Independent social workers were used extensively before the establishment in 1984 of panels of guardians *ad litem* and reporting officers to represent children in public law proceedings. They were appointed by solicitors, conscious of the need to receive expert social work advice which was independent of either the local authority or the child's parents. Independent social workers are expert social work witnesses who represent a view to the court about the best interests of the child. Although not so commonly used since 1984, they are still appointed in some cases where guardians *ad litem* are

---

61 See *The Case for an Independent Representative for a Young Person in Care who is in Secure Accommodation*, published by a Voice for the Child in Care (1989).

62 *General Principles Governing Interventions to Maintain Control* (April 1993), Department of Health, Section IX, para. 9.1. See also *Mental Health Act Code of Practice* (1993), HMSO, Mental Health Act Guidance on Time Out, paras 19.9 to 19.11; and Department for Education Circular No. 2, *The Education of Children with Emotional and Behavioural Difficulties* (December 1993); and Lyon, 'Legal issues arising from the care and control of children with learning disabilities who also present severe challenging behaviour: a Guide for Parents and Carers' (1994), The Mental Health Foundation.

not appointed and an independent social work expert is required, or where there is a query about the recommendations of the guardian involved in the case and one of the other parties introduces their own independent social work expert witness.

Guardians ad litem *and reporting officers*

Introduced in November 1976 in unopposed care cases only and extended to act in adoption and/or care related cases in May 1984 under S.64 of the Children Act 1975, their role was further extended under the provisions of the Children Act 1989 and, from October 14, 1991, guardians *ad litem* were appointed earlier in a wider range of proceedings, including S.25 applications for Secure Accommodation Orders. They were also given a significant case management role, emphasising their role as officer of the court as well as representative of the child. Their statutory duty is to represent the best interests of children before the courts and they are generally experienced social workers. Family Court welfare officers from the civil section of the probation department act in adoption cases only. From November 1, 1994, guardians *ad litem* may be appointed in applications under Section 30 of the Human Fertilisation and Embryology Act 1990 (Surrogacy Arrangements).

Summary

The provisions in S.26 of the Act are a response to a long-standing concern about the position of children entering and leaving care, as well as those who are in care. While abuse of children in their own homes has received considerable publicity in recent years, abuse of children in care has had a consistently lower profile in spite of a number of public enquiries into the conduct of homes like Kincora, Leeways, Spyways, The Hollies and, more recently, the Melanie Klein Home in Greenwich. Each of these reports recommended the establishment of complaints procedures. The Leeways Enquiry Report in 1985 stated that every local authority should have a procedure for handling complaints and resolving disputes on the way it carries out its responsibilities for particular children. However, as the British Association of Social Workers comment, 'although the importance of strengthening the consumer voice through formalised complaints procedures has long been recognised, little progress has been made in widespread adoption of effective procedures'.[63]

The National Children's Bureau 'Who Says?' Project stated that one of the key messages from recent work has been that children are only likely to be able to participate properly in decision making if they are given adequate information about rights and responsibilities, access to forums where decisions are made, entitlement to independent representation, and support and means of redress through complaints procedures. However, if those complaints

---

63 *Rights, Responsibilities and Remedies: A Model Complaints Procedure* (1989), British Association of Social Workers.

procedures are to be effective, they must be both robust enough and independent enough to allow solutions which are satisfactory, not just from the point of view of the local authority but from the point of view of the young person, who may otherwise feel that they have been led up a rather long and convoluted blind alley. The provisions and spirit of S.26 (Complaints Procedures) have yet to be fully absorbed and endorsed by staff in many residential establishments.

Part III
Welfare

Chapter 11
Children in Need, Children at Risk and Children in Care

A central guiding philosophy of the Children Act 1989 is that children are generally best looked after within their family of origin, without recourse to legal proceedings. To this end, local authorities are required to provide the range of service provision necessary to achieve this objective. Families are to be supported in carrying out their responsibilities in relation to their children.

Children in Need

The statutory requirements

Part 3 of the Children Act 1989 covers local authority support for children and families and establishes two key principles which govern service provision: firstly, to safeguard and promote the welfare of children who are in need; and secondly, so far as is consistent with that duty, to promote the upbringing of such children by their families, by providing a range and level of services appropriate to those children's needs.[1]

The specific duties and powers of each local authority are set out in Part 1 of Schedule 2: 'Any service provided by an authority, in the exercise of functions conferred on them by S.17, may be provided for the family of a particular child in need, or for any member of his family, if it is provided with a view to safeguarding and promoting the child's welfare.'[2] The services provided by local authorities may include giving assistance in kind or, in exceptional circumstances, in cash.[3] However, cash may be loaned, subject to repayment: 'Assistance may be unconditional or subject to conditions, as to the repayment of the assistance of its value (in whole or in part).'[4] Before

---

1 S.17(1)(a) and (b).
2 S.17(3).
3 S.17(6).
4 S.17(7)

giving any assistance or imposing any conditions, the local authority shall have regard to the means of the child concerned and of each of his parents.[5] However, those in receipt of income support or family credit, under the Social Security Act 1986, will not be liable for repayment of assistance.

The definition of a 'child in need' is set out in S.17(10):

> a child shall be taken to be in need if:
> (a) he is unlikely to achieve or maintain, or to have the opportunity of achieving or maintaining, a reasonable standard of health or development without the provision for him of services by a local authority under this Part;
> (b) his health or development is likely to be significantly impaired, or further impaired, without the provision for him of such services; or
> (c) he is disabled.

Family, in relation to such a child, includes any person who has parental responsibility for the child and any other person with whom he has been living. The definition of a child in need is quite specific, yet broad ranging. The inclusion of further impairment, as well as significant impairment, gives considerable scope for the provision of supportive services.

For the first time, children with disability are included in definitions of children in need and local authorities have taken on significant responsibilities for the provision of services to them. Vol. 6 of the Children Act 1989 Guidance and Regulations deals with children with disabilities.[6]

The extensive range of services which may be offered to children and families is spelled out in Schedule 2 under Local Authority Support for Children and Families. Local authorities have a duty to take reasonable steps to identify the extent to which there are children in need within their area and to publish information about services provided by them under S.17 (Provision of services for children in need, their families and others), S.18 (Day care for pre-school and other children), S.20 (Provision of accommodation for children in need) and S.24 (Advice and assistance for certain children, including those leaving care).

Services to children in need are not to be limited to the resources available in the social services department. S.27, which is arguably the most under-utilised of the Act, provides for co-operation between different local authority departments to ensure a co-ordinated provision of services through the resources of education, housing and health authorities, as well as social services departments. Where it appears to a local authority that any authority or other person mentioned in sub-section 3 (education, housing or health) could, by taking any specified action, help in the exercise of any of their functions, they may request the help of that other authority or person, specifying the action in question.

An authority whose help is so requested shall comply with the request, if it is compatible with their own statutory or other duties and obligations and does not unduly prejudice the discharge of any of their functions.[7] Thus, this section provides not only a facility on the part of the local authority to seek

---

5 S.17(8).
6 See also Baldwin and Carlisle, *Social Support for Disabled Children and their Families: A Review of the Literature* (1994).
7 S.27(1) and (2).

help, but imposes a responsibility on other local authority departments to provide the help if it is within their power and does not prejudice other duties. Theoretically, this means that no child should come into care because of homelessness. However, although the Act lays down a framework for inter-departmental co-operation, there are no practical mechanisms for ensuring that such co-operation takes place. Policies in relation to children in need are restricted to the social services department and are not co-ordinated through an audit of the combined resources of health, social security, housing and welfare. In many cases, the provision that is available may not be appropriately targeted.

The range of services potentially available to children under the Act is impressive, including emotional support for families under pressure, provision of respite care and the establishment of family centres, where families may attend for occupational, social, cultural or recreational activities, advice, guidance and counselling, or be provided with accommodation while they are receiving advice, guidance and counselling. Such centres continue to be in short supply. Where they do exist, they have been widely used for a variety of activities, not least to provide neutral and non-sterile surroundings for contact visits between children and their families.

Local authorities have powers to provide day care for any child under five not attending school.[8] However, in relation to services for children in need, it is a question of whether the local authorities have 'powers' or 'duties'. Duties provide a strong imperative, while powers have taken a significantly lower profile. In the same way, although local authorities have powers to provide training, advice, guidance and counselling for child-minders under S.18(3), these powers have not been widely used. Under S.19(1), local authorities do have a duty to review, with the education department, the day care provision in their area, including child-minding facilities for the under eights and to publish the results of the review.[9] The concept of family support is much wider than that of prevention and includes provisions to improve the quality of life for children, as well as to diminish the need for them to be received into care. Direct services may be provided to parents to help in their care of children, including, for example, home helps and laundry services, holidays and social and recreational activities.

Volume 2 of the Children Act 1989 Guidance and Regulations deals with family support, day care and educational provision for young children. The Guidance stresses children's rights to an environment which facilitates their development:

> an approach based on children's rights would encompass all the factors necessary for their development. However, depending upon the values held by society at large, the child may be regarded as having rights which go beyond the provision of an environment which can be inherently demonstrated to facilitate development. For example, children should have the right to be cared for as part of a community which values the religious, racial, cultural and linguistic identity of the child. The

---

8 S.18(2). See also Fergus Smith in consultation with Gillian Beasley LL.B, *Personal Guide To — Childminding and Day Care of 'Under Eights' in England and Wales (Children Act 1989)*, published by Children Act Enterprises, 7 Graham Road, Purley, Surrey CR8 2EN, 1991.
9 S.19(6).

justification for the awarding of such a right would be in terms of fostering the child's sense of identity. Children's sense of identity is a fundamental aspect of their development and so such a right could be included within a definition based upon the facilitation of child development. Other examples of rights which might be assigned to children include the right to health, individuality, respect, dignity, opportunities for learning and socialising with adults and children, freedom from discrimination — such as racism or sexism, and cultural diversity. The extent to which a day care setting fulfils these rights may be used in defining the quality of care for that setting. All these rights can be regarded as potentially contributing to children's physical, intellectual, social and emotional development.[10]

Practical approaches to the provision of services to children in need are examined in *Children in Need and their Families: A New Approach*.[11]

Children with disability

There are an estimated 360,000 children with a disability in Great Britain.[12] Disability is defined, according to the World Health Organisation, as 'a restriction or lack of ability to perform normal activities, which has resulted from impairment of a structure or function of body or mind'. The 1989 Act included for the first time children with disabilities in its definition of children in need. Some of these children may be doubly disadvantaged by being one of the more than three million children in Britain living in poor families. Families with a disabled child have, on average, 22 per cent lower incomes than equivalent families in the population as a whole.[13]

For the first time, the Act included children with disability in its definition of children in need:

> A child is disabled if he is blind, deaf or dumb or suffers from mental disorder of any kind or is substantially and permanently handicapped by illness, injury or congenital deformity or such other disability as may be prescribed; and in this part 'development' means physical, intellectual, emotional, social or behavioural development; and 'health' means physical or mental health.[14]

There appears to be a very high level of unidentified need in relation to these children. Only one in ten children with disabilities was registered as handicapped by social services departments in England, according to OPCS (Office of Population Census and Surveys) surveys. This very low level of identified need is a factor in the limited provision of services, such as respite care. The overwhelming majority of children with disabilities in Britain live in the community with their families. Only 1.5 per cent live in residential establishments.[15] The Children Act 1989 contains specific provisions in respect of services to children with disabilities: 'Where a local authority

---

10 Children Act 1989 Guidance and Regulations Vol. 2, para. 6.28.
11 (1991) University of Leicester and the Department of Health, HMSO.
12 *National Children's Homes Fact File: British Children in Need* (1993), p. 17.
13 *Ibid.*, p. 18.
14 Children Act 1989, s. 17(11).
15 *NCH Fact File, op. cit.*, p. 17.

provides accommodation for a child, whom they are looking after and who is disabled, they shall, so far as is reasonably practicable, ensure that the accommodation is not unsuitable to his particular needs.'[16]

Local authorities are required to open and maintain a register of children with disabilities in their area.[17] They may assess a child's needs for the purpose of the Children Act at the same time as any other assessment under certain other Acts.[18] They are required to provide services for children with disabilities which are designed to minimise the effects of the children's disabilities and to give them the opportunity to lead lives that are as normal as possible.[19] Services to children with disabilities are based on the principle that they are children first. The Guidance recognises that work with children with special needs requires the provision of services both in terms of suitable, experienced staff and relevant practical resources. The Children Act provides that assessment arrangements for children who may be in need can be carried out simultaneously with assessments under the Chronically Sick and Disabled Persons Act 1970, the Education Act 1981, the Disabled Persons Act 1986 or any other enactment.

Social services departments should discuss with local education authorities, district health authorities and, where appropriate, National Health Service (NHS) Trusts, arrangements for joint assessment in appropriate cases, and the provision of health services under the collaborative arrangements, in the light of the Children Act and the NHS reforms.[20] Importantly, children with disabilities have the same rights to have their views sought and taken into account as any other children whose welfare is covered by the provisions of the Act.[21]

Research reveals that comparatively little is known about the impact of disability from the point of view of the young persons themselves. The transition from childhood through adolescence to young adulthood is a particularly stressful time for young people with disability, representing often impossible challenges in terms of financial, physical and emotional independence at the same time as they are required to make the transition from paediatric to adult service provision, in itself a somewhat indeterminate path to define. At this stage, adolescents with disability:

- were less likely to have attained the goals of adult life;
- had lower self-esteem and less sense of personal control;
- felt restricted in their disability;
- had more restricted social lives, fewer friendships and sexual or 'romantic' relationships;
- were less likely to be in paid work;
- had less experience of going away or on holiday independently;

---

16 S. 23(8) and see also Children Act 1989 Guidance and Regulations Vol. 6, Children with Disabilities.
17 Sched. 2, para. 2.
18 Sched. 2, para. 3.
19 Sched. 2, para. 9.
20 Children Act 1989 Guidance and Regulations Vol. 6, para. 1.8.
21 Ibid., para. 1.6.

- were less likely to be treated as adult, that is, have separate consultations, by health and social service professionals;
- had not maintained contact with the services they had access to as children, particularly physiotherapy;
- were much more likely to have no weekday placement or activity than their non-disabled peers.[22]

Services for children with disability and their families should focus on the following areas:

- initial diagnosis, treatment and support;
- providing information and practical strategies for coping with the disability;
- help with the practical problems of caring — for example, washing, bathing and dressing (70 per cent of the most severely disabled children in one study were incontinent);[23]
- support for parents and carers experiencing emotional problems — high levels of anxiety associated with the prolonged hard physical work involved in the caring, in addition to the emotional stress, particularly evident in single parents;
- financial difficulties arising from the reduced ability of the carer (usually mothers) to maintain full-time employment. There is significant research evidence to indicate generally lower living standards and greater levels of financial stress among families with disabled children, 'and some very severely disabled children are living in conditions of extreme hardship, which are partly related to their condition and which must reduce their quality of life';[24]
- support for parents suffering marital stress and breakdown, both of which may be exacerbated by the long-term effects of coping with a child with disability;
- helping families to adapt coping strategies and gain access to resources to enable them to cope;
- services to offset the disadvantages associated with disability, in particular services to ensure that children with disability do not become unduly educationally disadvantaged;
- counselling services for parents, carers, the young person with disability and their siblings;
- advocacy services for young people with disability. Many young people with disability are not in care, yet are cared for in institutions where they may suffer physical, sexual and psychological abuse. There may be significant areas where the wishes of the young people with disability may be at odds with the rest of the family. In these situations, access to information, advice and advocacy services are of crucial importance to the potentially isolated young person who has long-term dependency needs.

---

22 Hirst and Baldwin in *Social Support for Disabled Children and their Families*, op. cit., p. 36.
23 Office of Population and Census Survey 1985.
24 'Living with Disability: The Experience of Parents and Children' in *Social Support for Disabled Children and their Families*, op. cit., p. 25. See also Middleton, *Children First: Working with Children and Disability* (1992).

Services for children from racial, linguistic and cultural minorities

The Children Act 1989 is unique in requiring that, in making any decision, the local authority shall give due consideration to the child's religious persuasion, racial origin and cultural and linguistic background.[25] A child's ethnic origin, cultural background and religion are important factors for consideration. It may be taken as a guiding principle of good practice that, other things being equal and in the great majority of cases, placement with a family of similar ethnic origin and religion is most likely to meet a child's needs as fully as possible, and to safeguard his or her welfare most effectively. Families of similar ethnic origin are usually best placed to prepare children for life as members of an ethnic minority group in a multi-racial society where they may meet with racial prejudice and discrimination. However:

> these principles should be applied in proper consideration for the circumstances of the individual case. There may be circumstances in which placement with a family of different ethnic origin is the best choice for a particular child. In other cases, such a placement may be the best available choice. For example, a child may have formed strong links with prospective foster parents or be related to them . . .[26]

Account must also be taken of the needs of children of mixed parentage, with attempts being made to find a placement which most nearly reflects the child's ethnic (and/or religious) origins. The aim is to place the child in a situation which will reinforce, sustain and develop the child's own sense of race, religion and culture. As the child's own perception of his needs is central in this process, the Guidance also stresses that the child should be consulted and the choice of placement 'influenced' by his wishes and feelings in the matter. An independent visitor of the same race, religion or culture as the child may play a useful role to reinforce the child's sense of identity, if appropriate.

The Guidance stresses the need to treat each child as an individual, with a unique collection of needs. Each case must be looked at separately and allowance made for the fact that what may be right for one child may be wrong for another child in an ostensibly similar situation.

Services to children in need

The Children Act 1989 has done a great deal to increase the potential for the provision of an extensive and welcome range of services for children and families, yet it has done little to increase the range of services available on the ground. In particular, the lack of direct service provision for young people leaving care has left hundreds of young people stranded at 16, lacking psychological, financial, emotional and educational support.

The Children Act Report 1992 found that nearly all the authorities who replied had adopted a common system for prioritising levels of need entitling access to services. It was clear that the highest priority was accorded to

---

25 S.22(5)(c) and Children Act 1989 Guidance and Regulations Vol. 3 on how 'due consideration' may be given.
26 Children Act 1989 Guidance and Regulations Vol. 3, paras 2.40–42.

children for whom authorities already had some existing responsibility, i.e. children covered by Parts IV and V of the Act. When describing their approach to children in the community, as opposed to those for whom they already had some responsibility, local authorities showed only limited identification of groups of problems. Only 23 local authorities identified children with special health needs as 'in need', reflecting the requirement for health services to be more proactive, through their screening and surveillance programmes, in bringing children with special health needs to the attention of social services. Similarly, only 19 authorities grouped drugs/solvent abusing children and only 21 authorities recognised children at risk of HIV AIDS (it could be argued that the latter was a new group which needed planning for, so the figure of 21 could be interpreted as encouraging). School truants are an established yet lowly rated group, as only 9 authorities regarded truants and 15 authorities regarded children excluded from school as children in need. It was noticeable that just over a third of local authorities included children with difficult family relations and 19 per cent and 10 per cent respectively considered children of homeless and unemployed parents as groups of children in need. Seventeen per cent of local authorities recognised children in families living in bed and breakfast accommodation and only eight per cent identified children in families whose gas/electricity or water had been disconnected as groups of children in need.[27]

First Key identified a very wide range of leaving care grants given by local authorities in 83 areas in England and Wales. Forty-three per cent of local authorities either gave no grant or were not prepared to say what they did give. Twenty per cent of local authorities gave up to £500, 30 per cent gave up to £1,000 and 7 per cent gave over £1,000. The maximum payment given to any individual child was £2,000, with a national average maximum figure of £731. The prime purpose of the grants is to assist young people to meet the necessary costs of setting up home, or entering employment or further education, yet local authorities are not bound to give anything at all, and very often do not. The Children Act Report for 1992 recorded its disappointment that only one-fifth of authorities had produced specific guidance for young people leaving care, although a further one-third apparently had such guidance in hand.[28]

The Act and the Guidance place great emphasis on services to children in need, not as a reactive response but as a proactive programme of support and preventive strategies to prevent children coming into care. This is a view further endorsed by the Children Act Advisory Committee in their 1992 report and by the Audit Commission who carried out a survey on the allocation of resources in Health and Social Services Departments.[29]

The provisions regarding children in need are seen as 'an important innovation' by the Department of Health. A survey commissioned by the

---

27 Children Act Report 1992, Department of Health, paras 3.7, 3.8 and 3.9.
28 *Ibid.*, paras 7.12 and 7.13, and Fig. 7.2.
29 *Ibid.*, para. 3.10 and 'Seen — But Not Heard — Co-ordinating Community Child Health and Social Services for Children in Need — Detailed Evidence and Guidelines for Managers and Practitioners', Audit Commission, HMSO, 1994.

Department in 1993 looked for sample local authorities and identified five key decision-making points in responding to children with family support needs. They were:

- Recognition
- Investigation
- Assessment of needs
- Prioritisation, and
- Response.

Recognition of a referral of a 'case' of a child in need is an interpretative act requiring professional judgment about the gravity of needs and the impact on individuals. Prescriptive lists or categories of children or their states do little to assist practitioners in making those interpretative judgments. On the other hand, illustrative materials on the conditions or features which may be found in cases do seem to be helpful to practitioners. Likewise, arrangements for prioritising cases that exhibit certain conditions or states seem supportive of those professional judgments. In exercising professional judgment in recognising a 'case', a number of considerations come into play:

- Is the inquiry a social services responsibility?
- Does, or should, another agency carry responsibility?
- Will advice and assistance be a sufficient response to the referral (recognising that this can require substantial and sustained involvement)?
- Can the need be met by the person receiving the referral?
- Can the referral be dealt with by time limited involvement?
- How does the referral fit with the current priorities of the team if the involvement is to be more than transitory?

The results of the survey confirmed the impression that services to children in need are focused around child protection, rather than more general preventive work at an early stage. Although some good quality services are being provided to children and families with needs outside of the threshold of significant harm, such work is perceived to be under heavy pressure of being relegated by child protection cases. The survey concludes that:

> as yet there is little evidence of local quality assurance measures to test whether practice has been influenced by the new legislation and subsequent local policies. Nor is there much evidence of local mechanisms to ensure that policy developments locally reflect, to any great extent, the experience and requirements of the practitioners. In the absence of such mechanisms routinely applied, the priority given to support for children in need and their families will vary, depending upon the perception of professionals and their subjective judgements.[30]

---

30 *Children in Need: Definition Management and Monitoring* (1993), Social Information Systems Ltd for the Department of Health. See also *Putting Assessment Systems into Practice* (1992), Social Services Inspectorate and National Health Service (Management Executive), Department of Health, and Hardiker *et al.*, *Policies and Practices in Preventive Child Care* (1991). See also 'Seen — But Not Heard', Note 29 above, which also confirms the comparative over-emphasis on child protection rather than family support.

Children at Risk

Working together: a framework for child protection

Britain has a legalistic approach to child protection as opposed to the psycho-social approach adopted by many other countries, for example, Holland. A great deal of attention is focused on incidents of abuse and the removal of the child from the family, after which crisis point social work attention wanes. This results in a microscopic approach, isolating an incident or collection of incidents even though these occur as facets of the total framework of the child's life. Children are often lifted out of their environment, examined minutely over a relatively short period and then expected to struggle on in an environment and family network which may have totally changed as a result of the disclosure. However, child abuse procedures have become more sophisticated following implementation of the Children Act 1989.[31] Part V of the Act deals with the protection of children and establishes that the court may only make an Order if it is satisfied:

> that there is reasonable cause to believe that the child is likely to suffer significant harm if:
> (i) he is not removed to accommodation provided by or on behalf of the applicant; or
> (ii) he does not remain in the place in which he is then being accommodated.[32]

The criteria for the making of the Order are that:

● the applicant has reasonable cause to suspect that a child is suffering or is likely to suffer significant harm;
● the applicant is making enquiries with respect to the child's welfare; and
● those enquiries are being frustrated by access to the child being unreasonably refused to a person authorised to seek access and the applicant has reasonable cause to believe that access to the child is required as a matter of urgency.

Working Together, a guide to arrangements for inter-agency co-operation for the protection of children from abuse,[33] lays great emphasis on inter-disciplinary and inter-agency work as essential processes in the task of attempting to protect children from abuse. It provides important guidance on all aspects of child protection and brings together a body of valuable experience and expertise. The guidance it contains is issued under S.7 of the Local Authority Social Services Act 1970 and, although it does not have the full force of statute, it should be complied with unless local circumstances indicate exceptional reasons which justify variation. Although the key responsibilities of each agency are identified, primary responsibility for the protection of the child falls to the social services department.

---

31 For a comprehensive examination of both the civil and criminal law relating to child protection, see Lyon and de Cruz, *Child Abuse* (2nd ed., 1993). See also 'The Challenge of Partnership in Child Protection. A Practice Guide' (1995), Department of Health and Social Services Inspectorate.
32 S.44(1)(a).
33 (1991), HMSO.

The investigation of abuse and neglect are covered by Ss.37, 41, 47(1) and 47(8) and Schedule 2 para. 4 of the Children Act 1989. Local authorities have a statutory duty to investigate, where they have reasonable cause to suspect that a child is suffering or is likely to suffer significant harm, and to assess the needs of the child and the family, including the likelihood of significant harm and the need for protection.

Working Together identifies the following categories of child abuse:

- *Neglect* — the persistent or severe neglect of a child or a failure to protect a child from exposure to any kind of danger, including cold and starvation, or extreme failure to carry out important aspects of care, resulting in the significant impairment of the child's health or development, including non-organic failure to thrive.
- *Physical injury* — actual or likely physical injury to a child or failure to prevent physical injury (or suffering) to a child, including deliberate poisoning, suffocation and Munchausens syndrome by proxy.
- *Sexual abuse* — actual or likely sexual exploitation of a child or adolescent. The child may be dependent and/or developmentally immature.
- *Emotional abuse* — actual or likely severe adverse effect on the emotional and behavioural development of a child caused by persistent or severe emotional ill-treatment or rejection. All abuse involves some emotional ill-treatment. This category should be used where it is the main or sole form of abuse. (Emotional abuse may be further defined as behaviour which diminishes the child as a person; for example, perpetual criticism, verbal abuse, withholding of normal affection and communication, and scapegoating within the family.)
- *Organised abuse* — a generic term which covers abuse which may involve a number of abusers, a number of abused children and young people involving an element of organisation through, for example, paedophile or pornographic rings. Some organised groups may use bizarre or ritualised behaviour, sometimes associated with particular 'belief' systems which may or may not involve the use of satanic rituals. The guidance emphasises that it is incorrect to classify ritualised and organised abuse as the same phenomena.[34] Unlike the other categories of child abuse, organised abuse is not registrable.

Significant harm

Significant harm may be viewed from both a legal (necessarily shorter term) and a psychodynamic (longer term) point of view.

At the point of intervention by the investigating (who are also the helping) agencies, the legal focus is a three-pronged procedure. Firstly, whether, on the balance of probabilities, the child concerned is suffering, or is likely to suffer,

---

34 *Ibid.*, para. 5.26(1) and (2).

significant harm. Then, secondly, that the harm, or likelihood of harm, is attributable to:

● the care given to the child, or likely to be given to him if the Order were not made, not being what it would be reasonable to expect a parent to give to him, or
● the child being beyond parental control.

Thirdly, if these first two criteria are satisfied, then the minimum intervention, or positive advantage principle, comes into play. The court must ask itself whether making an Order will be better than making no Order at all.[35] This judgment will be based on an examination of the matters outlined in the welfare checklist.[36]

Then, and only then, will the court go on to consider which of the Orders available under the Act should be made. Clearly, the guardian *ad litem*'s recommendation will be heavily relied upon by the court in making their decision. The guardian will have had an early opportunity to scrutinise the local authority's application, the supporting evidence and the evidence of the other parties, and will have made their own independent assessment of the course of action which will be the best for the child, in view of all the circumstances. 'If the court overrides the guardian *ad litem*'s recommendation, they must give their reasons.'[37]

This is the shorter term legalistic timetable. Perhaps less attention is paid to the psychodynamic longer term effects of intervention and its accumulative effect on the family network. Young people may be stranded by legal decisions taken some years before. For example, a child may, quite appropriately, have no contact with an abusing parent for a number of years, but may at 14 or 15 wish to see the parent again and attempt to integrate the events of the past into an approach to the future. The end of the process is just as important to the child as the beginning, and there are still few social work resources available for young people attempting to survive a childhood of abuse and to come to terms with the reality of their continuing family relationships. Too often, the only choice is complete isolation and estrangement, not only from the abuser but also from any positive elements of that family network, in particular grandparents, aunts, uncles and cousins who may have lost touch with the young child following the abuse and subsequent intervention.

This is not an argument against protecting children from abuse, it is an argument for taking a more practical approach to the longer term welfare of the child and of the young adult that child will become. Abuse is not an isolated incident, it is a continuing blight on a young life and the capacity to form relationships. The risk of secondary abuse arising from the multi-disciplinary intervention, and clearly identified in the Cleveland Enquiry Report, must be honestly assessed. Young people themselves must be allowed to participate and have some control over the 'protective' events and their longer term consequences. Children want the abuse to cease: they do not necessarily want their entire life within their family to come to an abrupt end.

---

35 S.1(5).
36 S.1(3).
37 *S. v. Oxfordshire County Council* [1993] 1 F.L.R. 452.

Case conferences: participation of parents and children

The Guidance encourages the participation of children and family adults at both the initial child protection conference and subsequent child protection reviews. There are a variety of practical ways in which the participation of children and adults in the family at conferences can be encouraged and made less difficult. For example, conferences should be held at a time and place which is convenient for the family, as well as for the professional workers. The family should be prepared for the conference by the professional worker with whom they have the closest relationship. Parents and caring adults should meet the chair in advance and should be made aware of the issues to be discussed at the conference so that they can seek advice and prepare their points of view. The size of the professional group should be limited to those who really need to attend and comfortable waiting facilities should be available. These details should be addressed by area child protection committees in their local procedures.[38]

Children and parents do not have an absolute right to attend conferences.[39] However, their attendance is positively encouraged in the interests of promoting open and honest relationships between local authorities and families. There may be exceptional occasions when it will not be right to invite one or other parent to attend a case conference, in whole or in part. Exclusions should be kept to a minimum and must be justified. The procedure should lay down criteria for this, including the evidence required. Evidence of a strong risk of violence by the parents towards professionals or the child might be one example, as would be evidence that the conference would be likely to be disrupted. The possibility that one of the parents may be prosecuted for an offence against the child does not in itself justify exclusion.[40] The decision to exclude a parent, carer or a child from a child protection conference should rest with the chair of the conference, who should base his or her decision on the exclusion criteria in the local child protection procedures.[41] While parents are encouraged to bring a friend or supporter, the attendance of a legal representative is not encouraged: 'the conference is not a tribunal to decide whether abuse has taken place and legal representation is therefore not appropriate'.[42]

As part of the local authority's specific duty to promote the welfare of the child and to ascertain, as far as is practicable, his or her wishes and feelings and give due consideration to them, having regard to his or her age and understanding, a child should be encouraged to attend conferences. It is acknowledged that children may feel more able to do this if there is a friend or supporter present. This is a role that children's advocates have sometimes fulfilled. If a child does not wish to attend, or his or her age or understanding makes this inappropriate, the conference should be provided with a clear and up-to-date account of the child's views by the professionals who are working

---

38 *Working Together, op. cit.*, para. 6.23.
39 *Ibid.*, para. 6.14.
40 *Ibid.*, para. 6.15.
41 *Ibid.*, para. 6.16.
42 *Ibid.*, para. 6.18.

with the child. The conference should expect the key worker to be able to inform them about the views of a child who is not attending the meeting. Equally, the professional who is working most closely with the child should keep the child informed about the decisions and recommendations reached at the conference and about any changes in the inter-agency protection plan.[43]

Working Together makes no comment about the desirability, or otherwise, of guardians *ad litem* attending case conferences on behalf of the child. In general, their attendance has been discouraged on the grounds that they are not part of the decision-making process and should not get drawn into discussion about the case, as this may prejudice their independence. The *Manual of Practical Guidance*, however, envisages that there may be certain situations, for example case conferences held after the taking of an Emergency Protection Order, in which it may be desirable for the guardian to attend:

● to facilitate matters, through a swift exchange of information at the case conference;
● to ensure an adequate representation of the child's wishes and feelings, in relation to the application.[44]

However, the fact that guardians are now involved at a much earlier stage in proceedings does not mean that they should be drawn into the decision-making process and they should make it clear to the chair of the case conference that they are attending as observers, not key participants. The observer status of the guardian attending the conference should be recorded in the minutes and should be made clear to all those involved, in particular the other parties to the proceedings, who must be able to see the guardian as an independent person of credibility.

The guidance in *Working Together* is supported by regulation 7(2) of the Review of Children's Cases Regulations 1991,[45] which require the responsible authority, where they consider it appropriate, to involve the child and his parents in review meetings. The possibility of a child being accompanied by a friendly supporter should also be considered.

Summary of key messages in Working Together

● The safety and welfare of the child must be the most important consideration at all times.
● All work in the area of child protection should be based on inter-agency co-operation.
● Most cases should not require the intervention of the courts, but be dealt with in partnership with the child and family.
● Except when a child is in acute physical danger, the timing of any removal from home should be considered in the light of the best interests of the child and the need to work in partnership with the whole family.

---

43 *Ibid.*, para. 6.13.
44 Timms, *Manual of Practice Guidance for Guardians ad Litem and Reporting Officers* (1992), p. 86.
45 S.I. 1991 No. 895.

● All those involved in investigative interviews should approach each case with an open mind.

Unallocated cases

On June 30, 1992, the total number of cases unallocated by local authorities was 1,543 or 2.9 per cent of the total numbers of children looked after. What was particularly worrying was that the London authorities accounted for 40 per cent of the unallocated cases, but only 16.7 per cent of the number of children looked after. This imbalance has been commented on by guardians *ad litem* working on London panels who, in some cases, have found themselves providing the only social work input to children. On that day, the total number of unallocated child protection cases in 104 authorities was 1,110, or 3.2 per cent of the 38,600 children on the child protection register. A child protection case is categorised as allocated only if there is a named social worker who has the responsibility of key worker and who undertakes the social work aspects of the child protection plan.[46] Children are placed on the child protection register for one of three reasons:

● they are thought to be at risk of a specific form of significant harm;
● they are subject to a multi-agency child protection plan;
● their situation is subject to regular reviews with the family, to be revised as change is achieved.[47]

Clearly, if children on child protection registers have no allocated social workers, the social services department is substantially failing in its statutory duties in relation to those children. This is a matter which is the subject of continued monitoring by the Social Services Inspectorate.[48] In July 1992, the Social Services Inspectorate reported that over 600 children in London who were assessed as at risk of abuse had no social worker allocated, in spite of the requirements in *Working Together* that each child on the register must have a named social worker to implement the child protection plan, encourage full parental participation and to take into account the views of the child.[49]

The manner of the child's removal from home

Events in Cleveland, Orkney and Rochdale aroused particular public and media concerns about children being removed in dawn raids by both police and social workers. At 6 a.m. on February 27, 1991, four teams of social workers and police officers gathered at the police station at Kirkwall on the

---

46 The Children Act Report 1992, para. 2.47.
47 *Ibid.*, para. 2.45.
48 See *Survey of Management Arrangements for Child Care* (June 1993), reported in the Children's Act Report 1993. This showed that, of 21 authorities, 5 had levels of unallocated child protection cases which exceeded 10 per cent, while 9 had levels between 2 per cent and 10 per cent. Thus, 14 out of 21 authorities had levels of unallocated cases of over 2 per cent of the total of their child protection cases (Children's Act Report 1993, para. 3.26).
49 *Children Now* (1992), Children's Society and National Children's Bureau, p. 55.

island of Orkney. The plan was that all four teams should arrive simultaneously at 7 a.m. The team for the removal of the 'B' children consisted of
four social workers and four police officers — police officers being in plain
clothes. Mrs B. had got up as usual between 6.15 and 6.30, in order to wake
her son in time to catch the school bus. She heard the noise of the cars outside
the house. She had received no warning of the imminent removal of the
children. The account in the report of the removal of the children is both
disturbing and distressing. Some of the children had nothing to eat or drink
and were not allowed to take anything with them. There were confusions
about whether another child had necessary medication. One child protested
that her parents would not harm her and she was worried for her mother's
health, lest the experience would hurt her (her mother at this stage was
extremely distressed). For one of the children, leaving home and her medical
examination were the worst parts. For another it was saying goodbye to her
mother. She understood that separation would be for seven days (the length of
the Place of Safety Order) — in fact, the separation was for several months.[50]

Reading the accounts, no one could ever believe that such traumatic
removals could be anything but a brutalising and terrifying experience for the
children and families involved. *Working Together* gives specific guidance on
this matter:

> The removal of children from their home gives rise to public and professional
> concern, causes great distress if not handled sensitively and can be damaging both
> for the child and the rest of the family. Therefore, except when a child is in acute
> physical danger, it is essential that the timing of the removal of the children from
> their homes should be agreed, following consultation with all appropriate
> professionals. They should weigh up the likely immediate and long-term effects of
> removing the child against the possibility of harm if they leave the child at home and
> balance this with the need to secure evidence of criminal offences and, in some cases,
> to arrest the suspects. In many cases, there will be no need to remove a child and
> simultaneously arrest a suspect living in the same house. In other cases, however,
> particularly those involving several children and adults in different households, it
> may be important to prevent suspects from communicating with each other or
> destroying evidence. In those cases, it may be necessary for co-ordinated police
> action, distressing though this may be, at a time of day when the whole family is at
> home. In other cases, although early morning police action might secure better
> forensic evidence, such action may not be crucial to the overall welfare of the
> child(ren) and they should not therefore be part of the plan for an investigation. In
> all cases, the long-term protection of and well-being of the child will be the
> overriding concern, though the likelihood of securing the child's well-being through
> the courts will be an important consideration.[51]

A *child-centred approach*

The first thing that must be borne in mind in considering the position of
children at risk is that approximately 80 per cent of those children will return
home eventually and, while the professionals may have mentally crossed off
the family at the point of the child's removal, the child has to continue to live

---

50 The Report of the Inquiry into the Removal of Children from Orkney in February 1991
   (October 1992), Edinburgh, HMSO.
51 *Working Together, op. cit.*, para. 3.5.

with what has happened and to incorporate existing and ongoing relationships within the future fabric of a fragmented and traumatised life. In such situations, children are often amazingly loyal and adept at separating the abusive behaviour from other aspects of the abuser's personality. Professionals can sometimes be guilty of imposing their view of the alleged abuser as someone not worth taking into account in future planning for the child. The child may have a different view. Social workers can be somewhat cavalier with children's relationships, as is apparent when some of the outcomes of residential care are borne in mind. It is painful for social workers to have to acknowledge that in some cases life for children in care may be more hazardous than staying at home.

Ray Wyre's work with perpetrators of sexual abuse, at the Gracewell Clinic (now the Faithful Foundation), shows clearly that the abuse experience is not confined to the act of abuse. The victim may well have been on the receiving end not only of abuse, but of a whole battery of tactics to prevent disclosure. If, despite all this, the victim manages to disclose to a trusted adult, it is vital:

● that the disclosure be taken seriously; and
● that the child be allowed to maintain some control of an immensely frightening situation, by being involved in the planning (as far as possible) and by being given, firstly, reassurances that he will be protected and, secondly, information about when, how, where and for how long.

Children's evidence

Common myths about children's evidence are:

● children's memories are unreliable;
● children are egocentric;
● children are highly suggestible;
● children have difficulty distinguishing fact from fantasy;
● children make false allegations, particularly of sexual abuse.

In fact, false allegations tend to be instigated more by adults than by children, frequently in the context of a contact dispute.[52] Where children do make false allegations, it is usually for identifiable reasons and the major problem is not one of false allegations but of false retractions.[53] Children are no more likely to lie than adults. However, young children may not be so good at it as adults and are more likely to be detected.[54] In relation to children's evidence, the Pigot Committee (the Home Office Advisory Group on Video Evidence), reporting in 1989, said that, 'we understand, however, that, contrary to the traditional view, recent research shows that untruthful child witnesses are

---

52 Vizard and Tranter, 'Helping children describe experiences of child sexual abuse', in Bertovim, Elton, Hildegrand, Tranter and Vizard (eds.), *Child Sexual Abuse within the Family: Assessment and Treatment* (1988), John Wright.
53 See Richardson and Bacon (eds.), *Child Sexual Abuse: Whose Problem? Reflections from Cleveland* (1991).
54 Perry, 'Child and Adolescent Development: A Psychological Perspective', in Myers, *Child Witness Law and Practice* (1987), Wiley.

comparatively uncommon and, like their adult counterparts, they act out of identifiable motives'.[55]

Weak links in the chain of child protection

Differential approaches to the disclosure of abuse, depending on whether the child is in their own home or in residential care. If children disclose abuse in their own home, they are much more likely to be believed than if they disclose abuse while in residential care, because that involves one professional accepting that a professional who is a colleague has perpetrated acts which may defy belief. When children allege abuse in their own home or in a residential setting, the allegation may well be interpreted in terms of their bad relationship with that particular worker and, in some circumstances, it has been suggested that the child should sit down with the alleged perpetrator in an attempt to sort out why the child is making malicious allegations. What is needed is a co-ordinated approach to child abuse, which means that the child has an equal chance of being believed wherever the abuse occurs, in care, at home or in a foster home.

Lack of an Ouster Order to enable the alleged perpetrator to be removed from the home. This is a significant lacuna in the provisions of the Children Act 1989. Although the non-abusing parent can apply to the County Court for a short-term ouster injunction under S.1 of the Domestic Violence and Matrimonial Proceedings Act 1976 or, if they are married, for an Exclusion Order under S.16 of the Domestic Proceedings and Magistrates Court Act 1978, there is no direct provision for local authorities to exclude alleged perpetrators. This throws the responsibility for the decision on a spouse or partner, at a time when the situation may be too fraught for them to contemplate such an action.

Inconsistent protection of children. The detailed analysis contained in *One Scandal Too Many*[56] revealed dangerous inconsistencies and gaps in the protection for children, despite the Children Act. The report emphasised the need for comprehensive legal reforms which would give children clear rights and safeguards wherever they are living (see also Chapters 9 and 10 above). Aimless surveillance and monitoring are ineffective if they are not part of a tightly focused child protection plan, which takes into account key elements of risk in that particular child's situation. Parents and children must understand why the social workers are there; the professionals involved must have sufficient expertise to interpret the material gained through observation and assessment; and they must all understand the importance of giving children full information about the options available to them, and the right to have their wishes and feelings considered.

---

55 See also *The Child Witness Pack* (1993), published by the NSPCC and others, and *Memorandum of Good Practice on Video Recorded Interviews with Child Witnesses for Criminal Proceedings* (1992), Department of Health. For an in-depth examination, see Spencer and Flin, *The Evidence of Children: The Law and the Psychology*, 2nd edn (1993).
56 *One Scandal Too Many: The Case for Comprehensive Protection for Children in all Settings* (July 1993), Report of a Working Party convened by the Gulbenkian Foundation.

Professional confusion regarding confidentiality. Although *Working Together* sets out clear guidelines for the sharing of relevant information between agencies, in certain situations key professionals have withheld information which has been critical to the welfare of the child. It is a question of volunteering information, not just answering questions. Inter-agency communication must overlap, not just meet. Health visitors, in particular, sometimes feel reticent about giving negative information about families, when they may be the only professionals who are welcomed into the house. However, even though that information may not seem of direct relevance to an individual professional, it may be the piece which completes a whole picture. This is a clear example of putting the rights of children to be protected before the rights of adults to have their confidentiality respected. These are difficult professional and ethical dilemmas, but those with statutory child care responsibilities have a duty to give the welfare of the child paramount consideration.

Fragmented services

> The recent reorganisation of health authorities into purchasers and trusts, along with opting out moves current in education, has led to considerable fragmentation in services to children. For example, the multi-agency approach to child protection — fundamental to government policy on this issue — is put in serious danger by the disassembly of the health and education services. Strategies must be developed to ensure that child protection can be developed co-operatively.[57]

A lack of accurate charting of information (for example about relevant medical details such as percentile ratings, properly charted) can distort critical information in relation to children who are failing to thrive. In particular, the considerable area of overlap between services to children and families, from both health and social services departments, requires clarification. For example, do social workers have access to relevant information recorded by the school nursing service? There are interfacing, if not directly overlapping, areas of responsibility between health and social services, and there should be clearer procedures for delineating areas of responsibility and exchange of information.

Problems regarding the interface between criminal and care proceedings. There are practical conflicts between the aims of a criminal justice and child welfare system. The prime concern of the criminal court is to determine guilt or innocence, whereas in the civil court the child's welfare is paramount. Examples of this conflict are given by the Association of Directors of Social Services and the Council for Family Proceedings in their messages to Parliament concerning children:

> Police and social services are asked to work together, but have different aims. For example, over the last year there has been a marked increase in the number of cases in criminal proceedings which have had to be disclosed to the defence. This has caused significant problems to those agencies engaged in child protection work, for example, with other professionals and families, as they become aware that information provided on a confidential basis may have to be disclosed in a criminal

57 Association of Directors of Social Services, *A Message to Parliament Concerning Children* (November 1993), National Children's Bureau.

court. Sometimes, defence lawyers have appeared to go on fishing expeditions in files and then distort the information so as to put the victims on trial.[58]

Guardians *ad litem*, in particular, have experienced difficulties in obtaining access to criminal evidence. Similarly, in some instances they have been perturbed by being asked to act as witnesses in criminal proceedings. The precise interface between criminal and care proceedings, the evidence needed for each and the burdens of proof necessary for criminal and civil cases are still areas of confusion, certainly for parents and also for some professionals.

Where care and criminal proceedings are running concurrently, it is unacceptable that the care proceedings should be delayed to await the outcome of the criminal proceedings. The child's welfare must be the paramount consideration. In this respect, post-Children Act practice has reinforced earlier decisions in *R. v. Exeter Juvenile Court, ex p. H. and H.*[59] In *Re S. (Child Abuse Cases: Management)*,[60] Thorpe J stated that care cases should only exceptionally be held up pending the outcome of criminal proceedings, thus endorsing the views set out in a Home Office Circular in 1982. Nevertheless, lawyers representing their clients accused of child abuse may still see the paramountcy of that child's welfare as a potential barrier to the pursuit of justice in the criminal court.

Confusion of fact and opinion. In looking at 40 child protection conferences in 1990, Higginson found that the basis of the decision is often subjective and at variance with the evidence presented. The experience of many guardians *ad litem*, looking at social services files in the course of their investigations, is that, often, there is not a clear separation of fact and opinion. Events which were originally hearsay may acquire the status of truth through frequent repetition. It is always worth asking about the behaviour or incident which led to a particular opinion being formed.

In one case, the guardian was told that the child wanted to live with the maternal grandmother who was not a suitable carer because she was a rather peculiar old lady who was obsessed with death. Tracking this observation back to the incident which had occurred, the guardian found that the maternal grandmother, who was 60, had taken her 12-year-old granddaughter to put a bunch of flowers on her mother's grave during a contact visit. She had then sat with her granddaughter and looked at family photographs, which included pictures of the child's mother who had sadly committed suicide. This was considered inappropriate and unnecessarily morbid behaviour by the social services department, whose interpretation of events controlled the planning for the child. She herself wanted to live with her grandmother, who was equally keen to have her. She was, however, unsuccessfully placed with three different sets of foster parents because her grandmother had been judged unsuitable. As a result of a reappraisal of the behaviour exhibited by the grandmother in relation to the death of her daughter, the child's wishes were taken into consideration and she was successfully reunited with her grandmother.

---

58 *Ibid.* See also Lyon and de Cruz, *Child Abuse*, 1993 (2nd edn), Chapters 6 and 7.
59 (1988) 2 F.L.R. 214.
60 [1992] F.C.R. 31.

Local authorities should not be selective in the evidence they submit to courts. In *Re B. (Minors)* (Care Proceedings),[61] a social worker called by the local authority had been selective in the material she culled from the records from which she made up her statement. When she was challenged about this in cross-examination, she said she had reported what supported the local authority's case for a Care Order. The way in which the social worker had prepared her statement was to be deprecated. Applicants such as a local authority must present the case in a balanced way, and not fail to refer to factors which pointed in a direction opposite to that desired by the authority. Such selectivity may be carried out on the basis of a value-based assumption about the welfare of the child, rather than the balance of the evidence, and can effectively skew the planning for the child inappropriately at an early stage in decision making.

Lack of suitably experienced and qualified child protection workers. The Central Council for the Education and Training of Social Workers have estimated that 25 per cent of newly qualified social workers are allocated child protection cases within the first year of qualifying. There are fundamental concerns about the gaps in experience and knowledge between the skills offered by a two-year social work training and the high degree of professional competence and statutory accountability required in child protection work. Both the British Association of Social Workers and the Association of Directors of Social Services support the establishment of an Accredited Social Worker in Child Care, in the same way as there are Approved Social Workers in Mental Health.[62]

Children in Care

Volume 4 of the Children Act 1989 Guidance and Regulations is concerned with residential care. Volume 3 deals with family placement. The general conduct of children's homes is dealt with in the Children's Homes Regulations 1991[63] and in the Arrangements for Placement of Children (General) Regulations 1991.[64]

A cause for concern

At the end of March 1991, there were approximately 62,260 children in care in England and Wales, with a further approximate 41,000 on child protection registers in England and Wales.[65] Research has identified that the majority of the care population consists of young people in the 13 to 16 age range and that young people in residential placements are generally older than those in the care population as a whole. In his review of residential care in 1991, Sir

---

61 [1994] 1 F.C.R. 471.
62 *A Message to Parliament Concerning Children: Accredited Social Workers in Child Care* (November 1993), National Children's Bureau, p. 10.
63 S.I. 1991 No. 1506.
64 S.I. 1991 No. 890.
65 *NCH Fact File, op. cit.*

William Utting referred to the 1985 Social Services Inspectorate Inspection of Community Homes, which identified many children who, in addition to family breakdown, had experienced sexual abuse, violence within the family, repeated rejection and numerous changes of carer prior to admission to local authority care.[66] Sadly, a pilot study undertaken by the National Association of Young People in Care (NAYPIC) in 1990/91 indicated that, once in care, young people are frequently abused, both physically and sexually. The study showed that it was common practice for young people to be moved from home to home and 90 per cent of the sample complained of failure to be consulted about the decisions made about their lives. Either they had not been consulted at all about placements and reviews, or they felt that the consultation that was carried out was a meaningless exercise. The research also identified a number of cases where brothers and sisters were denied access to siblings or family. Contact was, at best, infrequent and, at worst, non-existent. This has also been the conclusion of research from the Dartington Research Unit, in 1986, whose study *Lost in Care* showed that nearly three-quarters of children experienced great difficulty in maintaining contact with their parents, in spite of the fact that the majority of those children will eventually return home. In one-third of cases, this was as a result of restrictions placed by social workers on entry to the residential establishments. Two-thirds of children in the early days of placement can face barriers such as hostility, distance and inaccessibility.[67]

Between 1981 and 1991 the total number of children in care decreased by 35 per cent, from 92,270 to 59,834. However, although the overall figures have fallen, there has been a rise in the number of children subject to statutory rather than voluntary provisions, indicating that, certainly before implementation of the 1989 Act, the state was intervening more in family life generally and particularly in the family life of the poor (if one accepts the substantial research findings which indicate that poverty in all its manifestations renders children more likely to be received into care).

> There is a well-established link between deprivation and children coming into care. Put crudely, the majority of children in care are the children of the poor. This does not mean that parental poverty was the sole or sufficient cause of their coming into care; that would be to deny the responsibility of individual parents and the obvious fact that most children never have to receive local authority care, but poor families are more at risk. Evidence from Equality for Children emphasises this. Studies have shown that the majority of children in care come either from one parent families or from families with an unemployed head of household, or both. Social work intervention alone cannot be expected to combat the cycle of poverty, bad housing and indebtedness. Social work can, however, be expected to ensure that the full range of services provided by the state and others reach those most at risk. The timely provision of such services to those families identified as being most at risk could help avert unnecessary receptions into care.[68]

---

66 *Children in the Public Care: A Review of Residential Child Care* (1991), carried out for the Social Services Inspectorate by Sir William Utting, HMSO.
67 See Moss, Sharp and Faye, *Abuse in the Care System: A Pilot Study by NAYPIC* (1990).
68 House of Commons Second Report from the Social Services Committee, Session 1983/84, *Children in Care*, Vol. 1 (March 28, 1984), para. 36. See also *Children Act Report*, 1993, HMSO, Chapter 4: 'Children looked after by the Local Authority'; 'looked after' describes both children being accommodated by a local authority under a voluntary agreement with parents, and children who are the subject of a care order.

It is difficult to view the concept of children's rights in isolation from other factors of social, economic and financial policies, all of which have a bearing on whether or not a child is able to be maintained in its family of origin. There is little point in having rights without the resources to provide the services to ensure that those rights can translate into improvements in health, care, education and housing.

The following statistics show how the care experience can substantially increase the vulnerability of some children and young people:

- One-third of young homeless people aged 16 to 19 have been in care.
- 66 per cent of young male prostitutes have a care background.
- 23 per cent of the adult prison population and 38 per cent of young offenders have been in care.
- 80 per cent of young people leaving care are unemployed after 2½ years.
- 35 per cent of young people leaving care have no educational qualifications.[69]

Speaking in a debate in the House of Lords in 1992 on Children's Homes, Lord Ennals urged the Government, local authorities and Members of Parliament in both Houses to be more willing to listen to the views of children and to understand their attitudes towards the situation in which they exist. He added:

> We do not consult the children on their experience within the care system. Nor do we place a high value on quality staff by insisting on appropriate training and rewarding them with appropriate salary levels.[70]

Leaving care. Figures from the National Children's Bureau put the numbers of young people leaving care with no qualifications at 72 per cent against a national average of 11 per cent.[71] National Children's Bureau research also indicated that 23 per cent of young women leaving care are already mothers.

The provisions of the 1989 Act for the 11,000 or so young people annually leaving care are particularly weak and have attracted widespread criticism. They are based on the fallacious assumption that it is possible for young people to leave home physically, emotionally, educationally and financially all on the same day, instead of as part of a gradual movement towards independence, with frequent return visits to be topped up with cash, care and clean clothes. Local authorities are required to advise, assist and befriend children who are looked after with a view to promoting their welfare when they cease to be looked after.[72]

There is ample scope for a lack of tangible provision which renders these young people particularly vulnerable, falling foul of both the social security and the housing benefit legislation. In September 1988, the majority of 16 and 17-year-olds lost all entitlement to income support.[73] Guarantees of places on Youth Training Schemes for all in that age group who were not in full-time

---

69 'Children's Homes: Care and Aftercare', *Hansard*, House of Lords, Vol. 535, col. 1332 (February 19, 1992).
70 *Ibid.*, col. 1333.
71 *Children Now*, *op. cit.*, p. 55.
72 Children Act 1989, s. 24(1).
73 See also Social Security Act 1989, S.5 *re* liability of parents to maintain children under the age of 19 in respect of whom income support is paid.

education were not fulfilled, often due to the limited availability of places in many areas. In October 1992, Youthaid (Working for Youth Employment) estimated that there were 124,000 young people not in work, education or training. Department of Employment Statistics showed a higher figure, indicating that in the summer of 1992 an average of 195,000 16 and 17-year-olds were without work. This represents and unemployment rate of around 24 per cent.[74] Unemployment is a short step from homelessness. A survey carried out by Social Work Today in September 1992 found that 75 per cent of local authorities place young people leaving care in bed and breakfast accommodation. In October 1992, CHAR (Campaign for Homeless And Rootless) reported that local authorities are unable to meet their obligations to house homeless 16 and 17-year-olds whose welfare is at risk. Nearly one in five local authorities did not accept that homelessness means that young people's welfare is at risk.[75]

Children from minority ethnic groups. Children from minority ethnic groups face all the problems of white children, exacerbated by potential problems of discrimination on the basis of race and culture. Black British children face particular difficulties:

> Welfare and educational services appear to have no real understanding of Asian and Afro-Caribbean cultural processes, and expect black children to adopt a 'white mask'. The irony is that, when black children do become honorary whites, they continue to face discrimination and racism. They therefore miss out on their cultural processes and solidarity, and also fail to achieve in the white world.[76]

There is a lack of both basic research and statistical information on the numbers and particular problems encountered by children from ethnic minority groups. Many local authorities do not have precise information on how many children from which ethnic group they have in their care and this makes it difficult to make either appropriate or sufficient service provision. The problem is compounded by the fact that it is difficult to transfer information on proportions of children from each minority group from one authority to another because of major differences in the ethnic mix of populations. Only 6 out of 33 boroughs have any special services for black care leavers.[77]

The most striking research findings are those which relate to the marked over-representation of children of mixed parentage in the care system. They are two and a half times more likely to enter care as white young people and to

---

74 *UK Agenda for Children* (1994), Children's Right Development Unit, p. 74, para. 4.4.2. See also two publications by the National Children's Bureau: Biehal, Clayden, Stein and Wade, 'Prepared for Living? — A Survey of Young People Leaving the Care of Three Local Authorities', 1994, and Louise Garnett, 'Leaving Care and After'.

75 *Children Now, op. cit.*, p. 48.

76 Popple and Popple, 'Black Children's Rights' in Franklin (ed.), *The Rights of Children* (1986).

77 Bonnerjea, *Leaving Care in London* (March 1990), London Boroughs Regional Planning Committee.

have multiple admissions.[78] In contrast, children from Asian communities have much lower rates of admission to care. The question here is whether the family and community networks diminish the need for public care, or whether the services offered are considered inappropriate for Asian children.

Concern following a spate of enquiries into abuse of children in care led to a Review of Residential Care in 1991, in which Sir William Utting welcomed the 1989 Act as:

> the most important piece of legislation affecting children this century. Among other provisions, it both extends and clarifies the responsibility of the local authority for assisting children and families in need and protecting and caring for children at risk.[79]

Young runaways: incidents of children missing in the UK annually

Between July 1989 and July 1990, 102,000 children were notified missing in the UK. Key findings in a National Children's Homes Report were:

- 67 per cent of all runaways are aged between 14 and 16;
- 65 per cent of individual runaways ran away only once during the year; 35 per cent ran away more than once and accounted for 73 per cent of runaway incidents;
- 70 per cent of runaways in the sample had run away from home and 30 per cent from care. Since fewer than 1 per cent of children and young people in England and Scotland are in care, this means that runaways from care are highly over-represented within the runaway population;
- 62 per cent of runaways from residential care run away more than once, compared with only 23 per cent of runaways from home. Runaways from care therefore appear more likely to run away repeatedly.[80]

Enquiries into the abuse of children in residential care

There have been at least as many, if not more, enquiries into the abuse of children in residential care as there have been enquiries into the abuse of

---

78 Bebbington and Miles, 'The Background of Children Who Enter Local Authority Care', *British Journal of Social Work*, Vol. 19, No. 5 (October 1989); Rowe, Hundleby and Garnett, *Child Care Now* (1989), BAAF Research Series 6. Reported in *Patterns and Outcomes in Child Placement: Messages from Current Research and their Implications* (1991), HMSO, pp. 13–17.

79 *Children in the Public Care, op. cit.*, Introductory, paras 2, 3 and 4. See also *The Pindown Experience and the Protection of Children*, the Report of the Staffordshire Child Care Enquiry 1990, published by Staffordshire County Council (1991); the Ty Mawr, Gwent Enquiry 1992; the Leeways, Spyways, Hollies and Melanie Klein Enquiries and Clwyd, Cleveland and Leicestershire Social Service Departments enquiries into abuse of children in residential care; *Planning Long-Term Placements: A Study of Experiences in Local Authorities of Planning and Achieving Long-Term Placements for Children* (1994), Department of Health, Social Services Inspectorate; and the report of the National Survey of Children's Services Plans: Progress made during 1993, Department of Health, Social Services Inspectorate.

80 National Children's Homes, *Young Runaways Report* (1992); see also Newman, *Young Runaways: Findings from Britain's First Safe House* (1989); Stein, Rees and Frost, *Running the Risk: Young People on the Streets of Britain Today* (1994), The Children's Society.

children in their own homes. The first which achieved wide publicity was the Kincora Enquiry,[81] involving allegations of sexual abuse and prostitution in nine different boys' homes in Northern Ireland. Other enquiries include the Leeways, Spyways and Melanie Klein Homes, the Report of the Staffordshire Child Care Enquiry,[82] the Ty Mawr, Castle Hill, Leicester and Clwyd Enquiries.[83]

One of the most disturbing features of abuse of children in residential care is that this is often not carried out in secret, but with the knowledge, if not the collusion, of other members of staff, whose prime concern should be the welfare of the children in their care. What was extraordinary was that, in the cases of Frank Beck in Leicester and Tony Latham in Staffordshire, both had been able to establish regimes which masqueraded as treatment, regression therapy or behaviour modification and which, therefore, were not perceived as outright cruelty. The lack of full independent and effective complaints procedures also meant that the practices could continue, undetected by the wider public, for a frightening length of time. Frank Beck was convicted on 17 different counts of sexual and physical assault, receiving five life sentences and a total of 33 years imprisonment. The Pindown regime, established as a way of controlling difficult children, was based on 10 basic rules:

- Clothes must be removed and stored in the office on arrival, along with money, cigarettes and personal possessions.
- Each child must bathe and wash their hair, regardless of the time of day or night, on arrival.
- Residents are allowed nightwear, underwear and dressing gown — no footwear (or outer clothes) of any description.
- All meals must be eaten in the bedroom. If a child wishes to go to the bathroom, have a drink or impart information, they must knock on their bedroom door and wait for duty staff to answer.
- Residents must not communicate with each other.
- Residents are not allowed personal possessions, e.g. jewellery, books, make-up, etc.
- Residents are not allowed television, music, magazines, cigarettes or telephone calls. Visits from social workers are permitted by arrangement with the team leader. Parents wishing to visit must arrange this through the team leader.
- During the day, residents should complete any school work as set, adhering strictly to the 9.00 a.m. to 4.00 p.m. working day with appropriate meal/drink breaks. All books and working materials should be removed after 4.00 p.m.

---

81 The Hughes Report (1985).
82 *The Pindown Experience and the Protection of Children*, op. cit.
83 See Report of the Enquiry into the Conduct of Leeways Children's Home (1985), published by the London Borough of Lewisham; *The Pindown Experience and the Protection of Children*, op. cit., the Ty Mawr Community Home Enquiry 1992, published by Gwent County Council; *The Kirkwood Report*, the Leicestershire Enquiry 1992, published by Leicestershire Social Services (1993). See also *Enquiry into Police Investigation of Complaints of Child and Sexual Abuse in Leicestershire Children's Homes* (1993), Police Complaints Authority; and the enquiry into the treatment of children at the St Charles Youth Treatment Centre, Department of Health (1991).

- Residents rise at 7.00 a.m. (including weekends), have a bath and wash their hair.
- Residents must be in bed by 7.00 p.m. (including weekends), after taking a bath.

Small wonder that one of the girls subjected to this regime jumped from an upper window, barefoot and in her nightclothes, and went in search of help. It was only after she contacted a solicitor, who in turn contacted the Director of Social Services in Staffordshire, that the whistle was finally blown — not, significantly, by a member of staff or any of the adults who must have been aware of the regime.

A key element in enquiries into abuse in residential care is the classification of basic human rights as privileges. Telephone calls, contact visits, even food in one case, are privileges to be earned or withheld by staff who may be all powerful in their own abusive systems. This power is exercised not just in respect of vulnerable children, but also in respect of other adults and professionals who become seduced into a distorted and punitive system in the name of treatment and — dare it be said — the best interests of the child. This is a clear illustration of how rights can regulate and inform welfare. If the residential workers in Leicestershire and Staffordshire had had a clear grounding and awareness of children's rights, even if they did not agree with them, they would at least have hesitated before colluding with a system clearly in breach of so many different Articles of the UN Convention on the Rights of the Child.

In July 1991, the Gulbenkian Foundation convened a working group to produce a report summarising existing safeguards, following implementation of the Children Act 1989, and indicating the reforms needed to provide an adequate and consistent framework of protection for all children and young people throughout the UK from injurious and humiliating treatment and punishment. The subsequent report, One Scandal Too Many, was published in July 1993. The Report highlighted the extraordinary lack of coherence and co-ordination in safeguards for children and young people, and sought a programme of comprehensive rather than piecemeal reform, to anticipate rather than to react to further scandals. The Report made a series of recommendations which would give children access to advice and counselling, advocacy and effective complaints procedures:

> Children and young people in all settings should be told how they can contact an independent advocate or representative who can advise them on important matters, in confidence, and help them to seek redress for any wrongs that they are suffering, by guiding them through complaints procedures and, where appropriate, representing them. In particular, information on how to contact an independent advocate or representative should be available through helplines for children, and information about any complaints procedures they may use.[84]

A wide range of children's organisations contributed to the final draft of the Report and endorsed the following statement:

> We support the case made in One Scandal Too Many for comprehensive reform to provide adequate protection for children and young people against ill treatment and

---

84 One Scandal Too Many, op. cit., p. 202, para. 2.1.

abuse and arbitrary restriction of liberty in all settings. We share the working group's concern at current inconsistencies and gaps in protection and, above all, at the way in which the law and social attitudes continue to condone deliberately hurting children as a form of punishment or treatment. While not necessarily endorsing every detailed recommendation in the report, we do endorse its approach, based on principles in the UN Convention which the government is committed to implementing, and we hope that appropriate inter-departmental action will follow its publication.[85]

The Utting and Warner Reports

The Utting Report. The public concern about standards and practices in residential child care, following the publication of the Pindown Experience, led to the setting up of a special review to consider all matters bearing upon residential child care in England, including the availability of resources of all kinds. The review was chaired by Sir William Utting, who commissioned a survey to find out the state of qualification and experience amongst residential staff. The results were not encouraging. Twenty local authorities were asked to complete a questionnaire and the exercise was designed to ensure that the findings would be representative of the national picture. The survey showed that residential care staff themselves were a beleaguered group, being under-qualified, under-paid and under-resourced. Of all the officers in charge, 33 per cent held a Certificate of Qualification in Social Work (CQSW), 40 per cent held a Certificate in Social Services (CSS) and 6 per cent a social care qualification. The remaining 20 per cent had no qualifications. Fewer than 50 per cent of assistant officers in charge had a social work or social care qualification, 37 per cent had been in post for under two years. No more than 5 per cent of care staff held either the CQSW or CSS and a further 18 per cent held another social care qualification, leaving over 75 per cent with no qualifications. Forty-five per cent of care staff had been in post for under two years.

Overall, the survey showed that the vast majority, some 70 per cent of staff of local authority homes for children, were unqualified, with a significant number being unqualified and in post for under two years. Such information as exists suggests that the proportion of residential child care staff who possess a relevant qualification is no higher than it was 10 years ago, which would imply a net loss of trained staff from residential care. This situation was described as deplorable.[86] The review revealed a sad picture of children's homes, staffed by workers with low morale, low self-esteem and low expectations, both of themselves and of the children. Children in residential care may be difficult to manage and require endless patience and commitment, but they are not there to be contained and controlled. They are there because courts and local authorities have decided that this will be the best situation for them, a situation which purports to meet their educational, developmental,

---

85 *Ibid.*, p. xiii.
86 *Children in the Public Care*, op. cit., paras 5.8, 5.9 and 5.10. See also 'Accommodating Children — A Review of Children's Homes in Wales', Welsh Office with Social Information Systems Ltd, 1991, and 'Another Kind of Home: A Review of Residential Care', The Social Work Services Inspectorate for Scotland, The Skinner Report, HMSO, Edinburgh, 1992.

emotional and physical needs. Ninety-eight per cent of children are in residential establishments in their own best interests. Only 2 per cent of the whole population of children in care are there on a Care Order made as a result of a criminal offence.[87]

In the past 10 years, residential care has become a much less favoured option than foster care. Some authorities have closed down all their children's homes and rely completely on family placements. The population of children in residential care is now generally older, more difficult and may have had a history of disrupted placements. The implications of this changing population are not that the children should be subjected to more punitive and repressive regimes, but that more money and time should be invested in selecting and training staff who have the qualifications and experience to meet their needs. Many residential care staff are more geared to the care of younger children than difficult teenagers and have few resources themselves to meet the challenges posed by children who may be both distressed and traumatised, in addition to the problems experienced as a function of normal adolescent development. The culture of any residential establishment is very much dependent on the personality and skills of the officer in charge. If none of the other staff members is sufficiently qualified or experienced to question the regime established by the head of care, then things can go badly wrong, as they did in Staffordshire, Leicestershire and elsewhere.

In such a situation, independent complaints procedures and access to advocacy services are essential if there are to be any safeguards within the system. The Utting Report recommended that the Department of Health consider extending the role of the independent visitor, particularly in relation to children with disabilities, but also in relation to all children in residential care.[88] The Review also recommended that the Local Authority Associations should consider offering a service of independent adjudication in cases of intractable dispute between a child and a care authority.[89] The Review further recommended, in response to the deep concern about such a poorly qualified workforce, that the Department of Health, the Central Council for Education and Training of Social Workers (CCETSW) and the Local Authority Associations form an action plan within the strategy for social services training to obtain, within five years, the output from qualifying training to provide the numbers of qualified staff needed.[90]

The Warner Report. On November 29, 1991, following the trial and conviction of Frank Beck at Leicester Crown Court for numerous sexual and other offences against young people in a local authority children's home, a Committee of Enquiry was set up with the following frame of reference:

> to examine selection and recruitment methods and criteria for staff working in children's homes and recommend practical improvements, and to make such further examination as the committee may consider justified of management and other

---

87 *Ibid.*, para. 40; see also *Working with Troubled and Troublesome Young People in Residential Settings: A Directory of Training Materials* (1993), the Open University.
88 *Children in the Public Care, op. cit.*, paras 3.39 and 3.48.
89 *Ibid.*, para. 3.50.
90 *Ibid.*, Recommendation 16.5.

issues relevant to the protection of children and young people and to the support and guidance of staff in such homes, and to report with recommendations to the Secretary of State for Health.

The enquiry concentrated on the recruitment, selection and appointment of staff in children's homes and the closely related issue of the management of homes, including appraisal, supervision and staff development.[91] The enquiry revealed a significant change in the composition of residential care establishments, with a diminishing local authority and voluntary sector function and a very rapidly expanding private sector. The average age of the children in homes was 14. About two-thirds of all the children in homes were considered to be suffering from emotional or behavioural difficulties. The enquiry found that this was unsurprising, considering that about one-third of the children in homes are reported to have been sexually abused. Some children's homes today have high proportions of sexually abused and behaviourally disturbed children, many substance abusers and many victims of serious violence within their own families.

These children were being looked after by largely unqualified and sometimes untrained staff, although they were not particularly young or inexperienced. The average age of heads of homes was about 40 and that of care staff was over 30. Over 80 per cent of local authorities appear to have no statement of minimum training requirements for care staff, so they have not worked out what training the staff ought to have. Some of the most troubled and demanding children in our society are being looked after in children's homes by an inadequately trained and experienced staff.[92] The enquiry made the point that children with such particular and special needs require not only qualified staff, but specialist qualified staff, because of their emotional and behavioural difficulties, yet only about 40 per cent of local authority homes had access to specialist psychological, psychotherapeutic and psychiatric services on a monthly or more frequent basis. Some have no access at all. It was clear that, in some parts of the country, the National Health Service had largely abandoned providing specialist support to children's homes and local authority staff had given up asking for help.[93] The enquiry found that there were only a minority of establishments where staff were given the support and counselling that they needed to deal with the many stressful situations which they faced on a daily basis. The enquiry summarised their concerns as follows:

● an increasing number of difficult children to care for in homes;
● low esteem of homes and staff, and consequent staff morale and recruitment problems;
● a lack of sustained attention to children's residential care by employers, senior management and social services departments;
● non-existent or inadequate arrangements for staff appraisal and supervision in many places and other poor management practices;

---

91 *Choosing with Care*, the Report of the Committee of Enquiry into the Selection, Development and Management of Staff in Children's Homes (the Warner Report) (1992). See also the Howe Report: 'The Quality of Care', Report of the Residential Staffs Inquiry 1992, Local Government Management Board.
92 *Ibid.*, paras 10.4 and 10.5.
93 *Ibid.*, para. 10.12.

- deficient and sometimes unsafe employment practices, with a need for a more systematic and rigorous approach to the recruitment, selection and appointment of staff;
- inadequate knowledge and training to enable staff to cope with the children in their care;
- a shortage of specialist support services from the NHS for the children and staff in homes, and deficiencies in the educational services provided for children in residential care;
- inadequate definition of policy and standards at the national level and an absence of adequate joint planning arrangements at the local level.

The enquiry also revealed a general lack of supervision of staff and some rather lax systems of recruitment and appointment of staff members. The enquiry made the point that, in view of the circumstances and the conditions of work, many staff do a remarkable job in trying circumstances, with very little thanks or reward. However, there was a feeling that staff were being set up to fail rather than to succeed because of 'poor management, low self-esteem, deficiencies in supervision and appraisal, and poor employment practices, especially in relation to the selection of staff and patchy management that too often loses interest or fails to respond to problems'.[94]

In addition, there had been a significant shift away from the use of residential establishments run by local authorities or voluntary organisations and a growth in the use of private sector provision. In response to concerns raised about this development and the prevalence of small unregistered children's homes, the then Under Secretary of State commissioned a study of small unregistered children's homes in the northwest of England in March 1993.

The report provided the background for the circular LAC(93)(16), issued to local authorities in August 1993.[95] The conclusions of the study were that, while some of the small children's homes offered valuable services, generally there was a need to ensure that the Arrangements for Placement of Children (General) Regulations 1991[96] and the Review of Children's Cases Regulations 1991[97] are applied in a 'more robust and comprehensive fashion than inspectors observed to be the case during this study'.

The circular lays down specific standards for the supervision of placements, including requirements that the social worker sees the child alone at each visit, checks the child's bedroom and other facilities, and responds without delay if the child makes a complaint about his care or treatment, or when there is a concern about the child's welfare. Basic standards are laid down relating to the use of adequate washing facilities, availability of adequate meals and rights to make private phone calls. The circular specifically prohibits any deprivation of food or drink or visits from the child's family and friends.

---

94 *Ibid.*, para. 10.21.
95 See *The Children Act 1989: Small Unregistered Children's Homes* (1994), Report of a Study by the Social Services Inspectorate; and LAC(93)(16), Provision of Accommodation and Maintenance for Children Looked After.
96 S.I. 1991 No. 890.
97 S.I. 1991 No. 895.

In view of the findings in these two major reports, S.1(5) of the Children Act 1989, which requires courts not to make an Order unless it would be better than making no Order at all, takes on a new significance. One wonders how many members of the case conferences and area child protection committees are fully aware of the full implications of making a Care Order and how many social workers fully appreciate the pros and cons of removal from home against the reality of residential care. The Warner Committee attracted criticism and controversy by suggesting that a two-year diploma in social work may not be a suitable training for residential care as it is now emerging. It was the view of the Committee that residential child care today justifies the creation of a new professional qualification, covering a wider range of disciplines than social work. It was proposed that this new qualification 'must be the equivalent of the Diploma of Social Work and could be acquired through accumulated modules in a system of staggered secondment which would not involve impossibly lengthy absences from the workplace'.[98] The proposed new diploma would focus on the group care of children and young people and would be the preferred professional qualification for staff working in children's residential care. The enquiry was somewhat contradictory in identifying these specialist needs of children, thereby implying that 'the task had become more, not less, complex, while at the same time maintaining that not all staff in children's homes need to be qualified at diploma level, and not all will aspire to such qualifications'.[99]

Social workers who have fought hard to establish the equal status and training needs of residential and fieldwork staff felt less happy about the proposal to replace the diploma with what may be perceived as a lesser qualification. The enquiry was undoubtedly influenced by the need to increase the quotas of qualified staff as a matter of urgency, but the proposal smacked of short-term expediency.

The care experience

In 1985 the Department of Health published the results of nine research projects examining social work decisions in child care. Six of them dealt directly with children in care and the findings were illuminating:

● Far less attention was given to what was to happen after admission than to whether or not to admit and, if children stayed long in care, social work attention faded.
● Children in care were likely to experience many changes of placement.
● Discharge or remaining in care was not usually the result of social work planning.
● Family links were seldom given much consideration. As a result, circumstantial barriers to access often went unrecognised and little practical help was offered to encourage parental visits so that the chances of a child's return home were diminished.

---

98 *Choosing with Care*, *op. cit.*, para. 7.33.
99 *Ibid.*, para. 7.35.

- Difficulties in maintaining links were exacerbated for both children and social workers by the rapidity with which the families of children in care changed and reconstituted themselves.
- Parents of children in care often felt pushed aside and disillusioned.
- Tension and misunderstandings were often caused by differing values and attitudes to child rearing held by parents, social workers and residential staff.
- When parents felt that their problems and wishes were understood, they valued this highly.[100]

In 1991, the Department of Health published a second compendium of research,[101] which endorsed the findings of the Short Committee in 1984 by showing clear links between deprivation and reception into care, thus confirming the impression that children in care are predominantly the children of the poor.[102]

Being in residential care may well compound educational problems. Social workers appear to be remarkably blasé about the damaging effects of disrupted schooling.[103] 'In fact the health and educational needs of children in care and their future employment prospects are tackled relatively rarely.'[104] Certainly, care appears to render young people more vulnerable to homelessness and conviction on criminal offences. Paradoxically, while adolescence appears to be lasting longer in the general population, in terms of young people's dependency on parents for accommodation, financial and emotional support, young care leavers are being expected to achieve total physical, emotional, financial and educational independence at 16, thus setting up a situation where the least equipped to cope are expected to survive in the most difficult of circumstances, on a benefit income (for a 16 year old) in 1993 of £29.50.[105]

Links with parents

There is now a substantial body of research showing the benefit to children of maintaining links with their parents and wider extended family. The emphasis placed on the maintenance of contact at all stages of the care career is one of the strongest themes of post-Children Act practice. Frequent access to parents is associated with fewer fostering breakdowns.[106] Few placements broke

---

100 *Social Work Decisions in Child Care: Recent Research Findings and their Implications* (1984), Department of Health and Social Security, HMSO. See also Packman, Randall and Jacques, *Who Needs Care? Social Work Decisions about Children* (1986); Millham, Bullock, Hosey and Haak, *Children Lost in Care: The Family Contacts of Children in Care* (1985); Vernon and Fruin, *In Care: A Study of Social Work Decision Making* (1985); Fisher, Marsh and Phillips with Sainsbury, *In and Out of Care: The Experience of Children, Parents and Social Workers* (1986); Rowe, Caine, Handleby and Keene, *Long-Term Foster Care* (1984); and Sinclair, *Decision Making in Statutory Reviews on Children in Care* (1984).
101 *Patterns and Outcomes in Child Placement, op. cit.*
102 Bebbington and Miles, *op. cit.*
103 Berridge and Cleaver, *Foster Home Breakdown* (1987).
104 Diana Robbins, *Child Care Policy: Putting it in Writing* (1990), Department of Health Social Services Inspectorate.
105 See Bonnerjea, *Leaving Care in London* (March 1990), London Boroughs Regional Planning Committee; and Styne and Carey, *Leaving Care* (1986).
106 Berridge and Cleaver, *op cit.*

down when family links were maintained,[107] and those children whose links with their birth families had been maintained throughout placements with permanent substitute families were protected against the adverse effects of long periods in care.[108] The research also highlights the importance of maintaining sibling relationships.[109]

There are dangers in over-simplification of research findings. Child care professionals have a disturbing propensity to swing from one policy to another, according to the latest wind of change. Nowhere is this more evident than in the reconstituted attitude towards contact. Clearly, all research findings act as a general backcloth to inform, against which policy in practice evolves and develops. However, there is no substitute for looking at the particular needs of an individual child at a particular point in time in a particular situation. Too often, decision making may be skewed by blanket policies or ideological commitments to a particular form of service delivery. General policies can inform, but should not override all other considerations. The skill lies not just in providing services, but in providing the right services at the right time to the right child.[110]

Summary

The nature and quality of the public care of children depends on the social, economic and political climate in which it operates. The introduction of the internal market into the provision of health and welfare services has had a considerable impact on the organisational and managerial environment of child care services. In reviewing 30 years of change for children, as the National Children's Bureau celebrated its 30th anniversary, Gillian Pugh commented that 'the consensus on the role of the welfare state is being challenged by a concern that we can no longer afford this level of support'.[111] She pointed out that the statutory responsibilities of social workers were no longer underpinned by a general subscription to the view that an investment in children was an investment in the future of the country. Increasingly, children made demands on the diminishing resources of the welfare state and were seen as children in need of control rather than care (in this sense, 'control' often meant controlled expenditure). Children in need, children at risk and children in care and their families were seen as sapping the strength and health of the nation, rather than having any significant contribution to make towards it. The caring professions were, to some extent, included in this alienation from society. Those who have no direct contribution to make to the wealth of the

---

107 Thoburn and Rowe, 'Research: A Snapshot of Permanent Family Placement', *Adoption and Fostering*, Vol. 12, No. 3 (1988).
108 Wedge and Mantle, *Sibling Groups and Social Work* (1991).
109 Whittaker, *The Experience of Residential Care from the Perspectives of Children, Parents and Caregivers* (1985), University of York and Rowe *et al.* (1984), *op. cit.* See also Barbara Kahan, 'Growing Up In Groups', National Institute for Social Work Research Unit, HMSO (1994).
110 See also Paige and Clarke (eds.), *Who Cares? Young People in Care Speak Out* (1976); Gardener, *Who Says? Choice and Control in Care* (1987).
111 'Concern', *The Quarterly Journal of the National Children's Bureau* (Winter 1993), No. 87.

nation did not satisfy current criteria of productivity and effectiveness. In such a climate, care was becoming an increasingly anachronistic word.

If neither parents nor the state can be relied upon always to be able or willing to put the best interests of the child before their own, the recognition and enforcement of a core collection of rights as a primary source of protection for children assumes a higher profile. The statutory framework provides the potential for the development of a philosophy and provision of service unparalleled in the rest of Europe. Engaging with the reality of realising that potential is a much harder and longer task. Services for children in need have been strangled at birth through lack of resources. Services for children at risk remain essentially interventionist and crisis-orientated rather than providing support for families, while the position of many children in residential care should be a matter of concern to every citizen:

> The Act reflects a convergence of values about children as individuals in their own right — citizens enjoying legal protection, the parents of tomorrow's children and the future of our society. It is essential that practice in relation to children in the public care reflects those values. Hitherto, in spite of best intentions, such children have often been disadvantaged and stigmatised. The duty of public care is to deal with those children as if they were our own.[112]

---

112 *Children in the Public Care*, *op. cit.*, Introduction, paras. 3 and 4.

Appendix 1

Guidelines for the Development of Child Care Services

Appendix — 'Summarised List of Principles' from *The Care of Children: Principles and Practice in Regulations and Guidance* (1989), Department of Health, HMSO.

(To avoid tedious repetition, the terms 'children' and 'young people' are used interchangeably and either or both should be assumed to cover the whole age range 0 – 18 years.)

(1) Children and young people and their parents should all be considered as individuals with particular needs and potentialities.

(2) Although some basic needs are universal, there can be a variety of ways of meeting them.

(3) Children are entitled to protection from neglect, abuse and exploitation.

(4) A child's age, sex, health, personality, race, culture and life experience are all relevant to any consideration of needs and vulnerability and have to be taken into account when planning or providing help.

(5) There are unique advantages for children in experiencing normal family life in their own birth family and every effort should be made to preserve the child's home and family links.

(6) Parents are individuals with needs of their own.

(7) The development of a working partnership with parents is usually the most effective route to providing supplementary or substitute care for their children.

(8) Admission to public care by virtue of a compulsory order is itself a risk to be balanced against others. So also is the accommodation of a child by a local authority.

(9) If young people cannot remain at home, placement with relatives or friends should be explored before other forms of placement are considered.

(10) If young people have to live apart from their family of origin, both they and their parents should be helped to consider alternatives and contribute to the making of an informed choice about the most appropriate form of care.

(11) When out-of-home care is necessary, active steps should be taken to ensure speedy return home.

(12) Parents should be expected and enabled to retain their responsibilities and to remain as closely involved as is consistent with their child's welfare, even if that child cannot live at home either temporarily or permanently.

(13) Siblings should not be separated when in care or when being looked after under voluntary arrangements unless this is part of a well thought out plan based on each child's needs.

(14) Family links should be actively maintained through visits and other forms of contact. Both parents are important even if one of them is no longer in the family home and father should not be overlooked or marginalised.

(15) Wider families matter as well as parents — especially siblings and grandparents.

(16) Continuity of relationships is important, and attachments should be respected, sustained and developed.

(17) Change of home, caregiver, social worker or school almost always carries some risk to a child's development and welfare.

(18) Time is a crucial element in child care and should be reckoned in days and months rather than years.

(19) Every young person needs to develop a secure sense of personal identity and all those with parental or caring responsibilities have a duty to offer encouragement and support in this task.

(20) All children need to develop self-confidence and a sense of self-worth, so alongside the development of identity, and equally important, is self-esteem.

(21) Since discrimination of all kinds is an everyday reality in many children's lives, every effort must be made to ensure that agency services and practices do not reflect or reinforce it.

(22) Corporate parenting is not 'good enough' on its own.

(23) Young people should not be disadvantaged or stigmatised by action taken on their behalf, e.g. as a result of admission to care or to special residential provision.

(24) Children's long-term welfare must be protected by prompt, positive and pro-active attention to the health and education of those in both short and long-term care.

(25) Young people's wishes must be elicited and taken seriously.

(26) As young people grow up, preparation for independence is a necessary and important part of the parental role which child care agencies carry for young people in long-term care.

(27) In carrying out the duties and responsibilities laid upon them in the legislation and regulations, local authorities should put into practice the principles of good work with children and families which are set out in the previous section.

(28) The various departments of a local authority (e.g. health, housing, education and social services) should co-operate to provide an integrated service and range of resources even when such co-operation is not specifically required by law.

(29) The twin issues of confidentiality and access to records need to be addressed by all local authorities and child care organisations.

(30) Caregivers are entitled to have appropriate information about any child or young person placed in their charge and have a duty to keep this confidential.

(31) Letters and documents which are sent to parents and young people should be written in language which is fully comprehensible to them.

(32) Planning is a crucial responsibility for all agencies providing services to children and their families.

(33) Agencies have special, parental responsibilities for the minority of children who are in long-term out-of-home placements.

(34) When alternatives are being considered and/or decisions made, certain individuals or groups may need to be involved.

(35) Services to vulnerable children have to be largely provided through those who give them day-to-day care whether these are parents, relatives, residential social workers or foster carers. In each case, a balance must be struck between offering carers support (thus building confidence) and holding them accountable for the child's well-being.

(36) Caregivers — whether parents, foster carers or residential staff — need both practical resources and a feeling of being valued if they are to give of their best.

(37) Appropriate training should be provided for carers.

(38) There should be machinery for resolving differences of view or minor disputes, e.g. through involvement of a team leader, fostering officer or other appropriate individual, or through re-negotiating written agreements at the request of any of the signatories.

(39) Agencies have a responsibility to support placements which they have made.

(40) Registers and records must be maintained and kept up to date.

(41) Co-operation between organisations, departments and individuals is crucial in the provision of protection for vulnerable children and also in ensuring proper use of available resources.

(42) Foster homes and residential establishments used for the placement of children should be reviewed at regular and suitable intervals, though this needs to be done sensitively so as to avoid undermining carers' confidence or making children feel insecure.

Chapter 12
Best Interests and Empowering Children: An Integrated Approach

The Best Interests of the Child

While there is a general consensus about the importance of safeguarding the child's best interests, attempts to identify those best interests, in the case of a particular child, take practitioners into an ideological minefield in which notions of protection and welfare jostle for position with those of natural justice and children's rights. In the last 15 years, the concept of 'best interests' has been increasingly questioned.[1] There is no one formula or course of action which can guarantee a child's best interests, nor is there an interpretation of that best interest which can protect all children all of the time. Social workers deal with no more than a balance of probabilities. In discussing the lack of accuracy in determining standards of best interests, Mnookin and Szwed make the following points:

> The attractions of the best interests standards are not difficult to understand. On the surface it is an appealing principle for the decisions made in the area of child care. We are often reminded that our children are our future and, of course, we strive to do the best for our heirs. The phrase is so idealistic, virtuous and high sounding that it defies criticism and can delude us into believing that its application is an achievement in itself. Its mere utterance can trap us into the self-deception that we are doing something effective and worthwhile. However, the flaw is that, what is best for any child, or even children in general, is often indeterminate and speculative and requires a highly individualised choice between alternatives.[2]

1 Taylor, Lacey and Bracken, *In Whose Best Interests?* (1980); Morris, Giller, Geach and Szwed, *Justice for Children* (1980); and Freeman, 'The Rights and Wrongs of Children' in Pinter (ed.), *Who Knows Best? Child Rearing Decisions, Parents and the State* (1983).
2 Mnookin and Szwed, 'The Best Interests Syndrome and the Allocation of Power' in Geach and Szwed (eds.), *Providing Civil Justice for Children* (1983), p. 7.

The concept of the best interests of the child should be approached with caution by all concerned professionals, mindful that best interests can quickly become a camouflage for vested interest which may pave the way, in turn, for the insidious enactment of self-fulfilling prophecies. As every parent knows, there is no one infallible formula for the successful bringing up of children. Rapaport and Strelitz have drawn attention to the various influences which help to establish what is normal practice within society at any given time. These beliefs and practices may be communicated by child care professionals who have taken over where religion, the feudal system and extended family networks have left off. The culture thus produced is an 'amalgam of scientifically based knowledge, folk belief, plausible inference and extrapolation and sheer wish. Together they create expectations of parenthood, with variations for this or that social class, ethnic group or religion'.[3]

Parents may be bombarded with the current received wisdom, but there is no science of parenting which can guarantee successful outcomes. Similarly, there is no universally acknowledged body of research which informs local authority decision making in relation to the best interests of children. What is needed is greater acknowledgement of the largely subjective nature of some of the values on which decisions may be made, together with a more forensic approach to the concept of best interests, aimed at extracting and evaluating factors which are the key determinants of best interests, rather than relying on blind faith and a belief in positive outcomes, based on the fact that those making the decisions have the child's best interests at heart. Just as Parker's research[4] found that a 'liberal welfare' model can produce a more punitive form of juvenile justice than a straight tariff system, so the 'best interest' model may be producing a more punitive form of care than one which is formulated around children's rights.

The Children Act 1989 establishes the right of children to have their welfare considered by the court as a paramount consideration,[5] acknowledges the right to have their wishes and feelings taken into account when decisions are being made about their lives,[6] and tries to ensure that the state only intervenes in situations in which the intervention will produce a better outcome than non-intervention.[7] The legislative framework allows for the development of a participatory model of practice, which incorporates the child's wishes and feelings as a key component in welfare decision making. Essentially, the model seeks to make decisions with children, rather than about children. Such an approach depends upon courts and child care law professionals being prepared to accept the right of the child to be consulted, while being able to understand the importance and value of using the child's wishes and feelings to achieve an appropriate balance of power between family and state autonomy. This requires a change of culture, as well as a change of legislation.

---

3 Rapaport and Strelitz, *Fathers, Mothers and Others* (1975).
4 Parker, *Receiving Juvenile Justice* (1981).
5 S.1(1).
6 Ss.1(3) and 22(4).
7 S.1(5). For a discussion of family and state autonomy, see Freud *et al.*, *Before the Best Interests of the Child* (1929), which argues for minimum state intervention.

The family's view of best interests

The view of natural parents is usually abundantly clear. They feel that the child's best interests are served by being with them. Once a child has been removed and a parent has fallen below acceptable standards of child care, it is extremely difficult to regain those parental responsibilities. Standards of care have to rise to a higher level for the local authority to consider placing the child back home. Natural parents whose children have been removed often complain that other people in the area are parenting at a much lower standard than they are, yet their children are still with them. This may well be true. The other parents may be at a different level on a downward spiral, which may end in reception into care, while the mother who is being subjected to the rigours of an Orange Book Assessment[8] is required to meet a much higher standard than formerly if she wishes to have her children returned to her. Natural parents can be totally bewildered by differing standards set, often retrospectively, by social workers, who are in the tremendously powerful position of being able to project their own standards of good parenting onto their clients. At one stage, the stimulation school enjoyed a great popularity, to the extent that a young mother could spend weeks down on her knees desperately trying to establish eye contact with her child and stimulate his flagging interest with legions of Fisher Price play people, while the foster mother and social worker dispassionately assessed her performance and the foster mother's children rampaged happily around the garden. At the end of the period of assessment, the mother could be told that she had failed to reach the required standard, even though there was no precise definition of what that standard was.

Inevitably, child care professionals tend to criticise parents according to their own particular standards. In one case, the play group leader took the view that a mother's insistence on accompanying her toddler to the lavatory was stifling his need for autonomy and babying him, while the social worker observed that, on another occasion, the mother didn't bother to accompany her child to the lavatory, thus exhibiting lack of attachment. The 'sweet syndrome' neatly illustrates the classic double-bind of the situation. If a mother brings sweets on a contact visit, it is bribery; if she does not, she shows lack of interest and appropriate motherly feeling. Natural parents who have had their children removed from them do not have a choice about whether to take the advice, and frequently jump through hoops to behave in ways which may make little sense to them, either culturally or emotionally.

Many natural parents are ashamed and demoralised by losing their child. They feel that they have failed as parents and as human beings. In an effort to be a good parent, a mother may fight to maintain links with her children and may frequently find it impossible to accept that contact may potentially be harmful to her children. Such recognition would involve accepting herself as totally worthless to the child, and ultimately to herself. This is one of the little understood aspects of policy and practice in relation to contact, for insufficient attention is paid to the psychological and emotional condition of a parent following removal of a child. If the process of grief and mourning were more

---

8 *Protecting Children: A Guide for Social Workers Undertaking a Comprehensive Assessment* (1988), Department of Health.

sensitively handled and understood by all agencies involved with the family, then the prospect of working in partnership with parents, and coming to satisfactory and reasonable arrangements for contact, would be much improved.

The foster and adoptive parents' view of best interests

Although foster parents have few legal rights in relation to the children in their care, they nevertheless exert enormous influence over the child's environment and development and often feel, with some justification, that, as they have the care of the child, they have a moral right to have a say in what is in his best interests. This means that foster parents can wield tremendous power, particularly in relation to working in partnership with parents and maintaining contacts. They also work closely with social services departments and, in some cases, an unhelpful collusion between the local authority and the foster parent can develop, with a focus on the failings of the natural parents in meeting the needs of the child who may have arrived at the foster home grubby, dirty and distressed. Yet foster parents are in an immensely difficult position themselves, particularly following the implementation of the Children Act 1989, about which they received little information and scant preparation, even though they may now often be faced with much increased demands in terms of links with the natural parents and the wider extended family. In working with foster parents, it is important to recognise the conflicts which they face. Holman identified two sorts of foster carers — exclusive and inclusive. He expanded this view, showing that exclusive foster parents often wish to distance the natural parents, taking the view that they, themselves, are the real parents and the representatives of the child's best interests.[9]

Holman showed that most social workers subscribe to an inclusive model of fostering, believing in the theory that natural parents should be involved in plans for the child, but inhibited, in practice, by the fear that the placement may break down if pressure is put on foster parents to incorporate natural parents into their lives.[10] Yet Holman found that foster parents are mainly of the exclusive type, seeing themselves as the true 'psychological' parents and seeking to exclude the biological family from the child's life.[11] In contrast, inclusive foster parents can offer love without having to regard themselves as the real parent.

Differentiation must be made, too, between the administrative and the emotional status of foster parents. On paper they may have been approved as short-term or long-term foster parents and may have made an intellectual acceptance of the need to incorporate the child's existing links and family within their own daily life routines. Emotionally, what foster parents want may be very different. Many go into fostering because of their overwhelming commitment to meeting the needs of individual children, not to encompass what may be perceived as unreasonable or over-intrusive demands from the

9   Holman, 'Exclusive and Inclusive Fostering' in *Fostering Parental Contact* (1982).
10   See also George, *Foster Care Theory in Practice* (1970), p. 54.
11   Holman, *op cit.*, p. 53.

natural parents and other members of the wider extended family. It was a significant omission that foster parents were not sufficiently involved in training for implementation of the Children Act 1989 and that, for many, the new contact provisions were both alarming and unwelcome.

Recognition of the different approaches is important for two reasons: firstly, because they can set up great conflicts of loyalty in the child and, secondly, because foster parents, who may really wish the child to become a permanent member of their family, can effectively undermine any plans for rehabilitation while remaining convinced that they are defending the child's best interests. Social workers should beware of collusion with foster parents and of delegating to foster parents the unfair responsibility for assessing natural parents who may often have something to offer the child, particularly in relation to considerations of identity, however irritating, slap-happy and intrusive they may be. Being a foster parent can be a thankless task, but being convinced that you are acting in the child's best interests is no guarantee of unbiased opinion. The enormous demands now placed on foster parents have significant implications for their recruitment and training. The training must include a commitment to the principles which underpin the Children Act, including partnership with parents and an assumption of reasonable contact. Although this should not constitute a dramatic change in emphasis compared with pre-Children Act practice, some of the confusions which surround the precise meaning of permanence have meant that post-Children Act policy and practice have been experienced as a major change in orientation, rather than a confirmation of existing best practice, and a firm basis for the establishment of increasing openness in adoption.[12]

The local authority's view of best interests

Local authorities have a statutory responsibility to give paramount consideration to the welfare of the child and all their decision making is governed by this requirement. However, it may not always be that the local authority view and the best interests of the child are one and the same thing, although there is a prevailing fantasy to that effect which manifests itself in the assertion that any contradiction of the local authority view is, by definition, failing to give consideration to the welfare of the child. There is a confusion on this point which makes it difficult for local authorities to change direction in their work with children and families, partly for fear of being shown to have failed in their statutory duty for which they may be accountable to the court or the social services committee. Local authorities' tremendous powers in relation to children are underpinned by a basic vulnerability, created by a lack of resources and a lack of trained and experienced personnel to meet the ever-growing needs of child care social work. Social services departments are constantly attempting to do more with less. Since 1971, social workers have had increased management, but reduced professional supervision and support,

---

12 See Fratter, Rowe, Sapsford and Thoburn, *Permanent Family Placement: A Decade of Experience* (1991); Mullender (ed.), *Open Adoption: The Philosophy and the Practice* (1991); and Lindsay, *Open Adoption: A Caring Option* (1988), Morning Glory Press.

which might have enabled them to contemplate alternative approaches to the best interests of the child. It is significant that, having first felt threatened by the emergence of guardians *ad litem* to appraise their work in relation to children, many social workers now welcome the guardian's involvement as an opportunity to obtain a second professional view. Court proceedings offer an opportunity for a change of direction in a system which can be very inflexible once the heavy vehicle of bureaucratic decision making has been set in motion.

It is sometimes overlooked that each local authority is, in effect, a law unto itself, formulating its own policies, practices, procedures and guidelines. There is very little time for comparison of policies and practices with other local authorities, so policies in relation to children and families can vary dramatically within a comparatively small geographical area. In addition, 'The number of children in care is significantly affected by the policies and practices adopted by a number of other agencies, education, police, housing, supplementary benefits and magistrates. All of this will have a bearing on the local authority planning for the child.'[13]

Blanket child care policies, formed to meet the needs of the majority of children, can sometimes work against the best interests of a particular child. Concerns have been expressed about local authorities who have closed all their residential accommodation for children, having taken the view that the interests of the children in their care are best served by being placed with families.

Factors affecting decision making in the best interests of the child

These may be broadly divided into general and specific factors.

General factors

- *The legislative framework* — relating to health, education, housing, social security and welfare in particular.
- *Local authority child care, structures and policies* — relating to primary health care, services to children and families, policies in relation to homelessness and housing generally, social security legislation, including the availability or non-availability of discretionary and specific grants, education, including the choices available and the provision for the education of children with special needs, and welfare services, particularly support services to children in need and their families.
- *Local authority policy in relation to the establishment of priority services* and targeted areas of service delivery will have a major impact on local authority decision making.

---

13   Association of Directors of Social Services Preliminary Evidence to the House of Commons: Second Report from the Social Services Committee, *Children in Care* (1983).

- *Resources.* Many services to children and families are resource limited, rather than needs led. Recommendations about what is necessary to secure the best interests of the child are very often made within the confines of available resources. 'Resources' in this sense mean not just physical or material resources, but resources in terms of the availability of suitably experienced and trained staff to carry out assessments and provide ongoing support to children and their families.

- *The social worker or child care professional's own skill, values and knowledge base.* Professionals are in a powerful position to interpret welfare decision making in the light of their own life experiences and systems of values, which may vary tremendously from worker to worker. All professionals should strive for objectivity, but should also be aware that some of their judgments will be more subjective than others.

- *Relevant literature and research.* Child care professionals, parents and others may be influenced by particular pieces of research or the publication of a particular book. *Children Who Wait* and *Beyond the Best Interests of the Child* are both examples of publications which had a considerable impact on prevailing child care theory and practice.[14]

- *Society's expectations* — these are affected by the attitudes prevailing in society at any given time, which may be influenced by major child abuse enquiries, crimes by or against children and by media coverage of issues to do with children and young people. Attitudes and expectations imposed by the outside world can certainly affect child care professionals.

- *Public safety.* In certain exceptional circumstances, the local authority may place the safety of the public above their duty to protect the individual child's best interests. S.22(6) of the Children Act 1989 qualifies the local authority's duty towards the child, if it appears to them that it is necessary for the purpose of protecting members of the public from serious injury. Similarly, under S.22(7), the Secretary of State may give directions to a local authority for the purpose of protecting members of the public from serious injury and local authorities must comply with those directions, even though doing so may not be consistent with their other duties under this section of the Act.

Specific factors

- *The wishes and feelings of the child.* S.1(3) and S.22 of the Act, together with Article 12 of the UN Convention on the Rights of the Child, place great emphasis on ascertaining the wishes and feelings of the child before either the court or the local authority makes decisions about his best interests.

- *The wishes and feelings of parents and carers.* The local authority have a general duty, in relation to children looked after by them, to consider the wishes and feelings of parents and carers in making any decision in relation to the child's welfare.[15]

---

14   Rowe and Lambert, *Children Who Wait* (1973), and Freud, Solnit and Goldstein, *Beyond the Best Interests of the Child* (1973).

15   Ss.22(4)(b) and (c), and 22(5)(b).

- *The risk involved in any particular course of action.* The welfare checklist directs the court to consider any harm which the child has suffered or is at risk of suffering. Any decision affecting the best interests of the child, therefore, must include an assessment of risk, specifically the risk of physical, sexual or emotional abuse and neglect.[16]
- *The natural parents' capacity for change.* The welfare checklist directs courts to consider how capable each of his parents, and any other person in relation to whom the court considers the question to be relevant, is of meeting the child's needs. This will also involve identifying particular needs and making an objective assessment of the needs of the individual child. The question of 'good enough' parenting is a ripe area for dispute and less than objective judgments. The evidence on which these judgments are based must be available to the court and to the challenge of other parties.[17]
- *The child's physical, emotional and educational needs.*[18]
- *The characteristics of the child* — including age, sex, background, race, culture and religion.[19]
- *Secure attachments*, or the likely effect on the child of any change in circumstances.[20] The importance of secure attachments has been emphasised by health and welfare professionals. In particular, Freud, Solnit and Goldstein emphasised the importance of the 'psychological parent' as the parent who provides the day-to-day care of the child.[21] Courts are often reluctant to disturb the status quo.[22]
- *Identity.* The effect of a possible disruption in placements and secure attachments must be considered alongside the question of the establishment and maintenance of the child's core identity. This is a particularly relevant issue when contemplating adoption for older children. It is not a matter which is referred to in the welfare checklist.[23]
- *Passage of time.* There is considerable evidence to show that many cases are decided through passage of time rather than on the facts of the case. Decisions are made on the basis of what is the best outcome in the circumstances, rather than what one would ideally have liked for the child, if matters had been decided earlier.[24]
- *The options available to the court.* Judicial and bureaucratic decision making will depend on what options are available to the court to secure the welfare of the child.[25] The Children Act 1989 offers a much more flexible range of alternatives for children and thus makes a positive contribution towards obtaining outcomes which will be in the best interests of the child.

---

16 S.1(3)(e).
17 S.1(2)(f).
18 S.1(3)(b).
19 Ss.1(3)(d) and 22(5)(c).
20 S.1(3)(c).
21 *Beyond the Best Interests of the Child* (1973).
22 S.1(3)(d). See Eekelaar and Clive, *Custody After Divorce* (1977).
23 See Triseliotis, 'Identity and Security in Long-term Fostering and Adoption', *Adoption and Fostering*, Vol. 7, No. 1 (1993).
24 See *Practice in Progress* (1993), Regional Reports from the Guardian *ad Litem* and Reporting Officer Conferences, IRCHIN with the Department of Health.
25 S.1(3)(g).

All of these factors will have a direct impact on differential interpretations of the child's best interests.

The Right of Children to have their Welfare Considered

Children's wishes and feelings must be ascertained in an effort to make appropriate decisions about their welfare. However, children's rights to have their welfare considered are by no means universal. All of the following groups of children would benefit from effective independent representation in decision making forums. The list is far from exhaustive, but highlights some areas of particular concern.

Children and education

Under the Education Act 1944, all children aged between five and sixteen have a right to education. The Education Act 1993 (Part III) imposes a duty on local education authorities to identify, assess and make appropriate provision for children with special educational needs. 'Special educational need' may be defined as a learning difficulty requiring educational provision which is additional to, or different from, that generally provided in maintained schools. Parents may challenge the local authority assessment and the proposed provision through appeal to a special educational needs tribunal. The Department of Education have issued a draft code of practice on the identification and assessment of special educational needs which, it is hoped, will address some of the difficulties which have been identified in relation to imprecise formulation of provision of special educational needs in statements, resource limitations at local education authority level and the complex inter-relationship between the delegation of budgets under local management of schools and local education authority provision. The Children's Legal Centre reports that a number of special needs enquiries to their advice service

> relate to the refusal, by local education authorities, to grant parents their request for an out of county school for their child, where the professional advice has clearly indicated that a school of that character is required for the child and there is no such provision within the county. While the 1993 Act now clearly provides for parents to be able to express their preference for a particular school, the Children's Legal Centre are concerned that certain requests may continue to be refused for resource reasons, on the stated ground of incompatibility with the efficient use of resources.[26]

Children have no right of separate representation at the special educational needs tribunal, which is a particular problem for children in care who have no parents to advocate on their behalf. Many young care leavers have expressed

---

26 Children's Legal Centre, 'Response to the Department of Education's Draft Code of Practice on the Identification and Assessment of Special Educational Needs', *Childright* (March 1994), No. 104.

concern at the low priority given to their educational needs and their lack of power or opportunity to affect decisions made about their schooling. Children who have been emotionally affected by abuse may be wrongly assessed and receive an inappropriate education which does not allow them to reach their educational potential.[27]

The statementing process has been abandoned in some areas, because it is not thought that it is in the children's interest to be labelled 'special' or 'different'. Difficulties experienced in assessment and statementing procedures in special education lead to long delays in the process, leaving the child without appropriate education and with diminishing chances of being included in mainstream planning.

Furthermore, there is no multi-agency planning to address the education, training and employment needs of young persons with disability at transition from full-time education to further and higher education. Nor is there clarity about the new funding arrangements for further education or about adequate standards of assessment for pupils with disability after the age of 16.[28] Meeting children's special needs should not undermine the rights of all children (both those with disabilities and those without) to an integrated system of education with pupils of their own age and from their own community.

Under the provisions of the Children Act 1989, social services departments became responsible for inspecting independent boarding schools involving 750 schools and 100,000 children. Some schools are still awaiting an inspection, while it is not clear that all schools which have been inspected have been measured by the same yardstick.[29] The Association of Directors of Social Services have stated that it is essential that the requirements to inspect independent boarding schools are not abandoned.[30]

Young people and poverty

Sixteen- and seventeen-year-olds can no longer receive income support as of right and have to claim hardship and show estrangement from their parents, in order to be eligible for help. While this change was intended as a measure to increase parental responsibility in relation to children, in fact it has meant that many young care leavers and others have been precipitated into primary poverty. In April 1993, 67,500 young people had no job, no training and no visible legal income. In the slightly higher age group (those aged 18 to 24), the

---

27 See 'The Care Experience', Chapter 11 above.
28 All Party Parliamentary Group for Children, *A Message to Parliament Concerning Children from Interested Associations and Organisations* (November 1993), National Children's Bureau.
29 *Ibid.*, p. 5.
30 *Ibid.*, p. 16. See also The Children Act 1989: Guidance and Regulations, Volume 5, 'Independent Schools'; and Children's (Homes, Arrangements for Placement, Reviews and Representations) (Miscellaneous Amendments) Regulations 1993, S.I. 1993/3069, exempting independent schools that are children's homes within the Children Act 1989, S.63 from some of the regulations. These regulations came into force on January 1, 1994.

level of income support was £34.80 a week, as opposed to £44.00 for those over the age of 24. The introduction of the Social Fund and the abolition of discretionary grants has meant that young people can no longer obtain grants for deposits or rent in advance.[31]

Young people and homelessness

Although S.27 of the Children Act 1989 enables social services departments to seek the help of housing departments in carrying out their responsibilities to provide services to children in need, there is no corresponding provision in housing legislation to require housing authorities to consider the welfare of children involved while making decisions about housing allocation and transfer. Such a principle could protect children from random placement in bed and breakfast, or other temporary accommodation, and could reinforce the principle that no child should be received into care because of homelessness.

S. 20(3) of the Children Act 1989 requires local authorities to provide accommodation for children in need whose welfare is likely to be seriously prejudiced unless they are provided with accommodation by the local authority. Young homeless people between the ages of 16 and 19 who fall into this category have difficulty in obtaining help, because of lack of resources or an inability to convince the authority that their welfare will be seriously prejudiced. There appears, particularly, to be some confusion between this definition and the Housing Act term of 'vulnerable'.

SHELTER has estimated that around 150,000 16- to 19-year-olds experience homelessness each year:

> More than 50,000 of these are in London. Young people under the age of 25 occupy 40 per cent of the country's furnished, rented accommodation. Ten per cent of this accommodation is unfit to live in. 830,000 young people live in bedsit accommodation which is substandard or unfit for habitation.[32]

The Social Security Act 1986 was seen as contributing directly to the rise in homelessness amongst young people. There are fears that, if implemented, the Department of Environment's Consultation Paper on the Review of Homeless Legislation will result in more young people being forced onto the streets and more children being received into care following the break-up of families due to homelessness.[33]

Children who offend

There has been a fall in the rate of juvenile offending, from 137,600 juveniles offending between the ages of 10 and 16 in 1987 to 110,600 in 1990. In the older age range, in 1987, 130,600 young adults between 17 and 20 were found guilty or cautioned for indictable offences, as opposed to 124,700 in

---

31   *Ibid.*, p. 23.
32   SHELTER (1989).
33   'Government Review of Homeless Legislation', *Childright* (March 1994), No. 104.

1990. Reconviction rates remain high and, of 14 to 16-year-olds sentenced to detention centres, 72 per cent are reconvicted. Eighty per cent of 15 to 16-year-olds sent to youth custody also re-offend. In the 17 to 20 year range, 62 per cent are reconvicted after going to detention centres. Prisons in the UK contain a far higher proportion of young people (24 per cent) than all other countries in Europe (apart from Ireland with 29 per cent).[34]

The Criminal Justice Act 1991 extended the scope of the new Youth Courts to 17-year-olds, abolished custody for 14-year-old boys and generally tightened up the criteria for custodial sentences while increasing the alternatives to custody. However, the solid body of research which supports the view that locking up young people carries more risks than not locking them up has been put under considerable pressure by recent highly publicised episodes of juvenile offending, leading to a general moral panic and fear that young people are out of control.

The Criminal Justice and Public Order Act 1994 provides for:

● new sentences of up to 14 years for juveniles aged 10 to 13 years convicted of serious offences;
● new Secure Training Orders of six months to two years for persistent offenders aged 12 to 14. There will be five new centres accommodating up to 40 children each;
● the doubling up of maximum sentences for 15 to 17-year-olds from one to two years.

Five organisations, including the Association of Chief Probation Officers and the Association of Directors of Social Services, have come together to form a group called 'New Approaches to Juvenile Crime', chaired by Baroness Faithful. The group opposes the introduction of the new Order in favour of working towards constructive measures to divert young people from crime.[35]

The purposes of the increased secure accommodation provision are defined as a mixture of punishment, education and training — the concepts of treatment or the welfare of the child being conspicuous by their absence. The new proposals signal a change in attitude which draws a sharp definition between punishment and welfare. Paradoxically, both routes may lead to secure accommodation in the same unit.

Every court dealing with a child or young person who is brought before it, either as an offender or otherwise, shall have regard to his or her welfare.[36]

---

34   The disparities are very marked. In Belgium, the figure is 0.5 per cent, Italy 1 per cent and Austria 2 per cent. Each year there are a number of suicides of young inmates in British prisons — 46 in 1987 and 37 in 1988 (National Children's Homes Fact File, *Children in Britain* (1992), p. 74). See also S. Milham, R. Bullock, K. Hosie, *Locking Up Children*, Saxon House, 1978.

35   See further *Creating More Criminals: New Approaches to Juvenile Crime*, Briefing Paper 1994. The briefing paper cites research which shows that juvenile offenders involved in non-custodial, supervised activities programmes vary between reconviction rates of 45 and 55 per cent, comparing very favourably with those released from custody with reconviction rates of 70 to 80 per cent. See also 'Criminal Justice Bill Published: Group Offers New Approach to Juveniles', *Childright* (January/February 1994), No. 193.

36   Children and Young Persons Act 1933, S.44, as amended by the Children and Young Persons Act 1969, S.6.

However, the duty to have regard to the welfare of the child is not paramount, as in family proceedings.

The proposals for the extension of secure accommodation to a much younger age group have attracted widespread criticism, being seen as a seriously retrograde step leading to an increased chance of re-offending for a greater number of younger children.

There is also a children's rights issue. The government are committed to implementing the UN Convention on the Rights of the Child, which specifically states that secure accommodation should only be used as a measure of last resort and for the shortest appropriate period of time.[37] This, taken in conjunction with Article 4 which lays an obligation on the state to undertake all appropriate legislative, administrative and other measures for the implementation of the rights recognised in the Convention, provides a framework against which it is hard to justify the provisions of the Criminal Justice and Public Order Bill, particularly as the government has committed £100 million to the establishment of secure training centres and put the contracts out to tender to private companies of unknown quality and expertise.[38]

The message to parliament from the Association of Chief Officers of Probation and the National Children's Homes, in common with many other people and bodies, is that:

> if there is a need for further action in relation to seriously delinquent children, this should be met by building on the best of existing experience and not by setting up new establishments running conceptually threadbare regimes, most of them at vast differences from the homes and social environments of the children concerned. Our young people are no more vicious, criminally minded or more persistent in offending than other Europeans, yet in the face of all the evidence of negative outcomes we continue to lock up comparatively high numbers of young people in both prison departments and social services accommodation. If we want a safer society where young people stop offending for good, rather than one where they are stopped only for the period they are detained, we should recognise, resource and use the many valid initiatives being offered as an alternative to custody — at a cheaper cost — yet current proposals suggest that the trend away from custody is being reversed and we will see a massive increase in numbers locked up.[39]

In 1994 there was an increase in the number of 15-year-olds remanded or sentenced to prison custody. Often this is a direct result of the local authority refusing to pay for secure accommodation and is in direct conflict with the government's stated intention to phase out remands to custody for this age group. The Howard League for Penal Reform have suggested that an independent agent should investigate, on a case-by-case basis, the reason for each 15-year-old being remanded to prison and seek to secure a more positive method of dealing with him or her. Accordingly, the Trouble-Shooter Project was set up in collaboration with Feltham Young Offenders Institution and Remand Centre. While recognising that the project is swimming against the tide, those operating the scheme believe that 'the independent perspective

---

37 Art. 37(b).
38 Community Care, February 10, 1994, 'Seen and Not Heard' in *Community Care* (weekly journal for social workers).
39 All Party Parliamentary Group for Children, *op. cit.*, p. 21.

which it offers and the additional resource which it makes available is of even greater value than ever'.[40]

The position of 17-year-olds remanded to custody is also a matter of concern as, unlike those under 16, they are treated as youths for the purposes of sentencing, but not in relation to bail and remand. Moreover, criminal courts in England and Wales dealing with 17 and 18-year-old offenders are under no obligation to consider their best interests. The purpose of the proceedings within the criminal justice system is to establish beyond reasonable doubt whether or not the young person has committed the offence with which he or she is charged. The court is not directly concerned with the welfare of the young person. In this context, reference should be made to the government's initiative[41] which provided a range of alternatives to custodial sentences for young offenders. According to the Association of Directors of Social Services, this not only reduced the level of custodial sentences but also offered a more than adequate level of protection to young offenders and their local communities.[42]

Children and health

In spite of the considerable interface between the provisions of the National Health Service and Community Care Act 1990 and the Children Act 1989 in providing primary care of, and services to, families and children in need, there is no principle concerning the best interests of children in the legislative framework of the National Health Service. Considerations of the child's welfare rely on the general duty of the medical professionals to consider the patient's welfare, but such principles do not cover the administration of health institutions.[43]

Young people and unemployment

Between July 1990 and July 1992, unemployment amongst young people aged 16 to 17 increased by 72 per cent and for those aged between 16 and 24 years by 66 per cent. The effect of unemployment is to increase the likelihood that those young people who are unable to obtain support from their parents will become homeless.[44]

Young people and social security

Social security tribunals, which hear direct appeals from young people aged 16 and 17, and tribunal hearings which cover immigration and nationality

---

40   *Childright* (March 1994), No. 104, Children's Legal Centre.
41   LAC 83(3).
42   All Party Parliamentary Group for Children, *op. cit.*, p. 22.
43   See further Newall, *The UN Convention and Children's Rights in the UK: Best Interests of the Child* (1991).
44   All Party Parliamentary Group for Children, *op. cit.*, p. 24.

appeals and may affect children indirectly, are not bound by any best interest principle.[45]

HIV infection and children

There are particular concerns regarding HIV infection and children in need.[46] In 1991, the World Health Organisation reported that there were 3,000 cases of AIDS in Europe in children under the age of 13. At the end of January 1993 there were 444 children born to HIV infected mothers in the UK and Eire, and a further 262 had received blood or other products known to be HIV positive.

Children and surrogacy

The Human Fertilisation and Embryology Act 1990 was initially silent on the subject of the interests or rights of children born as a result of artificial methods of conception. However, S.13(5), as amended, does require that account must have been taken of the welfare of any child who may be born as a result of such treatment (including the need of that child for a father) and any other child who may be affected by the birth before providing treatment services to a woman.[47]

All of these groups of children and young people are theoretically covered by the requirements of Article 3 of the UN Convention on the Rights of the Child, which states that in all actions concerning children, whether undertaken by public or private social work institutions, courts of law, administrative authorities or legislative bodies, the best interests of the child shall be of primary consideration. Compliance with the UN Convention on the Rights of the Child (see Chapter 2 above) will involve the overhaul of all pieces of legislation which not only relate directly to children, but which have implications or impinge on matters concerning the welfare of the child, so that all services to children in whatever field, health, education or welfare, can be developed from a coherent and consistent legislative framework. Compliance with Articles 3 and 12 requires not only that children shall have their best interests considered, but that they will have a right of participation and consultation in the decision-making process.

The Context of Welfare

One of the messages from the more punitive approaches towards children and particularly juvenile offenders is that the public at large are losing faith in the ability of welfare professionals to deal satisfactorily with today's problems. Social workers have failed to prevent the break-up of families or stem the

---

45 See Newall, op. cit.
46 See Batty (ed.), HIV Infection and Children in Need (1993).
47 See Chapter 8 above, 'Children born as a result of surrogacy arrangements' and 'The role of the guardian ad litem in surrogacy arrangements'.

increasing flow of child abuse and have consistently shown that they are not able to provide universal solutions after only two years' training.[48] Ten years of swingeing cuts in departmental budgets have contributed to the problem. An article in *The Sunday Times* of July 18, 1993, entitled 'Clueless, Tactless or Hapless — what is a social worker?', was typical in its illustration of society's ambivalent feelings towards social work. Social work has been under attack from the state too, which, as Chris Jones and Tony Novak point out:

> has challenged its legitimacy and sense of identity. In the wake of this onslaught, social work has not only been thrown onto the defensive but has become characterised by a degree of demoralisation unparalleled in its history. In this context and driven by legislative and administrative reform, the relationship between social workers and their clients has also been critically changed to one that is increasingly characterised by antagonism and mistrust. While social workers feel and act like besieged gatekeepers to an inadequate and crumbling system of support, they have been pushed remorselessly towards practices of surveillance, monitoring and control.[49]

Child care social workers have been picked out for particular criticism in respect of child abuse. Attempting to achieve the correct balance between maintaining the integrity of the family (said by the Lord Chancellor to be a basic building block of a free and democratic society) and acting as the agents of state intervention into family life has always been the most complex and onerous job in any social services department. Public opinion is fickle and, in the past 20 years, child care social workers have had little support or encouragement from a press which has been remorseless in its criticisms, not just of the perceived results of social work intervention but of the concept of social work itself. Paradoxically, social workers attract criticism from both sides of the political spectrum. Social services departments are perceived by the right as an institutionalised manifestation of the dependency culture, staffed largely by politically correct young socialists who roll their own cigarettes and are a far cry from the days of the Lady Almoner with her white coat and neat felt 'Institute of Almoners' hat. Meanwhile, the left worries about social workers who act as agents of an essentially patriarchal interventionist state.[50]

The response of child care social workers has, sadly, been to retreat into a form of defensive social work practice, which has more to do with determining accountability for decisions taken than with the nature of the decisions themselves.

> A level three social worker in a children and families team reported that due to the pressure of media attention and the endless re-examination of practice ... the response ... from within the system has been to take out a place of safety order just in case, in order to cover your back. At least this is the advice of the management ...[51]

---

48 The British government have consistently rejected proposals from the profession to extend social work training to three years. The Diploma in Social Work is a two-year course.
49 Jones and Novak, 'Social Work Today', *British Journal of Social Work*, Vol. 23, No. 23 (June 1993), p.196.
50 See Campbell, *Unofficial Secrets* (1988).
51 Jones and Novak, *Social Work in Crisis* (1989), quoting NALGO, *op. cit.*, p. 203.

It is, therefore, a somewhat confused and demoralised workforce which is being called upon to deal with the major changes in the provision of social welfare which are being introduced by the National Health Service and Community Care Act 1990 and the 1989 Act, both of which reflect a change in culture away from a paternalistic form of welfare provision towards a more consumer-led service, in which service providers are increasingly accountable to service users. What we are seeing, according to Terry Bamford, Director of Social Services for Kensington and Chelsea, is:

> a retreat from direct service provision by the public sector, a shift to a regulatory role and the creation of a competitive market in social welfare provision. Within the health service, the NHS and Community Care Act is designed to create an internal market, with authorities buying services from one another and competing on cost. So, too, within the personal social services, the Government aims to create a mixed economy of welfare . . .[52]

The new legislation and the introduction of the purchaser/provider split are signalling not just a new wrinkle in existing policies, but a manifestation of major changes in social welfare provision, changes which are arguably more fundamental than those introduced by the Local Authorities Social Services Act in 1971. The introduction of compulsory competitive tendering emphasises the responsibility of local authorities to their finance departments, before their responsibility to service users. Without effective rights-based services, the paradoxical notion of contracts for care may mean that children and young people participate in decision making only as passive recipients of services which have been pre-packaged for their own good, according to a corporate formula of best interests.

Key Factors in Service Provision

Since the creation of the generic social work departments in 1971, social work with children and families has been provided as part of a local authority's general responsibility to provide services to a number of client groups. Pre-existing children's departments were incorporated into the new generic departments and social work training was reorganised to provide social workers with a general experience of all types of case rather than a specialist experience of more limited requirements. With the creation of the Certificate of Qualification in Social Work, basic social work training was cut to two, rather than three, years. The structure of the profession changed too. Instead of belonging to a particular professional association, such as the Association of Medical Social Workers or Child Care Officers, social workers were absorbed into the hierarchy of local government services. The new structure, with its clear bureaucracy of line management responsibility, progressively undermined the development of individual professional accountability. As one director of social services said: 'I don't think anyone working in any local authority feels that he operates as a fully autonomous professional. It's not the

---

52   Bamford, Address to the British Association of Social Workers (1992).

way local authorities are set up.'[53] Decisions within social services departments are usually reached by a collective process and it is possible to
sympathise with a member of an emergency night duty team who said: 'I like
working at night. It's the only way I can make a decision on my own.'

The plethora of procedures and guidelines accompanying the
implementation of the Children Act 1989 and the increasing requirement to fill
out forms of all descriptions are tacit acknowledgements of the fact that, after
nearly 25 years of life within the local government hierarchy, professional
social work is more a matter of quality control through inspection, monitoring
and measurement than the appropriate exercise of a proper professional
discretion by suitably trained and experienced practitioners.

The purchaser/provider split

The introduction of the purchaser/provider split into the provision of social
welfare has further compounded the problems in that it has imposed an alien
model of service provision on what has traditionally been a needs-led service.
In the new world, social workers are providers and are increasingly distanced
from the main purchasing power base. Social workers are seeking new careers
in care management and assessment, and are, increasingly, losing touch with
their traditional skills which were based in enhancing, rather than measuring,
the quality of human relationships.

Shortage of resources

Consistent cuts in public sector budgets in the last 15 years have led to the
establishment of resource-limited, rather than needs-led, services for children
and families. Grave concerns about the lack of resources for the proper
implementation of the Children Act were expressed consistently throughout
the passage of the Bill through both Houses. Supportive services to children
and families have been particularly resource starved, but there has been a
general lack of investment in the development of social work practice which
has led to a consistently low morale within the profession. Changes in
legislation in the last decade, such as the introduction of the Social Fund, the
establishment of the Child Support Agency and restrictions on the claiming of
unemployment, invalidity or incapacity benefit, have collectively eroded the
traditions of liberal welfare provision. Social workers are increasingly driven
into defensive forms of practice which revolve around crisis management
rather than long-term preventive care:

> Gatekeeping is no longer subtle. We lock the front doors and, if needs be, put on the
> ansaphone. The effect is frustrating for consumers and workers. Anger is seemingly
> more in evidence and so is desperation. There are many children in care without
> allocated workers, without, let me stress, allocated parents. I now often consider an
> admission to care more an abuse than remaining at home. Supervision orders are left
> to languish, as are the kids at the back of them. Social enquiry reports often cannot

53   Leo Goodman, Director of Wandsworth Social Services Department (1983). Reported in
      Social Work Today, Vol. 14 (May 24, 1983), p. 4.

be completed in Harringay due to severe staff cuts and local union action over unallocated work. The result for kids and their families: no result . . . The freezing of aids and adaptations budgets means that clients already waiting eighteen months for an occupational therapy service cannot have one after all.[54]

This graphic description sums up current pressures of child care social work.

Local authority accountability

Social services departments' collective decision-making processes, which arise as a function of their method of organisation, do not always work in favour of individual children. Many professionals may be involved with a child, in one case as many as 30, but each one views the child in the light of his own agency function or statutory responsibility. There is a lack of focus on the whole child, who may become compartmentalised into oblivion. In addition, local authorities have a limited accountability for their actions in relation to children in public care who, apparently, have no right to sue a local authority for its failure to protect them.

In a case in which children sued a local authority, through the Official Solicitor as their next friend, for damages as a result of negligence and/or a breach of statutory duty, it was held that parliament had not intended any private law right of action for the following reasons:

- following *A. v. Liverpool City Council*,[55] the only challenge to local authority discretion lay in judicial review and not in wardship. It therefore followed that there is no existence of a private law right.
- this has not been challenged by parliament and the Children Act 1989 supports this approach.
- if a local authority might be liable in private law for breach of statutory duty, so might other agencies involved in the decision-making process, such as police, health and education authorities. This could give rise to claims in the courts for contribution between them and was an indication that parliament had not intended that this should be so.

As regards negligence, no tort of negligence by a local authority was recognised in common law and compelling reasons of social policy had to exist before such a tort should be recognised. The court accepted the local authority's claim that it was contrary to public interest that such claims should be allowed. Private law actions would not assist local authorities to discharge their duties to others whom they should be assisting. Scarce resources would be diverted into investigations and record keeping might become guarded and defensive.[56]

---

54 Oppenheim (1987), quoted in Jones and Novak, 'Social Work Today', *British Journal of Social Work*, Vol. 23, No. 3 (June 1993), pp. 203–204.
55 [1982] A.C. 363.
56 *X. v. Bedfordshire County Council*, *The Times*, November 24, 1993 and reported in *Childright* (March 1994), No. 104.

It is regrettable that the decision in *A. v. Liverpool City Council*[57] continues to have such a negative impact on the ability of parents and children to challenge local authority decisions made in their 'best interests'. *A. v. Liverpool City Council* found its way to the Court of Appeal following a period in which local authority social workers in Liverpool had been on strike for a continuous period of more than six months. The question of how, or in whom, parental responsibility for children in care was vested during the period of the strike has never been satisfactorily answered. What happens when the local authority effectively abandons its children? Collective responsibility for individual children within local authority structures is exposed as a myth at the elected members level. It is often impossible to find out who bears the ultimate responsibility for individual children in care or, indeed, who was directly responsible for their welfare at any given time. Much depends on S.26 representations and complaints procedures being sufficiently robust and independent to challenge local authority decision making. This remains in doubt, particularly when it is children and young people who are attempting to initiate complex procedures without independent advocacy. The Secretary of State's S.84 default powers in relation to the failure of local authorities to comply with their statutory duty have yet to be fully explored.

It is within this general context of welfare that services to children in need, children at risk and children in care must be viewed.

Empowering Children

Involving children in decision making

In recent years there has been something of a growth industry in communicating with children, sometimes losing sight of the fact that such communication is not an end in itself, but the means to an end; namely, the identification of the child's stated wishes and feelings and an assessment of the impact of those wishes and feelings on plans for future care. There are clear advantages in involving children in future planning:

- involving children in decision making increases their sense of identity, self-esteem and personal autonomy. It enhances their sense of direction and gives them some element of control of what are often distressing and traumatic events;
- if children have been involved in the making of a decision, they have a sense of 'ownership' and an emotional investment in positive outcomes, which means that plans are more likely to succeed;

---

57 [1982] A.C. 363. See also *R v Kingston upon Thames Royal Borough ex p. T.* [1994] 1 F.C.R. 232 Q.B.D., which showed the court's reluctance to resort to judicial review on the basis that the representation procedure was a more appropriate remedy. Furthermore, the shortage of resources was something courts were entitled to take into account. See also *R v London Borough of Brent ex p. S.* [1994] 1 F.L.R. 203 (C.A.) This case concerned the duty of the local authority to provide suitable accommodation for an autistic child. In rejecting the boy's application for judicial review, the Court of Appeal considered that the decision was not 'Wednesbury' unreasonable, and the S.26 representations procedure would have been the appropriate course to pursue. Neither the boy nor his grandparents knew of the existence of the representations procedure.

- even if consultation does not lead to the outcome the child would have preferred, participation in the decision-making process can still leave the child with positive feelings about himself and the fact that he has been treated with respect;
- it is possible to allow children to have an input into the decision-making process without burdening them with the responsibility for making the decision;
- the child's perspective may encourage adults, or agencies, to think more flexibly or consider a wider range of alternatives.

Rights and responsibilities

There may be a tension between the responsibility of courts and welfare professionals to protect children and the right of children to have their wishes and feelings taken into consideration in decision making. It is a paradox that those who are the most successful advocates for the welfare of the child, in general terms, have the most difficulty with the concept of rights and responsibility. The right of children to have their wishes and feelings considered in decision making does not imply an accompanying right to determine the outcome of that decision making, nor does it imply that, by expressing a view, the child somehow assumes responsibility for the final outcome. Consulting children does not mean colluding with children, nor does it mean that children sacrifice their right to be protected by the courts and welfare agencies. On the other hand, the view that children cannot have rights, including rights to participate in decision making, without attendant responsibilities is an area of particular confusion. Children are not to be burdened with responsibility, yet they are not to be given the privilege of being consulted, because they cannot give a guarantee that they will make responsible decisions. It is this filtering of rights, through welfare, which can distort decision making in a particular case.

The only way to develop responsibility and responsible attitudes is through practice. The right to autonomy, with its attendant responsibility, is not something which happens at a particular age, but should rather be part of a dynamic process towards independence and self-realisation, which grows within an atmosphere of trust and mutual respect between parent and child from the moment that a toddler learns to tie his or her own shoelaces. The role of the adult in the child's world is to facilitate the child's growth and maturation by encouraging him to exercise free will in decisions which are appropriate to his age and understanding. In younger children, this process is geared around the attainment of physical independence and managing a physical environment. As the child gets older, it is concerned with the development of emotional autonomy. Of course, this will depend on responsible adults being prepared to relinquish aspects of their control over the child, to allow him to exercise free will and test the water of self-determination. Sometimes the young person will make mistakes — that is an inevitable part of the process. Mia Kelmer Pringle has emphasised the development of responsibility as a skill to be practised:

How can responsibility be given to the immature and to the irresponsible? There is no way out of the dilemma that, unless it is granted, the child cannot learn how to exercise it. Like every other skill, it needs to be practised under adult guidance, which then gradually diminishes during adolescence and adulthood. That it is worth taking the risks involved has been shown by the work of those who make this a central issue for their care for deprived, disturbed or delinquent young people.

Further, she says that:

Help needs to be given in defining the problem, providing the necessary information (or where it can be found) and assisting in the process of weighing up and predicting the likely consequences of alternative choices. Next, the decision must really be the young person's who, consequently, must also be allowed to cope with its outcome. Then the adult should not interfere, even if he disagrees with the choice made (unless the wrong decision would really be quite disastrous). At the same time, he should be prepared to stand by the adolescent if things do go wrong and give what help he can in putting things right.[58]

This sounds very much like a blueprint for the development of advocacy services and is certainly very similar to the approach adopted by children's advocates:

Advocacy is about empowerment. It is about supporting young people in speaking for themselves or presenting their views for them. It is about helping young people to make informed and free choices. It is about advising, assisting, supporting. It is not about pressurising or persuading.[59]

If things work well, young people become systematically empowered as part of the process of growing up in a supportive and trusted environment. This process is, of course, dependent on the good offices of adults, as children, generally, are a powerless group. However, children at risk, children in need and children in care, as well as the other groups of children discussed, are powerless because of their position, either in their family or in society, as well as being generally vulnerable as young people.

Involving young people in decision making is something that can be done on both an individual and a group basis. Children's advocates can help individual children or groups of children facing specific problems, like home closure, but in the wider context of society, compliance with Article 12 of the UN Convention would encourage children to participate in decision making in schools and residential establishments. Adults have some lessons to learn about how to involve children, as one 12-year-old boy found after attending a conference on children's rights which set out to encourage children to be involved in the day's events: 'In the workshops when I had something to say and all the adults were talking, they wouldn't take any notice of me, but when they thought I should say something they would say "now let's have a young person's opinion about this" . . . and I wouldn't have one.'[60]

If children's rights to be consulted are dependent upon whether or not those who have authority over them consider it is in their best interests to have those rights, then in fact they have no rights at all. In one case, a 15-year-old boy, in

---

58 Pringle, *The Needs of Children* (3rd ed., 1986), Routledge, pp. 56–7.
59 *Advocacy for Children and Young People* (1993), ASC (Advice, Advocacy and Representation Services for Children and Young People), p. 10.
60 *Ibid.*, p. 26.

the care of the local authority, asked to see a children's panel solicitor following an incident of alleged physical abuse by a member of staff. He was told that he could not see a solicitor because it was not in his best interests, a view which poses the question of whether or not a child in care has a right to seek legal advice. Clearly they have, but in such head-on collisions between rights and welfare, welfare may be used to ration rights in an unacceptable manner. Situations in which young people wish to return home to a potentially abusive situation are more problematic. Many of the problems which arise in relation to involving children in decision making arise because adults are not used to relinquishing any of their control in relation to children. In addition, the framework of services to children and families does not allow for participation in the decision-making process by the client. In reality, it is the children who carry the responsibility for the decisions being made by adults. They live with the reality of those decisions every hour, while the professionals go home at five o'clock and comfort themselves with the reassurance that whatever decisions they have made have been in the best interests of the child.

It is not necessary, or desirable, for children and young people to assume total responsibility for their own lives. This would be neither appropriate nor reasonable. What children want is not necessarily what children need, although these two aims need not be mutually exclusive and it is unfortunate that ascertaining children's wishes and feelings has become so clearly identified with a perceived corollary of commitment to children's rights. Children must not be left to the mercy of their rights — they have a right to protection. As Michael Freeman says:

> We would not be taking rights seriously if we only respected autonomy when we consider the agent was doing the right thing, but we also would be failing to recognise a child's integrity if we allowed him to choose an action, such as using heroin or choosing not to attend school, which could seriously, and systematically, impair the attainment of full personality and development subsequently. The test of irrationality must also be confined so that it justifies intervention only to the extent necessary to obviate the immediate harm, or to develop the capacities of rational choice by which the individual may have a reasonable chance of avoiding such harms. The question we should ask ourselves is, 'What sort of action, or conduct, would we wish, as children, to be shielded against, on the assumption that we would want to mature to a rationally autonomous adulthood, and be capable of deciding on our own system of events, as free and rational beings?' We would, I believe, choose principles that would enable children to mature to independent adulthood.[61]

On this analysis, it is possible to forge a middle ground which incorporates the child's right of self-determinism without sacrificing the child's right to be protected. As Freeman says, 'We need to change childhood, but this need not mean ignoring its existence.'[62]

Self-determinism need not be destructive. Such an approach draws on the principles of client-centred therapy, established by Carl Rogers, while theories about the self-realisation of the individual[63] take account not just of the best

---

61   Freeman, 'Taking Children's Rights More Seriously' in Olsten, Parker and Seymour (eds.), *Children's Rights and the Law* (1993), p. 67.
62   Freeman, *The Rights and Wrongs of Children* (1983), Pinter, p. 5.
63   See Store, *The Integrity of the Personality* (1960).

interests of the child that is, but of the long-term life goals and emotional health of the unique adult that child will become. It respects the truth of Rogers' assertion that 'every individual exists in a continually changing world of experience, of which he is the centre, and that the individual is the only one who can know how any experience is perceived. The world of experience is, for each individual, in a very significant sense, a private world'.[64]

Conclusion

The intervention of the law through adversarially based courts can be a clumsy instrument for determining matters of welfare.[65] One problem of any Bill of Rights for children (apart from the obvious difficulty of giving children the same rights as adults when they are still physically and emotionally in need of protection) is that while it is possible to legislate against abuse or physical neglect, which are both clearly visible, it is not possible to legislate *for* the individual love and understanding demanded by Principle 6 of the United Nations Declaration of the Rights of the Child, nor *for* the full opportunity for play and recreation and a healthy environment required by the Declaration's general rights. The state may be reluctant to intervene in family life,[66] but there will always be inadequate, selfish or cruel parents whose children will become dependent on the fragmented parenting skills of the local authority.

It is argued that adequate and independent social work and legal representation should be made available to all children in all decision-making forums, both in and out of court. The system in public law proceedings, in which children may be represented by both a guardian *ad litem* (presenting a view to the court about the child's welfare) and a children's panel solicitor (acting as an advocate for the child and presenting a view about his rights), is one which provides a unique balance between children's rights and children's welfare and which is both respected and envied by other countries. If this system were to be extended to cover private law proceedings and proceedings in all quasi-judicial procedures (for example, representations arising from S.26 of the 1989 Act), then a more healthy synthesis of rights and welfare would be achieved, while a foundation would be laid for a framework of decision making between children and adults which respects both the rights of one and the responsibilities of the other. This is not a new idea. In 1974, David Owen argued for the consideration of full party status and the separate representation of minors in any proceedings in which they are involved.[67]

The rights and lack of representation of the many thousands of children involved in their parents' divorce and separation is a subject of pressing concern. In particular, the proposals to establish a separately administered and

---

64 Rogers, *Child Centred Therapy: A Theory of Personality and Behaviour* (1951), p. 484.
65 This theme is explored in King and Trowel, *Children's Welfare and the Law: The Limits of Legal Intervention* (1992).
66 Freud *et al.* have argued for minimum state intervention and the adoption of the principle of the least intrusive alternative in the lives of substitute as well as biological families (Freud, Goldstein and Solnit, *Before the Best Interests of the Child* (1979)).
67 Children Bill 1974, clause 52.

funded support service for the family jurisdiction merit urgent consideration,[68] provided that any such services recognise the child as a primary client rather than the secondary subject of dispute resolution.

It is unfortunate that, within our social structure, courts are the main determinants of child welfare issues. Trowel and King argue that many cases need never come to court if adequate preventative facilities were made available. They make the important point that the law tends to intervene in the lives of children in an episodic way, rather than as part of a continuing process, focusing on service delivery rather than on dispute resolution.

There are practical and philosophical difficulties in espousing a mutually exclusive rights or welfare based approach to the best interests of children. The child may not be capable of exercising his rights in his own best interests in certain situations. Similarly, the imprecise science of best interests may itself constitute an abuse of children's rights if applied within a subjective rather than objective framework of welfare.

The Cleveland Inquiry in 1987 highlighted the risk of secondary systems abuse of the child during rescue, in addition to the original primary abuse. There are cogent reasons for allowing the child to participate in decision making, while building in safeguards to prevent him being overwhelmed by both the responsibility for making the decision and the consequences of making a mistake. The Children Act 1989 and the UN Convention provide a framework for such a synthesis by emphasising the right of the child to have both his welfare considered and his wishes and feelings taken into consideration. What is lacking is an incorporation of those principles into co-ordinated rights-based services. In the final analysis, the equation of children's rights to services, alongside those of other services users as part of a general framework of consumerism, is not satisfactory (see Chapter 12 above, 'The Context of Welfare').

It is not a necessary corollary of empowerment that children who are dignified with rights should also be burdened with responsibility at a time when their conceptual understanding is limited by immaturity. Nor should rights be seen as weakening or undermining the autonomy of family life. On the contrary, any group which recognises and respects the rights and needs of its individual members can only be strengthened and enriched.

For happy, healthy and secure children, rights are an insurance policy they may never need. For the many thousands of children who are disadvantaged, dispossessed, alone, unhappy and ill-treated, rights are their only hope and effective representation the only way of making their voice heard.

Ultimately, society's children are society's own creation. Trust and responsibility engender the same qualities in return, while the demeaning of action and aspiration may fuel a self-fulfilling prophecy of irresponsibility, based on a fundamental lack of respect for themselves and others.

---

68   Murch and Hooper, *The Family Justice System* (1992).

Index